Rendezvous

A PROSE READER

RENDEZVOUS
A Prose Reader

John J. McShea, O.S.A.

Joseph W. Ratigan

VILLANOVA UNIVERSITY

CHARLES SCRIBNER'S SONS, NEW YORK

In memory of our parents

Contents

PREFACE

THE PURPOSE of this book may be stated simply: the editors have tried to collect prose units which are readable, informative, and pertinent to literary studies. Fashions in readers come and go, and recently there has been a preference for the encyclopedic survey of all the related arts and sciences. With no wish to pass judgment on any but their own efforts, the editors feel that there is great advantage merely in gathering together matters directly relevant to English studies, with a latitude that does not extend too far.

A book of this kind is never wholly satisfactory, never pleasing to everyone, but it justifies itself if it introduces the student to literature, if it encourages further reading, if it fosters a curiosity about the authors included, and if it serves as a pattern for the writing of themes.

It has been the intention of the editors to avoid oversubtle criticism and experimental fiction. Accordingly, the critical articles are explicit and objective; they analyze their subjects in an orderly, logical fashion. In most instances the short stories have been considered for their themes which, it is hoped, lie within the ordinary range of experience of young men and women. The tone of the book is informal.

The selections have been taken from books, magazines, and newspapers. The full text of the original versions has been used throughout except for a few sentences or paragraphs omitted because their details might conceivably be irrelevant or misleading. Such deletions have been clearly marked by suspension points or asterisks. Moreover, every selection has been printed exactly as it appeared in the original source; thus the reader will notice some variation in American and British use of punctuation, spelling, and vocabulary, especially in writing of a century or two ago.

It should be stated that this book makes no pretensions toward a complete treatment of the four forms of communication: exposition, description, narration, and argumentation. Nor was it considered necessary merely for the sake of adornment to include "big name" authors because they are being widely heralded or are the subjects of contemporary discussion. Famous writers have been included because they fulfilled rigid standards of good writing. Writers not of major stature or well known have also been given recognition because they have poignantly portrayed life in one or more of its manifestations; because they have painted vivid portraits of places and people; and because they have interpreted characters in a moving and memorable manner.

An anthology such as this, it was felt, was needed to give students a keener insight into life and literature, to introduce them to new and fresh horizons, to challenge them to think more clearly and to write more effectively. For never before in the history of civilization was it so important that the student be articulate and literate as it is in these our days.

The editors of this anthology wish to express their appreciation to all the authors and publishers who permitted the reprinting of copyrighted material. All have been cooperative and gracious in lending assistance to this work. Mr. Ian Gilmour, editor of *The Spectator*, Mr. Hesketh Pearson, eminent English biographer, and the Rev. Thurston Davis, S.J., editor of *America*, have been of immeasurable help. The editors are especially grateful for the continued encouragement and many excellent suggestions given them by the Rev. Thomas F. Calpin, O.S.A., the Rev. Stephen F. Lanen, O.S.A., the Rev. Thomas F. Gilligan, O.S.A., and the Rev. Robert M. Sullivan, O.S.A. Many other persons, of course, notably Mrs. William J. Mannix and Mrs. Joseph W. Ratigan, should be cited for their assistance, but long lists are awkward, and the unnamed know they have the editors' true gratitude.

J. J. McS.
J. W. R.

Villanova, Pennsylvania
August 24, 1959

Rendezvous

A PROSE READER

EXPOSITION

EXPOSITION is that type of writing which explains or clarifies whatever it is considering. The object of its study may be a personality, an idea, a book, or just a random fancy that occurs to the active mind of a Charles Lamb, a Mark Twain, or a Freya Stark. In least complex forms, it is the most elementary species of expression, particularly when it answers the direct questions: "What comes next?" or "How do I use this part?" On such a level of exposition exist the Southern Italian cookbook and the list of instructions that accompanies a do-it-yourself "hi-fi" kit. In more ambitious and literary attempts, exposition extends to the biography, the essay (critical or personal), the book review, and the miscellaneous discussion that is intended to inform the reader.

This second kind of exposition is our immediate concern because it represents the artistry and skill of the process of explaining in advanced form. There was, no doubt, high sincerity in the reminiscing about his deceased neighbor by an early Greek or Etruscan farmer, but the best of these efforts was far inferior to the tidy characterizing of human activities by Plutarch. Not until forceful, learned writers set about commenting on the behavior of their predecessors and contemporaries did the readable and valuable biography emerge. Similarly, imaginative and fluent writers revealed their thoughts, their opinions, and their reveries and thereby developed the essay. And analytic, informed writers expounded their judgments on books and plays and produced the review, together with allied forms of criticism.

Long ago it was said that history is the study of fact and its meaning. Exactly the same basic purpose can be assigned to exposition, which starts with fact and proceeds to interpretation. The nature of biography is unusually pertinent in this respect. The individual items in a man's life—place of birth, opportunities, achievements, and death—lie within the province of recorded fact. But the listing of dates and occurrences is the business of a tombstone. Expository biography turns rather to the subject's character, to the sum total of distinctive traits possessed by no one else in this exact proportion. In the most explicit sense of the term the biographer *explains* best when he selects the most enlightening events and evaluates them intelligently. Efficient expository biography balances the brusque side of Jonathan Swift, who could satirize with splendid vengeance, and the tender manner of his recollection of Mrs. Johnson—a display, by the way, of intimate grief phrased in good taste with no taint of ostentation. With equal logic any adequate interpretation of James McNeill Whistler's career will note his aggressiveness toward some adults and his invariable fondness for children, his love of the beauty in simple things and his sophisticated wit of expression. On an occasion different from that recorded later in this section, he was called to court as a witness in a case based on the complaint that the buyer of a picture had been overcharged. There was the hint of collusion on

Whistler's part. After the usual preliminary queries, the counsel for the other side posed his question: "Mr. Whistler, it is reported that you received a goodly sum for this recommendation [that the purchaser buy the picture for £200]—is there anything in that?" Whistler answered: "Oh, nothing, I assure you"—and a prolonged yawn—"nothing but the indelicacy of the suggestion." In the few moments of this question-and-answer sequence, Whistler revealed himself as a curiously witty and resourceful person and extended a full-bodied portrayal of the personality that was his. Rather clearly, it is only from such an evenly poised presentation of biographical fact and interpretation, stated or implicit, that the reader can *understand* the subject thus outlined. And exposition, however varied its approach, is intended to be understood.

Eighteenth-century English literature provides the first instances of proficiency in virtually every category of exposition. The essays of Francis Bacon and Abraham Cowley reflect the virtue of innovation but the wooden, inflexible manner of the early attempt as well. After 1700 Richard Steele, Joseph Addison, Daniel Defoe, and Oliver Goldsmith brought essay composition to a point of eminence; besides, they broadened the scope of the essay to include satire (chiefly of a mild, kindly nature), judgment of people and their conduct, and informality in the discussion of almost every idea imaginable. They overlooked little of contemporary life in the course of their commentaries: the pretense and irresponsibility of the wealthy, the noise of London streets, and the value of those elements of gentility that make for genuine culture.

In biography and criticism, too, the eighteenth century made handsome advancements. In earlier centuries there had been the biographical efforts of William Roper, who recorded the life of St. Thomas More, his father-in-law; the intensely arresting self-revelations of Margery Kempe; and the studies by Isaac Walton of the calm and pleasant lifetime of George Herbert and the tortured existence of John Donne. But the eighteenth century produced the work of Samuel Johnson and James Boswell, who projected the people of their biographies with more clarity of outline and with more animation than anyone else before them had been capable of doing.

Criticism or literary exposition likewise attained a full maturity during the eighteenth century. To cite only a few of its exponents at this time, Johnson, Alexander Pope, and the unjustly belittled Thomas Rymer wrote with a personal intensity and a universality of theme unknown to the critics before them, except perhaps to John Dryden.

Exposition achieves its ends in many ways. But, though one form may predominate, there is usually a blending of methods in all but the shortest discussions.

First of all, exposition *defines*. Words and attitudes are most likely to need definition if they are to be understood with perfect clarity. In "On Wandering" Belloc offers a pointed definition of the terms *wander* and *travel*, sets their limitations, and fixes the degree of pleasure each is likely to produce.

For his part, Harold Nicolson defines urbanity at somewhat greater length and places the idea beyond misunderstanding. In effect, the Characters are definitions because they isolate their subjects from less eccentric and usually less unattractive humankind.

Second, exposition *compares* and *contrasts*. In his recollections of Chesterton and Belloc, Hesketh Pearson indicates the similarities and the disparities of temperament existing between two men so often united by identical tastes in politics and controversy. In Joseph Conrad's essay there is an implied, but poignant, contrast between the restrained celebration of Christmas at sea and the memory of that same day enjoyed at home with leisure and companionship.

Third, exposition *analyzes* or *separates the entire unit into its parts*. Samuel Taylor Coleridge's commentary on the characteristics of Shakespearean drama is a lucid analysis of eight separate components of the highest possible kind of genius in stagecraft. "The Art of the Short Story" by Sean O'Faolain is an expert resolution of a difficult and elusive creative activity into the elements that sustain it. Close, intelligent scrutiny of the parts which constitute any aggregate, artistic or scientific, is, of all the methods of exposition, most likely to enlighten the reader fully. A thorough analyst is generally the best expositor.

Fourth, exposition *supplies pertinent examples or details*. Arthur Daley's character sketches vivify "Bo" McMillin and James B. Connolly because of the richness, whether of humor or of seriousness, in the anecdotes recounted. Likewise, John T. Winterich succeeds in his portrait of A. S. W. Rosenbach largely because of the typical evidences of behavior in the citation of examples. Elizabeth Mongan's proficient study of the variety in William Blake's art develops by detailed reference to the separate drawings and engravings.

Exposition may progress in still other ways: by amplification or patient, studied clarifying of a difficult idea; by analogy or the ascertaining of resemblances of an accidental, rather than of a general, kind; and by the use of historical information that makes a modern problem more readily understandable.

Exposition has long preoccupied itself with criticism, but the qualifying and estimating of books and plays—and, now, of movies and television productions—is a development of the past century and a half. *The Edinburgh Review* and the *Quarterly Review* dramatized the function of criticism of current writings and, in passing, thundered at Lord Byron and Percy Bysshe Shelley—who threw back the bolts with anger and vigor. Today the large Sunday newspapers and most magazines present criticism of literary interest. The formidable bibliographies of articles about authors of great or even of little importance attest to the extent of critical examination today.

Modern criticism has evolved its own format. A century ago, as the examples of Thomas Babington Macaulay so clearly show, the critical essay was comprehensive and relatively long. Today the pattern is narrower: the review of a novel or a play tends to include a digest of plot, a notice of the plausibility of characterization, and expressed or implied approval or disapproval. The critic is regarded as an expositor, as one who acquaints the reader with the book's qualities.

Two attributes, however, do accompany first-class criticism and differentiate it from everything inferior. Distinguished criticism offers sharp perception, and it begets an enthusiasm on the part of the reader to obtain the book in question as soon as possible. The former of these attributes, that of a critical insight clarifying brilliantly or discovering new associations is illustrated in Alice Meynell's essay on Dickens. The critic singles out as a great, positive virtue Dickens' ability in "the telling what happened." She indicates that, unlike lesser novelists, Dickens "tells us what happened with a perfect speed which has neither hurry nor delays." The reader is thereby reacquainted with the fundamental importance of a novelist's primary task, that of putting events into sequence with the most imposing success. The fostering of a wholesome, rewarding enthusiasm is clear in Edward Weeks' review of Hesketh Pearson's biography of Walter Scott. A reader would be pathetically unresponsive if on reading the criticism he did not feel an eagerness, even a compulsion, to begin the books of Scott at once.

The selections which follow are planned to illustrate the many species of exposition. The biographical material includes the normal forms of presenting character: the anecdote, the memoir, the novel-like recreating of the subject's thoughts, the letter, the reconstruction of a personality long dead with the retrospective advantage of recording the achievements that live. The personal essays reflect the thoughtful, the amused, and the deeply interested surveys of the world and people by authors worthy of a hearing. The writings on art and diversions indicate the possibility of further fascination in byways the average reader has already located for himself. Finally, the opinions on literature represent the informed conclusions of critics who offer their views for rejection or acceptance.

A final word might be offered about the Characters. Originated by Theophrastus, a contemporary of Aristotle, the form had a somewhat extensive popularity in seventeenth-century England. The Character is general and synthetic: it does not depict a single person but a type of mankind, yet the composite is pieced together from traits which many individuals share. A further interest in the English writers of this form lies in the archaic phrasing remote from the idiom of today. John Earle and Joseph Hall remind us that seventeenth-century prose was still groping toward the smoothness to be attained in the next century.

Biography and Autobiography

HESKETH PEARSON

G. K. CHESTERTON
AND HILAIRE BELLOC*

In my young days there were four outstanding personalities in the literary world: Bernard Shaw, H. G. Wells, G. K. Chesterton, and Hilaire Belloc. We of the new generation admired them all, but though we recognised that Shaw was the most remarkable of the lot, both as man and writer, I think we were secretly fondest of Chesterton, who was not only lovable but had all the human frailties from which Shaw seemed to be so inhumanly free. Chesterton loved company, enjoyed a rousing song, relished a vulgar joke, drank good beer when he could get it and preferred bad beer to no beer at all. He would talk with anybody in a pub, either sense or nonsense according to the mood of the moment or the conversational atmosphere of the place. His laughter could be heard several houses away. He was a sort of Falstaff in bulk and wit, and like that notable character he laughed at his more serious followers. My first glimpse of him was in a Fleet Street pub in the summer of 1913, and I soon perceived that he was pulling the leg of his youthful companion, who looked so earnest that Chesterton's absurdities were probably uttered for the good of his soul.

'One should always drink port from a tankard', said G.K.C. 'Because one does not like to see that one is coming to the end of it. Also it takes on a richer hue. Also it has a mellower taste. Besides, one can *grasp* a tankard: and *drain* it. Now one can't drain a glass. One can only *sip* a glass'. To each of these statements the young man made affirmatory sounds, but as he was drinking from a glass he felt a little guilty and nodded his head dubiously when charged with sipping. This gave Chesterton a new idea. 'Glasses', he went on, 'are made to be smashed. It is said that those who live in glass houses should not throw stones. But what man, living in a glass house, would do anything else? It is the simplest way of getting out of a glass house. Indeed, if he throws a sufficient quantity of stones, it ceases to be a glass house'. He then ordered another tankard of port for himself and a glass of port for the young man.

The following year I was introduced to Chesterton and found him extremely amiable. His way of putting things appealed to me greatly in those days, and he chuckled with amusement when I said, parodying his own style, that Shaw's most serious limitation was that he preferred potatoes to potations. Some years later I published an imaginary conversation between him and Shaw, giving G.K.C. the phrase he had appreciated on that early occasion, and he wrote to say that as I could imitate his mannerisms so well perhaps I would like to do his next book for him.

The unique thing about Chesterton both as talker and writer was the way in which he could ridicule ideas by playing with words. My friend, Edward

* Reprinted from *The Listener* (June 28, 1956) by permission of the author.

Fordham, who was at St. Paul's School with him, tells me that they were once arguing as to whether some policy or other was good or bad. 'The word "good" ', said Chesterton, 'has many meanings. For example, if a man were to shoot his grandmother at a range of 500 yards I should call him a good shot but not necessarily a good man'. He was never stumped by an unexpected question. Following a debate on racial characteristics, he was chatting with Edward Fordham when an elderly lady whom neither of them knew came up and asked in a rather affected manner: 'Mr. Chesterton, I wonder if you could tell me what race I belong to?' Adjusting his glasses, he replied: 'I should certainly say, madam, one of the conquering races'.

His ability to adapt himself instantly to an unforeseen circumstance and make fun out of it was shown when his hat blew off one day in Fleet Street. A friend of mine witnessed the occurrence, saw him chasing the hat, and to save him trouble dodged the traffic and rescued it almost from under the wheels of a motor-bus. Returning to the pavement, he handed it to its owner who was puffing and panting from his exertion. 'That's very kind of you, very kind indeed', said G.K.C. 'But you shouldn't have taken the trouble. My wife has bought me a new hat, and she will be most disappointed when she hears that the old one has only just been saved from well-merited destruction'. 'In that case', protested my friend, a little vexed that he had uselessly imperilled his life, 'why on earth did *you* run after it?' 'It's an old friend', replied Chesterton with some emotion; 'I am fond of it, and I wanted to be with it at the end'.

Though he wrote a number of detective stories, G.K.C. struck me as the most absent-minded and unobservant person I had ever met. Yet he must have noticed people and things in a quick-glancing way, because when I met him again after a lapse of several years and mentioned my name in case he had forgotten me, he said: 'I remember you well. In fact you appear in one of my Father Brown stories'. Naturally I wanted to know which. 'Ah!' said he, 'it is a detective story and the least you can do is to detect yourself'. His absent-mindedness never worried him, though it caused much inconvenience to others, especially when he had promised to give a lecture at some distant spot. His wife once received a wire from him: 'Am at Wolverhampton. Where ought I to be?' On another occasion he arrived over an hour late at a meeting and apologised by saying: 'My wife always sees me into a train, but she is not there to see me out of it, and I left this one at a station further down the line'.

That aspect of his character displayed his other-worldliness. The acquisition of money meant nothing to him, and when he found money in his pocket he spent it or gave it away. He sold his books for a song. For one of the best, *The Napoleon of Notting Hill*, he received £100. His tastes were simple, and so were his pleasures. Just before going to a tea-party at his house a small girl was told by her mother that she would learn a lot from Mr. Chesterton, who was a very clever man. Afterwards the child revealed the nature of his lessons: 'He taught me how to throw buns in the air and catch them in my mouth'.

Even his pugnacity in print and on the platform was unworldly. He loved disputation and enjoyed a fight for its own sake, not for any kudos to be got out of it nor for the pleasure of scoring off an opponent. He probably never wanted to win, because that would have meant the end of the argument. He was once asked to stand for parliament, and replied that he would be delighted to do so if it were absolutely certain that he would be defeated.

In all these respects he was the exact opposite of his friend Hilaire Belloc, who went into battle to conquer, was punctilious in all his arrangements, prudent over money, selling his work for as much as he could get, and wholly conscious of what was going on around him. I was present at a public debate between Belloc and Shaw. With his invariable kindness Shaw frequently referred to Belloc's latest book, *The Cruise of the Nona*, and every time he did so Belloc looked sharply at the audience and said 'Buy it!'

I used to see Belloc in a bar near Ludgate Circus, debating, reciting in his high-pitched voice, laughing, telling Rabelaisian stories, and improvising lines of poetry that would not have been received with such shouts of merriment in a company of tea-drinkers. He was what is commonly called 'a man's man'—that is, he liked what most men are supposed to like: alcohol, argument, songs, jovial company, bodily exercise, ribald mirth, and rowdiness. In appearance he was shortish, thick-set, and might have passed for a red-faced medieval cardinal with mutton-shop whiskers. His habitual expression was severe and his conversation was precise. In telling someone how to get to a certain place, his instructions were so detailed that unless the other had an equally ordered mind he could not possibly follow them. I once heard him lay down a plan for reaching Paris from Sussex that so completely bewildered me that I should have found it easier to walk there. His systematic method, egotism, and indifference to the feelings of others, were exemplified on one of his many journeys to France. The incident may appear exaggerated, but his companion, a veracious person, assured me that it happened as here narrated.

Belloc arrived at Victoria Station carrying a number of books under both arms. He informed the clerk at the booking-office that he was in need of advice, and started off with a summary of his living expenses, during which a queue formed behind him and the clerk tried to interrupt his flow of statistics. But nothing could deter Belloc, who estimated his annual income, with possible fluctuations, the upkeep of his house, the scholastic requirements of his children, the cost of clothing, light, fuel and food. In the midst of his discourse an impatient member of the queue started to swear. Belloc paused, handed the fellow a book on trigonometry, and again addressed the booking-office clerk: 'I am on my way to Paris, and the question that is troubling me is this: am I, under all the circumstances I have mentioned, justified in taking a first-class ticket?'

Belloc's books are uneven in quality, and most of his historical works are vitiated by propaganda, but his essays, poems and travel books have a peculiar quality of their own that can only be called Bellocian. In June, 1947, my friend Hugh Kingsmill and I visited him at his home in Sussex and asked him several questions about his works, the answers to which surprised us. He seemed to think more of being a gentleman than of being a writer; but we did not deem it advisable to tell him, as Voltaire had told Congreve in a like situation, that we would not have travelled so far merely to meet a gentleman.

'I hate writing', he declared. 'I wouldn't have written a word if I could have helped it. I only wrote for money. *The Path to Rome* is the only book I ever wrote for love'.

'Didn't you write *The Four Men* for love?' I asked.

'No. Money'.

'*The Cruise of the Nona?*'

'Money'.

When he had also informed us that his best essays were written for money, we wished to know what profession he would have liked to follow. 'I was called to the bar', he answered. 'But what I wanted to be was a private gentleman. Lazing about doing nothing. Farm as a hobby perhaps. Keep someone to run it'.

We gathered from our talk with him that he had a poor opinion of the politicians of his time, dismissing most of them as superficial and brainless. One of his grievances was that none of them knew anything about France. Half French himself, Belloc had served in the French army for a little over a year; and when I asked how he had managed to get out of it so soon, he replied: 'I pulled strings. I had a cousin in the French Government'. So in one respect at least he had found a politician serviceable.

After we had left him Hugh Kingsmill and I discussed some of his delightful essays, and felt thankful that Belloc's desire to be a country gentleman had been thwarted by the necessity to earn a living.

W. SOMERSET MAUGHAM

FRAY LUIS DE LEON*

I⊤ is character too that makes Fray Luis de Leon a fascinating subject and in his case I feel that I have some justification for dwelling upon him for a little. He died in 1591, so the hero of my book could hardly have listened to his lectures, but I like to think that when he was studying at Salamanca he might have come in contact with the young Augustinian whom in Los

* Reprinted from *Don Fernando*, copyright 1935 by W. Somerset Maugham, by permission of Doubleday & Company, Inc. Permission for Canada granted by W. Somerset Maugham and William Heinemann, Ltd.

Nombres de Cristo, Fray Luis calls Juliano and from him heard something of the master of Spanish prose.

Salamanca is an agreeable place to linger in. It has a noble square, with arches all round it, and here towards evening the whole population perambulates, the men in one direction, the girls in the other, so that they may ogle one another as they pass. The town-hall, with its plateresque façade, is rose-coloured. The mass of the cathedral seen from a little distance is fine; it seems to be planted on the ground with a sort of solid arrogance; but when you approach you are repelled by its ugly reddish brown and the florid decoration. The interior is overwhelmingly magnificent. There are huge, lofty pillars that tower to a height that seems hardly believable. The choir is surrounded by elaborate bas-reliefs. It is all so grand and sumptuous, it reminds you of a Lord Mayor's banquet; it suggests a ceremonial, assured, opulent religion, and you ask yourself what solace in trouble the stricken heart could hope to find there.

At the University, sadly fallen from its ancient glory, I went to see the lecture-room of Fray Luis, a whitewashed room, large, dark and square, with a vaulted ceiling. Narrow benches and narrow desks fill the whole space, and at the side is a long, boxed-off passage where, it appears, the spectators stood. Over the pulpit at the back is a wooden hood somewhat like a great extinguisher. It is from this pulpit that Fray Luis, according to the legend, in which, however, the learned declare there is no truth, gave that lecture the first words of which have carried his name down to posterity more firmly than any of his works. After four years in the prisons of the Inquisition he was acquitted and returned to Salamanca. He was received to the sound of drums and trumpets by a great concourse of gentlemen, professors at the University and students, who came out on to the road from Valladolid to meet him. After a due interval he gave his first lecture. A crowd collected to hear him. They expected him to attack his accusers and once more to speak in his own defence. He began with the words: "As we were saying yesterday."

While he was in prison he wrote his most celebrated work. It is called De los Nombres de Cristo. This book is in the form of a dialogue between three friends in the Augustinian order whom the heat of summer has brought to the house of the community on the Tormes a few miles from Salamanca. It was called La Flecha. The scene of the various conversations is in the garden of this and on a little island in the river. I thought I should like to see a spot so celebrated in Spanish letters and having inquired the way, set out; but after driving for some time I began to think I had lost it. Presently I met a fat young priest, with a round, red face and spectacles, who was strolling along the road reading his breviary. I stopped the car and asked him if he could direct me. He seemed glad to do so. He was a poor parish priest, in a shabby cassock discoloured by sun and rain, and he talked in a high-pitched voice. He was very polite and when he got into the car and then out again took off his hat, but when he put it on seemed very uncertain which was the front and which the back. He never stopped smoking cigarettes he deftly rolled himself.

After a while he put up his hand and we stopped. A rough path led to the shady garden, surrounded by a hedge of box, where the friar sat and chatted with his friends. A brook ran by it, a tiny trickle of very clear water, and beyond was an orchard. It was a quiet and pleasant spot and the coolness was grateful in the heat of the Castilian summer. The priest showed me this place with a sort of proprietary air that I found very delightful and then he did a singular thing. He began to recite.

"Era por el mes de Junio, à las bueltas de la fiesta de San Juan, al tiempo que en Salamanca comiençan à cessar los estudios . . ."*

It was the beginning of the book, and the liquid, exquisitely balanced periods fell from his lips like music. On his fat, red face was a look of rapture.

"What a memory!" I cried, when at last he stopped.

"I have read it so often. I often have long walks to the farms in my parish, three and four and five leagues, and it shortens the way if I repeat to myself my favourite passages. No one ever wrote Spanish like my Fray Luis."

Then he said he would show me the island on which Fray Luis used to walk and we returned to the high road. This offered a wide prospect over the plain of Castile. In the distance the hills were diaphanous. We walked along the river, bordered with handsome, close-growing poplars, till we came to a farm built on the bank of the river, and here on a little terrace overlooking the water a woman with a handkerchief over her head was busy sewing. She greeted the shabby priest with affection and me with politeness and we passed through a mill on to the island. Beyond the mill-race the water seemed only just to flow. On the farther bank was a line of poplars and then the fields dry and brown after the harvest. A faint, pleasant breeze blew on the island, and here in a little circle of trees was a table where tradition says the friar sat and wrote. Now holiday-makers come on Sundays to picnic and the ground was strewn with old newspapers. The spot was exquisitely peaceful. The broad, placid river had a curious effect on one. One's mind was tranquil, but at the same time alert and buoyant.

But the recollection I brought away from the excursion was of this stolid peasant priest reciting line after line of that harmonious prose.

I have read the book from which he quoted, not every word of it, but a great deal. It consists of a series of homilies upon the appellations given to Jesus Christ in the scriptures, and I must admit I should have found it heavy going but for the charming descriptions with which the dialogues open, the digressions and illustrations, and the revelations here and there of the author's character. The reflections which are aroused in him by the subjects of his discourse do not seem to me of great subtlety. I should have thought them within the scope of any pious man who had an intimate acquaintance with theological literature.

* It was the month of June, about the time of the feast of St. John, the moment when studies in Salamanca begin to slacken off. . ,

To me there seems something extraordinarily modern about Luis de Leon. He was not all of a piece as so often appear the famous figures of the past. I do not suppose men then were any different from what they are now, but it looks as though to their contemporaries they seemed more homogeneous. Otherwise they could hardly have so often described them in terms of "humours." But Fray Luis was a contradictory creature in whom dwelt uneasily incongruous qualities and warring instincts. Pacheco, the father-in-law of Velazquez, has painted him in a few words: a little man, but well proportioned, with a big head covered with curly hair, a wide forehead, a round, rather than a long, swarthy face, and sparkling green eyes. He was vain and humble, arrogant and patient, sombre, peevish, bitter, loyal and chivalrous. He loathed fools and hypocrites. He was very tender to little children. He loved nature and truth. He was fearless. No matter what enmities he aroused he was always prepared to denounce tyranny; he would incur any danger to combat injustice. He was an ascetic, of great abstemiousness, and he seldom allowed himself the luxury of going to bed, so that the servitor who entered his cell in the morning found it as he had left it the night before. But he loved the fair things of life, the lovely, lulling sound of the Tormes flowing by La Flecha, the heavenly music of blind Salinas and the harmony and cadence of the Spanish tongue. He was quarrelsome, rude, violent, and he yearned above all else for peace. The cry for rest, rest from the turmoil of his thoughts, rest from the torment of the world, recurs in all his works. It gives his lovely lyrics a poignancy that pierces the artificiality of their Horatian manner. He sought for happiness and tranquility of spirit, but his temperament made it impossible for him to achieve them. They count him among the mystics. He never experienced the supernatural blessings which solace those that pursue the mystic way. He never acquired that aloofness from the things of the world that characterises them. He had an anxious longing for a rapture his uneasy nature prevented him from ever enjoying. He was a mystic only in so far as he was a poet. He looked at those snowcapped mountains and yearned to explore their mysteries, but he was held back by the busy affairs of the city. I always think that the phrase of his, no se puede vivir sin amar, one cannot live without loving, had for him an intimate, tragic meaning. It was not just a commonplace.

Fray Luis had something of the universal capacity that we wonder at in certain figures of the Italian Renaissance. He was a mathematician, an astrologer and a jurist. Untaught, he acquired considerable proficiency as a painter. He was not only deeply versed in theological literature, but also in the classics, and their dreams of the Golden Age never ceased to haunt him. He wrote some exquisite lyrics, after San Juan de la Cruz he is the best poet his country has produced, and I think all judges admit that nobody in Spain ever wrote prose so perfectly. Pen in hand Fray Luis was a scholar and a gentleman; he wrote with elegance, rather than with vigour. In La Perfecta Casada he quotes at length from Tertullian and even in the translation you can hardly fail to see how much more vivid, racy and virile was the African writer. But even a foreigner cannot but be sensible to the charm of Luis de Leon's liquid prose. It is as clear as the rivulet that runs through La Flecha. It is eloquent and at the same time colloquial; it is concise and yet abundant. It has a grave, playful music. To my cheerful mind the most attractive and diverting book of Fray Luis is The Perfect Wife. The reader, interested neither in theology nor in mysticism, can read it with entertainment. It offers sage counsel to a bride on her conduct in the various necessities of the married state. One cannot help feeling a certain amused astonishment at its curious mixture of simplicity, shrewdness and nobility. Incidentally it gives a pleasant glimpse of domestic life in the upper class and a hint here and there of circumstances which the conventional view of Spanish society would never have led you to suspect. Fray Luis was a Castilian gentleman of excellent family and his ideal of the good life was that of the landowner living on the produce of his estate. He does not seem to have considered the possibility that men might be born so unhappily as to have no broad acres to till. He had only scorn for such as engaged in commerce; it was not only disreputable, but gravely prejudicial to the soul's well-being. "The life of the field," he says, "and the cultivation of one's inheritance is a school of innocence and truth because one learns from those with whom one works and talks. And as the earth renders faithfully what is entrusted to it, and in its unchangeableness is stable and downright, bountiful in its fruits and generous of its riches, liberal and productive to well-doing; so it seems to engender and to impress in the breasts of them that work it a peculiar goodness and a simplicity of temper such as are found with difficulty in men of other kinds. So it teaches sincerity, true and faithful dealing and keeps in remembrance the good old customs."

The longest chapter is devoted to an attack, supported by abundant quotations from the classics and the fathers, on the unaccountable mania the women of his day had for dyeing their hair and painting their cheeks. (He thought, the good monk, that the beauty of a good woman resided not in the lineaments of her face, but in the secret virtues of her soul; and he was not sure that it became the perfect wife to be fair and lovely.) He admitted that not all women who painted had evil intentions. "It is politeness to think so," he remarks dryly. But if this mask on the face did not discover their bad desires, at all events it aroused those of their neighbours. This is how virtuous women should perform their toilet: "Let them hold out their hands and receive in them water poured from a jar, which their servant will pour from the washing-stand, and let them put it to their faces, and take some of it in their mouths and wash their gums, and rub their fingers over their eyes and in their ears, and behind the ears also, and let them not desist till their whole face is clean; and after that, letting the water be, let them cleanse themselves with a rough towel, and so will they remain more beautiful than the sun."

There is one chapter that is headed: "How important it is that women should not talk much and that they should be peaceable and of a gentle disposition." In this he has a phrase so modern that it makes one smile; he remarks that a "foolish and chattering woman, as foolish women generally are, whatever other merits she has, is an intolerable business." Further on he observes that the peculiarity of stupidity is that it is not aware of itself but contrariwise takes itself for wisdom. "And whatever we do it will be the greatest difficulty to instil common sense (into persons of this sort), for that is something you learn ill if you do not learn it with your mother's milk. . . . And the best advice we can give to such women is to beg them to hold their tongues; since there are few wise women they should aim at there being many silent ones." Before I leave this engaging work I should like to give an extract from the chapter entitled: "On the obligation of married couples to love one another and to assist one another in their labours." It is a quotation from St. Basil. "The viper, the most ferocious animal among reptiles, assiduously goes out to espouse the sea-lamprey, and having arrived, whistles, as though to give the signal that he is there, and attract her from the sea so that he may take her in his marital embrace. The lamprey obeys and rejoins the poisonous and savage beast without fear. What do I say to this? What? That however harsh and of savage qualities the husband may be, it is necessary for the wife to put up with it and that she should not allow peace to be disturbed for any cause."

That's talking, that is.

WILLIAM BUTLER YEATS

*GEORGE MOORE**

Moore had inherited a large Mayo estate, and no Mayo country gentleman had ever dressed the part so well. He lacked manners, but had manner; he could enter a room so as to draw your attention without seeming to; his French, his knowledge of painting, suggested travel and leisure. Yet nature had denied to him the final touch: he had a coarse palate. Edward Martyn alone suspected it. When Moore abused the waiter or the cook, he had thought, 'I know what he is hiding.' In a London restaurant on a night when the soup was particularly good, just when Moore had the spoon at his lip, he said: 'Do you mean to say you are going to drink that?' Moore tasted the soup, then called the waiter, and ran through the usual performance. Martyn did not undeceive him, content to chuckle in solitude. Moore had taken a house in Upper Ely Place; he spent a week at our principal hotel while his furniture was moving in: he denounced the food to the waiter, to the manager, went down to the kitchen and denounced it to the cook. 'He has written to the proprietress', said the manager, 'that the steak is like brown paper. How can you believe a word such a man would say, a steak cannot be like brown

* Reprinted from *The Autobiography of William Butler Yeats*, New York, The Macmillan Company, 1938, by permission of the publishers. Permission for Canada granted by Mrs. W. B. Yeats and The Macmillan Company of Canada.

paper.' He had his own bread sent in from the baker and said on the day he left: 'How can these people endure it?' 'Because', said the admiring head-waiter, 'they are not *comme il faut.*' A little later I stayed with him and wrote to Lady Gregory: 'He is boisterously enduring the sixth cook'. Then from Sligo a few days later: 'Moore dismissed the sixth cook the day I left—six in three weeks. One brought in a policeman, Moore had made so much noise. He dragged the policeman into the dining-room and said: "Is there a law in this country to compel me to eat this abominable omelette?"'

Sometimes Moore, instead of asking us to accept for true some monstrous invention, would press a spontaneous action into deliberate comedy; starting in bad blood or blind passion, he would all in a moment see himself as others saw him. When he arrived in Dublin, all the doors in Upper Ely Place had been painted white by an agreement between the landlord and the tenants. Moore had his door painted green, and three Miss Beams—no, I have got the name quite right—who lived next door protested to the landlord. Then began a correspondence between Moore and the landlord wherein Moore insisted on his position as an art critic, that the whole decoration of his house required a green door—I imagine that he had but wrapped the green flag around him—then the indignant young women bought a copy of *Esther Waters*, tore it up, put the fragments into a large envelope, wrote thereon: 'Too filthy to keep in the house', dropped it into his letter-box. I was staying with Moore, I let myself in with a latch-key some night after twelve, and found a note on the hall table asking me to put the door on the chain. As I was undressing, I heard Moore trying to get in; when I had opened the door and pointed to the note he said: 'Oh, I forgot. Every night I go out at eleven, at twelve, at one, and rattle my stick on the railing to make the Miss Beams' dogs bark'. Then I saw in the newspapers that the Miss Beams had hired organ-grinders to play under Moore's window when he was writing, that he had prosecuted the organ-grinders. Moore had a large garden on the other side of the street, a blackbird sang there; he received his friends upon Satur-day evening and made a moving speech upon the bird: 'I enjoy its song. If I were the bad man people say I am, could I enjoy its song?' He wrote every morning at an open window on the ground floor, and one morning saw the Miss Beams' cat cross the street, and thought, 'That cat will get my bird'. He went out and filled his pocket with stones, and whenever he saw the cat, threw a stone. Somebody, perhaps the typist, must have laughed, for the rest of the tale fills me with doubt. I was passing through Dublin just on my way to Coole; he came to my hotel. 'I remember how early that cat got up. I thought it might get the blackbird if I was not there to protect it, so I set a trap. The Miss Beams wrote to the Society for the Prevention of Cruelty to Animals, and I am carrying on a correspondence with its secretary, cat versus bird.' (Perhaps after all, the archives of the Society do contain that correspondence. The tale is not yet incredible.) I passed through Dublin again, perhaps on my way back. Moore came to see me in seeming great depression. 'Remember that trap?' 'Yes.' 'Remember that bird?' 'Yes.' 'I have caught the bird.'

Moore gave a garden party during the annual festival of the Gaelic League; there was a Gaelic play by Douglas Hyde based upon a scenario of Moore's, and to this garden party he invited the Catholic Archbishop, beginning the letter with: 'Cher confrère'. The Archbishop did not answer. He had already in a letter to the Press invited the Archbishop to institute a stage censorship. 'But, my dear Yeats, Archbishops are educated men. If there is some difficulty about a play, I will call upon him. I will explain. He will approve the play. No more mob rule. No more such trouble as we had about *The Countess Cathleen*. No more letters to the Press signed "Father of a Family".'

CHRISTOPHER DAWSON

ST. BONIFACE*

AFTER TWELVE hundred years it is high time that we remembered St. Boniface. For there is no doubt that he has been most shockingly neglected by his own countrymen. There is no standard English edition of his works; there has never been an adequate English biography of him and he was not even included in Newman's lives of the English saints where, at least, one would have expected to see him treated with especial care as the great representative of Anglo-Saxon missionary action. Yet there can be no question of his greatness both as a saint, a missionary and historical figure. As I wrote twenty-two years ago, he was a "man who had a deeper influence on the history of Europe than any Englishman who has ever lived," and though this seemed a paradox or an exaggeration, I still believe that it is strictly and literally true. No doubt he was no hero in Carlyle's sense. He was entirely lacking in that daimonic quality which the romantic historians and men of letters prized so highly. He was a servant rather than a master of his age—*servus servorum Dei*—but it was just because he was a faithful servant, accepting every charge that was laid upon him and never attempting to impress his personality on the course of history that he achieved such a great and enduring work, so that he deserves to be named with St. Benedict and St. Gregory the Great as the creator of medieval Christendom.

And the neglect of St. Boniface is the more astonishing because of all the men of his age, he is the one of whom we have the fullest, most personal and most intimate record. His letters, as Sir Frank Stenton has written, are "the most remarkable body of correspondence which has survived from the Dark Ages." This is not only because that part of the correspondence which deals with his relations with the Papacy and with the Frankish rulers is an authority

* Reprinted from *Saints and Ourselves*, P. J. Kenedy & Sons, New York, 1956, by permission of the publisher.

of the first importance for the history of his age. Even more remarkable is the correspondence with his friends in England and in Germany which reveal the rich background of personal relationships on which his work and his character were founded and which are also of the highest value for the history of Anglo-Saxon culture. Even men whose business it has been to study the history of that age have seldom appreciated sufficiently the character and achievement of that culture. What could be more surprising than this sudden flowering of Christian culture—even, one may say, of Christian humanism—in the midst of a barbarian society which had been pagan and illiterate and divorced from the higher culture of the Byzantine-Christian world only a century before? No doubt it was an aristocratic society. Boniface himself was of noble birth, perhaps the scion of one of those lesser tribal ruling families which had been absorbed by the growth of the West Saxon kingdom—and alike in Wessex and Northumbria and East Anglia the kings and princesses of the ruling families played a leading part in the development of the new culture. It was also a monastic society, which owed its high culture to the confluence of the two streams of monastic influence which flowed from Ireland to Lindisfarne and Malmesbury and from Rome to Canterbury and Jarrow and Ripon. The interest in culture and the apostolic spirit which inspired St. Boniface were common to both traditions, but it was the Roman tradition and the Benedictine spirit which gave the new Anglo-Saxon culture its distinctive character and made it a creative force in Europe. It was St. Willebrord and St. Boniface who took up the work of St. Gregory and St. Augustine and established that bond between the Papacy and the new Christian society of Western Germany and the Netherlands which was the corner stone of medieval Christendom. And they could never have accomplished this task unless both of them, but especially St. Boniface, had been not merely individual missionaries but creators and organizers of a great social movement which transplanted the new spiritual culture that had grown up in the Benedictine monasteries of Northumbria and Wessex to the barbarous lands and peoples beyond the Rhine.

It is clear from his letters that St. Boniface was a man with a genius for friendship who saw in every personal relationship an opportunity for the enrichment of the Christian life.

Thus at every stage in his career he associates his friends and relations and the church of his native land with his mission, and they repaid his affection with interest. Whatever the obstacles he met with—and we know that he suffered greatly from a sense of discouragement and frustration—his countrymen never let him down. For once the prophet was not without honour in his own country. And the letter which the Archbishop of Canterbury wrote to St. Lull on hearing of his martyrdom shows how the whole English church united to recognize his greatness and to canonize him as their patron along with St. Gregory the Great and St. Augustine of Canterbury—an almost unique example of the public and official cultus of a contemporary figure.

And yet his contemporaries cannot have realized the full significance of his achievement. They saw him as a great saint and a great missionary, but they could not have realized the extent to which his work was destined to change the face of Europe and the future of the world. There has never been an age in which the Western civilization and of Christianity itself seemed darker. Christendom was being attacked from every side and it seemed in danger of losing its internal cohesion and its power of resistance. During the generation before the birth of St. Boniface the whole of the Christian East had been conquered by Islam and the very existence of the Byzantine empire was in danger. During Boniface's youth conditions steadily deteriorated and the Christian world was sinking into a state of anarchy. Nor was the situation any better in the West. When Boniface was a monk at Nursling in 711-713 Spain was being conquered by the Saracens, and while he was beginning his mission to Germany the Saracens were beginning their invasions of France. The death of Pepin II, the protector of St. Willebrord, in 714 had left the Frankish realm without a master, and it was only after years of civil war that his bastard Charles Martel had succeeded in overcoming his rivals and their allies, the pagan Frisians, and was in a position to defend the West against the pagans of the North and the Saracens in the South.

Now Charles throughout his career until his death in 741 was the protector of St. Boniface in his missionary enterprises. He was no doubt acting in his own interests as the ruler of the Franks, while St. Boniface was obliged to work under his protection if he was to work at all. But beyond that the two men had nothing in common. Charles was essentially a warrior, a man of blood from his youth, like the heroes of the *chansons de geste*.* But he was ruthless and unscrupulous in the extreme in his dealings with the church, confiscating ecclesiastical property and using bishoprics and monasteries as fiefs to reward his relations and his captains like Milo, a good soldier, who received the bishoprics of Treves and Reims in payment of his services. But St. Boniface was a Christian after the manner of St. Paul who was entirely absorbed in his mission and who found the whole atmosphere of the court with its secularized bishops and greedy courtiers antipathetic. The more successful he was in creating a new Christian society among the northern barbarians based on the Anglo-Saxon monastic colonies, which were centres of culture as well as schools of the Christian life, the more glaring was the contrast with the moral and canonical anarchy of the Frankish church. Unless this process of corruption were checked, it must inevitably infect the new Christian society, and how could this be done, while the churches and monasteries of Southern Gaul were being ravaged by the Saracens so that the very existence of Christendom was in question?

In this dilemma St. Boniface turned to the Papacy as the only centre of stability and unity and order. From the beginning to the end of his career it was to Rome that he looked and throughout his correspondence we see how the intimate sense of his personal bond with the Apostolic See penetrated his whole work. The oath which he swore to Pope Gregory II in 722, which was the regular oath of a suburbicarian bishop of the Roman diocese,

* Old French epic poems glorifying historic deeds.

was to him no formality but a solemn personal obligation to which he remained faithful at all costs and in all circumstances during his mission of
more than thirty years.

Here I think we can see the action of that new spirit which was to transform the Christian Empire into medieval Christendom. The old Roman
pattern of hierarchy and law and obedience remained intact, but it was
renewed and transformed by the conception of homage and loyalty and
fidelity which were so deeply rooted in the heroic age of the Northern
Germanic and Celtic peoples. St. Boniface had become the "man" of St. Peter,
and he was bound in honour to set the interests of his lord before all else.
Hence it was not enough for him to carry out that missionary vocation on
which his heart was set. He forced himself against his natural inclination to
undertake the vast and ungrateful task of the reform of the whole Frankish
church, when the death of Charles Martel at last opened the way to a new
order in church and state. Charles's successors, Pepin and Carloman, were
men of a different type from their father, especially Carloman who now
ruled Germany and the East Frankish Kingdom and was prepared to do all
in his power to forward the work of St. Boniface. It was at his request that
St. Boniface held the first of the reforming councils in 742, and thence-
forward the prince and the saint worked together to carry out a far-reaching
programme of ecclesiastical reform and to bring the Frankish Church into
closer unity with the Papacy. In 744 the movement was extended with the
co-operation of Pepin to the West Frankish kingdom, and finally in 747 the
work was completed by a great council of the whole Frankish Church,
the proceedings of which are described in St. Boniface's letter to Archbishop
Cuthbert of Canterbury.

The work of these five years is of decisive importance in the history of the
West, for they laid the foundations of that threefold alliance of the monastic
reformers, the Papacy and the Frankish monarchy which was the basis not
only of Carolingian culture but of medieval Christendom itself.

As soon as the West Frankish Church was also committed to the principle
of reform, Carloman resigned his kingdom to his brother and became a Benedictine monk at Soracte and Monte Cassino, while St. Boniface turned back
to his missionary vocation and to the development of Fulda as a centre of
Christian culture for the new lands. The work which Boniface and Carloman
had begun passed to Pepin and to the Papacy which was now fully aware of
the importance of the Frankish alliance. The change of dynasty which
inaugurated the Carolingian kingdom and Empire was not the work of St.
Boniface, though his English disciple St. Burchard played a certain part in it.
But I think it is possible that the new ceremony of coronation and unction,
which was performed by St. Boniface himself in 751, may have also been
due to him, since it is not of Frankish origin while it has an obvious affinity
with the spirit of St. Boniface and the Anglo-Saxon culture which were
deeply permeated by Scriptural tradition and imagery. On the other hand it
is extremely unlikely that St. Boniface had anything to do with the policy of

Frankish intervention on behalf of the Pope against the Lombards, a policy to which his patron and disciple Carloman was actively opposed.

Ever since 747 St. Boniface had been withdrawing from public affairs in the Frankish kingdom and turning back to the field of his original missionary activities.

Thus when Pope Stephen crossed the Alps to conclude his alliance with King Pepin, Boniface had already washed his hands of temporal affairs and set forth on his last missionary journey to Frisia. He had already written to Pepin's adviser Fulrad, the abbot of St. Denis, begging him to secure the protection of the king for the Anglo-Saxon monks whom he was leaving behind him: "almost all strangers, some of them priests set in many places to minister to the Church and the people, some monks placed in cells to teach children their letters, some of them old men who have lived and laboured with me. For all of them I am anxious that they should not be lost after my death, but may have your counsel and royal protection and should not be scattered like sheep without a shepherd, and that the peoples who dwell by the pagan frontier may not lose the law of Christ."

He went on his last missionary journey fully conscious that there would be no return, commanding his disciple and successor St. Lull to send his shroud with him in the box of books which was his most precious possession. Finally before his departure he sent for St. Lioba, the abbess of Bischofsheim on the Tauber, who of all the English missionaries was nearest to him in spirit and culture. He charged her not to return to England after his death but to remain at her post as long as she lived, commending her to the protection of St. Lull and the abbey of Fulda and asking that she should be buried with him in the same grave, so that "as they had served Christ with the same desire and affection during their lives, so their bodies might await the day of resurrection together."

This last request is very typical of the consideration and affection which St. Boniface always showed in his personal relations. But it is more than that. It was also an acknowledgement to posterity of the help that he had received from his fellow country-women in his apostolate. Today we regard it as a matter of course that nuns should play an important part in all missionary activities. But it was not so in the past, either in antiquity or in the Middle Ages or in the missions of the sixteenth and seventeenth centuries. Thus the part taken by the Anglo-Saxon nuns, like St. Lioba, St. Walburga, St. Thecla and the rest, in the conversion and teaching of the German converts is almost unique. They brought to the German lands that high tradition of Christian feminine culture which had been formed during the preceding century by the great royal abbesses of Whitby and Ely and Thanet, and Barking and Wimborne, a tradition which was to live on in the abbeys of the Carolingian and German Empires after the Anglo-Saxon monastic culture had itself been swept away by the Danish invasions. In this tradition St. Lioba herself holds a central place, for she became the close friend of Queen Hildegard, the wife of Charlemagne and the mother of Louis the Pious, so that the authentic

Bonifacian tradition of spirituality and culture was carried on into the Carolingian age.

But St. Boniface himself had no thought even for posthumous success. His whole mind was concentrated on the culminating point of his apostolate. For him there could be no turning back and no resting on his achievement. Therefore his martyrdom near Dokkum in Frisia on 5 June, 754, was the only appropriate conclusion to his career. All his life he had prepared himself for such a consummation. Years before, he had written to St. Lioba asking her to pray that God would give him the spirit of a chief, so that when the wolf came he would not fly but would give his life for the sheep. And so when he and all his great following were massacred by a pagan mob, the Christian world received the news not with horror and dismay, but with a sense of triumphant achievement.

I have already mentioned the letter which Cuthbert, the Archbishop of Canterbury, wrote to St. Lull on this occasion, and we may well recall his words today. "We give thanks to the unspeakable goodness of God that the English people which dwells in Britain has deserved to send forth to spiritual conflict before the eyes of all men so great a scholar and soldier of Christ with the disciples that he trained and educated, for the salvation of many souls . . . wherefore, after the apostles and the evangelists, we hold and venerate him among the greatest doctors of the orthodox faith. And so in our general synod we have decided to celebrate the day when he and his companions suffered martyrdom by a solemn annual feast, since we hope and trust to have him, together with St. Gregory and St. Augustine, as our special patron before Christ the Lord, Whom he so loved in his life and Whom he so glorified in his death."

JOHN C. CALPIN

MATT TALBOT*

A CHILD shouted at play on darkening Summerhill Street, Dublin, the year 1884. At that precise instant, worn threads parted in the pocket of a workman trudging by with purposeful stride. His lone shilling escaped through the hole and slipped to the wet pavement, the tiny sound of the Queen's shilling tinkling among the cobbles drowned out by the childish voice. The man, bone-weary, thinking only of the drink of whiskey his shilling was to get him, heard it not.

Whoever found the coin rejoiced briefly and went his way. The loser was never afterward the same. The events to come changed the course of his life, his family. Men unborn were to be caught up in his story, their lives changed. Nor is the finish yet in view. The laborer was Matt Talbot, twenty-

* Written especially for this book.

eight years old, a carefree, gregarious Irishman, unmarried, barely able to read; a heavy drinker—even a drunkard—since he was twelve years old, when he got his first job in a winery.

That evening, moving along with that long stride and swinging walk peculiar to the Irish workman, he was intent only on his first drink. "Small, stooped, and bony, weighing about 128 lbs.," he is described by his principal biographer, Sir Joseph Glynn, though Matt would have no inkling that anyone would ever write his life. Talbot was hurrying along to Flaherty's bar, there to spend his shilling—that was his future.

It was a better place than he was used to, for his small income as a hod carrier was more fitted for dark little backrooms, with sawdust on the floor, where a glass of porter was a penny and a glass of fiery whiskey not much more.

His thirst this day was such that he had to get the most for his money, and damn the quality. But he couldn't wait to get to "Piggy" O'Neil's, where he could buy twice as much. He needed that drink in a hurry. Last night had been a doozer.

"Whiskey," he told the man behind the taps. "No trust to you, Talbot." "I have a shilling," Talbot answered. He reached for the potion and gulped it, and reached, also, for the shilling and found the hole. "I had it and it's gone!" he told Flaherty, with a sickly smile meant to be ingratiating. "You're a cheat and a sot, Talbot," Flaherty said and swiped him viciously across the face. Blood spurted from Talbot's nose and he fell. The burly tavern owner picked him up and threw him bodily into Summerhill Street.

Covering his injured face and hoping the bleeding would stop, Matt scurried home. There, he found that all members of the Talbot brood were absent. His mother, Elizabeth, had gone to church, probably to pray for this man who never missed a day at work or a night of drinking. He threw himself on his bed and wept like a child. Then the gnawing of the desire for a drink was on him, doubly strong.

> I must get some money, I must. I must. What happened to that shilling? That accursed shilling? It must have been accursed. Maybe that hole was put there by the devil, or by—No, I can't think that. Why did I save that one shilling when I spent the rest of the money from the fiddle—? Ah, the fiddle. That fiddle. I wish I'd never seen it.

Last night, he had used up the last of the eighteen shillings he had given the barmaid at Gillen's, as he did every payday. He drank each night "against" the little sum. With care, it could hold out until Wednesday. But one drink extra each night had wiped out his "tab" and last night he had gone for hours drinkless. Then came the fiddle. A poor fiddler, putting his instrument aside while he drank his glass of porter, looked up to find it gone. Talbot, from a window, had seen the violin, slipped in, snatched it up, and walked out with it. Old Isaac would give him a few bob on it. Many's the time he had pawned his boots with Isaac and walked home in his stocking feet.

> I hocked it with Ol' Isaac and then I started to drink it up. I bought drinks for the whole shebang. I was the toast of Biddy Murphy's "blind pig," all right. But I kept out one shilling. Why?
>
> I have to have a drink. I can't stand this. This is the worst I've ever been. I can't stand it one night, can't I? You big lug, you can't. Where will I get one shilling? Even a tripenny bit? I'll get up and go to Barney's, he'll trust me. No, I tried Barney last week. Sloan's? No more trust, he told me. Biddy Murphy's again? No, I don't like the way she looks at me. I have not come to that, yet.
>
> Not a barkeep will give me credit. I've sunk low, all right. Ma ought to have a few pence in her purse. Ah, now I'm thinking of stealing from my mother and I have not given her a shilling in an age. Maybe she'll loan me a shilling. I've done that before and I'll do it again. I'm her son, ain't I? But I don't want her to see me like this.

Talbot got up from bed and started walking. He walked for hours, staggering from fatigue, not from whiskey. It was a long, long night. At daybreak he came home. His mother fed him and he went off to the brickyard.

A day and a night without drink and Talbot had the shakes so bad he couldn't stack a brick at Maher's. Red Maher curtly told him to go home, as the second stack tumbled and raised a cloud of dust. Once more he scurried home, shaking like a man with the palsy or the ague. The thoughts that he had kept at bay by work, came unbidden as he headed home.

> Maybe Casey will buy me a drink? Many the one I bought for him. No, he turned on me last week. Haggerty? Finley? Gaffigan? They all said they had no pity on me anymore. Pity? God knows I need it now. My uncle Ned? Shall I try Pap once more, that righteous man? Or I'll get Phil, who has looked after me so often. Nah, soon, I'll make him as bad as myself. My little sister, Mary, who'd buy me shoes or books but no whiskey? No, I can't ask her.

At home, he pushed wordlessly by his mother, who wept at the sight of him. Stretched out on his bed, he couldn't sleep or lie still. He tossed and turned, trying to blot out the thoughts of a glass of porter or anything wet. For hours, the inner battle went on, hours of torture, hours of twisting pain, of agony. One by one, the brothers in whose room he slept, came in, looked quizzically at him, shrugged shoulders, said their night prayers and turned in.

Shortly, he got up and walked outside in the cool night air. He walked along Gardiner Street to O'Connell, to Nassau, to the gray walls of Trinity College. And the thoughts came.

> Maybe I can walk this off, if I stay out of the lights of the pubs and the sight of them. I'll hide in the shadows of the wall. Will I ever stop shaking? And this head of mine, will it stop pounding? My belly is crawling. Why did this suddenly come on me? I've been no bargain over the years. Why, now? God help me. That sounded as if I was prayin'. I've blasphemed but I have not prayed for a long time.

Maybe God is watching me now. What would He be saying if He talked to His Blessed Mother about me? He'd say, "Talbot stole a fiddle from a poor man, who used it to make a livin'. And he sold it to buy drink. And he's never given his mother more than a shilling a week since he went to work. He's a poor creature of a man," He'd say.

But He'd also say, for the Christian Brothers taught us that He had Mercy, that I am one of *His* children and He wouldn't turn His face away from me.

Would You say that, Lord? Can I talk to You, God? Will You help me, Lord? If I try to keep the pledge, will You help me, Lord? If You help me, Jesus, I'll try. I'll try. I'll try.

Let me get through this night and I'll take the pledge in the morning and I'll go to confession and the Sacraments. Jesus, Mary and Joseph, help me. Jesus, Mary and Joseph! That's the first time I've said that in a long time.

He slept. Next morning, Father Nevin gave him the "Pledge," with pity and compassion in his eyes, but without comment, forbearing a sermon. But he wondered, "Will Talbot last out even the day?" Talbot did.

Would confession and Communion be stretching it too far? I'm no great shakes as a Catholic, but should I go to the rail with a taste like the inside of Houlihan's boot in my mouth, for the lack of a drink? Huh, I made a joke. That's the first one in two days. But am I worthy? Is that my conscience saying that, or the Devil? I've begun remembering some more of the things the Brothers told us. There must be a devil to make us do the things they do.

I can't go to the altar today. I'll go tomorrow. I'll try. I'll try tomorrow. But, if I wait, I might take a drink. I'll go today and maybe Jesus will understand. I'll try.

He did, although he had to make three attempts, in three different churches. And he shook and he sweated from the effort of avoiding a public house; and his guts twisted, but he held to his pledge. Another day. Another week, and he was going to Mass and Communion daily.

September, 1884. Three months he had kept the pledge. But the craving was still with him. He had stopped smoking the dark tobacco because it made him thirsty and he needed nothing to whet his drinking appetite. Also, the pennies could be used to pay off debts of long standing. He has lost eight of the 128 pounds which covered his small frame. He was still not eating, and his mother, that loving soul, worried for fear his new-found moral strength threaten his physical body. A change had come over him, too. The happy, carefree man of drink, the party man, the "proper bowsie" was a somber introvert. More and more time he spent in the churches: St. Francis Xavier's, St. Laurence O'Toole's, the Pro-cathedral, St. Saviour's. He knew the Augustinians, the Jesuits, the Dominicans. But the craving never left him The daily battles went on and on and on.

> Dear God, I am trying, trying hard. I will take the pledge for three more months. I have paid off thirty-nine shillings of debt. I have given my mother twelve shillings a week. But I never found the fiddler and I got the fiddle back from Old Isaac. I wish I could get rid of it. It reminds me of that night. I try to forget it, but I can't.

June, 1886. It was two years since "that night." Talbot had kept the pledge, although it meant a daily battle of his will and his thirst. He had worked out a prayer to the Blessed Virgin which gave him great solace. He went to Mass daily, at 5:30 A.M. It had become a daily necessity.

For months now, he never once had deviated from the practice of hurrying home, eating a pitiful meal of vegetables or a few potatoes, washed down with weak tea or weaker cocoa, and going to his room. Fearing a fall from grace, he prayed from 6:30 P.M. to 10:30 P.M., on his knees. After a few hours sleep on a wooden plank placed above his already hard pallet, he would arise, often at 2 A.M., and pray, prostrate, until it was time to go to Mass. Then home for a bit of dry bread and a cup of tea and off to the hod of mortar or bricks. The hod felt like a yoke, but a welcome yoke. He had learned to accept pain and adversity, rain, fog, or hard frost. The lack of sleep made his feet drag and his eyes droop in the early days, but the penance he forced on himself, a limit even of sleep, became an inescapable part of the saintly round into which life had turned. Later, he could not sleep more than three hours, even if he tried.

And he became intolerant, too, but only because he feared for himself.

> When I drank, so did my brothers. Now, I can't stand to see anyone swill it. They have a right, I know. It's there for the taking and it's good for some, but not for me. How can I tell Phil and Joe and John to stay away from the drink? When they come near me and I can smell it on them—I must pray for them and for myself. Blessed Virgin, give me strength to do the will of God.
>
> My beloved sister, Mary, thinks I'm daft, I know. She found the planks on my bed and wonders why I sleep on them. Must I tell her that I must do penance? Am I going out of my head that pain takes the place of drink? No, that can't be it. Even one as stupid as I knows that the pain should drive me to drink, if I hadn't God's help. I must leave this house for the good of all, mother, brothers and sisters. I'll look for a room tomorrow.

He did move from his parents' home and took a small room on nearby Gloucester Street. He moved back home for a time, but, after the death of his father, he and his mother moved to poor lodgings on Upper Rutland Street. For the first time in his life, he voluntarily changed jobs. Better to be able to attend early Mass, he took a laboring job in a lumberyard on the River Liffey.

There was another important thing. He learned to read fluently. Almost like a miracle (maybe it was) he began to be able to make out the meaning of the words, and their sense. He started on the church papers, on a missal given him by a Jesuit confessor, and on religious pamphlets. One of the first was *Leaves from St. Augustine*.

> Tolle lege. Sounds like Gaelic but Father Nevin says it is the Latin for "take up and read." That's what St. Augustine wants us to do. Take up and read. Take up and read. Help me, Blessed Mother, to read. I can pray but I cannot understand all that the books say. I can pray for the tipplers like myself and I can pray for all the working people. But I want to know more so that I can pray more. Give me help, Jesus.

The books began to multiply. One, two, four, six, in broken bindings. In paper covers. Some without covers. Then there came the *Secret of Mary* and, later, *Treatise on the True Devotion to the Blessed Virgin*, both by St. Louis Marie de Montford. From these, apparently, he developed his strong devotion to the Blessed Virgin. Too, he apparently took from these beautiful books another penance, revealed in his death, of his practice of wearing chains, around his waist, his arms, and below one knee. When they rusted, they were changed for new. The chain on his knee scourged his flesh as he knelt, hour after hour, day after day.

A phrase in a book impressed him, and he often spoke of it. It was: "The Kingdom of Heaven was promised not to the sensible and the educated but to such as have the spirit of little children." He hoped that this applied to himself and he prayed to the Sacred Heart, to make it so.

As the years passed, there were dark and unhappy days for Ireland. Talbot went on strike with his fellows and staunchly defended them but did not picket. He supported the 1916 uprising and the Civil War but did not carry a gun. He prayed for the dead and wounded, the widows and orphans, of that bloody time.

Little notice of him was taken, except by those who saw him lift his bowler hat and pray softly at the first hint of blasphemy, or when the Angelus sounded, or by those who saw him kneel on the hard steps outside the churches before Mass, or by those who pitied him because the knees were slit in his worn trousers. To his neighbors, he was Matt Talbot, that odd little man who bothered no one and prayed for all.

But when he fell dead one Trinity Sunday morning, in little Granby Lane near St. Saviour's Church, his sanctity came to light. Then they remembered his way of life and the things he had said, and before long Granby Lane became a sort of shrine and the Sodality raised a cross over his grave in Glasnevin Cemetery, so that it wouldn't be lost, as so many others had.

They said that Talbot was a lay apostle, perhaps the greatest of modern times. But that will wait. His cause has been taken up by the Church. The body was exhumed in 1952 and reinterred in a new coffin.

The papal decree posted in Ireland says in part: "May God grant that the example of this Servant of God may preserve workmen from the teachings of those who are trying to upset the social order."

And the carving over his new tomb calls him, too, "The Servant of God, Matthew Talbot."

WASHINGTON IRVING

THE ARICKARA INDIANS*

THE WEALTH of an Indian of the far west consists principally in his horses, of which each chief and warrior possesses a great number, so that the plains about an Indian village or encampment are covered with them. These form objects of traffic, or objects of depredation, and in this way pass from tribe to tribe over great tracts of country. The horses owned by the Arickaras are, for the most part, of the wild stock of the prairies; some, however, had been obtained from the Poncas, Pawnees, and other tribes to the southwest, who had stolen them from the Spaniards in the course of horse-stealing expeditions into the Mexican territories. These were to be known by being branded, a Spanish mode of marking horses not practiced by the Indians.

As the Arickaras were meditating another expedition against their enemies the Sioux, the articles of traffic most in demand were guns, tomahawks, scalping-knives, powder, ball, and other munitions of war. The price of a horse, as regulated by the chiefs, was commonly ten dollars' worth of goods at first cost. To supply the demand thus suddenly created, parties of young men and braves had sallied forth on expeditions to steal horses; a species of service among the Indians which takes precedence of hunting, and is considered a department of honorable warfare.

While the leaders of the expedition were actively engaged in preparing for the approaching journey, those who had accompanied it for curiosity or amusement found ample matter for observation in the village and its inhabitants. Wherever they went they were kindly entertained. If they entered a lodge, the buffalo robe was spread before the fire for them to sit down; the pipe was brought, and while the master of the lodge conversed with his guests, the squaw put the earthen vessel over the fire, well filled with dried buffalo meat and pounded corn; for the Indian in his native state, before he has mingled much with white men, and acquired their sordid habits, has the hospitality of the Arab: never does a stranger enter his door without having food placed before him; and never is the food thus furnished made a matter of traffic.

The life of an Indian when at home in his village is a life of indolence and amusement. To the woman is consigned the labors of the household and the field; she arranges the lodge; brings wood for the fire; cooks; dresses the skins of the animals killed in the chase; cultivates the little patch of maize, pumpkins, and pulse, which furnishes a great part of their provisions. Their time for repose and recreation is at sunset, when, the labors of the day being ended, they gather together to amuse themselves with petty games, or hold gossiping convocations on the tops of their lodges.

As to the Indian, he is a game animal, not to be degraded by useful or menial toil. It is enough that he exposes himself to the hardships of the chase

* Reprinted from *Astoria*, 1836.

and the perils of war; that he brings home food for his family, and watches and fights for its protection. Everything else is beneath his attention. When at home he attends only to his weapons and his horses, preparing the means of future exploit. Or he engages with his comrades in games of dexterity, agility, and strength; or in gambling games in which everything is put at hazard, with a recklessness seldom witnessed in civilized life.

A great part of the idle leisure of the Indians when at home is passed in groups, squatted together on the bank of a river, on the top of a mound on the prairie, or on the roof of one of their earth-covered lodges, talking over the news of the day, the affairs of the tribe, the events and exploits of their last hunting or fighting expedition; or listening to the stories of old times told by some veteran chronicler; resembling a group of our village quidnuncs and politicians, listening to the prosings of some superannuated oracle or discussing the contents of an ancient newspaper.

As to the Indian women, they are far from complaining of their lot. On the contrary, they would despise their husbands could they stoop to any menial office, and would think it conveyed an imputation upon their own conduct. It is the worst insult one virago can cast upon another in a moment of altercation. "Infamous woman!" will she cry, "I have seen your husband carrying wood into his lodge to make the fire. Where was his squaw that he should be obliged to make a woman of himself?"

Mr. Hunt and his fellow-travelers had not been many days at the Arickara village when rumors began to circulate that the Sioux had followed them up, and that a war party, four or five hundred in number, were lurking somewhere in the neighborhood. These rumors produced much embarrassment in the camp. The white hunters were deterred from venturing forth in quest of game, neither did the leaders think it proper to expose them to such risk. The Arickaras, too, who had suffered greatly in their wars with this cruel and ferocious tribe, were roused to increased vigilance, and stationed mounted scouts upon the neighboring hills. This, however, is a general precaution among the tribes of the prairies. Those immense plains present a horizon like the ocean, so that any object of importance can be descried afar, and information communicated to a great distance. The scouts are stationed on the hills, therefore, to look out both for game and for enemies, and are, in a manner, living telegraphs conveying their intelligence by concerted signs. If they wish to give notice of a herd of buffalo in the plain beyond, they gallop backward and forward abreast, on the summit of the hill. If they perceive an enemy at hand, they gallop to and fro, crossing each other; at sight of which the whole village flies to arms.

Such an alarm was given in the afternoon of the 15th. Four scouts were seen crossing and recrossing each other at full gallop, on the summit of a hill about two miles distant down the river. The cry was up that the Sioux were coming. In an instant the village was in an uproar. Men, women, and children were all brawling and shouting; dogs barking, yelping, and howling. Some of the warriors ran for the horses to gather and drive them in from the prairie, some for their weapons. As fast as they could arm and equip they sallied forth; some on horseback, some on foot. Some hastily arrayed in their war dress, with coronets of fluttering feathers, and their bodies smeared with paint; others naked and only furnished with the weapons they had snatched up. The women and children gathered on the tops of the lodges and heightened the confusion of the scene by their vociferation. Old men who could no longer bear arms took similar stations, and harangued the warriors as they passed, exhorting them to valorous deeds. Some of the veterans took arms themselves and sallied forth with tottering steps. In this way, the savage chivalry of the village, to the number of five hundred, poured forth, helter-skelter, riding and running, with hideous yells and war-whoops, like so many bedlamites or demoniacs let loose.

After a while the tide of war rolled back, but with far less uproar. Either it had been a false alarm, or the enemy had retreated on finding themselves discovered, and quiet was restored to the village. The white hunters continuing to be fearful of ranging this dangerous neighborhood, fresh provisions began to be scarce in the camp. As a substitute, therefore, for venison and buffalo meat, the travelers had to purchase a number of dogs to be shot and cooked for the supply of the camp. Fortunately, however chary the Indians might be of their horses, they were liberal of their dogs. In fact, these animals swarm about an Indian village as they do about a Turkish town. Not a family but has two or three dozen belonging to it of all sizes and colors; some, of a superior breed, are used for hunting; others, to draw the sledge, while others, of a mongrel breed, and idle vagabond nature, are fattened for food. They are supposed to be descended from the wolf, and retain something of his savage but cowardly temper, howling rather than barking; showing their teeth and snarling on the slightest provocation, but sneaking away on the least attack.

The excitement of the village continued from day to day. On the day following the alarm just mentioned, several parties arrived from different directions, and were met and conducted by some of the braves to the council lodge, where they reported the events and success of their expeditions, whether of war or hunting; which news was afterward promulgated throughout the village, by certain old men who acted as heralds or town criers. Among the parties which arrived was one that had been among the Snake nation stealing horses, and returned crowned with success. As they passed in triumph through the village they were cheered by the men, women, and children, collected as usual on the tops of the lodges, and were exhorted by the Nestors of the village to be generous in their dealings with the white men.

The evening was spent in feasting and rejoicing among the relations of the successful warriors; but sounds of grief and wailing were heard from the hills adjacent to the village: the lamentations of women who had lost some relative in the foray.

An Indian village is subject to continual agitations and excitements. The next day arrived a deputation of braves from the Cheyenne or Shienne nation;

a broken tribe, cut up, like the Arickaras, by wars with the Sioux, and driven to take refuge among the Black Hills, near the sources of the Cheyenne River, from which they derive their name. One of these deputies was magnificently arrayed in a buffalo robe, on which various figures were fancifully embroidered with split quills dyed red and yellow; and the whole was fringed with the slender hoofs of young fawns, that rattled as he walked.

The arrival of this deputation was the signal for another of those ceremonials which occupy so much of Indian life; for no being is more courtly and punctilious, and more observing of etiquette and formality than an American savage.

The object of the deputation was to give notice of an intended visit of the Shienne (or Cheyenne) tribe to the Arickara village in the course of fifteen days. To this visit Mr. Hunt looked forward, to procure additional horses for his journey; all his bargaining being ineffectual in obtaining a sufficient supply from the Arickaras. Indeed nothing could prevail upon the latter to part with their prime horses, which had been trained to buffalo hunting.

* * * * *

On the 9th of July, just before daybreak, a great noise and vociferation was heard in the village. This being the usual Indian hour of attack and surprise, and the Sioux being known to be in the neighborhood, the camp was instantly on the alert. As the day broke Indians were descried in considerable number on the bluffs, three or four miles down the river. The noise and agitation in the village continued. The tops of the lodges were crowded with the inhabitants, all earnestly looking toward the hills, and keeping up a vehement chattering. Presently an Indian warrior galloped past the camp toward the village, and in a little while the legions began to pour forth.

The truth of the matter was now ascertained. The Indians upon the distant hills were three hundred Arickara braves returning from a foray. They had met the war party of Sioux who had been so long hovering about the neighborhood, had fought them the day before, killed several, and defeated the rest with the loss of but two or three of their own men and about a dozen wounded; and they were now halting at a distance until their comrades in the village should come forth to meet them, and swell the parade of their triumphal entry. The warrior who had galloped past the camp was the leader of the party hastening home to give tidings of his victory.

Preparations were now made for this great martial ceremony. All the finery and equipments of the warriors were sent forth to them, that they might appear to the greatest advantage. Those, too, who had remained at home, tasked their wardrobes and toilets to do honor to the procession.

* * * * *

It was near noon that a mingled sound of voices and rude music, faintly heard from a distance, gave notice that the procession was on the march.

The old men and such of the squaws as could leave their employments hastened forth to meet it. In a little while it emerged from behind a hill, and had a wild and picturesque appearance as it came moving over the summit in measured step and to the cadence of songs and savage instruments; the warlike standards and trophies flaunting aloft, and the feathers, and paint, and silver ornaments of the warriors glaring and glittering in the sunshine.

The pageant had really something chivalrous in its arrangement. The Arickaras are divided into several bands, each bearing the name of some animal or bird, as the buffalo, the bear, the dog, the pheasant. The present party consisted of four of these bands, one of which was the dog, the most esteemed in war, being composed of young men under thirty, and noted for prowess. It is engaged on the most desperate occasions. The bands marched in separate bodies under their several leaders. The warriors on foot came first, in platoons of ten or twelve abreast; then the horsemen. Each band bore as an ensign a spear or bow decorated with beads, porcupine quills, and painted feathers. Each bore its trophies of scalps, elevated on poles, their long black locks streaming in the wind. Each was accompanied by its rude music and minstrelsy. In this way the procession extended nearly a quarter of a mile. The warriors were variously armed, some few with guns, others with bows and arrows, and war clubs; all had shields of buffalo hide, a kind of defense generally used by the Indians of the open prairies, who have not the covert of trees and forests to protect them. They were painted in the most savage style. Some had the stamp of a red hand across their mouths, a sign that they had drunk the life-blood of a foe!

As they drew near to the village the old men and the women began to meet them, and now a scene ensued that proved the fallacy of the old fable of Indian apathy and stoicism. Parents and children, husbands and wives, brothers and sisters met with the most rapturous expressions of joy; while wailings and lamentations were heard from the relatives of the killed and wounded. The procession, however, continued on with slow and measured step, in cadence to the solemn chant, and the warriors maintained their fixed and stern demeanor.

Between two of the principal chiefs rode a young warrior who had distinguished himself in the battle. He was severely wounded, so as with difficulty to keep on his horse; but he preserved a serene and steadfast countenance, as if perfectly unharmed. His mother had heard of his condition. She broke through the throng, and rushing up, threw her arms around him and wept aloud. He kept up the spirit and demeanor of a warrior to the last, but expired shortly after he had reached his home.

The village was now a scene of the utmost festivity and triumph. The banner, and trophies, and scalps, and painted shields were elevated on poles near the lodges. There were war feasts and scalp dances, with warlike songs and savage music; all the inhabitants were arrayed in their festal dresses; while the old heralds went round from lodge to lodge, promulgating with loud voices the events of the battle and the exploits of the various warriors.

Such was the boisterous revelry of the village; but sounds of another kind were heard on the surrounding hills; piteous wailings of the women, who had retired thither to mourn in darkness and solitude for those who had fallen in battle. There the poor mother of the youthful warrior who had returned home in triumph but to die, gave full vent to the anguish of a mother's heart. How much does this custom among the Indian women of repairing to the hill-tops in the night, and pouring forth their wailing for the dead, call to mind the beautiful and affecting passage of Scripture, "In Rama was there a voice heard, lamentation, and weeping, and great mourning, Rachel weeping for her children, and would not be comforted, because they are not."

MOGENS LIND

WE DANES*

Our Culture

THE DANES display a possibly surprising conviction that they are a thoroughly civilized nation. The reasons for this must be that most of them speak foreign languages more or less badly, that many of them have read *Hamlet*, that they are all endowed with an infinite curiosity (which, as we know, can lead to wisdom or to dangerous adventures), and that they each and every one love romance—whether of the Hans Christian Andersen kind or of their own making.

They feel so closely bound up with Hans Christian Andersen's fairy tales—Thorvaldsen's statues—the East Asiatic Company—the Round Tower in Copenhagen—Roskilde Cathedral—Osterlars church on the island of Bornholm—Burmeister and Wain's ships—Professor Niels Bohr—and the Viking planes that they almost believe themselves to be the creators, inventors, builders, organisers, or in some way responsible for the whole lot. They seem to be on most intimate terms with Bishop Absalon, who put Copenhagen on the map in 1167; and they really genuinely regard themselves as related to Christian IV, who turned Copenhagen into a beautiful city, and to Christian X, who reigned during the period when it transformed itself from a provincial town into one of the world's great cities—in a small way.

Then, of course, it is a matter of no small pride that among the four million inhabitants of Denmark there are only two persons (some people contend there are double this number) who can neither read nor write. On the other hand, there are still two thousand Danes who have never written a book or a play or painted a picture, but this figure is steadily diminishing.

Denmark is stacked with Art, old and new. There are, for example, the

---

* Reprinted from the travel booklet *We Danes and You* by permission of the author and the Danish National Travel Office. This pamphlet was issued in 1954.

Pearls of Architecture distributed evenly over the countryside. Among these Pearls are our castles and manors. Nobody can afford to live in them today, but they are attractive all the same.

Night Falls on Denmark

How does one pass one's evening in Denmark?

You stay at home or you go out. In the country there are fields and parks or gardens for those whose fancy lives in an eternal spring. In town you can go down to the harbour and look at the ships and such like; you can go to the railway station to see who is arriving or departing; you can walk in the municipal park and listen to the music; you can visit the theatre or the cinema. In short, you behave as in all other towns in all other countries.

But there is one difference. From the middle of May until well into August, if you go out, it is into nights which hardly get dark. Light nights can have a dangerous effect on sensitive persons of both sexes.

In Copenhagen and the other large towns you can go to the theatre. If you understand Danish, you have a most enjoyable time. If you don't—well, there are always more visual shows or you will easily find a place to dance, eat Smorrebrod, and drink Danish Snaps, until it dawns on you either a) that you have drunk too much of the stuff, or b) that it is stronger than you thought. In practice it hardly matters whether you decide on a) or b) or both.

In Copenhagen you can go to the Royal Theatre for an opera or ballet or a classical play with which you are already familiar so that you can forgive the Danes for speaking Danish on their stage. But if you are in raptures about the summer, then there's Tivoli, which the Danes claim to be unique in Europe, doubtless because it is unique in Europe. Or you can go to Dyrehavsbakken with its merry-go-rounds and rollercoasters, spend a pleasant evening at a seaside hotel, or wander up to the Hermitage Lodge in the middle of the night in pursuit of a romantic feeling.

There is absolutely no reason for claiming that Denmark is more beautiful than any other country on a summer's evening; but the Danes say it is undoubtedly true, and the curious thing is that occasionally they convince foreigners of it too. An American once said that Miami and Waikiki were dreary compared with a summer's evening at Klampenborg, the Skaw, or Fano. Probably he had good grounds for this contention, but they are not on record.

Manners

Two words crop up a great deal in the Danish language. One is "I" and the other "Thank you". People say "Thank you" when they get their ticket in a bus or a train. They say "Thank you" when they are given their change.

When they buy anything in a shop they say "Thank you" at least three times. Variations of "Thank you" are "Many thanks", "Hearty thanks" and "A thousand thanks". The two latter are used more particularly if you really mean it.

When you are invited out to a Danish house you begin by saying "Thank you for inviting me"; go on to "Thank you for the food" when dinner is over; departing, you mutter "Thank you for this evening"; and at the next meeting rush out with "Thank-you-for-the-last-time-we-were-together".

These "thanks" are usually accompanied by a prolonged and hearty hand-shake, which must in any case be given on arrival, on departure, and after dinner or any kind of meal.

At parties guests are introduced to each other and shake hands all around. The hostess or the host or the guests themselves mumble their names indistinctly and nobody hears what is being said so the evening slips away in finding out who is who and who is married to whom. The sensible thing to do is to listen in the first place—or to ask the person to whom you have just been introduced to repeat his or her name. This will ensure more time for eating and other activities.

It is not unusual for ladies to stand up when they are introduced either to ladies or gentlemen. It is not unknown, however, for Danish men to continue to sit happily on their chairs when a lady comes into the room. This should not be set down hastily to mere rudeness. The man may have got hold of a good chair and be afraid of losing it to someone else. He may even be tired, or he may just not know any better. From which it will be seen that the Danes are not particularly polite or formal—although, kind hearts being more than coronets, it may perhaps be mentioned that they will cheerfully rush all over the town to do something for a visitor or drive him 20 miles into the country if he wants to see a memorial or an inn.

It is customary to bring a few flowers with you on being invited to a Danish home for the first time. An alternative is to send them beforehand with a card. It may be comforting to know that there is no compulsion about asking your host and hostess back within a week.

One need have no scruples about staying too long when asked out to dinner or for the evening. In many homes the host and hostess do not think the party has been a success if the guests leave before midnight or just after. This may have something to do with calling the evening meal "Middag".

It is always wise to bear in mind that the Danes often have an ironical way of expressing themselves. They say it's "wonderful weather" when it's pouring with rain; they hint delicately that it's "a trifle chilly" when it's stifling hot. They are also quite capable of being positively rude about each other's manners or appearance, and it is not an uncommon thing for them to tell their hosts with glee that the food is terrible. This kind of thing is not recommended to our guests—at any rate not until they are absolutely familiar with its use.

Odd Information

Going to bed in Denmark entails covering oneself with a "Dyne". This is a sort of cushion, rather bigger (as a rule) than oneself and stuffed with feathers. Those unaccustomed to a "Dyne" run the risk of the illusion—it is, we repeat, an illusion—that you are being attacked by it in the middle of the night. Unless you firmly remember this and quietly adjust it you will, inevitably, be forced to give battle to the monster.

It does not do to assume, as a matter of course, that one can get a room with a bath in the smaller Danish hotels. Many cautious visitors take a bath before setting out—and then rely on the sea.

Just after midnight it is general for Danes to break into English whether they can or not.

At parties Danes love making speeches for their guests, for each other, and for themselves. In spite of this, it is customary for the guests to reply in another speech. It doesn't matter in the least what is said, but it is pleasanter for everybody if the speech is short—unless the guest likes making speeches too, when it is just pleasanter for the others.

Women do not smoke in the streets in Denmark. They smoke everywhere else. Some smoke cheroots and cigars. This indicates nothing at all except that they like the cheroots and cigars better than cigarettes.

If Danes experience difficulty in making themselves understood by a foreigner they simply shout louder—just like the foreigner.

Children are nearly always present at table in Danish homes. Most of them take an unflagging part in the conversation, to the infinite delight of their proud parents and to other people's astonishment.

Copenhagen's night clubs are the cheapest in the world. You can order a sandwich and a glass of beer in the best of them—and let it end at that, if you like.

The official rate of tipping is 12½ per cent; but 15 per cent ensures better service, which is why many people give 17 per cent.

When drinking beer, wine, or spirits one says "Skaal" to one's companion. Nobody seems to know precisely why it should be "Skaal"; but it is friendly and, therefore, necessary.

For reasons unknown, an announcer is called a "Speaker" in Danish, a dinner jacket a "Smoking" and a cap a "Sixpence."

Fresh air is regarded with enthusiasm as very, very healthy. In railway carriages, however, it is not fresh air because it instantly becomes a draft.

Some people believe the streets are clean because the wind immediately blows away the dirt. They are mistaken. The streets are swept and washed every morning like all nice children. Some even say that the trees are combed! At any rate, they are trimmed!

The Danes have a pronounced sense of humor. It is so strong that it makes them laugh at things which are definitely not funny.

There are many dogs in Denmark—but very few Great Danes. To make the confusion complete we call them "Grand Danois."

Denmark was never intended to be inhabited in winter, but it is lovely in spring, summer and autumn.

A visitor from Florida once said that Copenhagen had two winters, a white one and a green one. That statement is a bit unjust.

The Danish national drink is beer. The Danish national weakness is another beer.

The Danes worship anything foreign and everything Danish.

WILLIAM MAKEPEACE THACKERAY

GOETHE IN HIS OLD AGE*†

LONDON, *April* 28, 1855.

DEAR LEWES,—I wish I had more to tell you regarding Weimar and Goethe. Five-and-twenty years ago, at least a score of young English lads used to live at Weimar for study, or sport, or society—all of which were to be had in the friendly little Saxon capital. The Grand Duke and Duchess received us with the kindliest hospitality. The Court was splendid, but yet most pleasant and homely. We were invited in our turns to dinners, balls, and assemblies there. Such young men as had a right appeared in uniforms, diplomatic and military. Some, I remember, invented gorgeous clothing—the kind old Hof-Marschall of those days, Monsieur de Spiegel (who had two of the most lovely daughters eyes ever looked on), being in nowise difficult as to the admission of these young Englanders. Of the winter nights we used to charter sedan-chairs, in which we were carried through the snow to those pleasant Court entertainments. I for my part had the good luck to purchase Schiller's sword, which formed a part of my Court costume, and still hangs in my study, and puts me in mind of days of youth the most kindly and delightful.

We knew the whole society of the little city, and but that the young ladies, one and all, spoke admirable English, we surely might have learned the very best German. The society met constantly. The ladies of the Court had their evenings. The theatre was open twice or thrice in the week, where we assembled, a large family party. Goethe had retired from the direction, but the great traditions remained still. The theatre was admirably conducted; and besides the excellent Weimar company, famous actors and singers from various parts of Germany performed "Gastrolle"‡ through the winter. In that winter I remember we had Ludwig Devrient in Shylock, "Hamlet," Falstaff, and the "Robbers;" and the beautiful Schröder in "Fidelio."

---

* Reprinted from *Essays and Reviews*, Thomas Nelson and Sons, 1909, London and New York.

† This letter was written by W. M. Thackeray in answer to a request from G. H. Lewes for some account of his recollections of Goethe. It is printed in Lewes's "Life of Goethe," p. 560.   ‡ What in England are called "starring engagements."

After three-and-twenty years' absence I passed a couple of summer days in the well-remembered place, and was fortunate enough to find some of the friends of my youth. Madame de Goethe was there, and received me and my daughters with the kindness of old days. We drank tea in the open air at the famous cottage in the Park,* which still belongs to the family, and has been so often inhabited by her illustrious father.

In 1831, though he had retired from the world, Goethe would nevertheless very kindly receive strangers. His daughter-in-law's tea-table was always spread for us. We passed hours after hours there, and night after night, with the pleasantest talk and music. We read over endless novels and poems in French, English, and German. My delight in those days was to make caricatures for children. I was touched to find that they were remembered, and some even kept until the present time; and very proud to be told, as a lad, that the great Goethe had looked at some of them.

He remained in his private apartments, where only a very few privileged persons were admitted; but he liked to know all that was happening, and interested himself about all strangers. Whenever a countenance struck his fancy, there was an artist settled in Weimar who made a portrait of it. Goethe had quite a gallery of heads, in black and white, taken by this painter. His house was all over pictures, drawings, casts, statues, and medals.

Of course I remember very well the perturbation of spirit with which, as a lad of nineteen, I received the long-expected intimation that the Herr Geheimrath would see me on such a morning. This notable audience took place in a little antechamber of his private apartments, covered all around with antique casts and bas-reliefs. He was habited in a long grey or drab redingote, with a white neckcloth and a red ribbon in his button-hole. He kept his hands behind his back, just as in Rauch's statuette. His complexion was very bright, clear, and rosy; his eyes extraordinarily dark,† piercing, and brilliant. I felt quite afraid before them, and recollect comparing them to the eyes of the hero of a certain romance called "Melmoth the Wanderer," which used to alarm us boys thirty years ago—eyes of an individual who had made a bargain with a Certain Person, and at an extreme old age retained these eyes in all their awful splendour. I fancy Goethe must have been still more handsome as an old man than even in the days of his youth. His voice was very rich and sweet. He asked me questions about myself, which I answered as best I could. I recollect I was at first astonished, and then somewhat relieved, when I found he spoke French with not a good accent.

Vidi tantum. I saw him but three times—once walking in the garden of his house in the *Frauenplan;* once going to step into his chariot on a sunshiny day, wearing a cap and a cloak with a red collar. He was caressing at the time a beautiful little golden-haired granddaughter, over whose sweet fair face the earth has long since closed too.

* The *Gartenhaus.*
† This must have been the effect of the position in which he sat with regard to the light. Goethe's eyes were dark brown, but not very dark.

Any of us who had books or magazines from England sent them to him, and he examined them eagerly. *Fraser's Magazine* had lately come out, and I remember he was interested in those admirable outline portraits which appeared for awhile in its pages. But there was one, a very ghastly caricature of Mr. Rogers, which, as Madame de Goethe told me, he shut up and put away from him angrily. "They would make me look like that," he said; though in truth I can fancy nothing more serene, majestic, and *healthy-*looking than the grand old Goethe.

Though his sun was setting, the sky round about was calm and bright, and that little Weimar illumined by it. In every one of those kind salons the talk was still of Art and Letters. The theatre, though possessing no very extraordinary actors, was still conducted with a noble intelligence and order. The actors read books, and were men of letters and gentlemen, holding a not unkindly relationship with the *Adel.** At Court the conversation was exceedingly friendly, simple, and polished. The Grand Duchess (the present Grand Duchess Dowager), a lady of very remarkable endowments, would kindly borrow our books from us, lend us her own, and graciously talk to us young men about our literary tastes and pursuits. In the respect paid by this Court to the Patriarch of letters, there was something ennobling, I think, alike to the subject and sovereign. With a five-and-twenty years' experience since those happy days of which I write, and an acquaintance with an immense variety of human kind, I think I have never seen a society more simple, charitable, courteous, gentlemanlike than that of the dear little Saxon city where the good Schiller and the great Goethe lived and lie buried.

Very sincerely yours,

W. M. THACKERAY.

JOHN T. WINTERICH

DR. ROSENBACH:

THE TYCOON OF RARE BOOKS†

Doctors of philosophy in chemistry, physics, and related areas of knowledge are doing very well for themselves these days, but only one American that I know of has ever parlayed a doctorate of philosophy in English literature into a fortune.

His name was Abraham Simon Wolf Rosenbach, and at the peak of his career that name was familiar to most of his fellow-countrymen (including, probably, a good many illiterates) and to much of the rest of the world. A London messenger boy of the 1920s, stopping to explore an outdoor book-bin, saw something to his taste and called to the proprietor within:

"How much?"

* The nobles.
† Reprinted from *Harper's Magazine* (March, 1956) by permission of the author.

"Four-pence," said the proprietor. The boy tossed the book back.

"Who do you think I am?" he yelled. "Dr. Rosenbach?"

For Dr. Rosenbach was the man who, more than any other in bibliophilic history, put rare books on the front page and kept them there. That he lined his well-tailored pockets abundantly in the process was beside the point—he helped line the pockets of other booksellers too, because you cannot advertise Jones' Gin without advertising all gin. He was the autocrat of the literary auction room, the czar of his highly specialized and esoteric calling. He lived a life of Lucullan luxury and Medicean splendor, and played Maecenas by stealth, nor blushed if word of his kindnesses got out—because word didn't get out unless he wanted it to, and when he did want it to, it got out big.

His beginnings were modest. His father, a Philadelphia cotton broker, had prospered during the Civil War, but by the time Abraham was born, in 1876, cotton was no longer king—out of a considerable family, Abraham was the only child to go to college. His mother was a sister of Moses Polock, a long-established Philadelphia bookseller, who greatly influenced the boy.

Young Rosenbach edited Central High School's magazine, *Argus*, during his senior year, and the issue for February 1894 enshrines his first appearance in print—a paper called "Bibliomania." The twig was bent. Seven months later he entered the University of Pennsylvania where his idol—a sort of stand-in for Uncle Moses, now nearing eighty—became Professor Felix E. Schelling, a dedicated and voluminous expositor of Elizabethan letters. Schelling probably suggested, and certainly endorsed, Rosenbach's choice of subject for his eventual doctoral thesis: "The Influence of Spanish Literature in the Elizabethan and Stuart Drama."

The thesis was a capable and, within its strict acreage, an important accomplishment. It offered evidence that a Spanish tragi-comedy called *Celestina*, first published not later than 1499, provided the impulse that produced the first non-morality English drama, *Calisto and Melibea*, published in London not later than 1536. The author of neither work has ever been identified. It is noteworthy, in view of Rosenbach's subsequent eminence in his chosen field, that each of these publications is known, in its earliest form, by a single copy.

In 1901 Rosenbach earned the right to put Dr. in front of his name. For two years he continued to serve as an assistant in the English department at Pennsylvania. Then in the summer of 1903 Uncle Moses died, naming his twenty-seven-year-old nephew administrator of his estate and willing him his remarkable collection of early American children's books. It was not exactly a case of taking over a business, for there was little business to take over. But there was an abundance of good will, and there was the memory of a good man who had led a good life in a good calling.

Two Philadelphians of substance, Clarence S. Bement and Joseph M. Fox, agreed to back Rosenbach. Bement, in fact, became a silent partner, and during the next few years fed not only money but his notable library into the Rosenbach establishment.

Rosenbach's modest Catalogue Number One, dated March 15, 1904, was a grab bag of miscellanies, 208 lots in all, at prices ranging from $1 to $750. The most expensive item was a Book of Hours in Latin and French—a manuscript on vellum, elaborately bound, which once belonged to Henry IV of France, he of Navarre, and Gabrielle d'Estrées. John Fleming, who acquired the Doctor's stock after his death, pointed to this entry recently and remarked: "We still have that, and the price is still $750."

When Rosenbach set up shop, Philadelphia had (as it still has) several wealthy collectors. The difficulty was that most of them were too old to make good disciples. Rosenbach's first important client who was also his junior was Harry Elkins Widener, then a Harvard undergraduate. Widener had already assembled a remarkable library, and as he had virtually unlimited funds at his disposal, his collection expanded rapidly under Rosenbach's inspired tutelage. In the spring of 1912 Widener was in London buying books. Among his purchases was a copy of the second (1598) edition of Bacon's *Essaies* (the first, of the previous year, is known by only six copies, all in institutional collections). As he was arranging to have his acquisitions shipped home, he said to his London agent:

"I think I'll take this little Bacon with me in my pocket, and if I'm shipwrecked it will go with me."

He sailed on the *Titanic*.

During the next few years, Rosenbach built up a sound business without attracting much attention outside his native city. He believed in Philadelphia as devoutly as he did in the influence of Spanish literature on the Elizabethan drama. Eventually he added a New York establishment, but it was always strictly a flag stop.

But even the Doctor had to admit that New York was the capital of the American book world, and that George D. Smith was first among American booksellers. Smith died suddenly in 1920 when the high-powered collectors of the country were at the flood tide of acquisitiveness. On the roster were names familiar beyond the confines of book nooks. Rosenbach knew who they were, and they knew who he was—they were doing business with him. If Smith had lived, the book world might have been jolted by just such a battle of the giants as used to shake Wall Street when the great railroad barons (some of them sound bookmen) threw down the gage of battle.

Rosenbach owed much of his early propulsion toward wealth and immortality to his friend and fellow-Philadelphian A. Edward Newton, who in 1918 published *The Amenities of Book-Collecting and Kindred Affections*. It was a $5 book in a day when you could buy a fat 500-page novel for $1.50. Price and subject matter considered, or even ignored, *The Amenities* sold handsomely, and eventually won the accolade of inclusion in the Modern Library, carrying to its readers, among much light-hearted zealotry, a full-page halftone of the Doctor and numerous laudatory passages, of which this was the first:

> The most scholarly bookseller in this country today is Dr. Rosenbach—"Rosy" as we who know him well call him. It was not his original intention to deal in rare books, but to become a professor of English, a calling for which few have a finer appreciation; but mere scholars abound. He must have felt that we collectors needed some one to guide our tastes and deplete our bank accounts. In both he is unequaled.

The decade of the twenties was the Doctor's harvest time. But he did not do badly in the thirties and forties, either. Eventually he maintained two bachelor establishments in Philadelphia, two in New York, and two at Corson's Inlet, New Jersey, where he also kept his 38-foot cabin-cruiser *First Folio* and his deep-sea fishing gear. These six *pieds-à-terre* were kept functioning by a staff of from fifteen to twenty servants. Breakfasting with his protégé John Fleming one morning, the Doctor hazarded the guess that the cup of coffee he was drinking had set him back around $25. Fleming got the idea that the Doctor thought it was well worth it.

His bachelorhood was nominal. He enjoyed the society of women, intellectual and otherwise, but he did not flaunt them as if they were choice items ripe for the shelving. No surviving evidence points to a frustrated romance in his youth; he was too busy being the bibliophile to play the philanderer. He numbered few booksellers among his intimates, but his special friends—Mitchell Kennerley, president of the Anderson Galleries in the great days, Christopher Morley, and Jo Davidson, among others—were far from unbookish.

The Doctor was in his element in the great sequence of auctions that followed the first world war. A book auction is like no other exchange of goods on earth. It has none of the frenetic informality of the barnyard vendue, none of the machine-gun briskness of the tobacco and fur markets. It is both decorous and businesslike. The lay spectator is likely to wonder where the bids are coming from, for here art conceals art. Dealer A is bidding as long as his pencil is behind his ear. Dealer B is bidding as long as his fingers clutch his lapel. Dealer C, an excitable sort, is bidding as long as his face continues to be suffused. The universally respected James F. Drake once sat beside his friend Walter Hill, dean of Chicago dealers, at a New York auction. Drake had his right arm across the back of Hill's chair. Hill was bidding vocally and vigorously. The hammer fell.

"Sold—Drake."

"How the devil—" began Hill, and stopped. Drake and the auctioneer were chuckling. Drake had been bidding by elevating his right thumb alongside Hill's right ear.

Rosenbach would have none of this coy semaphoring. His bids were visible and audible. Bidding made drama in the auction room, and the Doctor, who owed his doctorate to the drama, was all for it. Arthur Swann, who at eighty is Nestor of the New York auction world, remarked recently that Rosenbach would rather have bought a book at auction for $2,000 than by private treaty for $1,000. If a book on which Rosenbach was bidding reached a figure which he did not choose to exceed (a situation as rare as most of the things he went after), he would never retire gracefully from the field, or even ungracefully. With an imperious gesture he would have an attendant bring him the book. He would examine the binding searchingly, inspect the title-page, and then hand the book back with a shake of the head and a knowing smile. The feeblest-minded spectator could not miss the implication. It was as if the Doctor had turned and addressed the gathering:

"To think that an expert of my caliber just missed being taken in by this palpable and egregious cripple!"

Yet the biggest single deal the Doctor ever engineered was consummated quietly, undramatically, and expeditiously. Sometime in the 1920's, somewhere between the Rio Grande and Tierra del Fuego, the Doctor acquired a huge mass of manuscript material documenting the conquests of Cortés and Pizarro. Just where he picked up this trove, and exactly how much he paid for it, are details that have never been disclosed—the antiquarian book trade does not wear its ledgers on its sleeves. The impression persists, however, that the Doctor did not extend himself heavily in making the haul.

There was a curtain-raiser to the Cortés-Pizarro non-drama. In 1926 the copy of the Gutenberg Bible which for four and a half centuries had been the property of the Benedictine abbey at Melk, Austria, was put up for auction at the Anderson Galleries. Dinner jackets were numerous in a sell-out audience, a tribute not so much to the Scriptures in their first appearance in print as to the thumping sum they were likely to bring. The book trade enjoys making pools whenever a crown jewel is about to go on the block, and the most ambitious guess put down for the Melk Bible was $75,000.

The Doctor, of course, was among the dinner-jacketed. His stomach, with good capon lined, was invariably thrust well to the front in his own despite; to compensate for the bulge, he always drove his chest forward as well. The effect was much enhanced when the Doctor exposed a sea of stiff white shirt-bosom; the irreverent book trade used to allude to him, thus clad, as the Penguin. (Even when the Doctor wasn't wearing his penguin suit, he was a commanding figure. He always dressed conservatively, in dark clothes; he always wore a stiff white collar and rimless pince-nez. But the effect was not quite so 1910 as it may sound. Though he was only of average height, perhaps five feet nine or ten, and slightly heavier than his physician probably recommended, he seemed taller, and certainly heavier. But not when he moved, which was most of the time, for he was light and quick on his feet, alert in his gestures.)

The bidding on the Gutenberg Bible opened at $50,000—a ladies-first gesture to Belle da Costa Greene, director of the Pierpont Morgan Library (which already had two complete Gutenberg Bibles plus an Old Testament).

"May I have fifty-five?" inquired Tony Bade, the gentle-voiced auctioneer.

He got it from an expected quarter—Gabriel Wells. Wells, a subscription-book salesman who had become a big-time antiquarian dealer second only to Rosenbach, was known in the auction world as the Great Underbidder—and the underbidder is the darling of the salesroom. Rosenbach bid $56,000, Wells $56,500. The bidding progressed in small-change spurts of $500 and $1,000 to $83,000, at which point Wells dropped out. But it was not Rosenbach who bid $83,500. It was a new voice—the voice, recognized by few at the time, of W. Evarts Benjamin, a wealthy Episcopalian layman.

The audience quivered with ecstasy. The bidding continued to inch ahead. When Benjamin carried it to $100,000, the assemblage forgot its manners and broke into applause (clapping at a book auction is as indecorous as clapping during a rally at a national tennis championship match). Never before had a book reached so high a figure at auction. And the end was not yet. Dr. Rosenbach upped the figure to $100,500. The audience gasped. There were more inchings, until Benjamin reached $105,000. The Doctor added $1,000. The rest was silence.

A few days later it was announced that the Bible had been sold to Mrs. Edward S. Harkness—"at God knows what price," declared a *Fortune* writer six years later. The price was $116,600—cost plus the 10 per cent fee which the dealer customarily charges for executing an auction commission. Mrs. Harkness gave the Bible to Yale University.

(It should be noted, in passing, that twenty-one years later, on January 28, 1947, the Rosenbach Company broke its own record when it paid $151,000 at auction for the Prince-Crowninshield-Stevens-Brinley-Vanderbilt-Whitney copy of *The Whole Booke of Psalmes*, popularly known as *The Bay Psalm Book*, put in type at Cambridge, Massachusetts, in 1640—the first book printed in what became the United States. The Doctor, aging and unwell, was not present, and the sale was effected by his capable and well-schooled deputy, John Fleming. *The Bay Psalm Book* is now at Yale too, the gift of a band of bibliophilic alumni plus a University of Pennsylvania alumnus named A. S. W. Rosenbach, whose contribution to the kitty was around $40,000. That was not quite the way the Doctor had planned it, but that was the way it worked out.)

Acquisition of the Melk Bible put the Doctor closely *en rapport* with Mr. and Mrs. Edward S. Harkness. Mr. Harkness' *Who's Who in America* entry modestly limited his interests to directorships in eight railroads and membership in two sound New York clubs and the Presbyterian Church. This example of verbal economy did not blind the Doctor, or anybody else, to the fact that Edward S. Harkness was the son of an early Rockefeller partner and one of America's wealthiest citizens. And when the Doctor acquired the Cortés-Pizarro papers, the Harknesses were his number one prospect.

Both the Philadelphia and the New York Rosenbach establishments regularly closed on Columbus Day. But on October 11, 1928, the Doctor asked

John Fleming to help him out on the holiday. Mr. Harkness was coming in to look at the Cortés-Pizarro collection.

The Columbus Day dialogue was not tape-recorded, but as the Doctor played it back to Fleming a few minutes after Harkness' departure, the client had inspected the temptingly displayed documents (a Fleming creation) and listened courteously to the Doctor's lecture—the Ph.D. was at the gallop again. Then Mr. Harkness asked how much. The Doctor said $985,000. Mr. Harkness seemed mildly embarrassed. He could pay only half of that at the moment, he explained; would it be all right if the balance were split into three equal installments at two, four, and six months? It would.

By an inexcusable clerical inadvertence that was readily excused, the Rosenbach Company, on November 1, 1928, billed Edward S. Harkness for $492,500. At the Harkness office, too, ineptitude reared its ugly head, and a check for $492,500 went to the Rosenbach Company by return mail.

The Harkness Cortés-Pizarro collection is not at Yale. It is in the Library of Congress.

My own contacts with the Doctor were infrequent, casual, and invariably cordial, though my total outlay as a Rosenbach client was $17.50 (seven-tenths of a cup of coffee). When I first entered the Doctor's premises he was at 273 Madison Avenue, the New York outpost he had set up in 1920—an ornate old stone mansion which has long since vanished.

On this occasion, as always thereafter, I visited the shop only to see one of the Doctor's underlings. It was something like going to the big house to play with the coachman's boy. My host took me down into the vault. On a table stood a silver tray holding two glasses, a pitcher of water, a bucket of ice cubes, and a decanter of Scotch. The glasses were cloudy with the dew of recent use, and I wondered how many hundreds or even thousands of dollars had been built into the upset price of some coveted item on the strength of one highball.

Scotch was the Doctor's favorite drink; he took it as if it were wine. Those who knew him well ascribed his addiction, which grew stronger as he grew older, either to his basic shyness or to the almost filial awe which characterized his attitude toward his older brother Philip. Taken to task once for his affinity to Scotch, Rosenbach exclaimed: "What would I ever have done if I didn't drink?" Possibly he was right; certainly the Scotch did not slow him down until the weight of advancing years caught up with it.

Some years after the first excursion to the Doctor's establishment, I had a striking illustration of his offhand, but invariably bullish, pricing technique. His New York branch now occupied an imposing residence at 15 East 51st Street. My host—again an underling—led me past the cage containing the parrot Josephine and the thickly carpeted stairway to the second floor. The Doctor happened to be passing.

"Hello, there!" he called, extending his hand. "Glad to see you. How have you been? What are you working on now?"

I hastened to frame a bibliophilic answer; I was, I said, investigating the eccentricities of early printings of *The Ballad of Reading Gaol.*

"Splendid, splendid!" cried the Doctor. "I'm certain I have something that will help you. Miss Brown, will you bring me the Oscar Wilde folder, please?"

Miss Brown fetched the Wilde folder and put it on a table. The Doctor sat down and opened the folder. He began to study the contents, laying each examined document face down on the left side of the folder. The folder must have held half a hundred units—letters and manuscripts of varying length, all in Wilde's involute but oddly legible hand. Each unit was priced lightly in pencil in the upper right corner.

"These figures certainly have not been checked in some time," said the Doctor.

"Ridiculous," he muttered as he came to the fourth or fifth unit. (In defiance of all the etiquette manuals, I was looking squarely over his shoulder.) He picked up a pencil. The item under immediate view was marked $150. A flick of the pencil turned the 1 into a 4. The next lot was marked $300. A slightly more involved bit of penciling turned the 3 into an 8. A superb poetical manuscript bore a $750 tag. It was an elementary business to convert the 7 into a 2 and stick a 1 in front of it.

I tiptoed away, leaving the Doctor making money hand over fist.

He could raise prices, too, for purely disciplinary reasons. Once a client, glancing over the Doctor's shelves, saw a fine copy of the first Edinburgh (1787) edition of *Burns' Poems, Chiefly in the Scottish Dialect* marked $150.

"Isn't this a little high?" asked the client. He did not know it, but he had committed the sin against the Holy Ghost. The Doctor said nothing. The client made the circuit of the room, seeing nothing else that he wanted. At the end of half an hour, feeling, perhaps, as so many people do in bookshops, church bazaars, and one-man art shows that he really shouldn't leave without buying something, he went back to the Burns and took it off the shelf. Before saying "I'll take this" to the Doctor he glanced at the price again. It was now $250. The client reshelved the book and went away.

Toward his fellows in the antiquarian trade, the Doctor adopted the Borgias' blazon of "Caesar or nothing." "You train him for me and I'll take him over when he's educated," he would say to a lesser member of the brotherhood who had managed to collar a promising prospect. He had various ways of applying this principle. A dealer had a client who was heavily interested in a popular Victorian author. The Doctor had a magnificent star cluster of pertinent material, and both dealer and collector knew he had it. The collector, not wanting to go over the dealer's head, asked him to find out how much the Doctor wanted for it. The Doctor said $60,000. The dealer urged the collector to see what direct negotiation might accomplish. The Doctor was the soul of amiability, sweet reason, and large discounts. The collector could have the material for $35,000. He took it.

Another of the Doctor's artifices was to play down a book about which another dealer consulted him. A young bookseller once discovered an apparently unrecorded Franklin item. He spent several days consulting printed authority, discussed it with special librarians, and described it to Franklin collectors of unimpeachable omniscience. No one had ever heard of it. In his mental catalogue the young bookseller altered the description "apparently unrecorded" to "unrecorded and unique." (When a rare-bookseller says unique he means unique.)

Many dealers who made discoveries of this magnitude called on the Doctor, who had outlets far beyond the range of the lesser fry. They called on him even though they were well aware that every Rosenbach catalogue carried on the back cover the unequivocal warning of Proverbs xx, 14: "It is naught, it is naught, saith the buyer, but when he is gone his way, then he boasteth." (On several early catalogues the quotation had inaccurately read "hath gone," but some friend or enemy tipped the Doctor off.)

The young dealer who made the Franklin discovery consulted the Doctor. The Doctor inspected the find with what seemed to be unstudied indifference.

"An interesting piece," he pronounced. "And not common. Not at all common. I don't think I've handled a copy in over a year. The last one I had I sold to William Smith Mason of Chicago."

Burning a hole in the young bookseller's pocket was a letter from William Smith Mason declaring flatly that he had never heard of the item. It took all the bookseller's strength to withdraw the letter, unfold it, and lay it on the Doctor's desk. The Doctor read it without a quiver.

"Oh, yes," he said. "What I sold Mason was something similar to this." He described it in elaborate bibliographical detail. "But this lot you have here is extremely interesting. You won't have any trouble getting rid of it."

The dealer didn't have any trouble at all. And he also had the satisfaction—almost unique—of jockeying the Doctor into a position where the latter would have lost face if he had shown an eagerness to acquire the item.

Another young dealer once acquired a fine copy of Poe's *Tales of the Grotesque and Arabesque*, published at Philadelphia in two volumes in 1840. A well-to-do newcomer to the collecting scene was actively interested in it, though the asking price of $800 exceeded anything he had yet spent in one lump for a book.

"You're sure it's all right?" he asked the dealer. The dealer assured him that it was. The dealer was then, as he still is, knowledgeable, discriminating, and conscientious. But the new collector wanted a verdict from what he regarded as higher authority.

"How about letting Dr. Rosenbach take a look at it?" he suggested.

The dealer was not in a position to say "Take it or leave it." He expressed a willingness, if not quite an eagerness, to wait on the Doctor. The Doctor listened to the story, accepted the book, and took it to a window. He studied the title pages, riffled the gatherings, held the preliminary leaves up to the light. After several minutes of this elaborate expertizing, he handed down his decision:

"New end-papers."

A book published as recently as 1840 with new end-papers would have as high a degree of acceptance in the antiquarian market as a young lady with three eyes in a Miss America contest.

The dealer protested, but the Doctor refused to depontificate. Dealer and client went their way. Fortunately for their side, the story has a happy ending. The dealer persuaded the client to consult half a dozen other authorities, in and out of the trade. All of them said, without hesitation, that the original end-papers had not been tampered with.

I discussed the Doctor's attitude toward his brothers in the bond with an alert bookman on New York's Fourth Avenue, the heart of the American antiquarian book market.

"Look at it this way," he said. "I never had any dealings with Rosenbach. I'm above the battle, or below it, so I can be objective. This business still operates on a competitive basis, with all the advantages and disadvantages that such a situation implies. There are no supermarkets in the antiquarian field, thank God—no mergers, no cartels, no chains. With us it's literally every man for himself. Rosenbach, with ample means at his disposal and with the power those means supplied, could be for himself more effectively than the rest of us. He could afford a battleship, and we had to fight back with bows and arrows. If we could have afforded battleships, you can bet your life we'd have bought some."

But in the Doctor's neatly compartmented universe, scholars were accorded diametrically opposite treatment to booksellers. From the eager seeker after knowledge the Doctor demanded only the credentials of dedication to learning and a reasonably high IQ. The shelves of the Rosenbach Foundation in Philadelphia, endowed in perpetuity as a memorial to the Doctor and his older brother Philip (who was the firm's expert on furniture, *objets d'art*, and such), are lined not only with the world's great rarities but also with scores of literary studies inscribed to the Doctor by research students who were beneficiaries of his altruism. One example is typical.

Early in 1935, John D. Gordan, a Virginian who had recently got his A.B. at Harvard, enrolled in the graduate school with the aim of winning his doctorate with a dissertation on Joseph Conrad. Professor Hyder E. Rollins endorsed the project, but told Gordan he would have to consult several Conrad manuscripts which Rollins believed were available somewhere in America—he recalled reading about their sale at auction some years previously. He suggested that Gordan consult *American Book-Prices Current*, an annual publication giving the auction records of literary property, and then ask the auction house that had sold the manuscripts for the names of the buyers.

Gordan learned that in 1923 the manuscript of *Almayer's Folly* had sold for $5,300, of *Lord Jim* for $3,900, and of *The Nigger of the Narcissus* for $4,500. He wrote the Anderson Galleries in New York, where the sale had been made, and was informed that the purchaser of all three manuscripts had been Dr. A. S. W. Rosenbach. It is significant that while Gordan had never previously heard of *American Book-Prices Current* or the Anderson Galleries, he *had* heard of Dr. Rosenbach.

Easter vacation was approaching, and Gordan planned to drive to Virginia. He wrote to the Doctor in Philadelphia and asked if he might call on him on the way. The Doctor said yes.

The Doctor proved to be the essence of accommodation. It was arranged that Gordan should come to Philadelphia again at the end of the college year and devote his summer to a study of the manuscripts. The only evidence the Doctor had of Gordan's good faith and capability was his obvious earnestness and competence and the fact that his letter had been written on the letterhead of the Harvard English Department.

Just as Gordan was preparing for his Philadelphia sojourn he received an offer of an apartment in New York for the summer at five dollars a week. If he went to Philadelphia, his expenses would inevitably be much higher. He decided to lay the facts before the Doctor, and the Doctor agreed to have the manuscripts transferred to New York. (Gordan, today Dr. Gordan, curator of the Berg Collection at the New York Public Library, has no idea how the delivery was effected—probably by messenger, and the Doctor himself may well have been the messenger, clutching a pair of fat briefcases for the contents of which he had paid out $13,700.)

In mid-June Gordan reported at the New York office of the Rosenbach Company. He was given a desk and told he could make all the local telephone calls he wanted, but that he must restore the manuscripts to the vault at the end of the day's work. (Quite a ceremonial was made of this.) The Doctor, commuting over from Philadelphia, exchanged the time of day with him, but this was the extent of his attentions. It is worth noting that Gordan had consulted two New York dealers who had fragments of Conrad manuscript; each asked him if he was in a position to buy the material (a reasonable demand); when he said no, they placed it at his disposal. But Dr. Rosenbach did not ask that question.

Gordan read Conrad and filled notebooks until the end of August. When *Joseph Conrad: The Making of a Novelist* appeared over the imprint of Harvard University Press in 1940, it was dedicated "to all those who have made this book possible and especially to my wife, John Archer Gee [of Yale], Hyder E. Rollins, and A. S. W. Rosenbach."

Before Rosenbach's death in 1952, just three weeks short of his seventy-sixth birthday, he had become a doctor several times over—in 1927 the University of Pennsylvania added an honorary degree to the one he had earned there twenty-six years earlier—and had established the Rosenbach Fellowship in Bibliography "to bring to the University of Pennsylvania distinguished scholars in the field," an annual lecture series that has produced several important published studies.

Following the death of the Doctor and, eight months later, of his brother Philip, the name and corporate entity of the Rosenbach Company were

erased as quickly as due process of law could effect the annihilation. John
Fleming acquired the considerable stock that remained, and, with Inc. after
his name, is carrying on at the old company's third and final New York
address, 322 East 57th Street. His letterhead is permitted to declare that he
was "formerly associated with Dr. A. S. W. Rosenbach."

The Doctor's will left the bulk of his estate to the Rosenbach Foundation.
Cash bequests to friends, employees, charities, and religious organizations
totalled $122,500, and Philip and another brother, Moses, benefited by sub-
stantial annuities. Under the terms of the will, the value of the estate was not
to be made public, and it has not been—the executor, the Doctor's friend
Morris Wolf, said it was "large" and let it go at that.

Philadelphia newspaper and wire-service reports of the filing of the will
quoted the Doctor as having once estimated, presumably late in life, that
he had bought "more than $75,000,000 worth" of literary property since his
first purchase, at the age of eleven, of a not very early *Reynard the Fox* for
$24. If all of these transactions had been at auction (which they were not),
Rosenbach's commissions would have amounted to $7,500,000; on his non-
auction purchases he must have averaged much better than 10 per cent. In
both groups, too, were many treasures which went into his private collection,
now housed permanently in the Rosenbach Foundation. Some of his de-
tractors were wont to suggest that the Doctor's "private collection" was
made up of the things he was stuck with, but this was not true. Philadelphia
Central High School's ranking bibliomaniac remained a bibliomaniac to the
end.

HARRIET MARTINEAU

*MRS. WORDSWORTH**

THE LAST thing that would have occurred to Mrs. Wordsworth would have
been that her departure, or anything about her, would be publicly noticed
amidst the events of a stirring time. Those who knew her well, regarded
her with as true a homage as they ever rendered to any member of the
household, or to any personage of the remarkable group which will be for
ever traditionally associated with the Lake District: but this reverence,
genuine and hearty as it was, would not, in all eyes, be a sufficient reason for
recording more than the fact of her death. It is her survivorship of such a
group which constitutes an undisputed public interest in her decease. With
her closes a remarkable scene in the history of the literature of our century.
The well-known cottage, Mount, and garden at Rydal will be regarded
with other eyes, when shut up, or transferred to new occupants. With
Mrs. Wordsworth, an old world has passed away before the eyes of the

* Reprinted from *Biographical Sketches,* 1877.

inhabitants of the District, and a new one succeeds which may have its own delights, solemnities, honours, and graces, but which can never replace the familiar one that is gone. There was something mournful in the lingering of the aged lady—blind, deaf, and bereaved in her latter years; but *she* was not mournful, any more than she was insensible. Age did not blunt her feelings, nor deaden her interest in the events of the day. It seems not so very long ago that she said that the worst of living in such a place (as the Lake District) was its making one unwilling to go. It was too beautiful to let one be ready to leave it.

Within a few years, the beloved daughter was gone; and then the aged husband, and then the son-in-law; and then the devoted friend, Mr. Wordsworth's publisher, Mr. Moxon, who paid his duty occasionally by the side of her chair; then she became blind and deaf. Still her cheerfulness was indomitable. No doubt, she would in reality have been "willing to go" whenever called upon, throughout her long life; but she liked life to the end. By her disinterestedness of nature, by her fortitude of spirit, and her constitutional elasticity and activity, she was qualified for the honour of surviving her household—nursing and burying them, and bearing the bereavement which they were vicariously spared. She did it wisely, tenderly, bravely, and cheerfully, and she will be remembered accordingly by all who witnessed the spectacle.

It was by the accident (so to speak) of her early friendship with Wordsworth's sister that her life became involved with the poetic element, which her mind would hardly have sought for itself in another position. She was the incarnation of good sense, as applied to the concerns of the every-day world. In as far as her marriage and course of life tended to infuse a new elevation into her views of things, it was a blessing; and, on the other hand, in as far as it infected her with the spirit of exclusiveness which was the grand defect of the group in its own place, it was hurtful; but that very exclusiveness was less an evil than an amusement, after all. It was a rather serious matter to hear the Poet's denunciations of the railway, and to read his well-known sonnets on the desecration of the Lake region by the unhallowed presence of commonplace strangers; and it was truly painful to observe how the scornful and grudging mood spread among the young, who thought they were agreeing with Wordsworth in claiming the vales and lakes as a natural property for their enlightened selves. But it was so unlike Mrs. Wordsworth, with her kindly, cheery, generous turn, to say that a green field with buttercups would answer all the purposes of Lancashire operatives, and that they did not know what to do with themselves when they came among the mountains, that the innocent insolence could do no harm. It became a fixed sentiment when she alone survived to uphold it; and one demonstration of it amused the whole neighbourhood in a good-natured way. "People from Birthwaite" were the bugbear—Birthwaite being the end of the railway. Mrs. Wordsworth's companion told her (she being then blind) that there were some people in the garden . . . "Boys from

Birthwaite," said the old lady. . . . When the strangers were gone, it appeared that they were the Prince of Wales and his companions. Making allowance for prejudices, neither few nor small, but easily dissolved when reason and kindliness had opportunity to work, she was a truly wise woman, equal to all occasions of action, and supplying other persons' needs and deficiencies.

In the "Memoirs of Wordsworth" it is stated that she was the original of

"She was a phantom of delight,"

and some things in the next few pages look like it; but for the greater part of the Poet's life it was certainly believed by some who ought to know that that wonderful description related to another, who flitted before his imagination in earlier days than those in which he discovered the aptitude of Mary Hutchinson to his own needs. The last stanza is very like her; and her husband's sonnet to the painter of her portrait in old age discloses to us how the first stanza might be so also, in days beyond the ken of the existing generation. Of her early sorrows, in the loss of two children and a beloved sister who was domesticated with the family, there are probably no living witnesses. It will never be forgotten by any who saw it how the late dreary train of afflictions was met. For many years Wordsworth's sister Dorothy was a melancholy charge. Mrs. Wordsworth was wont to warn any rash enthusiast for mountain walking by the spectacle before them. The adoring sister would never fail her brother; and she destroyed her health, and then her reason, by exhausting walks, and wrong remedies for the consequences. Forty miles in a day was not a singular feat of Dorothy's. During the long years of this devoted creature's helplessness she was tended with admirable cheerfulness and good sense. Thousands of Lake tourists must remember the locked garden gate when Miss Wordsworth was taking the air, and the garden chair going round and round the terrace, with the emaciated little woman in it, who occasionally called out to strangers, and amused them with her clever sayings. She outlived the beloved Dora, Wordsworth's only surviving daughter. After the lingering illness of that daughter (Mrs. Quillinan), the mother encountered the dreariest portion, probably, of her life. Her aged husband used to spend the long winter evenings in grief and tears—week after week, month after month. Neither of them had eyes for reading. He could not be comforted. She, who carried as tender a maternal heart as ever beat, had to bear her own grief and his too. She grew whiter and smaller, so as to be greatly changed in a few months: but this was the only expression of what she endured, and he did not discover it. When he too left her, it was seen how disinterested had been her trouble. When his trouble had ceased, she too was relieved. She followed his coffin to the sacred corner of Grasmere churchyard, where lay now all those who had once made her home. She joined the household guests on their return from the funeral, and made tea as usual. And this was the disinterested spirit which carried her through the last few years, till she had just reached the ninetieth. Even then, she had strength to combat disease for many days. Several times she rallied and relapsed; and she was full of alacrity of mind and body as long as exertion of any kind was possible. There were many eager to render all duty and love—her two sons, nieces, and friends, and a whole sympathizing neighbourhood. . . .

Not one is left now of the eminent persons who rendered that cluster of valleys so eminent as it has been. Dr. Arnold went first, in the vigour of his years. Southey died at Keswick, and Hartley Coleridge on the margin of Rydal Lake; and the Quillinans under the shadow of Loughrigg; and Professor Wilson disappeared from Elleray; and the aged Mrs. Fletcher from Lancrigg; and the three venerable Wordsworths from Rydal Mount.

The survivor of all the rest had a heart and a memory for the solemn *last* of everything. She was the one to inquire of about the last eagle in the District, the last pair of ravens in any crest of rocks, the last old dalesman in any improved spot, the last round of the last pedlar among hills where the broad white road has succeeded the green bridle-path. She knew the District during the period between its first recognition, through Gray's "Letters," to its complete publicity in the age of railways. She saw, perhaps, the best of it. But she contributed to modernise and improve it, though the idea of doing so probably never occurred to her. There were great people before to give away Christmas bounties, and spoil their neighbours as the established almsgiving of the rich does spoil the labouring class, which ought to be above that kind of aid. Mrs. Wordsworth did infinitely more good in her own way, and without being aware of it. An example of comfortable thrift was a greater boon to the people round than money, clothes, meat, or fuel. The oldest residents have long borne witness that the homes of the neighbours have assumed a new character of order and comfort, and wholesome economy, since the Poet's family lived at Rydal Mount. It used to be a pleasant sight when Wordsworth was seen in the middle of a hedge, cutting switches for half-a-dozen children, who were pulling at his cloak, or gathering about his heels: and it will long be pleasant to family friends to hear how the young wives of half a century learned to make home comfortable by the example of the good housewife at the Mount, who was never above letting her thrift be known.

Finally, she who had noted so many last survivors was herself the last of a company more venerable than eagles, or ravens, or old-world yeomen, or antique customs. She would not in any case be the first forgotten. As it is, her honoured name will live for generations in the traditions of the valleys round. If she was studied as the Poet's wife, she came out so well from that investigation that she was contemplated for herself; and the image so received is her true monument. It will be better preserved in her old-fashioned neighbourhood than many monuments which make a greater show.

THEOPHRASTUS

*THE OSTENTATIOUS AND THE DISSEMBLER**

The Ostentatious

THE ABSURD vanity of the purse-proud man leads him to make as many false pretensions to wealth as the veriest knave who lives by seeming to be what he is not. A boaster of this sort frequents the Exchange; and, while he gathers strangers around him, talks of the rich cargos which he pretends to have on the seas: then he tells what loans he has abroad, and what is the amount of interest on them. Or you may see him stalking along the road, while he lolls on the arm of a chance companion, whom he informs that he was one of those who served in the expedition into Asia under Alexander; and that, in the spoil which fell to his share, there were many costly vessels studded with gems. This leads him to talk of eastern magnificence; and he stoutly contends that the artificers of Asia are incomparably superior to those of Europe. He pretends to have received letters from Antipater, stating that the victorious king had just returned to Macedonia. He declares, that although he possesses the costly license for exporting timber, he has forborne to make use of it, lest he should give occasion to the malicious remarks of some who would envy him his privilege. In a company of strangers he recounts, that during the late scarcity he expended more than five talents in corn, to be distributed among the poorer citizens; and doubting whether he may not have underrated the sum, he requests one of the company to assist him in going through a calculation, by making a list of those who were the objects of his munificence, and the relief afforded to each; when, pretending to name above six hundred persons, the result proves that, instead of five, he must actually have expended not less than ten talents on the occasion. Nor does he include in this computation the maintenance of his galleys, nor sundry disbursements consequent on the gratuitous discharge of public business. He goes to the stalls where the finest horses are exposed for sale, and pretends to bid for them: or, at the shop of the robe-maker, he requests a cloak to be shown to him of the value of two talents; and then takes occasion to reprove his attendant for not being furnished with gold. He lives in a hired house; yet he assures a visitor, ignorant of his affairs, that he inherited the house from his father; but that, finding it too small for the entertainment of his friends, he intends to sell it.

The Dissembler

Every word, and every action, of the Dissembler is an artifice by which he labors to conceal some evil intention. A man of this sort approaches his enemy with professions of friendship; he flatters those against whom he is secretly plotting mischief; and he condoles with them in the day of their

* Reprinted from *The Characters of Theophrastus* translated anonymously in 1836.

calamity: to one who has defamed him he proffers his forgiveness: he receives contumely with patience; or he soothes with blandishments those who resent the injuries they have sustained from his villainy.

The Dissembler, from mere habit, will evade any direct application that may be made to him: 'Call on me to-morrow,' says he, to one who seeks to converse with him on business that admits of no delay. To elude inquiry, he will pretend that he is but just returned from a journey; that he came home only last evening; or that he is too ill to attend to business. He never acknowledges that he has actually commenced an undertaking; but professes to be still deliberating on the affair. He tells those who would borrow money of him, or who demand the sum he has subscribed to a contribution, that he has not taken a sixpence of late: but when trade is dull, he boasts of his dealings. He feigns not to have attended to what he has heard: he professes not to have observed what passed before his eyes; and he takes care to forget his promises. He is fertile in evasions: now, he purposes to take an affair into consideration: now, he knows nothing of the business: he is amazed at what is told him: or it accords exactly with his own opinion. He makes himself remarkable by his frequent use of certain phrases; such as, 'I am fain to doubt it;'—'I don't take your meaning;'—'I'm vastly surprised:'—or, if it suits his purpose, he will say, 'I am not the man you take me for: no such thing has been said to me before: what you say is incredible.—Prithee find some one else to whom you may tell this tale: truly, I know not whether to think you or him the impostor.'

But beware thou of one who employs these artfully-woven and often-repeated phrases, which commonly serve to cloak the worst designs. A man in whose manners there is no simplicity, and whose every word seems to have been studied, is more to be shunned than a viper.

JOHN EARLE

THE YOUNG MAN OF THE UNIVERSITY*

Is one that comes there to wear a gown, and to say hereafter, he has been at the university. His father sent him hither because he heard there were the best fencing and dancing schools; from these he has his education, from his tutor the oversight. The first element of his knowledge is to be shown the colleges, and initiated in a tavern by the way, which hereafter he will learn of himself. The two marks of his seniority, is† the bare velvet of his gown, and his proficiency at tennis, where when he can once play a set,

---

* Reprinted from *A Book of Characters*, compiled by Richard Aldington. Published by George Routledge & Sons, Ltd., London, 1924.
† This use of *is* was not uncommon when Earle wrote in 1638. The lack of a uniform grammar was due to the continued use of local dialects in some of which the singular verb was used with the plural subject.

he is a freshman no more. His study has commonly handsome shelves, his books neat silk strings, which he shews to his father's man, and is loth to untie, or take down for fear of misplacing. Upon foul days for recreation he retires thither, and looks over the pretty books his tutor reads to him, which is commonly some short history, or a piece of Euphormio,* for which his tutor gives him money to spend the next day. His main loitering is at the library, where he studies arms and books of honour, and turns a gentleman critic in pedigrees. Of all things he endures not to be mistaken for a scholar, and hates a black suit though it be made of satin. His companion is ordinarily some stale fellow, that has been notorious for an ingle† to gold hatbands, whome he admires at first, afterwards scorns. If he have spirit or wit he may light of‡ better company, and may learn some flashes of wit, which may do him knight's service in the country hereafter. But he is now gone to the inns-of-court,§ where he studies to forget what he learned before, his acquaintance and the fashion.

JOSEPH HALL

THE TRUE FRIEND**

His affections are both united and divided: united, to him he loveth; divided, betwixt another and himself: and his own heart is so parted, that, while he hath some, his friend hath all. His choice is led by virtue, or, by the best of virtues, religion; not by gain, not by pleasure: yet not without respect of equal condition, of disposition not unlike: which, once made, admits of no change; except he, whom he loveth, be changed quite from himself; nor that suddenly, but after long expectation. Extremity doth but fasten him; while, he, like a well-wrought vault, lies the stronger, by how much more weight he bears. When necessity calls him to it, he can be a servant to his equal, with the same will wherewith he can command his inferior; and, though he rise to honour, forgets not his familiarity, nor suffers inequality of estate to work strangeness of countenance: on the other side, he lifts up his friend to advancement with a willing hand; without envy, without dissimulation. When his mate is dead, he counts himself but half alive: then his love, not dissolved by death, derives itself to those orphans, which never knew the price of their father: they become the heirs of his affection and the burden of his cares. He embraces a free community of all

* A general reference to fiction. Euphormio is a character in John Barclay's *Euphormionis Satyricon*, a satirical novel written in Latin.
† An *ingle* was a companion; gold hatbands were ornaments worn by young nobles as indication of their social rank.
‡ The English Dialect Dictionary defines *light of* as meet with or find.
§ *Inns-of-court* were law schools.
** Reprinted from *A Book of Characters*, compiled by Richard Aldington. Published by George Routledge & Sons, Ltd., London, 1924.

things; save those, which either honesty reserves proper, or nature: and hates to enjoy that, which would do his friend more good. His charity serves to cloak noted infirmities; not by untruth, not by flattery; but by discreet secrecy: neither is he more favourable in concealment, than round in his private reprehensions; and, when another's simple fidelity shews itself in his reproof, he loves his monitor so much the more, by how much more he smarteth. His bosom is his friend's closet, where he may safely lay up his complaints, his doubts, his cares: and look, how he leaves, so he finds them; save for some addition of seasonable counsel for redress. If some unhappy suggestion shall either disjoint his affection or break it, it soon knits again; and grows the stronger, by that stress. He is so sensible of another's injuries, that, when his friend is stricken, he cries out, and equally smarteth untouched; as one affected, not with sympathy, but with a real feeling of pain: and, in what mischief may be prevented, he interposeth his aid; and offers to redeem his friend, with himself: no hour can be unseasonable, no business difficult, nor pain grievous, in condition of his ease; and what either he doth or suffereth, he neither cares nor desires to have known, lest he should seem to look for thanks. If he can, therefore, steal the performance of a good office unseen, the conscience of his faithfulness herein is so much sweeter, as it is more secret. In favours done, his memory is frail; in benefits received, eternal: he scorneth, either to regard recompense, or not to offer it. He is the comfort of miseries; the guide of difficulties; the joy of life; the treasure of earth; and no other than a good angel clothed in flesh.

Personal Essays

ON PRAISE*

To go to the grave, or even to the gallows, without being praised must be difficult. Somewhere along the line the dimmest, the most homicidal of us can hardly have failed to hear some other member of the human race 'express' (as the dictionary puts it) 'warm approbation of, commend the merits of' himself or herself. It may have happened only in our childhood; but we have all been praised.

Praise is an interesting commodity. Go on getting enough of it, and you achieve fame. But fame is perishable. It can be lost; it can be forfeited; it can fade away. It is conferred rarely, sometimes arbitrarily, and quite often post-humously. Praise is the pennies or threepenny bits which every child puts into its money-box; fame is the more complex basis of a millionaire's prosperity.

The other day I asked a man of great sensibility what were the nicest words he remembered being spoken to him in the course of his varied and distinguished career. He thought for a moment, then quoted a compliment which a great man had bestowed on him. It was phrased with felicity and delivered with conviction; it was the highest praise, and I said so.

Its recipient agreed. 'But if only,' he added with a sigh, 'more people had been there to hear it!'

I found that I was vaguely puzzled by these words. Praise has always struck me as a private matter, whose value is not necessarily increased, and may indeed be lowered, if it is publicly bestowed. If a banquet were given in my honour at the Guildhall (a mercifully though rather unaccountably remote contingency) I should not at all enjoy listening to the eulogy which the Lord Mayor would feel impelled to pronounce on my character and attainments. I should not glow as he went booming on; I should wince, fidget, stare at the tablecloth, quite possibly perspire. If on the other hand the Lord Mayor had stopped me in the street and had said 'Look, you don't know me from Adam and it's the most awful cheek, but I simply *had* to say how much I enjoyed your book about pond-life in Staffordshire,' I would be very much gratified and would, however ephemerally, glow.

I suspect, though I cannot be sure, that we place a higher value on spoken praise than on praise in writing. The latter may have a more permanent utility, but the former makes a stronger impact. There is something about all

* Reprinted from *The Spectator* (March 21, 1958) by permission of Ian Gilmour, editor.

testimonials which causes them to fade, to lose very quickly the power to please us as much as they did when we first read them.

'The evening was a triumph for Mr. Snooks, whose performance can only be described as a *tour de force.*' 'Golly!' thinks Mr. Snooks when he reads these golden words; he is as pleased as Punch. But somehow time tarnishes them. Pasted into his press-cutting album they will continue to give him grounds for complacency, to sustain him in moments of disappointment. Yet there is something dead, something bygone about them. They lack that quality of perennial freshness which in his memory will always transfigure a single sentence of percipient commendation uttered by a stage-hand as he came off after the second act.

One would expect praise in writing to give more pleasure when it is published than when it is read only by the recipient and anyone he cares to show it to; but I am not sure that this is always so.

For one thing, to be praised (or blamed) in print is in certain careers an occupational hazard. Athletes, actors, authors, musicians and philanthropists must become partially inured to favourable comment in the press, the more so since it tends to arrive in bulk and to be repetitive. If for instance you made a century in a Test Match, do you think you would read through *all* the tributes to your prowess in *all* the morning papers, evening papers, provincial papers, Sunday papers and weeklies? After a successful first night even a dramatist, for whom the critics' praise has a quasi-commercial value, must, once he has read what the half-dozen most important ones have to say, find scrutiny of the remainder a rather insipid task.

It is different if some person, a total stranger to the limelight, earns printed praise for (say) a deed of heroism; but even then the accounts of what he did, how he came to be on the scene, what he said afterwards, and what his old mother in Builth Wells thinks about it all will vary so radically from each other, will be so full of inaccuracies and so interlarded with pure tosh, that they are likely to engender in him as much of astonishment and irritation as of pure pleasure.

On the other hand written praise which is privately communicated may (I imagine) be more highly valued by the recipient than a sackful of press-cuttings. A letter from someone whose opinion he respects, commending him for something he has done, is potentially more glow-producing than the most ecstatic headline, even though the letter is read at only one breakfast table and the headline at millions.

There are several reasons for this. The letter is unexpected, the newspaper comment (save sometimes to an author) is not. The letter is spontaneous; its writer did not have to write it and was not paid for doing so. It is—like, I suspect, all the praise that people really care about and remember—direct and personal. The fact that, being private, it can do nothing, or very little, to enhance in the eyes of the world the reputation of the person praised is neither here nor there. The child dropping coins into its money-box is not disappointed because the threepenny bit makes less of a clink than the pennies.

Those of us who cannot readily call to mind the last time we were praised, those of us who after a promising start ('But for Ragwort's doughty efforts in goal, the 2nd XI's 14–0 defeat might have become a veritable rout') have somehow not very often seen our names in print—for such there is comfort in the thought that people are constantly being praised behind their backs, *in absentia*, unawares. At this very moment somebody may be saying of you, my long-suffering reader, or even conceivably of me: 'Now there is a really first-class man! If only he could be induced to go into public life! I shall never forget——' And so on. No one can prove that this is impossible.

But it is a possibility on which it would be unwise to dwell for too long. Let it pass reassuringly but swiftly through your mind, then turn elsewhere for solace before it occurs to you that, if praise is often given *in absentia*, so—and much more frequently—is blame.

FREYA STARK

*MEMORY**

Some words come heavily jeweled out of their history. Feelings and thoughts have been encrusted on them in their passage through centuries and nations, and Oxus

> Rejoicing, through the hush'd Chorasmian waste
> Under the solitary moon . . .†

carries a siren magic; there is, as it were, a patina of old bronze produced by use and time. This jeweled quality of language gives richness to literature. It gives to words the same atmosphere that a house acquires by being loved and lived in—whose magnificence is not expressed but latent, and belongs neither to the builder nor to the present user of the dwelling; but has been gathered unconsciously by those who, in careless generations, have played and used and left the mark of their lives upon their symbols.

Pleasure, too, has the acquired quality, the polish of repeated use, so that there is difference like that of childhood and age between new and remembered delight. I have never been able to determine their respective claims. Whether for instance, on a holiday, it is better to revisit or to explore? The passing of time decides for us; and part of the contentment of age with its own walks and gardens comes from an increase of riches, the accumulated capital, as it were, which the mind in its journey has collected; so that every note of the small instrument we play on becomes an orchestra in itself, and

* From *Perseus in the Wind*, Beacon Press, Boston, 1956. Reprinted by permission of the publisher. Permission for Canada granted by John Murray Publishers, Ltd.
† Matthew Arnold, *Sohrab and Rustum*.

links and wreathes into a wealth of undertones the melodies and half-for-
gotten snatches of our past.

> No nightingale did ever chaunt
> Such welcome notes to weary bands
> Of travellers in some shady haunt
> Among Arabian sands:
> Such thrilling voice was never heard
> In spring-time from the cuckoo-bird,
> Breaking the silence of the seas
> Among the farthest Hebrides.*

In Kurdistan I have heard the sudden call of the cuckoo from some dell
encircled and sheltered by precipices and hidden in walnut trees, among
hills white in the sun like bones. The poor notes, shrill and naked in themselves, brought an English edge of woodland and lush paths, and the afternoons that slope to twilight with the lengthening days; and in the train of
these, the songs of poets and echo of that pleasure which their words first
gave. Now to all this richness is added the Kurdish landscape with its gaunt
ridges and warlike remote life, that comes to me when the cuckoo sings in
June among the Asolo hills.

Such is pleasure, so linked and enriched with all that goes before it until,
like a piece of embroidery, the stuff on which it is stitched is hidden beneath
the silken threads—threads of our own life's countless moments, and threads
of gold, spoken or sung or painted by those immortals who weave themselves into our pattern regardless of time. The pleasure which first we feel
is a storehouse for all the repetitions of itself. And it is well to take our feelings as fully and as deeply and in as great a variety as we can in our youth,
since they are the capital on whose interest the rest of our life will flourish:
for kind dispensation has permitted nearly all agreeable things to gain an
access of grace through memory, while the disagreeable withhold their
unpleasantness and, unaided, are easily and soon forgotten.

The charm of presents, for instance, lies in a magic only accidentally connected with the object, whatever it may be. I am particularly delighted with
scented things that one can use daily, and in their little shock of repeated
delight think kindly of the sender: without such personal addition, there is
a poverty in the most ravishing perfume; and I daresay it is this feeling of
delight enriched by memory and so easily repeated which has made perfume
acceptable as a gift to women from the days of the Queen of Sheba and
before.

Among the peoples of the world, memories held in common, that build
themselves like coral islands from generation to generation, create a barrier
of nationalism: for what is there in human beings to differentiate one from
another in their essential qualities except their past? Like the words of their
speech, the flags of nations go by heavy with encrusted meanings, the dust

* William Wordsworth, "The Solitary Reaper."

and stains of battlefields whose history is forgotten though the marks remain; they hang in the cathedrals of their people, whom they stir because of those old rents of war; and a new flag speaks as little as a new-coined word to the heart.

In smaller, more familiar things, memory weaves her strongest enchantments, holding us at her mercy with some trifle, some echo, a tone of voice, a scent of tar and seaweed on the quay; we have all been explorers in our time, even if it was only when we learned to walk upon unsteady feet on the new carpet of our world; and it is those forgotten explorations that come back, intruding all about us in the ordinary routine of our lives. This surely is the meaning of home—a place where every day is multiplied by days before it. The edifice can be created at any age, by an accumulation of happiness and time; but it is rare in later life to drink such draughts as we do in childhood of the world's wonder, whose first depth remains through all our days.

In Devonshire, where my parents lived for many years, old oak woods and fir plantations stretched up from the back of the house towards the moors. The oak trees were mossy with comfortable branches, and a yellow-green light filtered there in a friendly way, hanging as in cathedral aisles among the fretted leaves and airy domes; but the fir plantations were silent and private, little inhabited by birds and too closely grown for winds to toss or sun to visit; a fear, a sort of taboo brooded in their straight darkness carpeted with moss and starred with still and muddy pools; and beyond them, the heart lifted at a sudden clearing, where boulders of speckled granite were piled in a weather-beaten wall against the moors. Here the bracken washed up the hillside with fronds shiny as the sea, and young shoots unfolded in a Byzantine curl of waves, and the whole expanse bent when the south wind blew; and at one step from the path the serrated canopies met above one's head, opening in fanlike traceries like the vaulting at Christ Church, and leading in endless avenues of stems to the Unknown. No exploration I have ever shared in has been more rich than this in delight and wonder, which still linger when I see the bracken in a woodland clearing, though tame now and flat and shrunken in my sight.

Love, too, and even more so friendship, are built by memory in this small persistent way. After our first vision of them, the persons we care for become composite beings, altered by every meeting as it comes so that they really exist less in the present than in the past, and are embodiments not only of their own but also of *our* departed days: the ingredients of them, as far as we are concerned, are all the gathered occasions, mostly forgotten, in which our lives have joined.

This is what makes absence so dangerous a menace to love, for the creature we meet again is no longer the one whose image lay like the sleeping princess in our heart; she is awake, and alarmingly different; and who can blame anyone for being unable to live on memories that have ceased to tally with the facts? The wise lover follows the French poet:

J'ai trouvé le secret
De t'aimer
Toujours pour la première fois.*

Constancy is a static virtue; the delight which we have seen moving like wind through our loves and pleasures is here recollected in a state of apotheosis and apt to be deified into stone. "All the privilege I claim for my own sex," says Anne Elliot, in that memorable conversation with Captain Harville, ". . . is that of loving longest, when existence or when hope is gone!"†

Even the most inconstant are faithful in their way, and through the varied pageant of their loves see and pursue again and again the first and fleeing splendor. To most of us some stranger, in the press of the world, with a mere glance, a gesture, an expression, will suddenly wring our heart out of the depths of its days; dead love, like a drowned face, then rises to the surface of our stream. There is no rule for constancy: if recollection is rich enough to satisfy, that is happiness sufficient: if the harvest is poor, if bare patches begin to appear in those private fields so often tilled—why then let us remember that Experience is like the marshal's baton, a potential fortune at the bottom of every knapsack in the world, a treasure of which hope is the key. So Dr. Johnson appeared to think, when on the subject of widowers and wives. The truth is that constancy of a sort is an unescapable virtue; for the things that the heart is seeking, if they are multiple at all, are very few; they are found and lost many times over with changing names: the young explorer looks for them and the old lover remembers; and the difference between them is not so great.

For when its wonder of infancy was over, Memory began to take all human things, and warmed them and made them pliable as wax, and modeled them anew; altering the meaning of words and of banners, and the buildings of love; giving a value to pleasure and a halo to sorrow and joy. In the garment of memory man is encased like a grain of wheat in the sheaf of the ear, and the two are indistinguishable in the russet of the harvest.

FRANCIS X. CONNOLLY

WE WENT TO MEXICO‡

As recently as fifteen years ago, to cross the International Bridge from the United States to Mexico, from Laredo to Nuevo Laredo, was to move from relative efficiency to chaos, from sanitation to squalor, from energy to lassitude. Dilapidation, stench, indifference, a nation dead at its extremities—

* I have found the secret of loving you always for the first time. From "Toujours pour la Première Fois" by André Breton.
† Jane Austen, *Persuasion*.
‡ Reprinted from *America* (January 18, 1958) by permission of the editor and of the author.

this was the first impression of Mexico. Nor did the impression change as one traversed the bleak border country. The scraggly mesquite and cactus mothered a few herds of stunted Chihuahua range cattle and skinny goats. Villages looked like faintly organized mud-piles. Red-painted slogans on white-washed schools screamed reform. Monterrey, the Pittsburgh of Mexico, sprawled in ugly confusion in its cradle between the mountains.

Now the contrast between south Texas and the neighboring Mexican zone is less pronounced. Nuevo Laredo blends almost imperceptibly with old Laredo. A broad new boulevard leads from the border city—*a México*. Near Monterrey one passes a sparkling new airport, the beginnings of a new university city, an army camp with the military neatness of the forts around San Antonio, an industrial park, modernistic villas. Mexican border guards wear natty uniforms and, when addressed in Spanish, a gleaming smile.

As one moves farther south, through those tropical areas where, as the tourist books say, life has not changed much for 2,000 years, one still sees oxen, burros and mules, villages that begin with a circle of mud and thatched huts and peter out suddenly in a brown puddle that is the water supply, the laundry and the drainage pool.

Yet even here there is change. A Pemex gas station thrusts its 20th-century face out of the primeval jungle; trucks and buses spit and choke on the indigestible Mexolina gas on roads where once one met only burros and burdened porters; a new rural school, named for Obregón or Alemán or some local revolutionary hero, proclaims the continuing struggle for literacy and progress. Alongside the *ejidos*, those semi-Communist collective farms that replaced the estates several decades ago, are new, thousand-acre ranches of Santa Gertrudis cattle, neat fruit plantations and fields of sugar cane. Occasionally one encounters some small individual farms, thanks to a new law that permits peons to buy 110 to 150 *hectares* from the Government over a ten-year period. Private ownership has returned—not, one gathers, because of an ideological shift, but because it is more productive, and Mexico needs all the food she can raise.

Today Meets Yesterday

All these symptoms of change prepare one for the dazzling spectacle of Mexico City. (Damage wrought by the earthquake of last July 28 has all been repaired.) Now the fourth largest city in the Western Hemisphere, with a metropolitan population of 4.5 million, the capital presents all the appearances of phenomenal growth. The old section of the city remains the same, the plaza imperishable in its Spanish colonial splendor, the markets splashy with gaudy fruits and flowers, the narrow streets vivid with a brown swarm of buyers and sellers. The business district, for all its renovations and chattering traffic, retains a sedate 19th-century air.

But as one moves from the center toward the Paseo de la Reforma, past the innumerable statues, along the wide, tree-lined boulevard, one walks into a new world of tall, modern office buildings, chic shops, glittering hotels, Parisian restaurants. Still farther out, rows of Renaissance palaces, protected by high walls and iron gates, yielding only a passing glimpse of their green gardens and tiled fountains, flank the road to Chapultepec Castle and its surrounding park. Beyond Chapultepec is the district called the Lomas of Chapultepec. Here the new rich and the rising middle class have built even more splendid villas. From hillside terraces they can see the spires of the glittering city, and beyond, the snowy tops of the guardian mountains.

In another direction the city streams out—along other broad boulevards to the equally sumptuous suburbs of Alvaro Obregón, San Angel and the Pedregal, near the showcase of modern Mexico, the handsome but forbidding National University. On the campus an heroic statue of former President Alemán, more like Stalin than the President, gazes with satisfaction on concrete rectangles that somehow mingle the mystique of Aztec primitivism with that of modern science.

At first glance, too, the spirit of the city seems as bright as its appearances. A new confidence, born of political maturity and steady economic progress, is evident in new enterprises, in the relaxed gaiety of evening strollers in the Alameda and along the Paseo, in the tone of newspaper comment. Mexicans quietly rejoice in the fact that they have not had a "shooting election" for some time, and that, by standards of the past, their Government is stable and reasonably honest. If their democratic conscience is pricked by a one-party system, unobtrusively managed by ex-Presidents and provincial *jefes*, they console themselves with the fact that the Party of Revolutionary Institutions, like the French Radicals, has grown conservative with the years.

Revolution Grown Reasonable

Emphatically the party, now celebrating the centenary of La Reforma, wants no nonsense in the practical order. Officially an organ of a secular state, it encourages its orators and philosophers to yell all they want about the sagacity of Juárez and the perfidy of Díaz. Officially it sanctions radical artists like Juan O'Gorman and Diego Rivera, who depict their (to foreign eyes) wildly improbable versions of Mexican history in all the best public places. It still casts the United States as the thief of Texas. It is still proud of a huge monument it erected to commemorate the expropriation of the foreign oil companies.

But unofficially, Mexico—that is, the governing party—encourages foreign investments by its bland tax policy, desires an increasing collaboration with the United States, deplores the divisive tendencies of its factions on the extreme left. It even tolerates a token representation of other parties in the National Congress.

Indeed, one of the most ambiguous features of contemporary Mexican life is the contrast between its official stringencies and its unofficial compromises. Nowhere is this paradox more evident than in the mixed attitude toward religion. Though none of the harsh legislation against the Church has been repealed, the Church is, on the surface, a respected institution. Approximately a third of the people are devout Catholics, and a large majority are at least passively religious.

In the museums, the Church is crudely painted as the handmaiden of a foreign conqueror, and *Mexicanidad* is identified with the pre-Columbian races. Nevertheless, the Government does not interfere with Christian pieties. Churches are crowded, even on weekdays. The shrine at Guadalupe, as ever the heart of Mexican piety, throbs with a tangible fervor. The movements of the Archbishop of Mexico City are reported with cordial respect in all the newspapers.

Because of the acute shortage of schools, the Government tolerates "private" schools, undisguisedly conducted by nuns, brothers and priests. One meets representatives of these religious groups, invariably dressed in lay fashion, some of them indeed as smartly as the professional society of the city itself. Prudent, yet zealous, they have won great respect by their competence as educators and their sensitive adjustment to the Mexican reality. The serious people, including members of the Government, send their children to the "private" schools, thus encouraging the belief that, at some future date, official toleration may ripen into a more benign attitude.

Common sense, orderly progress, concentration on such practical ends as improving roads, increasing the food supply, extending social aids, encouraging tourism, playing down factional disputes—all these emollient attitudes seem to have replaced the revolutionary rancor that was still evident fifteen or twenty years ago.

Of necessity, too, the new tone is favorable to a mild materialism—the instinct of the shopkeeper for a fast peso, of the official for "grease" to lubricate the wheels of public business, of the student to learn those subjects—English especially—that will help him get a better job. Contrary to the romantic view, Mexicans adore supermarkets, Woolworths, Sears Roebuck, air conditioning, drug stores, family cars, radios, comic books and movies; and they dream with innocent envy of the way of life enjoyed by the American worker.

Hence, they have moved, in a psychological sense, closer to the United States. They are disposed to intensify the economic, political and social connections that officials of both nations have carefully forged in recent years. The United States wants Mexico's friendship at all costs, as we demonstrated last year by buying up Mexico's surplus cotton. That Mexico responds to this attitude is clear in her willingness to destroy cattle infected by the hoof-and-mouth disease, an heroic gesture indeed in the light of her social and economic situation. These two acts symbolize the increasing collaboration between the two countries, a collaboration that was thought impossible before World War II.

Though Mexico is more modern, less "foreign" than in the past, we should not ignore the fact that Mexico is still a land of paradox, where potentially dangerous divisions exist between rich and poor, between blueblood and Indian, between political party and social community, between Christian piety and Socialist materialism, between legal theory and legal practice, between relaxed federalism and doctrinaire centralism. In many ways these paradoxes are not rooted in the healthy pluralism or diversity that most North Americans regard as the condition of their unity. Rather, they are the results of many inconclusive revolutions, of unresolved tensions, of abortive reforms, of sometimes ingenious improvisations, of what border residents used to call a series of Mexican stand-offs.

The Mexican economy is shaky. The Indians want shoes, education, land. It is not inconceivable that they may learn how to put pressure behind their demands. How long will laborers be satisfied with a wage of 8oc a day when a young engineer earns $27? The persistent voice of communism, now hushed by the disgrace of Hungary, may again sound beguiling if nine-tenths of the nation remains underpaid, undereducated and undernourished.

Mexico boasts—and rightly so—that she tolerates no social distinctions. The laws permit no segregation or discrimination. In her showplaces—the National Museum, Chapultepec Palace, the National University, her public squares and circles—she exalts the Indian and the mestizo, and depreciates, sometimes vilely, her European heritage. The best families, clearly not Indian in their ancestry, proclaim their Mexicanism in language that suggests a greater identity with Montezuma than with Cortez.

But at bottom a vast distinction exists among the classes. For the residents of the Lomas of Chapultepec, the Indians are still a *gente sin razón,** fit to hew wood and draw water. Dark skins rarely marry into the best families. A caballero whose ancestry might be suspected often wears a flourishing mustache to proclaim that he is not an Indian. The Mexican social structure, no less than her economic life, is shaky.

The Virgin and the Eagle

In the long run, neither economic, nor political nor social forces are likely to give Mexico the kind of unity that will ensure her continued progress. Indeed, the only strong bonds among Mexican citizens are the Spanish language and the Catholic religion, the one uniting the minds and the other the soul of a heterogeneous population. Of the two, Catholicism is clearly the more powerful link, forging a supernatural unity that can and does overcome natural divisions and instinctive animosities. It has been said that of the two chief symbols of Mexico—the Virgin of Guadalupe and the Aztec Eagle—it is the Virgin, as universal mother, who unites all her different children, and it is the Eagle, with its primitivism and retaliation, that divides them.

That our Lady's role is no mere fancy is something one can see and feel and breathe all through Mexico. The Virgin is everywhere. Her image stands in church portal and in house window; it dangles in the cabs of trucks and jingles on the arms of brown girls. No day passes without a huge pilgrimage

* A race beneath consideration.

to her shrine at Guadalupe. Some come in Cadillacs from the Lomas of Chapultepec and the villas of Cuernavaca, some in buses from middle-class dwellings in Mexico City. And always, winding down from the mists of the brown hills, bearing its banners and images, a whole village is walking, who knows how many miles, to the basilica on the hill of Tepeyac.

At Guadalupe the great church our Lady commanded to be built is at once a sanctuary of her Son, an enormous hostel for the countless brothers and sisters of Juan Diego, a wordless school of love and a place of communion where all Mexicans and all Christians can repossess their common brotherhood. At Guadalupe one cannot doubt that our Lady is Queen of Mexico, the protectress of this beautiful land, the silent unraveler of its dark and often bloody complexities.

HILAIRE BELLOC

ON WANDERING*

I HAVE WANDERED all my life, and I have also travelled; the difference between the two being this, that we wander for distraction, but we travel for fulfilment.

A man wanders in order to entertain himself with new discoveries and experiences, the stranger the better, and if beautiful, why then better still. But he travels in order to visit cities and men, and to get a knowledge of the real places where things happened in the past, getting a knowledge also of how the mind of man worked in building and works now in daily life. The two things overlap, do wandering and travel. In all travel there is some element of wandering, though often very little travel in wandering is undertaken for its own sake. Yet are the two distinct.

A man travels most fully if he has already learned much of the place he would visit. The goal of his journey when he reaches it, is thus already furnished for him; yet however thoroughly he knows a place in this secondary way it will be still quite new to him when he discovers it in reality. There is nothing more striking about travel than this: that not only scenes and buildings with which a man is—or thinks himself to be—familiar from much reading, but even those which have been reproduced a thousand times until they are quite hackneyed, turn out, upon discovery of them, to be new and unsuspected things.

There is a landscape which is perhaps the most repeated in the world, and which modern men have seen in photography reproduced in series. It is the sight of Vesuvius seen from the shoulder of the hill of Naples. Yet when I saw it for the first time in my thirtieth year I found it to be a thing quite different from what I was awaiting. The volcano seemed to overhang all the

* Reprinted from *Places* by permission of A. D. Peters, literary agent for the Belloc estate. *Places* was published in 1941.

city and the plain about it; it was the person of that country, and Naples was but an attendant thereto. There was a slight wisp of smoke from the crater, such as I had read of I know not how often, but to *see* it was to see a wholly novel thing. It was as though in all that lay before one the mountain alone was sombrely alive. This novelty about a distant place actually experienced at last through the senses is not due to the addition of sight and sound and scent, temperature, and the movement of the actual air. It is not the filling in of an outline or the embodiment of a vision hitherto vague, it is what I have called it, a discovery. So much is it a discovery that for each newcomer it is a discovery of his own.

I have known men who have gone so far in their fear of disappointment and their disgust with mere repetition that they deliberately avoided visiting whatever had filled modern fiction and illustration, especially whatever had been hammered in by advertisements. One such went out of his way to miss the Pyramids. They who act thus are comprehensible enough, yet they are wrong. If the man who had avoided the Pyramids had seen those great kilns, he would probably have come back with something quite new which would remain fresh with him to the end of his life. He might, for instance, have found them disappointingly small, though I am told that the largest of them would cover Lincoln's Inn Fields.

As for the Acropolis of Athens, I knew yet another man who, determining to avoid it, thought he had seen it rising in splendid fashion through the half light from the harbour of the Piraeus a little before true dawn had come, and while things were still grey. He was profoundly moved; he repented of his foolish and deliberate isolation, and became inspired with something like worship. As the light broadened, the outline puzzled him, and long before it was full day he discovered the sacred rock to be, in fact, a neighbouring warehouse, with a penthouse for the Parthenon and a few chimney-pots for columns. Yet when he came to see the true Acropolis later on that same day he was very pleased. For he had the good fortune to come upon it from the North, in which aspect it is a rock indeed. But famous things seen in travel are most effective, I think, when they are unexpected. Let me repeat here such an experience of travel long ago.

I was in a train, travelling through the raw and chilly air of the very early morning before the spring had come upon Tuscany. I was intent upon reaching, for dull political reasons, a further place where it was my duty to discuss dull political things in a dull exposition which I knew well would bear no fruit. Happily for me, the train stopped in the middle of a wide expanse through some small accident or other. I was told that we had at least an hour to wait, and there began the noise of distant hammering. With other passengers I got out of the train, to taste the freshness of the air, and I saw, almost on a level with my eye, the level line of water under hills which marks a lake. I asked of a fellow-traveller, native to that country, what the name of that mere might be—it was only curiosity; I hardly wanted to know—when he replied with a word which struck me like a clap of thunder: "Trasimene."

I was to see that famous lake many, many a time in later years; I was even to go carefully over the supposed site of the battle between the shore and the lifted land beyond, but no further acquaintance, no increase of detail, came near to that first revelation.

The moral would seem to be, travel with an object, travel with exact intention, and be certain that you will be rewarded on the way by some discovery inward and outward much beyond your expectation.

That is one of the fifteen or sixteen hundred ways in which passage through the places of the earth is like passage through a human life and in which travel so closely follows the pattern of living. For in life we both know and do not know what it is that we approach, and find accidental revelation perpetually, as well as accidental disappointment.

I take it that the wise are those who do not too much allow natural frailty to emphasize the disappointments, but who are careful to record for their own enrichment the happier accidents along with the less happy. Though there is, it is true, this trouble about the better things, that they do not last. So it is with the worse, as well as the better. But we forget that consolation.

Perhaps the best relaxation for the mind is the recollection of normal and familiar travel not too far from home. It is one of the worst of the minor evils attaching to great modern wars that they cut men off from recreative travel. Cultivated British people of a past and happier generation never showed their taste and wisdom more than in their fashion of travel. The Victorian period was full of wise use in this respect, and the conversation of my elders was filled with experience of the Continent, more civilised than their own land. From the beginning of the railway era, and even before, there was no better or stronger cultural influence than this occupation of leisure by travel.

Even before the catastrophe of 1914 and the opening of the first Great War of our time, travel had become less valuable.

It was deteriorating. Much larger numbers travelled and they travelled less intelligently because they forgot more and more the object of travel, which is a mixture of information, novelty and enlargement. These are most fully obtained when men and women already sufficiently instructed in the past go from one European town to another, staying in those inns and hotels which are full of local custom and tradition.

Today we mark with regret the contrast between those older days of our early youth and the first years of the twentieth century. The big cosmopolitan hotels of that later time were no centres for real travel. The French have a generic term for such hotels, the term "palace," and I think it would be well to have a generic term for them all over Europe. They gave the same cooking pretty well everywhere, and it was mediocre. They had much the same furniture. They had the same atmosphere of regular and mechanical living, which was death to all hospitality and to all domestic feeling. Therefore the wise continued to patronise such of the older hostelries as were left;

but these also dwindled one by one and the first sign of death in them was the appearance of the American bar.

I am not sure that travelling by stage-coach, of which we have made a romance nowadays, was better worthwhile than the slower kind of Victorian travel by train. I talked a good deal with my elders when I was young about their stage-coach experiences and they were never enthusiastic about them. They nearly all agreed that the railway had come as a relief. Even those who were wealthy enough to use the post-chaise—such as that in which my English grandfather travelled over a great part of France and Italy with my mother in her youth—did not feel the coming of the railway to be a loss of opportunity save in one point: that of landscape.

I have heard men and women of that generation say that no one has really appreciated Italy since the Alps were pierced. Crossing the mountains by the high summer roads one saw the new vision of the southern land open before one and there was the right interval between the North and South. But except in this point of international travel, all but a few of that generation agreed that the railway, which they came to use more and more during and after the 'fifties, had given them a greater possession of Europe than had the older forms of travel.

I cannot help feeling also that the guide-books of the Victorian time made better reading and told one much more than those of our day. I preserve and, so long as travel was possible, used in travel the old Murrays and Baedekers which I had inherited. They were well written; they told one the things one really wanted to know. So did the travel books of those days, which were a time of discovery after a fashion: notably a discovery of what mountains could mean. One of the best books ever written in that connection was Whymper's *Scrambles Among the Alps*. There was a sense of height and majesty in his illustrations which we do not get today. But I am afraid the best of all that travel period—the end of which I well remember, for by the end of the century and of the reign I had already experienced my best travel years from the time when I was only seventeen—can never be restored.

One can often still go off by a side-track to some little-known district and recover in part the atmosphere of those days. One can have in many country-sides the full tradition of a quiet and happy civilisation with a prosperous agriculture for its background and a long tradition of architecture showing upon every side. But one cannot get away from the wireless or from the gramophone. You will suffer even in the remotest hamlets that assault on the nerves which is a permanent character of modern competitive publicity.

I remember once in a barber's shop of the most primitive kind up in the high Pyrenees, where there was no road but only a rough stone mule-track leading to the little group of houses, having before me while I was being shaved a violently-coloured picture imploring me in American to buy a particular brand of bicycle. What tenacious travelling salesman could have planted such a thing in such a place? There it was and I have always remembered it—which after all was what the advertiser wanted me to do, I suppose.

JOSEPH CONRAD

CHRISTMAS DAY AT SEA*

THEOLOGICALLY Christmas Day is the greatest occasion for rejoicing offered to sinful mankind; but this aspect of it is so august and so great that the human mind refuses to contemplate it steadily, perhaps because of its own littleness, for which, of course, it is in no way to blame. It prefers to concentrate its attention on ceremonial observances, expressive generally of goodwill and festivity, such, for instance, as giving presents and eating plum-puddings. It may be said at once here that from that conventional point of view the spirit of Christmas Day at sea appears distinctly weak. The opportunities, the materials too, are lacking. Of course, the ship's company get a plum-pudding of some sort, and when the captain appears on deck for the first time the officer of the morning greets him with a "Merry Christmas, sir," in a tone only moderately effusive. Anything more would be, owing to the difference in station, not correct. Normally he may expect a return for this in the shape of a "The same to you" of a nicely graduated heartiness. He does not get it always, however.

One Christmas morning, many years ago (I was young then and anxious to do the correct thing), my conventional greeting was met by a grimly scathing "Looks like it, doesn't it?" from my captain. Nothing more. A three days' more or less thick weather had turned frankly into a dense fog, and I had him called according to orders. We were in the chops of the Channel, with the Scilly Isles on a vague bearing within thirty miles of us, and not a breath of wind anywhere. There the ship remained wrapped up in a damp blanket and as motionless as a post stuck right in the way of the wretched steamboats groping blindly in and out of the Channel. I felt I had behaved tactlessly; yet how rude it would have been to have withheld the season's greeting from my captain!

It is very difficult to know what is the right thing to do when one is young. I suffered exceedingly from my gaucherie; but imagine my disgust when in less than half an hour we had the narrowest possible escape from a collision with a steamer which, without the slightest warning sound, appeared like a vague dark blot in the fog on our bow. She only took on the shape of a ship as she passed within twenty yards of the end of our jib-boom, terrifying us with the furious screeching of her whistle. Her form melted into nothing, long before the end of the beastly noise, but I hope that her people heard the simultaneous yell of execration from thirty-six throats which we sent after her by way of a Christmas greeting. Nothing more at variance with the spirit of peace and goodwill could be imagined; and I must add that I never saw a whole ship's company get so much affected by one of those "close calls" of the sea. We remained jumpy all the morning and con-

* Reprinted from *Last Essays*, 1926, by permission of J. M. Dent & Sons, Ltd., trustees of the Joseph Conrad estate, and Doubleday & Company, Inc.

sumed our Christmas puddings at noon with restless eyes and straining ears as if under the shadow of some impending marine calamity or other.

On shore, of course, a calamity at Christmas time would hardly take any other shape than that of an avalanche—avalanche of unpaid bills. I think that it is the absence of that kind of danger which makes Christmas at sea rather agreeable on the whole. An additional charm consists in there being no worry about presents. Presents ought to be unexpected things. The giving and receiving of presents at appointed times seems to me a hypocritical ceremony, like exchanging gifts of Dead Sea fruit in proof of sham good-fellowship. But the sea of which I write here is a live sea; the fruits one chances to gather on it may be salt as tears or bitter as death, but they never taste like ashes in the mouth.

In all my twenty years of wandering over the restless waters of the globe I can only remember one Christmas Day celebrated by a present given and received. It was, in my view, a proper live sea transaction, no offering of Dead Sea fruit; and in its unexpectedness perhaps worth recording. Let me tell you first that it happened in the year 1879, long before there was any thought of wireless messages, and when an inspired person trying to prophesy broadcasting would have been regarded as a particularly offensive nuisance and probably sent to a rest-cure home. We used to call them mad-houses then, in our rude, cave-man way.

The daybreak of Christmas Day in the year 1879 was fine. The sun began to shine some time about four o'clock over the sombre expanse of the Southern Ocean in latitude 51; and shortly afterwards a sail was sighted ahead. The wind was light, but a heavy swell was running. Presently I wished a "Merry Christmas" to my captain. He looked still sleepy, but amiable. I reported the distant sail to him and ventured the opinion that there was something wrong with her. He said, "Wrong?" in an incredulous tone. I pointed out that she had all her upper sails furled and that she was brought to the wind, which, in that region of the world, could not be accounted for on any other theory. He took the glasses from me, directed them towards her stripped masts resembling three Swedish safety matches, flying up and down and waggling to and fro ridiculously in that heaving and austere wilderness of countless water-hills, and returned them to me without a word. He only yawned. This marked display of callousness gave me a shock. In those days I was generally inexperienced and still a comparative stranger in that particular region of the world of waters.

The captain, as is a captain's way, disappeared from the deck; and after a time our carpenter came up the poop-ladder carrying an empty small wooden keg, of the sort in which certain ship's provisions are packed. I said, surprised, "What do you mean by lugging this thing up here, Chips?"— "Captain's orders, sir," he explained shortly.

I did not like to question him further, and so we only exchanged Christmas greetings and he went away. The next person to speak to me was the steward.

He came running up the companion-stairs: "Have you any old newspapers in your room, sir?"

We had left Sydney, N.S.W., eighteen days before. There were several old Sydney *Heralds, Telegraphs,* and *Bulletins* in my cabin, besides a few home papers received by the last mail. "Why do you ask, steward?" I enquired naturally. "The captain would like to have them," he said.

And even then I did not understand the inwardness of these eccentricities. I was only lost in astonishment at them. It was eight o'clock before we had closed with that ship, which, under her short canvas and heading nowhere in particular, seemed to be loafing aimlessly on the very threshold of the gloomy home of storms. But long before that hour I had learned from the number of the boats she carried that this nonchalant ship was a whaler. She was the first whaler I had ever seen. She had hoisted the Stars and Stripes at her peak, and her signal flags had told us already that her name was: "*Alaska*—two years out from New York—east from Honolulu—two hundred and fifteen days on the cruising ground."

We passed, sailing slowly, within a hundred yards of her; and just as our steward started ringing the breakfast-bell, the captain and I held aloft, in good view of the figures watching us over her stern, the keg, properly headed up and containing, besides an enormous bundle of old newspapers, two boxes of figs in honour of the day. We flung it far out over the rail. Instantly our ship, sliding down the slope of a high swell, left it far behind in our wake. On board the *Alaska* a man in a fur cap flourished an arm, another, a much be-whiskered person, ran forward suddenly. I never saw anything so ready and so smart as the way that whaler, rolling desperately all the time, lowered one of her boats. The Southern Ocean went on tossing the two ships like a juggler his gilt balls, and the microscopic white speck of the boat seemed to come into the game instantly, as if shot out from a catapult on the enormous and lonely stage. That Yankee whaler lost not a moment in picking up her Christmas present from the English wool-clipper.

Before we had increased the distance very much she dipped her ensign in thanks, and asked to be reported "all well, with a catch of three fish." I suppose it paid them for two hundred and fifteen days of risk and toil, away from the sounds and sights of the inhabited world, like outcasts devoted, beyond the confines of mankind's life, to some enchanted and lonely penance.

Christmas Days at sea are of varied character, fair to middling and down to plainly atrocious. In this statement I do not include Christmas Days on board passenger ships. A passenger is, of course, a brother (or sister) and quite a nice person in a way, but his Christmas Days are, I suppose, what he wants them to be: the conventional festivities of an expensive hotel included in the price of his ticket.

NOEL PERRIN

THE NIGHTINGALE SONG*

In Madingley Wood, near Cambridge, England, there is a grove famous for nightingales. Nettles grow thick under the trees there, and the nettles attract the nightingales—just why, nobody is quite sure, though last year my supervisor at Cambridge, where I was then doing graduate work in English, said it was because the nightingales want to sting themselves. In the Middle Ages, he pointed out, nightingales were constantly impaling themselves on thorns; they believed that the pain made them sing better. Modern nightingales, too degenerate for the thorn technique, try to encourage their melody with nettles.

One night last May, a careful observer might have seen me in the Wood, standing under a large copper-beech tree, near a patch of nettles. I was waiting to hear the nightingales sing, and I was standing because an English wood is nearly always too wet to sit down. It wasn't just some idle love of birds that had drawn me there. It was my duty as an American citizen. I had just written a paper on the poetry of T. S. Eliot, and, among other things, I'd remarked that, for a modern poet, Eliot shows rare accuracy in his descriptions of nature.

"Bosh!" my supervisor had said when he returned the paper to me. "What about Eliot's *nightingales?* ' "Jug Jug" to dirty ears,' he quotes them in 'The Waste Land.' 'Jug Jug' to *tin* ears, perhaps. No nightingale ever made the noise 'Jug Jug' in his life, and so much for Mr. Eliot's rare accuracy. He'd better leave English birds to English poets."

My pride of country was aroused. As soon as I left the supervisor's rooms, I rushed to my college library and took down an enormous "Dictionary of Birds." It was no help at all. "The song of the European or English nightingale (*Luscinia megarhyncha*) is indescribable," wrote the author evasively. Well, at least Eliot had done better than *that*. But to uphold the honor of American poetry, so must I. I decided to go and actually hear the bird for myself.

By eight o'clock that same evening, I had walked the four miles out to Madingley and was standing under my tree, listening hard. By eight-thirty, I had heard nothing but a lovesick crow. There was no use hoping for nightingales while he was around, so I sat down (getting my pants wet instantly) and returned to the literary approach. What *English* poets, I asked myself, had committed themselves on the voice of the nightingale?

Shakespeare was the obvious one to start with, but I could come up with nothing better than Bottom's boast "I will roar you as 'twere any nightingale." Bottom's ears were obviously the wrong sort for hearing nightingales, so I passed on to Shelley. Once I'd realized that the skylark was the

---

only bird he ever wrote an ode to, I tried Keats. Of course! In "Ode to a Nightingale," Keats must have given the bird the best description it has ever had. What does Keats say? Well, as far as I could remember, Keats says that nightingales sing of summer in full-throated ease and that the time to hear them is at midnight.

It seemed a long while to wait.

When I got back to Cambridge, at about two o'clock, I was soaking wet from the hard rain that had started at twelve-thirty. My hands ached from nettle stings, and my shoes were full of mud. I was through relying on Keats for bird lore; midnight had passed without a sound. And I had made no progress toward the vindication of American poetry.

In the morning, my roommate asked me what on earth I'd done to my hands, and I told him the whole story. "Oh, well, it wouldn't have mattered if you had heard a nightingale," he said cheerfully. "Still be your word against the supervisor's, wouldn't it? Besides, the old boy is right. Nightingales don't go 'Jug Jug,' they go 'tsoo tsoo.' See Edward Thomas on this."

So I saw Edward Thomas. I went back to my college library and looked up his collected poems. "Tsoo," his nightingales cry. The sub-librarian heard me cursing softly and came over to me. I told *him* the whole story. "But Mr. Eliot's quite right," he said. "Nightingales do have a note that sounds very much like 'Jug Jug.' Beautiful it is, sir. I think you'll find it quoted in Samuel Taylor Coleridge—'The Nightingale, A Conversation Poem,' from 'Lyrical Ballads.' That should satisfy your supervisor, sir."

I carried "A Conversation Poem" with me to my next supervision, and pointed out the lines to my supervisor. He read them aloud:

> "And murmurs musical and swift jug jug.
> And one low piping sound more sweet than all—

Well, Perrin, true enough," he said easily. "But the 'Jug Jug' counts for no more than the preliminary cough of a Wagnerian tenor. That 'low piping sound' is the real *song* of the nightingale. It's as if Eliot had announced that he was going to describe a violin concerto and then had written, 'The violins tune up, "Squeak Squeak" to dirty ears.' "

Two days later, I went to Oxford for the weekend and attended a literary tea. After the third cup, I found myself telling the whole story to my host, a sympathetic don of Lincoln College. He rubbed his hands with pleasure. "What curious nightingales you have at Cambridge," he said. "All that tuning up. Your birds must suffer from sore throats, like your lecturers. A healthy, normal nightingale—the one that lives in my garden, for example —doesn't need to warm up. He just opens his beak and starts singing. And 'Jug Jug' is an integral part of what he sings. If I were you," he concluded, pouring me a fourth cup of tea, "I should look at John Lyly's 'The Songs of Birds,' from 'Campaspe,' the edition of 1584. Then I'd have a word with my supervisor."

I couldn't wait until I got back to Cambridge to speak to my supervisor. That same night, I posted him a card from Oxford. It read:

> Jug, Jug, Jug, Jug, tereu shee cryes,
> And still her woes at Midnight rise.
> —J. Lyly

When I returned to Cambridge on Monday, there was a note waiting for me.

> DEAR PERRIN [my supervisor had written]: I didn't realize you were so serious about nightingales. I fear you are leaning on a feeble reed in John Lyly, however. His bird cries are pure literary artifice, and not even original.
>
> Look up the Latin version of the Greek myth of Philomela, who was turned into a nightingale, and of King Tereus, who was responsible. Then tell me if you still believe in Lyly's "tereu"s—or in his "Jug, Jug"s.

Underneath, he had inscribed the following:

> Every thing did banish moan
> Save the nightingale alone.
> She, poor bird, as all forlorn,
> Leaned her breast up-till a thorn,
> And there sung the dolefull'st ditty,
> That to hear it was great pity.
> *Fie, fie, fie,* now would she cry,
> *Teru, teru,* by and by,
> That to hear her so complain
> Scarce I could from tears refrain.
> —Richard Barnfield (1574-1627)

I was still smarting from this blow when a fresh note came on Tuesday.

> DEAR PERRIN [it began]: I've been doing a little research on literary references to the nightingale, myself. There weren't many major poets rash enough to try to reproduce his characteristic song. But there was one: Lord Tennyson.
>
> Unlike your Mr. Eliot, Tennyson *does* have an extraordinarily accurate ear. I quote from a minor poem of his called "The Grandmother":
> The moon like a rick on fire was rising over the dale.
> And whit, whit, whit, in the bush beside me chirrupt the nightingale.

The next morning, I presented myself at the Cambridge University Library precisely at nine-thirty, opening time. About eleven, I emerged from its bowels, grimy to the elbows from handling old books, and bearing a sheet of paper. On it were written these words from a poem titled "To Mistress Isabel Pennell," by the reasonably major poet John Skelton:

> To hear this nightingale
> Among the birdes smale
> Warbeling in the vale,
> Dug, dug,
> Jug, jug,
> Good year and good luck,
> With chuck, chuck, chuck, chuck.

In the entrance hall, I ran into my supervisor. He, too, was grimy and had a slip of paper. Silently we exchanged. "Walther von der Vogelweide," his said. "Early German minnesinger. From 'Unter den Linden':

> Near the woods, down in the vale,
> *Tandaradi!*
> Sweetly sang the nightingale."

My supervisor spoke first. "Perrin, suppose you meet me at Madingley pub at eight," he said. "It's going to be a long evening. We might as well start with a pint of beer."

SAMUEL LANGHORNE CLEMENS

THE PETRIFIED MAN*

Now, TO SHOW how really hard it is to foist a moral or a truth upon an unsuspecting public through a burlesque without entirely and absurdly missing one's mark, I will here set down two experiences of my own in this thing. In the fall of 1862, in Nevada and California, the people got to running wild about extraordinary petrifactions and other natural marvels. One could scarcely pick up a paper without finding in it one or two glorified discoveries of this kind. The mania was becoming a little ridiculous. I was a brand-new local editor in Virginia City, and I felt called upon to destroy this growing evil; we all have our benignant, fatherly moods at one time or another, I suppose. I chose to kill the petrifaction mania with a delicate, a very delicate satire. But maybe it was altogether too delicate, for nobody ever perceived the satire part of it at all. I put my scheme in the shape of the discovery of a remarkably petrified man.

I had had a temporary falling out with Mr. ——, the new coroner and justice of the peace of Humboldt, and thought I might as well touch him up a little at the same time and make him ridiculous, and thus combine pleasure with business. So I told, in patient, belief-compelling detail, all about the finding of a petrified man at Gravelly Ford (exactly a hundred and twenty miles, over a breakneck mountain trail from where —— lived); how all the savants of the immediate neighborhood had been to examine it (it was notorious that there was not a living creature within fifty miles of there,

* Reprinted from *Sketches New and Old*, Harper and Brothers, New York, 1907.

except a few starving Indians, some crippled grasshoppers, and four or five buzzards out of meat and too feeble to get away); how those savants all pronounced the petrified man to have been in a state of complete petrifaction for over ten generations; and then, with a seriousness that I ought to have been ashamed to assume, I stated that as soon as Mr. ——— heard the news he summoned a jury, mounted his mule, and posted off, with noble reverence for official duty, on that awful five days' journey, through alkali, sagebrush, peril of body, and imminent starvation, to *hold an inquest* on this man that had been dead and turned to everlasting stone for more than three hundred years! And then, my hand being "in," so to speak, I went on, with the same unflinching gravity, to state that the jury returned a verdict that deceased came to his death from *protracted exposure.* This only moved me to higher flights of imagination, and I said that the jury, with that charity so character-istic of pioneers, then dug a grave, and were about to give the petrified man Christian burial, when they found that for ages a limestone sediment had been trickling down the face of the stone against which he was sitting, and this stuff had run under him and cemented him fast to the "bed-rock"; that the jury (they were all silver-miners) canvassed the difficulty a moment, and then got out their powder and fuse, and proceeded to drill a hole under him, in order to *blast him from his position,* when Mr. ———, "with that delicacy so characteristic of him, forbade them, observing that it would be little less than a sacrilege to do such a thing."

From beginning to end the "Petrified Man" squib was a string of roaring absurdities, albeit they were told with an unfair pretense of truth that even imposed upon me to some extent, and I was in some danger of believing in my own fraud. But I really had no desire to deceive anybody, and no expectation of doing it. I depended on the way the petrified man was *sitting* to explain to the public that he was a swindle. Yet I purposely mixed that up with other things, hoping to make it obscure—and I did. I would describe the position of one foot, and then say his right thumb was against the side of his nose; then talk about his other foot, and presently come back and say the fingers of his right hand were spread apart; then talk about the back of his head a little, and return and say the left thumb was hooked into the right little finger; then ramble off about something else, and by and by drift back again and remark that the fingers of the left hand were spread like those of the right. But I was too ingenious. I mixed it up rather too much; and so all that description of the attitude, as a key to the humbuggery of the article, was entirely lost, for nobody but me ever discovered and compre-hended the peculiar and suggestive position of the petrified man's hands.

As a *satire* on the petrifaction mania, or anything else, my Petrified Man was a disheartening failure, for everybody received him in innocent good faith, and I was stunned to see the creature I had begotten to pull down the wonder-business with, and bring derision upon it, calmly exalted to the grand chief place in the list of the genuine marvels our Nevada had pro-duced. I was so disappointed at the curious miscarriage of my scheme, that at first I was angry, and did not like to think about it; but by and by, when the exchanges began to come in with the Petrified Man copied and guilelessly glorified, I began to feel a soothing secret satisfaction; and as my gentleman's field of travels broadened, and by the exchanges I saw that he steadily and implacably penetrated territory after territory, state after state, and land after land, till he swept the great globe and culminated in sublime and unimpeached legitimacy in the august London *Lancet*, my cup was full, and I said I was glad I had done it. I think that for about eleven months, as nearly as I can remember, Mr. ——'s daily mail-bag continued to be swollen by the addition of half a bushel of newspapers hailing from many climes with the Petrified Man in them, marked around with a prominent belt of ink. I sent them to him. I did it for spite, not for fun. He used to shovel them into his back yard and curse. And every day during all those months the miners, his constituents (for miners never quit joking a person when they get started), would call on him and ask if he could tell them where they could get hold of a paper with the Petrified Man in it. He could have accommodated a continent with them. I hated —— in those days, and these things pacified me and pleased me. I could not have gotten more real comfort out of him without killing him.

HAROLD NICOLSON

*URBANITY**

A friend of mine has recently sent me two articles published in a periodical called *Books and Art* and written by a zestful man under the pseudonym of 'Humphry Clinker.' In these articles I am reproved not so much for my prose style, as for my attitude towards life. One can always profit by criticism and I therefore read these articles with appreciation and care. I was distressed to discover that, owing in all probability to a disparity of age, I was unable to grasp the full force of 'Mr. Clinker's' indictment.

His accusations in the first place were inconsistent. At one moment he referred to me as 'an amply paid professional journalist' and at another point as 'an amateur.' At one moment he blames my colleague Mr. John Davenport for referring to Anthony Powell's previous novels, and at the next he rates Mr. Cyril Connolly for admitting that he had not yet read Richard Church's admirable autobiography *Over the Bridge*. I do not quite see how I can err by being both an amateur and a professional or why my fellow reviewers should be abused, the one for mentioning other books that he has read by the same author, and the other for remarking that he had failed so far to read a previous work by the same author. Ignoring these perplexing inconsistencies, I settled down to study the crimes for which I was being assailed.

* Reprinted from *The Spectator* (March 28, 1958) by permission of *The Spectator*, Ian Gilmour, editor.

There were five main delinquencies which had earned me 'Mr. Clinker's' displeasure. I was accused of being a 'virtuoso,' a word the full significance and purpose of which I do not fully understand. It is, I suppose, intended to be a term of abuse almost as destructive as the kindred term 'intellectual.' I was also accused of being 'cultured,' 'urbane,' 'snobbish' and 'an amateur.' Here again I find it difficult to penetrate to the inner core of 'Mr. Clinker's' meaning.

Of course I am cultured, having received an expensive education both at home and abroad, and having read and written a large number of books during the last fifty years. For me to pretend not to be cultured would be as gross an imposition and affectation as if I were to simulate a passionate interest in football pools or to adopt a Yorkshire accent. I may be mistaken in supposing that it is a creditable thing to be cultured, but I am certainly of the opinion that a certain amount of learning is an asset to those who write history or review the historical works of others. What is discreditable is to pretend to be more cultured than one really is, and this is a crime to which, I earnestly hope, I am not addicted. I probably dislike every bit as much as does 'Mr. Clinker' the writer who flaunts knowledge that his readers are unlikely to possess. But, then, I do not write for the uneducated public: I write for the educated public: and I take it for granted that they can recognise the allusions that I employ.

I admit that the epithet 'urbane' is one that sends an arrow to my heart. It is not used to indicate that I am tolerant, gentle and overflowing with the milk of human kindness. It is meant to suggest that both the manner and the matter of my writing are as placid, smooth, and oleaginous as a tin of face-cream. I am stung when I read, as I frequently do read, this wounding epithet applied to my style. But I am too old to change my placidity for violence or to become angry, vindictive or harsh. Those who hate calm styles must seek for stimulus in someone else.

The adjective 'snobbish' is one that I find salutary but bewildering. When I was a boy at school and at the university I was abominably snobbish, being more impressed by a duke than a viscount, by a baron than a knight. But since I have reached adult age my snobbishness has considerably declined. I should not, today, regard it as one of my major faults. It may be, of course, that what 'Mr. Clinker' intended when hurling this jagged stone at my head, was not social snobbishness but intellectual snobbishness. Yet here again I do not see that it is a grave crime to be fastidious: to prefer intelligent people to stupid people, good books to bad books, good cooking to bad cooking, or comfortable mattresses to uncomfortable mattresses.

I suspect that 'Mr. Clinker' is annoyed with me for being detached from 'the dust and roar of life.' In the past I have experienced a great deal of dust and frequent roars. But, after all, I write generally for a sober Sunday news-paper and the readers of that newspaper spend their lives amid the rattle of modern traffic and actually prefer, on the Day of Rest, to read something that is composed in dulcet tones. I suspect also that what 'Mr. Clinker' objects to is that I and my fellow virtuosi do not possess 'the common touch.' But there are many periodicals and daily newspapers which possess, cultivate and exploit that touch: these are readily available to those readers who prefer the rough to the smooth: and it would be ungainly for me to pretend to be common when I am not.

'Mr. Clinker' again accuses me of being 'an amateur.' Yet he must know that I earn my living by journalism, that I have written several hundred articles and some thirty books. It is this accusation that gives me some clue to the real burden of his indictment. What irritates him is that I and my fellows should be more interested in literature than in news. 'Instead,' he writes, 'of squatting alone in his study and speculating over a book's purpose or provenance [sic]' I ought to 'hunt out' the author and ask him how and why he wrote it. Were I a popular author, I should be infuriated if what 'Mr. Clinker' calls 'a new-style literary columnist' were to 'hunt me out' and probe for news. Being an unpopular writer, I remain unmolested in my ivory tower, more concerned with ideas than with personalities. 'Mr. Clinker' urges me to grasp the telephone and thereby to get into touch with the great authors of the age. Shall I telephone this morning to Mr. T. S. Eliot or Dame Edith Sitwell, ceasing, thereby, to be either considerate or urbane? I shall do nothing of the sort.

I am grateful to 'Mr. Clinker' for the attention that he has paid me and for the polite terms in which he has veiled his attack. But it is not for me suddenly to start barking at younger writers in the columns of the *Observer*. I will make this concession to 'Mr. Clinker.' I agree with him that contemporary criticism, as compared to the good old days, is inclined to be mealymouthed. It needs more vigour; and 'Mr. Clinker' and his generation will assuredly provide it.

JACQUES MARITAIN

AMERICAN MODESTY*

THE POPULAR image of the Yankee boasting that he has the biggest car or runs the biggest business in the world is, in my opinion, utterly misleading. My experience with American students taught me quite another thing. I was struck by their modesty—even, sometimes, surprised at the slight value they seemed to attach to their own personal opinion as long as they had not examined the various views of all the experts in the matter.

My experience with many of my colleagues led me to the same conclusion. One of my most distinguished students at the Graduate School at Princeton was a Jesuit Father; and the members of the department seemed to be, at

* Reprinted from *Reflections on America*, Charles Scribner's Sons, New York, 1958. Copyright 1958 by Jacques Maritain. Reprinted by permission of the publisher.

the beginning, as intimidated by him as he was by them. That was the first, I assume, that a Jesuit Father had got his doctorate in philosophy at Princeton with a (quite remarkable) dissertation on Thomas Aquinas. But mutual esteem and appreciation grew rapidly between him and them, and a professor, who is a good friend of mine, said to me one day: "I like your Jesuit Father very much. I enjoy my talks with him. His way of thinking is really American; he doesn't have all the answers; he is able to say, 'I don't know.' . . ."

Finally I came to realize that this distrust of self-assertion and self-reliance was a general feature of the American mind. Of course I know there are still some people in this country who pass judgment on European nations with all the more contempt and severity as they know nothing or almost nothing about them. If my present reflections are true, we should say that in doing so these people (they are fewer and fewer, I hope) show an un-American mental attitude. In actual fact there is an American modesty before life and reality which is a great moral virtue and a dynamic quality of considerable efficacy.

It originates, I think, in a sense of the complexity of things; of the fluidity of life which escapes our concepts; and of the multiple aspects of reality which make our judgments precarious. Hence, a circumspection before taking a stand or reaching a conclusion; a passion for blueprints; a slowness (which is an exasperating surprise for European visitors) in preparatory processes, and an extreme boldness and rapidity in execution; an extraordinary power of unceasing change, renewal, and adaptation to the growth of history.

This modesty is essentially linked with what might be called the *experiential approach*, in which it is necessary to get all factual data, all points of view and all possible opinions before making a judgment—itself tentative.

Now, let me say, a single idea, if it is right, saves us the labor of an infinity of experiences. (That is why a Frenchman starts with his own idea.) Yes, but the idea must be right. If it is wrong, it involves us in infinite trouble. Thus it is that a sound distrust of ideology seems quite advisable in practical matters, especially if we remember that the discovery of new true ideas is, as a rule, prodded on by some alluring folly which preys upon them.

In this country the general distrust of ideology proceeds from the modesty before reality to be grasped—and to be improved—the eager modesty of which I am speaking, rather than from sheer empiricism.

Yet—and here is the dark side of the picture—it is liable to veer toward empiricism, and to a general and systematic Fear of ideas. If this cast of mind—Fear of ideas, and of intellectual intuition—became prevalent, it would involve the danger of impairing intellectual creativity; the risk, for instance, of making, not new applications, but new fundamental discoveries, much more difficult in the field of science.

There would be a risk, also, of imperiling the deep-rooted intellectual convictions, rationally founded, which man needs for the comfort of his life.

In particular, the moral tenets of a free people—justice; freedom; equality;

human rights—would risk becoming a matter of feeling and national tradition, or adjustment to the environment, instead of being held as objective values, justifiable in reason.

Then, on the one hand, these moral tenets would lose their inner vigor in each individual. They would become more or less relativized, subjectivized. And on the other hand, they would lose their intelligible universality, and communicability, their impact on the minds of other peoples, that persuasive, illuminating, apostolic power which is peculiar to ideas.

Here I come to a point which is, to my mind, of especial interest, namely the need, with respect to genuine human communication, for a proper ideology—better to say, a proper intellectual expression—or an explicit philosophy and an explicitly formulated ideal.

It is through ideas that we communicate with other minds. It is through ideas that anything we have achieved or discovered in concrete life is made known to others, and even to ourselves.

Now the distrust of ideas, the too great ideological modesty of which I am speaking,* involves a serious risk: the risk of intellectual isolation, the risk of making American reality, and the greatest human and social achievements of the American people, non-communicable to other nations, and walled up in themselves, as long as ideology or philosophy remains far behind real and actual behavior.

* This modesty is partly responsible, it seems to me, for another kind of harm: I mean the spreading of the notion (imported from Germany) that only specialists have a right to think—and that each one of them, moreover, is all the more competent in his own field, and all the more reliable, as he shuns knowing anything outside the field in question.

Art

ELIZABETH MONGAN

THE ART OF WILLIAM BLAKE*

WILLIAM BLAKE was born 28 November, 1757, at 28 Broad Street, Carnaby Market, Golden Square, London. His father, James, was a moderately successful hosier, who brought up his five children in a highly respectable manner. According to Benjamin Heath Malkin, who in 1806 wrote the first account of Blake's life in "A Father's Memoirs of His Child," Blake was sent at the age of ten to Henry Pars' drawing school in the Strand. Pars' method of instruction consisted almost entirely in training his pupils to copy from plaster casts. It is revealing to note that even when his son was so young, James Blake bought for him casts of the Gladiator, the Hercules, the Medici Venus, and various heads, hands, and feet. He also supplied him with money for the purchase of prints. Apparently the young Blake began to haunt the print shops and auctions, his precocious eye already fixed on prints after Raphael, Michelangelo, Marten Heemskerck, Dürer and Giulio Romano. Langford, an auctioneer, called him "his little connoisseur." When he was fourteen, Blake was apprenticed for seven years to the well known engraver James Basire. Basire was a Royal Academician, and engraver to the Antiquarian Society. A conventional, academic engraver, he got on very well with Blake for a number of years, since at this time they had many tastes in common. Blake's first years with Basire were spent in learning the practice of formal engraving as it was then taught. But after two years Blake, who was not too sympathetic to the other apprentices, was sent out by his master to make drawings of what were, then, neglected works of art, called "Gothic monuments." He copied the monuments of the Kings and Queens in Westminster Abbey, especially those near the Chapel of King Henry III. "All these he drew in every point he could catch, frequently standing on the monuments, and viewing the figures from on top." Thus, Blake, from his earliest training, was "gothicized" and fed upon British antiquities. He also spent long hours in the British Museum poring over early illuminated manuscripts. These facts were taken from a man who knew Blake in 1803.

With such a formal background in drawing, collecting, and study at a very early age, it is quite evident that Blake did not spring suddenly into genius—alone, ignored and untaught. He was taught and he did know how to draw correctly and engrave. At the age of 21, his apprenticeship over, he went out to make a living as an engraver. This he might easily have done, but his heart, mind, and hand were set on the "ancients," so he changed his course.

Blake's first known engraving, in its early state, *Joseph of Arimathea*

* From *The Art of William Blake*, National Gallery of Art, Smithsonian Institution, Washington, 1957. Reprinted by permission of the author.

among the Rocks of Albion, was made when he was sixteen years old, and still a student of Basire. On an impression of the early state (belonging to Sir Geoffrey Keynes) Blake wrote "engraved when I was a beginner at Basires from a drawing by Salviati after Michel Angelo." Several things are interesting about the engraving. The figure of Joseph of Arimathea was derived from one of the "ancients" whom Blake always admired. The subject was one that he was to return to in later life and the engraving itself was kept by the artist to be reworked and strengthened when he was more mature and certain, ca. 1810. He often first lightly sketched a theme on paper, composing with just a few brief pencil lines. Later, sometimes years later, the idea was reconsidered, and refashioned into a more complete and harmonious composition. An outstanding example of the method is to be seen in the great "Job" cycle. The first drawings for "Job" were apparently conceived about 1785. A water color of *The Complaint of Job* was done in 1793. The final noble series of 21 engravings for the "Book of Job" was finished for John Linnell, his patron, six years before Blake's death in 1821. Throughout the artist's life the same subject was frequently repeated in different media: pencil, water color, tempera and prints, over long periods of time until the culmination was reached, or even occasionally over-reached.

Blake's water colors are without doubt the chief glory of his art. It was not for nothing that he had pored over the mediaeval manuscripts in the British Museum when he was young. From a study of the manuscripts he learned a number of things that were in accord with his own creative bent. In brief, a two dimensional composition, drawn with intensity and illuminated with wonderful colors to illustrate that a faith can result in a very high form of art. Line, vision, color were sufficient. The core, the essence of art or faith, (they were the same to Blake), was to be sought and found in the binding line. "What does Precision of Pencil mean? If it does not mean outline, it means nothing." "Broken colours, Broken lines & Broken Masses are Equally Subversive of the Sublime." (Blake—*Annotations to Reynolds,* pp. 32 and 43). Blake's linear designs were complicated not by the means employed—a flat surface and a "wirey," bounding line,—but by the number of figures drawn in a small scale with flowing grace to illustrate what he believed to be profound truths, i.e., revealed, imagined scenes. The compositions were then decorated or illuminated with colored washes, in infinite variety, depending on the subject, his mood or his age. Sometimes the water colors are light, variegated, "Tulip-like" and sparkling, as in the illustration of Milton's *L'Allegro,* ("Mirth"). In other cases the color is deepened in intensity for more visionary scenes, *The Woman Clothed with the Sun and the Great Red Dragon,* from "Revelations." Even the distortion of the human figure, as is seen in some 12th century English manuscripts, must have had an influence on Blake, consciously or unconsciously. He adopted distortions, they became with him almost mannerisms, to form an individual style which he forced to tell his story. For Blake was essentially an illustrator, though an exceptional and often baffling one, to be sure. The extraordinary number of recent books on the interpretation of his designs proves, aside from the fact that the artist has a strong appeal for the contemporary mind, that he was primarily a visionary story teller. Each picture has a meaning. The pen, the brush, the graver, were always subservient to the mind and the imagination. It is probably the reason why that, except in the case of a few very free pencil drawings, like *Time's Triple Bow*, from "Jerusalem," or the *Stoning of Achan*, so little plastic sense is to be found in his work. Blake's art underneath is essentially didactic—he was explaining his world, or inventing a theology. It is a literary art, not one where plastic values or painter-like surfaces have any place for themselves. In Blake's mind such values were highly meretricious and false. His passionate defense of his own position runs through all his commentaries in his *Annotations to Reynolds, Public Address* and *Descriptive Catalogue*.

But, since Blake was so obsessed with his own ideas, and furthermore, since he was a dedicated, incredibly hard working artist, he became almost inevitably an innovator, a man given to experiment in certain mechanical techniques. It matters little whether he received the recipe for stereotype printing, as he claimed, in a dream from his dead brother Robert, or whether modifications of the technique had been used gropingly by other artists earlier. Blake labored over the process until he bound it to his will, from the early tentative "There is No Natural Religion," 1788, on through the "Songs of Innocence and Experience," 1789–94, to the magnificent late books, "Milton," "Urizen" and "Jerusalem."

Few, if any, artists were engaged in making monotypes during Blake's lifetime. Yet Blake developed a very telling method of procedure in the process. He used large crude mill boards, drew on them directly with pen and ink, laid on color and then pulled an impression which he touched up with water color or tempera. *Christ Appearing to His Disciples After the Resurrection* and *Elijah in the Fiery Chariot* are examples of the technique. Some of Gauguin's monotypes were done in a very similar way.

Lithography, invented in 1789 by the Bavarian, Senefelder, was introduced into England by J. André. In 1803, André brought out a portfolio called "Specimens of Polyautography." For this portfolio, or the edition of 1806, Blake made one now very rare lithograph, *Enoch*, reminding one that his Spanish contemporary, Goya, also turned to the new medium late in life. Blake never pursued lithography further. Possibly, since he was sensitive and prophetic, he foresaw that lithography as a medium would take a direction contrary to his canons of the law of art.

It is not surprising that, when Blake was commissioned in 1820 to illustrate a children's text of Thornton's "Eclogues of Virgil" with woodcuts, he chose the "white line" technique, which is the most expressive, and the one that requires the hand of the artist on the block. Blake cut on a very small scale a series of 17 charming oblong designs which contain a deceptively simple Arcadian mood.

The sources of inspiration for Blake show the depth and perception of his spirit: the Bible, particularly the "Book of Job" and the "Book of Revelations," Spenser, Chaucer, Milton, Shakespeare, Homer, Virgil and Dante. Blake meant it when he said that he was "Drunk with intellectual vision." He seized upon the most abstract or intangible literary images and, with a daring unknown in English art, translated the verbal concepts into visual form. "Pity like a Naked, New-Born Babe" from Shakespeare becomes an unforgettable picture in his large color-printed drawing. "Come pensive Nun" from Milton's *Ode to Melancholy*, an illusive haunting poem, is turned without loss of rhythm into a moving, graphic water color. Perhaps this gift for visualizing abstract words or phrases in human form was the reason Blake had little feeling for landscape in the usual sense. "The grain of Sand," the "Caterpillar on the Leaf" were so insistent in their presence that broad vistas or distant hills had little meaning for him. Blake said that "Nature puts me out."

If the great poets were always at hand for Blake as sources of inspiration, so also his own lyrical genius poured forth a torrent of ideas, that cried out for illumination. The unique quality of Blake's art lies in the fact that he was able to interpret with fire the inventions of his own imagination. He created both in words, and drew a vast cosmos, in which the dark, satanic forces of evil, i.e., reason, struggled continuously with the joys of free untrammelled creation, i.e., imagination. That Blake had for himself no personal doubt of the outcome of such a strife is clear. On his death bed he was busily and happily engaged in coloring an impression of the *Ancient of Days*, or *The Act of Creation*, as it is sometimes called, for one of his friends, Robert Tatham. Years before in a prophetic discourse, he had written his own epitaph: "Inspiration & Vision was then, now & is, & I hope will always Remain, my Element, my Eternal Dwelling place."

ELIZABETH AND JOSEPH PENNELL

WHISTLER vs. *RUSKIN**

THE COURT was crowded. Mr. Serjeant Parry and Mr. Petheram were counsel for the plaintiff, and the Attorney-General (Sir John Holker) and Mr. Bowen for the defendant. Mr. Serjeant Parry opened the case for Whistler, "who has followed the profession of an artist for many years, while Mr. Ruskin is a gentleman well known to all of us, and holding perhaps the highest position in Europe or America as an art critic. Some of his works are destined to immortality, and it is the more surprising, therefore, that a gentleman holding such a position could traduce another in a way that would lead that other to come into a court of law to ask for damages. The jury, after

* Reprinted from *The Life of James McNeill Whistler*, J. B. Lippincott Company, Philadelphia, Pennsylvania, New and Revised Edition, 1919.

hearing the case, will come to the conclusion that a great injustice has been done. Mr. Whistler, in the United States, has earned a reputation as a painter and an artist. He is not merely a painter, but has likewise distinguished himself in the capacity of etcher, achieving considerable honours in that department of art. He has been an unwearied worker in his profession, always desiring to succeed, and if he had formed an erroneous opinion, he should not have been treated with contempt and ridicule. Mr. Ruskin edits a publication called *Fors Clavigera*, that has a large circulation among artists and art patrons. In the July number of 1877 appeared a criticism of the pictures in the Grosvenor, containing the paragraph which is the defamatory matter complained of. Sir Coutts Lindsay is described as an amateur, both in art and shopkeeping, who must take up one business or the other. Mannerisms and errors are pointed out in the work of Burne-Jones, but whatever their extent, his pictures 'are never affected or indolent. The work is natural to the painter, however strange to us, wrought with the utmost conscience and care, however far, to his or our desire the result may seem to be incomplete. Scarcely so much can be said for any other pictures of the modern schools. Their eccentricities are almost always in some degree forced, and their imperfections gratuitously, if not impertinently, indulged. For Mr. Whistler's own sake, no less than for the protection of the purchaser, Sir Coutts Lindsay ought not to have admitted works into the gallery in which the ill-educated conceit of the artist so nearly approaches the aspect of wilful imposture. I have seen and heard much of cockney impudence before now, but never expected to hear a coxcomb ask two hundred guineas for flinging a pot of paint in the public's face.' Mr. Ruskin pleaded that the alleged libel was privileged as being a fair and *bona fide* criticism upon a painting which the plaintiff had exposed to public view. But the terms in which Mr. Ruskin has spoken of the plaintiff are unfair and ungentlemanly, and are calculated to do, and have done him, considerable injury, and it will be for the jury to say what damages the plaintiff is entitled to."

Whistler was the first witness. He said: "I studied in Paris with Du Maurier, Poynter, Armstrong. I was awarded a gold medal at The Hague. . . . My etchings are in the British Museum and Windsor Castle collections. I exhibited eight pictures at the Grosvenor Gallery in the summer of 1877. No pictures were exhibited there save on invitation. I was invited by Sir Coutts Lindsay to exhibit. The first was a *Nocturne in Black and Gold—The Falling Rocket*. The second, a *Nocturne in Blue and Silver* [since called *Blue and Gold—Old Battersea Bridge*]. The third, a *Nocturne in Blue and Gold*, belonging to the Hon. Mrs. Percy Wyndham. The fourth, a *Nocturne in Blue and Silver*, belonging to Mrs. Leyland. The fifth, an *Arrangement in Black—Irving as Philip II. of Spain*. The sixth, a *Harmony in Amber and Black*. The seventh, an *Arrangement in Brown*. In addition to these, there was a portrait of Mr. Carlyle. That portrait was painted from sittings Mr. Carlyle gave me. It has since been engraved, and the artist's proofs were all subscribed for. The Nocturnes, all but two, were sold before they went to the Grosvenor Gallery. One of them was sold to the Hon. Percy Wyndham for two hundred guineas—the one in *Blue and Gold*. One I sent to Mr. Graham in lieu of a former commission, the amount of which was a hundred and fifty guineas. A third one, *Blue and Silver*, I presented to Mrs. Leyland. The one that was for sale was in *Black and Gold—The Falling Rocket*."

Curiously, the only one for sale was pounced on by Ruskin. The coxcomb was trying to get two hundred guineas, and the British commercial critic spotted it.

Asked whether, since the publication of the criticism, he had sold a Nocturne, Whistler answered: "Not by any means at the same price as before."

The portraits of Irving and Carlyle were produced in court, and he is said to have described the *Irving* as "a large impression—a sketch; it was not intended as a finished picture." We do not believe he said anything of the sort.

He was then asked for his definition of a Nocturne: "I have perhaps, meant rather to indicate an artistic interest alone in the work, divesting the picture from any outside sort of interest which might have been otherwise attached to it. It is an arrangement of line, form, and colour first, and I make use of any incident of it which shall bring about a symmetrical result. Among my works are some night pieces; and I have chosen the word Nocturne because it generalises and simplifies the whole set of them."

The Falling Rocket, though it is difficult here to follow the case, was evidently produced at this point upside down; Whistler describing it as a night piece, said it represented the fireworks at Cremorne.

Attorney-General: "Not a view of Cremorne?"

Whistler: "If it were called a view of Cremorne, it would certainly bring about nothing but disappointment on the part of the beholders. (Laughter.) It is an artistic arrangement."

Attorney-General: "Why do you call Mr. Irving an *Arrangement in Black?*" (Laughter.)

The judge interposed, though in jest, for there was more laughter, and explained that the picture, not Mr. Irving, was the *Arrangement*.

Whistler: "All these works are impressions of my own. I make them my study. I suppose them to appeal to none but those who may understand the technical matter."

And he added that it would be possible to see the pictures in Westminster Palace Hotel close by, where he had placed them for the purpose.

Attorney-General: "I suppose you are willing to admit that your pictures exhibit some eccentricities. You have been told that over and over again?"

Whistler: "Yes, very often." (Laughter.)

Attorney-General: "You send them to the gallery to invite the admiration of the public?"

Whistler: "That would be such vast absurdity on my part that I don't think I could." (Laughter.)

Attorney-General: "Can you tell me how long it took you to knock off that Nocturne?"

Whistler: "I beg your pardon?" (Laughter.)

Attorney-General: "I am afraid that I am using a term that applies rather perhaps to my own work. . . ."

Whistler: . . . "Let us say then, how long did I take to 'knock off'—I think that is it—to knock off that Nocturne; well, as well as I remember, about a day. . . . I may have still put a few more touches to it the next day if the painting were not dry. I had better say, then, that I was two days at work on it."

Attorney-General: "The labour of two days, then, is that for which you ask two hundred guineas?"

Whistler: "No; I ask it for the knowledge of a lifetime."

Attorney-General: "You don't approve of criticism?"

Whistler: "I should not disapprove in any way of technical criticism by a man whose life is passed in the practice of the science which he criticises; but for the opinion of a man whose life is not so passed, I would have as little regard as you would if he expressed an opinion on law."

Attorney-General: "You expect to be criticised?"

Whistler: "Yes, certainly; and I do not expect to be affected by it until it comes to be a case of this kind."

The Nocturne, the *Blue and Silver*, was then produced.

Whistler: "It represents Battersea Bridge by moonlight."

The Judge: "Is this part of the picture at the top Old Battersea Bridge? Are those figures on the top of the bridge intended for people?"

Whistler: "They are just what you like."

The Judge: "That is a barge beneath?"

Whistler: "Yes, I am very much flattered at your seeing that. The picture is simply a representation of moonlight. My whole scheme was only to bring about a certain harmony of colour."

The Judge: "How long did it take you to paint that picture?"

Whistler: "I completed the work in one day, after having arranged the idea in my mind."

The court adjourned, and the jury went to see the pictures at the Westminster Palace Hotel. When, on their return, the *Nocturne in Black and Gold —The Falling Rocket*, was produced, the Attorney-General asked:

"How long did it take you to paint that?"

Whistler: "One whole day and part of another."

Attorney-General: "What is the peculiar beauty of that picture?"

Whistler: "It would be impossible for me to explain to you, I am afraid, although I dare say I could to a sympathetic ear."

Attorney-General: "Do you not think that anybody looking at the picture might fairly come to the conclusion that it had no particular beauty?"

Whistler: "I have strong evidence that Mr. Ruskin did come to that conclusion."

Attorney-General: "Do you think it fair that Mr. Ruskin should come to that conclusion?"

Whistler: "What might be fair to Mr. Ruskin, I cannot answer. No artist of culture would come to that conclusion."

Attorney-General: "Do you offer that picture to the public as one of particular beauty, fairly worth two hundred guineas?"

Whistler: "I offer it as a work that I have conscientiously executed and that I think worth the money. I would hold my reputation upon this, as I would upon any of my other works."

*   *   *   *   *

Arthur Severn wrote us that, at the Ruskin trial, he "was on the opposite side, although my sympathies were rather with Whistler, whose *Nocturne in Black and Gold* I knew to be carefully painted. Whenever we met he was most courteous, understanding my position. During the trial one of the Nocturnes was handed across the court over the people's heads, so that Whistler might verify it as his work. On its way, an old gentleman with a bald head got a tap from the frame, then the picture showed signs of falling out of its frame, and when Serjeant Parry turned to Whistler and said 'Is that your work, Mr. Whistler?' the artist, putting his eyeglass up and with his slight American twang, said, 'Well, it was, but if it goes on much longer in that way, I don't think it will be.' And when Ruskin's Titian was shown, 'Oh, come, we've had enough of those Whistlers,' said a juryman. I thought Whistler looked anxious whilst the jury was away. Another trial came on so as not to waste time. The court was dark, and candles had to be brought in— it seemed to be about some rope, and huge coils were on the solicitors' table. A stupid clerk was being examined. Nothing intelligent could be got out of him, and at last Mr. Day, one of the counsel (afterwards the judge), said, 'Give him the rope's end,' which produced great laughter in court, in which Whistler heartily joined. Then, suddenly, a hush fell; the jury returned a verdict for Whistler, damages one farthing."

ROBERT SENCOURT

*EL GRECO**

Although Velazquez occasionally painted a religious picture, his triumphs are interesting because they are not the triumphs of religious genius. His religious paintings illustrate Newman's warning, for they are indeed profane. The very lack of spirituality added assurance to his gifts, and left it to other

* Reprinted from *The Consecration of Genius*, Hollis and Carter, Ltd., 1947. Copyright 1947 by Hollis and Carter. Used by permission of the publishers.

painters to strain at effects which he had abandoned. Yet without an idea of how he surpassed, how can we estimate their successes?

The most arresting of them had preceded him. Domenico Theotocopuli had been born in Crete, and had first studied Byzantine art, of which the seriousness and formality always haunted him: he had arrived at Venice when Titian was the master of her painters. He went on from there to Rome, and was finally attracted by Philip II to work at the Escorial and Toledo. His paintings can be seen in Paris, in London, in certain American and German collections: but, except for the Royal Collection at Bucharest, all his masterpieces are in Spain. We cannot know him till we have been to the Prado, to the Escorial and to Toledo. We see then that he is not merely a painter of skies, of soot, of clouds like icebergs, of mournful lights and morbid ecstasies, of elongated limbs and features, or of tip-tilted noses in holy women. The Prado shows him a painter of stately portraits: he has given them the quality of his own attitude towards life by outlining their heads with a thin, faint line of light. Just as Veronese often gives vividness to his subjects by outlining them with a faint shadow, this outline of light gives an elusive hint of a halo, so that each appears to emerge from an atmosphere of spiritual brightness. El Greco belonged to an age which both discerned holiness and studied earth.

His two most famous pictures are the "St. Maurice" in the Escorial, and the "Burial of the Conde de Orgaz" at Santo Thomé in Toledo. The "St. Maurice" has already left far away the Venetian influences which are so marked in "The Purification of the Temple" at Richmond or "The Annunciation" in the Prado. . . . And this picture tells a story: St. Maurice and his Theban legion were Christians, but had sworn fealty to a Pagan Emperor who commanded the worship of the gods. Unable to forfeit either their allegiance or their faith, their only prospect was death: but death was a gateway to the skies, and the martyr's banner is roseate like the hues of dawn.

This was El Greco's preparation for his masterpiece, the famous "Burial of the Conde de Orgaz": a Spanish nobleman who had left as a perpetual charge on his estates the provision of certain charities for the poor. When his relations disputed the will and lost their case, El Greco was commanded to paint. Going back to the example of Raphael, he again showed on one canvas scenes of both heaven and earth. The clouds are as unsuccessful as ever; they seem like wind-blown sheets, but their lines give powerful aid to the composition, at the summit of which the Redeemer, clothed in fine linen white and clean, beams austerely over the Virgin and the Baptist, and a shining company of the heavenly host, while below two figures, one a Bishop, one a deacon, lift the dead body into its tomb before a company of friars and hidalgos. The Bishop was held to be St. Augustine, the deacon St. Stephen.

In this composition we see the soul of Spain: we see types characteristic of a people, solemn, serene and noble, looking into the very grave and gate of death, and seeing in it the end and purpose of their lives. Death invests daily life with religion, and frames it in eternity. This picture of a burial arrests us like the tones of the trumpet blown among the sepulchres to drive us before the judge's throne. For though the scene on earth is full of peace, and the peace is itself illumined with a silent joy, as at the arrival of a beloved companion in the place of prayer, the *Gloria*, as we call the heavenly vision above it, is restless and disquieting.

The "Burial of the Conde de Orgaz", says Don Manuel Cossío, is indeed one of the truest pages of the history of Spain. "I hold it very difficult", he writes, "to picture to oneself the soul and body of the society of Castile in the last years of the reign of Philip II in other guise, or with more authentic accuracy than is seen here. The true dignity of a miracle in Spain, a solemn office for the dead, an austere company of highly strung and well-born men in mourning between priests on one side and friars on the other, and each of these not simply chosen for the design but faithful portraits: forms rooted up out of the ground of actual experience, and more alive than when they breathed; they are edged instruments which engrave deep in our souls the melancholy impression of those last miserable days of the sixteenth century in Spain, when the Sovereign, who was the most genuine representative of his people, was dying in his room at the Escorial", meditating on the mysteries of the life beyond the grave, the sacred truths of faith, and the glory of the Mass. Here is a picture of a nation's soul "more real than living man"; it is instinct with that immediacy which made Aristotle say poetry is truer than history. It has what Goethe saw was the essential of a work of art when he wrote that they "should live in our fancy". They are as intimate to a Spaniard as his own soul.

For out of the arid plains and rocky sierras of his country, out of its bracing air, its blaze of sun, its piercing winds, he has drawn austerity of manners and opulence of taste: he lives by contrasts. Courteous in general, he makes the fiercest of enemies; patient in repose, his impulses of fury are as torrential as his streams: his moods vary between mildness, whether in melancholy or fun, and a fierce excitement of blood and brain. His eyes shine with the lights of life and death.

In a country of this character, El Greco was at home. He understood it, not in its fierceness, but in its mysticism, not in its blandishments, but in its suffering. Interpreting Spain in repose, he bathes every personage in the contemplative concentration of St. John of the Cross. Each has passed through the dark night of the soul to the living flame of love: each dwells in an interior castle and finds his entertainment there. Not all have suffered: some may have eaten too much: for the Spaniards are fed on heavy dishes, and many of the children are already victims of an overloaded stomach. But whether fed or fasting, they are gentlemen; they know how to bear themselves on all occasions: though touched, they are not abashed at the sudden appearance of Saints. On the contrary, their demeanour is as sensitive as it is calm. Those eyes, so dark and tender, have long since learned to weep with them that weep. Those hands, so slender and nervous, delineate natures and moods more truly than any face.

It was said of El Greco by Palomino that "what he did well none did better: what he did badly none did worse". The saying has been thought to receive complete illustration in this one picture. Few could cavil at the portraits: but it needs a taste, or a wisdom, of a peculiarly excellent kind to enjoy the *Gloria,* and Madrazo could not attain to it: he said that the man who painted it was mad. Yet it is exactly these qualities, so special, so typical and—must we not add?—so eccentric, that now make his admirers most enthusiastic. If we could know El Greco, as Señor Cossío knew him, the peculiarities take their inevitable place in our understanding of the painter, and show him nearer to common men than he seems.

He was, like Michelangelo, very highly strung: he had strong affinities to the religious temperament: he was scarcely normal. He had no fear, nor need to fear

> . . . lest love should ride the wind
> With Spain's dark-glancing daughters.*

In fact, his was a temperament with many resemblances to that of Michelangelo. The great Florentine habitually gave to his representations of the saints the weight of his own suffering, El Greco likewise stamped his saints with his own temper: in the contemplation of a certain elevated type of congenial men his nerves were calm, his appreciation exalted, his fervour strong, though all his own: but if he let his imagination loose, either amid the muscles of men, the personalities of women, or the life beyond the grave, he could not remain serious. The fine features coarsen, the shining eyes fade, the lips thicken, the point of the nose turns upward, and the expression becomes pert, vulgar, rather fatuous; and nothing illustrates more clearly both the passion and exaltation of his temper than his "Sacred and Profane Love".

These rather idiotic stares of ecstasies upon the face go with an extreme sensuousness, sometimes delicate, sometimes coarse, in the naked forms below. Once the balance of his tense nature was disturbed, a morbidity, that some confuse with madness, caused him to veer between genius and ineptitude. It is because he strains, in all sincerity, at an effect beyond his gifts that he, like Cézanne, is felt to be so touching and even great. Cézanne, said M. Maurice Denys, reminds us of El Greco, and "tel est le desarroi de notre temps qu'il semble nous ouvrir une renaissance classique en nous proposant un idéal voisin de la décadence de Venise."†

Shall we admire El Greco, then, for what he aspired to and was not? Perhaps the extravagances that come very near being silly are the proof of genius. Señor Cossío traces a further complication, purely technical. It was an attempt at sincerity in the treatment of colours: an effort to escape from a splendid but inapplicable convention to paint lights and hues that up to then had escaped the artist. He sought in the very clouds something congenial

* Lord Byron, *Childe Harold's Pilgrimage.*
† Such is the disarray of our time that it seems to disclose to us a classical renascence while proposing to us an ideal close to the decadence of Venice.

to those human bodies which gave him sharp longings for he knew not what: for something which appealed intensely to his heart and which he felt only the unseen life could satisfy. His pictures transcend his aims, and base their most powerful appeal not on his genius, but on the weakness of his temperament. "Such", says Cossío, "is the condition of the work of art, and perhaps of every human work. It is executed deliberately as though the spirit made it: and yet in it there is something more and sometimes very different from what the artist desired to give it, elements which traversed his intention for which alone he is responsible, elements which arise without him suspecting it from the great subconsciousness in which the mind moves, and which can come to light by the slow, undisturbed assimilation and the propitious point of vantage which come with time." Perhaps we can discern now something of what puzzled earlier ages: the man had the most acute sense of spirituality as shown in character, and yet could find assurance neither in sacred history nor in visions of a life beyond shared with the Saviour and His saints. He understood the mystics without sharing their faith.

PHILIP GILBERT HAMERTON

IMAGINARY PORTRAITS*

ONE OF the most interesting characteristics of the human mind is the pleasure that it has in pure make-believe, in self-deception of which it still remains perfectly conscious. An artist paints or carves a portrait of somebody that he never saw, and concerning whose person he possesses no documents whatever, the chances are millions to one that there is not the slightest trace of resemblance to the supposed original, yet we look upon the work with quite genuine satisfaction if only it answers in some degree to our notion of what the original might possibly have been like. Novelists and playwrights have occasionally turned into ridicule the propensity of a few self-made men to invent ancestors for themselves, and to have imaginary portraits of them on their walls. If ever this has been done in real life for the satisfaction of an individual, he only followed a precedent set for him by humanity at large. Unable to rest content with what is really known about the past, we encourage the painter or the sculptor to travel beyond the confines of the known and bring back for us rich spoils out of the abyss of emptiness. He is to go, like Lord Bacon, and rediscover the lost Atlantis.

The most remarkable of our inconsistencies in the love of imaginary portraits is that we accept them when contradictory of each other. We accept a King Alfred from the invention of one artist, and another King Alfred from another artist, the two being entirely incompatible, yet we have a kind of satisfaction in both. Our mind accommodates and adjusts itself to different inventions as it does to different effects of light in landscape.

* Reprinted from *Men in Art*, Macmillan and Company, London, New York, 1892.

If we are descended from some historical personage of whom there is no authentic portrait, and if some painter or sculptor makes an imaginary portrait of him, we are drawn to it by an irrational but irresistible curiosity. We know that it is only the portrait of some model, more or less idealised, yet the mere choice of the name (which may have been decided upon at the last moment after the work was done) is enough of itself to act upon our own sympathy and imagination. It was perfectly natural, perfectly in accordance with this human instinct, that the Duke of Westminster should have set up a colossal statue of his ancestor Hugh Lupus in the grounds of Eaton Hall. Nobody knows what Hugh Lupus was like, but Mr. Watts, with his gift of imagination, is supposed to know, and reveals him to us stalwart in his armour of bronze. Our pedigrees are often mere catalogues of names; they would be more real for us if an artist enriched them with miniatures or medallions throughout the ages. Thackeray touched playfully upon this desire to realise what can never be made visible when he described young Clive Newcome as drawing ideal sketches of his reputed ancestor the "barber-surgeon."

It is a vast advantage for ideal portraiture that we should not possess any record of the reality. When Rubens made his portraits of the Magi he was free to choose the most majestic models. If the Church had possessed photographs of her prophets and apostles, Michael Angelo would have been so hampered by them, and by the priestly desire for a reverent fidelity, that his imaginative production of sublime personages would have been made impossible. It is curious, but indisputable, that we owe the overpowering Moses of Michael Angelo and his awful prophets and his stately and authoritative apostles and evangelists not to his great imaginative genius merely, but to the universal ignorance about the real men which left his genius free to do its best. This is but one of the many artistic advantages that we owe to our ignorance of the past, for if we knew it familiarly as we do the England of the newspaper age, it would be difficult indeed for any public man, however strong in intellect and pure in character, to preserve that ideal grandeur which the genius of Michael Angelo realised.

There is an interesting example in art-history of a kind of portraiture which is not entirely fictitious, as the artist had access to materials, but which, nevertheless, is in a certain degree fictitious, as the materials were inadequate for paintings in which the artist affected to know more than had come down to him. When Titian undertook the portraits of the Twelve Caesars for Federico Gonzaga, Duke of Mantua, he could refer to many statues, busts, and medals or gems; but a little reflection soon makes us perceive how far these materials are from supplying the *life* in the eyes and complexion, in the colour of the hair, and in the qualities of the living tissues that interest a painter, and most especially a colourist. The commission for this series was a strange and not altogether a prudent commission to give. The impulse that prompted it was the common desire to know more about the past than can ever now be ascertained, along with a semi-belief that Titian could somehow gain access to it and reveal it.

A nearer approach to this kind of truth might be possible for artists if they were aided, as they have been in some cases, by the light thrown on slender artistic materials by literary description, but this would lead us away from imaginary portraiture to historical. However, the imagination of a portrait-painter may sometimes find vigorous exercise in the endeavour to realise a face that the artist has never seen, but for which he has some slight memoranda. In such a case the kind of imagination exercised appears to be purely scientific and reconstructive within the limits of positive consistency and truth. Portraiture of this kind, applying known laws to the reconstruction of a human face, and to the bestowal of new life, is far from being an idle employment of a painter's knowledge and ability.

Here is a case in which the imagination may be employed in the revival of the past. A contemporary portrait exists, but although it answers almost every question we might ask about the physical appearance of an ancestor who lived, let us say, in the time of Queen Elizabeth—although it tells us plainly what was the shape of his face, the colour of his hair and complexion and of his eyes, the trimming of his beard and the fashion of his dress—still, the work is stiff and hard, it is insufficiently modelled, and even the dress itself is without quality and texture as a piece of painting, though nothing could be clearer and more explicit as a mere piece of information *about* the costume our ancestor wore. In a case of this kind a modern artist might be called in, not to touch upon the old painting, which, however poor, is sacred, but to realise it over again, on another canvas, with the help of his greater technical accomplishment and his better knowledge of the life. Here the exercise of imagination would simply be in imparting vitality to the face and reality to the costume. By a process resembling in some degree the transfusion of living blood, the artist would take a certain quantity of life out of his own century (this *present*, in which life is superabundant) and carry it back to the Elizabethan age that life has quitted long ago. Such a process is so common in modern literature that it has ceased to attract attention. The modern biographer of a man who lived in the distant past brings to his task a knowledge of life acquired from his observation of the living, and he is more exposed to anachronism than a painter, as there is clear evidence that the minds of men have changed more than their bodies.

Drama

CHARLES LAMB

PLAY-HOUSE MEMORANDA*

I ONCE SAT in the Pit of Drury-lane Theatre next to a blind man, who, I afterwards learned, was a street musician, well known about London. The play was *Richard the Third*, and it was curious to observe the interest which he took in every successive scene, so far more lively than could be perceived in any of the company around him. At those pathetic interviews between the *Queen* and *Duchess of York*, after the murder of the children, his eyes (or rather the places where eyes should have been) gushed out tears in torrents, and he sat intranced in attention, while every one about him was tittering, partly at him, and partly at the grotesque figures and wretched action of the women, who had been selected by managerial taste to personate those royal mourners. Having no drawback of sight to impair his sensibilities, he simply attended to the scene, and received its unsophisticated impression. *So much the rather her celestial light shone inward.* I was pleased with an observation which he made, when I asked him how he liked Kemble, who played *Richard*. I should have thought (said he) that that man had been reading something out of a book, if I had not known that I was in a play-house.

I was once amused in a different way by a knot of country people who had come to see a play at that same Theatre. They seemed perfectly inattentive to all the best performers for the first act or two, though the piece was admirably played, but kept poring in the play-bill, and were evidently watching for the appearance of one, who was to be the source of supreme delight to them that night. At length the expected actor arrived, who happened to be in possession of a very insignificant part, not much above a mule. I saw their faint attempt at raising a clap on his appearance, and their disappointment at not being seconded by the audience in general. I saw them try to admire and to find out something very wonderful in him, and wondering all the while at the moderate sensation he produced. I saw their pleasure and their interest subside at last into flat mortification, when the riddle was at once unfolded by my recollecting that this performer bore the same name with an actor, then in the acme of his celebrity, at Covent-Garden, but who lately finished his theatrical and mortal career on the other side of the Atlantic. They had come to see Mr. C——, but had come to the wrong house.

Is it a stale remark to say, that I have constantly found the interest excited at a play-house to bear an exact inverse proportion to the price paid for admission? Formerly, when my sight and hearing were more perfect, and my purse a little less so, I was a frequenter of the upper gallery in the old Theatres. The eager attention, the breathless listening, the anxiety not to

* Reprinted from *Works of Charles Lamb*, ed. by Thomas Hutchinson, Oxford University Press, 1924.

lose a word, the quick anticipation of the significance of the scene (every sense kept as it were upon a sharp look out), which are exhibited by the occupiers of those higher and now almost out-of-sight regions (who, going seldom to a play, cannot afford to lose any thing by inattention), suffer some little diminution, as you descend to the lower or two-shilling ranks; but still the joy is lively and unallayed, save that by some little *incursion* of *manners*, the expression of it is expected to abate somewhat of its natural liveliness. The oaken plaudits of the trunkmaker would *here* be considered as going a little beyond the line.—In the pit first begins that accursed critical faculty, which, making a man the judge of his own pleasures, too often constitutes him the executioner of his own and others'! You may see the *jealousy of being unduly pleased*, the *suspicion of being taken in to admire;* in short, the vile critical spirit, creeping and diffusing itself, and spreading from the wrinkled brows and cloudy eyes of the front row sages and newspaper reporters (its proper residence), till it infects and clouds over the thoughtless, vacant countenance of John Bull tradesmen, and clerks of counting-houses, who, but for that approximation, would have been contented to have grinned without rule, and to have been pleased without asking why. The sitting next a critic is contagious. Still now and then a *genuine spectator* is to be found among them, a shopkeeper and his family, whose honest titillations of mirth, and generous chucklings of applause, cannot wait or be at leisure to take the cue from the sour judging faces about them. Haply they never dreamed that there were such animals in nature as critics or reviewers; even the idea of an author may be a speculation they never entered into; but they take the mirth they find as a pure effusion of the actor-folks, set there on purpose to make them fun. I love the unenquiring gratitude of such spectators. As for the Boxes, I never can understand what brings the people there. I see such frigid indifference, such unconcerned spectatorship, such impenetrability to pleasure or its contrary, such being *in the house* and yet not of it, certainly they come far nearer the nature of *the Gods*, upon the system of Lucretius at least, than those honest, hearty, well-pleased, unindifferent mortals above, who, from time immemorial, have had that name, upon no other ground than situation, assigned them.

Take the play-house altogether, there is a less sum of enjoyment than used to be. Formerly you might see something like the effect of a novelty upon a citizen, his wife and daughters, in the Pit; their curiosity upon every new face that entered upon the stage. The talk of how they got in at the door, and how they were crowded upon some former occasion, made a topic till the curtain drew up. People go too often now-a-days to make their ingress or egress of consequence. Children of seven years of age will talk as familiarly of the performers, aye and as knowingly (according to the received opinion) as grown persons; more than the grown persons in my time. Oh when shall I forget first seeing a play, at the age of five or six? It was *Artaxerxes*. Who played, or who sang in it, I know not. Such low ideas as actors' names, or actors' merits, never entered my head. Thy mystery of delight was not cut open and dissipated for me by those who took me there. It was *Artaxerxes* and *Arbaces* and *Mandane* that I saw, not Mr. Beard, or Mr. Leoni, or Mrs. Kennedy. It was all enchantment and a dream. No such pleasure has since visited me but in dreams. I was in Persia for the time, and the burning idol of their devotion in the temple almost converted me into a worshipper. I was awe-struck, and believed those significations to be something more than elemental fires. I was, with Uriel, in the body of the sun.— What should I have gained by knowing (as I should have done, had I been born thirty years later) that that solar representation was a mere painted scene, that had neither fire nor light in itself, and that the royal phantoms, which passed in review before me, were but such common mortals as I could see every day out of my father's window? We crush the faculty of delight and wonder in children, by explaining every thing. We take them to the source of the Nile, and shew them the scanty runnings, instead of letting the beginnings of that seven-fold stream remain in impenetrable darkness, a mysterious question of wonderment and delight to ages.

JOHN CHAPMAN

O'NEILL'S "LONG DAY'S JOURNEY INTO NIGHT"*

Eugene O'Neill's tremorous illness had been progressing with the steadiness of doom. Sometimes his wife, Carlotta Monterey O'Neill, would help him move about by turning her back to him, draping his arms over her shoulders, lifting him by bending, and thus carrying him to where he wanted to go. Almost always she kept a cheerful countenance toward him. There had been no new O'Neill play for many years, not a revival of an old one, and so his income was slight; they were living on a moderate income of hers.

One day he discovered on her a thoughtful look and he asked, "What are you worrying about?" She confessed. "Money."

"Don't worry," he said. "Remember, we have a nest egg—*Long Day's Journey.*" She looked at him in surprise and said, "But you said this wasn't to be done until twenty-five years after your death."

The playwright answered, "Oh, that was for Gene, and Gene's dead now."

This, as Mrs. O'Neill told it to me one afternoon late in 1956, was the beginning of the public history of the dramatist's greatest play. It had had a private history: When he had finished it in July 1941 he showed it to his son, Eugene, Jr., a bearded, brilliant classical scholar who was an assistant

---

* This article by John Chapman is from his book, *Broadway's Best*, 1957. Copyright (c) 1957 by Doubleday & Company, Inc. Reprinted by permission of the publisher. The play, "Long Day's Journey into Night," copyright as an unpublished work, 1955, by Carlotta Monterey O'Neill; copyright, 1955, by Carlotta Monterey O'Neill; published by the Yale University Press, 176 pages.

professor of Greek at Yale University. The son told his father he did not think this play should be produced or published because it put him, the son, in a bad light—showed the kind of family he came from. Almost offhand, the elder O'Neill wrote on a card and slipped the card into the script; it read, "Not to be published or produced until twenty-five years after my death."

Then, in the fall of 1950, Eugene O'Neill, Jr., killed himself in his summer cottage.

Soon after *Long Day's Journey into Night* struck Broadway with shattering impact, there arose debate as to whether this drama *did* represent the "kind of family" Gene, Jr., had sprung from. Obviously O'Neill had used the dramatist's privilege of compression and arrangement, for he presented and developed his four principal characters and told what happened to and within them in the time lapse of a single day. This, obviously, was not realism in a reportorial sense. But there were some—old actors, old neighbors in New London among them—who insisted that the characters themselves were not realistic. They said that Eugene's father, the great James O'Neill, was neither a drunkard nor a miser, but a kindly family man and a genial good neighbor.

There is no doubt, though, that the Tyrone family in the play—father, mother, and two sons—is the O'Neill tribe: James, the father, Ella, the mother, and sons James, Jr., and Eugene. After he finished his play O'Neill dedicated it to his wife on their twelfth wedding anniversary, July 22, 1941. He wrote, in his tight, small longhand, "I give you the original script of this play of old sorrow, written in tears and blood. A sadly inappropriate gift, it would seem, for a day celebrating happiness. But you will understand, I mean it as a tribute to your love and tenderness which gave me the faith in love that enabled me to face my dead at last and write this play—write it with deep pity and understanding and forgiveness for all the four haunted Tyrones."

In November 1956 Mrs. O'Neill wrote me: "That particular play is—to me—far different from all O'Neill's other plays. He *had* to write it. It was as if he were bedevilled. In the writing he was tortured. After his day's stint he would come out of his study with sunken cheeks, eyes red from weeping—& physically & mentally exhausted. . . Thus the play was written—it was a very large part of him! His whole life & thought were influenced by those early years."

Eugene O'Neill died November 27, 1953, in Boston, leaving his estate to his wife with the behest that certain of his papers and manuscripts be given to Yale University. Mrs. O'Neill became mindful of one important document—*Long Day's Journey into Night*. Remembering that her husband had, in effect, released the play after his son's death, she felt that this drama should become part of O'Neill's public record. The finally revised and typed playscript was reposing in the safe of O'Neill's publisher, Random House.

Mrs. O'Neill called the publisher and suggested the drama be published. She explained that the twenty-five-year restriction no longer held, and sent her lawyers to the publisher's lawyers to show that, as executor of her husband's estate, she could do as she would with the script. Even so, Random House, according to Mrs. O'Neill, declined to bring out the play. She then thought of Yale, her husband's beneficiary, and asked the university's librarian if he knew of someone who might publish it. He said he thought the Yale University Press would bring it out. The drama was published in February, 1956 and a year later it had reached the fifty-thousand mark in sales—an unusual figure for a theatre piece.

Once the play was published, it meant that it was available for stage production. Although he had never seen any of his plays done in Swedish, O'Neill had always felt that the Royal Theatre in Stockholm, which had devoted itself to his works over the years, had given his plays their finest productions. Mrs. O'Neill gave the Royal Theatre the opportunity to present the world premiere of *Long Day's Journey into Night*. This production was an international sensation, and it whetted the already keen appetites of Broadway managers.

Many established managers pleaded for the privilege of producing *Long Day's Journey*. It is said that Mrs. O'Neill asked one of them, "What are you going to do it with—elephants?" She fended them off. Then one day she sent for thirty-two-year-old, Panama-born, Spanish-Italian Jose Quintero and forthwith asked him if he would like to produce the play. He reeled a moment, asked for time to think, went out of Mrs. O'Neill's New York hotel, and had a drink at a bar. Thus calmed and fortified, he went back to the widow and said "Yes."

The selection of Quintero, a semipro, over many well-established and highly regarded Broadway professionals, was not a quixotic one. In the season of 1946–1947 the Theatre Guild had made a production of the newest O'Neill play, *The Iceman Cometh*, with the late Dudley Digges as Harry Hope, the saloon keeper, and James Barton as Hickey, the salesman. It was not altogether an artistic success and it was a commercial failure. Ten years later Quintero and his two partners, Theodore Mann and Leigh Connell, who operated a small, arena-style theatre in Greenwich Village called the Circle in the Square, obtained permission to make a modest revival of *The Iceman* in their little show shop.

The revival was directed by Quintero, who had begun directing at the little playhouse because he and his partners, when they first went into business, could not afford the fee of a professional director. *The Iceman* was an immediate success, artistically and at the box office, on its second time around. Many critics declared it was closer to O'Neill and better than the original Broadway production. It also offered a bravura performance by an unknown young actor, Jason Robards, Jr.—son of an old-time movie star—in the role of salesman Hickey. At this writing, the Village revival of *The Iceman* has run more than a year and is still running—even though Robards is no longer in it. Robards now is in *Long Day's Journey into Night*, playing the embittered and alcoholic elder son of the haunted Tyrones. The opportunity to produce *Long Day's Journey* was offered Quintero solely on the artistic strength of the off-Broadway production of *The Iceman*.

Once the course is set for a play to be presented on Broadway, there are two main problems: Who is going to put up the money? Who will act it? Money was no problem for Quintero and his partners, nor was acting.

Fund-raising for today's theatre often is a long and harrowing task, occasionally embracing more drama and comedy than does the play for which the money is being assembled. The problem of financing O'Neill's drama was one of whom *not* to include among the investors, for, following the Stockholm success, many people wanted a "piece." One stage-struck tycoon, a gentleman of high reputation in the theatre as well as in the realm of finance, offered to put up the entire production cost, no matter what it might be, but his offer was respectfully declined. Quintero & Co., sensing that this was their main chance, decided to let in on the production as many people as possible—all the old friends and backers and actors who had helped them in their early Greenwich Village struggles. So the shares of *Long Day's Journey into Night* were sliced in many pieces and widely distributed.

The casting also offered few obstacles. Many stars had hankered for roles in the drama, and from the outset Fredric March and his wife, Florence Eldridge, were eager for the parts of the elder Tyrones. There was no question on the part of the young producing partners as to who should play the dissolute elder son of this couple: He would be Jason Robards, Jr., who had been playing for so long in *The Iceman Cometh*. Two parts remained to be filled—a serving girl and the younger Tyrone son. By now Quintero's acquaintance with and knowledge of actors was considerable, and he had no particular difficulty in choosing Katherine Ross, who had already appeared in two of his downtown productions, as the servant. Finding an actor to play the ailing and neurotic younger Tyrone, Edmund, was a task to be approached with care—for here, purportedly, was the young Eugene O'Neill himself. Quintero listened to upwards of two hundred actors before engaging Bradford Dillman, a young ex-Marine and Yale drama student, who had appeared in one Broadway play and in several off-Broadway and summer-stock productions.

The still-young season had offered few presentations of quality by early November 1956: there had been a charming English drawing-room comedy, *The Reluctant Debutante;* Terence Ratigan's tour de force for actors, *Separate Tables;* a young Shakespeare repertory company from the Old Vic; Rosalind Russell's peppermint candy stick, *Auntie Mame;* and two theatrically solid Shaw revivals—*The Apple Cart* and *Major Barbara*. The evening of November 7, 1956, was electrifying, for it was then that *Long Day's Journey* had its premiere at the Helen Hayes Theatre on West Forty-sixth street.

My own report on the event began: "Let us now forget something that everybody knows by now, that Eugene O'Neill's *Long Day's Journey into Night* is about himself, his parents, and his brother. This is a mere detail. . . . The news this morning is that *Long Day's Journey into Night* is a magnificent work, and last evening it was given a magnificent performance by Florence Eldridge, Fredric March, Jason Robards, Jr., and Bradford Dillman. It exploded like a dazzling skyrocket over the humdrum of Broadway theatricals." This first-night notice concluded: "Last evening at the Helen Hayes was a great evening for the American theatre, and the first-night audience was spellbound and enraptured."

There were few reservations expressed by the critics of the other daily journals. Brooks Atkinson reported in the New York *Times*, "*Long Day's Journey into Night* has been worth waiting for. It restores the drama to literature and the theatre to art." In the *Herald Tribune*, Walter Kerr called it "a stunning experience." In the New York *Post*, Richard Watts, Jr., called it "magnificent and shattering." However, although they acknowledged the strength of the drama, two of the next-day critics did not go all out. In the *Mirror*, Robert Coleman called it rugged and sprawling and added, "It is carved from granite. Perhaps that's why it never really touches the heart, though, in all its facets, it excites admiration. It is over-long Chekhov, with a vengeful bite and too little compassion. But it is emotional dynamite for those with the patience to wait for its eventual explosion." Tom Donnelly, of the *World-Telegram* and *The Sun*, concurred with Coleman in his reservations as to the length of the drama. But O'Neill, who began as a short-play writer (his *The Emperor Jones* is a masterpiece of tight writing) never was one to be bothered by length, as such marathons as *Strange Interlude* and *Mourning Becomes Electra* testify. He rewrote his plays painfully and painstakingly, but once he felt he could do no more for them, they stood. He would not permit any cuts, nor will his widow now. One time, the Theatre Guild begged O'Neill to shorten a play, arguing that as it stood it would run so late that commuters would find it difficult to get home. "I'm not writing for commuters," the playwright said flatly. *Long Day's Journey into Night* is so long that it has no matinees and plays only six performances a week. The curtain goes up at seven-thirty p.m. and comes down well after eleven. However, director Quintero did manage to shorten the play by ten minutes—by eliminating one intermission.

RICHARD HAYES

*THE BEAUTIFUL GALATEA (REVIEW OF "MY FAIR LADY")**

Pygmalion, so Ovid tells us in Mr. Rolfe Humphries' translation of the gentle *Metamorphoses*,

> . . . . made, with marvelous art, an ivory statue,
> As white as snow, and gave it greater beauty

* Reprinted from *The Commonweal* (April 27, 1956) by permission of Edward S. Skillin, editor.

Than any girl could have, and fell in love
With his own workmanship . . .
He pays her compliments, and brings her presents
Such as girls love, smooth pebbles, winding shells,
Little pet birds, flowers with a thousand colors,
Lilies, and painted balls and lumps of amber . . .
A necklace, and earrings, and a ribbon for her bosom,
And all of these become her.

But no life warms that marble beauty, until "golden Venus" hears the young man's prayer, and shows her presence, and

Pygmalion came
Back where the maiden lay, and lay beside her
And kissed her, and she seemed to glow,
. . . . and (he) felt the ivory soften
Under his fingers, as wax grows soft in sunshine. . .

In "My Fair Lady," however, Messrs. Lerner and Loewe have brought their subtle blandishments not to an ivoried perfection, but to a play as quick, as pungent and flushed with blood as any this century has produced, and one, moreover, which enshrines the great dramatic image of a purely personal relationship. For Shaw's "Pygmalion" is surely nothing less: we may have ascended (and descended) more grandly with Pirandello, with Chekhov, even with "Saint Joan" and "Major Barbara," yet no single human relationship in the modern drama—unless perhaps, on a different level, that of Stanley and Blanche in "Streetcar"—lives in the mind with such zest and grittiness and ardent tenacity as that of the willful Professor Higgins and the mucky guttersnipe fished out of the trampled violets of Covent Garden.

There is, too, a special happiness in watching this fabulous relationship work again its remembered mesmerism on the audiences at "My Fair Lady": pleasure in realizing that Mr. Lerner's finest wit issues from the Shavian fountainhead, that Mr. Loewe's richest song comments on the Shavian scheme. Conversely, the occasion abdicates its high splendor when the adaptors sweeten Shaw's wryness into the honeyed jam of sentiment. (One often met unicorns in the garden of Ayot St. Lawrence, but rarely did they weep the easy tears of love.) Yet surely it is possible to see what prompted Messrs. Lerner and Loewe to soften the conclusion of "Pygmalion," for along with the other great cry-babies of this world, I too have never been able to down the bitter solution in which Shaw washes the play's finale: something resists that sober draught of evangelical rigor: one feels that art and life have subtly been confused. And who is to say that we are wrong, for does not even Bradley in his *Shakespearean Tragedy*—writing on that wider, deeper, greater play *Lear*—say that the heart is bruised by the wanton deaths imposed on Cordelia and the old king at the last (the tragic demands already having been satisfied), and does he not suggest that the later Shakespeare of *The Tempest* would have confessed and corrected such an excess? The beauty of the Pygmalion-Galatea relationship—its fertilizing command of the imagination—lies in its ultimate anchoring in myth, the concerns of which diverge from those of a Protestant reality. Shaw translates the myth from Paphos to Piccadilly, but the thing will not undergo a sea-change, and we sense that he does violence to some profound demand of the spirit (however fully he satisfies *other* demands) in allowing the clammy air of an ideology of personality to descend on the play's resolution. Still, one must confess that the figure, in "My Fair Lady," of a lovesick Higgins lamenting his lost goddess of the dropped aitches, is not one of dignity.

I shall say nothing further about the pleasures of "My Fair Lady," most of which have been bruited about so noisily by our ever-busy critics that one wonders what may remain for the delectation of a clamorous public. One would wish, however, to pay tribute to Mr. Rex Harrison for a capital, liverish Higgins, and to Mr. Cecil Beaton, who enfolds the myth in his own parti-colored cocoon of Edwardian *chic*. But of the rest, nothing. For the pleasures of theater, as Mr. Eric Bentley has observed, are more directly sensuous than criticism can suggest: they are not so much above it, as beyond it. And if you take this to be an evasion of the critical task, I can only agree with you. But tell me then: how does one fix and capture the moment when Miss Julie Andrews, all radiance and pearly luster, glides imperceptibly out of a grotesque wit into the shimmer and grace of melody? What shall one say? It is the lark. . . .

Yet the great musical comedy—and particularly the one drawn from a great play—always leaves me with a heightened but instructive melancholy. For while I can conceive no limit to the various and possible existences of "Pygmalion," the beauty of "My Fair Lady" seems to me, subtly, the flower of this moment in time. I cannot imagine another age recreating its heady and potent charms. The history of musical comedy, Mr. Virgil Thomson once noted, is written in the secret emotional life of every man and woman. Its triumphs are ever hostages to fortune, the buried treasure of time: in nothing so much as these joys do we read the unmistakable pattern of our mortality.

JACK GOULD

TV: "LITTLE MOON OF ALBAN"*

A PLAY of stirring poignancy and beauty, superbly acted by Julie Harris and Christopher Plummer, was presented Monday night on "Hallmark Hall of Fame" over Channel 4.

The work was James Costigan's original drama "Little Moon of Alban," a searching and sensitive study of the turmoil of a human soul, a lovely Irish

* Reprinted from *The New York Times* (March 26, 1958) by permission of *The New York Times*.

girl, who is driven to God by fear but ultimately achieves full dedication through selfless love.

Mr. Costigan told his story against a background of the waning hours of the Irish rebellion against the English in the Nineteen Twenties. In the midst of the violence and emotional strife he related with tenderness and delicacy the moral struggle between two individuals uncertain of their faith.

Mr. Costigan's words frequently achieved almost a poetic quality in their deep reverence and awareness of man's frailty. It was a most moving ninety minutes, certainly deserving of prize consideration.

The central figure of "Little Moon of Alban" is Brigid Mary, who sees her fiancé killed by the English and seeks the comfort of the Daughters of Charity. Upon taking the vows for a year she is assigned to a hospital for the English. There it is her lot to nurse a wounded English lieutenant who himself has lost faith and fears death.

Through the girl's care and prayers he survives miraculously and asks her to leave the religious community and become his wife. But she realizes that by believing with her heart in God she has now found her own salvation, which dictates their separation.

Miss Harris' interpretation of the Sister was a glowing achievement. She conveyed the complete sincerity of faith yet the inner struggle of the individual who questions her own strength. Her performance was utterly compelling.

Mr. Plummer, as the English lieutenant, gave a magnificent portrayal of a soldier wounded in soul as well as body. The man's superficial cynicism, his halting search for a faith and his appreciation of the heart-rending situation was conveyed with fine conviction and meticulous discipline.

In the tradition of the "Hallmark Hall of Fame" the supporting cast was excellent. Nora O'Mahoney's performance as the girl's mother was a gem of characterization. Barry Jones played the overworked English field physician with great understanding, and Frank Conroy had many touching scenes as the family priest.

George Schaefer directed "Little Moon of Alban" with exquisite attention to detail and complete sensitivity. The camera work was superb. So were the settings.

"Little Moon of Alban" was more than a television program; as good theatre should be, it also was an experience.

CHARLES J. ROLO

A REVIEW OF "THE ELDER STATESMAN"*

In Hugh Kenner's critical study, *The Invisible Poet: T. S. Eliot* (Mc-Dowell, Obolensky), there is an illuminating discussion of Eliot's recent plays,

* Reprinted from *The Atlantic Monthly* (June, 1958) by permission of Charles J. Rolo.

the latest of which is *The Elder Statesman* (Farrar, Straus & Cudahy). Mr. Kenner is an extremely learned and ingenious critic whose previous work, by and large, has struck me as rich in pretentiousness and obscurantism. His book on Eliot is a study for the specialist, and a reviewer pressed for space cannot come to grips with it decently. But the final chapter on Eliot's theater is sharp, succinct, and exceptionally interesting—an admirable piece of criticism—and by way of preface to *The Elder Statesman* I propose to summarize briefly some of its findings.

The Eliot play, Mr. Kenner observes, is on its way to becoming a distinct dramatic genre, in which "a special language, a corresponding moral climate, and a whimsically melodramatic plot irradiate one another's possibilities." What is special about the language is its "inimitable explicitness." Eliot's people talk with preternatural efficiency and wit, as though people were capable of saying exactly what they wanted; and as they talk, they advance toward a discovery of their real identity. Eliot has cunningly contrived a stage verse "which *shall set the characters free*" and enable him to construct his plot around the theme of self-discovery and liberation. In these plots, the unemphatic use of incidents in which one is not really expected to believe directs attention to the inner drama. At the beginning we see only what is normally seen in the drawing room, and a person's drawing-room personality is normally an invention. But the invention is challenged by the return of ghosts—a woman who knows the secret of the character's parentage or people who have shared the past which his contrived self has obliterated. And in the third act, the character comes to terms with some hitherto elusive self—joins a religious nursing order or drops a financial career to become a church organist.

Claverton ran over a man and failed to stop. Gomez claims that Claverton was the author of his corruption: that he took up a poor undergraduate whose admiration tickled his love of power and led him on to form expensive tastes beyond his means. Mrs. Carghill, formerly Maisie Montjoy, had an affair with Claverton, her first, when she was a very young actress; and she feels he betrayed her love by letting his father buy her off. These suavely vindictive ghosts are seeking a subtle revenge: what they want is not money but Claverton's "friendship"—the pleasure of his company. If he refuses it, they will discredit him in the eyes of his children—Monica, who is so devoted to him that she cannot bring herself to leave him to marry the man she loves, and Michael, who bitterly resents the high standards he has been expected to live up to.

But Claverton outfaces his blackmailers. He makes a full confession to his children, and he recognizes that he has always wanted to dominate them and others—has used people to bolster his pretenses. By confession and contrition, he exorcises the ghosts which, he realizes, have "always been with me." And though his son rejects him and he knows that he is close to death, he feels at peace: "I've only just now had the illumination/Of knowing what love is. . . ./ In spite of everything, in defiance of reason,/I have been brushed by the wing of happiness."

The Elder Statesman has not, I think, the tantalizing brilliance or the originality of *The Cocktail Party*, but it is a highly satisfying and entertaining work. Certainly the mellowest of Eliot's plays, it speaks continually of love, and, in contrast to its predecessors, it proclaims that human love can be self-sufficient, provided that the parties to it have shown their true self to each other. *The Elder Statesman* is also the most unambiguous of Eliot's plays. It affirms that we cannot escape the past or ultimately evade responsibility; and that to find "the truth that shall set you free," we must strip ourselves of all pretenses.

Diversions

JOSEPH STRUTT

WRESTLING, GOFF, AND FOOT-BALL*

Wrestling

THE ART of wrestling, which in the present day is chiefly confined to the lower classes of people, was, however, highly esteemed by the ancients, and made a very considerable figure among the Olympic games. In the ages of chivalry, to wrestle well was accounted one of the accomplishments which a hero ought to possess.

Wrestling is a kind of exercise that, from its nature, is likely to have been practised by every nation, and especially by those the least civilized. It was probably well known in this country long before the introduction of foreign manners. The inhabitants of Cornwall and Devon have, we are well assured, from time immemorial been celebrated for their expertness in this pastime, and are universally said to be the best wrestlers in the kingdom. To give a Cornish hug is a proverbial expression. The Cornish, says Fuller, are masters of the art of wrestling, so that if the Olympian games were now in fashion, they would come away with the victory. Their hug is a cunning close with their fellow-combatants, the fruits whereof is his fair fall or foil at the least. They learn the art at an early period of life, for you shall hardly find, says Carew, an assembly of boys in Devon and Cornwall, where the most untowardly among them will not as readily give you a muster (or trial) of this exercise as you are prone to require it.

The citizens of London, in times past, are said to have been expert in the art of wrestling, and annually upon St. James's day they were accustomed to make a public trial of their skill. In the sixth year of Henry III, they held their anniversary meeting for this purpose near the hospital of St. Matilda, at St. Giles's in the fields, where they were met by the inhabitants of the city and suburbs of Westminster, and a ram was appointed for the prize; the Londoners were victorious, having greatly excelled their antagonists, which produced a challenge from the conquered party, to renew the contest upon the Lammas day following at Westminster: the citizens of London readily consented, and met them accordingly, but in the midst of the diversion, the bailiff of Westminster and his associates took occasion to quarrel with the Londoners, a battle ensued, and many of the latter were severely wounded in making their retreat to the city. The unjustifiable petulance of the bailiff gave rise to a more serious tumult, and it was several days before the peace could be restored. Stow informs us, that in the thirty-first year of Henry VI, A.D. 1453, at a wrestling match near Clerkenwell, another tumult was excited against the lord mayor, but he does not say upon what occasion it rose.

* From "Strutt's Sports." Reprinted from *The Sports and Pastimes of the People of England*, Chatto and Windus, London, 1898. As the style indicates, however, the book was first published in 1801.

In old time, says Stow, wrestling was more used than it has been of later years. In the month of August, about the feast of St. Bartholomew, adds this very accurate historian, there were divers days spent in wrestling; aldermen and sheriffs being present in a large tent pitched for that purpose near Clerkenwell; upon this occasion the officers of the city, namely, the sheriffs, serjeants, and yeomen, the porters of the king's beam or weighing-house, and others of the city, gave a general challenge to such of the inhabitants of the suburbs as thought themselves expert in this exercise; but of late years, continues he, the wrestling is only practised on the afternoon of St. Bartholomew's day. The latter ceremony is thus described by a foreign writer, who was an eye-witness to the performance: 'When,' says he, 'the mayor goes out of the precincts of the city, a sceptre, a sword, and a cap, are borne before him, and he is followed by the principal aldermen in scarlet gowns with golden chains; himself and they on horseback. Upon their arrival at a place appointed for that purpose, where a tent is pitched for their reception, the mob begin to wrestle before them two at a time.' He adds a circumstance not recorded by the historian: 'After this is over, a parcel of live rabbits are turned loose among the crowd, which are pursued by a number of boys, who endeavour to catch them with all the noise they can make.'

From the time that wrestling became unfashionable and was rarely practised by persons of opulence, it declined also among the populace, but by slower degrees; and at present is seldom seen except at wakes and fairs, where it still continues to be partially exhibited. ****

Goff

There are many games played with the ball that require the assistance of a club or bat, and probably the most ancient among them is the pastime now distinguished by the name of goff. In the northern parts of the kingdom goff is much practised. It requires much room to perform this game with propriety, and therefore I presume it is rarely seen at present in the vicinity of the metropolis. It answers to a rustic pastime of the Romans which they played with a ball of leather stuffed with feathers, called paganica, because it was used by the common people: the goff-ball is composed of the same materials to this day: I have been told it is sometimes, though rarely, stuffed with cotton. In the reign of Edward III, the Latin name cambuca was applied to this pastime, and it derived the denomination, no doubt, from the crooked club or bat with which it was played; the bat was also called a bandy, from its being bent, and hence the game itself is frequently written in English bandy-ball.

Goff, according to the present modification of the game, is performed with a bat, not much unlike the bandy: the handle of this instrument is straight, and usually made of ash, about four feet and a half in length; the curvature is affixed to the bottom, faced with horn and backed with lead; the ball is a little one, but exceedingly hard, being made with leather, and, as before observed, stuffed with feathers. There are generally two players, who have each of them his bat and ball. The game consists in driving the ball into certain holes made in the ground; he who achieves it the sooner, or in the fewest number of strokes, obtains the victory. The goff-lengths, or the spaces between the first and last holes, are sometimes extended to the distance of two or three miles; the number of intervening holes appears to be optional, but the balls must be struck into the holes, and not beyond them. It should seem that goff was a fashionable game among the nobility at the commencement of the seventeenth century, and it was one of the exercises with which Prince Henry, eldest son to James I, occasionally amused himself, as we learn from the following anecdote recorded by a person who was present: "At another time playing at goff, a play not unlike to pale-maille, whilst his schoolmaster stood talking with another, and marked not his highness warning him to stand farther off, the prince thinking he had gone aside, lifted up his goff-club to strike the ball; mean tyme one standing by said to him, 'beware that you hit not master Newton:' wherewith he drawing back his hand, said, 'Had I done so, I had but paid my debts.'" ****

Foot-ball

Foot-ball is so called because the ball is driven about with the feet instead of the hands. It was formerly much in vogue among the common people of England, though of late years it seems to have fallen into disrepute, and is but little practised. I cannot pretend to determine at what period the game of foot-ball originated; it does not, however, to the best of my recollection, appear among the popular exercises before the reign of Edward III, and then, in 1349, it was prohibited by a public edict; not, perhaps, from any particular objection to the sport in itself, but because it cooperated, with other favourite amusements, to impede the progress of archery.

When a match at foot-ball is made, two parties, each containing an equal number of competitors, take the field, and stand between two goals, placed at the distance of eighty or an hundred yards the one from the other. The goal is usually made with two sticks driven into the ground, about two or three feet apart. The ball, which is commonly made of a blown bladder, and cased with leather, is delivered in the midst of the ground, and the object of each party is to drive it through the goal of their antagonists, which being achieved the game is won. The abilities of the performers are best displayed in attacking and defending the goals; and hence the pastime was more frequently called a goal at foot-ball than a game at foot-ball. When the exercise becomes exceeding violent, the players kick each other's shins without the least ceremony, and some of them are overthrown at the hazard of their limbs.

The danger attending this pastime occasioned King James I, to say, 'From this court I debarre all rough and violent exercises, as the foot-ball, meeter for lameing than making able the users thereof.'

The rustic boys made use of a blown bladder without the covering of leather by way of foot-ball, putting peas and horse beans withinside, which occasioned a rattling as it was kicked about.

'It had been the custom,' says a Chester antiquary, 'time out of mind, for the shoemakers yearly on the Shrove Tuesday, to deliver to the drapers, in the presence of the mayor of Chester, at the cross on the Rodehee, one ball of leather called a foote-ball, of the value of three shillings and fourpence or above, to play at from thence to the Common Hall of the said city; which practice was productive of much inconvenience, and therefore this year (1540), by consent of the parties concerned, the ball was changed into six glayves of silver of the like value, as a reward for the best runner that day upon the aforesaid Rodehee.'

ARTHUR DALEY

BO AND HIS BOYS*

ALVIN (Bo) McMILLIN was a man of character and class. He had a delightful drawl, an infectious grin and a warm, bubbling personality. His place in football history is secure. He will rank as one of the game's great players although he never gained equal stature as a coach despite his Coach of the Year honors one season. The genuinely beloved Bo died yesterday but his death was not unexpected. It had been an open secret in sports circles for a year that his days were numbered, ever since it had been discovered that he had cancer.

The discovery came shortly after he had succeeded Greasy Neale as the coach of the Philadelphia Eagles. Bo got to do little work on that job. He went home to wait for the end, unafraid and at peace with his God. Bo was always a God-fearing man. He never used profanity. He never took a drink. He never smoked. His was a model life.

In Search of Material

The white-thatched McMillin delighted to tell a story of his boyhood days in Fort Worth, and Bo was a magnificent story-teller, much in the Will Rogers manner. He was on his way to church one Saturday afternoon—or so he drolly claimed—when he heaved a rock through a store window. A policeman collared him instantly.

"Why did you do that?" sternly asked the gendarme.

"Well, officer," drawled Bo, turning on the charm. "I wuz on my way to confession and I reckon I wuz jes' a mite short of material."

It's an apocryphal tale, of course, but Bo was never shy about going after

* Reprinted from *The New York Times* (April 4, 1952) by permission of *The New York Times*.

material when he was a college coach. He pursued it with great industry. Once he tried to woo away a player from Pitt back in the days when the dour Jock Sutherland was turning out powerhouses for the Panthers.

The wily Bo phoned the boy's home. "Hello," snapped a voice at the far end of the wire. Bo went into his spiel, reciting the greater educational advantages that Indiana had to offer over Pitt. Bo thought he was convincing but soon began to get uneasy at the strange and uncomfortable silence at the Pittsburgh end of the line.

"Do you know whom you're talking to?" asked the voice. There was a note of asperity to it. Also a faint Scottish burr. The quick-witted Bo recognized it as belonging to Jock Sutherland himself.

"Yes, sir," he chuckled. "Now I do." He hung up.

His Pore Li'l Boys

The gracious McMillin was a success as long as he remained in college coaching, but when he yielded a virtual lifetime tenure at Indiana for a fling at the professionals, he overreached himself. He just wasn't gaited for the play-for-pay boys and he failed with the Detroit Lions.

Bo belonged with the colleges. The younger collegians adored him, drank in his blarney and responded to the inspirational force he offered. His face was innocent and guileless. His humor was sharp and contagious. He always could evoke sympathy, even though it occasionally had to be larded with laughter.

He moaned long and loud before the start of the 1945 season about his "pore li'l boys," but his fertile brain improvised a style of attack for Indiana which he described as "the cockeyed T-formation." It was, in the main, an early model of the Winged-T which was to gain prominence later. He used his backs interchangeably with variations of the single wing to make it more confusing. He won the Big Ten championship for Indiana with it, the first such title the Hoosiers had achieved in forty-five years.

His Rich, Big Boys

Among the professionals, however, Bo discovered a different situation. These weren't impressionable boys whom he could mold at will. These were mature men. They resented his strict training rules, rules so strict that even smoking was forbidden. They sneered at his improvisations, the same sort of improvisations which delighted and intrigued his collegians. The squad split into cliques and so did the seventy-odd members of the syndicate which owned the Lions. For the first time in his life Bo had the material he craved but he couldn't make it click. Buddy Parker, who succeeded him, took the same material and almost won the divisional championship, losing on the final day.

There can be no doubt, however, about Bo's qualities as a player. He was just a little fellow with a pug nose and a sharp football brain when he went from Texas to unknown Centre College in the Kentucky hills, but the Praying Colonels were to electrify the football world by upsetting mighty Harvard in 1921. It was a carefully plotted 35-yard run by McMillin which produced the 6–0 score, but before that Walter Camp had recognized his greatness by naming him to his 1919 All-American team.

He was a true builder of character. But the best job he did in that respect was in building his own.

A TRUE OLYMPIAN*

THE FIRST Olympic champion was Coroebus of Elis. He won the great foot race in a meadow beside the river Alpheus at Olympia in 776 B. C. The Emperor Theodosius halted the Olympic Games by decree in 394 A. D.

Fifty-five years ago this week James Brendan Connolly, a red-haired Bostonian, joined Coroebus as a historic first. He became the first Olympic champion of the modern era, winning the hop, step and jump, the opening event of the 1896 games at Athens.

Even today James B. Connolly is a lot prouder of that exploit than he is of many books he has written—books that have made him the most distinguished author of sea stories in the land. It was a bitter choice he had to make in order to win his championship and he still doesn't regret it.

Young Jim was a student at Harvard in those days and a fine athlete. He had won the triple jump at the National A. A. U. title meet and was an avid reader of the classics, completely fascinated by Chapman's translation of Homer. When he also read that the Olympic Games were being revived after a lapse of 1,500 years, he just couldn't resist, particularly since they were to be held on the ancient sites of which Homer had spoken with such eloquence and elegance.

Volunteers Only

There was no formal American Olympic team in those days. It was strictly a catch-as-catch-can operation and anyone who could pay his own way was eligible. The Boston A. A. and Princeton University were the only groups represented. The clubmen paid their own expenses and the collegians were financed by Bob Garrett, who was to find it a profitable investment because he himself won two Olympic crowns.

Presumably Princeton raised no objection to the Garrett expedition, but Harvard definitely frowned on Connolly's.

---

* Reprinted from *The New York Times* (April 4, 1951) by permission of *The New York Times*.

He applied for a two-month leave of absence and was told stiffly that he could resign if he wished and then apply later for reinstatement. No concessions would be made.

"I'm not resigning and applying for reinstatement later," said the redhead, flaring into the redheaded rage he'd inherited from the Aran Island fisherfolk who'd been his ancestors. "I'm quitting now."

Almost an Afterthought

This much must be said for Harvard, however. The Cantabs did give Connolly his major H for winning the Olympic championship. But Jim didn't receive that letter until the fiftieth anniversary of his graduating class in 1949—which is a pretty long delay even for Harvard.

The Boston A. A. group worked its way to Athens on a cattle boat, figuring that the athletes would have twelve days for practice and acclimatization. But the Greeks had inconsiderately used the Hellenic calendar instead of the Roman one. Instead of twelve days to spare, they had none whatsoever. Connolly had to compete on the very day he arrived.

Even that arrival was quite an undertaking. In Naples the carrot-top from Boston lost his wallet in a cab. Not only did this leave him penniless but the train ticket to Athens was also in the wallet. The carabinieri nailed the cabbie after he'd spent the cash but before he'd disposed of the ticket. Connolly grabbed it and raced for the train. Only by sprinting down the platform did he make it, willing hands hauling him into the compartment.

His First Jump

They reached Athens in time for breakfast. Not until then did Jim discover that he was competing that very afternoon. Nor did his dismay diminish when he first saw the jumping runway. It wasn't sleek and hard-packed cinders but loose soil, heavy underfoot.

Connolly was the last man to try of all the contestants. He raced down and hopped, stepped and jumped 45 feet. An excited roar cascaded out of the stands.

"What's that racket for?" asked the startled Connolly as he lay in the pit. "By Jove, man," answered a rueful British rival. "You're a mile in front!"

Actually it was only three feet, not a mile. But Connolly's leap of 45 feet was sufficient to bring victory and a traditional wreath of olives to this latterday Coroebus.

How good was Connolly? Well, he later did 49 feet ½ inch in the triple jump and that endured as a world record for thirteen years.

James B. Connolly would be a great man if he had done no more than write his fascinating tales of the Gloucester fishing banks. But as the first of the modern Olympic champions he's extra special, a true champion in sports as well as literature.

JOHN ARLOTT

*BRONCHO**

Rodrigo Marcos, although a Spaniard of Spain, was clearly unaccustomed to the type of heat that Brisbane calls normal. In his own land, the sun may burn, but there is always escape into the shade. In the hot-house humidity of Queensland, where pineapples grow like weeds, the only corrective to irritability is air-conditioning.

Brisbane, however, is slightly more temperate than the Queensland back-block township of Mareeba on the Atherton Tableland, known—in so far as it is known at all—as the air-base for the Battle of the Coral Sea and the postal address of Donald Johnson. Johnson is known as "Broncho" to the five thousand observers of boxing who compress themselves, every Friday night, into the Brisbane Stadium. There, under the arc-lamps and the dark weight of ceiling, they conspire with the normal climate of the city to create an atmosphere in which the mere act of breathing acts as a perspiration pump, and all voluntary movement is reduced to a gingerly minimum.

Johnson is not taken entirely seriously by the local spectators. To be sure, he was amateur middleweight boxing champion of Australia before he became a professional to relieve his family's temporary financial difficulties by undertaking five fights, in a booth, for a total 'purse' of five shillings. His training consists largely of tree-felling in intervals of rough-riding, horse-breaking and the staging of rodeos in the sparsely populated areas of North Queensland. His wife is purely of the first Australian people and, when her husband's various employments take him from home, she and their two children travel in the caravan attached to the rear of his car. One of the major difficulties of arranging fights for the Broncho is that from time to time he will decide to 'go walkabout,' as the aboriginals call it, so that he cannot be found for several weeks.

In appearance Johnson is more remarkable than impressive. His vast mop of black hair continues down his cheeks in two fanshaped side whiskers; the remains of the beard he removes for appearance in the boxing ring. His dressing gown is decorated with a large picture of a bucking horse and, when he takes it off, his body appears no more than serviceable. His chest is not deep nor his arms thick: his legs look unathletic and the size of his feet gives more promise of balance than suggestion of aesthetically pleasing proportion.

Rodrigo Marcos, undefeated welterweight champion of Spain, has added weight until he fights at eleven stone four pounds, but he looks an athlete. He is powerfully built, with strong shapely legs, firm arms and a sturdy neck: his face has a cast of breeding; it is lively and little marked by his trade. Johnson versus Marcos was the main match of the evening.

---

* Reprinted from *The Spectator* (January 7, 1955) by permission of Ian Gilmour, editor.

The spectator in front of me wore the wide-brimmed trilby hat and the half-sleeved shirt, open at the neck, which mark the Australian on a sporting occasion. Turning round to the rows of faces which shone and steamed back into the darkness of the five-shilling seats, he shouted, with little hope, 'I'll bet five to one.' He had no need to indicate that he was laying odds against Johnson. The appearance of the two boxers in the ring was already enough to promise a one-sided fight.

It was confirmed by the first round, in which the Spaniard gave a skilful demonstration of attacking boxing. It was marred—without discredit to the demonstrator—only by the fact that Johnson would not play his part. Instead of giving ground, he continued to advance, however hard he was hit, in a belligerent shuffle towards his opponent. From time to time, indeed, he came close enough to him to embrace him, and grind his stubby jaw, with a half-tender roll of the head, into the hollow of Marcos' shoulder while seeming to congratulate him with slaps on the back of the neck and over the kidneys. He had a habit of breaking from clinches with his right hand cupped over his ear as if he were straining to hear some whisper from Marcos. His body reddened under quick, whippy punches and a swing peeled his nose like a tomato.

Yet, as the gong went for the end of the round, Johnson drew himself up, and breathing in the greatest possible volume of the oxygen-starved air his lungs could contain, swaggered with a self-conscious air of mastery to his corner.

For one three-minute round after another, Johnson walked determinedly if ungracefully towards Marcos and Marcos punched him. Perhaps once in a round Johnson landed a punch: Marcos landed a dozen. Four times Johnson's upswinging fist made a strange angular line in the space where Marcos had been a moment before. Tobacco smoke had turned the steam-heat into a swamp mist. Punches landed with the sound of a boot slapped into a puddle. Gloves stamped against Johnson's guarding arms and hands, against his face and ribs.

It was a gladiatorial certainty that he could not last four rounds. Yet he swaggered only a little wearily back to the ice-water and ironic sympathy of his seconds after the seventh round. He had barely moved from his stool for the eighth round when Marcos ran at him and hit him and hit him again and again with a feminine intensity. Johnson could not fall down, the ropes were at his back. He started to walk towards Marcos, through the blows. Then he put his arms round him, pinioning his arms and, resting his gritty chin again on Marcos' shoulder, put out his tongue. 'He's tough,' said an Australian, 'you can't knock him down except with an axe.' 'Johnson's knees is wobbling,' tore a bugle voice in my ear, 'the Broncho's had it, he can't take another punch.' Someone—was it me?—said, 'A pound he doesn't go down.'

In the ninth round, Johnson still walked towards Marcos, and Marcos, in intervals of almost hysterical punching, leant on Johnson. Late in the tenth round Johnson hit Marcos: not very hard, for he was tired. Marcos staggered, partly fell through the ropes. Johnson pressed forward, stumbled, hit Marcos again, off one knee: the gong sounded. Johnson swaggered to his corner, Marcos went slowly to his: the referee followed him. He was jaunty but he was a cold grey colour. He could not come to his feet for the eleventh round. The referee raised Johnson's hand as the winner. Johnson acknowledged the applause with a perfunctory smile and a wave.

Then Johnson, who is used to the Queensland climate, bathed and changed and waited the long three-quarters of an hour until Marcos had recovered from his chilled fatigue. The Broncho's vocabulary and style of speech stem purely from the Bible. He declared himself well pleased with the fight and so valiant an opponent. He received the sum of £400 for the fight. It is said in Brisbane that Broncho Johnson is a showman.

ROGER BANNISTER

ALL BREAK RECORD IN '1500'*

THE OLYMPIC 1,500-metre final today surpassed all expectations. It was a magnificent struggle in which every competitor broke the Olympic record.

When less than two seconds separates the best times of all the runners, the victor needs ability, good judgment and tactics, but he also needs luck.

Twelve finalists lined up in glorious sunshine and were lucky to get away first time, after even the Marathon runners an hour earlier had taken a false start. The diminutive Murray Halberg had the inside position, the three British runners—Brian Hewson, Ken Wood and Ian Boyd—next to him, with John Landy of Australia and Ron Delany of Ireland towards the outside of the track.

Halberg, wearing the black New Zealand colours that Lovelock carried to his 1,500-metre victory in the Berlin Olympics, shot into the lead, but no one really wants to lead from a field like this. Hewson, tall and pale, now with a crisper stride than he had in Britain, did well to slip in behind him.

Then came a block of runners three abreast, protecting their insecure positions with their elbows. John Landy, on whom all Australian eyes were focused, ran most conspicuously last—for him, a most unusual position.

The first lap was completed in 58.8 seconds, fast enough to bring a world record within reach.

Merv Lincoln, the 23-year-old Australian schoolmaster, moved into the lead after one and a half laps, with Ian Boyd trailing him. Just before the race Lincoln required injections for a painful foot. He is a stumpy runner, with unbounded competitive ability, who seems to defy the laws of nature

* "All Break Record in '1500'" appeared in the December 2, 1956 edition of *The Sunday Times*, London. Reprinted by permission of the author and *The Sunday Times*.

by sprinting all the way. He led past the half-mile in 2 min. 0.2 sec. and was still leading at the bell.

The rest of the field uncomfortably jostled each other, no one anxious to take the lead yet no one willing to be last. Then Klaus Richtzenhain of Germany, who recently ran an impressive 1,500 metres in Britain, was at Lincoln's shoulder, with Hewson and Boyd just behind him.

At the bell in the 1,500 metres the jumble begins to sort itself out. Every split second is crucial in the shuffling of leading positions.

At the bell, each runner must gauge the depth of his dwindling reserves of energy to decide the moment he should attempt to get away from the field. Once he starts his finish the die is cast and he must never let up.

He exposes in a moment his strength or his weakness to the rest of the field. If he starts too soon, he will be caught by the field as he crawls across the line. If he leaves it too late, another runner may snatch four or five yards that he can never regain.

In my experience, the first runner to attempt to jump the field seldom gets away with it. Most runners start too soon; that is, if they are able to take the lead at all. The best chance lies with the runners who, merely by increasing their pace, keep with the leaders for a finishing burst. It takes courage to wait.

Round the second-to-last bend in today's 1,500 metres, six runners wrestled with this problem—the trickiest in middle-distance running. They were Lincoln, Hewson, Richtzenhain, Boyd, Delany and Landy.

Lincoln was still leading, but looked a spent force. Hewson was the most anxious of the six and the least able to restrain himself. He sprang into the lead at the three-quarter mile mark, which was passed in 3 min. 1.5 sec.— not quite fast enough for a world record. Not that it mattered in a race of this calibre.

But Hewson was too tired to escape and stole a bare two yards from his rivals. Richtzenhain was the second to make his effort, but his moment of glory was short-lived. Delany, the stringy, quick-striding Irishman, watched the field closely. Round the bend he paused and checked Landy, who was running at his shoulder, for a few strides. Then, as the finishing straight approached, Delany with perfect timing pounced on Richtzenhain and led by four yards a hundred yards from the tape.

But in this field even the last bend may be too soon to start a finishing burst. The crowd rose to their feet as John Landy, running his first big race from behind, tore towards Richtzenhain and Delany with the air of a man astonished by his own performance. For a moment it looked as though we might see the most impossible victory of the Games, but Delany was too good for Landy and drew ahead over the last 30 yards.

Landy crossed the finish abreast of Richtzenhain, who gained second place on a photo finish. Tabori, one of the few Hungarians to produce any form in these Olympics, was fourth and Hewson, who fought with waning strength over the last few yards, came fifth and, like Boyd, who came eighth, ran his best 1,500 metres yet.

Could Landy have won? He ran as though he knew he could not win; he ran for a place and not for a gold medal.

Had he regained his confidence before the race and, by chance or good planning, held Delany's position on the last bend, I think the story might have ended differently.

Could Hewson have won? Only he knows how much reserve he had left at the three-quarter mark. But I suspect he might more wisely have left his finish until the last bend.

Ron Delany, by running a last lap in 54 seconds, had outstripped the greatest field of 1,500-metre runners yet assembled, even remembering the regrettable absence of Roszavolgyi of Hungary, the world record-holder, eliminated in the heats.

Afterwards Delany said, "I never felt so happy in my life." He had won Ireland's first gold medal since Tisdall won the 400-metre hurdles in 1932. When asked afterwards by an American correspondent if he received a check during the race, he momentarily wondered if we were discussing the old amateur problem.

Then he emphatically denied any obstruction in a broad Irish-American brogue in which Irish still dominates. "The track is rather small for 12 people. Everyone had trouble getting through and, if you got too near a person, you were as likely as not to get a wallop."

* * * * *

We all liked the way he ran today but we took him to our hearts when he said, "It was John Landy who taught me how to relax and, if I didn't win myself, I wanted John Landy to."

BRUCE CATTON

THE GREAT AMERICAN GAME*

BY THE carefully repeated definition of men who stand to make money out of its acceptance, baseball is the Great American Game. The expression was invented long ago and it has been rammed home by talented press agents ever since, even in times when most Americans seemed to be interested very largely in something else. But what has given the phrase its sticking power is not the fact that a big industry has kept plugging it, or the allied fact that unceasing repetition has dinned it into an unreflecting public's ears for generations, but simply the fact that in its underlying essence it is perfectly true.

* Reprinted from *American Heritage* (April, 1959) by permission of *American Heritage, The Magazine of History.*

Baseball is the American game, great or otherwise, because it reflects so perfectly certain aspects of the American character that no other sport quite portrays.

It has few of the elements of pure sportsmanship, as that dubious word is commonly accepted, and it is not notably a game for gentlemen. But it does embody certain native-born fundamentals, including above all others the notion that the big thing about any contest is to win it. It is also built upon the idea that anything you can get away with is permissible, and it is the only sport (at least the only one since the Roman populace sat in the thumbs-down section at the gladiatorial games) that puts an invitation to homicide in one of its enduring sayings: "Kill the umpire!" (The thing has actually been attempted, too, more than once.) It is pre-eminently the sport for the professional rather than for the amateur, the sport in which the well-intentioned duffer neither is given nor especially wants a part.

Almost everyone in the country has played it at one time or another, but almost nobody except the professional dreams of going on playing it once full manhood has come. It is a spectator sport in which each spectator has had just enough personal experience to count himself an expert, and it is the only pastime on earth that leans heavily on the accumulation of page upon page of inherently dry statistics. It is also an unchanging pageant and a ritualized drama, as completely formalized as the Spanish bullfight, and although it is wholly urbanized it still speaks of the small town and the simple, rural era that lived before the automobile came in to blight the land-scape. One reason for this is that in a land of unending change, baseball changes very little. There has been no important modification of its rules for well over half a century. The ball in use now will go farther when properly hit, and the gloves worn on defense are designed to do automatically what personal skill once had to do, but aside from these things the game is as it was in the early 1900's. Even the advent of night baseball, which seemed like pure sacrilege when it was introduced two decades ago, has made little difference; the pictorial aspect of the game—which is one of its most important features—has perhaps even gained thereby. The neat green field looks greener and cleaner under the lights, the moving players are sil-houetted more sharply, and the enduring visual fascination of the game—the immobile pattern of nine men, grouped according to ancient formula and then, suddenly, to the sound of a wooden bat whacking a round ball, break-ing into swift ritualized movement, movement so standardized that even the tyro in the bleachers can tell when someone goes off in the wrong direction —this is as it was in the old days. A gaffer from the era of William McKinley, abruptly brought back to the second half of the twentieth century, would find very little in modern life that would not seem new, strange, and rather bewildering, but put in a good grandstand seat back of first base he would see nothing that was not completely familiar.

But that is only the surface part of it. Baseball, highly organized, pro-fessionalized within an inch of its life, and conducted by men who like dollars better than they like sport, still speaks for the old days when nine young men in an open park somehow expressed the hot competitive instincts of everybody and spoke for home-town pride.

And perhaps the central part of all of this is the fact that in its essence baseball is still faintly disreputable and rowdy. Its players chew tobacco, or at least look as if they were chewing it; many of them do not shave every day; and they argue bitterly with each other, with their opponents, and with the umpires just as they did when John McGraw and Ed Delehanty were popular idols. They have borrowed nothing from the "sportsmanship" of more sedate countries; they believe that when you get into a fight you had better win, and the method by which you win does not matter very much. Anything goes; victory is what counts.

This John McGraw, for example. When he was playing third base and there was a runner there, and someone hit a fly to the outfield, McGraw would unobtrusively hook his fingers in the player's belt so that the take-off for the plate, once the ball was caught, would be delayed by half a second or so. He got away with it, too, and no one thought the worse of him, until one day a baserunner unbuckled his belt in this situation and, legging it for home, left the belt dangling in McGraw's hand, tangible evidence of crime. Note, also, that baseball knows about the bean ball—the ball thrown at the batter's head to drive him away from the plate and hamper his hitting process. A big leaguer was once killed by such a pitch; it has been condemned by everybody ever since then, and it is still a regular feature of the game.

In its essentials, then, baseball is plebeian, down-to-earth, and robustious. Even half a century ago it was dwindling to the rank of secondary sport in the colleges. Professors who have adjusted themselves to the presence on the campus of soi-disant students who are paid to attend college so that they may play football have a way of considering the football player one cut above the baseball player. The former may be a hulking behemoth of pure muscle, wholly incapable of differentiating between Virgil's Eclogues and Boyle's law, but he does not seem quite as uncouth as the baseball player— who, in his own turn, may also be on the campus as a paid hand, the difference being that he is being paid by some major-league team that wants to see his athletic skills developed, while the football player gets his from ardent alumni who want to see the college team beat State on Homecoming Day next fall. There has never been any social cachet attached to skill on the diamond.

The reason, obviously, is that baseball came up from the sand lots—the small town, the city slum, and the like. It had a rowdy air because rowdies played it. One of the stock tableaux in American sports history is the aggrieved baseball player jawing with the umpire. In all our games, this tableau is unique; it belongs to baseball, from the earliest days it has been an integral part of the game, and even in the carefully policed major leagues today it remains unchanged. Baseball never developed any of the social niceties.

In the old days, when (as we suppose, anyway) most of us lived in small towns, or at least in fairly small cities, the local baseball team represented civic pride, to say nothing of representing at the same time the dreams of a great many young men who wished to be much more athletic than they actually were. In very small towns, its games were usually held in Farmer Jones's pasture, where the difficulty, in a hot moment of split-second play, of distinguishing between third base and some natural cow-pasture obstacle sometimes led to odd happenings; and in slightly larger places the county fairground or a recreational park at the end of the streetcar line provided the arena. In any case, muscular young men, wearing the singularly unbecoming uniforms that were standardized 75 years ago, presently took their positions on the grass, and the game was on.

It was, and still is, hotly competitive, and within reasonable limits anything goes. If the umpire (there was just one, in the old days) could be suborned to give all vital judgments in favor of the home side, all well and good; no one ever blushed to accept a victory that derived from an umpire's bias. If he could be intimidated, so that close decisions would go as the spectators wanted them to go, that also was good. This often happened; an umpire who decided a crucial play against the home team was quite likely to be mobbed, and few pictures from the old-time sports album are more authentic or more enduring than the vision of an umpire frantically legging it for the train, pursued by irate citizens who wished to do him great bodily harm. It took physical courage to render impartial judgments in old-time small-town baseball, and not all umpires were quite up to it.

If the umpire could be deceived while the game was on, that also was good. A man running from first to third on a base hit would cut twenty feet short of second base if he thought he could get away with it, and no one dreamed of censuring him for it. If an opposing player could be intimidated, so that he shirked his task, that was good, too. Not for nothing was the greatest baseball player who ever lived, Ty Cobb, famous for sitting on the bench just before the game sharpening his spikes with a file. An infielder, witnessing this, and knowing that Cobb was practically certain to ram those spikes into his calf or thigh in a close play, was apt to flinch just a little at the moment of contact, and out of that split second of withdrawal Cobb would gain the hair's edge of advantage that he needed. It was considered fair, too, to denounce an opponent verbally, with any sort of profane, personal objurgation that came to mind, on the off-chance that he might become unsettled and do less than his best. (This still goes on, like practically all of the other traditional things in baseball, and the "bench jockey"—the man who will say anything at all if he thinks it will upset an enemy's poise— can be a prized member of a big-league team even now.)

Baseball is conservative. What was good enough in Cap Anson's day is good enough now, and a populace that could stand unmoved while the federal Constitution was amended would protest with vehemence at any tampering with the formalities of baseball. It looks as it used to look; the batter still grabs a handful of dust between swings, the catcher still slams the ball over to third base after a strike-out, and the umpire still jerks thumb over right shoulder to indicate a putout. (Dismayingly enough, some umpires now grossly exaggerate this gesture, using an elaborate full-arm swing, but possibly the point is a minor one.)

An inning begins; the pitcher takes his warm-up tosses, now as in the days half a century ago, and after three, four, or five of these he steps aside and the catcher whips the ball down to second base. The second baseman tosses it to the shortstop, two yards away, and the shortstop throws it to the third baseman, who is standing halfway between his own base and the pitcher's box; the third baseman, in turn, tosses it over to the pitcher, and the inning can get started. To vary from this formula is unthinkable; from the little leaguers up to Yankee Stadium, it is as one with the laws of the Medes and the Persians.

Then action: players shifting about, pounding their gloves, uttering cries of encouragement (which, like all the rest, are verbatim out of the script of 1900); and the batter approaches the plate, swinging two bats (another ironclad requirement), tossing one aside, planting his feet in the batter's box, and then swinging his single bat in determined menace. The fielders slowly freeze into fixed positions; for a moment no one anywhere moves, except that the pitcher goes into his stretch, takes a last look around, and then delivers—and then the frozen pattern breaks, the ball streaks off, men move deftly from here to there, and the quick moments of action are on.

In all of this there is unending fascination, coupled with the knowledge that wholly fantastic athletic feats may at any moment be displayed by any one of the players. Even an easy fly ball to the outfield or a simple grounder to short can call forth a nonchalant, effortless expertness that a man from another land would find quite incredible. (I once took an Englishman to see his first baseball game, and he was dumfounded by the simplest plays, marveling at what all the rest of us took for automatic outs.) In no contest can the split second be so important. A routine double play can make both outs with no more than half a second to spare, and if the half second is lost anywhere, the player who lost it will be derided for a clumsy oaf.

Primarily a team game, baseball is also the game for the individualist. The team play is essential, and when you watch closely you can see it, but the focus is usually on one man. A base runner streaks for second with the pitch, falls away while in full stride, and slides in in a cloud of dust, baseman stabbing at him with gloved hand, umpire bending to peer through the murk and call the play; an outfielder runs deep and far, arching ball coming down—apparently—just out of his reach, trajectories of fielder and baseball coming miraculously together at the last, gloved hand going out incredibly to pick the ball out of the air; a pitcher who has been getting his lumps looks about at filled bases, glowers at the batter, and then sends one in that is struck at and missed . . . always, some individual is trying for an astounding feat of athletic prowess and, now and then, actually accomplishing it.

Hence baseball celebrates the vicarious triumph. The spectator can identify himself completely with the player, and the epochal feat becomes, somehow, an achievement of his own. Babe Ruth, mocking the Chicago Cubs, pointing to the distant bleachers and then calmly hitting the ball into those bleachers, took a host of Walter Mittys with him when he jogged around the bases. (There is some dispute about this, to be sure; he was jawing with the Cubs, but purists say he did not actually call his shot. This makes no difference whatever.) It was the same when old Grover Cleveland Alexander, the all-but-washed-up veteran of many baseball wars, came into the seventh inning of a decisive World Series game, found the bases filled with Yankees, and struck out Tony Lazzeri, going on to win game and Series; and this was after a wearing night on the tiles, Alexander having supposed that his work was over until next spring. Many an aging fan shared in Old Alex's triumph.

These things are part of baseball's legend, for the game never forgets its gallery of immortals. That it actually has a tangible Hall of Fame, with bronze plaques to commemorate the greatest, is only part of the story; the noble deeds of the super-players are handed down in barside stories, year after year, losing nothing in the telling. Some of the heroes have been super-men, in a way, at that. There was, for instance, Shoeless Joe Jackson, barred from baseball in mid-career because he let himself be bribed to help lose a World Series. (He did not do very well at losing; even under a bribe, he batted .375 in that Series—a natural hitter who just couldn't make himself miss even when paid to do so.) A sand-lot pitcher tells of a day, a whole generation later, when, pitching for a textile-mill team in the Carolinas, he found on the opposing team none other than Jackson—a pathetic, fat, doddering wreck in his late fifties, with a monstrous belly like some disreputable Santa Claus, still picking up a few odd bucks playing semi-pro ball under an assumed name. The young pitcher figured Jackson would be easy; a low inside curve, coming in close to the overhang of that prodigious paunch, was obviously the thing to throw. He threw, Jackson swung, and swung as he used to thirty years earlier, and the ball went far out of the park, one of the most authoritative home runs the young pitcher ever witnessed. Old Jackson lumbered heavily around the bases, and halfway between third and home he turned to accost the young pitcher. "Son," he said, "I always could hit them low inside curves."

There were others cast in similar molds . . . Rube Waddell, the wholly legendary character who, when cold sober, which was not often, may have been the greatest pitcher of them all: the man who now and then, on a whim, would gesture the entire outfield off the premises and then retire the side without visible means of support; Walter Johnson, who once pitched fifty-odd consecutive scoreless innings, and who to the end of his days had nothing much in his repertoire except an unhittable fast ball; Tris Speaker, who played such a short center field that he often threw a batter out at first on what ought to have been a legitimate down-the-middle base hit; and lean Satchel Paige, who in his great days in the Negro leagues had a way of pointing to the shortstop and then throwing something which the batter must hit to short, and who then would go on around the infield the same way, compelling the opposition to hit precisely where he wanted it to hit. The legends are, in some ways, the most enduring part of the game. Baseball has even more of them than the Civil War, and its fans prize them highly.

Under the surface, baseball is always played to a subdued but inescapable tension, because at any second one of these utterly fabulous events may take place. The game may be distressingly one-sided, and the home team may come up in the ninth inning five runs behind, and in a clock game like football or basketball the margin would be physically unbeatable; but in baseball anything can happen, and the tiniest fluke can change everything. (Remember the World Series game the Yankees won when a Brooklyn catcher dropped a third strike with two men out in the ninth?) A commonplace game can turn into a hair-raiser at any moment, and things do not actually need to happen to create the suspense. A free-hitting, high-scoring game may be most eventful, but few strains are greater than the strain of watching a pitcher protect a 1–0 lead in the late innings of a routine game. Nothing, perhaps, actually happens—but every time the ball is thrown the game may turn upside down, and nobody ever forgets it.

All of this is built in, for the spectator. Built in, as well, is the close attention to records and statistics. Batting averages and pitchers' records are all-important; to know that a Rogers Hornsby, for instance, could bat more than .400 in three different years—that is, could average getting two hits for every five times he came to the plate, 154 games a year, for three years— is important. It has been suggested, now and then, that big league playing schedules be reduced from 154 games to some small figure, and the suggestion has always been howled down: it would upset all the averages. Unthinkable; how do you compare today's pitcher with Walter Johnson or Lefty Grove if today's pitcher plays in fewer games every year?

The circumstances under which baseball is played nowadays have changed greatly, to be sure. Less than half a century ago, every town that amounted to anything at all was represented in some league of professional players, and these leagues—the minor leagues, of hallowed memory—have been dissolving and vanishing, as more and more spectators get their games by television or by radio and ignore the local ball park. The Little Leagues have come up, and semi-subsidized sand-lot leagues, and even college baseball is here and there enjoying a new lease on life—after all, the new players in the big leagues have to come from somewhere, and besides, young Americans still like to play baseball; but the old pattern is gone, and even the major leagues themselves have undergone profound changes and, to a purist from the old days, are all but unrecognizable. Where are the St. Louis Browns, or the Philadelphia Athletics, or the Boston Braves—or, for the matter of that, even the magnificent New York Giants, and the Brooklyn Dodgers? Gone forever, to be sure, with new cities taking over, and with a few old-timers muttering that the last days are at hand.

Actually, the last days are probably a long, long way off, for baseball even in its modern guise has not changed in its essentials. It is a rough, tough game, encased by rules that were made to be broken if the breaking can be accomplished smoothly enough, a game that never quite became entirely respectable, a game in which nobody wants to do anything but win. It will undoubtedly be around for a good time to come, and it will continue, in spite of its own press agents, to be in truth the great American game.

Or so, at least, believes one old-time fan.

Literary Opinions and Criticism

JEAN DIETRICK CONNORS

*HAWTHORNE**

Because of his association with Emerson and Thoreau, Nathaniel Hawthorne has been actively identified with the transcendental movement by most literary historians. Unlike his fellow transcendentalists, however, Hawthorne was singularly unimpressed by the pantheistic view of the divine goodness in man's nature. Instead, his attitude seemed to reflect the Calvinism inherited from his Puritan forebears, with its insistence that human nature is radically corrupt. As Henry James phrased it: "To him, as to them, the consciousness of sin was the most importunate fact of life; and if they had undertaken to write little tales, this baleful substantive . . . could hardly have been more frequent in their pages than in those of their faithful descendant."

Actually, it was not sin itself which absorbed Hawthorne, but its psychological effect upon the sinner. The characters he created, after the commission of their crimes, fashioned their own hells of remorse and ceaseless retribution. Temptation, sin, punishment, retribution—these were the major chords in the Hawthorne symphony.

His use of themes of crime and punishment grew naturally from his interest in the complexities of the individual soul. His ability to combine the scientific detachment of a doctor with the sympathetic understanding of a priest for penitents has made him one of America's foremost psychological writers. In *The Blithedale Romance*, his own words defined his attitude toward his characters when he wrote, "Of all possible observers, methought a woman like Zenobia and a man like Hollingsworth (the principals of the novel) should have selected me . . . True, I might have condemned them. Had I been judge as well as witness, my sentence might have been as stern as that of destiny itself. But, still, no trait of original nobility of character, no struggle against temptation—no iron necessity of will on the one hand, nor extenuating circumstances to be derived from passion and despair on the other—no remorse that might co-exist with error, even though powerless to prevent it—no proud repentance that should claim retribution as a meed—would go unappreciated. True, again, I might give my full assent to the punishment which was sure to follow. But it would be given mournfully, and with undiminished love. And after all was finished, I would come, as if to gather up the white ashes of those who had perished at the stake, and to tell the world—the wrong being now atoned for—how much had perished there which it had not yet known how to praise."

The most significant part of the passage is the inevitability found in the line, "the punishment which was sure to follow." Those seven words form

* Reprinted from *Perspective* (Winter, 1948) by permission of John J. Mulloy, editor of *Perspective*, and the author.

143

the keynote of his four most famous novels, and throughout all of them, in the characters of Hargrave, Kenyon, Coverdale and Chillingworth, Hawthorne plays the part of observer of fallen human nature.

The House of the Seven Gables traces the effects of a crime through succeeding generations of heirs to an old Salem mansion. Visibly, the effect is the strangely recurring hereditary Pyncheon malady, probably hemorrhage, which causes a peculiar gurgle in the throat of the sufferer. Invisibly, the Pyncheon family is afflicted by an insatiable desire for wealth and power, as exemplified originally by the greed of Colonel Pyncheon, and finally by that of the inexorable Judge Pyncheon. Clifford, a cousin of the judge, gives the framework of the story in these words: "A man will commit almost any wrong—he will heap up an immense pile of wickedness, as hard as granite, and which will weigh as heavily upon his soul to eternal ages—only to build a gloomy, dark-chambered mansion for himself to die in and for his posterity to be miserable in. He lays his own dead corpse beneath the underpinning, as one might say, and hangs his frowning picture on the wall, and after thus converting himself into an evil destiny, expects his remotest great-grandchildren to be happy there!"

Colonel Pyncheon commits the original crime by branding old Matthew Maule a witch and stealing his land. Hawthorne has hinted that Maule makes advantageous use of his knowledge of the family disease in framing his famous curse, which reflects a seemingly deterministic view that evil pursues the family like fate. The colonel pays for his sin by dying dramatically on the very day when his new house is opened to Salem society.

The Pyncheon penchant for stealing other people's property blossoms occasionally during later generations, and finally culminates in the avarice of the judge. "Maule's blood" is again heard in a Pyncheon throat as retribution is exacted from the judge for his successful attempt to "frame" his cousin, Clifford. The dramatic climax which Hawthorne achieves is superb, in his description of the dead man slumped in his best parlor chair. Again, as the cat leaps to the window to gaze in at the moonlit parlor, the emphasis in on fire and brimstone. "Is it a cat watching for a mouse, or the devil for a human soul?"

In *The Scarlet Letter*, the personification of evil in Roger Chillingworth is developed even more masterfully. Hawthorne says of him: "In a word, Roger Chillingworth is a striking evidence of a man's faculty of transforming himself into a devil, if he will only, for a reasonable space of time, undertake a devil's office." Chillingworth's self-appointed task seems to be to drag the good Mr. Dimmesdale to perdition with him. In the conception of his character, the author seems to personify his own idea of the Prince of Darkness. A glare in Chillingworth's eyes mirrors the hell-fire in his soul, despite his best efforts to conceal it behind a mask of benignity. In his character as devil's advocate, he exacts retribution from his unfaithful wife, Hester Prynne, and her lover, minister Arthur Dimmesdale. No word is left unturned to show how these two souls are seared by their crime.

The scarlet letter "A" which Hester must wear on the bosom of her dress becomes a symbol of their penance. Because she must acknowledge her sin openly, Hester is able to purge her soul of its debt and rise to new heights of nobility. But Dimmesdale, who poses as a pure angel of the Lord, is torn between the longing to confess his shame and a desire for the almost idolatrous esteem of his congregation. It is upon Dimmesdale that Chillingworth has his vengeance—prying and playing upon his sensitive being until he finally ferrets out the guilty secret of the scarlet "A" that lies hidden on the minister's breast. Again the "A" burns in the sky in meteoric warning to Dimmesdale to confess his crime. Hawthorne has been criticized for this excessive use of symbolism, but the device may be justified by its morbid success in amplifying his theme of the far-reaching effects of sin.

In *The Blithedale Romance*, Hawthorne comes closer to reality. The background for the story was provided by the Brook Farm project, an impractical application of the basic tenets of transcendentalism. Hawthorne had an active interest in the project, and in the novel which grew out of it, took a more active role (in the person of Miles Coverdale) than in any of his other novels. In the words of Coverdale, he regrets that the exhaustive demands of physical labor left too little time for the speculation and study which were to have formed an integral part of community life, yet he seems to have found ample time to observe the influence of evil on human destiny.

The plot of the novel concerns itself with the degeneration of the philanthropic impulses of a fictional fellow-reformer, Hollingsworth. Sin and retribution are repeated in Zenobia's suicide and Hollingsworth's subsequent life of remorse. The crime is Hollingsworth's in that he rejects Zenobia's love because she refuses to submit to the dominance of his will. One might ask, "What crime is that?" and the question is difficult to answer except by referring the questioner to the novel. Certainly Hollingsworth feels himself responsible for Zenobia's death. The ghastly scene in which her body is dragged from the sinister water of the brook so burns itself on his brain that he becomes a premature and remorseful old man.

Hawthorne has denied that any of his *Blithedale* characters were real, but there is no doubt that the background was. Because the novel was based on a phase of the author's life, one begins to seek clues to the degree of his belief in the transcendental theories which were put to the test at Brook Farm. Unlike Emerson and Thoreau, who contented themselves with sporadic visits to the place, Hawthorne spent a summer there. Whatever his acceptance of transcendentalism might have been, by the end of summer he seems to have found the Brook Farm scheme woefully inadequate. In lapsing into Fourierism, he claimed it failed to be true to its first high ideals, and the original projectors finally yielded the field to the town paupers. "Alas, what faith is requisite," he wrote, "to bear up against such results of generous efforts."

A desire to trace the author's life and feelings through his work becomes even stronger in *The Marble Faun*. Anyone who has read Hawthorne's journal of his days in Rome will find it simple to identify the origins of the story. His descriptions of the carnival, of the church of the Capuchins, of Beatrice Cenci's portrait and her prison room in the Castle of Saint Angelo, Hawthorne's reaction to the sight of a fellow tourist at confession (". . . I . . . finding nothing attractive in the picture, take my departure. Protestantism needs a new apostle to convert it into something positive . . ."), and most of all the description of the Faun of Praxiteles, form the unmistakable framework of the novel. The following passage about the Faun indicates the beginning of the plot:

". . . It seems to me that a story, with all sorts of fun and pathos in it, might be contrived on the idea of their species having become intermingled with the human race; a family with the faun blood in them having prolonged itself from the classic era till our own days. The tail might have disappeared, by dint of constant intermarriages with ordinary mortals; but the pretty hairy ears should occasionally reappear in members of the family; and the moral instincts and intellectual characteristics of the faun might be most picturesquely brought out without detriment to the human interest of the story."

With his characteristic morbidity, Hawthorne forgot the fun and concentrated on the pathos. The Faun becomes Donatello, half man, half elf. The characters are primarily symbols, Donatello of pagan sensualism, Miriam of Jewish oriental mystery, and Hilda of a Christianity just emerging from Puritanism to a fuller type of religion. In the murder of Miriam's mortal enemy, the Capuchin monk, she and Donatello forfeit any possibility of subsequent happiness. Their remorse and repentance form the psychological expression of Hawthorne's crime and atonement *motif*. Into this design he originally inserted the idea that sin is valuable because the suffering caused by it develops character, since Donatello's personality matures under the influence of his remorse for his crime. But Hawthorne must have sensed the danger of such a theory, for he rejected it immediately.

A study of the novel tempts a thoughtful reader to read the opinions of Hawthorne into the character of Hilda. Clinging to the Puritan heritage of his Salem forebears, Hawthorne thunders against "that mass of unspeakable corruption, the Roman Church," yet in the same chapter he admires the "attractions of a faith which so marvellously adapts itself to every human need."

As in the case of many another unsolvable question, much print and paper have been wasted in speculating whether Hawthorne would eventually have become a Catholic if he had lived a little longer. In his *American Renaissance*, F. O. Matthiessen adequately summarizes the whole question when he says:

> Many passages in his European notebooks . . . attest to his interest in Catholicism. His tenor frequently accords with that of his first impression of a service at the Madeleine in Paris, that the ceremonies of the Church "were a superb work of art, or perhaps a true growth of man's religious nature; and so long as men felt their original mean-

ing, they must have been full of awe and glory." But, like Kenyon, he dwelt on the many corruptions of the visible church; and he gave the background for his belief that Hilda was right in her rejection when he said, "Generally, I suspect, when people throw off the faith they were born in, the best soil of their hearts is apt to cling to its roots!" Further evidence of how deeply Hilda's problem had absorbed his family circle is furnished by the fact that neither of his daughters was able to find peace in their father's indifference to dogma, and both, like many other troubled New Englanders of their day, took the solution opposite to Hilda's. Una . . . accepted the Anglican faith after a long struggle, and devoted herself to works of charity until she died while on a visit to a Protestant convent. Rose married George Parsons Lathrop, and both she and her husband were finally converted to Catholicism. After his death she became a nun under the name of Sister Alphonsa and, haunted no less than her father by the existence of suffering, founded in New York a sisterhood for relief of victims of incurable cancer.

The question, "What is the significance of Hawthorne's work in the light of Catholic morality?" is far more important to the Catholic critic than any speculation on his possible conversion. What is the value of his "sense of sin," or of his literary amplification of the text, "The wages of sin is death"? To the psychologist, to the social reformer, to the realistic novelist, Hawthorne's novels contain sound elements of instruction. In his conception of the havoc sin creates in individual lives, in his doctrine of the inevitable retribution exacted for wrong-doing, in his strong sense of the possibility of damnation, this descendant of the Puritan divines forces us to reconsider the tragedy of Eden. But the hell to which the unrepentant evil-doer is committed is more than a psychological hell of his own consciousness. Many sinners have successfully circumvented that inferno. Rather, it is the unremitting hell of the gospels. Properly speaking, hell is not a psychological but an eschatological fact.

SAMUEL TAYLOR COLERIDGE

RECAPITULATION AND SUMMARY
OF THE CHARACTERISTICS OF SHAKSPEARE'S DRAMAS*†

HAVING INTIMATED that times and manners lend their form and pressure to genius, let me once more draw a slight parallel between the ancient and modern stage, the stages of Greece and of England. The Greeks were polytheists; their religion was local; almost the only object of all their knowledge, art and taste, was their gods; and, accordingly, their productions were,

---

* Reprinted from *Shakespeare Criticism*, introduction by D. Nichol Smith, Oxford University Press, London, 1936.
† Noteworthy is Coleridge's spelling of the dramatist's name.

if the expression may be allowed, statuesque, whilst those of the moderns are picturesque. The Greeks reared a structure, which in its parts, and as a whole, filled the mind with the calm and elevated impression of perfect beauty and symmetrical proportion. The moderns also produced a whole, a more striking whole; but it was by blending materials and fusing the parts together. And as the Pantheon is to York Minster or Westminster Abbey, so is Sophocles compared with Shakspeare; in the one a completeness, a satisfaction, an excellence, on which the mind rests with complacency; in the other a multitude of interlaced materials, great and little, magnificent and mean, accompanied, indeed, with the sense of a falling short of perfection, and yet, at the same time, so promising of our social and individual progression, that we would not, if we could, exchange it for that repose of the mind which dwells on the forms of symmetry in the acquiescent admiration of grace. This general characteristic of the ancient and modern drama might be illustrated by a parallel of the ancient and modern music;—the one consisting of melody arising from a succession only of pleasing sounds,—the modern embracing harmony also, the result of combination and the effect of a whole.

I have said, and I say again, that great as was the genius of Shakspeare, his judgment was at least equal to it. Of this any one will be convinced, who attentively considers those points in which the dramas of Greece and England differ, from the dissimilitude of circumstances by which each was modified and influenced. The Greek stage had its origin in the ceremonies of a sacrifice, such as of the goat to Bacchus, whom we most erroneously regard as merely the jolly god of wine;—for among the ancients he was venerable, as the symbol of that power which acts without our consciousness in the vital energies of nature,—the *vinum mundi*,*—as Apollo was that of the conscious agency of our intellectual being. The heroes of old under the influences of this Bacchic enthusiasm performed more than human actions;—hence tales of the favorite champions soon passed into dialogue. On the Greek stage the chorus was always before the audience; the curtain was never dropped, as we should say; and change of place being therefore, in general, impossible, the absurd notion of condemning it merely as improbable in itself was never entertained by any one. If we can believe ourselves at Thebes in one act, we may believe ourselves at Athens in the next. If a story lasts twenty-four hours or twenty-four years, it is equally improbable. There seems to be no just boundary but what the feelings prescribe. But on the Greek stage where the same persons were perpetually before the audience, great judgment was necessary in venturing on any such change. The poets never, therefore, attempted to impose on the senses by bringing places to men, but they did bring men to places, as in the well known instance in the Eumenides, where during an evident retirement of the chorus from the orchestra, the scene is changed to Athens, and Orestes is first introduced in the temple of Minerva, and the chorus of Furies come in afterwards in pursuit of him.

In the Greek drama there were no formal divisions into scenes and acts;

* Wine of the world.

there were no means, therefore, of allowing for the necessary lapse of time between one part of the dialogue and another, and unity of time in a strict sense was, of course, impossible. To overcome that difficulty of accounting for time, which is effected on the modern stage by dropping a curtain, the judgment and great genius of the ancients supplied music and measured motion, and with the lyric ode filled up the vacuity. In the story of the Agamemnon of Aeschylus, the capture of Troy is supposed to be announced by a fire lighted on the Asiatic shore, and the transmission of the signal by successive beacons to Mycenae. The signal is first seen at the 21st line, and the herald from Troy itself enters at the 486th, and Agamemnon himself at the 783rd line. But the practical absurdity of this was not felt by the audience, who, in imagination stretched minutes into hours, while they listened to the lofty narrative odes of the chorus which almost entirely fill up the interspace. Another fact deserves attention here, namely, that regularly on the Greek stage a drama, or acted story, consisted in reality of three dramas, called together a trilogy, and performed consecutively in the course of one day. Now you may conceive a tragedy of Shakspeare's as a trilogy connected in one single representation. Divide *Lear* into three parts, and each would be a play with the ancients; or take the three Aeschylean dramas of Agamemnon, and divide them into, or call them, as many acts, and they together would be one play. The first act would comprise the usurpation of Aegisthus, and the murder of Agamemnon; the second, the revenge of Orestes, and the murder of his mother; and the third, the penance and absolution of Orestes;— occupying a period of twenty-two years.

The stage in Shakspeare's time was a naked room with a blanket for a curtain; but he made it a field for monarchs. That law of unity, which has its foundations, not in the factitious necessity of custom, but in nature itself, the unity of feeling, is every where and at all times observed by Shakspeare in his plays. Read *Romeo and Juliet*;—all is youth and spring—youth with its follies, its virtues, its precipitancies;—spring with its odours, its flowers, and its transiency; it is one and the same feeling that commences, goes through, and ends the play. The old men, the Capulets and the Montagues, are not common old men; they have an eagerness, a heartiness, a vehemence, the effect of spring; with Romeo, his change of passion, his sudden marriage, and his rash death, are all the effects of youth;—whilst in Juliet love has all that is tender and melancholy in the nightingale, all that is voluptuous in the rose, with whatever is sweet in the freshness of spring; but it ends with a long deep sigh like the last breeze of the Italian evening. This unity of feeling and character pervades every drama of Shakspeare.

It seems to me that his plays are distinguished from those of all other dramatic poets by the following characteristics:

1. Expectation in preference to surprise. It is like the true reading of the passage;—'God said, Let there be light, and there was *light*;'—not there *was* light. As the feeling with which we startle at a shooting star, compared with that of watching the sunrise at the pre-established moment, such and so low is surprise compared with expectation.

2. Signal adherence to the great law of nature, that all opposites tend to attract and temper each other. Passion in Shakspeare generally displays libertinism, but involves morality; and if there are exceptions to this, they are, independently of their intrinsic value, all of them indicative of individual character, and, like the farewell admonitions of a parent, have an end beyond the parental relation. Thus the Countess's beautiful precepts to Bertram, by elevating her character, raise that of Helena her favorite, and soften down the point in her which Shakspeare does not mean us not to see, but to see and to forgive, and at length to justify. And so it is in Polonius, who is the personified memory of wisdom no longer actually possessed. This admirable character is always misrepresented on the stage. Shakspeare never intended to exhibit him as a buffoon; for although it was natural that Hamlet, —a young man of fire and genius, detesting formality, and disliking Polonius on political grounds, as imagining that he had assisted his uncle in his usurpation,—should express himself satirically,—yet this must not be taken as exactly the poet's conception of him. In Polonius a certain induration of character had arisen from long habits of business; but take his advice to Laertes, and Ophelia's reverence for his memory, and we shall see that he was meant to be represented as a statesman somewhat past his faculties,—his recollections of life all full of wisdom, and showing a knowledge of human nature, whilst what immediately takes place before him, and escapes from him, is indicative of weakness.

But as in Homer all the deities are in armour, even Venus; so in Shakspeare all the characters are strong. Hence real folly and dullness are made by him the vehicles of wisdom. There is no difficulty for one being a fool to imitate a fool; but to be, remain, and speak like a wise man and a great wit, and yet so as to give a vivid representation of a veritable fool,—*hic labor, hoc opus est.** A drunken constable is not uncommon, nor hard to draw; but see and examine what goes to make up a Dogberry.

3. Keeping at all times in the high road of life. Shakspeare has no innocent adulteries, no interesting incests, no virtuous vice;—he never renders that amiable which religion and reason alike teach us to detest, or clothes impurity in the garb of virtue, like Beaumont and Fletcher, the Kotzebues of the day. Shakspeare's fathers are roused by ingratitude, his husbands stung by unfaithfulness; in him, in short, the affections are wounded in those points in which all may, nay, must, feel. Let the morality of Shakspeare be contrasted with that of the writers of his own, or the succeeding, age, or of those of the present day, who boast their superiority in this respect. No one can dispute that the result of such a comparison is altogether in favour of Shakspeare;—even the letters of women of high rank in his age were often coarser than his writings. If he occasionally disgusts a keen sense of delicacy, he never injures the mind; he neither excites, nor flatters, passion, in order to degrade the subject of it; he does not use the faulty thing for a faulty purpose, nor carries on warfare against virtue, by causing wickedness to

* This is the effort made; this, the task to be accomplished.

appear as no wickedness, through the medium of a morbid sympathy with the unfortunate. In Shakspeare vice never walks as in twilight; nothing is purposely out of its place;—he inverts not the order of nature and propriety, —does not make every magistrate a drunkard or glutton, nor every poor man weak, humane, and temperate; he has no benevolent butchers, nor any sentimental rat-catchers.

4. Independence of the dramatic interest on the plot. The interest in the plot is always in fact on account of the characters, not *vice versa*, as in almost all other writers; the plot is a mere canvass and no more. Hence arises the true justification of the same stratagem being used in regard to Benedict and Beatrice,—the vanity in each being alike. Take away from the *Much Ado About Nothing* all that which is not indispensable to the plot, either as having little to do with it, or, at best, like Dogberry and his comrades, forced into the service, when any other less ingeniously absurd watchmen and night-constables would have answered the mere necessities of the action;—take away Benedict, Beatrice, Dogberry, and the reaction of the former on the character of Hero,—and what will remain? In other writers the main agent of the plot is always the prominent character; in Shakspeare it is so, or is not so, as the character is in itself calculated, or not calculated, to form the plot. Don John is the main-spring of the plot of this play; but he is merely shown and then withdrawn.

5. Independence of the interest on the story as the ground-work of the plot. Hence Shakspeare never took the trouble of inventing stories. It was enough for him to select from those that had been already invented or recorded such as had one or other, or both, of two recommendations, namely, suitableness to his particular purpose, and their being parts of popular tradition,—names of which we had often heard, and of their fortunes, and as to which all we wanted was, to see the man himself. So it is just the man himself, the Lear, the Shylock, the Richard, that Shakspeare makes us for the first time acquainted with. Omit the first scene in *Lear*, and yet every thing will remain; so the first and second scenes in the *Merchant of Venice*. Indeed it is universally true.

6. Interfusion of the lyrical—that which in its very essence is poetical—not only with the dramatic, as in the plays of Metastasio, where at the end of the scene comes the *aria* as the *exit* speech of the character,—but also in and through the dramatic. Songs in Shakspeare are introduced as songs only, just as songs are in real life, beautifully as some of them are characteristic of the person who has sung or called for them, as Desdemona's 'Willow,' and Ophelia's wild snatches, and the sweet carollings in *As You Like It*. But the whole of the *Midsummer Night's Dream* is one continued specimen of the dramatized lyrical. And observe how exquisitely the dramatic of Hotspur;—

> Marry, and I'm glad on't with all my heart;
> I had rather be a kitten and cry—mew, &c.

melts away into the lyric of Mortimer;—

I understand thy looks: that pretty Welsh
Which thou pourest down from these swelling heavens,
I am too perfect in, &c.

HENRY IV. *part i act iii. sc. i.*

7. The characters of the *dramatis personae,* like those in real life, are to be inferred by the reader;—they are not told to him. And it is well worth remarking that Shakspeare's characters, like those in real life, are very commonly misunderstood, and almost always understood by different persons in different ways. The causes are the same in either case. If you take only what the friends of the character say, you may be deceived, and still more so, if that which his enemies say; nay, even the character himself sees himself through the medium of his character, and not exactly as he is. Take all together, not omitting a shrewd hint from the clown or the fool, and perhaps your impression will be right; and you may know whether you have in fact discovered the poet's own idea, by all the speeches receiving light from it, and attesting its reality by reflecting it.

Lastly, in Shakspeare the heterogeneous is united, as it is in nature. You must not suppose a pressure or passion always acting on or in the character;—passion in Shakspeare is that by which the individual is distinguished from others, not that which makes a different kind of him. Shakspeare followed the main march of the human affections. He entered into no analysis of the passions or faiths of men, but assured himself that such and such passions and faiths were grounded in our common nature, and not in the mere accident of ignorance or disease. This is an important consideration, and constitutes our Shakspeare the morning star, the guide and the pioneer, of true philosophy.

ALICE MEYNELL

DICKENS*

IT was said for many years, until the reversal that now befalls the sayings of many years had happened to this also, that Thackeray was the unkind satirist and Dickens the kind humorist. The truth seems to be that Dickens imagined more evil people than did Thackeray, but that he had an eager faith in good ones. Nothing places him so entirely out of date as his trust in human sanctity, his love of it, his hope for it, his leap at it. He saw it in a woman's face first met, and drew it to himself in a man's hand first grasped. He looked keenly for it. And if he associated minor degrees of goodness with any kind of folly or mental ineptitude, he did not so relate sanctity; though he gave it, for companion, ignorance; and joined the two, in Joe Gargery,

* Reprinted from *Hearts of Controversy,* Burns, Oates and Washbourne, Ltd., 1917, by permission of the publishers.

most tenderly. We might paraphrase, in regard to these two great authors, Dr. Johnson's famous sentence: 'Marriage has many pains, but celibacy has no joys.' Dickens has many scoundrels, but Thackeray has no saints. Helen Pendennis is not holy, for she is an egoist in love; Lady Castlewood is not holy, for she too is cruel; and even Lady Jane is not holy, for she is jealous; nor is Colonel Newcome holy, for he is haughty; nor Dobbin, for he turns with a taunt upon a plain sister; nor Esmond, for he squanders his best years in love for a material beauty; and these are the best of his good people. And readers have been taught to praise the work of him who makes none perfect; one does not meet perfect people in trains or at dinner, and this seemed good cause that the novelist should be praised for his moderation; it seemed to imitate the usual measure and moderation of nature.

But Charles Dickens closed with a divine purpose divinely different. He consented to the counsels of perfection. And thus he made Joe Gargery, not a man one might easily find in a forge; and Esther Summerson, not a girl one may easily meet at a dance; and Little Dorrit, who does not come to a day's sewing; not that the man and the woman are inconceivable, but that they are unfortunately improbable. They are creatures created through a creating mind that worked its six days for the love of good, and never rested until the seventh, the final Sabbath. But granting that they are the counterpart, the heavenly side, of caricature, this is not to condemn them. Since when has caricature ceased to be an art good for man—an honest game between him and nature? It is a tenable opinion that frank caricature is a better incident of art than the mere exaggeration which is the more modern practice. The words mean the same thing in their origin—an overloading. But as we now generally delimit the words they differ. Caricature, when it has the grotesque inspiration, makes for laughter, and when it has the celestial, makes for admiration; in either case there is a good understanding between the author and the reader, or between the draughtsman and the spectator. We need not, for example, suppose that Ibsen sat in a room surrounded by a repeating pattern of his hair and whiskers on the wall-paper, but it makes us most exceedingly mirthful and joyous to see him thus seated in Mr. Max Beerbohm's drawing; and perhaps no girl ever went through life without harbouring a thought of self, but it is very good for us all to know that such a girl was thought of by Dickens, that he loved his thought, and that she is ultimately to be traced, through Dickens, to God.

But exaggeration establishes no good understanding between the reader and the author. It is a solemn appeal to our credulity, and we are right to resent it. It is the violence of a weakling hand—the worst manner of violence. Exaggeration is conspicuous in the newer poetry, and is so far, therefore, successful, conspicuousness being its aim. But it was also the vice of Swinburne, and was the bad example he set to the generation that thought his tunings to be the finest 'music'. For instance, in an early poem he intends to tell us how a man who loved a woman welcomed the sentence that condemned him to drown with her, bound, his impassioned breast against hers, abhorring. He might have convinced us of that welcome by one phrase of the profound exactitude of genius. But he makes his man cry out for the greatest bliss and the greatest imaginable glory to be bestowed upon the judge who pronounces the sentence. And this is merely exaggeration. One takes pleasure in rebuking the false ecstasy by a word thus prim and prosaic. The poet intended to impose upon us, and he fails; we 'withdraw our attention', as Dr. Johnson did when the conversation became foolish. In truth we do more, for we resent exaggeration if we care for our English language. For exaggeration writes relaxed, and not elastic, words and verses; and it is possible that the language suffers something, at least temporarily—during the life of a couple of generations, let us say—from the loss of elasticity and rebound brought about by such a strain. Moreover, exaggeration has always to outdo itself progressively. There should have been a Durdles to tell this Swinburne that the habit of exaggerating, like that of boasting, 'grows upon you'.

It may be added that later poetry shows us an instance of exaggeration in the work of that major poet, Mr. Lascelles Abercrombie. His violence and vehemence, his extremity, are generally signs not of weakness but of power; and yet once he reaches a breaking-point that power should never know. This is where his Judith holds herself to be so smirched and degraded by the proffer of a reverent love (she being devoted to one only, a dead man who had her heart) that thenceforth no bar is left to her entire self-sacrifice to the loathed enemy Holofernes. To this, too, the prim rebuke is the just one, a word for the mouth of governesses: 'My dear, you exaggerate.'

It may be briefly said that exaggeration takes for granted some degree of imbecility in the reader, whereas caricature takes for granted a high degree of intelligence. Dickens appeals to our intelligence in all his caricature, whether heavenly, as in Joe Gargery, or impish, as in Mrs. Micawber. The word 'caricature' that is used a thousand times to reproach him is the word that does him singular honour.

If I may define my own devotion to Dickens, it may be stated as chiefly, though not wholly, admiration of his humour, his dramatic tragedy, and his watchfulness over inanimate things and landscape. Passages of his books that are ranged otherwise than under those characters often leave me out of the range of their appeal or else definitely offend me. And this is not for the customary reason—that Dickens could not draw a gentleman, that Dickens could not draw a lady. It matters little whether he could or not. But as a fact he did draw a gentleman, and drew him excellently well, in Cousin Feenix, as Mr. Chesterton has decided. The question of the lady we may waive; if it is difficult to prove a negative, it is difficult also to present one; and to the making, or producing, or liberating, or detaching, or exalting, of the character of a lady there enter many negatives; and Dickens was an obvious and positive man. Esther Summerson is a lady, but she is so much besides that her ladyhood does not detach itself from her sainthood and her angelhood, so as to be conspicuous—if, indeed, conspicuousness may be properly predicated of the quality of a lady. It is a conventional saying that sainthood and angelhood include the quality of a lady, but that saying is not true; a lady has a great number of negatives all her own, and also some things positive that are not at all included in goodness. However this may be—and it is not important—Dickens, the genial Dickens, makes savage sport of women. Such a company of envious dames and damsels cannot be found among the persons of the satirist Thackeray. Kate Nickleby's beauty brings upon her at first sight the enmity of her workshop companions; in the innocent pages of *Pickwick* the aunt is jealous of the niece, and the niece retorts by wounding the vanity of the aunt as keenly as she may; and so forth through early books and late. He takes for granted that the women, old and young, who are not his heroines, wage this war within the sex, being disappointed by defect of nature and fortune. Dickens is master of wit, humour, and derision; and it must be confessed that his derision is abundant, and is cast upon an artificially exposed and helpless people; that is, he, a man, derides the women who miss what a man declared to be their 'whole existence.'

The advice which M. Rodin received in his youth from Constant—'Learn to see the other side; never look at forms only in extent; learn to see them always in relief'—is the contrary of the counsel proper for a reader of Dickens. That counsel should be, 'Do not insist upon seeing the immortal figures of comedy "in the round." You are to be satisfied with their face value, the fact of two dimensions. It is not necessary that you should seize Mr. Pecksniff from beyond, and grasp the whole man and his destinies.' The hypocrite is a figure dreadful and tragic, a shape of horror; and Mr. Pecksniff is a hyprocrite, and a bright image of heart-easing comedy. For comic fiction cannot exist without some such paradox. Without it, where would our laugh be in response to the generous genius which gives us Mr. Pecksniff's parenthesis to the mention of sirens ('Pagan, I regret to say'); and the scene in which Mr. Pecksniff, after a stormy domestic scene within, goes as it were accidentally to the door to admit the rich kinsman he wishes to propitiate? 'Then Mr. Pecksniff, gently warbling a rustic stave, put on his garden hat, seized a spade, and opened the street door, as if he thought he had, from his vineyard, heard a modest rap, but was not quite certain.' The visitor had thundered at the door while outcries of family strife had been rising in the house. ' "It is an ancient pursuit, gardening. Primitive, my dear sir; for, if I am not mistaken, Adam was the first of the calling. My Eve, I grieve to say, is no more, sir; but" (and here he pointed to his spade, and shook his head, as if he were not cheerful without an effort) "but I do a little bit of Adam still." He had by this time got them into the best parlour, where the portrait by Spiller and the bust by Spoker were.' And again, Mr. Pecksniff, hospitable at the supper table: ' "This," he said, in allusion to the party, not the wine, "is a Mingling that repays one for much disappointment and vexation. Let us be merry." Here he took a captain's biscuit. "It is a poor heart that never rejoices; and our hearts are not poor. No!" With such stimulants to merriment did he beguile the time and do the honours of the table.' Moreover it is a mournful thing and an inexplicable, that a man should be as mad as Mr. Dick. None the less is it a happy thing for any reader to watch Mr. Dick while David explains his difficulty to Traddles. Mr. Dick was to be employed in copying, but King Charles the First could not be kept out of the manuscripts; 'Mr. Dick in the meantime looking very deferentially and seriously at Traddles, and sucking his thumb.' And the amours of the gentleman in gaiters who threw the vegetable-marrows over the garden wall. Mr. F's aunt, again! And Augustus Moddle, our own Moddle, whom a great French critic most justly and accurately brooded over. 'Augustus, the gloomy maniac,' says Taine, 'makes us shudder.' A good medical diagnosis. Long live the logical French intellect!

Truly, Humour talks in his own language, nay, his own dialect, whereas Passion and Pity speak the universal tongue.

It is strange—it seems to me deplorable—that Dickens himself was not content to leave his wonderful hypocrite—one who should stand imperishable in comedy—in the two dimensions of his own admirable art. After he had enjoyed his own Pecksniff, tasting him with the 'strenuous tongue' of Keats's voluptuary bursting 'joy's grape against his palate fine', Dickens most unfairly gives himself the other and incompatible joy of grasping his Pecksniff in the third dimension, seizes him 'in the round', horsewhips him out of all keeping, and finally kicks him out of a splendid art of fiction into a sorry art of 'poetical justice', a Pecksniff not only defeated but undone.

And yet Dickens's retribution upon sinners is a less fault than his reforming them. It is truly an act denoting excessive simplicity of mind in him. He never veritably allows his responsibility as a man to lapse. Men ought to be good, or else to become good, and he does violence to his own excellent art, and yields it up to his sense of morality. Ah, can we measure by years the time between that day and this? Is the fastidious, the impartial, the non-moral novelist only the grandchild, and not the remote posterity, of Dickens, who would not leave Scrooge to his egoism, or Grandgrind to his facts, or Mercy Pecksniff to her absurdity, or Dombey to his pride? Nay, who makes Micawber finally to prosper? Truly, the most unpardonable thing Dickens did in those deplorable last chapters of his was the prosperity of Mr. Micawber. 'Of a son in difficulties'—the perfect Micawber nature is respected as to his origin, and then perverted as to his end. It is a pity that Mr. Peggotty ever came back to England with such tidings. And our last glimpse of the emigrants had been made joyous by the sight of the young Micawbers on the eve of emigration; 'every child had its own wooden spoon attached to its body by a strong line', in preparation for Colonial life. And then Dickens must needs go behind the gay scenes, and tell us that the long and untiring delight of the book was over. Mr. Micawber, in the Colonies, was never again to make punch with lemons, in a crisis of his fortunes, and 'resume his peeling with a desperate air'; nor to observe the expression of his friends' faces during Mrs. Micawber's masterly exposition of the financial situation or of the possibilities of the coal trade; nor to eat walnuts out of a paper bag what time the die was cast and all was over. Alas! nothing was over until Mr. Micawber's pecuniary liabilities were over, and the perfect comedy turned into dullness, the joyous impossibility of a figure of immortal fun into cold improbability.

There are several such late or last chapters that one would gladly cut away: that of Mercy Pecksniff's pathos, for example; that of Mr. Dombey's installation in his daughter's home; that which undeceives us as to Mr. Boffin's antic disposition. But how true and how whole a heart it was that urged these unlucky conclusions! How shall we venture to complain? The hand that made its Pecksniff in pure wit, has it not the right to belabour him in earnest—albeit a kind of earnest that disappoints us? And Mr. Dombey is Dickens's own Dombey, and he must do what he will with that finely wrought figure of pride. But there is a little irony in the fact that Dickens leaves more than one villain to his orderly fate for whom we care little either way; it is nothing to us, whom Carker never convinced, that the train should catch him, nor that the man with the mustache and the nose, who did but weary us, should be crushed by the falling house. Here the end holds good in art but the art was not good from the first. But then, again, neither does Bill Sikes experience a change of heart, nor Jonas Chuzzlewit; and the end of each is most excellently told.

George Meredith said that the most difficult thing to write in fiction was dialogue. But there is surely one thing at least as difficult—a thing so rarely well done that a mere reader might think it to be more difficult than dialogue; and that is the telling *what happened*. Something of the fatal languor and pre-occupation that persist beneath all the violence of our stage—our national undramatic character—is perceptible in the narrative of our literature. The things the usual modern author says are proportionately more energetically produced than those he tells. But Dickens, being simple and dramatic and capable of one thing at a time, and that thing whole, tells us what happened with a perfect speed which has neither hurry nor delays. Those who saw him act found him a fine actor, and this we might know by reading the murder in *Oliver Twist*, the murder in *Martin Chuzzlewit*, the coming of the train upon Carker, the long moment of recognition when Pip sees his guest, the convict, reveal himself in his chambers at night. The swift spirit, the hammering blow of his narrative, drive the great storm in *David Copperfield* through the poorest part of the book—Steerforth's story. There is surely no greater gale to be read of than this: from the first words, ' "Don't you think that," I said to the coachman, "a very remarkable sky?" ' to the end of a magnificent chapter. 'Flying clouds tossed up into most remarkable heaps, suggesting greater heights in the clouds than there were depths below them. . . . There had been a wind all day; and it was rising then with an extraordinary great sound. . . . Long before we saw the sea, its spray was on our lips. . . . The water was out over the flat country, and every sheet and puddle lashed its banks, and had its stress of little breakers. When we came within sight of the sea, the waves on the horizon, caught at intervals above the boiling abyss, were like glimpses of another shore, with towers and buildings. . . . The people came to their doors all aslant, and with streaming hair.' David dreams of a cannonade, when at last he 'fell—off a tower and down a precipice—into the depths of sleep'. In the morning, 'the wind might have lulled a little, though not more sensibly than if the cannonading I had dreamed of had been diminished by the silencing of half a dozen guns out of hundreds.' 'It went from me with a shock, like a ball from a rifle,' says David in another place, after the visit of a delirious impulse; here is the volley of departure, the shock of passion vanishing more perceptibly than it came.

The tempest in *David Copperfield* combines Dickens's dramatic tragedy of narrative with his wonderful sense of sea and land. But here are landscapes in quietness: 'There has been rain this afternoon, and a wintry shudder goes among the little pools in the cracked, uneven flag-stones. . . . Some of the leaves, in a timid rush, seek sanctuary within the low-arched cathedral door; but two men coming out resist them, and cast them out with their feet.' The autumn leaves fall thick, 'but never fast, for they come circling down with a dead lightness.' Again, 'Now the woods settle into great masses as if they were one profound tree.' And yet again, 'I held my mother in my embrace, and she held me in hers; and among the still woods in the silence of the summer day there seemed to be nothing but our two troubled minds that was not at peace.' Yet, with a thousand great felicities of diction, Dickens had no *body* of style.

Dickens, having the single and simple heart of a moralist, had also the simple eyes of a free intelligence, and the light heart. He gave his senses their way, and well did they serve him. Thus his eyes—and no more modern man in anxious search of 'impressions' was ever so simple and so masterly: 'Mr. Vholes gauntly stalked to the fire, and warmed his funereal gloves.' ' "I thank you," said Mr. Vholes, putting out his long black sleeve, to check the ringing of the bell, "not any." ' Mr. and Mrs. Tope 'are daintily sticking sprigs of holly into the carvings and sconces of the cathedral stalls, as if they were sticking them into the button-holes of the Dean and Chapter.' The two young Eurasians, brother and sister, 'had a certain air upon them of hunter and huntress; yet withal a certain air of being the objects of the chase rather than the followers.' This phrase lacks elegance—and Dickens is not often inelegant, as those who do not read him may be surprised to learn—but the impression is admirable; so is that which follows: 'An indefinable kind of pause coming and going on their whole expression, both of face and form.' Here is pure, mere impression again: 'Miss Murdstone, who was busy at her writing-desk, gave me her cold finger-nails.' Lady Tippin's hand is 'rich in knuckles'. And here is vision with great dignity: 'All beyond his figure was a vast dark curtain, in solemn movement towards one quarter of the heavens.'

With that singleness of sight—and his whole body was full of the light of it—he had also the single hearing; the scene is in the Court of Chancery on a London November day: 'Leaving this address ringing in the rafters of the roof, the very little counsel drops, and the fog knows him no more.' 'Mr. Vholes emerged into the silence he could scarcely be said to have broken, so stifled was his tone.' 'Within the grill-gate of the chancel, up the steps surmounted loomingly by the first-darkening organ, white robes could be dimly seen, and one feeble voice, rising and falling in a cracked monotonous mutter, could at intervals be faintly heard . . . until the organ and the choir burst forth and drowned it in a sea of music. Then the sea fell, and the dying voice made another feeble effort; and then the sea rose high and beat its life out, and lashed the roof, and surged among the arches, and pierced the heights of the great tower; and then the sea was dry and all was still.' And this is how a listener overheard men talking in the cathedral hollows: 'The word "confidence", shattered by the echoes, but still capable of being pieced together, is uttered.'

With humour, derision—to each of these words we assign by custom a part in the comedy of literature; and (again) those who do not read Dickens —perhaps even those who read him a little—may acclaim him as a humorist and not know him as a wit. But that writer is a wit, whatever his humour, who tells us of a member of the Tite Barnacle family who had held a sine-cure office against all protest, that 'he died with his drawn salary in his hand'. But let it be granted that Dickens the humorist is foremost and most precious. For we might well spare the phrase of wit just quoted rather than the one describing Traddles (whose hair stood up), as one who looked 'as though he had seen a cheerful ghost.' Or rather than this:

> He was so wooden a man that he seemed to have taken his wooden leg naturally, and rather suggested to the fanciful observer that he might be expected—if his development received no untimely check—to be completely set up with a pair of wooden legs in about six months.

Or rather than the incident of the butcher and the beef-steak. He gently presses it, in a cabbage leaf, into Tom Pinch's pocket. ' "For meat", he said with some emotion, "must be humoured, not drove." '

A generation, between his own and the present, thought Dickens to be vulgar; if the cause of that judgment was that he wrote about people in shops, the cause is discredited now that shops are the scenes of the novelist's research. 'High life' and most wretched life have now given place to the little shop and its parlour, during a year or two. But Dr. Brown, the author of *Rab and His Friends*, thought that Dickens committed vulgarities in his diction. 'A good man was Robin' is right enough; but 'He was a good man, was Robin' is not so well, and we must own that it is Dickensian; but assuredly Dickens writes such phrases as it were dramatically, playing the cockney. I know of but two words that Dickens habitually misuses, and Charles Lamb misuses one of them precisely in Dickens's manner; it is not worth while to quote them. But for these his English is admirable; he chooses what is good and knows what is not. A little representative collection of the bad or foolish English of his day might be made by gathering up what Dickens forbore and what he derided; for instance, Mr. Micawber's portly phrase, 'gratifying emotions of no common description,' and Littimer's report that 'the young woman was partial to the sea.' This was the polite language of that time, as we conclude when we find it to be the language that Charlotte Brontë shook off; but before she shook it off she used it. Dickens, too, had something to throw off; in his earlier books there is an inflation—rounded words fill the inappropriate mouth of Bill Sikes himself—but he discarded them with a splendid laugh. They are charged upon Mr. Micawber in his own character as author. See him as he sits to hear Captain Hopkins read the petition in the debtors' prison 'from His Most Gracious Majesty's unfortunate subjects'. Mr. Micawber listened, we read, 'with a little of an author's vanity, contemplating (not severely) the spikes upon the opposite wall'. It should be remembered that when Dickens shook himself free of everything that hampered his genius he was not so much beloved or so much applauded as when he gave to his cordial readers matter for facile sentiment and for humour of the second order. His public were eager to be moved and to laugh, and he gave them Little Nell, and Sam Weller; he loved to please them, and it is evident that he pleased himself also. Mr. Micawber, Mr. Pecksniff, Mrs. Nickleby, Mrs. Chick, Mrs. Pipchin, Mr. Augustus Moddle, Mrs. Jellyby, Mrs. Plornish, are not so famous as Sam Weller and Little Nell; nor is Traddles, whose hair looked as though he had seen a cheerful ghost.

We are told of the delight of the Japanese man in a chance finding of something strange-shaped, an asymmetry that has an accidental felicity, an interest. If he finds such a grace or disproportion—whatever the interest may be—in a stone or a twig that has caught his ambiguous eye at the roadside, he carries it to his home to place it in its irregularly happy place. Dickens seems to have had a like joy in things misshapen or strangely shapen, uncommon or grotesque. He saddled even his heroes—those heroes are, perhaps, his worst work, young men at once conventional and improbable—with whimsically ugly names; while his invented names are whimsically perfect: that of Vholes for the predatory silent man in black, and that of Tope for the cathedral verger. A suggestion of dark and vague flight in Vholes; something of old floors, something respectably furtive and musty, in Tope. In Dickens, the love of lurking, unusual things, human and inanimate—he wrote of his discoveries delightedly in his letters—was hypertrophied; and it has its part in the simplest and the most fantastic of his humours, especially those that are due to his child-like eyesight; let us read, for example, of the rooks that seemed to attend upon Dr. Strong (late of Canterbury) in his Highgate garden, 'as if they had been written to about him by the Canterbury rooks and were observing him closely in consequence'; and of Master Micawber, who had a remarkable head voice—'On looking at Master Micawber again I saw that he had a certain expression of face as if his voice were behind his eyebrows'; and of Joe in his Sunday clothes, 'a scarecrow in good circumstances'; and of the cook's cousin in the Life Guards, with such long legs that 'he looked like the afternoon shadow of somebody else'; and of Mrs. Markleham, 'who stared more like a figure-head intended for a ship to be called the Astonishment, than anything else I can think of'. But there is no reader who has not a thousand such exhilarating little sights in his memory of these pages. From the gently grotesque to the fantastic run Dickens's enchanted eyes, and in Quilp and Miss Mowcher he takes his joy in the extreme of deformity; and a spontaneous combustion was an accident much to his mind.

Dickens wrote for a world that either was exceedingly excitable and sentimental, or had the convention or tradition of great sentimental excitability. All his people, suddenly surprised, lose their presence of mind. Even when the surprise is not extraordinary their actions are wild. When Tom Pinch calls upon John Westlock in London, after no very long separation, John, welcoming him at breakfast, puts the rolls into his boots, and so forth. And this kind of distraction comes upon men and women everywhere in his books—distractions of laughter as well. All this seems artificial to-day, whereas Dickens in his best moments is the simplest, as he is the most vigilant, of men. But his public was as present to him as an actor's audience is to the actor, and I cannot think that this immediate response was good for his art. Assuredly he is not solitary. We should not wish him to be solitary as a poet is, but we may wish that now and again, even while standing applauded and acclaimed, he had appraised the applause more coolly and more justly, and within his inner mind.

Those critics who find what they call vulgarisms think they may safely go on to accuse Dickens of bad grammar. The truth is that his grammar is not only good but strong; it is far better in construction than Thackeray's, the ease of whose phrase sometimes exceeds and is slack. Lately, during the recent centenary time, a writer averred that Dickens 'might not always be parsed', but that we loved him for his, &c., &c. Dickens's page is to be parsed as strictly as any man's. It is, apart from the matter of grammar, a wonderful thing that he, with his little education, should have so excellent a diction. In a letter that records his reluctance to work during a holiday, the word 'wave' seems to me perfect: 'Imaginary butchers and bakers wave me to my desk.' In his exquisite use of the word 'establishment' in the following phrase, we find his own perfect sense of the use of words in his own day; but in the second quotation given there is a most beautiful sign of education. 'Under the weight of my wicked secret' (the little boy Pip had succoured his convict with his brother-in-law's provisions) 'I pondered whether the Church would be powerful enough to shield me . . . if I divulged to that establishment.' And this is the phrase that may remind us of the eighteenth-century writers of prose, and among those writers of none so readily as of Bolingbroke: it occurs in that passage of Esther's life in which, having lost her beauty, she resolves to forgo a love unavowed. 'There was nothing to be undone; no chain for him to drag or for me to break.'

If Dickens had had the education which he had not, his English could not have been better; but if he had had the *usage du monde** which as a young man he had not, there would have been a difference. He would not, for instance, have given us the preposterous scenes in *Nicholas Nickleby* in which parts are played by Lord Frederick Verisopht, Sir Mulberry Hawke, and their friends; the scene of the hero's luncheon at a restaurant and the dreadful description of the mirrors and other splendours would not have have been written. It is a very little thing to forgive to him whom we have to thank for—well, not perhaps for the 'housefull of friends' for the gift of whom a stranger, often quoted, once blessed him in the street; we may not wish for Mr. Feeder, or Major Bagstock, or Mrs. Chick, or Mrs. Pipchin, or Mr. Augustus Moddle, or Mr. F's aunt, or Mr. Wopsle, or Mr. Pumble-chook, as an inmate of our homes. Lack of knowledge of the polite world is, I say, a very little thing to forgive to him whom we thank most chiefly for showing us these interesting people just named as inmates of the comedy homes that are not ours. We thank him because they are comedy homes, and could not be ours or any man's; that is, we thank him for his admirable art.

JOHN W. SIMONS

CERVANTES AND HIS INGENIOUS KNIGHT†

IT IS now more than four centuries since the birth of Europe's first novelist, Miguel Saavedra de Cervantes. Over the years the critics of all lands have paid their customary tribute of encomiastic essays. Yet, the fact remains that Don Quixote, formerly a "must " book for all literate peoples, has relatively few readers in our own times. "Quixoticism" survives in our language both as a word and symbol, but its magnificent context has to a great extent faded from popular memory.

The great work has its readers, of course. Indeed, when we compare its fate with that of other classics and pseudo-classics, we can claim for it a consoling margin of survival. Nevertheless, few youngsters of high-school age are familiar with *Don Quixote's* riot of humorous incident, and few adults of average education have acquaintance with its resonant overtones. In point of fact, our contemporary novelists themselves, concerned as many of them are with fastidious economy of craft, are inclined to be impatient with a novel which wanders aimlessly for the duration of more than a thousand pages. They have forgotten, it seems, that so scrupulous a crafts-man as Flaubert claimed to find his origins in *Don Quixote*.

* Worldly outlook.
† "Cervantes and His Ingenious Knight" appeared in *America* (September 13, 1947). Re-printed by permission of the author and the editor of *America*.

I suppose the chief reason why Cervantes' novel is no longer an intimate part of the reading experience of most people is that the public appetite for comedy is amply satisfied through other media—the movies, the comic strip and television. Besides, conditioned as we are to reading in quick, asthmatic gasps, the sheer bulk of *Quixote* is a discouragement. It is not a little ironical that an age which is so intolerant of bowdlerization should give such incontinent welcome to digests and abstracts.

What was Cervantes really up to when he penned his *Don Quixote?* An answer to this question may give some indication of the difference between high comedy and low, between the comedy which aspires to be literature and the comedy which achieves no more than a transient (and frequently vulgar) titillation. For Cervantes was no mere literary buffoon. That he took his parody seriously as art is proved by the fact that, when some contemporary hack took the more obvious characteristics of the ridiculous knight and his gross squire and produced a sequel to their adventures, Cervantes felt the necessity of refuting his clumsy and clownish endeavors. It is to this accident that we owe the second and more artistically self-conscious part of *Don Quixote*. It constitutes an *apologia* for the comedian as artist.

Cervantes' immediate purpose in writing *Don Quixote* was to satirize the romances of chivalry, those impossible *libros de caballerías* which were so much in the fashion. That he did so with lethal efficiency is a fact of literary history, but in the very act of annihilation he created a new and invulnerable thing. His method was satire but, because it was the satire of a humanist and not of a misanthrope, the victims transcend their burden of parody. Despite his ludicrous antics, Don Quixote has the affection, not only of the author and reader, but of Sancho Panza, his earthly antitype, as well.

It would be altogether too simple an explanation to maintain that the spindly knight is the visionary and his obese squire the realist. What Cervantes is trying to do is to strike an equilibrium between warring tensions. The besetting sin of the knight is not that he has noble ideas, but that these ideals are largely illusory or mischievous. He has lived so long with his books —books of the Amadizing* romantic school—that he confuses the realm of the imagination with the realm of reality.

Don Quixote, because he abdicates reason for fancy, is unfit to cope with the uncompromising world of fact. Windmills become giants, a barber's basin becomes Mambrino's golden helmet, shoddy taverns become castles, squadrons of sheep become armies of knights, a stable-smelly country wench becomes the incomparable Princess Dulcinea del Toboso. It is chivalrous, but dangerous, to free the king's prisoners. And it is ridiculous to give florid discourses to a gathering of famished goatherds on the coming of the Golden Age.

At the opposite pole is Don Quixote's pot-bellied *escudero*,† Sancho Panza. He is concerned primarily, almost exclusively, with money, food and sleep.

* Amadis was the hero of popular romances, chiefly in the sixteenth century.
† Squire.

He has a fund of practical wisdom, quotes apposite folk aphorisms, and manifests cunning in extricating himself from difficult situations. When we are introduced to him he is a creature pretty much on the animal level. He becomes Quixote's squire for definitely materialist reasons: he wants the islands which his master has promised as a reward for services rendered. His very hedonism protects him against hallucination, for his ideas are never allowed to wander beyond the frontiers of sense behavior.

The truly remarkable feature of this impossible *liaison* is that what began as expediency endures through affection. Even after Sancho Panza is convinced that his master is mentally *desvencijado*,* that he himself will never see—much less occupy—the promised islands, and that his association with Quixote is physically hazardous and legally ambiguous—even after these discoveries, he continues faithfully at the side of his knight-aberrant.

It is the anomaly of this idealist-materialist relationship which constitutes the chief humor of the novel. It is the same anomaly, however, which constitutes its underlying pathos and deep humanity. Ridicule can never become derision when love steps in to blur the black-and-white antinomies. And this is precisely what happens. We discover that each element in the relationship is susceptible to the influence of the other, and that the chemistry of their mutual affection works a subtle, almost imperceptible, transformation. In the end we are not surprised that something of the squire's skepticism passes into Don Quixote. Neither are we surprised that something of the knight's idealism passes into Sancho Panza.

One of the knight's most frequent expressions, delivered magisterially to his mundane squire, is, "Don't think small thoughts." The "small thoughts" were usually intensely practical thoughts, calculated to forestall imminent embarrassment. How amusing it is, then, suddenly to come upon this very expression in the mouth of Sancho Panza as he repudiates the common-sense advice of his wife. It is but one symbol of the change which the relationship has effected. In like manner, when we hear the impractical knight venture the opinion that the laws of knight-errantry, were they to become the laws of the land, would lead to endless mischief, we know that he has succumbed, if only tentatively and momentarily, to the plain peasant wisdom of his squire.

Thus we come to the gradual realization that these two characters, though marvelously self-subsistent, are facets of a single identity. It occurs to us at last that Cervantes gives his full allegiance neither to the one nor the other except in the realm of his splendid art, and that we, the readers, are expected to temper the relationship into a workable ideal for practical living. He himself refuses to be our instructor, but it is clear in the end that the so-called realism of Sancho Panza is every bit as reprehensible as the illusory idealism of Don Quixote. I do not wish to overstress the didactic value of *Quixote* or bury the comedy in a homily, but I think we cannot avoid the conclusion that behind the panorama of hilarious incident there is an implied philosophy.

* Rickety, tottering.

It is small wonder that Cervantes felt compelled to write the second part of his novel. He wanted, so he has told us, to rinse his mouth of the bad taste left by the tawdry vaudeville of the psuedo-*Quixote*.

In speaking of the lack of serenity in the humor of Byron's *Don Juan*, Mark Van Doren suggests that, though Byron was very sensitive to the folly of the world, he had no philosophy by which to conquer the world. As a result Byron's laughter tends to the sardonic, and his criticism of folly tends to pure destruction. This serenity is a quality which the comedy of Cervantes (and of Chaucer, too) possesses in a marked degree, and I submit that this quality is a legacy of Catholic humanism. Cervantes does have a philosophy which, while taking full account of the folly of men, leaves the world steady on its foundations.

Cervantes could not be surprised by the folly of men, because original sin was a primary datum of the world's experience. He could not be unduly pessimistic about man's folly, because the Incarnation made it certain that where sin had abounded grace would abound more. Moreover, hope was a Christian virtue, a spiritual weapon which could transform society more effectively than arms. A great deal of modern social criticism has a kind of millenarist tendency. It aims to transform the world completely and at once, and it is exasperated that men are so tardy in rallying to the "cause." Cervantes' profound grasp of human nature gave him an insight into the lethargy of history. And this lethargy, though it arises from man's limitations, is a good thing, for it allows causes to wane which the interim reveals to be either fallacious or absurd. Mankind needs to be rescued from its friends as well as from its enemies.

Cervantes' comic sense is rooted in a sound psychology, but this psychology is itself nourished on Catholic theology. In our day to be a fool is almost the same as to be a knave, but Cervantes could combine stupidity and nobility into a single lovable personality. The character of *Quixote* would have withered at Byron's cynic touch, but it flourishes in the sun of Cervantes' charity. At the peak of his grandiose delirium, when it would seem that all his thoughts were hopelessly beyond this world, Don Quixote does not forget the contemptible matter of Sancho's donkeys. The law of charity leavens artistic creation, and we share the confused anguish of the squire when we are ushered into the deathroom of the ingenious knight.

It would be wrong to assume that Cervantes sentimentalizes his hero. Cervantes is not Rousseau, and folly is not a virtue. Indeed, he abases Quixote almost to the point of cruelty, and exposes his folly with unremitting comic vigor. Thomas Mann, in his essay, "Voyage with Don Quixote," remarks on the author's readiness to exalt and abase his hero, and he justly concludes that abasement and exaltation are twin aspects of a single Christian essence:

> Their psychological union, their marriage in a comic medium, shows
> how very much Don Quixote is a product of Christian culture,
> Christian doctrine and Christian humanity. It shows as well what
> Christianity everlastingly means for the world of mind and of poesy

> and for the human essence itself and its bold expansion and libera-
> tion. . . . Say what you will, Christianity, the flower of Judaism,
> remains one of the two pillars upon which Western culture rests. . . .

The great German novelist, non-Christian eclectic though he is, touches the
paradox which is at the center of Christian psychology. Man is a cipher; yet
he is everything. He is the most fragile thing in nature; yet he is immortal.
He has the pedigree of the worm; yet he is destined to be a consort of the
divine nature. He works out his salvation between humiliation and ecstasy,
between his sense of sin and his sense of the deific power of grace. Don
Quixote, in his abasement as well as in his exaltation, gives clear witness to
his Catholic provenance.

It is important that Cervantes be rescued from those critics who only see
in the *Quixote* a rebellion against idealism. It is now fairly well established—
most recently in Aubrey F. G. Bell's scholarly biography—that Cervantes
was not opposed to the chivalric ideal as such but to its perversion in the
romances. On the other hand, the hard-headed realism which he advocates
is not a realism which precludes the loftiest idealism. St. Theresa of Avila
was a very great mystic, yet her literary style is racy and realist in the
extreme. Illusion was her great enemy, and Spanish critics have been quick
to see both a literary and psychological filiation in the writings of the mystic
and the ex-soldier.

The truth of the matter—as C. S. Lewis's *The Allegory of Love* proves
beyond cavil—is that there was in the chivalric ideal a confusion of Christian
and pagan elements. In certain of its aspects it was oriental, nihilistic, amoral
and anti-social. The cult of woman, in particular, had ethically dangerous
implications, and was in fact mere sensuousness clothed in a vaporous ecto-
plasm. Pre-Raphaelitism was but the nineteenth-century revival of its pseudo-
spirituality. Catholicism was never able wholly to acclimatize the chivalric
ideal, but the life and work of St. Francis of Assisi is a splendid example of
the faith's transforming vigor.

I do not mean to maintain that Cervantes was a thoroughgoing critic of
all these chivalric aberrations or even that he was conscious of their full
danger. That he did see their basic illusoriness, however, is beyond question,
and I believe it was his Catholic orthodoxy which permitted him such dis-
cernment. It is necessary to stress this because there is a school of thought
which persists in seeing Cervantes as unfriendly to the Church, and his great
book as a valedictory to the superstitions of the Middle Ages. It was not
the Church which fostered the fanciful hyperbole which Cervantes attacks.
It was the *avant-garde littérateurs* and the high-brow cenacles which
flourished about such dubious personalities as Eleanor of Aquitaine. The
mockery of Cervantes is in his book, not in his life; and when, in his later
years, he became a member of the Third Order of St. Francis, he was committing, not an act of extravagance, but a sincere and humble act of religion.

Yes, Cervantes has much to teach. Above all else he can teach us the function of high comedy and its power of human revelation. We have had

piddling, and pawkish comedy, farce and satire aplenty. But all these have tended either to evaporate into trivial sentimentality or to boil to a viscous hatred. Modern novelists, when they are serious artists, give themselves over almost exclusively to the tragic muse, and they portray man in an atmosphere of unrelieved or exaggerated gloom. *"L'ignoble bal masqué qu'on appelle le monde,"** says Stendhal, and his successors continue to underscore the lie. It is significant that Cervantes never once allows his hero to laugh. This absence of laughter is the indubitable sign of Quixote's folly. Catholic novelists would do well to study the theology of Cervantes' laughter. When they have absorbed the lesson, there will be less rending of garments and more dancing before the indestructible Ark.

MANYA HARARI

ON TRANSLATING FROM THE RUSSIAN†

In Russian a great many different words can be formed from the same root by adding prefixes or suffixes, and in general many fewer words are needed to make up a sentence than in English.

Russian construction is also infinitely freer than that of most Western languages. Words and even clauses can be put in almost any order, and strings of adjectives can both precede and follow nouns. In English you can say 'I was there yesterday' or 'Yesterday I was there' or even 'There I was, yesterday'; but in Russian these four words can be put together in any of their sixteen possible combinations and still make good sense.

Great Suppleness

This freedom gives great suppleness to the language. Not only can the written sentence convey every inflexion of the human voice, but many sentences can be used as clauses or strung together into passages of almost indefinite length. Vladimir Nabokov in his brilliant study of Gogol has shown how this can lead to a proliferation not only of ideas and images but, in Gogol's handling, even of a whole race of background characters as short-lived as summer flies.

On the other hand, together with the absence of the link words which help to give precision in English, it can lead to a confusing vagueness. In one of Pasternak's early works—one of the stories which he now dismisses as 'immature'—he describes a boy, Seryozha, who has just arrived at his sister's house and is washing after the journey; transliterated, the sentence runs on:

* The sordid masquerade dance that is called the world.
† Reprinted from *The Listener* (February 26, 1959) by permission of the author. This article was originally written for *The Twentieth Century* but was abridged for *The Listener*.

'And here, towel over shoulder, sister noticed how Seryozha had grown'. If this means anything in English, it suggests that it was the sister who had a towel over her shoulder, but it is impossible to tell from the Russian whether it was not, in fact, the brother.

Pasternak would be most unlikely to write this today. For it is not that construction is a matter of indifference in Russian—only that it is determined by sense and sound rather than by academic rules. At the same time, where usage does influence the word order, the Russian usage is often the opposite of the English. Thus in English you would say, 'He was cross, angry, furious', rather than 'He was furious, angry, cross', but in Russian you might get the same impact by using the reverse sequence.

These differences are not, however, the worst of the translator's headaches. Most real problems arise from the lack of a common background between the Russian and the English reader. 'Black' is *chorny* both visually and morally. But 'blue' is either *siny*—'dark blue'—or *goluboy*—'light blue'. *Goluboy* is not 'azure' (which is *lazurny*) but very like it; however, it is etymologically connected with *golub*—dove or pigeon—a bird for which the Russians have a tender feeling (we all know the Russian use of 'little pigeon' as an endearment). Probably because of these associations with skies and pigeons, *goluboy* has a pleasant, cheerful, festive sound in which 'light blue' is disappointingly defective.

Malinovy, which is derived from *malina*—raspberry—is not raspberry red but a pale mulberry mauve. The mood associated with it is also associated with a sound: a certain gentle, solemn ringing of church bells is a *malinovy zvon*—a red-mauve ringing. This is sometimes explained as a corruption of Malines, the Belgian town famous for its carillon, but if this derivation is correct it has been forgotten. What is certain is that *malinovy zvon* is as familiar and meaningful to Russians as 'mauve ringing' is alien and obscure to English readers.

Krasny is red. But while red has only a visual or a political or occasionally an angry meaning (as in 'seeing red'), *krasny* has the same root as *krasota*—beauty. Segal's Russian-English dictionary actually translates *krasny* as 'red, serene, fine, nice, fair, beautiful, handsome, republican, revolutionary, extremist', and Dahl—the Russian equivalent of the Oxford Dictionary—adds the meaning 'strange' or 'half-mad'.

The Red Square

The Red Square in Moscow is usually supposed by foreigners to have been so named at the revolution; in fact it was always called the Red Square, for it was always known as the 'fine', or 'handsome', or 'main' square of the town. The 'red corner', if you find it in a Soviet novel, is not a corner but a rest room—say, in a workers' club—where propaganda pamphlets and portraits of the leaders are kept; it has merely derived its name from the 'red corner' in an Orthodox household: this is traditionally the corner of the room where the icons hang and which is regarded as a place of honour—a guest coming into the room bowed in its direction before speaking to his host. Clearly in all these cases, whatever English words are used, they will not convey the exact aura of the Russian words.

Vladimir Nabokov has an unforgettable chapter on the word *poshlost* (which he spells 'posh-lust'). The usual translation, 'vulgar', is weak, for *poshlost* has a murderous way of pinpointing bad faith as well as bad taste. The fact, he says, that this word does not exist in English does not necessarily mean that the concept is lacking but only that 'it is split among several English words'. This does, however, mean that the unified Russian concept is difficult to convey.

Slavny means glorious, and no Soviet communiqué during the war failed to use it of Soviet armies, victories, people, or achievements. But in Russian you can also speak of a *slavny* child, a *slavnaya* woman, or a *slavny* cat, or say to anyone for whom you feel affection 'You are *slavny*' meaning 'You are a dear'. Nor does a *slavnaya* girl have the *poshlust*—vulgarity—of a 'glorious girl'. It would be possible to write a book on this association of ideas and even include a chapter on the glory of God in the tradition of the Eastern Church. But in the meantime *slavny* remains a barrier to understanding.

If there is no word for *poshlost* there is certainly no word for *toska*. It can be used descriptively or by itself, as an ejaculation, and, as such, be a sufficient comment on an infinite variety of situations or on the imperfection of life itself. It can mean the mildest sadness or the depths of metaphysical despair, and it exhausts all the meanings of the existentialist *angoisse*. The translator can only be guided by the Russian speaker's mood, and perhaps, to be successful, he should even have a sense of the Russian landscape with its capacity to stress the isolation of man and to reflect his boredom as well as his exuberance.

But when it comes to visual background, what may be lacking is not a word or concept but an object familiar in both countries. Thus houses, buildings, flats, all exist in Russian, but when we leave the *gleichgeschaltet* urban world we come upon *izba*. To me this brings a detailed image of a cabin made of caulked logs with a roof of thatch or wooden slats, with or without a raised porch, and carved and painted ornaments round the windows. Such houses have existed immemorially over the greater part of European Russia, but if the translator wishes to reproduce this image, what, in English, can he say? 'Cottage' is too bourgeois, 'peasant hut' or 'house' too general, a chalet suggests Switzerland, and a log cabin Canada. You can, of course, put *izba* in italics and with a footnote. This is informative and may be pleasing, for the reader of a foreign book is rather like a traveller in a foreign land: he is curious about the sights and likes to add exotic words to his vocabulary.

Mint Biscuit or Gingerbread?

But a novel is not a travel book. In trying to draw the reader into the centre of a human situation, the novelist assumes him to know the scenic background. It may even be necessary for his purpose that the reader should feel thoroughly at home in it, and so he will bring in a word or an object which he has known since childhood just because it is familiar and makes for intimacy. In such a case an italicized exotic word in the translation, with or without a footnote, breaks the mood of the original passage. All Russian children know what a *myatny prianik* is: it is a kind of mint biscuit which I have never tasted outside Russia. If the author has brought in a *myatny prianik* to remind the reader of his childhood and so touch off his sensibility in as direct a way as possible, then it seems to me that the substitution of a piece of English gingerbread may sometimes be legitimate.

Many critics would disagree with me, yet such liberties are taken for granted in dialogue. Few people would give a word-for-word translation of foreign slang: they would look for the equivalent slang expression. The difficulty is only to know what the equivalent is. What, for instance, is the right equivalent for a slang dialogue between two boys from a good Moscow high school? Is it public school slang? Or will the result be as confusing for the reader as the accompanying image of boys in Eton collars and top hats boarding a Moscow bus? And is Scottish or Welsh the proper equivalent for Caucasian or Ukrainian?

Names and Their Diminutives

Nor is it the custom now to transliterate such forms of address as 'little brother' or 'little friend'. On the other hand the infinite variety of Russian names is usually kept, to the confusion of the reader. And yet what else can be done? In Russia, if you have just made the acquaintance of Nikolay Nikolayevich Ivanov you address him as 'you' and as Mr. or Comrade Ivanov; if you go on seeing him, you will soon call him Nikolay Nikolayevich; if you get to know him well enough you will say 'thou' and call him Nikolay; and then, depending on your mood and the degree of your affection, you will say Kolya, or Kolenka or even Kolka. (If he is a small boy, Kolya or Kolenka or Kolka is all he can be.) Kolya is the diminutive of Nikolay, Kolenka is the affectionate diminutive of Kolya, while Kolka is grammatically pejorative—it should mean that you are cross with Kolya, but in fact it usually implies merely a good-tempered familiarity. To dodge the issue by never referring to Kolka-Kolenka-Kolya-Nikolay Nikolayevich Ivanov as anything but Nicholas or Ivanov is to dodge the whole character of Russian dialogue. Yet to leave them all in means bespattering the page with rows of letters which drive the reader frantic.

Putting dialogue aside, Russian prose in general is more colloquial than English. Inevitably, the translator has to choose between literal exactness and the naturalness of his tone—but a natural tone should not be dull. How do you translate? 'His eyes shone with the fire of the soul'. Should you say? 'His eyes shone with an inward fire'. This is very homely; on the other hand the Russian sentence is not in the least startling. But this is partly because the soul has greater currency in Russian than in English. Incidentally, it often replaces the English heart: A Russian knows in his soul what an Englishman knows in his heart.

Pasternak's style is as colloquial as Dostoevsky's, but his is a new colloquialism. His language is never mannered or vulgar, yet in it thieves can curse, witches cast their spells, and intellectuals discuss abstractions. It can be earthy, violent, and it can rise from one moment to the next to the height of lyricism. He has, too, a poet's mastery of prose rhythm—a rhythm unbroken by changes of mood or theme or by transition from description to dialogue, yet it always fits the subject and the speaker and is infinitely variable. He uses its variations to speed up or to slow down the pace, to create excitement or leisure, having, so he implies, learnt the art of doing this from Shakespeare.

He is never commonplace, and yet he is a master of clichés; he uses them as boldly as he uses words from peasant language and old Russian and the rarest as well as the most current terms, and their vitality in his text supports his theory that literary language refreshes and re-creates itself by contact with the language of the street. Needless to say, the English version of *Dr. Zhivago* loses much of the richness of the original. In some instances this seems to me inevitable.

The Rowanberries

I have referred to the associations of the Russian word for 'red'. In peasant language the expression 'You are my little red berry' is an endearment and is in no way ridiculous. In *Zhivago* there is a rowan tree which stands for love and kindly magic to the hero. The tree feeds the birds in winter 'like a foster-mother'. A witch asks it to protect Zhivago and to scatter its berries in the wind so that one of them should reach Lara as a message of love and hope. It plays a part in Zhivago's escape from the partisans, and its berries are like sugared fruit and like drops of blood. Blood has already stained the snow when a procession was scattered by Cossacks at the beginning of the book, and soon after this red rowanberry wine appears in sparkling bottles at a party; later, when Zhivago is dangerously ill, he sees dawn shining through the hoar frost on his window like red wine through cut glass, and this precedes the coming of Lara, who is to save him—Lara whose arms are also the arms of heaven as well as the branches of the tree. Earlier, just before his capture by the partisans, Zhivago, in his daydream of being on his way to Lara, sees the icon lights inside the houses reflected like red berries in the puddles in the streets; and towards the end of the story, when Lara's husband shoots himself, drops of blood are scattered in the snow 'like rowanberries'.

Buried in all this symbolism about history, life, death, resurrection, love, Sophia, blood, wine and the tree of life, is the small red berry of folk legend and endearment and the colour red with its multiple associations.

But at least in this case the reader can discover the connecting symbols in the end. In other cases this is impossible. The novel opens with the funeral of Zhivago's mother. Passers-by join the funeral procession out of curiosity and ask:

'Who is being buried?'

'Zhivago.'

'Oh, I see . . .'

'It isn't him, it's his wife.'

Further on, on the same page, we learn that the dead woman has left a son, Yura. What the reader needs to know is that the word Zhivago has the same root as *zhivoy*, the masculine form of 'alive'. The accusative of *zhivoy* is *zhivovo;* 'He was buried alive' is *pogrebli zhivovo.* But *zhivovo* is spelt *zhivogo* and its earlier form was *zhivago.* So here, at the very outset, the reader is given a strong hint about the book; it is a book about life and death; its hero is a man who, above all else, is alive, a man who will be so defeated by circumstances as to be virtually 'buried alive', but whose defeat will not be ultimate for he is Yury—George, the killer of dragons, the killer of death. How, in English, to convey these hints which are so important, yet which are veiled by the fact that Yury is only one of the Russian forms of George and that Zhivago is not a name invented by the author but an existing surname, though admittedly a rare one?

Creating an Impression of Life

Fortunately not all Pasternak's verbal clues are equally untranslatable, for the importance in his work of language, and by this I mean also voice and tone, can hardly be exaggerated. Fortunately, too, he has expressed his own views on translation. In his essay on translating Shakespeare he says that 'As much as the author the translator must confine himself to a vocabulary which is natural to him . . . Like the original text, the translation must create an impression of life and not of verbiage'.

SEAN O'FAOLAIN

THE ART OF THE SHORT STORY*

THE MOST misleading thing about the short story is its name. The word 'story' continues to suggest to most readers and to all too many editors and writers what I have no other word for except a 'yarn'; that is, some ingenious anecdote with, if possible, an arresting beginning, a dramatic middle, and, above all, a surprising end. The purest form of this kind of story is the limerick; and the best retailers of such stories are the fellows who buttonhole us down at the club with: 'I heard a very good one today . . .'

* Reprinted from *The Listener* (August 9, 1956) by permission of the author.

Limerick and Fireside-Yarn

The limerick and the fireside-yarn at the club are, indeed, generally arresting or amusing tales, and all the more so since they are supposed to be recorded directly from life. I suppose they are the modern version of the folk-tale told by the *shanachee* beside the cottage fire. But that is perhaps also precisely why they do not make and can rarely be made into short stories in our modern sense of the word. Since they are meant to be heard, not to be read—let alone re-read—the essence of them is action or event, and they have to make a clear and quick impact which is easily picked up by the casual ear. They may, of course, have their own sort of stylistic merit. One teller of yarns will do it better, more vividly, more dramatically than another. Yet essentially what we are held by is our interest in 'what happened next'— the yarn, or sheer sequence of anecdotal event.

The written story is a refinement, or rather a whole series of refinements, of this sort of entertainment. One such refinement is the plot. As a matter of literary history, the oldest fireside tales never contain any plot; they just proceed from event to event in a sequence of adventures which are limited in number only by the inventiveness of the story-teller or the patience or interest of the listeners. The plot is essentially a literary invention. It is a simple way of boiling down or compressing the diffuse and wandering saga. But this is merely where the art of story-writing begins—and I stress the word 'begins'. Because what we have to ask ourselves is: 'To what end or purpose is this boiling down process undertaken?' It is not done just for the mere sake of brevity. Certainly it is done in part for our entertainment. Or it would be more accurate to say that it is done in part for the entertainment of a sophisticated audience—an audience that enjoys such things as shape and form, that likes to see a story being rounded featly, given suspense or surprise, brought to a point of neat emphasis.

Device of The Plot

But still the question remains: 'What is the purpose of this?' There is no one single answer, unless, greatly daring, we venture on some large generalisation; such as that the plot-story purposes to illuminate the vagaries of human nature, or—to be still more vague—the vagaries of society in general. If, for example, we think of a Boccaccio short story we will see at once that while we undoubtedly get the kick, or relish, of the ingenious plot, the amusing situation, the expected or unexpected *dénouement*, the real relish comes with our laughter at the odd ways of human nature which the story reveals. The condensed plot is presumably there to draw the perspective of the story to this point and this effect. That is its purpose. It is its sole justification. Otherwise we get a pointless club-fire anecdote which records an event without any ulterior significance. In short, the plot is a device, one device among many, not an end in itself.

James Joyce gives an example—adapted from Aristotle—of an event which has no ulterior significance and which therefore could never be used for any artistic purpose. A young woman was driving through London in a cab when a lorry collided with the cab and made a star-shaped hole in the window. A long, fine sliver of glass from the window pierced her heart like a dagger and killed her immediately. The incident was described by a journalist as a tragic death. But the death was, in terms of art, not tragic. It was outside tragedy in the realms of fatal chance. It had no significance, no meaning, no point other than the melancholy truth that many pointless fatalities occur in life.

What I am saying, then, is that the essence of a story is not what happens but the revelation of the larger significance of what happens. It is this significance that must chiefly be considered in weighing the merits of a short story. I know that I am here using debatable terms. What does significance mean? And how does this significance get into a short story? Where does the writer find it? How does he know whether he has found it or not? To such questions there can be no answer. It is one of the things nobody can be taught and that nobody can learn. It is why all those courses in 'How to Write Short Stories' are in the long run a snare and a delusion. You might as well have courses in 'How to Write Poetry'. For the truth is that neither a short story nor a poem can be completely translated into any other words except its own words. The technique and the content are united into a single entity by the personality of the author. All the technique is there for is to hypnotise us into accepting that what the writer is describing is actually happening to us, as it were vicariously, or by proxy, in order that we may feel life in the manner in which the writer feels it. A story is therefore never really about anything—it is about the writer's view of life; his personal *manière de voir*.

The Writer's Subject and Personality

It is true that we can say that Shelley's poem is about a skylark, and that Maupassant's *La Parure* is about a woman who lost a borrowed necklace. But the poem is not really so much about the skylark as about Shelley, and that hour, and that day and all his life, and all his tumbled dreams and all his jumbled feelings and half-articulated perceptions. It is about the essence of what, for short, we choose to call his heart. Likewise Maupassant's story is about Maupassant. It is the way of saying 'That's life!'—meaning, 'That's how I see life'. He could just as easily have confined himself to writing about Norman peasants—and he did, over and over again. It really does not matter what thing a man writes about so long as the subject and his personality are in concordance; so long as the subject appealed strongly to something in him; let him say something that he felt deeply. I need hardly say that he will never know clearly what it is that he feels, what it is that he wants to say. All he will know is that this thing hit something inside him and he had to get it out. Plot? Character? Anecdote? He does not think of plot. He does not think of anything. All he is aware of is that he feels and that because he feels so much he must overflow. He may write comically, tragically, fantastically. That does not matter, either. So long as there is a bit of feeling and personality in it, that is all that primarily matters. Without feeling and personality a short story is a dud. A sewing-machine could have written it.

When you come to write down the thing you have felt, a complete transformation must take place. The 'you' with which the story began must appear to disappear. You retire into the background. The thing that hit you is all we want now. When we look at Botticelli's 'Primavera' we do not think of Botticelli—he has transformed himself into a painted canvas. Likewise the writer is translated into his picture, its mood, its scent, its indescribable quality. This is why, as far as is possible, no short-story writer ever utters a personal opinion. To say, for example, "Andrew McLaughlin was a very fine fellow' is an unforgivable intrusion. That would be your opinion of Andy McLaughlin. Show us Andy doing something, and let us draw our own conclusions. A direct statement in a short story is as intrusive as if Botticelli wrote across his canvas: 'This is spring. This is a breezy day. These are vernal flowers. This lady has a very charming figure'. Convey, suggest, imply, infer, but never say. I agree that it is quicker to say, and be done with, but saying never persuades half so effectively as the suggestion or the hint. Indeed one reason why I do not happen to care for plot-stories is that the plot seems to me to be an emphatic and obvious way of making a point, and it brings the author very much into the foreground. 'What a clever fellow he is!', we are inclined to say as we finish reading his story.

Some of you may have been reading Mr. V. S. Pritchett's recently published volume of collected stories. I mention it because it contains so many good examples of the type of story which is at once suggestive and significant without undue emphasis of this sort. One such is called 'Many Are Disappointed'. It is overtly about a few chaps cycling through the country and looking forward eagerly to a halt at a country tavern several miles ahead where they will be rewarded by a well-deserved drink. When they come there they find to their dismay that it is no longer a tavern and that nothing is available but tea. Disconsolately they accept the tea and fall into casual talk with the woman and child who seem to be the sole residents of the isolated house. There is apparently nothing at all to the story except the mood created in their minds by the flaccid, feeble, damp domesticity of this lonely house, so utterly removed from the warm expectations with which they had approached it. Their response to the atmosphere of the place is no more than suggested. And yet when they get on their bicycles again and drive away, heads down, full of boisterous good cheer, we are somehow or other not only deeply touched by this brief communion of human nature but have the sensation that a chord has been touched for all of them at the heart of the ineluctable loneliness of life.

'Like a Conjurer'

I need not say that I am doing utter injustice to the story by trying to convey in this explicit way an effect that it manages to impart so casually that it is not until we re-read it that we become aware of its unobtrusive skill. But then that is the whole art of the short-story writer—to produce an effect without our knowing how it has happened, like a conjurer making a lovely cloud of pigeons come out of a tall hat.

What comes out of the short-story writer's hat? A little event—a story, yarn, an anecdote by all means, if you like it that way. Something slight: it does not matter how slight, so long as it is human, so long as behind the story there is a light falling on the landscape of life, like the sun throwing down its searchlight through the clouds.

One of the commonest delusions of readers and writers of short stories is that interesting characters make good stories and that all good stories must contain clearly elaborated characterisation. All you have to do to see that this is not so is to read a half-dozen good short stories. In the first place there is no time for elaborate characterisation, and we find that any story that indulges in it runs to length. In the second place character in a short story, because of the limitation in length, has an awkward way of ending up as caricature if it is not handled very lightly indeed. All any short story can do is to pick out whatever characteristic quality or weakness in the protagonists is essential to the theme. Many of the finest stories do not even do so much. After all, we have to remember that one great difference between the story and the novel is that in the novel there is room for development of character whereas in a story—unless one believes in lightning conversations—a character may be suddenly revealed to us (and to himself) but he cannot change. A short story deals with a point of crisis, which is why it so often happens that the Aristotelian unities seem to be specially applicable to this craft. The short story generally locates itself in one place for a brief period, among two, three, or four people.

'The Essence of a Thing'

Chekhov's 'The Chorus Girl' or Hemingway's 'The Light of the World' are classical examples of this compactness, and the main thing that strikes us about them is the simplification of the characters. They are the merest outlines of persons. As I see it, the reason for this simplification is that a short story is the essence of a thing. It boils down a whole lot of complexities, and ambiguities, and inconclusions, and pros and cons about a man, or a woman, or a human relationship, or some aspect of living, such as childhood's fears, or the pathos of age, or jealousy, or self-deception, or anything that interests the writer—it boils everything about any one thing down to—to, I was going to say a sonnet, but I will say the final couplet of a sonnet. I do not—heaven forbid that I should be so silly—suggest for a moment that it boils down to a conclusion, or to a moral: a mood suffices; a little note of music heard in the air; something that puts us into a mood like to the mood of the author when he wrote, a mood in which we see life, for a few revealing moments, through his eyes, in its essence, or quintessence, pith, marrow, sap, sum, substance, call it what you like.

I hope I do not appear solemn or pompous in all this. It is as true of comic stories as of tragic stories. Whether we put a story down with a laugh or a sigh, either result is a tribute to the purity or clarity of the writer's view of life. We do not have to agree with him. The truth of his observation is irrelevant. All that matters is whether he has got down to the essence of his viewpoint so clearly that we, for the moment, borrow his eyes, to feel with his heart.

ALLEN TATE

EMILY DICKINSON*

1

GREAT POETRY needs no special features of difficulty to make it mysterious. When it has them, the reputation of the poet is likely to remain uncertain. This is still true of Donne, and it is true of Emily Dickinson, whose verse appeared in an age unfavorable to the use of intelligence in poetry. Her poetry is not like any other poetry of her time; it is not like any of the innumerable kinds of verse written today. In still another respect it is far removed from us. It is a poetry of ideas, and it demands of the reader a point of view—not an opinion of the New Deal or of the League of Nations, but an ingrained philosophy that is fundamental, a settled attitude that is almost extinct in this eclectic age. Yet it is not the sort of poetry of ideas which, like Pope's, requires a point of view only. It requires also, for the deepest understanding, which must go beneath the verbal excitement of the style, a highly developed sense of the specific quality of poetry—a quality that most persons accept as the accidental feature of something else that the poet thinks he has to say. This is one reason why Miss Dickinson's poetry has not been widely read.

There is another reason, and it is a part of the problem peculiar to a poetry that comes out of fundamental ideas. We lack a tradition of criticism. There were no points of critical reference passed on to us from a preceding generation. I am not upholding here the so-called dead-hand of tradition, but rather a rational insight into the meaning of the present in terms of some imaginable past implicit in our own lives: we need a body of ideas that can bear upon the course of the spirit and yet remain coherent as a rational instrument. We ignore the present, which is momently translated into the

* Reprinted from *Collected Essays* by Allen Tate by permission of the publisher, Alan Swallow. Copyright 1959 by Allen Tate.

past, and derive our standards from imaginative constructions of the future. The hard contingency of fact invariably breaks these standards down, leaving us the intellectual chaos which is the sore distress of American criticism. Marxian criticism has become the latest disguise of this heresy.

Still another difficulty stands between us and Miss Dickinson. It is the failure of the scholars to feel more than biographical curiosity about her. We have scholarship, but that is no substitute for a critical tradition. Miss Dickinson's value to the research scholar, who likes historical difficulty for its own sake, is slight; she is too near to possess the remoteness of literature. Perhaps her appropriate setting would be the age of Cowley or of Donne. Yet in her own historical setting she is, nevertheless, remarkable and special.

Although the intellectual climate into which she was born, in 1830, had, as all times have, the features of a transition, the period was also a major crisis culminating in the war between the States. After that war, in New England as well as in the South, spiritual crises were definitely minor until the First World War.

Yet, a generation before the war of 1861-65, the transformation of New England had begun. When Samuel Slater in 1790 thwarted the British embargo on mill-machinery by committing to memory the whole design of a cotton spinner and bringing it to Massachusetts, he planted the seed of the "Western spirit." By 1825 its growth in the East was rank enough to begin choking out the ideas and habits of living that New England along with Virginia had kept in unconscious allegiance to Europe. To the casual observer, perhaps, the New England character of 1830 was largely an eighteenth-century character. But theocracy was on the decline, and industrialism was rising—as Emerson, in an unusually lucid moment, put it, "Things are in the saddle." The energy that had built the meeting-house ran the factory.

Now the idea that moved the theocratic state is the most interesting historically of all American ideas. It was, of course, powerful in seventeenth-century England, but in America, where the long arm of Laud could not reach, it acquired an unchecked social and political influence. The important thing to remember about the puritan theocracy is that it permeated, as it could never have done in England, a whole society. It gave final, definite meaning to life, the life of pious and impious, of learned and vulgar alike. It gave—and this is its significance for Emily Dickinson, and in only slightly lesser degree for Melville and Hawthorne—it gave an heroic proportion and a tragic mode to the experience of the individual. The history of the New England theocracy, from Apostle Eliot to Cotton Mather, is rich in gigantic intellects that broke down—or so it must appear to an outsider—in a kind of moral decadence and depravity. Socially we may not like the New England idea. Yet it had an immense, incalculable value for literature: it dramatized the human soul.

But by 1850 the great fortunes had been made (in the rum, slave, and milling industries), and New England became a museum. The whatnots groaned under the load of knick-knacks, the fine china dogs and cats, the pieces of Oriental jade, the chips off the leaning tower at Pisa. There were the rare books and the cosmopolitan learning. It was all equally displayed as the evidence of a superior culture. The Gilded Age had already begun. But culture, in the true sense, was disappearing. Where the old order, formidable as it was, had held all this personal experience, this eclectic excitement, in a comprehensible whole, the new order tended to flatten it out in a common experience that was not quite in common; it exalted more and more the personal and the unique in the interior sense. Where the old-fashioned puritans got together on a rigid doctrine, and could thus be individualists in manners, the nineteenth-century New Englander, lacking a genuine religious center, began to be a social conformist. The common idea of the Redemption, for example, was replaced by the conformist idea of respectability among neighbors whose spiritual disorder, not very evident at the surface, was becoming acute. A great idea was breaking up, and society was moving towards external uniformity, which is usually the measure of the spiritual sterility inside.

At this juncture Emerson came upon the scene: the Lucifer of Concord, he had better be called hereafter, for he was the light-bearer who could see nothing but light, and was fearfully blind. He looked around and saw the uniformity of life, and called it the routine of tradition, the tyranny of the theological idea. The death of Priam put an end to the hope of Troy, but it was a slight feat of arms for the doughty Pyrrhus; Priam was an old gentleman and almost dead. So was theocracy; and Emerson killed it. In this way he accelerated a tendency that he disliked. It was a great intellectual mistake. By it Emerson unwittingly became the prophet of a piratical industrialism, a consequence of his own transcendental individualism that he could not foresee. He was hoist with his own petard.

He discredited more than any other man the puritan drama of the soul. The age that followed, from 1865 on, expired in a genteel secularism, a mildly didactic order of feeling whose ornaments were Lowell, Longfellow, and Holmes. "After Emerson had done his work," says Mr. Robert Penn Warren, "any tragic possibilities in that culture were dissipated." Hawthorne alone in his time kept pure, in the primitive terms, the primitive vision; he brings the puritan tragedy to its climax. Man, measured by a great idea outside himself, is found wanting. But for Emerson man is greater than any idea and, being himself the Over-Soul, is innately perfect; there is no struggle because—I state the Emersonian doctrine, which is very slippery, in its extreme terms—because there is no possibility of error. There is no drama in human character because there is no tragic fault. It is not surprising, then, that after Emerson New England literature tastes like a sip of cambric tea. Its center of vision has disappeared. There is Hawthorne looking back, there is Emerson looking not too clearly at anything ahead: Emily Dickinson, who has in her something of both, comes in somewhere between.

With the exception of Poe there is no other American poet whose work so steadily emerges, under pressure of certain disintegrating obsessions, from the framework of moral character. There is none of whom it is truer to say that the poet *is* the poetry. Perhaps this explains the zeal of her admirers for her biography; it explains, in part at least, the gratuitous mystery that Mrs. Bianchi, a niece of the poet and her official biographer, has made of her life. The devoted controversy that Miss Josephine Pollitt and Miss Genevieve Taggard started a few years ago with their excellent books shows the extent to which the critics feel the intimate connection of her life and work. Admiration and affection are pleased to linger over the tokens of a great life; but the solution to the Dickinson enigma is peculiarly superior to fact.

The meaning of the identity—which we merely feel—of character and poetry would be exceedingly obscure, even if we could draw up a kind of Binet* correlation between the two sets of "facts." Miss Dickinson was a recluse, but her poetry is rich with a profound and varied experience. Where did she get it? Now some of the biographers, nervous in the presence of this discrepancy, are eager to find her a love affair, and I think this search is due to a modern prejudice: we believe that no virgin can know enough to write poetry. We shall never learn where she got the rich quality of her mind. The moral image that we have of Miss Dickinson stands out in every poem; it is that of a dominating spinster whose very sweetness must have been formidable. Yet her poetry constantly moves within an absolute order of truths that overwhelmed her simply because to her they were unalterably fixed. It is dangerous to assume that her "life," which to the biographers means the thwarted love affair she is supposed to have had, gave to her poetry a decisive direction. It is even more dangerous to suppose that it made her a poet.

Poets are mysterious, but a poet when all is said is not much more mysterious than a banker. The critics remain spellbound by the technical license of her verse and by the puzzle of her personal life. Personality is a legitimate interest because it is an incurable interest, but legitimate as a personal interest only; it will never give up the key to anyone's verse. Used to that end, the interest is false. "It is apparent," writes Mr. Conrad Aiken, "that Miss Dickinson became a hermit by deliberate and conscious choice"— a sensible remark that we cannot repeat too often. If it were necessary to explain her seclusion with disappointment in love, there would remain the discrepancy between what the seclusion produced and the seclusion looked at as a cause. The effect, which is her poetry, would imply the whole complex of anterior fact, which was the social and religious structure of New England.

The problem to be kept in mind is thus the meaning of her "deliberate and conscious" decision to withdraw from life to her upstairs room. This simple fact is not very important. But that it must have been her sole way of acting out her part in the history of her culture, which made, with the variations of circumstance, a single demand upon all its representatives—this

* Simon Binet developed an intelligence test for children.

is of the greatest consequence. All pity for Miss Dickinson's "starved life" is misdirected. Her life was one of the richest and deepest ever lived on this continent.

When she went upstairs and closed the door, she mastered life by rejecting it. Others in their way had done it before; still others did it later. If we suppose—which is to suppose the improbable—that the love affair precipitated the seclusion, it was only a pretext; she would have found another. Mastery of the world by rejecting the world was the doctrine, even if it was not always the practice, of Jonathan Edwards and Cotton Mather. It is the meaning of fate in Hawthorne: his people are fated to withdraw from the world and to be destroyed. And it is one of the great themes of Henry James.

There is a moral emphasis that connects Hawthorne, James, and Miss Dickinson, and I think it is instructive. Between Hawthorne and James lies an epoch. The temptation to sin, in Hawthorne, is, in James, transformed into the temptation not to do the "decent thing." A whole world-scheme, a complete cosmic background, has shrunk to the dimensions of the individual conscience. This epoch between Hawthorne and James lies in Emerson. James found himself in the post-Emersonian world, and he could not, without violating the detachment proper to an artist, undo Emerson's work; he had that kind of intelligence which refuses to break its head against history. There was left to him only the value, the historic rôle, of rejection. He could merely escape from the physical presence of that world which, for convenience, we may call Emerson's world: he could only take his Americans to Europe upon the vain quest of something that they had lost at home. His characters, fleeing the wreckage of the puritan culture, preserved only their honor. Honor became a sort of forlorn hope struggling against the forces of "pure fact" that had got loose in the middle of the century. Honor alone is a poor weapon against nature, being too personal, finical, and proud, and James achieved a victory by refusing to engage the whole force of the enemy.

In Emily Dickinson the conflict takes place on a vaster field. The enemy to all those New Englanders was Nature, and Miss Dickinson saw into the character of this enemy more deeply than any of the others. The general symbol of Nature, for her, is Death, and her weapon against Death is the entire powerful dumb-show of the puritan theology led by Redemption and Immortality. Morally speaking, the problem for James and Miss Dickinson is similar. But her advantages were greater than his. The advantages lay in the availability to her of the puritan ideas on the theological plane.

These ideas, in her poetry, are momently assailed by the disintegrating force of Nature (appearing as Death) which, while constantly breaking them down, constantly redefines and strengthens them. The values are purified by the triumphant withdrawal from Nature, by their power to recover from Nature. The poet attains to a mastery over experience by facing its utmost implications. There is the clash of powerful opposites, and in all great poetry—for Emily Dickinson is a great poet—it issues in a tension between abstraction and sensation in which the two elements may be, of course, distinguished logically, but not really. We are shown our roots in Nature by examining our differences with Nature; we are renewed by Nature without being delivered into her hands. When it is possible for a poet to do this for us with the greatest imaginative comprehension, a possibility that the poet cannot himself create, we have the perfect literary situation. Only a few times in the history of English poetry has this situation come about, notably, the period between about 1580 and the Restoration. There was a similar age in New England from which emerged two talents of the first order—Hawthorne and Emily Dickinson.

There is an epoch between James and Miss Dickinson. But between her and Hawthorne there exists a difference of intellectual quality. She lacks almost radically the power to seize upon and understand abstractions for their own sake; she does not separate them from the sensuous illuminations that she is so marvellously adept at; like Donne, she *perceives abstraction* and *thinks sensation*. But Hawthorne was a master of ideas, within a limited range; this narrowness confined him to his own kind of life, his own society, and out of it grew his typical forms of experience, his steady, almost obsessed vision of man; it explains his depth and intensity. Yet he is always conscious of the abstract, doctrinal aspect of his mind, and when his vision of action and emotion is weak, his work becomes didactic. Now Miss Dickinson's poetry often runs into quasi-homiletic forms, but it is never didactic. Her very ignorance, her lack of formal intellectual training, preserved her from the risk that imperiled Hawthorne. She cannot reason at all. She can only *see*. It is impossible to imagine what she might have done with drama or fiction; for, not approaching the puritan temper and through it the puritan myth, through human action, she is able to grasp the terms of the myth directly and by a feat that amounts almost to anthropomorphism, to give them a luminous tension, a kind of drama, among themselves.

One of the perfect poems in English is "The Chariot," and it illustrates better than anything else she wrote the special quality of her mind. I think it will illuminate the tendency of this discussion:

> Because I could not stop for death,
> He kindly stopped for me;
> The carriage held but just ourselves
> And immortality.

> We slowly drove, he knew no haste,
> And I had put away
> My labor, and my leisure too,
> For his civility.

> We passed the school where children played,
> Their lessons scarcely done;
> We passed the fields of gazing grain,
> We passed the setting sun.

We paused before a house that seemed
A swelling of the ground;
The roof was scarcely visible,
The cornice but a mound.

Since then 'tis centuries; but each
Feels shorter than the day
I first surmised the horses' heads
Were toward eternity.

If the word great means anything in poetry, this poem is one of the greatest in the English language. The rhythm charges with movement the pattern of suspended action back of the poem. Every image is precise and, moreover, not merely beautiful, but fused with the central idea. Every image extends and intensifies every other. The third stanza especially shows Miss Dickinson's power to fuse, into a single order of perception, a heterogeneous series: the children, the grain, and the setting sun (time) have the same degree of credibility; the first subtly preparing for the last. The sharp *gazing* before *grain* instills into nature a cold vitality of which the qualitative richness has infinite depth. The content of death in the poem eludes explicit definition. He is a gentleman taking a lady out for a drive. But note the restraint that keeps the poet from carrying this so far that it becomes ludicrous and incredible; and note the subtly interfused erotic motive, which the idea of death has presented to most romantic poets, love being a symbol interchangeable with death. The terror of death is objictified through this figure of the genteel driver, who is made ironically to serve the end of Immortality. This is the heart of the poem: she has presented a typical Christian theme in its final irresolution, without making any final statements about it. There is no solution to the problem; there can be only a presentation of it in the full context of intellect and feeling. A construction of the human will, elaborated with all the abstracting powers of the mind, is put to the concrete test of experience: the idea of immortality is confronted with the fact of physical disintegration. We are not told what to think; we are told to look at the situation.

The framework of the poem is, in fact, the two abstractions, mortality and eternity, which are made to associate in equality with the images: she sees the ideas, and thinks the perceptions. She did, of course, nothing of the sort; but we must use the logical distinctions, even to the extent of paradox, if we are to form any notion of this rare quality of mind. She could not in the proper sense think at all, and unless we prefer the feeble poetry of moral ideas that flourished in New England in the eighties, we must conclude that her intellectual deficiency contributed at least negatively to her great distinction. Miss Dickinson is probably the only Anglo-American poet of her century whose work exhibits the perfect literary situation—in which is possible the fusion of sensibility and thought. Unlike her contemporaries, she never succumbed to her ideas, to easy solutions, to her private desires.

Philosophers must deal with ideas, but the trouble with most nineteenth-century poets is too much philosophy; they are nearer to being philosophers than poets, without being in the true sense either. Tennyson is a good example of this; so is Arnold in his weak moments. There have been poets like Milton and Donne, who were not spoiled for their true business by leaning on a rational system of ideas, who understood the poetic use of ideas. Tennyson tried to mix a little Huxley and a little Broad Church, without understanding either Broad Church or Huxley; the result was fatal, and what is worse, it was shallow. Miss Dickinson's ideas were deeply imbedded in her character, not taken from the latest tract. A conscious cultivation of ideas in poetry is always dangerous, and even Milton escaped ruin only by having an instinct for what in the deepest sense he understood. Even at that there is a remote quality in Milton's approach to his material, in his treatment of it; in the nineteenth century, in an imperfect literary situation where literature was confused with documentation, he might have been a pseudo-philosopher-poet. It is difficult to conceive Emily Dickinson and John Donne succumbing to rumination about "problems"; they would not have written at all.

Neither the feeling nor the style of Miss Dickinson belongs to the seventeenth century; yet between her and Donne there are remarkable ties. Their religious ideas, their abstractions, are momently toppling from the rational plane to the level of perception. The ideas, in fact, are no longer the impersonal religious symbols created anew in the heat of emotion, that we find in poets like Herbert and Vaughan. They have become, for Donne, the terms of personality; they are mingled with the miscellany of sensation. In Miss Dickinson, as in Donne, we may detect a singularly morbid concern, not for religious truth, but for personal revelation. The modern word is self-exploitation. It is egoism grown irresponsible in religion and decadent in morals. In religion it is blasphemy; in society it means usually that culture is not self-contained and sufficient, that the spiritual community is breaking up. This is, along with some other features that do not concern us here, the perfect literary situation.

II

Personal revelation of the kind that Donne and Miss Dickinson strove for, in the effort to understand their relation to the world, is a feature of all great poetry; it is probably the hidden motive for writing. It is the effort of the individual to live apart from a cultural tradition that no longer sustains him. But this culture, which I now wish to discuss a little, is indispensable: there is a great deal of shallow nonsense in modern criticism which holds that poetry—and this is a half-truth that is worse than false—is essentially revolutionary. It is only indirectly revolutionary: the intellectual and religious background of an age no longer contains the whole spirit, and the poet proceeds to examine that background in terms of immediate experience. But the background is necessary; otherwise all the arts (not only poetry) would have to rise in a vacuum. Poetry does not dispense with tradition; it probes the deficiencies of a tradition. But it must have a tradition to probe. It is too bad that Arnold did not explain his doctrine, that poetry is a criticism of life, from the viewpoint of its background: we should have been spared an era of academic misconception, in which criticism of life meant a diluted pragmatism, the criterion of which was respectability. The poet in the true sense "criticizes" his tradition, either as such, or indirectly by comparing it with something that is about to replace it; he does what the root-meaning of the verb implies—he *discerns* its real elements and thus establishes its value, by putting it to the test of experience.

What is the nature of a poet's culture? Or, to put the question properly, what is the meaning of culture for poetry? All the great poets become the material of what we popularly call culture; we study them to acquire it. It is clear that Addison was more cultivated than Shakespeare; nevertheless Shakespeare is a finer source of culture than Addison. What is the meaning of this? Plainly it is that learning has never had anything to do with culture except instrumentally: the poet must be exactly literate enough to write down fully and precisely what he has to say, but no more. The source of a poet's true culture lies back of the paraphernalia of culture, and not all the historical activity of an enlightened age can create it.

A culture cannot be consciously created. It is an available source of ideas that are imbedded in a complete and homogeneous society. The poet finds himself balanced upon the moment when such a world is about to fall, when it threatens to run out into looser and less self-sufficient impulses. This world order is assimilated, in Miss Dickinson, as medievalism was in Shakespeare, to the poetic vision; it is brought down from abstraction to personal sensibility.

In this connection it may be said that the prior conditions for great poetry, given a great talent, may be reduced to two: the thoroughness of the poet's discipline in an objective system of truth, and his lack of consciousness of such a discipline. For this discipline is a number of fundamental ideas the origin of which the poet does not know; they give form and stability to his fresh perceptions of the world; and he cannot shake them off. This is his culture, and like Tennyson's God it is nearer than hands and feet. With reasonable certainty we unearth the elements of Shakespeare's culture, and yet it is equally certain—so innocent was he of his own resources—that he would not know what our discussion is about. He appeared at the collapse of the medieval system as a rigid pattern of life, but that pattern remained in Shakespeare what Shelley called a "fixed point of reference" for his sensibility. Miss Dickinson, as we have seen, was born into the equilibrium of an old and a new order. Puritanism could not be to her what it had been to the generation of Cotton Mather—a body of absolute truths; it was an unconscious discipline timed to the pulse of her life.

The perfect literary situation: it produces, because it is rare, a special and perhaps the most distinguished kind of poet. I am not trying to invent a new critical category. Such poets are never very much alike on the surface; they show us all the varieties of poetic feeling; and like other poets they resist all classification but that of temporary convenience. But, I believe, Miss Dickinson and John Donne would have this in common: their sense of the natural world is not blunted by a too rigid system of ideas; yet the ideas, the abstractions, their education or their intellectual heritage, are not so weak as to let their immersion in nature, or their purely personal quality, get out of control. The two poles of the mind are not separately visible; we infer them from the lucid tension that may be most readily illustrated by polar activity. There is no thought as such at all; nor is there feeling; there is that unique focus of experience which is at once neither and both.

Like Miss Dickinson, Shakespeare is without opinions; his peculiar merit is also deeply involved in his failure to think about anything; his meaning is not in the content of his expression; it is in the tension of the dramatic relations of his characters. This kind of poetry is at the opposite of intellectualism. (Miss Dickinson is obscure and difficult, but that is not intellectualism.) To T. W. Higginson, the editor of *The Atlantic Monthly*, who tried to advise her, she wrote that she had no education. In any sense that Higginson could understand, it was quite true. His kind of education was the conscious cultivation of abstractions. She did not reason about the world she saw; she merely saw it. The "ideas" implicit in the world within her rose up, concentrated in her immediate perception.

That kind of world at present has for us something of the fascination of a buried city. There is none like it. When such worlds exist, when such cultures flourish, they support not only the poet but all members of society. For, from these, the poet differs only in his gift for exhibiting the structure, the internal lineaments, of his culture by threatening to tear them apart: a process that concentrates the symbolic emotions of society while it seems to attack them. The poet may hate his age; he may be an outcast like Villon; but this world is always there as the background to what he has to say. It is the lens through which he brings nature to focus and control—the clarifying medium that concentrates his personal feeling. It is ready-made; he cannot make it; with it, his poetry has a spontaneity and a certainty of direction that, without it, it would lack. No poet could have invented the ideas of "The Chariot"; only a great poet could have found their imaginative equivalents. Miss Dickinson was a deep mind writing from a deep culture, and when she came to poetry, she came infallibly.

Infallibly, at her best; for no poet has ever been perfect, nor is Emily Dickinson. Her precision of statement is due to the directness with which the abstract framework of her thought acts upon its unorganized material. The two elements of her style, considered as point of view, are immortality, or the idea of permanence, and the physical process of death or decay. Her diction has two corresponding features: words of Latin or Greek origin and, sharply opposed to these, the concrete Saxon element. It is this verbal conflict that gives to her verse its high tension; it is not a device deliberately seized upon, but a feeling for language that senses out the two fundamental components of English and their metaphysical relation: the Latin for ideas and the Saxon for perceptions—the peculiar virtue of English as a poetic language.

Like most poets Miss Dickinson often writes out of habit; the style that emerged from some deep exploration of an idea is carried on as verbal habit when she has nothing to say. She indulges herself:

> There's something quieter than sleep
> Within this inner room!
> It wears a sprig upon its breast,
> And will not tell its name.
>
> Some touch it and some kiss it,
> Some chafe its idle hand;
> It has a simple gravity
> I do not understand!
>
> While simple hearted neighbors
> Chat of the "early dead,"
> We, prone to periphrasis,
> Remark that birds have fled!

It is only a pert remark; at best a superior kind of punning—one of the worst specimens of her occasional interest in herself. But she never had the slightest interest in the public. Were four poems or five published in her lifetime? She never felt the temptation to round off a poem for public exhibition. Higginson's kindly offer to make her verse "correct" was an invitation to throw her work into the public ring—the ring of Lowell and Longfellow. He could not see that he was tampering with one of the rarest literary integrities of all time. Here was a poet who had no use for the supports of authorship—flattery and fame; she never needed money.

She had all the elements of a culture that has broken up, a culture that on the religious side takes its place in the museum of spiritual antiquities. Puritanism, as a unified version of the world, is dead; only a remnant of it in trade may be said to survive. In the history of puritanism she comes between Hawthorne and Emerson. She has Hawthorne's matter, which a too irresponsible personality tends to dilute into a form like Emerson's; she is often betrayed by words. But she is not the poet of personal sentiment; she has more to say than she can put down in any one poem. Like Hardy and Whitman she must be read entire; like Shakespeare she never gives up her meaning in a single line.

She is therefore a perfect subject for the kind of criticism which is chiefly concerned with general ideas. She exhibits one of the permanent relations between personality and objective truth, and she deserves the special attention of our time, which lacks that kind of truth.

She has Hawthorne's intellectual toughness, a hard, definite sense of the physical world. The highest flights to God, the most extravagant metaphors of the strange and the remote, come back to a point of casuistry, to a moral dilemma of the experienced world. There is, in spite of the homiletic vein of utterance, no abstract speculation, nor is there a message to society; she speaks wholly to the individual experience. She offers to the unimaginative no riot of vicarious sensation; she has no useful maxims for men of action. Up to this point her resemblance to Emerson is slight: poetry is a sufficient form of utterance, and her devotion to it is pure. But in Emily Dickinson the puritan world is no longer self-contained; it is no longer complete; her sensibility exceeds its dimensions. She has trimmed down its supernatural proportions; it has become a morality; instead of the tragedy of the spirit there is a commentary upon it. Her poetry is a magnificent personal confession, blasphemous and, in its self-revelation, its honesty, almost obscene. It comes out of an intellectual life towards which it feels no moral responsibility. Cotton Mather would have burnt her for a witch.

MARTIN C. D'ARCY

BERNARD SHAW'S ST. JOAN*

MANY, like myself, must have disliked intensely the idea of Bernard Shaw writing a play on St. Joan. Courtesy and chivalry were demanded of all who would speak or write of her, and now she was to fall into the hands of a second Anatole France, while this time the mocking would be less delicate and more offensive. The bad taste so evident in *Androcles and the Lion,* with its cheap and incompetent criticism of Christ and Christianity, had forced those who love reverence to regard Mr. Shaw as little better than a mountebank with a glib tongue and abounding assurance. Moreover, there was reason for thinking that he would not make even a good stage play out of this subject. His *Back to Methuselah* showed obvious signs of a decline in his power. The dialogue, save for one or two passages, was tedious, the action of the play uninteresting, the ideas silly.

Then *St. Joan* was performed and, to one's surprise, all who saw it concurred in praising it as a play. Some had no fault to find at all, others admitted that this St. Joan was not their conception of the Saint but liked the character, because she was a heroine and no caricature. Others again felt something wrong, and a few, while owning the fascination of the play, saw intended an insidious attack upon the Catholic Church. At any rate, one's worst fears were not realized; St. Joan was not made a target for witty shafts; in fact it looked as if, at long last, an old and genuine affection had found expression and produced a better play than any the author had hitherto written.

* Reprinted from *The Month* (May, 1923) by permission of the editor.

And now the publication of the play in book form with the customary long preface confirms this impression. The play does stand, perhaps, supreme among his many others, and for the very reason that one would have thought impossible, the justice he has rendered to a saintly character. Of course the old Adam is still alive in Mr. Shaw; he is still at the mercy of a clever wit, still an iconoclast. The characters talk Shavinese, and St. Joan has lost that supernatural beauty which few save the Catholic-minded can appreciate. There are times when, despite his satire against those who ignore the spirit of the mediaeval world, he himself is irredeemably modern. Cauchon actually talks of a "Will to Power" as if he had sat at Shaw's feet; the Archbishop throws off remarks about the Greek "Hubris" and its chastisement; an organ plays the people out of the nave after the coronation of the Dauphin! Details these, which may be easily forgiven, because the sincerity of the play as a whole is beyond question, and the author has taken great pains to capture the spirit of the time.

In his Preface, and it is with the Preface, as being the expression of his mind, that we are mainly concerned, the ideals of the Mediaeval Church and Feudalism are trenchantly contrasted with the boasted excellence of our own times. Catholics will purr with contentment and Protestants rub their eyes when they read the following:

> "Perhaps I had better inform my Protestant readers that the famous Dogma of Papal infallibility is by far the most modest pretension of the kind in existence. Compared to our infallible democracies, our infallible medical councils, our infallible astronomers, our infallible judges, and our infallible parliaments, the Pope is on his knees in the dust confessing his ignorance before the throne of God, asking only that as to certain historical matters* on which he has clearly more sources of information open to him than anyone else his decision shall be taken as final."

While those who are made perfect in a little while by reading modern text books will not know which way to look when they are asked which would be the saner Joan,—

> "the one who told them the story of the angel and Mary, or the one who questioned them as to their experiences of the Edipus Complex? the one to whom the consecrated wafer was the very body of the virtue that was her salvation, or the one who looked forward to a precise and convenient regulation of her health and her desires by a nicely calculated diet of thyroid extract, adrenalin, thymin, pituitrin, and insulin, with pick-me-ups of hormone stimulants, the blood being first carefully fortified with antibodies against all possible infections by inoculations of infected bacteria and serum from infected animals, and against old age by surgical extirpation of the reproductive ducts or weekly doses of monkey gland? . . . Which is the healthier mind, the saintly mind or the monkey-gland mind?"

* Mr. Shaw evidently includes the fact and content of revelation as belonging to History.

Polemically and as a counterblast this is excellent; but it remains to be seen whether the exaggeration apparent in this outburst does not distort also his vision of the Middle Ages and the Maid. And on the answer to this question hangs the truth of his thesis,—for, as usual, it is a thesis he is exploiting in the play.

According to him, St. Joan was in her convictions and character the pro-tagonist of private judgment, of what he calls Protestantism. Consequently she came into conflict with the feudal and ecclesiastical ideas of her time. The Church which claimed to be the ultimate court of appeal in religion, the sole authority in matters of conscience, had to suspect the strange girl who preferred her voices to the Pope and Cardinals, and appealed directly to the will of God. The feudal lords, also, who barred kingly supremacy and the principle of nationality, were incensed at the simple faith of St. Joan in kingship and in the right of the French to rule in France, no matter what feudal right the English might claim. Both sides acted rightly according to their lights; there were no villains in the piece, and the tragedy lay in the fact that there was no way out for the Church save to burn St. Joan for heresy. In keeping with the idea St. Joan is a simple, downright, pure Christian with an unquestioning belief in her voices. She never mentions the authority of the Church; she makes no appeal to the Pope, and the sole accu-sation that carries weight, for which she is condemned, is heresy. Cauchon is whitewashed; he is not the creature of tradition, in the pay of the English and disgracing his office, but a Bishop sensible of his duty to the Church and of the danger of heresy, and too proud, however much tempted, to put political considerations first. The Dominican Inquisitor, Brother John Le-maitre, again, personifies the zeal of the Catholic Church; he is severe but just, high-minded if narrow, while a fellow Dominican, Ladvenu, is skilfully delineated as a saintly and merciful man, who does all in his power to save Joan from the burning. On one point alone is he adamant, the duty of sub-mitting one's judgment to the Church.

In his Preface, Mr. Shaw frankly acknowledges that he has touched up the characters of Cauchon, Lemaitre and Warwick, but this sacrifice of verisimilitude was required to mark, within the short compass of a play, the true bearing of St. Joan's story. This would be sufficient justification, if the truth of the story were helped, but the danger is that the touching-up is made to suit Shaw's interpretation. The characters are made to stand for certain types, and in the play they are conscious of what they stand for. Now Shaw admits that in fact they would have been "as unconscious of the peculiarities of the Middle Ages as the atomic formula they breathed"; but he has to make them conscious, not only of those peculiarities, but of what he considers to be the centuries-later development of those peculiarities. This invites error and gives a touch of unreality to the dialogue. To mention feudalism first; there was no such clear-cut division between feudalism and nationalism as Warwick is made to state. One has only to pick up the thirteenth-century chronicle of de Joinville and read of Sir William Long-sword to see that feudal conceptions did not run counter to a true sentiment of nationality. It is simply untrue to say that "Nationalism is essentially anti-Catholic and anti-Christian; for the Catholic Church knows only one realm and that is the realm of Christ's Kingdom." There is an anti-Christian nationalism, certainly; but it is unmistakably a false conception. A similar error, unless I am mistaken, underlies Warwick's assertion that the Maid's ideal of kingship is anti-feudal. Shaw, with some justification, seems to be confusing Absolute Monarchy, a Protestant gift, which Joan never dreamt of, with the perfectly legitimate kingship of the Middle Ages based on rights and duties.

Warwick, the mediaeval baron, is therefore not true to type, and the same criticism holds of Cauchon and the Church party. It is extremely improbable that Cauchon would have likened Joan to Mahomet as an equally pernicious champion of private judgment,—two mighty pillars of Protestantism! Such exaggeration and simplification may provide a good story, but please let us give up calling it historical truth. Forced by his thesis, Shaw is compelled unconsciously to emphasize and omit facts and so give a false perspective, despite the best of intentions to be faithful to the facts. For instance, he makes much of the accusation of heresy and minimizes the superstitious fear of the Maid and the many incidents in the trial which showed its irregularity and the preponderating influence of fear, spite and hatred. St. Joan, it is implied, set her voices against the Church, recks nothing of its authority, whereas so steeped was she in the spirit of Catholicism, so simple in her faith, that she failed to understand the point of the accusation, and in her innocence appealed to the Pope as a sure judge of her fidelity and guiltlessness. There is no mention of this appeal; instead, the tribunal which convicted her, a tribunal in no way immune from error, but local and prejudiced, is made to stand for the authority of the Church of God. There was nothing inconsistent in the Pope rehabilitating the Maid and condemning the unfair trial of 1431.

In his portrait of St. Joan, Mr. Shaw labours under a difficulty. He admires her intensely and makes us too admire her; but he has to see her as a saint thoroughly Catholic and mediaeval and yet as no saint and a stout Protestant. Hence he has to explain away her voices and yet defend them, for, as usually happens with Catholic saints, their lives are integral; they have to be taken whole or not at all. He calls the voices hallucinations, but healthy hallucinations, the kind of experience that people who are visualizers are apt to enjoy or suffer. He dismisses their reality on the ground that they failed her during the trial, an argument as convincing as that of the sceptic who denies the validity of perception because we sometimes mistake a friend approaching. Instead then of accepting them he falls into the very vice he upbraids in his Preface,—the over-credulity of the modern; he shows himself the victim of an hallucination, the hallucination of unproved psychology,—though Francis Galton, whose word he takes, is not such a "high panjandrum" as he thinks, and is, truth to tell, rather antiquated. He ignores many facts which tell against the facile theory of hallucination; so far from desire producing the message of the voices, Joan did not want to go on her crusade and fight; it took years before she was finally persuaded. Then her "hallucination" did succeed in making her prophesy victory, give a secret sign to the Dauphin which settled his doubts, discover an ancient sword buried in the chapel of Ste. Catharine de Fierbois, and foretell, as we know from a letter of Sire de Rotslaer, dated April, the actual events of the summer. This Joan, who by trusting her voices, saw and did what was more than natural, who spent hours in prayer, who was approved at the beginning of her career at Poitiers by a learned gathering of bishops and doctors, differs from the Protestant born out of due time who figures in the play.

And this coupling of her name with Protestanism brings us to the crucial point in Mr. Shaw's thesis. It is best stated in his own words. He says that "an irresistible force met an immovable obstacle and developed the heat that consumed poor Joan." Joan stood for the supremacy of free thought, for Protestantism, while the Church ever stands uncompromisingly for authority, for intolerance of free thought and the law of change. "The saints and prophets, though they may be accidentally in this or that official position or rank, are always really self-elected, like Joan." . . . "All evolution in thought and conduct must at first appear as heresy and misconduct." Therefore, if the Church is to be a perfect body, it must admit "that no official organization of mortal men whose vocation does not carry with it extraordinary mental powers, can keep pace with the private judgment of persons of genius . . ." Mr. Shaw continues:

> "A Church which has no place for free-thinkers, nay, which does not inculcate and encourage free-thinking with a complete belief that thought when really free, must by its own law take the path that leads to the Church's bosom, not only has no future in modern culture, but obviously has no faith in the valid science of its own tenets, and is guilty of the heresy that theology and science are two different and opposite impulses, rivals for human allegiance."*

And so Mr. Shaw sees some hope in the Church's canonization of Joan of Arc, for it "was a magnificently Catholic gesture, as the canonization of a Protestant saint by the Church of Rome."

Such is Mr. Shaw's thesis, and at first sight it may sound very plausible. But let us examine it carefully. There is first an ambiguity to be noticed. A

---

* Notice that in this passage the Church is taken to be a purely natural institution, just in fact what it says it is not. If Shaw were right it would lose its raison d'être and not bother to live on. If it is right, the whole of Shaw's argument is wide of the mark. His attitude is rationalism and does not entertain the idea of the supernatural or even of Theism; for, if God existed, He could easily guide His Church in truth; and the Church could test free-thought and take over what is true in it and reject the false, as it does. The conflict then Shaw speaks of, so far from being necessary, would simply not exist. Yet as Shaw, to judge from the words quoted, now sees and respects the possibilities of the Catholic Church, please God he may come to see that there is still more in it than he suspects.

And so Mr. Shaw sees some hope in the Church's canonization of Joan of Arc, for it "was a magnificently Catholic gesture, as the canonization of a Protestant saint by the Church of Rome."

Protestant saint has been canonized by the Church of Rome! But does Shaw really mean Protestant? The use of such an epithet must inevitably call up in the mind that species of Christianity which Luther and Calvin started,—a form which, if it does not signify something specifically Christian, signifies nothing at all. But Shaw in many places means by Protestantism something quite different. In his mind it stands for free-thought, for the unfettered supremacy of reason, for the law of evolution and change. I wonder whether Protestants will be pleased at finding that the Christianity they have preached and practiced and defended these three and more centuries turns out to be nothing else than free-thinking. Whatever they feel, it is clear that Mr. Shaw has "queered the pitch" by his application of the word to the naturalistic rationalism which is the secular foe of Catholicism. This free-thought is coloured, moreover, by a curious philosophy. The gospel of Man and Superman still makes itself heard, the gospel of a vague Power behind the forces of nature, which pursues its mysterious purpose in life, driving men to knowledge and power and issuing in remarkable personages, like St. Joan. He calls it in the Preface "The Evolutionary Appetite." I mention this only to make definite Shaw's argument and to submit that St. Joan would have listened in amazement to such doctrine and despite her lack of learning given it short shrift with her tongue.

Forget this peculiar philosophy, and the conflict of free-thought and Catholicism as stated by Shaw turns out to be nothing but the old, familiar dispute between the Church's claim to the possession of unchanging truth and the counter-claim of the non-Catholic philosopher, scientist and rationalist that truth is never absolute, but progresses and suffers a change in each succeeding age. The position of the Church on this subject is clear and well known, and, to the Catholic, impregnable. She is the representative of the Divine Word which descended from Heaven, the word of Truth shining in a human and therefore necessarily confused world. This Word is still being pronounced and ever will be to the end of time, and the Church would commit suicide and make Christianity a fable were she to admit that God's Revelation through her could suffer substantial change or emendation by the exercise of the human mind. Even in natural philosophy she maintains that it is in the accidents of life that change occurs and not in the fundamental truths, for, if man be man, he must, whatever age he live in, have some abiding truth to live by.

But, we may grant that to the accidents of life the Church may give at times inadequate attention; she may be slow to accept a new scientific discovery, slow to adopt a new political theory. Were she not conditioned by her human constitution, she might reach the ideal of being abreast of all the learning of the world, because her interests are world-wide, and she alone can gather up all the fragments of truth from any particular science into a complete and shining system. But even granted her overcaution, dilatoriness and conservatism, her essential life remains intact as long as she sets forth to every age the faith once delivered to the saints.

It is a pity to drag St. Joan into such a discussion, for St. Joan's life has nothing to do with it, not even if we limit the exercise of free-thought to the sphere of religion, as Mr. Shaw inclines to do. St. Joan had no creed like Luther's opposed in its essence to that of the Catholic Church. A sharp distinction must be drawn between those who propound a new faith, setting up their own authority against the divinely-guaranteed doctrine of the Church, and those who, within the Church, receive special gifts from God for a definite purpose. With these latter the Church surely does not act unwisely. The authorities admit private revelation, particular missions, for there is nothing contrary there to the rule of faith given by God once and for all.* Yet such revelations must be tested. Nowadays we do not need to be told how easily delusion might creep in, and how impotent the highly-stimulated mind may be to distinguish the true from the false. Therefore the value of the vision or revelation must first be established, and then the moral character of the prophet or visionary put to the trial, for unless such virtues as humility, patience and wisdom be conspicuous, there is little chance of the message being divinely-inspired. Mistakes in policy, too, may be made by ecclesiastical authority; even ugly blunders: the history of the Church shows not a few instances of such blunders, the most glaring of all, perhaps, being the burning of St. Joan at the instance of an episcopal court. But as there is no question here of infallibility, no question of heretical teaching denounced authoritatively, such blunders in no way make against the claims of the Catholic Church.

Where heresy is publicly taught, the case is different, and no doubt Bernard Shaw is thinking of doctrinal teaching at variance with that of the Church put forward on private authority. "Our Churches must admit that no official organization of mortal men . . . can keep pace with the private judgment of persons of genius . . ." "It is not possible that an official organization of the spiritual needs of millions of men and women, mostly poor and ignorant, should compete successfully in the selection of its principals with the direct choice of the Holy Ghost, as it flashes with unerring aim upon the individual." This might hold true if the organization were merely human, but it is emphatically not true of a Church, which is founded by God, instructed in the wisdom of God and divinely assisted by the Spirit of God. And the proof is that no one can point to a single new religious truth which has sprung up and become a part of Catholic faith, independently of Catholicism and in defiance of it. Every heresy has, sooner or later, been rightly anathematized as a mutilation of God's truth, and history has shown it to be such by its rapid decay or reabsorption into other beliefs. The "genius" of the heretic has manifested no traces of the work of the Holy Ghost, and Mr. Shaw is far too clever a man to believe that Luther's doctrine of faith, Calvinism, Quakerism or Mormonism are advances upon the Catholic ideal. Indeed, Catholicism has from the beginning triumphantly

---

* Such, for instance, as those of St. Juliana of Liège which gave rise to the festival of Corpus Christi, and of St. Margaret Mary which made devotion to the Sacred Heart more universal in the Church.

asserted that its ideal can never be surpassed, for it is an ideal which in its
very fabric betrays the mark of Divinity, the ideal made Flesh! And therefore it is that the Church has been able to include in her fold the long series
of religious geniuses, Augustine, Hugh of St. Victor, Peter the Hermit,
Bernard, Francis, Ruysboeck, Teresa and Joan, many of them saints, and all
of them gifted with special individual graces of the Holy Spirit. They were
none of them prophets of revolt; their inner experiences were always brought
to the test of Catholic tradition; they were far from thinking that the prompt-
ings of the Holy Ghost could be against the work of the one and the same
Spirit in the Church; and thus they give the lie to any worked-up theory
about the incompatibility of religious genius with organized religion. Mr.
Shaw, for all his powers of intuition, has still much to learn about the essence
of Catholicism. We thank him for his sympathy with St. Joan, but we protest
against his making her a "Protestant." In life as in death she was an obedient
child of her Mother, the Church, who by canonizing her has put that fact
beyond dispute.

RONALD KNOX

FATHER BROWN*

WHEN YOU met Chesterton in life, the physical bigness of the man made
him seem out of scale; he overflowed his surroundings. And the same thing
is true, in a curious way, of his literary output; he never really found his
medium, because every medium he tried—and how many he tried!—was too
small a receptacle for the amount of himself he put into it. He stood alone
in the remarkable generation to which he belonged in being perfectly inte-
grated; he had a philosophy of life, and not of this life only, which was all
of a piece, and it so possessed him that he could not achieve, in any particular
form of writing, mere literary perfection. His life of Dickens is an admirable
performance, but it is really the Chestertonian philosophy as illustrated by
the life of Dickens; his *History of England* is a brilliant *résumé*, but it is a
history of Chesterton rather than of England. Shaw kept on urging him to
write plays, but when *Magic* was produced it was too good for the stage;
an after-dinner audience was not capable of the intellectual effort demanded
of it. Even *The Ballad of the White Horse*, one of his certainly immortal
works, cannot be graded among English epics because it is so much more
than an epic. And the same fate pursued him in that fortunate moment when
he took to writing detective stories. When we founded the Detection Club,
he was appointed, without a dissentient voice, as its first president; who else
could have presided over Bentley and Dorothy Sayers and Agatha Christie

* Reprinted from *Literary Distractions*, copyright 1958, by Evelyn Waugh. Published
  by Sheed and Ward, New York, N. Y. Reprinted by permission of Sheed and Ward,
  Inc.

and those others? Yet the Father Brown stories cannot really be graded among mystery stories; they are mystery stories with a difference. As usual, the box has been so tightly packed that the clasps will not fasten; there is too much meat in the sandwich.

When you take to writing detective stories, the measure of your success depends on the amount of personality you can build up round your favourite detective. Why this should be so, is not immediately obvious; it might have been supposed that this kind of fiction had a merely mathematical appeal. But, whether because Sherlock Holmes has set the standard for all time, or because the public does not like to see plots unravelled by a mere thinking-machine, it is personality that counts. You are not bound to make your public *like* the Great Detective; many readers have found Lord Peter Wimsey too much of a good thing, and I have even heard of people who were unable to appreciate the flavours of Poirot. But he must be real; he must have idio-syncrasies, eccentricities; even if he is a professional policeman, like Hanaud, he must smoke those appalling cigarettes, and get his English idioms wrong. And if possible—perhaps that is where Lord Peter fails—he must appeal to us through weakness; when he appears on the scene of the tragedy, the general reaction must be "A man like that will never be able to get at the truth." It is because he drops his parcels and cannot roll his umbrella, because he blinks at us and has fits of absent-mindedness, that Father Brown is such a good publisher's detective. He is a Daniel come to judgment.

He was "based", as we say, on Monsignor John O'Connor of Bradford; it was he who later received Chesterton into the Church. The occasion on which Father Brown came into being is well documented, both in Chester-ton's autobiography and in Monsignor O'Connor's memoir of him; and it should serve for a specimen of what is meant when we are told that such and such a character in a book was "based" on such and such a figure in real life. Two young acquaintances of Chesterton's, having been introduced by him to this new clerical friend, expressed surprise afterwards that a man trained in the seminary should possess such knowledge of the world, espe-cially of the criminal world. Chesterton was delighted with their *naïveté*; was it not to be expected (he said to himself) that a man who spent three hours every Saturday listening to the tale of other people's sins should have some acquaintance with the by-ways of human depravity? And this reflection was incorporated bodily in the first of the Father Brown stories, *The Blue Cross:*

> "How in Tartarus," cried Flambeau, "did you ever hear of the spiked bracelet?"
> "Oh, one's little flock, you know," said Father Brown.

That was all, really; nobody who had met Monsignor O'Connor would have put him down as "a clerical simpleton". He may have had difficulties about folding his umbrella; but instinctively you felt that this priest was a shrewd judge of men, with a reading of history and literature beyond the common. The owlish eyes blinking at you, the wooden indifference to appearances, the prosaic trudge in pursuit of his day-to-day tasks—all that was not Monsignor O'Connor as Chesterton saw him, but Father Brown as Chesterton invented him. He simply decided that for his own purposes— if I may put it in that way—he wanted a detective as unlike Lord Peter Wimsey as possible.

There was to be nothing of the expert about Father Brown; he should have no knowledge of obscure poisons, or of the time required to let the *rigor mortis* set in; he was not to be the author of any treatise about the different kinds of cigarette ashes. All his knowledge was of the human heart; he explains, in *The Secret of Flambeau*, that he is only capable of detecting murder mysteries because he was the murderer himself—only, as it were, *in petto*. "What I mean is that, when I tried to imagine the state of mind in which such a thing would be done, I always realized that I might have done it myself under certain mental conditions, and not under others; and not generally the obvious ones. And then, of course, I knew who really had done it; and he was not generally the obvious person." He could put himself inside the other man's skin. He could even put himself inside an animal's skin—no, the dog did not know the murderer by instinct and spring at him, that was sentimental mythology. The important thing about the dog was that it howled when the sword-stick was thrown into the sea—howled because the sword-stick didn't float.

The real secret of Father Brown is that there is nothing of the mystic about him. When he falls into a reverie—I had almost said, a brown study— the other people in the story think that he must be having an ecstasy, because he is a Catholic priest, and will proceed to solve the mystery by some kind of heaven-sent intuition. And the reader, if he is not careful, will get carried away by the same miscalculation; here, surely, is Chesterton preparing to shew the Protestants where they get off. Unconsciously, this adds to the feeling of suspense; you never imagine that Poirot will have an ecstasy, or that Albert Campion will receive enlightenment from the supernatural world. And all the time, Father Brown is doing just what Poirot does; he is using his little grey cells. He is noticing something which the reader hasn't noticed, and will kick himself later for not having noticed. The lawyer who asks "Where was the body found?" when he is told about the Admiral's drowning has given himself away as knowing too much, already, about the duck-pond; if he had been an honest man, he would have assumed that the Admiral was drowned at sea. The prophet who goes on chanting his litany from the balcony, when the crowd beneath is rushing to the aid of the murdered woman, gives himself away as the murderer; he was expecting it. We had all the data to go upon, only Father Brown saw the point and we didn't.

What is the right length for a mystery story? Anybody who has tried to write one will tell you, I think, that it should be about a third of the length of a novel. Conan Doyle uses that formula in *A Study in Scarlet*, and in *The Valley of Fear*, filling up the rest of the book with a long story which does not really affect the plot. The modern publisher expects a full-length novel (which demands either a second murder or a great deal of padding), or else a short story (in which it is difficult for the author to give us the full conditions of the problem). Father Brown began life as short stories in the *Saturday Evening Post,* and short stories he remained; for an author so fertile in ideas, perhaps it was the simplest arrangement. But it must be confessed that this enforced brevity produces a rather breathless atmosphere; the more so, because Chesterton was an artist before he became an author, and occupies a good deal of his space with scene-painting. And the scene-painting takes up room—valuable room, the pedantic reader would tell us.

What scene-painting it is! The Norfolk Broads, and the house full of mirrors standing on its lonely island; or that other island on the Cornish estuary, with its wooden tower—you would expect the second of these pictures to be little more than a repetition of the first, but in fact it is nothing of the kind; in the one case you have the feeling of being in Norfolk, in the other you have the feeling of being in Cornwall. The atmosphere of that dreadful hotel in *The Queer Feet;* the atmosphere of a winter-bound summer resort in *The God of the Gongs;* the (quite irrelevant) effect of bitter cold in *The Sign of the Broken Sword*—what a setting they give to the story! Flambeau explains, at the beginning of *The Flying Stars,* that in his criminal days he was something of an artist; "I had always attempted to provide crimes suitable to the special seasons or landscapes in which I found myself, choosing this or that terrace or garden for a catastrophe"; and if the criminal, so limited in his choice of means, can be expected to provide a suitable *décor,* how much more the writer of stories! Yet it is only Chesterton who gives us these effects, the "topsy-turvydom of stone in mid-air" as two men look down from the tower of a Gothic church; the "seas beyond seas of pines, now all aslope one way under the wind" on the hill-side of Glengyle; the "green velvet pocket in the long, green, trailing garments of the hills" on to which Mr. Harrogate's coach overturns, ready for the coming of the brigands. Did Chesterton pick out these landscapes with his artist's eye, and then, like Flambeau, invent crimes to suit them?

But it does take up room. And, if only because the canvas is so over-crowded, you must not expect in these stories the mass of details which you would expect of Freeman Wills Crofts; the extracts from Bradshaw, the plan of the study with a cross to shew where the body was found. Hence the severely orthodox readers of detective stories, who love to check and to challenge every detail, must be prepared for a disappointment; Chesterton will not be at pains to tell us whether the windows were fastened; how many housemaids were kept (in defiance of modern probabilities), and which of them dusted the room last; whether a shot in the gun-room would be audible in the butler's pantry, and so on. Even the unities of time and place are neglected; you can never be quite sure whether it is next morning, or a week later, or what. Consequently, you never quite feel "Here am I, with all the same data at my disposal as Father Brown had; why is it that his little grey cells work, and mine don't?" Not that there is any deliberate concealment of clues, but the whole picture is blurred; the very wealth of detail confuses you. All you can do is to set about eliminating the impossible characters in the hope of finding, by a process of exhaustion, the villain. Women can be ruled out; there is only one female villain in the whole series —it is part of Chesterton's obstinate chivalry that he hardly ever introduces you to a woman you are meant to dislike. People with Irish names (how unlike Sherlock Holmes!) are fairly certain to be innocent. But, even so, the characters of the story elude you; you do not feel certain that you have been told quite enough about them.

For Chesterton (as for Father Brown) the characters were the really important thing. The little priest could see, not as a psychologist, but as a moralist, into the dark places of the human heart; could guess, therefore, at what point envy, or fear, or resentment would pass the bounds of the normal, and the cords of convention would snap, so that a man was hurried into crime. Into crime, not necessarily into murder; the Father Brown stories are not bloodthirsty, as detective stories go; a full third of them deal neither with murder nor with attempted murder, which is an unusual average nowadays; most readers demand a corpse. The motives which made it necessary for Hypatia Hard to elope with her husband, the motives which induced the Master of the Mountain to pretend that he had stolen the ruby when he hadn't—the reader may find them unimpressive, because there is no black cap and no drop at the end of them. But, unless he is a man of unusual perspicacity, he will have to admit that he also found them unexpected.

The truth is that what we demand of a detective story is neither sensations, nor horrors, but ingenuity. And Chesterton was a man of limitless ingenuity. What really contents us is when we see at last, and kick ourselves for not having seen before, that the man who was murdered in the Turkish bath without any trace of a weapon was stabbed with an icicle; that the poisoner did drink the tea which accounted for her victim, but took a stiff emetic immediately afterwards; that the time of a particular incident was given wrongly, not because the witness was in bad faith, but because she saw, not the clock, but the reflection of the clock in a looking-glass. All those brilliant twists which a Mason and an Agatha Christie give to their stories, Chesterton, when he was in the mood for it, could give to his. How to dispose of the body? If it was only for a short time, you could hang it up on the hat-stand in a dark passage; if you wanted to get rid of it altogether, you could bury it in the concrete floor of a new set of flats. A ship could be lured to its doom by lighting a bonfire which would confuse the appearance of the lights in the tideway; you could gag a ruler so securely that he would be unable to answer the challenge of his own sentries, and would be shot. They are all ideas we might have thought of, and didn't.

Whether such expedients would be likely to be adopted in real life is perhaps more questionable. But then, how far is the writer of mystery stories bound by the laws of probability? Nothing could be more improbable than Father Brown's habit of always being on the spot when a crime is committed; but he shares this curious trick of ubiquity with Hercule Poirot. The thing is a literary convention; it may not be a good one, but it is well worn. No, when we open a detective story we leave the world of strict probability behind us; we must be prepared for three or four quite independent pieces of shady business happening to happen in the same country house on the same evening. And Chesterton's imagination was flamboyant; he was like a schoolboy on holiday, and could sit as light to realism as P. G. Wodehouse. If you meet him on his own ground—that is, halfway to fairyland—you will have to admit that for sheer ingenuity he can rival Miss Sayers herself. Cast your mind back to your first reading of the Father Brown stories, and ask yourself whether you saw what was the missing factor which linked all the various exhibits in Glengyle Castle, or why *The Insoluble Problem* was insoluble.

No, if we are to judge the Father Brown cycle by the canons of its own art, we shall not be disposed to complain that these are something less than detective stories; rather, that they are something more. Like everything else Chesterton wrote, they are a Chestertonian manifesto. And it may be reasonably maintained that a detective story is meant to be read in bed, by way of courting sleep; it ought not to make us think—or rather, it ought to be a kind of *catharsis*, taking our minds off the ethical, political, theological problems which exercise our waking hours by giving us artificial problems to solve instead. If this is so, have we not good reason to complain of an author who smuggles into our minds, under the disguise of a police mystery, the very solicitudes he was under contract to banish?

I am inclined to think that the complaint, for what it is worth, lies against a good many of the Father Brown stories, but not all, and perhaps not the best. Where the moral which Chesterton introduces is vital to the narrative, belongs to the very stuff of the problem, the author has a right, if he will, to mystify us on this higher level. In the over-civilized world we live in, there are certain anomalies which we take for granted; and he may be excused if he gently mocks at us for being unable, because we took them for granted, to read his riddle. There is something artificial in a convention which allows us to say that nobody has entered a house when in fact a postman has entered it, as if the postman, being a State official, were not a man. There is something top-heavy about a society in which a fellow guest is indistinguishable from a waiter if he cares to walk in a particular way. And there is something lacking in the scientific investigator who can be taken in when his own secretary disguises himself in a false beard, simply because he has sat opposite his secretary day after day without noticing what he looked like. But it must be confessed that in some of the stories, especially the later ones, the didactic purpose tends to overshadow, and even to crowd out, the detective interest: such stories as *The Arrow of Heaven*, and *The Chief Mourner of Marne*. If we read these with interest, it is not because they are good detective stories, but because they are good Chesterton. When he wrote *The Incredulity* and *The Secret* (*of Father Brown*), Chesterton had perhaps rather written himself out, and publishers pressed him for copy faster than even he could supply it. At the end of his life, he seemed to get a second wind, and *The Scandal of Father Brown* contains some of his most ingenious plots. But how seldom does an author manage to spin out a formula indefinitely; how signally Conan Doyle failed to do it! But—those first six stories Chesterton contributed to the *Saturday Evening Post*! How could that level have been maintained?

Reviews and Comment

GERALD WEALES

A REVIEW OF

THE YEARS WITH ROSS

BY JAMES THURBER*

Wнем тне Thurber pieces that go to make up *The Years with Ross* first
began to appear in the *Atlantic Monthly*, I assumed that the amorphous
Harold Ross would finally be pinned down, be put on paper so clearly that
an inquisitive outsider—even one as far out as I am—could come to understand
the father of the *New Yorker*. After several months and installments, with
Ross still a vague but busy figure in the magazine's pages, I assumed that the
editor would not emerge until the pieces were all brought together in a
single book where there need be no month's wait between settings, where
one could walk all around the man in a few hours and come away with a
likeness in depth. Now the book is at hand, but the great Harold Ross
mystery is still unsolved. "Who Was Harold, What Was He?" asks Thurber
in one of his chapter headings, but he plainly cannot answer the question for,
as he says of Ross at the beginning of the book, "He won't sit still in anybody's mind long enough for a full-length portrait."

There are actually not one, but two unbelievable Rosses—the professional
Ross and the personal Ross. The difficulty with the first is that it is so hard
to believe that the hero of all the country-bumpkin anecdotes and the Phil-
istine stories, in and out of the Thurber book, could have been the prime
mover of the *New Yorker*, which, whatever its drawbacks, became under
his hands one of the most literate magazines in the country. Ross comes out
of these pages as a man who could not read poetry and chose not to read
prose, except for *True Detective*, one on whom the most obvious literary
allusion was lost, one who was so unimaginative that he questioned metaphors
for their factual validity, one whose ear for the rhythm of a sentence was
as likely to go wrong as it was to come right.

Thurber records his own obvious pleasure in Ross's good opinion of his
work and quotes other *New Yorker* writers who treasure the editor's sentences of praise, but there are practically no stories that show that Ross had
any critical judgment, no indication of why Ross's praise should be worth
much. There is, in fact, the suggestion that Ross was sparing with his approbation except when he was trying to force an indolent author back to his
typewriter. There is ample evidence—as in the account of how E. B. White
forced Thurber's drawings on Ross—that the editor had to be talked into
accepting contributors who later became staples of the magazine. The only
extended example of editorial astuteness that Thurber includes is his reprinting of "Theory and Practice of Editing *New Yorker* Articles" and that
remarkable document was written by Wolcott Gibbs, not Ross.

* Reprinted from *The Commonweal* (July 17, 1959) by permission of the editor.

The reader is forced finally to one of two conclusions. Either Ross, for all his literary gaucheness, knew how to spot talent and so drew to himself the writers and artists who finally made the *New Yorker,* or he was a compulsive force whose energy drove the band-wagon onto which a cluster of homeless authors and cartoonists clambered. Thurber leans to the second view, for he says, "I think the moths deserve most of the credit for discovering the flame." In the end, Thurber can only insist that Ross was a great editor without showing the how, when and where of that still untold story.

Ross the man is as hard to accept as Ross the editor. Thurber's fondness for him is evident throughout the book, particularly in the moving pages about Ross's death, but although he makes clear that some people—many people apparently—loved Ross, he does not make the man likable. In many of the stories, Ross seems much less the lovable old curmudgeon than he does the bad-mannered ruffian. I can see a group of Ross's friends sitting around reminiscing, shaking their heads affectionately, taking turns at "Do you remember . . ." and under such conditions the anecdotes might become fond and foolish. In cold print, however, Ross's primness is vaguely creepy, his brusqueness sounds brutal, his naiveté becomes ignorance.

In his chapter on the friendship and feud of Ross and Alexander Woollcott, Thurber explains that he never fell under the fabled spell of the latter, although he occasionally came close enough for the legendary aura to spill over him. I understand just how Thurber feels. The Alexander Woollcott who comes through the collection of anecdotage about him appears to be a kind of androgynous monster, a tasteless dictator of taste, but Ross, I am afraid, does not come off much better. I went into *The Years with Ross* quite willing to be charmed by the hero, but although there are occasional endearing glimpses of him, I came out with the feeling that Thurber must still know something that he has failed to tell me. Actually the knowledge is only affection, and anyone with a friend who is still not housebroken knows how impossible a quality that is to communicate.

Thurber says in the Foreword to the book that he has no intention of writing a formal biography of Ross, that "the unity I have striven for, whether I have achieved it or not, is one of effect," by which he means that he has looked at several of the many faces of Ross and hopes that they all add up to one. I have already indicated that the man still seems to be missing. In place of a fully realized Ross there are a host of anecdotes, some of them funny, some of them just Rossiana, divided into categories: Ross and money, Ross and sex, Ross and artists. Thurber gets so involved in stories that often he relaxes and embraces the irrelevant, and his method is finally self-defeating; by the end of the book there are just a few too many anecdotes.

Now, having carped for four paragraphs, I would like to say that *The Years with Ross* is often fascinating, that one listens to most of the Ross stories with the same open-eared wonder that one gives to literary gossip heard in the flesh. What is more, many of the early chapters are full of the workings of the *New Yorker* in the precarious twenties, when a steady stream of editors marched through the offices of the infant weekly, and these chapters add up to a good informal history of the launching of the magazine.

There are, as well, many incidental virtues to *The Years with Ross;* it is just that with such an author and such a subject, I somehow expected a great deal more.

EDWARD WEEKS

A REVIEW OF

SIR WALTER SCOTT

BY HESKETH PEARSON*

HESKETH PEARSON's biography, *Sir Walter Scott* (Harper), is one of the pleasantest books I have read in years. Mr. Pearson is an experienced and skillful delineator; he has written the best books we have had thus far on Whistler, Disraeli, Oscar Wilde, Sydney Smith, and Bernard Shaw—to mention five of his seventeen biographies; and in this new volume he is working with a subject whose buoyant and attractive personality pervades every page. Walter Scott—"Wattie," as his mother used to call him—was the son of a respectable Edinburgh lawyer, and he was only eighteen months old when he was struck and crippled by infantile paralysis. The infant was given the usual treatment of the time, and the blistering naturally had little effect on his crippled leg; he was sent to his grandfather's farm at Sandyknowe in the Border Country, and there the fresh air, his rugged constitution, and his grandfather's infinite patience pulled him through.

Mr. Pearson rightly stresses the aftereffects of this illness: how the boy was thrown on his own resources and neglected by his older brothers, who had no patience with his limp; how he filled his mind with the action and violence of Border affrays and found his consolation in the local history where "every mountain had its fable, every valley its legend, every stream its song, every castle its story." On fair days Wattie would be carried out and laid beside the shepherd minding his flock; later, as he grew older, he was given a Shetland pony to navigate with; he read early and fearlessly— Pope's translation of Homer and Milton's *Paradise Lost* at the age of six, Shakespeare at seven—and was an avid listener whenever there were Scottish veterans or seafarers to be heard. Thus out of his physical limitation came the seeding and impetus for his writing.

"All men who have turned out worth anything have had the chief hand in their own education," he once wrote, and this was certainly true of Walter Scott. When Walter entered Edinburgh University in 1783, a professor of Greek, at the end of the first term, informed him that he was a dunce and

* Reprinted from *The Atlantic Monthly* (January, 1955) by permission of *The Atlantic Monthly*.

would never be anything else. This did not deter him from his omnifarious reading, and now what he craved was books of poetry and chivalry, Shakespeare, Spenser, and the old ballads. The classroom bored him; so did the law courts for which his father insisted that he be prepared. It was the Highlands that claimed him; and although he walked with a stick, he was indefatigable on the climbs and even more so on a horse. So it was that in rebellion against the law and in pursuit of his boyhood dreams he began to collect the ballads and minstrelsy which were to establish him, first as an editor and collector, and then, with his publication of *Marmion*, as a national poet.

It might be said that Scott sidled into literature. Edinburgh had long rated him a good-natured failure at law before it woke up to the fact that he could write. He had been collecting ballads for years before it ever occurred to him to publish them between covers; when his own poetry became popular, he was as surprised as anyone, and his first novel he published anonymously. Then fame and royalties descended upon him, his life became more spacious, and the claims on his time multiplied. He moved to his beloved manor at Abbotsford, and here came friends, dukes, dogs, impecunious poets, charlatans, clansmen, servants, and the Prince of Wales. Mr. Pearson, who is much at ease in the nineteenth century, has brought out Scott's generosity, his intrepidity, his deep sentiment for his clan and his country (but not necessarily for women or great persons), his tolerance of his rascally publishers, and his kindness toward anyone who wrote. "Life," Scott once wrote, "is too short for the indulgence of animosity." And he could not bear to criticize his contemporaries even when reason must occasionally have told him that what they wrote was rubbish. Zestful, a prodigious worker, and greatly beloved, he stands straight and true in this admirable book.

Scott's books, uneven because they were often hastily written, receive at Mr. Pearson's hands a long-needed and persuasive re-evaluation which sets *Rob Roy* at the head of the list, *The Betrothed* at the bottom; which finds dullness in *Ivanhoe* and much pure gold in *The Lay of the Last Minstrel* and *Marmion*.

RUSSELL KIRK

THE MEASURE OF ABRAHAM LINCOLN:

A REVIEW OF *Abraham Lincoln* BY BENJAMIN THOMAS AND *The Ethics of Rhetoric* BY RICHARD WEAVER *

"WHATEVER THE result of the convulsion whose first shocks were beginning to be felt, there would still be enough square miles of earth for elbow-room; but that ineffable sentiment made up of memory and hope, of instinct and

* Reprinted from *The Month* (April, 1954) by permission of the editor.

tradition, which swells every man's heart and shapes his thought, though perhaps never present to his consciousness, would be gone from it, leaving it common earth and nothing more. Men might gather rich crops from it, but that ideal harvest of priceless associations would be reaped no longer; that fine virtue which sent up messages of courage and security from every sod of it would have evaporated beyond recall. We should be irrevocably cut off from our past, and be forced to splice the ragged ends of our lives upon whatever new conditions chance might leave dangling for us."

So James Russell Lowell wrote in his essay on Lincoln. In truth, Abraham Lincoln's election to the presidency of the United States is the great line of demarcation in the history of America; for the triumph of the North during the four terrible years that followed swept away the American society from which Lincoln arose, and Reconstruction, the Gilded Age, and material aggrandizement made it certain that the United States would not look upon his like again. A man very unlike Lincoln in his origins, but markedly like him in heart—Nathaniel Hawthorne—wrote, in the last year of his life (the year of Gettysburg), of "the hurricane that is sweeping us all along with it possibly into a Limbo where our nation and its polity may be as literally the fragments of a shattered dream as my unwritten Romance." Both the New England of Hawthorne and the backwoods Illinois of Lincoln were effaced by the whirlwind of fanaticism which had first stirred in their youth, had wailed onward to Sumter, and then had raved triumphant from Manassas to Appomattox. From that hurricane-fanned conflagration of reforming enthusiasm and sinful appetite which became Civil War and Reconstruction, American moral and political conservatism has not yet recovered, and perhaps never can. With Lincoln dead, the obligations of conservative restoration lay with the mind of the victorious North; but the Northern intellect, which practically was the New England intellect, faltered before this tremendous task, being ill-equipped for it. The crabbed conservative strain which wound through New England character, reaching its most humane expression in Hawthorne, was in essence a conservatism of negation; after 1865, burdened with the necessity for affirmation and reconstruction, the New England mind shied and groaned and cursed at these perplexities. For years earlier, the masters of New England—not the State Street men, but leaders like Charles Francis Adams and Sumner and Everett and Parker and Emerson, the men of speculation and statecraft—had been engaged in a perilous, self-righteous flirtation with radicalism, political abstraction, and that kind of fanatic equalitarianism which Garrison represented. Their conservative instincts were bewildered by the passion of this moral crusade, the Civil War, and by the influence of Transcendentalism; they scarcely remembered where to look for the foundations of a conservative order; and power slipped from their grasp during the administration of Ulysses S. Grant. The ruined South, in that age, could not afford the luxury of any species of thought—there, every nerve was strained, for decades, to deal hastily with exigencies, somehow to make a dismembered economy stir again, in some fashion to reconcile negro emancipation with social stability; her disfranchised leaders were employed, half dazed, in writing apologia, like Davis and Stephens, or in mending resignedly the fabric of civilization, like Lee. Lincoln's successor, Andrew Johnson, had neither the mind nor the temper to save his country from the rapacity and the folly of the age of Reconstruction, though he did all he could to realize the wise and moderate policies which Lincoln had outlined. American conservatism never has recovered wholly from that blight. To-day, however, the United States, wakening to the vastness of its moral responsibilities throughout the world, seeks with increasing earnestness for conservative principles and examples. This present conservative yearning of the American nation gives a renewed interest to study of the mind and policies of Abraham Lincoln.

Two recent books* contribute something toward this subject. Mr. Thomas' one-volume life of Lincoln, the best short biography since Lord Charnwood's, has no power of style; but it is a plain, sound, honest, impartial account of one of the strangest and most appealing figures ever to rise to great political authority. Mr. Weaver's long essay is a closely-reasoned exercise in criticism, designed to prove Seneca's observation that "As a man speaks, so is he"; for our present purpose, the most significant chapters are those on Burke and Lincoln, in which Mr. Weaver comes to the conclusion that Lincoln was a sounder conservative than was Burke. "What is conservatism?" Lincoln himself asked, before he was president. "Is it not adherence to the old and tried, against the new and untried?" Conservatism is that, but it is also a great deal more, as these two books suggest. Mr. J. G. Randall, Lincoln's most scholarly biographer, thinks of his subject as a liberal. But as Mr. Stanley Pargellis, in 1945, pointed out with cogency, in his cast of mind, his policies, and his empiricism, Lincoln was strongly conservative; and Mr. Weaver, for rather different reasons, holds the same opinion. Moreover, Lincoln's original allegiance was to the Whigs, then the conservative party of the United States; and, says Mr. Weaver, "It is no accident that Lincoln became the founder of the greatest American conservative party, even if that party was debauched soon after his career ended. He did so because his method was that of the conservative." There are some stirrings of true conservatism in the Republican party nowadays; and it is time, probably, that Republican leaders began to understand their founder, as well as to praise him.

> Among the lessons taught by the French Revolution there is none sadder or more striking than this, that you may make everything else out of the passions of men except a political system that will work, and that there is nothing so pitilessly and unconsciously cruel as sincerity formulated into dogma. It is always demoralizing to extend the domain of sentiment over questions where it had no legitimate jurisdiction; and perhaps the severest strain upon Mr. Lincoln was in re-

---

* *Abraham Lincoln* by Benjamin Thomas (Eyre & Spottiswoode, London). *The Ethics of Rhetoric* by Richard Weaver (Henry Regnery, Chicago). Both books were published in 1953.

sisting a tendency of his own supporters which chimed with his own private desires, while wholly opposed to his convictions of what would be wise policy.

This is Lowell again, writing with high truth and justice. Lincoln never was a doctrinaire; he rose from very low estate to very high estate, and he knew the savagery which lies so close beneath the skin of men, and he knew that most men are good only out of obedience to routine and convention. The Fire-eater and the Abolitionist were abhorrent to him; yet he took the middle path between them not out of any misapplication of the doctrine of the golden mean, but because he held by the principle that the unity and security of the United States transcended any fanatic scheme of uniformity. As Mr. Weaver observes, "he is astonishingly free from tendency to assume that 'the truth lies somewhere in between.' " Here he was very like Burke; yet it is improbable that he ever read Burke, or any other political philosopher except Blackstone; his wisdom came from the close observation of human nature, and from the Bible and Shakespeare. The Radical Republicans detested him as much as the Southern zealots did. In his great conservative end, the preservation of the Union, he succeeded; and he might have succeeded in a conservative labour equally vast, the restoration of order and honesty, had not Booth's pistol put an end to the charity and fortitude of this uncouth, homely, melancholy, lovable man.

Sentimental adulation has done much harm to the memory of the real Lincoln; and the man who reads Carl Sandburg's biography may do well to balance it with the bitter criticisms of Donald Davidson in *The Attack on Leviathan*. Mr. Thomas, however, writes with a painstaking seriousness, sedulous to clear away the cobwebs of legend even at the expense of every shred of the picturesque.

There emerges the form of a man who, until late in his life, seemed thoroughly unlikely ever to be a leader of opinion or of party, let alone a statesman—a man who entered politics simply with the modest hope of making a tolerable living out of political office, clumsy always, often feckless, declaring in his debates with Douglas that it is "better to be a live dog than a dead lion," defeated for years in every endeavour to influence politics on a national scale, a self-taught back-country lawyer, sunk in melancholy, married to a neurotic woman, eclipsed in his own party by men whose talents seemed to outshine his immeasurably. We see him (through the eyes of his partner Herndon) enduring the excesses of his disorderly children, who "soon gutted the room—gutted the shelves of books—rifled the drawers and riddled boxes—battered the points of gold pens against the stove—turned over the ink-stands on the papers—scattered letters over the office and danced over them." We see him apparently unfit for regular business of any description, his office all higgledy-piggledy, amid its confusion an envelope marked, in Lincoln's hand, "When you can't find *it* anywhere else, look into this." We see him, only three years before he won the presidential election, still an obscure and gawky Western attorney, attending court in Cincinnati, in his rumpled clothes, a blue cotton umbrella in his hand, snubbed by Stanton and the other distinguished lawyers. The man still seemed pathetic at best, if not downright ludicrous; all the majesty and loneliness of his tragedy was yet to come.

So Lincoln seemed to the casual observer, at least. For all that, ever since his boyhood his friends had perceived in this curious being some element of greatness. Lincoln possessed the incongruous dignity that was Samuel Johnson's, too. Here was a man of sorrows. It has always been true that melancholy men are the wittiest; and Lincoln's off-colour yarns, told behind a log barn or in some dingy Springfield office, were part and parcel of his consciousness that this is a world of vanities. The attempts of Herndon and other biographers to find the source of this brooding sorrowfulness in some early blighted love are puerile, and Mr. Thomas shows what slight foundation those notions have. "What? Would you cry for a little girl?" Epictetus asks. So it was with Lincoln. He was no woman's man, of course, and his marriage was made tolerable only by his own vast charity and tenderness; but he never was the man to weep over his own blemishes or errors. The vanity of human wishes: Lincoln's awareness of unalterable reality, combining with his knowledge of all the weaknesses of poor sinning mortality, made the man noble in his sadness, and gave him the strength to endure with humility and generosity the terrible burdens of his office. When Chief Justice Taney, "old, shrunken, and shrivelled like 'a galvanized corpse'," administered the inaugural oath to the first Republican President, *sic transit gloria mundi* was stamped across the face of the strange giant in the new black suit, whose lacklustre eyes stared down upon the crowd, the soldiers, and the cannon from a rough platform built against the unfinished Capitol.

Once I heard a popular speaker declare that what modern America needs is "old-fashioned religion, the sort of religion that Washington and Lincoln had." Now that would be a most imperfect sort of religion: for Washington's eighteenth-century conformity was scarcely more than moralism, and Lincoln was a Christian only in the vaguest of senses, if a Christian at all. Every American president employs the phrases of Christian piety; but very few presidents have been conspicuously devout. Lincoln began as a naive sceptic; he received next to no religious instruction of any description; solitary reading of the Bible gave majesty to his mind and his style, but never brought to him any faith less cloudy and austere than a solemn theism. Yet there have been few Americans more thoroughly graced with the theological virtues, charity most of all. The New Testament shines out from his acts of mercy, and the Old from his direction of the war. We all know the high piety of his Gettysburg Address; and in some of his letters there looms up a great and stern Christian justice, as in his order appointing Hooker to the command of the Army of the Potomac:

> I have placed you at the head of the Army of the Potomac. Of course
> I have done this upon what appear to me to be sufficient reasons.
> And yet I think it best for you to know that there are some things in

regard to which I am not quite satisfied with you. I believe you to be a brave and skilful soldier, which, of course, I like. I also believe you do not mix politics with your profession, in which you are right. You have confidence in yourself, which is a valuable, if not an indispensable quality. You are ambitious, which, within reasonable bounds, does good rather than harm. But I think that during Gen. Burnside's command of the Army, you have taken counsel of your ambition, and thwarted him as much as you could, in which you did a great wrong to the country, and to a most meritorious and honourable brother officer. I have heard, in such a way as to believe it, of your recently saying that both the Army and the Government needed a Dictator. Of course it was not for this, but in spite of it, that I have given you the command. Only those generals who gain successes, can set up dictators. What I now ask of you is military success, and I will risk the dictatorship. The government will support you to the utmost of its ability, which is neither more nor less than it has done, and will do, for all the commanders. I much fear that the spirit which you have aided to infuse into the Army, of criticizing their commander, and withholding confidence from him, will now turn upon you. I shall assist you, as far as I can, to put it down. Neither you, nor Napoleon, if he were alive again, could get any good out of an army, while such a spirit prevails in it.

And now, beware of rashness. Beware of rashness, but with energy, and sleepless vigilance, go forward, and give us victories.

This prophetic majesty was not Lincoln's constant mood, nor did it predominate in his character until the War called forth the latent greatness in the back-country politician. When, at the beginning of his administration, Lincoln called Charles Francis Adams to Washington to appoint him minister to England, the dignified and nearly humourless son of John Quincy Adams was confounded by the boorish and almost inane manner of the head of the Republic. The President, lounging heavily in his office, addressed a few brusque and inconsequential remarks to the representative of the greatest family in America, about to assume the most important diplomatic post in the world; then, as if forgetting Adams' very existence, he turned aside to discuss some obscure postmastership with a member of his Cabinet. Lincoln was, indeed, a puzzle. Nearly all the leaders of his own party hated him, or despised him, or thought he would be the ruin of the Republicans. "We asked for a rail-splitter, and we have got one." It was a surprise to nearly everyone that he was nominated for the presidency, and a surprise that he was elected. He won only by a plurality of the popular vote—nothing like a majority. But here, unknown to almost everyone, was a man for the ages. The war made Lincoln great—not by chance, but by summoning forth the noble fortitude and gravity that had no more than peeked out timidly from him in his Illinois years. How far Lincoln himself was conscious that a Providential purpose worked through him, we cannot be sure; yet some such apprehension rings from the phrases of his speeches and letters between 1861 and 1865. Here was a man; and as the best of life is tragic, and as the highest reward of virtuous life is a noble end, so this man was fortunate in the hour of his death.

Lincoln was struck down at the height of his powers, having endured with meekness and resignation all the agony of the war years; he died at the moment all his hopes were rewarded and all his acts justified. He passed from life unblemished by the rancour and corruption of the Reconstruction era, so that the intended evil of Booth's bullet was in reality, for Lincoln, a great relief and blessing.

Misunderstood in life, Lincoln the statesman has been generally misunderstood during the eighty-nine years which have elapsed since his death. He never was an Abolitionist, and the act for which he is most celebrated, the Emancipation Proclamation, he undertook simply as a measure of military expediency, not as a moral judgment. If he could have preserved the Union, short of war, by tolerating slavery forever, he would have done so. He was no fanatic reformer of society. Acton, in his essay on "The Causes of the American Revolution" (1861), touches upon the perplexed nature of the slavery question in America—or rather of the negro question, which the Civil War and Reconstruction did not solve, and which is nowhere near solution to-day; Acton writes of the abstractions of modern revolutionaries, and adds:

> Very different is the mode in which the Church labours to reform mankind by assimilating realities with ideals, and accommodating herself to times and circumstances. Her system of Christian liberty is essentially incompatible with slavery and the power of masters over their slaves was one of the bulwarks of corruption and vice which most seriously impeded her progress. Yet the Apostles never condemned slavery even within the Christian fold. The sort of civil liberty which came with Christianity into the world, and was one of her postulates, did not require the abolition of slavery. If men were free by virtue of their being formed after the image of God, the proportion in which they realized that image would be the measure of their freedom. Accordingly, St. Paul prescribed to the Christian slave to remain content with his condition. . . .

> The Secession movement was not provoked merely by the alarm of the slave-owners for their property, when the election of Lincoln sent down the price of slaves from twenty-five to fifty per cent, but by the political danger of Northern preponderance; and the mean whites of the Southern States are just as eager for separation as those who have property in slaves. For they fear lest the republicans, in carrying emancipation, should abolish the barriers which separate the negroes from their own caste. At the same time, the slaves show no disposition to help the republicans, and be raised to the level of the whites. There is a just reason for this fear, which lies in the simple

fact that the United States are a republic. The population of a republic must be homogeneous. Civil equality must be founded on
social equality, and on national and physiological unity. This has
been the strength of the American republic. Pure democracy is that
form of government in which the community is sovereign, in which,
therefore, the State is most nearly identified with society. But society
exists for the protection of interests; the State for the realization of
right—"concilia coetusque hominum *jure* sociati, quae civitates ap-
pelantur." The State sets up a moral objective law, and pursues a
common object distinct from the ends and purposes of society. This
is essentially repugnant to democracy, which recognizes only the
interests and rights of the community, and is therefore inconsistent
with the consolidation of authority which is implied in the notion of
the State. It resists the development of the social into the moral
community. If, therefore, a democracy includes persons with separate
interests or an inferior nature, it tyrannizes over them. There is no
mediator between the part and the whole; there is no room, therefore,
for differences of class, of wealth, of race; equality is necessary to the
liberty which is sought by a pure democracy.

Lincoln, by birth a Southern poor-white, perceived distinctly the complexity of this problem, as Acton suggests it; while Senator Sumner, for
instance, eminent among the New England illuminati, remained oblivious
to all the gargoyle faces that huddled slyly behind fanatic Abolition. For a
long time, Lincoln resisted the importunities of the Radicals in favour of
negro emancipation; he yielded, at length, out of the desperate necessities
of the Union cause; and once the thing was done, he engaged in a number
of unsuccessful endeavours to settle the freed negroes in the West Indies or
in Latin America. He tried to persuade the members of his Cabinet to agree
to a monetary compensation of former slaveholders out of the federal
treasury, and was profoundly saddened at their refusal to support him in this.
His proposals for Reconstruction in the South—carried out by Johnson so
far as Johnson had the power to enforce them—saved the Southern states
from much of the ignominy, and some of the material ruin, which the
Radicals would have inflicted upon them; and had his moderate projects for
the gradual improvement of the freedmen been made effectual, the whole
present problem of race in America might be a good deal less distressing.

In this, for the most part, as in much else, Abraham Lincoln was a conservative statesman of a high order. Lincoln himself remarked of the founders
of American independence (as Mr. Weaver reminds us),

> They meant to set up a standard maxim for free society, which
> should be familiar to all, and revered by all; constantly looked to,
> constantly laboured for, and even though never perfectly attained,
> constantly approximated, and thereby constantly spreading and deep-
> ening its influence and augmenting the happiness and value of life to
> all people of all colours everywhere.

To this ideal of liberty under law, Lincoln added his own example, which has worked incalculable good in the altered America which has followed 1865. His greatness came from his recognition of enduring moral principle. I cannot do better than to conclude in the words of Mr. Weaver:

> Let it be offered as a parting counsel that parties bethink themselves of how their chieftains speak. This is a world in which one often gets what one asks for more directly or more literally than one expects. If a leader asks only consequences, he will find himself involved in naked competition of forces. If he asks only circumstance, he will find himself intimidated against all vision. But if he asks for principle, he may get that, all tied up and complete, and though purchased at a price, paid for. Therefore, it is of first importance whether a leader has the courage to define. Nowhere does a man's rhetoric catch up with him more completely than in the topics he chooses to win other men's assent.

Abraham Lincoln, knowing that there is a Truth above the advantage of the hour, argued from definition, on most occasions.

> In the present civil war (he wrote in 1862), it is quite possible that God's purpose is something different from the purpose of either party. . . . The will of God prevails. In great contests each party claims to act in accordance with the will of God. Both may be, and one must be, wrong. God cannot be for and against the same thing at the same time.

This is a long way from the big battalions; it is also a long way from Jacobin abstraction. Lincoln's strength, and his conservatism, did not arise from an affection for the excluded middle, which he called a "sophistical contrivance." He knew that what moved him was a power from without himself; and, having served God's will according to the light that was given him, he received the reward of the last full measure of devotion.

J. DONALD ADAMS

SPEAKING OF BOOKS*

MARTHA'S VINEYARD, *Mass.*

SOMETIMES GREAT pieces of writing are recognized at once for what they are; sometimes they wait for full discovery. The most obvious example of the delayed reaction, I suppose, is the Gettysburg Address. There seems to be no doubt that Ernest Hemingway's new story belongs in the larger group of immediate reception. And like most pieces of great writing, its impact is

* Reprinted from *The New York Times* Book Review Section (September 21, 1952) by permission of *The New York Times*.

not only immediate but cumulative as well. I have already read "The Old Man and the Sea" three times, and that, I know, is not simply because I happen at the moment to be living beside the sea. Last year at this time I was high in the Selkirks of British Columbia, but there, too, I am sure the power of this writing would be felt no less. When I went sailing in a small boat off Edgartown the other day, Hemingway's old man of the sea was with me, but he will be with me for a long time, wherever I am.

Because of him, I take up this column again at the same point where I left it several weeks ago. When I left New York for the haven which this island is, I was talking about tragedy and the persistence of frustration as a literary theme. I spoke of the fact that tragedy greatly presented is never depressing in effect, as inferior handling of similar material inevitably is, and that the theme of frustration, which has been constant since men set pen to paper, would always be freshly worked whenever a writer was artist enough to heighten, through his mastery of language and the prism peculiar to his personality, our awareness of an ancient truth.

In both respects, the Hemingway story meets the test. It is a tragic story, but its effect is elevation, not depression. It increases, not lessens, one's appetite for life, and that is one reason why Hemingway, at his best, is a greater writer than Faulkner. No great art can diminish life, because art and life are at bottom synonymous. One of the great characteristics of the Hemingway story is that it is so pervadingly alive. Each time I read it I was aware of vitalities I had missed before. Sometimes they are little things, but deceivingly little, spreading out into wider circles, like those made by a pebble thrown into water.

Thus, for example, as Malcolm Cowley observed in one review, there is a sentence of twenty-eight words which evokes the life of a whole community: "They walked down the road to the old man's shack and all along the road, in the dark, barefoot men were moving, carrying the masts of their boats." That kind of writing may look easy, but is not; many years of arduous discipline lie behind it. Or take the passage I have used in today's Treasure Chest;* it has Hemingway's own peculiar descriptive magic, and I doubt whether anyone else could have written it.

It has already been observed that Hemingway's story is classical in spirit and design. It doesn't sprawl; it is rigidly confined; as Robert Gorham Davis remarked in his review, "the line of dramatic action * * * curves up and

---

* "In the dark the old man could feel the morning coming and as he rowed he heard the trembling sound as flying fish left the water and the hissing that their stiff set wings made as they soared away in the darkness. He was very fond of flying fish as they were his principal friends on the ocean. He was sorry for the birds, especially the small delicate dark terns that were always flying and looking and almost never finding, and he thought, 'The birds have a harder life than we do except for the robber birds and the heavy strong ones. Why did they make birds so delicate and fine as those sea swallows when the ocean can be so cruel? She is kind and very beautiful. But she can be so cruel and it comes so suddenly and such birds that fly, dipping and hunting, with their small sad voices are made too delicately for the sea.'"
[From *The Old Man and the Sea*, copyright 1952 by Ernest Hemingway. Page 31.]

down with a classic purity of design to delight the makers of textbooks."

The old Greeks, to whom I was recently referring, would have liked and understood Hemingway's handling of his story. More than one reviewer has remarked that the old fisherman is barely individualized. I think part of the story's strength derives from that fact, because although he is, like every novelist's hero, a part of the writer, sea, in this story, is Everywoman. Hemingway has accomplished here what I recently quoted Sean O'Faolain as asking for: liberation, in the delineation of character, from the photographic reality. Hemingway has, in this tale, got back to literature's roots in epic and folksong.

Too many of our young writers today are caught in what O'Faolain described as "the tangle of sophistication." Literature recurrently falls into that tangle, and to renew itself, needs to get back to the basic things, as Hemingway has done in "The Old Man and the Sea." He has here, even more successfully than in "For Whom the Bell Tolls," reached back to what O'Faolain spoke of as "a dignity that depends largely on the oneness of man."

There is also, in this story, to a degree which I think has been absent before in Hemingway, in spite of his always acutely sensuous response to the natural world, the sense of man's oneness (largely lost) with nature. The old man's attitude toward the great fish with which he has been battling is precisely that which would have been held by an American Indian, had his life been lived on the sea. He too would have seen the marlin as a part of nature with himself, and would have understood completely the old man's need for apology that time when he killed a female and watched the male circling about the boat while his mate was gaffed and clubbed. He would have understood, too, the old man's respect and sympathy for his adversary as they fought their long battle, exhausting to them both, in the Gulf Stream.

Robert Gorham Davis, in his excellent review in these pages* a fortnight ago, has already given the other reasons why this book will bulk so large in Hemingway's career. Certainly it is his most mature work, both in craft and attitude. He thinks that himself, and he is right.

* Cf. *The New York Times* Book Review Section (September 7, 1952).

Description

DESCRIPTION

DESCRIPTION may be defined as the type of writing which undertakes to transfer to the mind of the reader a picture of a person, a scene, a situation, or the impressions stimulated by the objects viewed as they present themselves to the writer; description attempts to reconstruct a similar image or sympathy in the consciousness of the reader. In specifying that much of the new construction in Madrid uses "the lovely yellowish rose brick which is baked in the neighborhood," Gerald Brenan not only portrays in words the peculiar tint of the buildings but adds his approval of the color's warmth and beauty as well. John Ruskin writes of "a blue, deep, desolate hollow of darkness" and "the cold, deadly shadows of the twilight" and projects a feeling of melancholy along with a vividly delineated scene.

The content of description is supplied by the five senses: sight, hearing, touch, smell, and taste. Sight (color, outline, bulk) and hearing (tone of voice, train whistles, symphonic music) offer the fewest difficulties in the reproduction of the original sensations. Samuel Johnson's mustard-colored coat is readily visible, and the watery swish of a tire on a wet street is a sound commonly enough experienced and shared. But describing the taste of a mango or the feeling of a handful of manila rope is a more exacting feat that requires a sharper degree of selectivity and vocabulary. And, although all successful description should be concrete in its naming of details, the reporting of touch, taste, and smell frequently needs comparison or association. As a result, description often recruits the simile and the metaphor to establish its point. Thus we could say that a Mexican tortilla tastes like fried cardboard and the surface of balsa wood resembles the texture of a banana skin.

The commonest tool of description, is, of course, the adjective. But the noun and the verb have an aptitude of their own in the pictorial function. Rhetoricians have invariably recommended the use of all the parts of speech in the general descriptive task.

Very rarely does description constitute a full unit of writing in itself, but rather it accompanies one of the other types. For this reason it has been called an auxiliary form of expression. To narration, especially, it is of artistic service whether it appears generously or sparingly. The *Canterbury Tales* are explicitly narrative, but they owe much to the considerable strength of the separate descriptions of the pilgrims in the Prologue. Without the lively, descriptive depictions of the Wife of Bath, the Knight, and the Prioress, the *Tales*, however excellent in themselves, could never have attained the totality of success they actually incorporate. In addition, one of the delights of meeting a new character in a novel by Charles Dickens or Joseph Conrad is the foreknowledge that the newcomer will be vividly and pointedly described. Henceforth that personality will have a substantial existence in the reader's imagination. But, if the value of description cannot be overestimated, it must be repeated that this type of composition rarely if ever occurs as an independent form. At most a sketch or an essay can be termed descriptive if in large measure the description be of unusual competence or of somewhat extended length. The descriptive selections in this section satisfy those general requirements.

Good, careful writers are usually adept at description. Edmund Spenser, to cite one example, made his *Faerie Queene* as memorable for its descriptive passages as for its allegory. William Shakespeare's masterly account of the barge in *Antony and Cleopatra* has the same spirited quality of the remainder of the play. More recently, historical novelists have used description to create the pageantry that is an inevitable, visual part of their technique—and frequently the best part. In our own century, W. Somerset Maugham, Thomas Wolfe, Graham Greene, and Ernest Hemingway have produced a large degree of the vitality of their novels through the use of expert description. Greene and Hemingway have even evolved a casual method, almost unobtrusive in its effect, which Evelyn Waugh has called the style of the movies. On the first page of *This Gun for Hire* Greene presents his character Raven in movement with a minimum of descriptive details, and even those details are more of a commentary nature than they are a definition. But the succession of Raven's activities proceeds by accumulation to the formation of a personality the reader can realize: the indifferent attitude to murder, the coat collar turned up against the wind, the swinging of the attaché case, the putting on of gloves, the cutting of the telephone wire, and the ringing of the doorbell. Almost as though a camera were following him with curiosity, Raven grows into an individual isolated from all mankind. Much the same descriptive process appears in Hemingway's story, "The Undefeated." After his humiliating interview with Don Miguel Retana, who mixes greed and compassion in his hiring of bullfighters, Manuel Garcia goes to a cafe, orders coffee and brandy, listens to the gossip and judgments of the waiters, and falls asleep at the table. The gestures and the dialogue describe Manuel in the peculiar desperation of his predicament: the reader sees a tired, forgotten, nearly defeated shadow of a once moderately successful matador. By a series of glimpses Hemingway has here achieved the end of all description: a visible, clearly outlined and understood person.

The overlong and dull descriptions of landscape favored by James Fenimore Cooper are no longer fashionable or, for that matter, even necessary. Modern description is more economical and selective. There is clearly more vigor and descriptive freshness in the brief reference to "the wedding cake churches" of Lisbon than there could conceivably be in a stone by stone record of those same churches in prolonged detail. Effective description is generally sparse and concentrated, and occasionally a character is vitalized by the simple means of identifying him with a single mannerism. And the best of description contains a poetic or striking power of suggestion. At the end of Chapter LVII of *The Moon and Sixpence* by W. Somerset Maugham there is a discussion of the blues, reds, yellows, and greens in a still life picture by the incredibly amoral Charles Strickland, the primitive painter. They are not, however, ordinary static colors but "sombre blues" and "reds *shrill* like the berries of holly." It can be conceded that nature has a mysterious fondness for mating red flowers with green stalks and leaves, for doing in effect what theoretic fashion designers would never permit in clothing combinations. But is there not a poetic felicity and the implication of startling contrast about the word *shrill* to define the red berry against its shining green and finely carved leaf? Is there not the hint in all this that the sensation of sight has been surprised?

The following sketches are primarily descriptive because they emphasize the transfer to the reader of sense experience, memory, sentiment, and state of mind. Charles Dickens describes London during the early hours when the city slowly returns to its metropolitan variety; Robert Louis Stevenson examines Edinburgh as a city in which the present and the past are entangled beyond the possibility of separation. The visual present, with considerable overtones of history, is depicted by R. B. Cunninghame Graham (the upper part of South America), by Ralph Adams Cram (the Near East), and by Henry James (a French bridge and its surroundings). Henry David Thoreau's reflections on the night and James Russell Lowell's impressions of the sea and its lonely horizons are virtually essays stimulated by huge but common aspects of nature. Emily Brontë presents the setting for a macabre story. For his part, James Anthony Froude offers the portrait of a man who was the most important spirit in nineteenth-century English ecclesiastical life. The value of Froude's recollections is underscored by the vigor and success of his purpose: he has imparted to the modern reader something of the unforgettable spell with which young men of all centuries respond to genuine, if barely tangible, greatness.

HENRY DAVID THOREAU

NIGHT AND MOONLIGHT*

CHANCING TO TAKE a memorable walk by moonlight some years ago, I resolved to take more such walks, and make acquaintance with another side of nature: I have done so.

According to Pliny, there is a stone in Arabia called Selenites, "wherein is a white, which increases and decreases with the moon." My journal for the last year or two has been *selenitic* in this sense.

Is not the midnight like Central Africa to most of us? Are we not tempted to explore it,—to penetrate to the shores of its Lake Tchad, and discover the source of its Nile, perchance the Mountains of the Moon? Who knows what fertility and beauty, moral and natural, are there to be found? In the Moun-

* Reprinted from *Excursions, Poems, and Familiar Letters*, Houghton Mifflin Company, Boston, 1929.

tains of the Moon, in the Central Africa of the night, there is where all Niles have their hidden heads. The expeditions up the Nile as yet extended but to the Cataracts, or perchance to the mouth of the White Nile; but it is the Black Nile that concerns us.

I shall be a benefactor if I conquer some realms from the night, if I report to the gazettes anything transpiring about us at that season worthy of their attention,—if I can show men that there is some beauty awake while they are asleep,—if I add to the domains of poetry.

Night is certainly more novel and less profane than day. I soon discovered that I was acquainted only with its complexion, and as for the moon, I had seen her only as it were through a crevice in a shutter, occasionally. Why not walk a little way in her light?

Suppose you attend to the suggestions which the moon makes for one month, commonly in vain, will it not be very different from anything in literature or religion? But why not study this Sanskrit? What if one moon has come and gone with its world of poetry, its weird teachings, its oracular suggestions,—so divine a creature freighted with hints for me, and I have not used her? One moon gone by unnoticed?

I think it was Dr. Chalmers who said, criticising Coleridge, that for his part he wanted ideas which he could see all round, and not such as he must look at away up in the heavens. Such a man, one would say, would never look at the moon, because she never turns her other side to us. The light which comes from ideas which have their orbit as distant from the earth, and which is no less cheering and enlightening to the benighted traveler than that of the moon and stars, is naturally reproached or nicknamed as moonshine by such. They are moonshine, are they? Well, then, do your night traveling when there is no moon to light you; but I will be thankful for the light that reaches me from the star of least magnitude. Stars are lesser or greater only as they appear to us so. I will be thankful that I see so much as one side of a celestial idea, one side of the rainbow and the sunset sky.

Men talk glibly enough about moonshine, as if they knew its qualities very well, and despised them; as owls might talk of sunshine,—none of your sunshine!—but this word commonly means merely something which they do not understand,—which they are abed and asleep to, however much it may be worth their while to be up and awake to it.

It must be allowed that the light of the moon, sufficient though it is for the pensive walker, and not disproportionate to the inner light we have, is very inferior in quality and intensity to that of the sun. But the moon is not to be judged alone by the quantity of light she sends to us, but also by her influence on the earth and its inhabitants. "The moon gravitates toward the earth, and the earth reciprocally toward the moon." The poet who walks by moonlight is conscious of a tide in his thought which is to be referred to lunar influence. I will endeavor to separate the tide in my thoughts from the current distractions of the day. I would warn my hearers that they must not try my thoughts by a daylight standard, but endeavor to realize that I speak out of the night. All depends on your point of view. In Drake's "Collection of Voyages," Wafer says of some albinos among the Indians of Darien: "They are quite white, but their whiteness is like that of a horse, quite different from the fair or pale European, as they have not the least tincture of a blush or sanguine complexion. . . . Their eyebrows are milk-white, as is likewise the hair of their heads, which is very fine. . . . They seldom go abroad in the daylight, the sun being disagreeable to them, and causing their eyes, which are weak and poring, to water, especially if it shines towards them, yet they see very well by moonlight, from which we call them moon-eyed."

Neither in our thoughts in these moonlight walks, methinks, is there "the least tincture of a blush or sanguine complexion," but we are intellectually and morally albinos, children of Endymion, such is the effect of conversing much with the moon.

I complain of arctic voyagers that they do not enough remind us of the constant peculiar dreariness of the scenery, and the perpetual twilight of the arctic night. So he whose theme is moonlight, though he may find it difficult, must, as it were, illustrate it with the light of the moon alone.

Many men walk by day; few walk by night. It is a very different season. Take a July night, for instance. About ten o'clock,—when man is asleep, and day fairly forgotten,—the beauty of moonlight is seen over lonely pastures where cattle are silently feeding. On all sides novelties present themselves. Instead of the sun there are the moon and stars; instead of the wood thrush there is the whip-poor-will; instead of butterflies in the meadow, fireflies, winged sparks of fire! who would have believed it? What kind of cool deliberate life dwells in those dewy abodes associated with a spark of fire? So man has fire in his eyes, or blood or brain. Instead of singing birds, the half-throttled note of a cuckoo flying over, the croaking of frogs, and the intenser dream of crickets. But above all, the wonderful trump of the bullfrog, ringing from Maine to Georgia. The potato vines stand upright, the corn grows apace, the bushes loom, the grain-fields are boundless. On our open river terraces once cultivated by the Indian, they appear to occupy the ground like an army, their heads nodding in the breeze. Small trees and shrubs are seen in the midst overwhelmed as by an inundation. The shadows of rocks and trees, and shrubs and hills, are more conspicuous than the objects themselves. The slightest irregularities in the ground are revealed by the shadows, and what the feet find comparatively smooth appears rough and diversified in consequence. For the same reason the whole landscape is more variegated and picturesque than by day. The smallest recesses in the rocks are dim and cavernous; the ferns in the wood appear of tropical size. The sweet-fern and indigo in overgrown wood-paths wet you with dew up to your middle. The leaves of the shrub oak are shining as if a liquid were flowing over them. The pools seen through the trees are as full of light as the sky. "The light of the day takes refuge in their

bosoms," as the Purana says of the ocean. All white objects are more remarkable than by day. A distant cliff looks like a phosphorescent space on
a hillside. The woods are heavy and dark. Nature slumbers. You see the
moonlight reflected from particular stumps in the recesses of the forest,
as if she selected what to shine on. These small fractions of her light remind
one of the plant called moonseed,—as if the moon were sowing it in such
places.

In the night the eyes are partly closed or retire into the head. Other
senses take the lead. The walker is guided as well by the sense of smell.
Every plant and field and forest emits its odor now, swamp-pink in the
meadow and tansy in the road; and there is the peculiar dry scent of corn
which has begun to show its tassels. The senses both of hearing and smelling
are more alert. We hear the tinkling of rills which we never detected before. From time to time, high up on the sides of hills, you pass through
a stratum of warm air, a blast which has come up from the sultry plains
of noon. It tells of the day, of sunny noontide hours and banks, of the laborer
wiping his brow and the bee humming amid flowers. It is an air in which
work has been done,—which men have breathed. It circulates about from
woodside to hillside like a dog that has lost its master, now that the sun
is gone. The rocks retain all night the warmth of the sun which they have
absorbed. And so does the sand. If you dig a few inches into it you
find a warm bed. You lie on your back on a rock in a pasture on the top
of some bare hill at midnight, and speculate on the height of the starry
canopy. The stars are the jewels of the night, and perchance surpass anything which day has to show. A companion with whom I was sailing one
very windy but bright moonlight night, when the stars were few and
faint, thought that a man could get along with *them*, though he was considerably reduced in his circumstances,—that they were a kind of bread
and cheese that never failed.

No wonder that there have been astrologers, that some have conceived
that they were personally related to particular stars. Dubartas, as translated by Sylvester, says he'll

> "not believe that the great architect
> With all these fires the heavenly arches decked
> Only for show, and with these glistering shields,
> T' awake poor shepherds, watching in the fields."
> He'll "not believe the least flower which pranks
> Our garden borders, or our common banks,
> And the least stone, that in her warming lap
> Our mother earth doth covetously wrap,
> Hath some peculiar virtue of its own
> And that the glorious stars of heav'n have none."*

* Joshua Sylvester translated *La Sepmaine* by Guillaume Du Bartas. The French poet's
surname is more commonly spelled as two words.

And Sir Walter Raleigh well says, "The stars are instruments of far greater use than to give an obscure light, and for men to gaze on after sunset;" and he quotes Plotinus as affirming that they "are significant, but not efficient;" and also Augustine as saying, "*Deus regit inferiora corpora per superiora.*" God rules the bodies below by those above. But best of all is this which another writer has expressed: "*Sapiens adjuvabit opus astrorum quemadmodum agricola terrae naturam:*" a wise man assisteth the work of the stars as the husbandman helpeth the nature of the soil.

It does not concern men who are asleep in their beds, but it is very important to the traveler, whether the moon shines brightly or is obscured. It is not easy to realize the serene joy of all the earth, when she commences to shine unobstructedly, unless you have often been abroad alone in moonlight nights. She seems to be waging continual war with the clouds in your behalf. Yet we fancy the clouds to be *her* foes also. She comes on magnifying her dangers by her light, revealing, displaying them in all their hugeness and blackness, then suddenly casts them behind into the light concealed, and goes her way triumphant through a small space of clear sky.

In short, the moon traversing, or appearing to traverse, the small clouds which lie in her way, now obscured by them, now easily dissipating and shining through them, makes the drama of the moonlight night to all watchers and night-travelers. Sailors speak of it as the moon eating up the clouds. The traveler all alone, the moon all alone, except for his sympathy, overcoming with incessant victory whole squadrons of clouds above the forest and lakes and hills. When she is obscured he so sympathizes with her that he could whip a dog for her relief, as Indians do. When she enters on a clear field of great extent in the heavens, and shines unobstructedly, he is glad. And when she has fought her way through all the squadron of her foes, and rides majestic in a clear sky unscathed, and there are no more any obstructions in her path, he cheerfully and confidently pursues his way, and rejoices in his heart, and the cricket also seems to express joy in its song.

How insupportable would be the days, if the night with its dews and darkness did not come to restore the drooping world. As the shades begin to gather around us, our primeval instincts are aroused, and we steal forth from our lairs, like the inhabitants of the jungle, in search of those silent and brooding thoughts which are the natural prey of the intellect.

Richter says that "the earth is every day overspread with the veil of night for the same reason as the cages of birds are darkened, viz., that we may the more readily apprehend the higher harmonies of thought in the hush and quiet of darkness. Thoughts which day turns into smoke and mist stand about us in the night as light and flames; even as the column which fluctuates above the crater of Vesuvius, in the daytime appears a pillar of cloud, but by night a pillar of fire."

There are nights in this climate of such serene and majestic beauty, so medicinal and fertilizing to the spirit, that methinks a sensitive nature would not devote them to oblivion, and perhaps there is no man but would be better and wiser for spending them out-of-doors, though he should sleep all the next day to pay for it,—should sleep an Endymion sleep, as the ancients expressed it,—nights which warrant the Grecian epithet ambrosial, when, as in the land of Beulah, the atmosphere is charged with dewy fragrance, and with music, and we take our repose and have our dreams awake,—when the moon, not secondary to the sun,—

> "gives us his blaze again.
> Void of its flame, and sheds a softer day,
> Now through the passing cloud she seems to stoop,
> Now up the pure cerulean rides sublime."*

Diana still hunts in the New England sky.

> "In Heaven queen she is among the spheres.
>   She, mistress-like, makes all things to be pure.
> Eternity in her oft change she bears;
>   She Beauty is; by her the fair endure.
>
> "Time wears her not; she doth his chariot guide;
>   Mortality below her orb is placed;
> By her the virtues of the stars down slide;
>   By her is Virtue's perfect image cast."†

The Hindoos compare the moon to a saintly being who has reached the last stage of bodily existence.

Great restorer of antiquity, great enchanter! In a mild night when the harvest or hunter's moon shines unobstructedly, the houses in our village, whatever architect they may have had by day, acknowledge only a master. The village street is then as wild as the forest. New and old things are confounded. I know not whether I am sitting on the ruins of a wall, or on the material which is to compose a new one. Nature is an instructed and impartial teacher, spreading no crude opinions, and flattering none; she will be neither radical nor conservative. Consider the moonlight, so civil, yet so savage!

The light is more proportionate to our knowledge than that of day. It is no more dusky in ordinary nights than our mind's habitual atmosphere, and the moonlight is as bright as our most illuminated moments are.

> "In such a night let me abroad remain
> Till morning breaks, and all's confused again."‡

Of what significance the light of day, if it is not the reflection of an inward dawn?—to what purpose is the veil of night withdrawn, if the morning reveals nothing to the soul? It is merely garish and glaring.

---

* From *The Seasons* ("Autumn") by James Thomson, an eighteenth-century poet.
† Sir Walter Raleigh, "Praised be Diana's fair and harmless light."
‡ Anne Finch, Countess of Winchilsea, "A Nocturnal Reverie."

When Ossian, in his address to the sun, exclaims,—

> "Where has darkness its dwelling?
> Where is the cavernous home of the stars,
> When thou quickly followest their steps,
> Pursuing them like a hunter in the sky,—
> Thou climbing the lofty hills,
> They descending on barren mountains?"*

who does not in his thought accompany the stars to their "cavernous home," "descending" with them "on barren mountains"?

Nevertheless, even by night the sky is blue and not black, for we see through the shadow of the earth into the distant atmosphere of day, where the sunbeams are reveling.

ROBERT LOUIS STEVENSON

EDINBURGH†

THE ANCIENT and famous metropolis of the North sits overlooking a windy estuary from the slope and summit of three hills. No situation could be more commanding for the head city of a kingdom; none better chosen for noble prospects. From her tall precipice and terraced gardens she looks far and wide on the sea and broad champaigns. To the east you may catch at sunset the spark of the May lighthouse, where the Firth expands into the German Ocean; and away to the west, over all the carse of Stirling, you can see the first snows upon Ben Ledi.

But Edinburgh pays cruelly for her high seat in one of the vilest climates under heaven. She is liable to be beaten upon by all the winds that blow, to be drenched with rain, to be buried in cold sea fogs out of the east, and powdered with the snow as it comes flying southward from the Highland hills. The weather is raw and boisterous in winter, shifty and ungenial in summer, and a downright meteorological purgatory in the spring. The delicate die early, and I, as a survivor, among bleak winds and plumping rain, have been sometimes tempted to envy them their fate. For all who love shelter and the blessings of the sun, who hate dark weather and perpetual tilting against squalls, there could scarcely be found a more unhomely and harassing place of residence. Many such aspire angrily after that Somewhere-else of the imagination, where all troubles are supposed to end. They lean over the great bridge which joins the New Town with the Old—that windiest spot, or high altar, in this northern temple of the winds—and watch the trains smoking out from under them and vanishing into the tunnel on a

---

* Ossian, according to James Macpherson, was a third-century Gaelic poet who was translated by Macpherson in the 1760's.
† Reprinted from *Edinburgh: Picturesque Notes* (1889).

voyage to brighter skies. Happy the passengers who shake off the dust of Edinburgh, and have heard for the last time the cry of the east wind among her chimney-tops! And yet the place establishes an interest in people's hearts; go where they will, they find no city of the same distinction; go where they will, they take a pride in their old home.

Venice, it has been said, differs from all other cities in the sentiment which she inspires. The rest may have admirers; she only, a famous fair one, counts lovers in her train. And indeed, even by her kindest friends, Edinburgh is not considered in a similar sense. These like her for many reasons, not any one of which is satisfactory in itself. They like her whimsically, if you will, and somewhat as a virtuoso dotes upon his cabinet. Her attraction is romantic in the narrowest meaning of the term. Beautiful as she is, she is not so much beautiful as interesting. She is pre-eminently Gothic, and all the more so since she has set herself off with some Greek airs, and erected classic temples on her crags. In a word, and above all, she is a curiosity.

The Palace of Holyrood has been left aside in the growth of Edinburgh; and stands grey and silent in a workman's quarter and among breweries and gas works. It is a house of many memories. Great people of yore, kings and queens, buffoons and grave ambassadors, played their stately farce for centuries in Holyrood. Wars have been plotted, dancing has lasted deep into the night, murder has been done in its chambers. There Prince Charlie held his phantom levées, and in a very gallant manner represented a fallen dynasty for some hours. Now, all these things of clay are mingled with the dust, the king's crown itself is shown for sixpence to the vulgar; but the stone palace has outlived these changes.

For fifty weeks together, it is no more than a show for tourists and a museum of old furniture; but on the fifty-first, behold the palace re-awakened and mimicking its past.

The Lord Commissioner, a kind of stage sovereign, sits among stage courtiers; a coach and six and clattering escort come and go before the gate; at night, the windows are lighted up, and its near neighbours, the work-men, may dance in their own houses to the palace music. And in this the palace is typical. There is a spark among the embers; from time to time the old volcano smokes. Edinburgh has but partly abdicated, and still wears, in parody, her metropolitan trappings. Half a capital and half a country town, the whole city leads a double existence; it has long trances of the one and flashes of the other; like the king of the Black Isles, it is half-alive and half a monumental marble. There are armed men and cannon in the citadel overhead; you may see the troops marshalled on the high parade; and at night after the early winter evenfall, and in the morning before the laggard winter dawn, the wind carries abroad over Edinburgh the sound of drums and bugles. Grave judges sit bewigged in what was once the scene of imperial deliberations.

Close by in the High Street perhaps the trumpets may sound about the stroke of noon; and you see a troop of citizens in tawdry masquerade; tabard above, heather-mixture trouser below, and the men themselves trudging in the mud among unsympathetic bystanders. The grooms of a well-appointed circus tread the streets with a better presence. And yet these are the Heralds and Pursuivants of Scotland, who are about to proclaim a new law of the United Kingdom before two score boys, and thieves, and hackney-coachmen. Meanwhile every hour the bell of the University rings out over the hum of the streets, and every hour a double tide of students, coming and going, fills the deep archways.

And lastly, one night in the spring-time—or say one morning rather, at the peep of day—late folk may hear the voices of many men singing a psalm in unison from a church on one side of the old High Street; and a little after, or perhaps a little before, the sound of many men singing a psalm in unison from another church on the opposite side of the way. There will be something in the words about the dew of Hermon and how goodly it is to see brethren dwelling together in unity. And the late folk will tell themselves that all this singing denotes the conclusion of two yearly ecclesiastical parliaments—the parliaments of Churches which are brothers in many admirable virtues, but not specially like brothers in this particular of a tolerant and peaceful life.

Again, meditative people will find a charm in a certain consonancy between the aspect of the city and its odd and stirring history. Few places, if any, offer a more barbaric display of contrasts to the eye. In the very midst stands one of the most satisfactory crags in nature—a Bass Rock upon dry land rooted in a garden, shaken by passing trains, carrying a crown of battlements and turrets, and describing its warlike shadow over the liveliest and brightest thoroughfare of the New Town. From their smoky beehives, ten stories high, the unwashed look down upon the open squares and gardens of the wealthy; and gay people sunning themselves along Princes Street, with its mile of commercial palaces all beflagged upon some great occasion, see, across a gardened valley set with statues, where the washings of the Old Town flutter in the breeze at its high windows. And then, upon all sides, what a clashing of architecture! In this one valley, where the life of the town goes most busily forward, there may be seen, shown one above and behind another by the accidents of the ground, buildings in almost every style upon the globe. Egyptian and Greek temples, Venetian palaces and Gothic spires, are huddled one over another in a most admired disorder; while, above all, the brute mass of the Castle and the summit of Arthur's Seat look down upon these imitations with a becoming dignity, as the works of Nature may look down upon the monuments of Art. But Nature is a more indiscriminate patroness than we imagine, and in no way frightened of a strong effect. The birds roost as willingly among the Corinthian capitals as in the crannies of the crag; the same atmosphere and daylight clothe the eternal rock and yesterday's imitation portico; and as the soft northern sunshine throws out everything into a glorified distinctness—or easterly mists, coming up with the blue evening, fuse all these incongruous features into one, and the lamps begin to glitter along the street, and faint lights to burn in the high windows across the valley—the feeling grows upon you that this also is a piece of nature in the most intimate sense; that this profusion of eccentricities, this dream in masonry and living rock is not a drop-scene in a theatre, but a city in the world of everyday reality, connected by railway and telegraph-wire with all the capitals of Europe, and inhabited by citizens of the familiar type, who keep ledgers, and attend church, and have sold their immortal portion to a daily paper. By all the canons of romance, the place demands to be half-deserted and leaning towards decay; birds we might admit in profusion, the play of the sun and winds, and a few gypsies encamped in the chief thoroughfare; but these citizens, with their cabs and tramways, their trains and posters, are altogether out of key. Chartered tourists, they make free with historic localities, and rear their young among the most picturesque sites with a grand human indifference. To see them thronging by, in their neat clothes and conscious moral rectitude, and with a little air of possession that verges on the absurd, is not the least striking feature of the place.

And the story of the town is as eccentric as its appearance. For centuries it was a capital thatched with heather, and more than once, in the evil days of English invasion, it has gone up in flame to heaven, a beacon to ships at sea. It was the jousting-ground of jealous nobles, not only on Greenside or by the King's Stables, where set tournaments were fought to the sound of trumpets and under the authority of the royal presence, but in every alley where there was room to cross swords, and in the main street, where popular tumult under the Blue Blanket alternated with the brawls of outlandish clansmen and retainers. Down in the palace John Knox reproved his queen in the accents of modern democracy. In the town, in one of those little shops plastered like so many swallows' nests among the buttresses of the old Cathedral, that familiar autocrat, James VI., would gladly share a bottle of wine with George Heriot the goldsmith. Up on the Pentland Hills, that so quietly look down on the Castle with the city lying in waves around it, those mad and dismal fanatics, the Sweet Singers, haggard from long exposure on the moors, sat day and night with "tearful psalms" to see Edinburgh consumed with fire from heaven, like another Sodom or Gomorrah. There, in the Grassmarket, stiff-necked, covenanting heroes offered up the often unnecessary, but not less honourable, sacrifice of their lives, and bade eloquent farewell to sun, moon, and stars, and earthly friendships, or died silent to the roll of drums. Down by yon outlet rode Grahame of Claverhouse and his thirty dragoons, with the town beating to arms behind their horses' tails—a sorry handful thus riding for their lives, but with a man at the head who was to return in a different temper, make a dash that staggered Scotland to the heart, and die happily in the thick of fight. There Aikenhead was hanged for a piece of boyish incredulity; there, a few years afterwards, David Hume ruined Philosophy and Faith, an undisturbed and

well-reputed citizen; and thither, in yet a few years more, Burns came from
the plough-tail, as to an academy of gilt unbelief and artificial letters. There,
when the great exodus was made across the valley, and the New Town
began to spread abroad its draughty parallelograms and rear its long frontage
on the opposing hill, there was such a flitting, such a change of domicile
and dweller, as was never excelled in the history of cities: the cobbler succeeded the earl; the beggar ensconced himself by the judge's chimney; what
had been a palace was used as a pauper refuge; and great mansions were so
parcelled out among the least and lowest in society, that the hearthstone of
the old proprietor was thought large enough to be partitioned off into a
bedroom by the new.

CHARLES DICKENS

THE STREETS—MORNING*

THE APPEARANCE presented by the streets of London an hour before sunrise, on a summer's morning, is most striking even to the few whose
unfortunate pursuits of pleasure, or scarcely less unfortunate pursuits of
business, cause them to be well acquainted with the scene. There is an air of
cold, solitary desolation about the noiseless streets which we are accustomed
to see thronged at other times by a busy, eager crowd, and over the quiet,
closely-shut buildings, which throughout the day are swarming with life
and bustle that is very impressive.

The last drunken man, who shall find his way home before sunlight, has
just staggered heavily along, roaring out the burden of the drinking song of
the previous night: the last houseless vagrant whom penury and police
have left in the streets, has coiled up his chilly limbs in some paved corner,
to dream of food and warmth. The drunken, the dissipated, and the
wretched have disappeared; the more sober and orderly part of the population have not yet awakened to the labours of the day, and the stillness of
death is over the streets; its very hue seems to be imparted to them, cold
and lifeless as they look in the grey, sombre light of daybreak. The coach-
stands in the larger thoroughfares are deserted: the night-houses are closed;
and the chosen promenades of profligate misery are empty.

An occasional policeman may alone be seen at the street-corners, listlessly
gazing on the deserted prospect before him; and now and then a rakish-
looking cat runs stealthily across the road and descends his own area with
as much caution and slyness—bounding first on the water-butt, then on the
dust-hole, and then alighting on the flag-stones—as if he were conscious
that his character depended on his gallantry of the preceding night escaping
public observation. A partially opened bedroom window here and there,

* Reprinted from *Sketches by Boz*, 1836.

bespeaks the heat of the weather, and the uneasy slumbers of its occupant; and the dim scanty flicker of the rushlight, through the window-blind, denotes the chamber of watching or sickness. With these few exceptions, the streets present no sign of life, nor the houses of habitation.

An hour wears away; the spires of the churches and roofs of the principal buildings are faintly tinged with the light of the rising sun; and the streets, by almost imperceptible degrees, begin to resume their bustle and animation. Market-carts roll slowly along: the sleepy waggoner impatiently urging on his tired horses or vainly endeavouring to awaken the boy, who, luxuriously stretched on the top of the fruit-baskets, forgets, in happy oblivion, his long-cherished curiosity to behold the wonders of London.

Rough, sleepy-looking animals of strange appearance, something between ostlers and hackney-coachmen, begin to take down the shutters of early public-houses; and little deal tables, with the ordinary preparations for a street breakfast, make their appearance at the customary stations. Numbers of men and women (principally the latter), carrying upon their heads heavy baskets of fruit, toil down the park side of Piccadilly, on their way to Covent Garden, and, following each other in rapid succession, form a long straggling line from thence to the turn of the road at Knightsbridge.

Here and there, a bricklayer's labourer, with the day's dinner tied up in a handkerchief, walks briskly to his work, and occasionally a little knot of three or four school-boys on a stolen bathing expedition rattle merrily over the pavement, their boisterous mirth contrasting forcibly with the demeanour of the little sweep, who, having knocked and rung till his arm aches, and being interdicted by a merciful legislature from endangering his lungs by calling out, sits patiently down on the door-step, until the house-maid may happen to awake.

Covent Garden Market, and the avenues leading to it, are thronged with carts of all sorts, sizes, and descriptions, from the heavy lumbering waggon, with its four stout horses, to the jingling coster-monger's cart, with its consumptive donkey. The pavement is already strewed with decayed cabbage-leaves, broken haybands, and all the indescribable litter of a vegetable market; men are shouting, carts backing, horses neighing, boys fighting, basket-women talking, piemen expatiating on the excellence of their pastry, and donkeys braying. These and a hundred other sounds form a compound discordant enough to a Londoner's ears, and remarkably disagreeable to those of country gentlemen who are sleeping at the Hummums for the first time.

Another hour passes away, and the day begins in good earnest. The servant of all work, who, under the plea of sleeping very soundly, has utterly disregarded 'Missis's' ringing for half an hour previously, is warned by Master (whom Missis has sent up in his drapery to the landing-place for that purpose), that it's half-past six, whereupon she awakes all of a sudden, with well-feigned astonishment, and goes downstairs very sulkily, wishing, while she strikes a light, that the principle of spontaneous combustion would extend itself to coals and kitchen range. When the fire is lighted, she opens the street-door to take in the milk, when, by the most singular co-incidence in the world, she discovers that the servant next door has just taken in her milk too, and that Mr. Todd's young man over the way, is, by an equally extraordinary chance, taking down his master's shutters. The inevitable consequence is, that she just steps, milk-jug in hand, as far as next door, just to say 'good-morning' to Betsy Clark, and that Mr. Todd's young man just steps over the way to say 'good-morning' to both of 'em; and as the aforesaid Mr. Todd's young man is almost as good-looking and fascinating as the baker himself, the conversation quickly becomes very interesting, and probably would become more so, if Betsy Clark's Missis, who always will be a followin' her about, didn't give an angry tap at her bedroom window, on which Mr. Todd's young man tries to whistle coolly, as he goes back to his shop much faster than he came from it; and the two girls run back to their respective places, and shut their street-doors with surprising softness, each of them poking their heads out of the front-parlour window, a minute afterwards, however, ostensibly with the view of looking at the mail which just then passes by, but really for the purpose of catching another glimpse of Mr. Todd's young man, who being fond of mails, but more of females, takes a short look at the mails, and a long look at the girls, much to the satisfaction of all parties concerned.

The mail itself goes on to the coach-office in due course, and the pas-sengers who are going out by early coach, stare with astonishment at the passengers who are coming in by early coach, who look blue and dismal, and are evidently under the influence of that odd feeling produced by travelling, which makes the events of yesterday morning seem as if they had happened at least six months ago, and induces people to wonder with considerable gravity whether the friends and relations they took leave of a fortnight before, have altered much since they have left them. The coach-office is all alive, and the coaches which are just going out, are surrounded by the usual crowd of Jews and nondescripts, who seem to consider, Heaven knows why, that it is quite impossible that any man can mount a coach with-out requiring at least sixpenny-worth of oranges, a penknife, a pocket-book, a last year's annual, a pencil-case, a piece of sponge, and a small series of caricatures.

Half an hour more, and the sun darts his bright rays cheerfully down the still half-empty streets, and shines with sufficient force to rouse the dismal laziness of the apprentice, who pauses every other minute from his task of sweeping out the shop and watering the pavement in front of it, to tell another apprentice similarly employed, how hot it will be to-day, or to stand with his right hand shading his eyes, and his left resting on the broom, gazing at the 'Wonder' or the 'Tally-ho,' or the 'Nimrod,' or some other fast coach, till it is out of sight, when he re-enters the shop, envying the passengers on the outside of the fast coach, and thinking of the old red-brick house 'down in the country,' where he went to school; the miseries of the milk and water, and thick bread-and-scrapings, fading into nothing before the pleasant recollection of the green field the boys used to play in, and the green pond he was caned for presuming to fall into, and other schoolboy associations.

Cabs, with trunks and bandboxes between the drivers' legs and outside the apron, rattle briskly up and down the streets on their way to the coach-offices or steam-packet wharfs; and the cabdrivers and hackney-coachmen who are on the stand polish up the ornamental part of their dingy vehicles —the former wondering how people can prefer 'them wild beast cariwans of homnibuses, to a riglar cab with a fast trotter,' and the latter admiring how people can trust their necks into one of 'them crazy cabs, when they can have a 'spectable 'ackney cotche with a pair of 'orses as von't run away with no vun;' a consolation unquestionably founded on fact, seeing that a hackney-coach horse never was known to run at all, 'except one, and *he* run back'ards.'

The shops are now completely opened, and apprentices and shopmen are busily engaged in cleaning and decking the windows for the day. The bakers' shops in town are filled with servants and children waiting for the drawing of the first batch of rolls—an operation which was performed a full hour ago in the suburbs; for the early clerk population of Somers and Camden Towns, Islington, and Pentonville, are fast pouring into the City, or directing their steps towards Chancery Lane and the Inns of Court. Middle-aged men, whose salaries have by no means increased in the same proportion as their families, plod steadily along, apparently with no object in view but the counting-house; knowing by sight almost everybody they meet or overtake, for they have seen them every morning (Sundays excepted) during the last twenty years, but speaking to no one. If they do happen to overtake a personal acquaintance, they just exchange a hurried salutation, and keep walking on, either by his side, or in front of him, as his rate of walking may chance to be. As to stopping to shake hands, or to take the friend's arm, they seem to think that as it is not included in their salary, they have no right to do it. Small office lads in large hats, who are made men before they are boys, hurry along in pairs, with their first coat carefully brushed, and the white trousers of last Sunday plentifully be-smeared with dust and ink. It evidently requires a considerable mental struggle to avoid investing part of the day's dinner-money in the purchase of the stale tarts so temptingly exposed in dusty tins at the pastry-cooks' doors; but a consciousness of their own importance and the receipt of seven shillings a week, with the prospect of an early rise to eight, comes to their aid, and they accordingly put their hats a little more on one side, and look under the bonnets of all the milliners' and staymakers' apprentices they meet—poor girls!—the hardest worked, the worst paid, and too often, the worst used class of the community.

Eleven o'clock, and a new set of people fill the streets. The goods in the shop-windows are invitingly arranged; the shopmen in their white neckerchiefs and spruce coats, look as if they couldn't clean a window if their lives depended on it; the carts have disappeared from Covent Garden; the waggoners have returned, and the coster-mongers repaired to their ordinary 'beats' in the suburbs; clerks are at their offices, and gigs, cabs, omnibuses, and saddle-horses are conveying their masters to the same destination. The streets are thronged with a vast concourse of people, gay and shabby, rich and poor, idle and industrious; and we come to the heat, bustle, and activity of NOON.

RALPH ADAMS CRAM

WHITE MAGIC*

WHITE CITIES. The phrase is almost meaningless to us, the vision it evokes nebulous and insubstantial, for such things lie outside our ken, unless indeed we venture far past the Pillars of Hercules into the once well-travelled roads of the Adriatic and Ionian and Aegean Seas. We live in grayness and our eyes are nourished (so to speak) on dun coloured towns; the mud-browns and gross gray-greens, faded and sullen, of mill towns, the harsh reds and clay-drabs of industrial plants, the rust of iron and the black of coal smoke.

One writes "If you will visualize Cadiz you must write the word 'white' with a white pencil on blue paper" but the vision still remains aloof and intangible. That swift-rushing line from "Lepanto": "They have dared the white republics up the capes of Italy" flashes a sudden gleam of light across customary shadow; it hardly achieves permanence, but fades on the moment leaving only a wistful wonder as to what these white things may be. Our own industrial cities we know—but what are "white cities" and in what fabulous land do they lift their walls and towers above blue seas and against violet hills?

Nor does the nearer Europe aid us much. Gray and red and brown achieve a certain transfiguration in England where old villages blend in with older groves of great trees and immemorial meadows. France—the old France of lords and peasants—lifts the key a little, and increasingly southward, with Spain and Italy, the possibility becomes more real, with Segovia and Cadiz and Umbrian hill towns in the sun, but always the undertone of gray and brown asserts itself and—Spain apart—leaves only a mitigated whiteness and a wonder as to what the absolute may be.

It is a real wonder and an abiding desire. Why is the white city so evocative in its name and why is "white" in itself so far more than a word and the denomination of a tincture? It is so, beyond question, and even to the walls of the New Jerusalem we attribute the living effulgence of luminous ivory

* Reprinted from *Convictions and Controversies,* Boston, Marshall Jones Company, 1935, by permission of Mrs. R. W. Cram.

and the pale radiance of mother-of-pearl. Memory or anticipation? Who knows? but the dream and the desire are always there, and if, by the grace of God, eyes blurred by the gray clay and the dull mud of familiar housing open suddenly on the radiant vision of apocalyptic white in a setting of blue, violet and gold—given sea, mountains, verdure—heart and soul answer with the thrill of revelation, the caught breath of ultimate fulfillment.

It is in the far eastern Mediterranean that the white cities still linger in isolation and merciful forgetfulness on the part of a world alien in temper and in impulse. Beyond the brave approximations of the Adriatic and the Ionian Sea, you must go to the coasts of Greece and to the islands of the Aegean and the shores of Anatolia. The littoral of North Africa also, to Morocco and Algeria, to Tunis and Tripoli, but this alluring land I do not know. I can tell only of some of the white things seen in cruising over the seas and along the lands where once Minoan ships and Egyptian, Phoenician and Carthaginian, Greek and Roman, Byzantine and Frank and Venetian and Moslem, cut the blue waters and contended with the wild winds in ceaseless and tangled traffic. The sea is unchangeably the same and the fanciful land-masses; snow crowned mountains and violet headlands, opal island-peaks and the lavender walls of strange continents. Tall cities have risen with each successive culture only to fall before ruthless devastation and vanish utterly away save for heaped debris, and the racked platforms and sagging steps of temples and palaces and theatres. Knossos and Mykenae, Troy and Halicarnassus, Alexandria, Antioch, Athens, Nicæa, Thessalonica, Mistrá, all have passed and their stones have been used over and over again after strange and alien ways, only to fall at last in final abandonment. Even the multitudinous castles of Franks and Venetians and Genoese and Crusaders, with their churches and palaces, are fast disintegrating, and Cyprus and the Morea show only shattered vestiges of a civilization that held sway for two hundred years.

It may be a lesser culture that survives and for its own housing has built its white cities of the stolen marble of great temples, and of rubble and plaster instead of the moon-white stone of Paros and Pentelicus, but the whiteness lasts and, ever and again renewed by washings of lime, still offers the simulacrum of the gleaming marble of a civilization that would not accept the substitute for the reality.

Sailing south from Piræus past the silver columns of Sunium on its high cliff—hail and farewell of Athens to its mariners—and threading a devious way through a city of mauve islands on a rippling plain of lapis lazuli, it was the marble island of Paros that began to weave the white magic of white cities. The goal was not this, nor was it dreamed of. It was only the "Church of an Hundred Gates," known vaguely for its unique archaeological qualities and because of its founding by the Empress Helena. The church itself proved disappointing in a measure, for it had been largely rebuilt after an earth-quake in the eighteenth century (earthquakes and fires and bombardments should never have been permitted by a kindly Providence later than the sixteenth century if the circumstances implied attempts at restoration) but as the yacht—a "white city" in itself—steamed slowly into the little harbour of Parœchia compensation, and more, revealed itself, for all along the sea rose a slender but faintly pyramidal town, whiter than the snow crown of Helicon, silhouetted against the Parian peak, and bubbling into little white domes on and round its old Acropolis. Landing in the midst of wind-mills and wine casks, with a vine-hung trattoria in front and a snow-white and domed little chapel to the left, with the great pale dome of the hundred-gated church further away, it was the path to the town that lured, and that fulfilled the promise of the silvery apparition from the sea. White, yes, the whole town, with its narrow and climbing streets, its pavements and curbstones and house steps of white marble, but "white" means so much more than snow. Once inside the town it appeared that the little houses with their outside stairs and their flat roofs, were of all possible hues, rose and mauve and pale ochre and cobalt blue mingling with the vivid white of lime-wash, and with the round white domes rising in every vista. Cleaner than clean, the blue-shadowed, narrow streets were shaded by luxuriant vines trained from side to side, translucent gold and emerald under the high sun. Fragments of Parian marble everywhere, spoil of the dismantled Acropolis and its temples, and mingled with them Mediæval statues set in niches on the arched stairs to upper stories. Strangest of all, a half ruinous castle of the Frankish domin-ion, built wholly of temple marble: architraves and pilasters laid in level courses, alternating with the drums of Greek and Roman columns set end-wise in the walls in uncouth patterning. On the very crest of the Acropolis, a little white-domed church, a part of the walls the lower courses of the cella of the vanished temple, a diminutive Gothic-arched cloister on one side and within the intricately carved iconostas all dull gold around its painted icons.

And the arcaded fore-court of the Church of an Hundred Gates was no less white than tiny Parœchia. Spotless and gleaming, with clear blue shadows under its procession of wide arches, and in the midst flowers and tall bronze cypresses, black against the dazzling church and the sequent arcades.

A white town in the midst of golden vineyards and orchards of orange and pomegranate, with the blue sea below and the blue mountain peak rising behind. The whiteness of a life that may have forgotten Hellas and its Parian symbol of white life, but had not known the drabness and the murk of the culture of coal and iron and all that they imply. Yes, one could live there well in the white lights and the blue shadows and the golden gleams of vine leaves.

In the open sea again, now "wine-dark" under driving winds though the sun is bright. Ahead a lavender silhouette grows slowly, clearer and more definite, Santorin, of old the island of Thera. As we come nearer the blue

wall shows a narrow cleft and suddenly to the left one headland blooms
into a vision of ivory and white and gold under the low sun. From the very
edge of the tumultuous sea the white begins, walls and terraces, and domes
like great pearls, mounting irregularly up the steep slope, a full thousand
feet, to the very crest where it spreads out into a wide city around the
silver of a crowning Mediæval castle. Maxfield Parrish may have made this
picture, but otherwise, so fantastical is it, it has no other reality.

The yacht slips through the purple gates and the dream-city is gone, all
too soon. Within there is a quiet inland sea, walled by astounding cliffs
eleven hundred feet high, the vast crater of a volcano once, some fifteen
hundred years B.C., greater than Aetna. The towering walls are almost vertical, a cross section of volcanic deposits, striated in many layers and every
shade of tan, cocoa-brown, ochre and puce. There is a huddle of white and
black at the one possible landing place on the edge of the water and zig-
zagging upward the thin line of a mule path cut in the face of the cliff,
ending at last on the very brim where, amazingly, there spreads a long
white city, again with its walls and terraces, domes and towers, luminous,
dazzling, like the icing on a giant layer cake, or a heavy fall of immaculate,
drifted snow. It is incredible, no less; outside all former experience.

The city itself, the snow crown of the crater cliffs, is not old enough to
be good nor new enough to be bad, but it is white, *white,* with its terraced,
flowery gardens creaming over the brink and dripping a little down the
sides of the abyss; its narrow and climbing streets in blue shadow, its
arcades and belfries, and its dim passages from one level to another. On
the crater side the fall is sheer to the blue disc of sea with the low black
hump of dead lava and scoriæ, the sluggish, intermittent crater of the still
extant volcano. On the other side the city ceases as abruptly but here the
long escarpment sweeps gently down to the island perimeter, gold-green
with vineyards and market gardens and orchards of orange and olive and
pomegranate. It is all exceedingly improbable. Why has no one told of this
strange thing before? At least one might have been warned, or was it better
to have this sudden revelation of a wonder unique in the world?

Shards of white cities along the coasts of Crete and Rhodes and Cyprus,
but fragments only. Desolated by modern civilization, both through destruction and reconstruction: Candia, Lindus, Rhodes, Larnaka, Famagusta: then
the amphitheatre of Symi with its circling tiers of new white houses, and
later the purple mountains of Doris and Ionia, leading on through the maze
of islands to incredible Halicarnassus.

Or rather, perhaps, one should say Boudrum, for the city of Mausolus
no longer exists, even as scattered stones amongst the olives. It is as though
it never had been; not even the fire-warped pavements of Phæstos or the
gaunt stylobate of Delphi. Only a green slope of gardens and gray Turkish
houses separated by dilapidated stone walls. "Boudrum." The name suggests
nothing, raises no anticipations of possible wonder, but as we neared the
mountain walls of Anatolia, here rather low and without marked diversity,

a line of whiteness along the sea extended itself, lifted in the centre and grew more luminous, and at last, as we cast anchor, revealed itself as an amazement. Another low-lying white city, or rather village, but in the midst, rising sheer from blue water, an enormous Mediæval castle with high battlemented ramparts, tier above tier, and many tall towers, turreted and crenelated, and all, not silver gray or tawny like the other castles we had seen in the Morea or the Cyclades, but dazzling white as though it were built of the marble of Paros or Pentelicus. And white marble it is, the whole amazing erection, and reared by the Franks from the white and chiselled spoil of the Mausoleum and the palace, the agora and the theatre of vanished Halicarnassus. Quite incredible, this white vision against the lavender hills; a dream castle that might have housed Lohengrin or guarded the Holy Grail. By rights a castle should look its warlike part; it should be steely gray like Ludlow, or black and ominous like Loches, but here in Greek lands under Moslem occupancy stands this Gothic castle white as moonlight and fanciful as a dream.

Until the Great War it stood absolutely intact, as complete an example of Mediæval military architecture as existed anywhere in the world. During the war every French battleship that passed towards the great and futile tragedy of the Dardanelles, threw a casual shell or two at the towering walls, bursting breaches here and there, splitting turrets from tower angles and piling marble wreckage in the courts and on the edge of the sea. Still the keep and most of the towers stand, though with gaping holes here and there, and from the sea the partial ruin seems almost intact, a silvery silhouette unreal, intangible. So should Camelot have seemed, or Joyous Gard or Montsalvat, the dream castle hoarding the Holy Grail.

From such a castle as this to Patmos of the Apocalypse is not so violent a transition after all, as it is no great distance over liquid sapphire amongst purple islands. Castle and monastery, workshop and cathedral and secret bower were all but varied showings of the same thing, a life that had, almost for the first time, fundamental unity. Fighting and worship and labour and love were all good things, each in its time and place. There was no real conflict for all were more frank and natural than now and none was blurred by psychoanalysis, blotted by a Manichæan puritanism or distorted out of all human shape by technological civilization. These things divide and destroy; the old life united and synthesized. Only its white memory remains and we can seek it best in these Aegean seas.

Patmos rises gaunt and barren to its low but dominating peak above a thin, deep, land-locked inlet of harbour. Here as always there is a low whiteness of quiet housings along the sea with a zig-zag of sun-baked road up to the gray fortress-like monastery on the high crest. High walls, sombre and unfriendly, militant rather than ascetic, but once through the gate the radiance of unblemished white is almost blinding when the sun shines down into little cloistered courts and through pointed arches that are apparently willful in their endless multiplication. Here the shadows are almost as blue as the sea but paler and more limpid. White stairways climb up past wandering galleries to flat white roofs where bronze bells hang in white belfries, arch upon arch, against the vivid sky. This is perhaps the whitest thing to be found anywhere, only the black habits of the old broad-bearded monks cutting into the hundred shades of what is in the end only white; but the little church is within all gold and the faded hues of old frescoes, and the brown of carved wood and the flicker of myriads of lamps and chandeliers of brass and crystal. The white light and the gold of the Revelation of St. John still seem to irradiate these courts and cloisters after the passing of nearly two thousand years.

So one goes on from one white thing to another in these Eastern waters, but it is to Athens one comes back in the end for final apotheosis. Not to the new Athens, a rather horrid place, reaching out and clutching the helpless country in every direction in jerry-built suburbs, not unlike the newer Detroit. A wilderness of tan and ochre plaster and streets of tawny dust driven by immoderate winds. A sad place and meaningless, swelling without conscious motive or sense of direction, rather pitiful when it tries to recover touch with its far past and sense of inheritance, through cheap architectural reproductions and plaster replicas of originals in Pentelic marble.

Out of this welter of fading yellow rises always the great rock of the Acropolis. Roman ruins and Greek huddle around its base, and thoughtfully the authorities have preserved some space of trees, here and there for measurable isolation. Busses and automobiles roar around the rock, and gasoline and cinema signs fight for nearer approximations, but at the base of the scarp civilization ceases and culture—or the memory of a culture, begins. Orthodox Christians, Moslems, Franks, Venetians, predatory amateurs and archæologists have sequently contributed their share of destructive energy, and now restoration comes in to play its part, but still some immortality fights down mortality, and the Acropolis, ruined, desecrated and defiled, still reveals and proclaims something in the life of man that had the whiteness of pure flame, a thing that could not die.

And yet there is no whiteness here as of snow or lime or deep-sea pearls. Rather it is all blue-silver and old ivory and amber from Samarkand. But the word means so much more than pure pallor, it embraces all these warm hues, that, as with the spectrum, together make the white fire of pure white. From the sea the Parthenon shows white against the mauve of Lycabettus and the blue of the Pentelican hills. It is white under the sun and white under the moon, but it is the white of some higher purity that transfigures its material accidents.

Approached as the Acropolis should be under a late sun on a cloudless day, the Propylæa is a towering wonder of clustered, truncated shafts of chiselled ivory glowing with an interior fire that makes these dead stones a living breath. I have never seen this before except once, long ago when, at his jubilee, Pope Leo XIII was borne into St. Peter's in his sedia gestatoria. How should marble of Pentelicus become ivory and how should this ivory grow into still flame? The chryselephantine statue of Athena in all its wonder of chiselled ivory and wrought gold is gone, refashioned perhaps into dice and traders' coins, but something of its soul has drifted down from the violet-crowned height to infuse these stones of the portal with their undying flame.

And through the last of the pale, fluted shafts, opens the bare, blue rock, like a broken pavement of tarnished silver with cobalt caught in the clefts and shadows. On one hand the girlish slenderness of the pearl-white Erech-theion, on the other hand, high, high as the hills, the Parthenon, supreme achievement of the highest intellect of man. Here also is the texture of old ivory so that the touch lingers and caresses, but the colour is of the honey of Hybla and of the wrought amber of Turkestan. Out of a giant stylobate of blue-silver it rises against purple Hymettus into a blue sky that is infinite depth; less colour than the radiant profundity of interstellar space.

Under the moon all colour is burned away and the Acropolis and all it sustains becomes burnished silver with shadows that are neither black nor violet, but something akin to both. Then Athens vanishes in the dark and becomes only a widespread star cluster, a fallen milky way of gleaming stars; the sky is impenetrable and the moon paints the ghost of Hellas in dark shadows on the pale silver of column, entablature and pavement. But the lasting memory is neither of ivory, nacre or amber, but of *white*, for it is this that is the indwelling spirit of the Acropolis.

I do not know the secret of this white magic that still lingers in these enclaves and islands and hidden places of the old East that saw the birth of the human world we know. It is more than what the eye sees, more than the joy of something clean and utterly pure. The final appeal is interior, mystical, taking hold, in some sort, of ultimate things. It is criticism and judgment, but it is also illumination. We know little enough of the Beatific Vision, but one thing we can safely assume and that is that it has that perfect whiteness that has its pale simulacrum in the white cities of the Aegean Sea.

JAMES ANTHONY FROUDE

NEWMAN AT OXFORD*

With us undergraduates Newman, of course, did not enter on such important questions, although they were in the air, and we talked about them among ourselves. He, when we met him, spoke to us about subjects of the day, literature, of public persons and incidents, of everything which was generally interesting. He seemed always to be better informed on common topics of conversation than any one else who was present. He was never condescending with us, never didactic or authoritative; but what he said carried conviction along with it. When we were wrong he knew why we

* Reprinted from *Short Studies on Great Subjects,* Charles Scribner's Sons, 1908.

were wrong, and excused our mistakes to ourselves while he set us right. Perhaps his supreme merit as a talker was that he never tried to be witty or to say striking things. Ironical he could be, but not ill-natured. Not a malicious anecdote was ever heard from him. Prosy he could not be. He was lightness itself—the lightness of elastic strength—and he was interesting because he never talked for talking's sake, but because he had something real to say.

Thus it was that we, who had never seen such another man, and to whom he appeared, perhaps, at special advantage in contrast with the normal college don, came to regard Newman with the affection of pupils (though pupils, strictly speaking, he had none) for an idolized master. The simplest word which dropped from him was treasured as if it had been an intellectual diamond. For hundreds of young men *Credo in Newmannum** was the genuine symbol of faith.

Personal admiration, of course, inclined us to look at him as a guide in matters of religion. No one who heard his sermons in those days can ever forget them. They were seldom directly theological. We had theology enough and to spare from the select preachers before the university. Newman, taking some Scripture character for a text, spoke to us about ourselves, our temptations, our experiences. His illustrations were inexhaustible. He seemed to be addressing the most secret consciousness of each of us—as the eyes of a portrait appear to look at every person in a room. He never exaggerated; he was never unreal. A sermon from him was a poem, formed on a distinct idea, fascinating by its subtlety, welcome—how welcome!—from its sincerity, interesting from its originality, even to those who were careless of religion; and to others who wished to be religious, but had found religion dry and wearisome, it was like the springing of a fountain out of the rock.

The hearts of men vibrate in answer to one another like the strings of musical instruments. These sermons were, I suppose, the records of Newman's own mental experience. They appear to me to be the outcome of continued meditation upon his fellow-creatures and their position in this world; their awful responsibilities; the mystery of their nature, strangely mixed of good and evil, of strength and weakness. A tone, not of fear, but of infinite pity runs through them all, and along with it a resolution to look facts in the face; not to fly to evasive generalities about infinite mercy and benevolence, but to examine what revelation really has added to our knowledge, either of what we are or of what lies before us. We were met on all sides with difficulties; for experience did not confirm, it rather contradicted, what revelation appeared distinctly to assert. I recollect a sermon from him—I think in the year 1839—I have never read it since; I may not now remember the exact words, but the impression left is ineffaceable. It was on the trials of faith, of which he gave different illustrations. He supposed, first, two children to be educated together, of similar tempera-

* I believe in Newman.

ment and under similar conditions, one of whom was baptized and the other unbaptized. He represented them as growing up equally amiable, equally upright, equally reverent and God-fearing, with no outward evidence that one was in a different spiritual condition from the other; yet we were required to believe, not only that their condition was totally different, but that one was a child of God, and his companion was not.

Again, he drew a sketch of the average men and women who made up society, whom we ourselves encountered in daily life, or were connected with, or read about in newspapers. They were neither special saints nor special sinners. Religious men had faults, and often serious ones. Men careless of religion were often amiable in private life—good husbands, good fathers, steady friends, in public honourable, brave, and patriotic. Even in the worst and wickedest, in a witch of Endor, there was a human heart and human tenderness. None seemed good enough for heaven, none so bad as to deserve to be consigned to the company of evil spirits, and to remain in pain and misery for ever. Yet all these people were, in fact, divided one from the other by an invisible line of separation. If they were to die on the spot as they actually were, some would be saved, the rest would be lost—the saved to have eternity of happiness, the lost to be with the devils in hell.

Again, I am not sure whether it was on the same occasion, but it was in following the same line of thought, Newman described closely some of the incidents of our Lord's passion; he then paused. For a few moments there was a breathless silence. Then, in a low, clear voice, of which the faintest vibration was audible in the farthest corner of St. Mary's, he said, 'Now, I bid you recollect that He to whom these things were done was Almighty God.' It was as if an electric stroke had gone through the church, as if every person present understood for the first time the meaning of what he had all his life been saying. I suppose it was an epoch in the mental history of more than one of my Oxford contemporaries.

JAMES RUSSELL LOWELL

*AT SEA**

THE SEA was meant to be looked at from shore, as mountains are from the plain. Lucretius made this discovery long ago, and was blunt enough to blurt it forth, romance and sentiment—in other words, the pretence of feeling what we do not feel—being inventions of a later day. To be sure, Cicero used to twaddle about Greek literature and philosophy, much as people do about ancient art nowadays; but I rather sympathize with those stout old Romans who despised both, and believed that to found an empire was as grand an achievement as to build an epic or to carve a statue. But though there might have been twaddle, (as why not, since there was a Senate?)

* Reprinted from *Literary Essays,* Vol 1, Fireside Edition, New York, 1890.

I rather think Petrarch was the first choragus of that sentimental dance which so long led young folks away from the realities of life like the piper of Hamelin, and whose succession ended, let us hope, with Chateaubriand. But for them, Byron, whose real strength lay in his sincerity, would never have talked about the "sea bounding beneath him like a steed that knows his rider," and all that sort of thing. Even if it had been true, steam has been as fatal to that part of the romance of the sea as to handloom weaving. But what say you to a twelve days' calm such as we dozed through in mid-Atlantic and in mid-August? I know nothing so tedious at once and exasperating as that regular slap of the wilted sails when the ship rises and falls with the slow breathing of the sleeping sea, one greasy, brassy swell following another, slow, smooth, immitigable as the series of Wordsworth's Ecclesiastical Sonnets. Even at his best, Neptune, in a *tête-à-tête*, has a way of repeating himself, an obtuseness to the *ne quid nimis,** that is stupefying. It reminds me of organ-music and my good friend Sebastian Bach. A fugue or two will do very well; but a concert made up of nothing else is altogether too epic for me. There is nothing so desperately monotonous as the sea, and I no longer wonder at the cruelty of pirates. Fancy an existence in which the coming up of a clumsy finback whale, who says Pooh! to you solemnly as you lean over the taffrail, is an event as exciting as an election on shore! The dampness seems to strike into the wits as into the lucifer-matches,† so that one may scratch a thought half a dozen times and get nothing at last but a faint sputter, the forlorn hope of fire, which only goes far enough to leave a sense of suffocation behind it. Even smoking becomes an employment instead of a solace. Who less likely to come to their wit's end than W. M. T. and A. H. C.?‡ Yet I have seen them driven to five meals a day for mental occupation. I sometimes sit and pity Noah; but even he had this advantage over all succeeding navigators, that, wherever he landed, he was sure to get no ill news from home. He should be canonized as the patron-saint of newspaper correspondents, being the only man who ever had the very last authentic intelligence from everywhere.

The finback whale recorded just above has much the look of a brown-paper parcel,—the whitish stripes that run across him answering for the pack-thread. He has a kind of accidental hole in the top of his head, through which he *pooh-poohs* the rest of creation, and which looks as if it had been made by the chance thrust of a chestnut rail. He was our first event. Our second was harpooning a sunfish, which basked dozing on the lap of the sea, looking so much like the giant turtle of an alderman's dream, that I am persuaded he would have let himself be made into mock-turtle soup rather than acknowledge his imposture. But he broke away just as they were hauling him over the side, and sank placidly through the clear water, leaving behind him a crimson trail that wavered a moment and was gone.

---

* Nothing too much.
† Lucifer was the trade name for a friction match produced in England in 1829.
‡ William Makepeace Thackeray and Arthur Hugh Clough.

The sea, though, has better sights than these. When we were up with the Azores, we began to meet flying-fish and Portuguese men-of-war beautiful as the galley of Cleopatra, tiny craft that dared these seas before Columbus. I have seen one of the former rise from the crest of a wave, and, glancing from another some two hundred feet beyond, take a fresh flight of perhaps as far. How Calderon would have similized this pretty creature had he ever seen it! How would he have run him up and down the gamut of simile! If a fish, then a fish with wings; if a bird, then a bird with fins; and so on, keeping up the light shuttle-cock of a conceit as is his wont. Indeed, the poor thing is the most killing bait for a comparison, and I assure you I have three or four in my inkstand;—but be calm, they shall stay there. Moore, who looked on all nature as a kind of *Gradus ad Parnassum,** a *thesaurus* of similitude, and spent his life in a game of What is my thought like? with himself, *did* the flying-fish on his way to Bermuda. So I leave him in peace.

The most beautiful thing I have seen at sea, all the more so that I had never heard of it, is the trail of a shoal of fish through the phosphorescent water. It is like a flight of silver rockets, or the streaming of northern lights through that silent nether heaven. I thought nothing could go beyond that rustling star-foam which was churned up by our ship's bows, or those eddies and disks of dreamy flame that rose and wandered out of sight behind us.

> 'Twas fire our ship was plunging through,
> Cold fire that o'er the quarter flew;
> And wandering moons of idle flame
> Grew full and waned, and went and came,
> Dappling with light the huge sea-snake
> That slid behind us in the wake.

But there was something even more delicately rare in the apparition of the fish, as they turned up in gleaming furrows the latent moonshine which the ocean seemed to have hoarded against these vacant interlunar nights. In the Mediterranean one day, as we were lying becalmed, I observed the water freckled with dingy specks, which at last gathered to a pinkish scum on the surface. The sea had been so phosphorescent for some nights, that when the Captain gave me my bath, by dousing me with buckets from the house on deck, the spray flew off my head and shoulders in sparks. It occurred to me that this dirty-looking scum might be the luminous matter, and I had a pailful dipped up to keep till after dark. When I went to look at it after nightfall, it seemed at first perfectly dead; but when I shook it, the whole broke out into what I can only liken to milky flames, whose lambent silence was strangely beautiful, and startled me almost as actual projection might an alchemist. I could not bear to be the death of so much beauty; so I poured it all overboard again.

Another sight worth taking a voyage for is that of the sails by moonlight.

* Steps to Parnassus.

Our course was "south and by east, half south," so that we seemed bound for the full moon as she rolled up over our wavering horizon. Then I used to go forward to the bowsprit and look back. Our ship was a clipper, with every rag set, stunsails, skyscrapers, and all; nor was it easy to believe that such a wonder could be built of canvas as that white many-storied pile of cloud that stooped over me or drew back as we rose and fell with the waves.

These are all the wonders I can recall of my five weeks at sea, except the sun. Were you ever alone with the sun? You think it a very simple question; but I never was, in the full sense of the word, till I was held up to him one cloudless day on the broad buckler of the ocean. I suppose one might have the same feeling in the desert. I remember getting something like it years ago, when I climbed alone to the top of a mountain, and lay face up on the hot gray moss, striving to get a notion of how an Arab might feel. It was my American commentary of the Koran, and not a bad one. In a New England winter, too, when everything is gagged with snow, as if some gigantic physical geographer were taking a cast of the earth's face in plaster, the bare knob of a hill will introduce you to the sun as a comparative stranger. But at sea you may be alone with him day after day, and almost all day long. I never understood before that nothing short of full daylight can give the supremest sense of solitude. Darkness will not do so, for the imagination peoples it with more shapes than ever were poured from the frozen loins of the populous North. The sun, I sometimes think, is a little *grouty* at sea, especially at high noon, feeling that he wastes his beams on those fruitless furrows. It is otherwise with the moon. She "comforts the night," as Chapman finely says, and I always found her a companionable creature.

In the ocean-horizon I took untiring delight. It is the true magic-circle of expectation and conjecture—almost as good as a wishing-ring. What will rise over that edge we sail towards daily and never overtake? A sail? an island? the new shore of the Old World? Something rose every day, which I need not have gone so far to see, but at whose levee I was a much more faithful courtier than on shore. A cloudless sunrise in mid-ocean is beyond comparison for simple grandeur. It is like Dante's style, bare and perfect. Naked sun meets naked sea, the true classic of nature. There may be more sentiment in morning on shore,—the shivering fairy-jewelry of dew, the silver point-lace of sparkling hoar-frost,—but there is also more complexity, more of the romantic. The one savors of the elder Edda,* the other of the Minnesingers.†

* A group of Icelandic poems of myth and religion belonging to the Middle Ages.
† Members of a group of German lyricists and singers of the Middle Ages.

HENRY JAMES

THE PONT DU GARD*

IT WAS a pleasure to feel one's self in Provence again,—the land where the silver-gray earth is impregnated with the light of the sky. To celebrate the event, as soon as I arrived at Nîmes I engaged a calèche to convey me to the Pont du Gard. The day was yet young, and it was perfectly fair; it appeared well, for a longish drive, to take advantage, without delay, of such security. After I had left the town I became more intimate with that Provençal charm which I had already enjoyed from the window of the train, and which glowed in the sweet sunshine and the white rocks, and lurked in the smoke-puffs of the little olives. The olive-trees in Provence are half the landscape. They are neither so tall, so stout, nor so richly contorted as I have seen them beyond the Alps; but this mild colorless bloom seems the very texture of the country. The road from Nîmes, for a distance of fifteen miles, is superb; broad enough for an army, and as white and firm as a dinner-table. It stretches away over undulations which suggest a kind of harmony; and in the curves it makes through the wide, free country, where there is never a hedge or a wall, and the detail is always exquisite, there is something majestic, almost processional. Some twenty minutes before I reached the little inn that marks the termination of the drive, my vehicle met with an accident which just missed being serious, and which engaged the attention of a gentleman, who, followed by his groom and mounted on a strikingly handsome horse, happened to ride up at the moment. This young man, who with his good looks and charming manner, might have stepped out of a novel of Octave Feuillet, gave me some very intelligent advice in reference to one of my horses that had been injured, and was so good as to accompany me to the inn, with the resources of which he was acquainted, to see that his recommendations were carried out. The result of our interview was that he invited me to come and look at a small but ancient château in the neighborhood, which he had the happiness—not the greatest in the world, he intimated—to inhabit, and at which I engaged to present myself after I should have spent an hour at the Pont du Gard. For the moment, when we separated, I gave all my attention to that great structure. You are very near it before you see it; the ravine it spans suddenly opens and exhibits the picture. The scene at this point grows extremely beautiful. The ravine is the valley of the Gardon, which the road from Nîmes has followed some time without taking account of it, but which, exactly at the right distance from the aqueduct, deepens and expands, and puts on those characteristics which are best suited to give it effect. The gorge becomes romantic, still, and solitary, and, with its white rocks and wild shrubbery, hangs over the clear, colored river, in whose slow course there is here and there a deeper pool. Over the valley, from side to side, and ever so high in the air, stretch the three tiers of the

* Reprinted from *A Little Tour in France,* Houghton Mifflin Company, Boston and New York, 1912.

tremendous bridge. They are unspeakably imposing, and nothing could be more Roman. The hugeness, the solidity, the unexpectedness, the monumental rectitude of the whole thing leave you nothing to say—at the time—and make you stand gazing. You simply feel that it is noble and perfect, that it has the quality of greatness. A road, branching from the highway, descends to the level of the river and passes under one of the arches. This road has a wide margin of grass and loose stones, which slopes upward into the bank of the ravine. You may sit here as long as you please, staring up at the light, strong piers; the spot is extremely natural, though two or three stone benches have been erected on it. I remained there an hour and got a complete impression; the place was perfectly soundless, and for the time, at least, lonely; the splendid afternoon had begun to fade, and there was a fascination in the object I had come to see. It came to pass that at the same time I discovered in it a certain stupidity, a vague brutality. That element is rarely absent from great Roman work, which is wanting in the nice adaptations of the means to the end. The means are always exaggerated; the end is so much more than attained. The Roman rigidity was apt to overshoot the mark, and I suppose a race which could do nothing small is as defective as a race than can do nothing great. Of this Roman rigidity the Pont du Gard is an admirable example. It would be a great injustice, however, not to insist upon its beauty,—a kind of manly beauty, that of an object constructed not to please but to serve, and impressive simply from the scale on which it carries out this intention. The number of arches in each tier is different; they are smaller and more numerous as they ascend. The preservation of the thing is extraordinary; nothing has crumbled or collapsed; every feature remains; and the huge blocks of stone, of a brownish-yellow (as if they had been baked by the Provençal sun for eighteen centuries), pile themselves, without mortar or cement, as evenly as the day they were laid together. All this to carry the water of a couple of springs to a little provincial city! The conduit on the top has retained its shape and traces of the cement with which it was lined. When the vague twilight began to gather, the lonely valley seemed to fill itself with the shadow of the Roman name, as if the mighty empire were still as erect as the supports of the aqueduct; and it was open to a solitary tourist, sitting there sentimental, to believe that no people has ever been, or will ever be, as great as that, measured, as we measure the greatness of an individual, by the push they gave to what they undertook. The Pont du Gard is one of the three or four deepest impressions they have left; it speaks of them in a manner with which they might have been satisfied.

I feel as if it were scarcely discreet to indicate the whereabouts of the château of the obliging young man I had met on the way from Nîmes; I must content myself with saying that it nestled in an enchanting valley,—*dans le fond*,* as they say in France,—and that I took my course thither on foot, after leaving the Pont du Gard. I find it noted in my journal as "an adorable little corner." The principal feature of the place is a couple of very ancient

* In the bottom,

towers, brownish-yellow in hue, and mantled in scarlet Virginia-creeper. One of these towers, reputed to be of Saracenic origin, is isolated, and is only the more effective; the other is incorporated in the house, which is delightfully fragmentary and irregular. It had got to be late by this time, and the lonely *castel* looked crepuscular and mysterious. An old housekeeper was sent for, who showed me the rambling interior; and then the young man took me into a dim old drawing-room, which had no less than four chimney-pieces, all unlighted, and gave me a refection of fruit and sweet wine. When I praised the wine and asked him what it was, he said simply, "C'est du vin de ma mère!"* Throughout my little journey I had never yet felt myself so far from Paris; and this was a sensation I enjoyed more than my host, who was an involuntary exile, consoling himself with laying out a *manège*,† which he showed me as I walked away. His civility was great, and I was greatly touched by it. On my way back to the little inn where I had left my vehicle, I passed the Pont du Gard, and took another look at it. Its great arches made windows for the evening sky, and the rocky ravine, with its dusky cedars and shining river, was lonelier than before. At the inn I swallowed, or tried to swallow, a glass of horrible wine with my coachman; after which, with my reconstructed team, I drove back to Nîmes in the moonlight. It only added a more solitary whiteness to the constant sheen of the Provençal landscape.

EMILY BRONTE

WUTHERING HEIGHTS‡

WUTHERING HEIGHTS is the name of Mr. Heathcliff's dwelling. 'Wuthering' being a significant provincial adjective, descriptive of the atmospheric tumult to which its station is exposed in stormy weather. Pure, bracing ventilation they must have up there at all times, indeed: one may guess the power of the north wind blowing over the edge, by the excessive slant of a few stunted firs at the end of the house; and by a range of gaunt thorns all stretching their limbs one way, as if craving alms of the sun. Happily, the architect had foresight to build it strong: the narrow windows are deeply set in the wall, and the corners defended with large jutting stones.

Before passing the threshold, I paused to admire a quantity of grotesque carving lavished over the front, and especially about the principal door; above which, among a wilderness of crumbling griffins and shameless little boys, I detected the date '1500' and the name 'Hareton Earnshaw.' I would

* "It is my mother's wine."
† A riding-school.
‡ Reprinted from Chapter I.

have made a few comments, and requested a short history of the place from the surly owner; but his attitude at the door appeared to demand my speedy entrance, or complete departure, and I had no desire to aggravate his impatience previous to inspecting the penetralium.

One step brought us into the family sitting-room, without any introductory lobby or passage: they call it here 'the house' pre-eminently. It includes kitchen and parlour, generally; but I believe at Wuthering Heights the kitchen is forced to retreat altogether into another quarter: at least I distinguished a chatter of tongues, and a clatter of culinary utensils, deep within; and I observed no signs of roasting, boiling, or baking, about the huge fire-place; nor any glitter of copper saucepans and tin cullenders on the walls. One end, indeed, reflected splendidly both light and heat from ranks of immense pewter dishes, interspersed with silver jugs and tankards, towering row after row, on a vast oak dresser, to the very roof. The latter had never been underdrawn: its entire anatomy lay bare to an inquiring eye, except where a frame of wood laden with oatcakes and clusters of legs of beef, mutton, and ham, concealed it. Above the chimney were sundry villainous old guns, and a couple of horse-pistols: and, by way of ornament, three gaudily painted canisters disposed along its ledge. The floor was of smooth, white stone; the chairs, high-backed, primitive structures, painted green: one or two heavy black ones lurking in the shade. In an arch under the dresser, reposed a huge, liver-coloured bitch pointer, surrounded by a swarm of squealing puppies; and other dogs haunted other recesses.

The apartment and furniture would have been nothing extraordinary as belonging to a homely, northern farmer, with a stubborn countenance, and stalwart limbs set out to advantage in knee-breeches and gaiters. Such an individual seated in his armchair, his mug of ale frothing on the round table before him, is to be seen in any circuit of five or six miles among these hills, if you go at the right time after dinner. But Mr. Heathcliff forms a singular contrast to his abode and style of living. He is a dark-skinned gypsy in aspect, in dress and manners a gentleman: that is, as much a gentleman as many a country squire: rather slovenly, perhaps, yet not looking amiss with his negligence, because he has an erect and handsome figure; and rather morose. Possibly, some people might suspect him of a degree of under-bred pride; I have a sympathetic chord within that tells me it is nothing of the sort: I know, by instinct, his reserve springs from an aversion to showy displays of feeling—to manifestations of mutual kindliness. He'll love and hate equally under cover, and esteem it a species of impertinence to be loved or hated again. No, I'm running on too fast: I bestow my own attributes over liberally on him. Mr. Heathcliff may have entirely dissimilar reasons for keeping his hand out of the way when he meets a would-be acquaintance, to those which actuate me. Let me hope my constitution is almost peculiar: my dear mother used to say I should never have a comfortable home; and only last summer I proved myself perfectly unworthy of one.

While enjoying a month of fine weather at the sea-coast, I was thrown into the company of a most fascinating creature: a real goddess in my eyes, as long as she took no notice of me. I 'never told my love' vocally; still, if looks have language, the merest idiot might have guessed I was over head and ears: she understood me at last, and looked a return—the sweetest of all imaginable looks. And what did I do? I confess it with shame—shrunk icily into myself, like a snail; at every glance retired colder and farther; till finally the poor innocent was led to doubt her own senses, and, overwhelmed with confusion at her supposed mistake, persuaded her mamma to decamp. By this curious turn of disposition I have gained the reputation of deliberate heartlessness; how undeserved, I alone can appreciate.

I took a seat at the end of the hearthstone opposite that towards which my landlord advanced, and filled up an interval of silence by attempting to caress the canine mother, who had left her nursery, and was sneaking wolfishly to the back of my legs, her lip curled up, and her white teeth watering for a snatch. My caress provoked a long, guttural snarl.

'You'd better let the dog alone,' growled Mr. Heathcliff in unison, checking fiercer demonstrations with a punch of his foot. 'She's not accustomed to be spoiled—not kept for a pet.' Then, striding to a side door, he shouted again, 'Joseph!'

Joseph mumbled indistinctly in the depths of the cellar, but gave no intimation of ascending; so his master dived down to him, leaving me *vis-à-vis* the ruffianly bitch and a pair of grim shaggy sheep-dogs, who shared with her a jealous guardianship over all my movements. Not anxious to come in contact with their fangs, I sat still; but, imagining they would scarcely understand tacit insults, I unfortunately indulged in winking and making faces at the trio, and some turn of my physiognomy so irritated madam, that she suddenly broke into a fury, and leapt on my knees. I flung her back, and hastened to interpose the table between us. This proceeding roused the whole hive. Half-a-dozen four-footed fiends, of various sizes and ages, issued from hidden dens to the common centre. I felt my heels and coat-laps peculiar subjects of assault; and, parrying off the larger combatants as effectually as I could with the poker, I was constrained to demand, aloud, assistance from some of the household in reestablishing peace.

Mr. Heathcliff and his man climbed the cellar steps with vexatious phlegm: I don't think they moved one second faster than usual, though the hearth was an absolute tempest of worrying and yelping. Happily, an inhabitant of the kitchen made more dispatch: a lusty dame, with tucked-up gown, bare arms, and fire-flushed cheeks, rushed into the midst of us flourishing a frying-pan: and used that weapon, and her tongue, to such purpose, that the storm subsided magically, and she only remained, heaving like a sea after a high wind, when her master entered on the scene.

'What the devil is the matter?' he asked, eyeing me in a manner I could ill endure after this inhospitable treatment.

'What the devil, indeed!' I muttered. 'The herd of possessed swine could have had no worse spirits in them than those animals of yours, sir. You might as well leave a stranger with a brood of tigers!'

'They won't meddle with persons who touch nothing,' he remarked, putting the bottle before me, and restoring the displaced table. 'The dogs do right to be vigilant. Take a glass of wine?'

'No thank you.'

'Not bitten, are you?'

'If I had been, I would have set my signet on the biter.'

Heathcliff's countenance relaxed into a grin.

'Come, come,' he said, 'you are flurried, Mr. Lockwood. Here, take a little wine. Guests are so exceedingly rare in this house that I and my dogs, I am willing to own, hardly know how to receive them. Your health, sir!'

I bowed and returned the pledge; beginning to perceive that it would be foolish to sit sulking for the misbehaviour of a pack of curs: besides, I felt loath to yield the fellow further amusement at my expense; since his humour took that turn. He—probably swayed by prudential considerations of the folly of offending a good tenant—relaxed a little in the laconic style of chipping off his pronouns and auxiliary verbs, and introduced what he supposed would be a subject of interest to me,—a discourse on the advantages and disadvantages of my present place of retirement. I found him very intelligent on the topics we touched; and before I went home, I was encouraged so far as to volunteer another visit to-morrow. He evidently wished no repetition of my intrusion. I shall go, notwithstanding. It is astonishing how sociable I feel myself compared with him.

R. B. CUNNINGHAME GRAHAM

THE PLAINS OF VENEZUELA*

Man has not staled their wildness, and they still stretch out along the Orinoco, the Apure, and the Arauca to the far-distant Meta, just as they first came from the Creator's hand when on the seventh day He rested from a work that He must surely now and then regret. A very sea of grass and sky, sun-scourged and hostile to mankind. The rivers, full of electric eels, and of caribes, those most ravenous of fish, more terrible than even the great alligators that lie like logs upon the sandbarks or the inert and pulpy rays, with their mortiferous barbed spike, are still more hostile than the land.

In the four hundred years the Llanos have been known to Europeans man has done little more than to endow them with herds of cattle and with bands of half-wild horses and of asses that roam upon them just as their ancestors roamed the steppes of Asia from the remotest times. Islets of stunted palm-

* From *Rodeo*. Copyright 1936 by Doubleday and Company, Inc. Reprinted by permission. Permission for Canada granted by John Johnson, author's agent.

trees break the surface of the plains, as the atolls peep up in the Pacific Ocean and also bear their palms. The sun pours down like molten fire for six months of the year, burning the grass up, forcing the cattle to stray leagues away along the river banks, or in the depths of the thick woods. Then come the rains, and the dry, calcined plains are turned into a muddy lake, on which the whilom centaurs of the dry season paddle long, crank canoes dug from a single log.

The Llanos, with their race of half-amphibious herdsmen, but little differing in features and in hue from their ancestors, the Achagua Indians, have been the scene of great events. They have had their days of glory, when they were almost household words in Europe during the great struggle for the independence of the Spanish Colonies, a hundred years ago. At the Queseras del Medio, by their aid, Paez, Prince of Llaneros, and almost the last good lance that villainous saltpetre has left to history, broke the cavalry of Spain. Out of the woods, sheltered behind the smoke of the dry grass they had set on fire, the saddleless, wild horsemen, half-naked, with but a rag or two tied round their bodies by a thong of hide, swooped on the uniformed, drilled, disciplined, brave, heavy-handed Spanish troopers, like the riders of the Valkyrie. Paez, himself as wild and savage in those days as any of his men, rode at their head upon a half-tamed colt. Those were not days of tactics, for personal prowess, perhaps for the last time in history, ruled everything. It must have been a glorious sight to see their charge, the flying hair, the tossing manes and tails, the dust, the shrill screams of the attacking horsemen, the answering shouts of "Viva España" of the Spanish troops, the frightened taotacos whirling above them uttering their harsh note, while in the sky the vultures sailed aloft, like specks against the sapphire blue, knowing a banquet was being set for them. To-day the Llanos that furnished the troops with which Paez so ably seconded Bolivar in his long fight for independence are almost depopulated. No one seems to know the cause.

Though much of the population has gone, enough remains to herd the cattle, the vast Llanos' only wealth. Unlike the Gauchos and the Mexicans, the Roman Butari, the Arabs of North Africa, the Western cowboy (before fell cinemas made a puppet of him), any old saddle, any clothes, content the dweller on the plains of the Apure. His horse is almost always thin, often sore-backed, and always looks uncared for, while the ungainly pace at which he rides, a shambling "pasitrote," or tied camel waddle, moving both feet on the same side at once, deprives him of all grace. Still few can equal, none excel, him for endurance. Nothing daunts him, neither the peril of the rivers, with all their enemies to mankind ever awake, to tear or numb the unlucky horseman who may come near their fangs or their electrically charged bodies or any other danger either by flood or field. He, of all wielders of the raw-hide noose, alone secures it, not to the saddle, but to his horse's tail, fishing for, rather than lassoing a steer, playing it like a salmon with a rope a hundred feet in length, instead of bringing it up with a smart jerk, after the fashion of the Argentines or Mexicans. Abominably slow and tedious in his methods to the eyes of commentators; still it is never wise, in matters of such deep import, to criticise or to condemn customs that use and wont have consecrated.

If the Llaneros have changed outwardly, the Llano has remained the same. No puffing steam engine or petrol-reeking car defiles its surface. Diligences it has never had, and the sole method for a caballero when he wants to traverse it is on a horse. Some indeed may have ridden mules. Camels and asses, with llamas, yaks, bullocks, and buffaloes, no doubt can carry man upon their backs, but on the horse alone can he be truly said to ride. So the Llanero still rides the Llano on his pacing horse, the reins held high, the stirrups dangling from his naked toe, his eyes fixed on the horizon, as a sailor, on his watch, looks out across the sea. The mirage still hangs castles in the air and cheats the eye in the terrific heat with pools of water, always just out of touch, as happiness is ever out of reach in life. The Promised Land is always a day's march ahead of us.

Unchanging and unchanged, the Llanos swelter in the sun as they first sweltered at the creation of the world, and as La Puebla saw them in the expedition that Maestre Diego Albeniz de la Cerrada describes, he who wrote, as it were in a mirage, his observation so minute, his gift of artistry so great, and with his dates, and trifles of that nature, all awry. So distant are the Llanos from our vainglorious, noisy, and evil-smelling civilization, as to be almost unaware that such a thing exists. They await the coming of the thing called progress, just as a girl may dream about her marriage night without exactly knowing what it means.

Meanwhile, through palm woods looking exactly like those of the Argentine Gran Chaco, through jungle and through woods, in dust, in rain, under a sun that blisters, if you touch an iron stirrup, the post of the republic carried in canvas bags on two grey mules accompanied by an apocalyptic horse, trails wearily across the plains. If in their pilgrimage the mules, the old white horse, and the dark half-breeds chance to light on a Velorio,* or a wedding at a rancho on the road, they join in it, for after all to-morrow is another day, and time is certainly not money, under the rule of him whose fellow-citizens style "El Benemerito." †

Even the garden by the Tigris could hardly have been fairer or more bird-haunted than the banks of the Apure, with its myriads of egrets making the trees as white as is a northern wood after a fall of snow. Legions of aquatic birds as black as jet sweep down the rivers in battalions, succeeding one another as if some feathered general was marshaling them to fight.

Flocks of flamingos rise from the waters, as Aphrodite rose up from the waves, rosy and beautiful. Piero di Cosimo alone could have dealt with them in paint, and if the painter of the "Death of Procris" had but visited the Apure, among his pelicans, his flamingos, and his swans, he would have placed new species, as fit to grace his theme and far more gorgeous than the

* Viewing of the dead.   † The Worthy One.

birds of the old world. In the freshness of the dawn, when a white mist bathes all the woods upon the rivers in a thin vaporous haze through which the trees show faintly, as a rich purple or green burnous tinges the fleecy whiteness of an Arab's haik, nature exults in the new birth of day.

The Llano for a brief moment turns to a tender green and stretches out like an interminable fresh field of corn. From the recesses of the woods along the river banks comes the harsh screaming of the parrot, and birds and insects raise their morning hymn of praise. Stilled are the voices of the prowling animals of prey, insistent during night. The jaguar no longer snarls, or whets his teeth against the tree trunks. The red, howling monkeys start their chorus, sounding as if a lion was raging in the everglades, and the shy tapir after a night passed feeding on the sedges and the grass swims to his lair, his head and back just showing, like a river horse, leaving a silvery trail behind him to mark his silent passage through the stream. Wild cattle troop back to the woods, before the vaqueros intercept them with their swift horses and their unerring noose.

Without an interval of crepuscule, the sun rises at once fierce, fiery, and inexorable, streaking the sky with rays of orange and of scarlet for an instant, then bursts upon the world like a fell enemy before whom fly all living things except the saurians, who bask somnolently upon the sandbanks, immune against his rays. Just at the break of dawn fish leap in shoals into the air, making the water boil, their silvery bodies for a moment springing like crescent moons into the air and falling with a splash into the deep. His well-greased lazo ready coiled in front of his right knee, his brown, bare toes sticking out through his alpargatas,* clutching the light Llanero stirrup with its crownlike prolongation underneath the foot, the Llanero scans the horizon as his horse paces rapidly along, leaving a well-marked trail upon the dewy grass. He sits so loosely in the saddle that one would think if his horse shied it must unseat him, but that he also shies. High on his vaquero† saddle, so straight and upright that a plummet dropped from his shoulder would touch his heel, he reads the Llano like a book.

Nothing escapes his sight, as keen as that of his Achagua Indian ancestors. Signs on the ground, almost undiscernible, he marks. If his horse, trippling along at its artificial gait, stumbles or pecks, he curses it, objurgating its female ancestry, gives a sharp pull with the bit, digs in his spurs, interrupts for a moment the interminable "galeron"‡ that he is crooning in a low voice, and pointing with his whip says, "Three horses passed along here early in the night. One is the big cream colour that always strays, for he is a little lame in the off hind foot, see where he has stepped short upon it." With an unerring eye he sights a steer with a strange brand. "That is one of General Atilio Pacheco's animals," he says, and turning to his companion, smiling, remarks, "If he stays too long in these parts he may stay for ever, for God is not a bad man, anyhow."

* Sandals.   † Cowboy.   ‡ Popular air.

As the sun rises higher in the heavens, the light distorting everything, magnifying or diminishing, according as its rays are refracted, dried tufts of grass appear as large as clumps of canes, and animals on the horizon as small as turkey buzzards. Then the vaquero heads for home, after assuring himself that no bullock has been killed by a tiger in the night, or has got wounded from any cause and requires treatment to prevent maggots from breeding in the wound. Clouds of dust rise on the horizon. The morning breeze dies out entirely during the hottest hours, and the plain shimmers in the heat. Bancos and mesas,* those curious sand formations that intersect the Llanos like striations in a rock, give back refracted heat to meet the heat descending from above. All nature groans. Only the lizards and iguanas seem to revel in it. Homing vaqueros, their "pelo de Guama"† hats coal-scuttled fore and aft against the enemy, lounge in their saddles. Their horses plod along, with drooping heads, too weary even to swish their tails against the flies. At the straw-thatched houses the riders get off with a sigh and seek the shade of the "caney."‡

As the heat waxes and the air quivers as if it came from some interior furnace, a deathly silence broods upon the plains. A sense of solitude creeps over everything, as if the world had been consumed by some unlooked-for cataclysm that had destroyed mankind. The weary horses, who endure the burden of their lives either parched with thirst, or forced to live a half-amphibious life during the periodical inundations, exposed year in, year out, to the perpetual torment of mosquitoes, horse-flies, ticks and all the "plagas"‡‡ of the insect world, with the off-chance of sudden death from the fangs of tiger or caiman, seek shelter where they can, under the scanty foliage of the Moriche palms. Cattle have long ago retired as far as possible into the reedy swamps. Nothing is stirring; not a sound breaks the afflicted silence of the sun-cursed plain, but the perpetual calling "Oh, ah ho" of the small, speckled doves. Gradually the heat decreases, a breeze springs up, and nature, after her long struggle with the sun, revives.

The animals, who have passed the hot hours under whatever shade that they could find, recommence eating and birds show signs of life. Parrots scream harshly. Flights of macaws, yellow and red and blue, the great white patches round their eyes making them look as if they all wore spectacles, soar like parti-coloured hawks, uttering their croaking cry. The interval of freshness is all too brief, for night falls without twilight on the Llanos; and the sun dips down under the horizon just as he does at sea.

Before the darkness closes in, flights of birds migrate towards the woods, fire-flies dart to and fro among the dark metallic leaves of the jungle fringing the river, and from the recesses of the forests the nightly chorus of the wild animals, silent through the day, breaks out. Then comes the miracle; the

---

* Small hills and plateaus.
† Literally, Guama fiber. The guama (usually not capitalized) is the fruit of the guamo tree.
‡ Log cabin.   ‡‡ Plagues.

miracle of miracles, unknown to those who have not journeyed on those interminable steppes or sailed upon the Apure or the Orinoco. No words can paint the infinite gradation of the scale of colour that leaves the spectroscope lacking a shade or two. Green turns to mauve, then back to green again; to scarlet, orange, and vermilion, flinging the flag of Spain across the sky. Dark coffee-coloured bars, shooting across a sea of carmine, deepen to black; the carmine melts into pale grey. Castles and pyramids spring up; they turn to cities; the pyramids to broken arches, waterfalls, and ships, with poops like argosies. Gradually pale apple-green floods all the heaven; then it fades into jade. Castles and towns and ships and broken arches disappear. The sun sinks in a globe of fire, leaving the world in mourning for its death.

Then comes the after-glory, when all the colours that have united, separated, blended and broken up, unite and separate again, and once more blend. A sheet of flame, that for an instant turns the Apure into a streak of molten metal, bathes the Llano in a bath of fire, fades gradually and dies, just where the plain and sky appear to join as if the grass was all aglow.

Argumentation

ARGUMENTATION

Aʀɢᴜᴍᴇɴᴛᴀᴛɪᴏɴ ʜᴀs long been one of the four traditional forms of communication; the other three are exposition, description, and narration. The function of exposition is to explain, to show or state something. Description attempts to create a vivid picture of persons, places, and things, and narration presents a story, factual or fictional, using chronology or time sequence.

Argument may be defined as the process by which one arrives at truth and persuades others to believe and act upon it. Argument is concerned with the gathering together and testing of facts, and attempts to proceed by applying reasons to these facts, in order to draw inferences as to their relationships and meanings.

Argumentation, then, is an attempt to try to convince or persuade ourselves and others of the truth of a certain proposition because every argument is based on a *proposition*. The subject and predicate are called *terms*. If there is a single *term*, there is no basis for argumentation. One cannot argue "Communism" or "Capitalism" or "Capital Punishment"; but one can argue "Communism is a success"; or "Communism is a failure." One can argue "Capitalism is the right way of life"; or "Capitalism is the wrong way of life." One can consider: "Capital punishment should be abolished"; or "Capital punishment should not be abolished."

It must be remembered, then, that there are always two sides to every discussion: one of affirmation, one of denial. If facts are one-sided, there is no argument; if the facts are evenly balanced, there is no conclusion. Both sides must be considered; the facts or evidence must be weighed, and an attempt be made to reach a justifiable conclusion.

Since time began, everyone has taken pleasure in arguing about virtually every subject, serious or amusing, of any interest to the mind of man. Orally or in writing, man has had his say.

In today's world people argue about everything of current interest. In groups of average persons one can hear about the merits and defects of rock and roll music, about the society of the beatniks, about baseball batting averages, and even about the place of religion in a pluralistic society. Discussions mostly about serious problems are heard daily on radio and television programs. But the editorial writers for the newspapers and magazines quite possibly exert the most influence in their attempts to persuade and convince the literate public on all major issues facing our nation and the world. These writers are now arguing the effects of nuclear fall-out, the race problem, juvenile delinquency, inflation, and many other grave and pressing problems. Most of these men of intelligence argue from evidence—a direct method; many non-writers argue merely from hearsay. The former argue from authority; the latter, quite often, argue from no evidence at all. Whatever the approach, man will continue to argue until time is no more.

The timely and argumentative essays which follow are worthy of analysis.

Ivor Brown's essay "In Praise of Clarity" details—although he may be guilty of overstatement—the importance of clearly-defined speech in this age which tries to confuse the reader through the use of esoteric and recondite language. Ananda K. Coomaraswamy's controversial "What Use is Art Anyway?" examines the value of art in modern society, and G. K. Chesterton's provocative article on "The Fallacy of Success" explodes a common twentieth-century myth. These articles are not presented with the intention of persuading the student to the writers' point of view, but rather with that of stimulating him to a critical response, whether of agreement or disagreement.

T. S. ELIOT

HAMLET AND HIS PROBLEMS*

Few critics have ever admitted that *Hamlet* the play is the primary problem, and Hamlet the character only secondary. And Hamlet the character has had an especial temptation for that most dangerous type of critic: the critic with a mind which is naturally of the creative order, but which through some weakness in creative power exercises itself in criticism instead. These minds often find in Hamlet a vicarious existence for their own artistic realization. Such a mind had Goethe, who made of Hamlet a Werther; and such had Coleridge, who made of Hamlet a Coleridge; and probably neither of these men in writing about Hamlet remembered that his first business was to study a work of art. The kind of criticism that Goethe and Coleridge produced, in writing of Hamlet, is the most misleading kind possible. For they both possessed unquestionable critical insight, and both make their critical aberrations the more plausible by the substitution—of their own Hamlet for Shakespeare's—which their creative gift effects. We should be thankful that Walter Pater did not fix his attention on this play.

Two writers of our time,† Mr. J. M. Robertson and Professor Stoll of the University of Minnesota, have issued small books which can be praised for moving in the other direction. Mr. Stoll performs a service in recalling to our attention the labours of the critics of the seventeenth and eighteenth centuries, observing that "they knew less about psychology than more recent Hamlet critics, but they were nearer in spirit to Shakespeare's art; and as they insisted on the importance of the effect of the whole rather than on the importance of the leading character, they were nearer, in their old-fashioned way, to the secret of dramatic art in general."

Qua work of art, the work of art cannot be interpreted; there is nothing to interpret; we can only criticise it according to standards, in comparison to other works of art; and for "interpretation" the chief task is the presenta-

* Reprinted from *Selected Essays* 1917–1932. Copyright, 1932, by Harcourt, Brace and Company, Inc. By permission of the publisher. For Canada, permission granted by Faber and Faber, Ltd.
† The present essay was written in 1919.

tion of relevant historical facts which the reader is not assumed to know. Mr. Robertson points out, very pertinently, how critics have failed in their "interpretation" of *Hamlet* by ignoring what ought to be very obvious; that *Hamlet* is a stratification, that it represents the efforts of a series of men, each making what he could out of the work of his predecessors. The *Hamlet* of Shakespeare will appear to us very differently if, instead of treating the whole action of the play as due to Shakespeare's design, we perceive his *Hamlet* to be superposed upon much cruder material which persists even in the final form.

We know that there was an older play by Thomas Kyd, that extraordinary dramatic (if not poetic) genius who was in all probability the author of two plays so dissimilar as *The Spanish Tragedy* and *Arden of Feversham;* and what this play was like we can guess from three clues: from *The Spanish Tragedy* itself, from the tale of Belleforest upon which Kyd's *Hamlet* must have been based, and from a version acted in Germany in Shakespeare's life-time which bears strong evidence of having been adapted from the earlier, not from the later, play. From these three sources it is clear that in the earlier play the motive was a revenge-motive simply; that the action or delay is caused, as in *The Spanish Tragedy*, solely by the difficulty of assassinating a monarch surrounded by guards; and that the "madness" of Hamlet was feigned in order to escape suspicion, and successfully. In the final play of Shakespeare, on the other hand, there is a motive which is more important than that of revenge, and which explicitly "blunts" the latter; the delay in revenge is unexplained on grounds of necessity or expediency; and the effect of the "madness" is not to lull but to arouse the king's suspicion. The altera-tion is not complete enough, however, to be convincing. Furthermore, there are verbal parallels so close to *The Spanish Tragedy* as to leave no doubt that in places Shakespeare was merely *revising* the text of Kyd. And finally there are unexplained scenes—the Polonius-Laertes and the Polonius-Reynaldo scenes—for which there is little excuse; these scenes are not in the verse style of Kyd, and not beyond doubt in the style of Shakespeare. These Mr. Robert-son believes to be scenes in the original play of Kyd reworked by a third hand, perhaps Chapman, before Shakespeare touched the play. And he con-cludes, with very strong show of reason, that the original play of Kyd was, like certain other revenge plays, in two parts of five acts each. The upshot of Mr. Robertson's examination is, we believe, irrefragable: that Shakespeare's *Hamlet*, so far as it is Shakespeare's, is a play dealing with the effect of a mother's guilt upon her son, and that Shakespeare was unable to impose this motive successfully upon the "intractable" material of the old play.

Of the intractability there can be no doubt. So far from being Shake-speare's masterpiece, the play is most certainly an artistic failure. In several ways the play is puzzling, and disquieting as is none of the others. Of all the plays it is the longest and is possibly the one on which Shakespeare spent most pains; and yet he has left in it superfluous and inconsistent scenes which even hasty revision should have noticed. The versification is variable. Lines like

> Look, the morn, in russet mantle clad,
> Walks o'er the dew of yon high eastern hill,

are of the Shakespeare of *Romeo and Juliet*. The lines in Act i, sc. ii,

> Sir, in my heart there was a kind of fighting
> That would not let me sleep . . .
> Up from my cabin
> My sea-gown scarf'd about me, in the dark
> Grop'd I to find out them: had my desire;
> Finger'd their packet;

are of his quite mature. Both workmanship and thought are in an unstable position. We are surely justified in attributing the play, with that other profoundly interesting play of "intractable" material and astonishing versification, *Measure for Measure*, to a period of crisis, after which follow the tragic successes which culminate in *Coriolanus*. *Coriolanus* may be not as "interesting" as *Hamlet*, but it is, with *Antony and Cleopatra*, Shakespeare's most assured artistic success. And probably more people have thought *Hamlet* a work of art because they found it interesting, than have found it interesting because it is a work of art. It is the "Mona Lisa" of literature.

The grounds of *Hamlet's* failure are not immediately obvious. Mr. Robertson is undoubtedly correct in concluding that the essential emotion of the play is the feeling of a son towards a guilty mother:

> "(Hamlet's) tone is that of one who has suffered tortures on the score of his mother's degradation. . . . The guilt of a mother is an almost intolerable motive for drama, but it had to be maintained and emphasized to supply a psychological solution, or rather a hint of one."

This, however, is by no means the whole story. It is not merely the "guilt of a mother" that cannot be handled as Shakespeare handled the suspicion of Othello, the infatuation of Antony, or the pride of Coriolanus. The subject might conceivably have expanded into a tragedy like these, intelligible, self-complete, in the sunlight. *Hamlet*, like the sonnets, is full of some stuff that the writer could not drag to light, contemplate, or manipulate into art. And when we search for this feeling, we find it, as in the sonnets, very difficult to localize. You cannot point to it in the speeches; indeed, if you examine the two famous soliloquies you see the versification of Shakespeare, but a content which might be claimed by another, perhaps by the author of the *Revenge of Bussy d'Ambois*, Act v, sc. i. We find Shakespeare's Hamlet not in the action, not in any quotations that we might select, so much as in an unmistakable tone which is unmistakably not in the earlier play.

The only way of expressing emotion in the form of art is by finding an "objective correlative"; in other words, a set of objects, a situation, a chain of events which shall be the formula of the *particular* emotion; such that when the external facts, which must terminate in sensory experience, are given, the emotion is immediately evoked. If you examine any of Shakespeare's more successful tragedies, you will find this exact equivalence; you will find that the state of mind of Lady Macbeth walking in her sleep has been communicated to you by a skilful accumulation of imagined sensory impressions; the words of Macbeth on hearing of his wife's death strike us as if, given the sequence of events, these words were automatically released by the last event in the series. The artistic "inevitability" lies in this complete adequacy of the external to the emotion; and this is precisely what is deficient in *Hamlet*. Hamlet (the man) is dominated by an emotion which is inexpressible, because it is in *excess* of the facts as they appear. And the supposed identity of Hamlet with his author is genuine to this point: that Hamlet's bafflement at the absence of objective equivalent to his feelings is a prolongation of the bafflement of his creator in the face of his artistic problem. Hamlet is up against the difficulty that his disgust is occasioned by his mother, but that his mother is not an adequate equivalent for it; his disgust envelops and exceeds her. It is thus a feeling which he cannot understand; he cannot objectify it, and it therefore remains to poison life and obstruct action. None of the possible actions can satisfy it; and nothing that Shakespeare can do with the plot can express Hamlet for him. And it must be noticed that the very nature of the *données* of the problem precludes objective equivalence. To have heightened the criminality of Gertrude would have been to provide the formula for a totally different emotion in Hamlet; it is just *because* her character is so negative and insignificant that she arouses in Hamlet the feeling which she is incapable of representing.

The "madness" of Hamlet lay to Shakespeare's hand; in the earlier play a simple ruse, and to the end, we may presume, understood as a ruse by the audience. For Shakespeare it is less than madness and more than feigned. The levity of Hamlet, his repetition of phrase, his puns, are not part of a deliberate plan of dissimulation, but a form of emotional relief. In the character Hamlet it is the buffoonery of an emotion which can find no outlet in action; in the dramatist it is the buffoonery of an emotion which he cannot express in art. The intense feeling, ecstatic or terrible, without an object or exceeding its object, is something which every person of sensibility has known; it is doubtless a subject of study for pathologists. It often occurs in adolescence: the ordinary person puts these feelings to sleep, or trims down his feelings to fit the business world; the artist keeps them alive by his ability to intensify the world to his emotions. The Hamlet of Laforgue is an adolescent; the Hamlet of Shakespeare is not, he has not that explanation and excuse. We must simply admit that here Shakespeare tackled a problem which proved too much for him. Why he attempted it at all is an insoluble puzzle; under compulsion of what experience he attempted to express the inexpressibly horrible, we cannot ever know. We need a great many facts in his biography; and we should like to know whether, and when, and after or at the same time as what personal experience, he read Montaigne, II. xii, *Apologie de Raimond Sebond*. We should have, finally, to know something which is by hypothesis unknowable, for we assume it to be an experience which, in the manner indicated, exceeded the facts. We should have to understand things which Shakespeare did not understand himself.

JOYCE CARY

VALUE AND MEANING*

THE GROWTH of every soul is mysterious and full of chances. It is the dream of every Utopian to throw luck out of the world—the luck of birth, of brains, of beauty, of fate—to make all destinies equal. That is a dream that can't be realised. The world is inescapably shot through with luck, because it is also shot through with freedom. It is in the field given over to luck, the field of the unconditioned, that the free soul operates, and one man's art is another's luck, one teacher's prejudice is the making or the ruin of a poet.

Luck remains and children will always have different abilities, different kinds of home, different fates, in experience. But it is still the duty of government and parents to battle with luck, to try to give the equal chance. And the front of that battle is education. The education of the writer is necessarily the education offered to other children, and what I am arguing is that it can't be too good, too definite. You can't preserve his youthful intuition. The child poet and writer, in my own experience, loses his powers even more quickly than the child painter. For he starts his education in the arts of the word, he is getting ideas about life, while the other is still being allowed to amuse himself with a colour-box.

No one, in short, escapes a conceptual and technical education in the use of words and ideas, and the only question is, how good should it be. I'm saying that it should be as good as possible. For the chance of destroying an original genius by too much scholarship, too rigid a conceptual drill, is much less than that of leaving him, when at last he is ready to do mature work, with a muddled mind and a feeble grasp of elementary technique.

The most sensible critic of the artistic education agrees to the absolute necessity of factual and conceptual knowledge and a dogmatic framework to give these facts value and meaning. But he says the trouble is not there but in the bias of the teachers who convey their own prejudices, who try to form their pupils' tastes, to bring them to be little copies of their teachers. This, he says, is the real disaster in academic education, not only for artists, but musicians, writers, architects. The old men who have a grip on all the schools, on all the universities, hate the original mind. They can't understand

* Reprinted from *Art and Reality*. Copyright 1958 by Arthur Lucius Michael Cary and David Alexander Ogilvie, executors of the estate of Joyce Cary. By permission of Harper and Brothers. For Canada, permission granted by Cambridge University Press.

it and, as pedants, they hate what they can't understand. Why not then get rid of this bias and find teachers without it? Let them teach without bias. Let them teach the facts, suggest a meaning for the facts, offer a theory to explain them, but not as an irrefutable dogma. For instance, let them say of poetry, 'This is Wordsworth's theory about good writing, but it was not Pope's. Take your choice.' Or of history, 'This is how Marx explains the march of events, and this is the Cambridge history. Here are the arguments, make up your own mind.'

There is a lot of truth and sense in this argument. For most teaching, especially in the arts, has a good deal of bias. The fact that students catch their tastes as well as their ideas from their teachers, that the pupils of an art school copy the style of some dominant master, is a commonplace. And there is no doubt it is a pretty common cause why some at least of them never form an original idea or style. But can your teacher hide his bias? If he does, will he be any good as a teacher? Is not the good teacher precisely a man of strong convictions who can put them over?

When I was at school, I wrote certain essays for which I was given prizes. And the two masters who chiefly encouraged me were both remarkable men. One had real genius, Grey. He taught the upper fourth. It consisted of lively young boys of fourteen or so, on their way to the fifth, and enormous block-heads of seventeen, tottering on the edge of superannuation, but mostly quite resigned to it. They weren't by any means all fools. A lot of them, for one reason or another, had simply decided to fight against education of any kind. Their chief glory was to be lowbrows. Yet Grey made some of them enjoy Shakespeare so much that they read the plays for themselves—one, I know, carried a Temple Shakespeare in his pocket for the rest of his life, and so far became not only an educated man but a very interesting person. Grey did this chiefly by reading the plays aloud. He would sit on his desk and act them for us. I had only one term with him, but he gave me an unforgettable and important experience.

The other remarkable man was Sydney Irwin, who opened his library to me. Irwin was a precise and careful scholar who did, I believe, a good deal of reviewing for *The Times* of that date. And he encouraged me to write. Unluckily, he was anxious not to impress his own judgments, he tried as far as possible to leave me to express my own ideas in my own way. The result was that I did not learn to use language with precision, and years later had to struggle with problems that I should have had solved for me at school. I found these prize essays some years ago, and they had the faults no school-boy should be allowed to commit, and what's more, their ideas were extremely conventional.

For I was perfectly aware that I had gone to school to learn, and Irwin, like Grey, had his preferences, his own formed taste. The only difference between them as teachers was that Grey made no secret of preferences, and Irwin sought to hide them. He succeeded too well. So, in my essays, I imitated anthology pieces.

Boys want an education as children seek knowledge. They want to know how and what to think, and it is not even certain whether, in the ages between ten and sixteen or later, they have any real creative energy in their imagination. I suspect it is largely taken up with growing, as their minds are taken up with gathering facts and technique.

Irwin, with all the good will in the world, gave me only encouragement. It was perhaps more valuable than I supposed. But I could have had the knowledge too, and I couldn't get that anywhere else. How could I know that I'd missed it? It is the tragedy of the world that no one knows what he doesn't know—and the less a man knows, the more sure he is that he knows everything.

I knew Grey only for a month or two, but he was an enthusiast, a man of the strongest literary prejudice. For him, Shakespeare was the only master that mattered. Often in his zest while reading, he obviously forgot all about us in the form. Grey gave me something of the profoundest value. As I say, he transformed lives, he saved some pretty hopeless lives. He had genius, and he had enthusiasm. But you don't have enthusiasm without bias.

In the same way, the man who taught me most about drawing in the art school was the one with strong prejudices. He liked only one kind of drawing, the classical. He would have loathed Picasso if he had ever heard of him. He would glance at my drawing of a model and say, 'You don't know what you're doing, do you? Here, what's that *mean?*' Pointing, say, at a shadow on the back. I would say, 'It's on the model,' and he would answer fiercely, 'But what is it—muscle or dirt? What's it *mean?*'

That was his cry all the time: 'What's it mean?' He would point at a knee and say, 'Look at that piece of boiled macaroni. What's that line mean there? Which leg is she standing on?'

'The left.'

'Then why don't you show the tension in the hamstrings?'

'It's in shadow.'

'What's that matter? You're not trying to be a camera. You're trying to tell us something,' and he'd take my pencil and do what I hated, slash in a line on top of my drawing. 'Now at least she can stand up on her own legs.'

I don't think this man had much enthusiasm for drawing. But he had a set of principles and he was perfectly sure they were right. He taught me exactly what I needed to know about drawing, the fundamental rules, the logic, the syntax. Teaching, in short, like everything else that conveys a meaning in words, is an art, and you can't be a good artist unless you believe you are giving a truth. The most effective teacher will always be biased, for the chief force in teaching is confidence and enthusiasm. To give merely information is to write on the sand. For it is his function to form a character of feeling about ideas and to do that he has to have pretty strong feelings himself, as well as clear ideas.

All the great painters of the past—Giotto, Rembrandt, Rubens, Watteau, Gainsborough, Reynolds—began as apprentices in a studio where they ground the colours and learnt by rote, like young plumbers. 'This is the right way to do the job, and there isn't any other.' They were expected to put in a background so like the master's that it would pass for his own work.

This, too, is the usual and universal education given to children in the nursery by parents of any strong and definite view, political or religious. The significant thing about Dostoevsky and Tolstoy, James Joyce and many more, is the permanent cast given to their minds and feelings by early religious training. Their genius was in their use of that training to make new and original works of art.

G. K. CHESTERTON

THE FALLACY OF SUCCESS*

THERE HAS appeared in our time a particular class of books and articles which I sincerely and solemnly think may be called the silliest ever known among men. They are much more wild than the wildest romances of chivalry and much more dull than the dullest religious tract. Moreover, the romances of chivalry were at least about chivalry; the religious tracts are about religion. But these things are about nothing; they are about what is called Success. On every bookstall, in every magazine, you may find works telling people how to succeed. They are books showing men how to succeed in everything; they are written by men who cannot even succeed in writing books. To begin with, of course, there is no such thing as Success. Or, if you like to put it so, there is nothing that is not successful. That a thing is successful merely means that it is; a millionaire is successful in being a millionaire and a donkey in being a donkey. Any live man has succeeded in living; any dead man may have succeeded in committing suicide. But, passing over the bad logic and bad philosophy in the phrase, we may take it, as these writers do, in the ordinary sense of success in obtaining money or worldly position. These writers profess to tell the ordinary man how he may succeed in his trade or speculation—how, if he is a builder, he may succeed as a builder; how, if he is a stockbroker, he may succeed as a stock-broker. They profess to show him how, if he is a grocer, he may become a sporting yachtsman; how, if he is a tenth-rate journalist, he may become a peer; and how, if he is a German Jew, he may become an Anglo-Saxon. This is a definite and business-like proposal, and I really think that the people who buy these books (if any people do buy them) have a moral, if not a legal, right to ask for their money back. Nobody would dare to publish a book about electricity which literally told one nothing about electricity; no one would dare to publish an article on botany which showed that the writer

* Reprinted from *All Things Considered*, Sheed and Ward, Inc., 1956, by permission of the publisher. For Canada, permission granted by Miss D. E. Collins, Mr. Chesterton's executrix, and the Messrs. Methuen and Co., Ltd.

did not know which end of a plant grew in the earth. Yet our modern world
is full of books about Success and successful people which literally contain
no kind of idea, and scarcely any kind of verbal sense.

It is perfectly obvious that in any decent occupation (such as brick-
laying or writing books) there are only two ways (in any special sense)
of succeeding. One is by doing very good work, the other is by cheating.
Both are much too simple to require any literary explanation. If you are
in for the high jump, either jump higher than any one else, or manage
somehow to pretend that you have done so. If you want to succeed at whist,
either be a good whist-player, or play with marked cards. You may want
a book about jumping; you may want a book about whist; you may want
a book about cheating at whist. But you cannot want a book about Success.
Especially you cannot want a book about Success such as those which
you can now find scattered by the hundred about the book-market. You may
want to jump or to play cards, but you do not want to read wandering
statements to the effect that jumping is jumping, or that games are won
by winners. If these writers, for instance, said anything about success in
jumping it would be something like this: "The jumper must have a clear
aim before him. He must desire definitely to jump higher than the other
men who are in for the same competition. He must let no feeble feelings
of mercy (sneaked from the sickening Little Englanders and Pro-Boers)
prevent him from trying to *do his best*. He must remember that a competition in jumping is distinctly competitive, and that, as Darwin has
gloriously demonstrated, THE WEAKEST GO TO THE WALL." That is the kind
of thing the book would say, and very useful it would be, no doubt, if
read out in a low and tense voice to a young man just about to take the
high jump. Or suppose that in the course of his intellectual rambles the
philosopher of Success dropped upon our other case, that of playing cards,
his bracing advice would run—"In playing cards it is very necessary to
avoid the mistake (commonly made by maudlin humanitarians and Free
Traders) of permitting your opponent to win the game. You must have
grit and snap and *go in to win*. The days of idealism and superstition are
over. We live in a time of science and hard common sense, and it has now
been definitely proved that in any game where two are playing IF ONE DOES
NOT WIN THE OTHER WILL." It is all very stirring, of course; but I confess
that if I were playing cards I would rather have some decent little book
which told me the rules of the game. Beyond the rules of the game it is
all a question either of talent or dishonesty; and I will undertake to provide
either one or the other—which, it is not for me to say.

Turning over a popular magazine, I find a queer and amusing example.
There is an article called "The Instinct That Makes People Rich." It is
decorated in front with a formidable portrait of Lord Rothschild. There
are many definite methods, honest and dishonest, which make people rich;
the only "instinct" I know of which does it is that instinct which theological
Christianity crudely describes as "the sin of avarice." That, however, is

beside the present point. I wish to quote the following exquisite paragraphs as a piece of typical advice as to how to succeed. It is so practical; it leaves so little doubt about what should be our next step—

"The name of Vanderbilt is synonymous with wealth gained by modern enterprise. 'Cornelius,' the founder of the family, was the first of the great American magnates of commerce. He started as the son of a poor farmer; he ended as a millionaire twenty times over.

"He had the money-making instinct. He seized his opportunities, the opportunities that were given by the application of the steam-engine to ocean traffic, and by the birth of railway locomotion in the wealthy but undeveloped United States of America, and consequently he amassed an immense fortune.

"Now it is, of course, obvious that we cannot all follow exactly in the footsteps of this great railway monarch. The precise opportunities that fell to him do not occur to us. Circumstances have changed. But, although this is so, still, in our own sphere and in our own circumstances, we *can* follow his general methods; we can seize those opportunities that are given us, and give ourselves a very fair chance of attaining riches."

In such strange utterances we see quite clearly what is really at the bottom of all these articles and books. It is not mere business; it is not even mere cynicism. It is mysticism; the horrible mysticism of money. The writer of that passage did not really have the remotest notion of how Vanderbilt made his money, or of how anybody else is to make his. He does, indeed, conclude his remarks by advocating some scheme; but it has nothing in the world to do with Vanderbilt. He merely wished to prostrate himself before the mystery of a millionaire. For when we really worship anything, we love not only its clearness but its obscurity. We exult in its very invisibility. Thus, for instance, when a man is in love with a woman he takes special pleasure in the fact that a woman is unreasonable. Thus, again, the very pious poet, celebrating his Creator, takes pleasure in saying that God moves in a mysterious way. Now, the writer of the paragraph which I have quoted does not seem to have had anything to do with a god, and I should not think (judging by his extreme unpracticality) that he had ever been really in love with a woman. But the thing he does worship— Vanderbilt—he treats in exactly this mystical manner. He really revels in the fact his deity Vanderbilt is keeping a secret from him. And it fills his soul with a sort of transport of cunning, an ecstasy of priestcraft, that he should pretend to be telling to the multitude that terrible secret which he does not know.

Speaking about the instinct that makes people rich, the same writer remarks—

"In olden days its existence was fully understood. The Greeks enshrined it in the story of Midas, of the 'Golden Touch.' Here was a man who turned everything he laid his hands upon into gold. His life was a progress amidst riches. Out of everything that came in his way he created the precious metal. 'A foolish legend,' said the wiseacres of the Victorian age. 'A truth,' say we of to-day. We all know of such men. We are ever meeting or reading about such persons who turn everything they touch into gold. Success dogs their very footsteps. Their life's pathway leads unerringly upwards. They cannot fail."

Unfortunately, however, Midas could fail; he did. His path did not lead unerringly upward. He starved because whenever he touched a biscuit or a ham sandwich it turned to gold. That was the whole point of the story, though the writer had to suppress it delicately, writing so near to a portrait of Lord Rothschild. The old fables of mankind are, indeed, unfathomably wise; but we must not have them expurgated in the interests of Mr. Vanderbilt. We must not have King Midas represented as an example of success; he was a failure of an unusually painful kind. Also, he had the ears of an ass. Also (like most other prominent and wealthy persons) he endeavored to conceal the fact. It was his barber (if I remember right) who had to be treated on a confidential footing with regard to this peculiarity; and his barber, instead of behaving like a go-ahead person of the Succeed-at-all-costs school and trying to blackmail King Midas, went away and whispered this splendid piece of society scandal to the reeds, who enjoyed it enormously. It is said that they also whispered it as the winds swayed them to and fro. I look reverently at the portrait of Lord Rothschild; I read reverently about the exploits of Mr. Vanderbilt. I know that I cannot turn everything I touch to gold; but then I also know that I have never tried, having a preference for other substances, such as grass, and good wine. I know that these people have certainly succeeded in something; that they have certainly overcome somebody; I know that they are kings in a sense that no men were ever kings before; that they create markets and bestride continents. Yet it always seems to me that there is some small domestic fact that they are hiding, and I have sometimes thought I heard upon the wind the laughter and whisper of the reeds.

At least, let us hope that we shall all live to see these absurd books about Success covered with a proper derision and neglect. They do not teach people to be successful, but they do teach people to be snobbish; they do spread a sort of evil poetry of worldliness. The Puritans are always denouncing books that inflame lust; what shall we say of books that inflame the viler passions of avarice and pride? A hundred years ago we had the ideal of the Industrious Apprentice; boys were told that by thrift and work they would all become Lord Mayors. This was fallacious, but it was manly, and had a minimum of moral truth. In our society, temperance will not help a poor man to enrich himself, but it may help him to respect himself. Good work will not make him a rich man, but good work may make him a good workman. The Industrious Apprentice rose by virtues few and narrow indeed, but still virtues. But what shall we say of the gospel preached to the new Industrious Apprentice; the Apprentice who rises not by his virtues, but avowedly by his vices?

JOHN CIARDI

THE MORALITY OF POETRY*

THE AMERICAN culture has developed a number of institutions that systematically encourage, and even give social prestige to, the shallowest possible view of poetry. Our Poetry Societies fluctuate between the society columns and the book-review page, but tend always to specialize in the frothy genteel. Some of our leading "quality" magazines still regularly publish as poetry a kind of counterfeit sentimentality that might once, with some minor changes of vocabulary, have made its way into the pages of *Godey's Lady's Book*. A number of our sovereign states still appoint a poet laureate—always, as far as I can determine, a writer from the vanity-press lists.

My acquaintance with the poetry features of our newspapers is far from total, but I have looked about me, and I have yet to find a single regular columnist or feature writer on any of our large-city newspapers who is competent to discuss more than the spelling of poetry. (I must certainly exclude that rare good man, Harvey Breit, from whom one can always expect both perception and wit.) Occasional reviews by guest specialists in the Sunday *New York Times* and *Tribune* begin to discuss poetry in viable terms. Yet after some years of sampling the editorial-page poems of the daily *Times* and *Tribune* I have not yet been able to find a poem that rises above a heavy-footed mediocrity. In fact, by a kind of Gresham's Law, the bad poetry drives out the good. Real poets refuse to submit their work to those pages.

The trouble with all of these institutions, and with their too-general endorsement by the School System, is that they make it possible for a well-intentioned person who is "interested in poetry" to be offered any number of socially endorsed counterfeits without ever experiencing a real poem. If the canvases at the Metropolitan and at the Museum of Modern Art were to be locked up, and made available only in newspaper reproductions, the consequent death of esthetic standards would be about comparable to what these institutions are doing to the sense of poetry in our culture.

If this sort of thing is what the "general reader" thinks he wants in the name of poetry, let him have it. The right to be wrong is a blessed democratic gift, and may the Constitution guarantee it forever. But if it is no offense to accept counterfeit money, it is still an offense to try to pass it on. Let the admirers and the writers of hobby-verse believe what they please, but they have no right to expect the poets to confirm their foolishness. Unless the poets hold counterfeit sentimentality in contempt, they become incapable of uttering their own devotions.

A stunning example of the poet's necessary contempt occurs in Yeats's "Adam's Curse." I am writing from Rome without my books about me and

* Reprinted from *The Saturday Review* (March 30, 1957) by permission of the author and *The Saturday Review*.

275

I must quote from memory throughout this article, but I believe I can avoid major misrepresentation:

> A line may take us hours maybe;
> Yet if it does not seem a moment's thought
> Our stitching and unstitching has been naught.
> Better get down upon your marrow bones
> And scrub a kitchen pavement, or break stones
> Like an old pauper in all kinds of weather;
> For to articulate sweet sounds together
> Is to work harder than all these and yet
> Be thought an idler by the noisy set
> Of bankers, schoolmasters, and clergymen
> The martyrs call the world.

Yeats is insisting clearly enough that the best of the world's work is done by the poets, whereas those spokesmen of the literal values, bankers-school-masters-clergymen, are no more than a "noisy set." W. H. Auden in his elegy "In Memory of W. B. Yeats" says it differently but says about the same thing. He notes the brokers "roaring like beasts on the floor of the Bourse" (the "noisy set" scorned) and carefully disassociates poetry from them:

> poetry makes nothing happen. It survives
> In the valley of its saying where executives
> Would never want to tamper. It flows south
> From ranches of isolation and the busy griefs,
> Raw towns that we believe and die in. It survives,
> A way of happening. A mouth.

And he adds later in the same poem that time, nevertheless, "Worships language and forgives/Everyone by whom it lives."

Yeats, in his poem, goes on to a related affirmation when he has one of his characters say:

> To be born woman is to know,
> Though it's not taught to us in school,
> That we must labor to be beautiful.

I take this to mean—among other things but emphatically—that the values Yeats defends have to do with the rescue of one's human attention from trivia and mindless conformity in order that that attention may be applied in a life-shaping way.

One could mine English poetry, past and present, for similar examples, but these will serve to make clear enough the existence of a basic difference between (in Yeats's terms, and I mean to keep those terms throughout the present discussion) the world on the one hand and poetry on the other.

If I have succeeded in establishing an acceptable distinction, I have attempted to do so in order to suggest that the real difference is a difference of morality. I have no ambition to define the world's morality for it, nor can I in any all-inclusive sense define the poet's for him. It may still be valuable, however, to discuss some principles of the poet's morality that are crucial to the success of a good poem while remaining generally unrecognized by the world as true primary values. An awareness of "this other morality," moreover, will provide one way of measuring the essential difference between the work of a poet and that of a hobbyist in metrics.

Let me skirt, for the moment, all argument for or against popular morality. I simply make the point here that poetry is independent of that morality, as it is of general good character or social standing. Villon, despite all his failures as measured by the world's morality, emerges as a poet, and Robert Southey—every reader's choice as the best Sunday-schoolteacher in English Literature—does not. If there ever was an original Tom o' Bedlam, his song is forever in the memory of the English language, but who reads the songs of Henry the Eighth? Baudelaire wrote "immoral" poetry and Swinburne found himself in serious trouble for translating it into Victoria's English, but Baudelaire will remain part of the indispensable knowledge of the human race long after students begin to forget which country Victoria was queen of in which century. Like it or not, poetry has never depended upon the approval of the world's morality, manners, or caste system. The fact seems to be, in fact, that more poems die of decency than of any other one cause.

Assume, if you please, that Baudelaire was indeed an immoral man. If, then, his work has become one of the values and resources of the race—a fact that seems clearly beyond argument at this point—what gives it value? To be sure, he was a poet and knew how to use words, metaphors, rhythms, and poetic structures to marvelous effect. But for the sake of the argument, let us even assume the monstrous untruth that poetic gift is merely ornamental and not of the essence. By what values did this "immoral" man seek the truth of his own life?

Peter Viereck's poem "Poet" contains some pertinent observations on this point. The poem is a tribute to Baudelaire based on two sentences taken from Baudelaire's "My Heart Stripped Bare": "All created form, even that created by man, is immortal. For the form is independent of the material, and it is not the particles that make up the form."

Clearly, this is a statement of devotion. In speaking of creation "even by man" Baudelaire is certainly putting man next to godliness by virtue of the fact that he, too, can give immortal shape to things, his own life among them. But to make a thing that will endure forever is a terrible responsibility. The very title of Baudelaire's piece—"My Heart Stripped Bare"—identifies one essential element of that responsibility: the maker must be uncompromisingly honest. Social niceties, received views on conduct, respect for established social habit, all the lures of easy sentiment must be brushed aside. Propriety and social glibness may be the measure of all things at a cocktail party or at the Thursday Group Meeting, but the human unconscious that reads the poem in the still midnight of immortal feeling is beyond social gesture. Be damned to all else: the poem must be real to its midnight.

And, exactly here, we may identify the first anti-social morality of the poet. It is, of course, anti-social only in short range terms. It is *against* its contemporary (and ever-shifting) proprieties in order to be *for* what is longest and truest in man's awareness of himself. The genteel, then as now, will not find Baudelaire bearable, but centuries from now that midnight-man will still be there to read and to learn some of his own life from the reading.

Viereck's treatment of this theme speaks the essence of that morality which compels the poet without quite being recognized as a morality by the world at large. In what precedes the passage I quote here, Viereck develops the theme that the poet, by the disciplines of his form and of his imagination, holds things in order. Viereck compares Baudelaire to a king who had ruthlessly driven all shabby elements from his court and kingdom. The instant the king dies the exiles begin to plot again the old chaos of the slovenly:

> Words that begged favor at his court in vain—
> Lush adverbs, senile rhymes in tattered gowns—
> Send notes to certain exiled nouns
> And mutter openly against his reign,
> While rouged clichés hang out red lights again,
> And refugees report from far-flung towns
> That exclamation marks are running wild,
> And prowling half-truths carried off a child.

The whole of Viereck's catalogue of esthetic (and intellectual) corruption is worth study, but it is especially to the point that he has selected clichés as the central prostitution. It has always been an astonishment to me that people of the highest moral principle in the world's terms will yet abandon themselves willingly to the immorality of the cliché.

For a cliché is not only a sinful slovenliness; it is an enemy of mind and hope, and it is not only a prostitution but a theft. Nor can the case be put, honorably and accurately, in milder terms. Every morality must be bound by both a blessing and a damnation, and on this point, within the morality of poetry, only damnation will serve. Our mass-media journalism, our collapsing educational system, and the insanities of the Madison Avenue-Hollywood axis have already put us in sufficient danger of becoming a mindless generation. If our poets and would-be poets are to be encouraged in such slovenly thefts within their own imaginations, then a primary cultured force for good intellectual order is seriously weakened. The ultimate sin of the mind is the failure to pay enough attention.

It is exactly at this point that one may locate the essential difference between the kind of morality that binds the poet and that which seems to operate in the general culture. The Christian tradition recognizes seven deadly sins, which I take to be another way of labeling seven moral failures. Of them, the culture at large seems to have an adequate sense of pride, envy, wrath, avarice, gluttony, and lust, but seems to be relatively unaware of Acedia. We translate Acedia as "sloth," but that translation tends to blur the essential meaning. "Sloth" tends to suggest mere physical slovenliness. Acedia is quite something else—it is the failure to pay sufficient attention to one's devotions. It has many faces, but its essence is an intellectual haphazardness that springs from not caring enough. In the Middle Ages, interestingly, it seems to have been the sin most feared by the monks: the fear that they had not paid enough attention to God.

No failure of poetic morality (and of artistic morality in general) can be more fundamental than the failure to pay enough attention to the nature and requirement of one's chosen form. To perform sloppily for high causes and high moral issues is both an affront to the cause and issue, and as thoroughly bad as performing in this way for low causes and issues.

So to the fundamental difference between one morality and the other: the world tends to recognize six deadly failures and to pay little attention to the seventh. The poet, finally, has to care only about the seventh. It is not at all necessary for him to scorn the other six, but granted that he has talent enough, his work will finally live or die on his ability to keep his attention in disciplined and self-consuming order.

Let the writers on "subjects"—and those would-be defenders of poetry who seek in it the loose affirmation of shabbily stated principles of high moral purport but low esthetic integrity—let them learn once and for all that the only subject of any poem is the kind of attention it brings to bear on the universe or on its least sliver. A poem may or may not have a "surface subject," but if it does not have as its central activation a motion of the attention that creates an ordered form then it is no poem, and what it does is shabbily done.

I have several times before used an example from the poetry of Elizabeth Bishop to illustrate what I mean at this point. The passage I have in mind is from a longish poem called "The Fish." Miss Bishop describes how she caught the fish, held it out of water, and began to look at it. Here is what she says about the fish's eye:

> I looked into his eyes
> which were far larger than mine
> but shallower and yellowed,
> the irises backed and packed
> with tarnished tinfoil
> seen through lenses
> of old scratched isinglass.

I read that passage to a convention of schoolteachers once and said that, as far as I knew, it was the best job of looking at a fish's eye in the whole range of English poetry. To which, of course, one teacher replied: "So what? What is so important about looking at a fish's eye?"

The fact is that anything significantly looked at is significant. And that is significant which teaches us something about our own life-capabilities. The function of detail when ordered by a human imagination is to illustrate the universe. One comes away from Elizabeth Bishop's poetry not simply with a miraculously observed and drawn image, but with a new idea of the possibilities of his own senses. The eye of the ignorant sees nothing. Only mind can apprehend the visible, and the eye can only register what the mind is able to perceive. Elizabeth Bishop's description literally lets us see a fish's eye, but beyond that literalness it teaches us what we ourselves will be capable of if we manage our imaginations with sufficient devotion, and if we are sufficiently ruthless toward any cheapening substitute for the real thing.

To achieve that ability to experience and to transmit experience in experienceable terms is the labor and the devotion and the morality of the poet —his "labor to be beautiful." An element of that morality is to scorn loose talk about the "large significances" of the poem. The poet is ready for "large significance" only as he has learned his art. To try to short-cut to the big-message by way of slurred details is to guarantee that the poem is a counterfeit. A poet is responsible for every last detail he allows into his poem. Nothing is too small to matter. There are accidentals, to be sure, but every accidental must be passed on by his principle of selection, and it is of the essence of this moral commitment that he insist on keeping that selection uncompromising. I submit it to be true of all of English poetry, that only those poets who have most cherished the close fact of things and the discipline of their art have been able to make enduring statements of human values. Art is the mentality of human passion. Without mind enough, which is to say without gift enough and discipline enough, passion is mush.

The true poet can have only scorn for those who call upon him to deliver pretty stereotypes. If that is what one wishes, he can buy it with four-color illustrations from Hallmark. One thinks, for instance, of those who cried throughout the war-years for another poem like "In Flanders Field"—as if the poets among those who were sitting in the blood or the boredom of the actual war could turn popular affirmations off and on at will like the smile of a politician.

The true poet can submit to anything before he can submit to the falsification of sentiment. But whether one concurs in the "surface subject" or not, if he cares at all about poetry he must realize that the surface subject is not the poem. I would grant, as in the case of a poet as talented as is Roy Campbell, that it is possible for the kind of mind offered in the poem to be so repulsive that one can almost regret the fragments of gift it possesses. That, however, must be left for another discussion, the basis of which would be that such a man as Campbell has gift but abuses it. The fact still remains that a poem written in true devotion to itself—rather than in some sort of split devotion to an over-riding sentiment—cannot be anything but an affirmation. There is no such thing as a negative creation if the creation is built on a ruthless devotion to order.

There is also society's reward in this, whether or not society is willing to be aware of it. The very fact that there have always been men among us who have chosen to be ruthlessly moral about language may well be the greatest single blessing a man inherits by being born into a civilization. No one guards the language as poets do—guards it, refreshes it, and restores it. (In speaking of language, one of course assumes the subject to include the perception and the discipline and the joy of what language is capable of expressing. One intends, in fact, nothing less than the total process of living with real awareness.) Without the poets to guard the language it would fall apart in the mouth, and with it the very possibility of social communication. When a language falls apart a nation is finished.

Let one example illustrate. I find hardly a schoolboy these days who can distinguish between "intra-" and "inter-" or between "democracy" and "republicanism." Yet almost all can distinguish meaningfully between "glory" and "grandeur." They can do so because Poe drew that distinction so well in "To Helen" that the words grew firm on the public tongue. May something teach that schoolboy—and his mother and father—more of the distinctions time will require of all of us. Poetry could do it, if the world would allow poetry to come to him as the real force and order of living that it is when it observes its own morality. It seems doubtful that the world is so inclined, and that fact must go down as the world's loss.

For poetry is no social ornament to be applied as part of a "finishing school" gloss. It is a way of life and it is a discrete and irreplaceable means of knowledge. It is as much a way of knowing as is science, and the kind of knowledge it vitalizes, stores, and makes available is forever beyond the range of science. It is rather for poetry to instruct science if humanity is to be rescued from its own pushbuttons.

Poetry takes as a primary value an awareness of one's own aliveness. A man becomes a man by learning the history and the miracle and the joy and the difficulty of his own attention and of his moral commitment to it. Poetry is what best makes available to a man exactly those life responses and that entrance into the possibilities and the devotions of his own attention—if he will guard it ruthlessly from everything including his own sentiments and his own surface decency. From the tribal chant to Genesis, and from Genesis to the next truly devoted and truly shaped poem to be created in human history, poetry has added and will add to the richness of man's awareness of what it is to be a human being on a tilted planet.

That awareness is no matter of "message." It is the life-dance of the poem, the shape and motion and force of the truly fulfilled form. A good poet does not take a poem: it takes him. He happens to it, and he does not know what has happened until it has been done. He goes into the poem and he comes out of it at some unpredictable point. But wherever he emerges, he emerges wiser and truer and more alive. And throughout the total process he lives ruthlessly by his trained attention, by his devotion to his principle of selection.

And only such devotion will serve him in his act of being a poet. For those who wish to flirt with the poem in easier and more passing terms the one critical mercy is to be silent. If, however, there comes a time to speak—then, as the sin is deadly, so must the judgment be damnation. That high moral affirmation battered into bad rhyme and slovened out of shape in the name of rhetorical-seriousness is not poetry but esthetic immorality. It blurs our apprehension of life itself. Ignorance is no excuse for it, and sincere good intention cannot plead for it. It pretends to care, it may believe it does care, but it simply does not care enough.

JOHN HENRY CARDINAL NEWMAN

KNOWLEDGE AND LEARNING*

Knowledge Viewed in Relation to Learning

7

A_{ND} NOW, if I may take for granted that the true and adequate end of intellectual training and of a University is not Learning or Acquirement, but rather, is Thought or Reason exercised upon Knowledge, or what may be called Philosophy, I shall be in a position to explain the various mistakes which at the present day beset the subject of University Education.

I say then, if we would improve the intellect, first of all, we must ascend; we cannot gain real knowledge on a level; we must generalize, we must reduce to method, we must have a grasp of principles, and group and shape our acquisitions by means of them. It matters not whether our field of operation be wide or limited; in every case, to command it, is to mount above it. Who has not felt the irritation of mind and impatience created by a deep, rich country, visited for the first time, with winding lanes, and high hedges, and green steeps, and tangled woods, and every thing smiling indeed, but in a maze? The same feeling comes upon us in a strange city, when we have no map of its streets. Hence you hear of practised travellers, when they first come into a place, mounting some high hill or church tower, by way of reconnoitring its neighbourhood. In like manner, you must be above your knowledge, not under it, or it will oppress you; and the more you have of it, the greater will be the load. The learning of a Salmasius or a Burman, unless you are its master, will be your tyrant. "Imperat aut servit"†; if you can wield it with a strong arm, it is a great weapon; otherwise,

Vis consili expers
Mole ruit sua.‡

You will be overwhelmed, like Tarpeia, by the heavy wealth which you have exacted from tributary generations.

Instances abound; there are authors who are as pointless as they are inexhaustible in their literary resources. They measure knowledge by bulk, as it lies in the rude block, without symmetry, without design. How many commentators are there on the Classics, how many on Holy Scripture, from whom we rise up, wondering at the learning which has passed before us,

---

* Reprinted from *The Idea of a University*, Doubleday, Doran & Co., New York, 1931.
† One either rules or is a slave.
‡ Physical force without a goal (or planned direction) falls of its own weight.

and wondering why it passed! How many writers are there of Ecclesiastical History, such as Mosheim or Du Pin, who, breaking up their subject into details, destroy its life, and defraud us of the whole by their anxiety about the parts! The Sermons, again, of the English Divines in the seventeenth century, how often are they mere repertories of miscellaneous and officious learning! Of course Catholics also may read without thinking; and in their case, equally as with Protestants, it holds good, that such knowledge is unworthy of the name, knowledge which they have not thought through, and thought out. Such readers are only possessed by their knowledge, not possessed of it; nay, in matter of fact they are often even carried away by it, without any volition of their own. Recollect, the Memory can tyrannize, as well as the Imagination. Derangement, I believe, has been considered as a loss of control over the sequence of ideas. The mind, once set in motion, is henceforth deprived of the power of initiation, and becomes the victim of a train of associations, one thought suggesting another, in the way of cause and effect, as if by a mechanical process, or some physical necessity. No one, who has had experience of men of studious habits, but must recognize the existence of a parallel phenomenon in the case of those who have over-stimulated the Memory. In such persons Reason acts almost as feebly and as impotently as in the madman; once fairly started on any subject whatever, they have no power of self-control; they passively endure the succession of impulses which are evolved out of the original exciting cause; they are passed on from one idea to another and go steadily forward, plodding along one line of thought in spite of the amplest concessions of the hearer, or wandering from it in endless digression in spite of his remonstrances. Now, if, as is very certain, no one would envy the madman the glow and originality of his conceptions, why must we extol the cultivation of that intellect, which is the prey, not indeed of barren fancies but of barren facts, of random intrusions from without, though not of morbid imaginations from within? And in thus speaking, I am not denying that a strong and ready memory is in itself a real treasure; I am not disparaging a well-stored mind, though it be nothing besides, provided it be sober, any more than I would despise a bookseller's shop:—it is of great value to others, even when not so to the owner. Nor am I banishing, far from it, the possessors of deep and multifarious learning from my ideal University; they adorn it in the eyes of men; I do but say that they constitute no type of the results at which it aims; that it is no great gain to the intellect to have enlarged the memory at the expense of faculties which are indisputably higher. . . .

Knowledge Viewed in Relation to Professional Skill

I

I have been insisting, in my two preceding Discourses, first, on the cultivation of the intellect, as an end which may reasonably be pursued for its own sake; and next, on the nature of that cultivation, or what that cultivation consists in. Truth of whatever kind is the proper object of the intellect;

its cultivation then lies in fitting it to apprehend and contemplate truth. Now the intellect in its present state, with exceptions which need not here be specified, does not discern truth intuitively, or as a whole. We know, not by a direct and simple vision, not at a glance, but, as it were, by piecemeal and accumulation, by a mental process, by going round an object, by the comparison, the combination, the mutual correction, the continual adaptation, of many partial notions, by the employment, concentration, and joint action of many faculties and exercises of mind. Such a union and concert of the intellectual powers, such an enlargement and development, such a comprehensiveness, is necessarily a matter of training. And again, such a training is a matter of rule; it is not mere application, however exemplary, which introduces the mind to truth, nor the reading many books, nor the getting up many subjects, nor the witnessing many experiments, nor the attending many lectures. All this is short of enough; a man may have done it all, yet be lingering in the vestibule of knowledge:—he may not realize what his mouth utters; he may not see with his mental eye what confronts him; he may have no grasp of things as they are; or at least he may have no power at all of advancing one step forward of himself, in consequence of what he has already acquired, no power of discriminating between truth and falsehood, of sifting out the grains of truth from the mass, of arranging things according to their real value, and, if I may use the phrase, of building up ideas. Such a power is the result of a scientific formation of mind; it is an acquired faculty of judgment, of clear-sightedness, of sagacity, of wisdom, of philosophical reach of mind, and of intellectual self-possession and repose,—qualities which do not come of mere acquirement. The bodily eye, the organ for apprehending material objects, is provided by nature; the eye of the mind, of which the object is truth, is the work of discipline and habit.

This process of training, by which the intellect, instead of being formed or sacrificed to some particular or accidental purpose, some specific trade or profession, or study or science, is disciplined for its own sake, for the perception of its own proper object, and for its own highest culture, is called Liberal Education; and though there is no one in whom it is carried as far as is conceivable, or whose intellect would be a pattern of what intellects should be made, yet there is scarcely any one but may gain an idea of what real training is, and at least look towards it, and make its true scope and result, not something else, his standard of excellence; and numbers there are who may submit themselves to it, and secure it to themselves in good measure. And to set forth the right standard, and to train according to it, and to help forward all students towards it according to their various capacities, this I conceive to be the business of a University.

2

Now this is what some great men are very slow to allow; they insist that education should be confined to some particular and narrow end, and should issue in some definite work, which can be weighed and measured. They argue as if every thing, as well as every person, had its price; and that where there has been a great outlay, they have a right to expect a return in kind. This they call making Education and Instruction "useful," and "Utility" becomes their watchword. With a fundamental principle of this nature, they very naturally go on to ask, what there is to show for the expense of a University; what is the real worth in the market of the article called "a Liberal Education," on the supposition that it does not teach us definitely how to advance our manufactures, or to improve our lands, or to better our civil economy; or again, if it does not at once make this man a lawyer, that an engineer, and that a surgeon; or at least if it does not lead to discoveries in chemistry, astronomy, geology, magnetism, and science of every kind.

This question, as might have been expected, has been keenly debated in the present age, and formed one main subject of the controversy, to which I referred in the Introduction to the present Discourses, as having been sustained in the first decade of this century by a celebrated Northern Review on the one hand, and defenders of the University of Oxford on the other. Hardly had the authorities of that ancient seat of learning, waking from their long neglect, set on foot a plan for the education of the youth committed to them, than the representatives of science and literature in the city, which has sometimes been called the Northern Athens, remonstrated, with their gravest arguments and their most brilliant satire, against the direction and shape which the reform was taking. Nothing would content them, but that the University should be set to rights on the basis of the philosophy of Utility; a philosophy, as they seem to have thought, which needed but to be proclaimed in order to be embraced. In truth, they were little aware of the depth and force of the principles on which the academical authorities were proceeding, and, this being so, it was not to be expected that they would be allowed to walk at leisure over the field of controversy which they had selected. Accordingly they were encountered in behalf of the University by two men of great name and influence in their day, of very different minds, but united, as by Collegiate ties, so in the clear-sighted and large view which they took on the whole subject of Liberal Education; and the defence thus provided for the Oxford studies has kept its ground to this day.

ANANDA K. COOMARASWAMY

WHAT USE IS ART ANYWAY?*

WE ARE familiar with two contemporary schools of thought about art. We have on the one hand a very small self-styled elite which distinguishes "fine" art from art as skilled manufacture, and values this fine art very

* Reprinted from the Christmas 1956 issue of the *Catholic Art Quarterly*. Reprinted by permission of Graham Carey.

highly as a self-revelation or self-expression of the artist; this elite, accordingly, bases its teaching of aesthetic upon style, and makes the so-called "appreciation of art" a matter of the manner rather than of the content or true intention of the work. These are our Professors of Aesthetics and of the History of Art, who rejoice in the unintelligibility of art at the same time that they explain it psychologically, substituting the study of the man himself for the study of the man's art; and these leaders of the blind are gladly followed by a majority of modern artists, who are naturally flattered by the importance attached to personal genius.

On the other hand we have the great body of plain men who are not really interested in artistic personalities, and for whom art as defined above is a peculiarity rather than a necessity of life, and who have, in fact, no use for art.

And over against these two classes we have a normal but forgotten view of art, which affirms that art is the making well, or properly arranging, of anything whatever that needs to be made or arranged, whether a statuette, or automobile, or garden. In the Western world, this is specifically the Catholic doctrine of art; from which doctrine the natural conclusion follows, in the words of St. Thomas, that "there can be no good use without art." It is rather obvious that if things required for use, whether an intellectual or a physical use, or under normal conditions both, are not properly made, they cannot be enjoyed, meaning by "enjoyed" something more than merely "liked." Badly prepared food, for example, will disagree with us; and in the same way autobiographical or other sentimental exhibits necessarily weaken the morale of those who feed upon them. The healthy patron is no more interested in the artist's personality than he is in his tailor's private life; all that he needs of either is that they be in possession of their art.

The present remarks are addressed to the second kind of man defined above, viz., to the plain and practical-minded man who has no use for art, as art is expounded by the psychologists and practised by most contemporary artists, especially painters. The plain man has no use for art unless he knows what it is about, or what it is for. And so far, he is perfectly right; if it is not about something, and not for anything, it *has* no use. And furthermore, unless it is about something *worth while*—more worth while, for example, than the artist's precious personality—and for something worth while to the patron and consumer as well as to the artist and maker, it has no real use, but is only a luxury product or mere ornament. On these grounds art may be dismissed by a religious man as mere vanity, by the practical man as an expensive superfluity, and by the class thinker as part and parcel of the whole bourgeois fantasy. There are thus two opposite points of view, of which one asserts that there can be no good use without art, the other that art is a superfluity. Observe, however, that these contrary statements are affirmed with respect to two very different things, which are not the same merely because both have been called "art." Let us now take for granted the historically normal and orthodox view that, just as ethics is the "right way of doing things," so art is the "making well of whatever needs making," or simply "the right way of making things"; and still addressing ourselves to those for whom the arts of personality are superfluous, ask whether art is not after all a necessity.

A necessity is something that we cannot afford to do without, whatever its price. We cannot go into questions of price here, beyond saying that art need not be, and should not be, expensive, except to the extent that costly materials are employed. It is at this point that the crucial question arises of manufacture for profit versus manufacture for use. It is because the idea of manufacture primarily for profit is bound up with the currently accepted industrial sociology that things in general are not well made and therefore also not beautiful. It is the manufacturer's interest to produce what we like, or can be induced to like, regardless of whether or not it will agree with us; like other modern artists, the manufacturer is expressing himself, and only serving our real needs to the extent that he *must* do so in order to be able to sell at all. Manufacturers and other artists alike resort to advertisement: art is abundantly advertised in schools and colleges, by "Museums of Modern Art," and by art dealers; and artist and manufacturer alike price their wares according to what the traffic will bear. Under these conditions, the manufacturer works in order to be able to go on earning; he does not earn, as he ought, in order to be able to go on manufacturing. It is only when the maker of things is a maker of things by vocation, and not merely holding down a job, that the price of things approximates to their real value; and under these circumstances, when we pay for a work of art designed to serve a necessary purpose, we get our money's worth; and the purpose being a necessary one, we *must* be able to afford to pay for the art, or else are living below a normal human standard; as most men are now living, even the rich, if we consider quality rather than quantity. Needless to add, the workman is also victimized by a manufacture primarily for profit; so that it has become a mockery to say to him that hours of work should be more enjoyable than hours of leisure; that when at work he should be doing what he likes, and only when at leisure doing what he ought—workmanship being conditioned by art, and conduct by ethics.

Industry without art is brutality. Art is specifically human. None of those primitive peoples, past or present, whose cultures we affect to despise and propose to amend, has dispensed with art; from the stone age onwards, everything made by man, under whatever conditions of hardship or poverty, has been made by art to serve a double purpose, at once utilitarian and ideological. It is we who, collectively speaking at least, command amply sufficient resources, and who do not shrink from wasting these resources, who have first proposed to make a division of art, one sort to be barely utilitarian, the other luxurious, and altogether omitting what was once the highest function of art, to express and to communicate ideas. It is long since sculpture was thought of as "the poor man's book." Our very word "aesthetics," from *aesthesis*, "feeling," proclaims our dismissal of the intellectual values of art.

If we called the plain man right in wanting to know what a work is about, and in demanding intelligibility in works of art, he is no less certainly wrong in demanding likenesses and altogether wrong in judging works of ancient art from any such point of view as is implied in the common expressions, "that was before they knew anything about anatomy," or "that was before perspective had been discovered." Art is concerned with the nature of things, and only incidentally, if at all, with their appearance; by which appearance the nature of things is far more obscured than revealed. It is not the artist's business to be fond of nature as effect, but to take account of nature as the cause of effects. Art, in other words, is far more nearly related to algebra than to arithmetic, and just as certain qualifications are needed if we are to understand and enjoy a mathematical formula, so the spectator must have been educated as he ought if he is to understand and enjoy the forms of communicative art. This is most of all the case if the spectator is to understand and enjoy works of art which are written, so to speak, in a foreign or forgotten language; which applies to a majority of objects in our museums.

This problem presents itself because it is not the business of a museum to exhibit contemporary works. The modern artist's ambition to be represented in a museum is his vanity, and betrays a complete misunderstanding of the function of art; for if a work has been made to meet a given and specific need it can only be effective in the environment for which it was designed, that is to say in some such vital context as a man's house in which he lives, or in a street, or in a church, and not in any place the primary function of which is to contain all sorts of art.

The function of an art museum is to preserve from destruction and to give access to such ancient works of art as are still considered, by experts responsible for their selection, to be very good of their kind. Can these works of art, which were not made to meet his particular needs, be of any use to the plain man? Probably not of much use at first sight and without guidance, nor until he knows what they are about and what they were for. We could rather wish, although in vain, that the man in the street had access to such markets as those in which the museum objects were originally bought and sold at reasonable prices in the everyday course of life. On the other hand, the museum objects were made to meet specific human needs, if not precisely our current needs; and it is most desirable to realize that there have been human needs other than, and perhaps more significant than, our own. The museum objects cannot indeed be thought of as shapes to be imitated, just because they were not made to suit our special needs; but in so far as they are good of their kind, as is presupposed by the expert selection, there can be deduced from them, when considered in relation to their original use, the general principles of art according to which things *can* be well made, for whatever purpose they may be required. And that is, broadly speaking, the major value of our museums.

IVOR BROWN

IN PRAISE OF CLARITY*

THE LITERARY fashion of these days is not to know what you mean and, if challenged, to shrug a careless shoulder and say that you write what you write and the reader must make his own interpretation. The author's observations are presumed to be pregnant; the reader is to be midwife and bring the child to birth. It is no business of genius to make itself plain.

This was the line taken up by T. S. Eliot in an interview given after the first production of "The Cocktail Party" (Harcourt, Brace) at the Edinburgh Festival of Arts in 1949. The play later acted with immense success in London and New York was, I think, a simplified and improved version of the original. But that does not affect Eliot's reply to the charge of being obscure and his tenet that the artist is under no obligation to be explicit. He projects his thoughts, feelings and fancies: on the task of interpretation the public must bring its own wits to bear.

I suggest in return that this attitude betrays either laziness or affectation. It is the abdication of authorship. It is the business of the literary artist to know his mind and to speak it. Mr. Eliot, after all, was dramatizing certain problems of conduct and of human relations and he presented a Psychotherapeutic Sage as moral preceptor. He was not just fetching up thoughts that lie too deep for tears; he was informing us about destiny and salvation, important matters on which we have a right to clear instruction. In that case we surely are entitled to know what his opinions on these great matters are. The fact that the play was written in what might be called conversational verse does not affect the proposition that an author is evading his responsibilities if he is not intelligible.

Swift shrewdly said that the true definition of style is "proper words in proper places." To this I would add "proper thoughts in proper order." There is nothing impossible about that. The greatest prose writers of our time are in my estimation Bernard Shaw and Somerset Maugham. Did either of them ever write a sentence that was vague?

If you are anti-Shavian you can accuse Shaw of writing every sort of nonsense, but you need never pause for a moment to wonder what sort of nonsense he intends. And as a model of lucid scrutiny of a life's experience and a life's conclusions Maugham's "The Summing Up" (Doubleday) is unsurpassed. Again, you need not agree with his judgments and valuations, but you know precisely what those judgments are.

Now let us have some examples of the muddled writing for which in my opinion there is no excuse. Mr. Henry Green's novels are now very much in the intellectual fashion, presumably because he so loftily disdains syntax,

* Reprinted from *Highlights of Modern Literature*, published as a Mentor Book. Reprinted by permission of the author and *The New York Times*.

grammar and punctuation. Here is a typical sentence from Page 1, of his much-praised story, modestly called "Nothing":

> It was wet then, did she remember he was saying, so unlike this he said, and turned his face to its dazzle of window, it had been dark with sad tears on the panes and streets of canals as he sat by her fire for Jane liked dusk, would not turn on the lights until she couldn't see to move, while outside a single street lamp was yellow, reflected over a thousand raindrops on the glass, the fire was rose, and Penelope came in.

Could anything be untidier? A schoolboy would be in trouble for such infantile, turbid, ill-punctuated stuff, with its flood of commas and contempt of all the rules of composition; those rules were not made to be a nuisance to writers but for the advantage of readers. As a reader I object to having this mess thrown at my head.

Then we have Mr. T. S. Eliot writing "Notes Towards a Definition of Culture." Note the timidity of the title. He is not offering to define culture; he is going to devote 124 pages to fidgeting round the edges of a definition. He includes sentences like this:

> The way of looking at culture and religion which I have been trying to adumbrate is so difficult that I am not sure I grasp it myself except in flashes or that I comprehend all its implications.

Now if an author can only "try to adumbrate" an opinion and then admits his own inability to understand his own point of view, I suggest that he should keep quiet until he has cleared up his own confusion. Can one imagine a master of thought and English faltering and fumbling in this way! But to cut one's way through mental fog is now to be called obvious, or trivial; to founder in it, confessing one's impotence, is taken to be profound.

Nobody can pretend that much of the poetry written in the last quarter of a century has not been obscure. That is one reason why in Great Britain the bulk of it has become unsalable. London publishers protest that, with the exception of Eliot and one or two others, it is ruin to print poetry, and the Arts Council, appealed to for help by the distraught bards, is busily considering what to do about the wilting Muse. Shall it endow with public funds publication of the poetry which the public is now so unwilling to read?

The defense of the Obscure poets who defy grammar, syntax and meaning as they eject their strained imagery is a mixed one. Some pleaders merely deny the charge; those who do not understand the tangled products of the Spasmodist Singers are accused of being lazy or stupid or both. The blame is laid on the boneheaded reader who will not puzzle the stuff out and work away at the verbal jigsaw provided. Another plea is that the contemporary world is so confused in its complex of economic, political, ethical and psychological problems that nobody who is true to his time can be expected to be lucid in the exposition of the age and its dilemmas.

The first excuse is a mere denial of guilt, which gets nowhere in a court of law. The second is an affirmation and defense of artistic impotence. Once more it is the abdication of the author. The more intricate the mass of our difficulties the greater is the need of minds able to cut into them like knives, get rid of jargon and give us meaning.

One habit of those unable to express themselves is to take cover under a long word which happens to be in vogue. Existentialism is an obvious case in point. Whenever somebody tells me that So-and-So is an Existentialist, with the implication that I am therefore to bow my head in awe and admiration, I immediately challenge him for a definition of Existentialism. I have never had the beginnings of a satisfactory reply.

Producers and actors of Existentialist plays are completely flummoxed if asked to cut the cackle and say exactly what they mean. So, in my experience, are literary critics. They wander off into some vague profundities about Essence and when asked to say exactly what that means they do not know.

To be vague may often be a short cut to a certain kind of popularity. It provides a debating point, and man is an argumentative animal. To write a poem, a play or a book which will become a dinner-table topic may be a profitable occupation. It is jam for the intellectual snobs who relish telling you what the author was really getting at. Because you do not know, and do not pretend to know, you are supposed to be a crude simpleton. The history of the Snob-Value of the Obscure deserves a book in itself. When Browning remarked that only the author knew the meaning of his "Sordello" and that he had forgotten it, he gave enormous joy to the Browning Societies of his day, who then got to work on unravelment and so displayed their own surpassing acumen and ingenuity.

Admittedly the poet is not quite in the same position as the writer of prose. He is working more on percept than on concept, more on feeling than on dialectic. But there is no reason why he should not be able to give an exact image in words of his perceptions and his emotions. The best poets have managed to do so. Do we know just what Keats felt about the nightingale or the Grecian urn? We do. He did not have to make war on syntax or turn his odes into a grammarian's funeral.

I have never had to scratch my head over the sweet melancholy of A. E. Housman or put wet towels round an aching brain in order to excavate the meanings from a poem of Tennyson. Sometimes a creative mind works so rapidly that his thought outruns his hand and the images become telescoped like the railway carriages in an accident: Shakespeare's immense fecundity sometimes led to this. But no great poet, at his best, is obscure.

The public as a whole—that is, the public barring the Intellectual Snobs—shows its sensible preference for having its artists in sufficient possession of their faculties to put us all, and immediately, in possession of their meaning. The artist who does not know his own intentions is a pretender. If he does know them and cannot express them he is merely incompetent. I hope I have made myself plain.

Narration

NARRATION

Narration may be defined as the art of telling an anecdote, an incident, or a story which may be true or made-up. Raconteurs have always been popular, for the urge to tell a story has been instinctive in man since the commencement of civilization.

Fiction is an author's presentation of life as he observes it or experiences it. Fiction may be imaginatively conceived, or it may be based on the real, or it may be a fusion of the real and the imaginative. The writer of fiction has a purpose: a story is never told accidentally or unconsciously. The writer gives an insight into life; he may attempt to please or amuse or even shock the reader; he may present his philosophy of life; or he may delight him with the beauty of his language or the magic of his imagination.

Three types of fiction are the novel, the novella, and the short story. The novel, a polymorphous form, has a limitless range of subject matter; it is, perhaps, the best genre for the delineation of character. The novella is a kind of literary hybrid; it is a compromise between the novel and the short story. Two excellent examples of this type of writing are Henry James' *An International Episode* and Jean Stafford's *A Winter's Tale*. The novella should have a much wider audience. The short story, now highly regarded in academic and non-academic circles, is possibly the most difficult form of artistic expression for the writer.

The short story is an account of a happening, and between the opening and closing of a story some significant event should take place. Edgar Allan Poe defined the short story as "a brief prose tale with a single or pointed effect." One often hears the question: "What is the story about?" But Sean O'Faolain in "The Art of the Short Story" says that "a story is really never about anything; it is the writer's view of life." The more the student reads, then, the more diversified will be the reactions to life that the short-story writers hold up to him.

The short story is generally concerned with one incident or situation. It employs only three or four characters, and considers them only super-ficially because of the spatial limitations of the story. Only one high point of interest is reached in the modern short story.

Like life itself, stories give an insight into human nature—at times, indeed, into depraved human nature. Like life itself, stories do not always end happily or pleasantly but often tragically. And like life itself, stories do not always have moral values, since literature, of which fiction is a genre, attempts to portray life as accurately as the writer sees it or experiences it.

There is a wide range of experiences and human emotions recorded in the stories that follow. There is a deep, warm feeling in John Campbell Smith's "Run, Run Away, Brother." There is a fantastic generosity in the timely story "The Credit Line" by Richard Young Thurman. There is the wild excitement of the young boy in Michael McLaverty's "The Wild Duck's

Nest." For many there is an evocative reminiscence in Nancy Hale's "A Slow Boat to China," and there is unquestionably a picture of futility and hope in Mary Deasy's "Morning Sun." Certainly there is an unforgettable loneliness pervading F. Scott Fitzgerald's "Babylon Revisited." These and other stories, it is hoped, will hold the interest and enthusiasm of readers, young and old.

OLIVER LA FARGE

THE HAPPY INDIAN LAUGHTER*

THREE MEN sat, each on one of three wooden steps. The one on the top step was young. His hair was cut short. He wore a fairly large, neat, light-gray Stetson, a blue Air Force officer's shirt, a blue silk scarf at his throat, neatly pressed Levis, and cowboy boots. He was waiting for something. He sat quietly as the others, but you could tell that he was waiting.

The two others were past middle age. Their large black felt hats were battered. One had a beadwork hatband, the other a hatband made of dimes. From under the hatbrims, just behind their ears, their braided hair hung down, wrapped in two colors of tape, crisscrossing. These two were not waiting for anything, they were just relaxing.

When a big blue convertible with the top up came around the corner at the end of the dusty street, all three looked up. The car seemed to hesitate, then came toward them slowly.

The man on the middle step said, "Tourists." He looked at the one below him, who was thin, and older than he. "Show your moccasins, brother; perhaps they'll pay to take your picture."

"Run tell your wife to weave a basket."

They both laughed. The young man's face had become blank.

The old man said, "Just one tourist—a woman, young. Perhaps we can be Apaches and frighten her."

The two laughed again—the pleasant, light laughter of Indians. The young man said, using a title of respect, "Grandfather, I know this woman. She was a friend to me when I was away in the Air Force."

The old man said, "Good. Let her walk in peace."

The girl had put up the top of her convertible when she encountered the penetrating dust of the road that led from the sad little town of Arenosa to the Indian Agency. The road appalled her. The dirt was hard, cut by ruts, and washboarded, and, for all its hardness, produced fine, clayey dust in quantity. She came to a cattle guard, a strong barbed-wire fence, and a sign reading, "Department of the Interior—U.S. Indian Service—Gohlquain Apache Indian Agency—No Trespassing." She stopped the car and studied

* From *A Pause in the Desert*, which was originally published in *The New Yorker* (August 6, 1955). Reprinted by permission of Houghton Mifflin Company.

the sign, half minded to turn back. Then, with a jerk, she started forward again. She had overcome too much opposition, in herself and from others, to turn back now.

The Agency was five miles inside the boundary, Ralph had written, and the high country of grass and trees not far beyond. She could see the high country ahead of her, blue and inscrutable. She'd find out soon enough what it was really like. She'd find out a lot, and above all the difference between a handsome—you could almost say beautiful—Air Force pilot with a bronze skin and an Apache cattleman. As she had pointed out to friends and relatives, he was a college man as well as a pilot, and he would be the same in any setting, with the same nice manners and the same humor. She wished now that she were sure of that.

The Agency was a village, strung out along a wide, straight section of the road. There were white wooden houses, some adobe ones, and a couple of dreary brick buildings. Ralph had written that he would be waiting for her in front of the Agency proper, which she could recognize by the sign over its door and the clock in the little tower on top. She came almost to a stop, looked about, then proceeded slowly.

She passed two women walking in the opposite direction, on her side of the road. Their hair hung, rich and black, over their shoulders. They wore calico blouses and full calico skirts. As she passed them, they did not glance but looked at her for a measurable time, their faces impenetrable, their eyes dismissing. So those were Apache women; even their manner of walking was alien.

She identified the Agency, which was one of the smaller structures—she had expected it to be large—and saw the three men sitting. That was surely Ralph on the top step, and by now he must have seen her Ohio license plates and recognized the car, but he did not get up. She felt a sudden anger.

The Agency building stood on the left-hand side of the street. She came to a stop opposite it, on the right. As she did so, the young man rose, came down the steps, and walked to the car, not hurrying. The two older men sat gazing at her. All three faces showed nothing but blankness it was difficult not to read hostility into.

Ralph stopped with his hand on the door. "You got here." The remark was neutral.

She said, "Did I?"

A trace of smile showed about his mouth. "Hard to tell in all this dust. You'd better let me drive; I know these roads, and I can take your car over them with less of a beating than you can."

She was within a hairbreadth of saying, "Thanks, I'm going back now," but she didn't, for the same reason that she hadn't turned back at the boundary, and because she remembered how guarded and withdrawn he had been, for all his wings and ribbons, the first time she took him to the country club. She said, "All right," and moved over.

He drove without speaking for nearly five minutes, handling the car carefully and well. Shortly beyond the Agency grounds, the road began to climb. Instead of the hard, dust-yielding baked mud, its surface was of a coarser, reddish earth, less dusty and less dramatically rutted. Scattered cactus and sagebrush on either hand were replaced by occasional piñons and junipers. The land seemed greener; she could not decide whether there was actually more vegetation or whether it was merely that the grass and small plants were not dust-coated and showed up more strongly against the warmer-colored earth.

The cowboy outfit was becoming to him. He was tanned, darker than when she had known him at the base. His nose was high and straight, his lips sculptured, his chin strong. There was the intriguing extra height of his cheekbones, and above them the dark eyes, slightly Oriental. They were not slanted, but at the outer corners of the upper lids there was a fascinating curve. All this was familiar, but the expressionless face remained strange.

They passed a single tall white pine by the side of the road. As if reaching that point released him, he looked at her and said, "You know, I didn't really believe you'd come until I saw the car." His face had come alive. This *was* Ralph, after all.

She was astonished to feel so much relief. "I wouldn't have missed it for anything. It isn't everyone who gets formally invited to spend a weekend with Indians."

"My dad was tickled with the whole idea. Mother said I was nuts; she said it would be too strange for you. Still, she's kind of looking forward to it. I think you'll find it interesting."

Of course, he had not mentioned the real purpose of her visit, any more than they were able to speak of it between themselves; it mattered so much and seemed so beyond reason. She wondered what that dark Apache mother was thinking, and the sisters—especially the one who had served in the Waves.

He slowed to a stop alongside a pickup truck parked by the road. The driver of the truck wore his hair in braids, heavy ones, the hair black and shiny where it was not wrapped. Ralph had told her once that long-haired Indians were mostly over forty. This one looked middle-aged. He had a blobby big nose in a broad, heavy face. As the two men talked, she thought he seemed a cheerful type.

The language sounded slurry, soft, with a good many "sh" and "l" sounds, punctuated by harsh, throaty consonants. There was a rise and fall of tone. The speech was milder than she had expected, faintly musical, and yet virile. She did not think she could ever hope to understand it.

Presently, the man in the truck laughed. Ralph turned to her. "This is my uncle, Juan Grijalva. He and Dad and I run our cattle together."

She smiled at the Indian, who studied her gravely. "You got a gun with you?" he asked.

She saw that his intent was humorous. "No. Do I need one?"

He shook his head. "These Inyans are mighty rough people. And these

Inyan veterans, now, you gotta watch them all the time. You need help, you let out a whoop and I'll come. I gotta keep my nephew in line."

He and Ralph laughed. She didn't think it particularly funny, but she liked the friendliness. She said, "Thanks, I'll remember that."

Ralph said to his uncle, in English, "All right. You'll bring up the salt then?"

"Yeh. Your friend ride?"

Ralph looked at her. She said, "Pretty well—that is, I've been on dude ranches."

Uncle Juan told Ralph, "You pick her out an easy horse, and we can take her along while we set out the salt, and let her view the configuration of the landscape."

As he said the last words, he was watching her closely and his eyes were dancing. Her mouth twitched.

Abruptly, he said, "Well, so long. *Ta'njoh*."

Ralph said, "*Ta'njoh*."

Both men started their cars and moved along.

"He took two years at Colorado A. & M.," Ralph told her. "He's really a fine cattleman; I'm learning from him right along. He's my dad's brother, so we kid each other all the time."

"Do uncles and nephews usually kid each other?"

"Only on your father's side. On your mother's side, you use respect. It's the custom."

"Oh." It sounded surprisingly complicated and artificial.

Pines were appearing among the smaller evergreens, and the grass was definitely richer. Presently Ralph said, "Anthropologists call it 'the joking relationship'—I mean relations who kid, like Juan and me. When I marry, he'll kid with my wife the same way. It's fun if you're used to it."

For a moment she stiffened, feeling the remark probe toward the central, unmentioned thing, the thing that had seemed possible at the officers' club, at the country club, in the city, and so totally impossible when the young man came down from the steps. She let time pass before speaking the thought that came to her, lest the connection be apparent. "You aren't going back into the Air Force?"

"Not unless they call me back. I belong here. These people are coming up, in the cattle business and a lot of other ways. There are only four of us in the tribe who've been all the way through college, besides maybe half a dozen like Juan, who went part way and then came back. Besides, it's good here. Look at it."

They had never ceased climbing. The air was fresher, the country greener and more rugged. At some distance to their right, a handsome bank of red cliffs paralleled the road, contrasting nicely with the pine and spruce at its base. They came into a long, wide, open meadow on which a score or more of beef cattle were grazing. It was good country.

He asked, "Did you bring a tent, and all?"

"Yes, one of those little green tents, and a cot."

"Good. It's not so long since we lived in tepees, and we're used to being kind of crowded together. There's five of us in the two rooms in Dad's house. You'll be more comfortable in a tent of your own."

When they had driven a little farther, he said, "I'll show you where I'm laying out my house. After the cattle sales this fall, I'll have enough cash to go ahead and build it. I'm going to put in butane gas for the kitchen, and there's a spring above it, so I can bring water in on straight gravity. I figure on three rooms and a bath to start with, and then build on later. Maybe you can give me some advice. There's good stone handy, as well as lots of timber; I don't know which to build in."

He could not possibly have sounded more casual, nor could she as she answered, "I'd like to see it."

Even so, she was relieved when he started reading brands on the cattle near the road and explaining to her which were good Herefords, which off-color or poorly made. As she already knew, he had delicacy; his capacity for perception and tact had surprised her friends.

Ralph's father's name was Pedro Tanitsin; she must find out, she thought, why Juan had a different surname. Tanitsin had put his house in a fairly narrow, craggy-sided valley with an outlook to the south. It was a simple, small frame house, slightly overdue to be repainted. There were no grounds —that is, no fenced area, smooth grass, or planting of any kind. At the east end of the house was a large, flat-topped shelter, its roof thickly covered with evergreen branches. Beyond that was the bare pole skeleton of a tepee. A heavy truck with a tarpaulin over the hood stood by the house. A hundred feet or so behind it, she made out the horizontal bars of a corral crossing the lines of the ruddy stems of the pines around it and she saw a horse move. Ralph parked the car beside the truck. Two dogs came skulking, but no human being came to meet them.

At the east end of the shelter was a wide opening. When they came to it, Ralph stopped, so she did, too, beside him and a step behind him. Inside were the people—Ralph's father, sitting on a bench, and his mother and his two sisters, standing. There was an interval of silence; she felt awkward, and saw before her the same blank, guarded faces that had repulsed her at the Agency. She was aware of a camp stove, a fire pit in the middle of the floor, some cooking utensils, and a large barrel, in addition to the bench.

Pedro Tanitsin's hair was braided, and he wore a brilliant beadwork vest over a bright flannel shirt, and Levis and moccasins. Ralph's mother wore the native dress; so did the older of his sisters, but instead of wearing her hair loose over her shoulders, she had it clubbed at the back of her neck. That must be Juanita, who had been in the Waves. The other, then, was Mary Ellen. Her hair was bobbed and curled, and she wore one of those gaudy silk blouses service men bring back from Japan, and slacks that had never been intended for outdoor life.

The mother spoke a single word, in Apache, and followed it with "Come een." Ralph moved forward, and the girl followed. She felt that she was moving against a wall of rejection. Ralph said something in his own tongue; then, gesturing, "This is my father."

She turned toward him. He nodded once, slowly.

Ralph said, "And this is my mother."

The older woman put out her hand, so the girl took it. The clasp was limp, there was no response to her motion of shaking, and the hand was quickly withdrawn. Then the mother spoke, ending with a laugh.

Ralph said, "She says—Well, you see, a while back one of the government women, some kind of social worker, came here, and she came in talking her head off before anybody had time to get used to her. You came in quietly, like an Indian. So she says, 'This one has good manners.'"

The woman laughed again. "Yes, not walk in talkin'."

The girl felt pleased and relieved. Then she saw that all of them were smiling except Mary Ellen.

Juanita gave her a somewhat firmer handclasp and said, "We were wondering whether you would really come here, to an Indian camp. I hope you like it." Mary Ellen's touch was limp and even more fleeting than her mother's; she kept her eyes down and did not speak.

It seemed that in summer they lived in the shelter, using the house only for sleeping and storage. Their housekeeping was easy and relaxed, rather like a well-organized picnic. She thought it better not to offer to help with getting supper; instead, she watched and took it easy. Hold back and go slow, she had decided, were essential elements of Apache etiquette. Cooking was well advanced when Pedro addressed some commonplace questions to her in heavily accented English. It was a little as if one of the pines had decided to speak, and the product, she thought, should have been less banal.

They all settled on the ground to eat, in a half circle. Ralph's mother insisted on giving her an angora skin, dyed deep blue, to sit on. The food was good, the utensils clean. In the middle of eating, to which the Indians devoted themselves with very little talk, Mary Ellen said something that made the others laugh. Juanita interpreted. "She says Ralph said that you were the kind who would wear Levis and sit on the earth, and you are."

She began to see that what she had taken for hostility in Mary Ellen was defensiveness, just as the inappropriate, pseudo-elegant costume was. The younger girl had not been out into the world, like her older brother and sister; nor had she the self-assurance, the satisfaction with plainly being Apache, of her parents. Her English was limited and unsteady. The presence of a strange white woman made her uneasy, and in an Indian, the visitor was beginning to see, uneasiness takes on the face of guarded enmity.

She herself was beginning to feel at home here. She looked around her. The incoming night air from beyond the shelter was chill. A generous fire burned in the central pit. About her were dark, friendly faces. In the air she breathed were the smells of smoke, food, coffee, pine needles, and the near-perfume of juniper boughs that had been brought up from lower country to make the walls of the shelter thicker and more fragrant. It was incredible that she should be here, at this moment, stirring the sugar in a fresh cup of coffee, listening to the musical rise and fall of a woman's voice saying something in that mysterious tongue. She looked sidelong at Ralph. In the shifting, reddening firelight, he was darker, at once familiar, loved, and alien, primitive. Could it be possible, after all? Was it anything more than a remnant of a madness that had seized her when she went visiting a friend who had married a fly-boy major?

By the end of the third day, she had to remind herself that all this was as strange as it was. Ralph planned to build a modern house, but the family's half-camping mode of life was agreeable; come winter, though, the inside of that little house would be on the grim side. The family were friendly, easy to be with, especially once Mary Ellen, feeling secure, had returned to native costume.

They had a radio, which they listened to chiefly for news, weather, and cattle-price reports, Ralph or Juanita translating for their parents. Mary Ellen read movie magazines. Juanita dipped into textbooks that would help her in college (the University of New Mexico had accepted her for next fall) and, for the same purpose, was struggling through "Vanity Fair." The white woman was able to help her there, realizing as she did so what a staggeringly broad context an educated white person moved and thought in, learned without effort, all of which an Indian had to grasp item by item. To speak English, read, and write were only the beginning.

Ralph and Uncle Juan, who visited daily, went in for bulletins from the extension service and agricultural colleges, reading them and then expounding their contents to Pedro. She was amused by the automatic gesture with which Uncle Juan would brush a braid back when it fell on the page. She had thought she had learned a little of the cattle business on a dude ranch near Tucson, where they made a big thing of running beef stock; not until now had she imagined it could be a bookish vocation with a highly technical vocabulary. Ralph and Juan turned to her to verify the meaning of "it is a far cry from," and in the same sentence were two words they had to explain to her. This amused Pedro greatly; he didn't know much English, but he had learned those.

Reading was occasional and in the daytime. After dinner, in the firelit dark, they told stories. Pedro, it turned out, was a noted storyteller in his own language. He talked and Ralph translated and explained. The stories had quality, and through them she saw that the Apaches, too, had a considerable context to be learned.

In her cot that night, with the sweet, cold air on her cheek, hearing the shushing rise and fall of a soft breeze in the high pines, she thought that it was possible, it could happen. It was just possible. Ralph in the saddle was magnificent. Uncle Juan sat his horse like a rock that had become one with the animal, but Ralph was fine-waisted live whalebone. They were fun to ride with—considerate, instructive, humorous.

As they went about the range, there was nothing that moved, nothing out of place, that they did not see, at the farthest distance to which good eyes could reach. They made no apparent effort, she was not conscious that they were scouting, but they saw everything and were not content until it was explained. A pinto horse, an over-age steer with long horns—whose? A truck, two mounted men—to her, when she finally made them out, no more than dots on a distant road—who were they? Where were they going?

It made her think of bygone days and Apaches on the warpath. Some of those warriors had still been alive when Ralph was a boy. The warpath training had not been dropped. It made her think, as well, of Ralph high in the air alongside the Yalu, and his record of kills. There was a closer link between a deadly grandfather with a painted face and the skilled pilot than one would have thought.

Nothing was quite what she had expected, and least expected of all was the constant thread of laughter—the happy Indian laughter running through everything, so light and so easily provoked. And it was possible, just barely possible—that is, if *they* accepted *her*. Before she came here, she had not thought of that. What was definite was that she was in love with Ralph. When she had fully faced that, tired as she was, she was long in falling asleep.

The following afternoon, Ralph told her, "There's a neighbor of ours had a curing ceremony a while back. What he had was a virus and a touch of pneumonia, and they cured that at the hospital, but he had a sing, too. They do that a lot. There's something to it; the doctor takes care of the physical end, and the medicine man takes care of the psychosomatic. Anyway, now he has to 'pick up' the ceremony, as they say. It's a kind of thanksgiving. He puts up a tepee, and they make *tulapai*—that's a kind of beer made from corn. The neighbors come in, and there's a little singing and a feast, and we drink *tulapai* and talk, then at the end everybody gets blessed."

She said, "It sounds interesting. Do they get drunk?"

"You'd have to work hard to get drunk on *tulapai*. It just makes everybody happy. While you're seeing the Apaches, you ought to see this, only— Well, it's kind of unsanitary. They fill a lard pail and pass it around. Of course, you're not an Indian, so it will be all right if you want to use a cup."

"I don't think that's necessary."

Ralph was pleased. "All right. Anyway, it will be just us and Uncle Juan's family, and this man's—his name is Pablo Horses. They're all healthy, and they're clean."

Near sundown, they drove the mile to Pablo's house in her car and the truck. That was her first sight of a real-life tepee; she was struck by its symmetry, the way in which the curved canvas caught the light, and the effect of the long, sloping white line against a green background. Inside, the tepee seemed even roomier than it had looked from the outside.

The door faced east. In the middle, there was a small, fragrant fire, and a kerosene lantern hung near the host's place at the back. The men sat on the south, the women on the north. All of them were wearing elements of Indian costume—items of buckskin, beadwork, Navaho silver, and Pueblo turquoise and shell. Pedro had his beaded vest on again; she knew now that his donning it that first day had been in honor of her. Ralph had put a wide band of beadwork around his hat, and at his throat, instead of his cowboy's scarf, he wore a broad choker of elk bone and beads. It was becoming.

All of them had blankets. Juanita had insisted that she take one, and had given her a handsome, soft expensive Pendleton. The idea of wearing it had embarrassed her, but now she felt that it helped her to blend in. She'd turn into an Apache yet, she thought.

Their host, a craggy man with definitely gray hair, was older than Pedro Tanitsin. Because this was a ceremony, he had an eagle feather tied to the top of his head.

All of them, and especially the women, were amused that a white woman should come to drink *tulapai*. There were comments and laughter. Juanita, sitting next to her, said, "You mustn't mind. It's good. You are giving people a good feeling, so that helps what we are doing."

Pablo Horses took up a rattle and began a chant, in which the older men joined. The time was slow and monotonous, the music narrow in range, and heavy. It was dull, and yet, as the girl listened, the monotonous rhythm and droning voices took hold of her. There was a curious power there.

After four songs, Pablo's daughter brought in a pail of *tulapai*, which was passed around solemnly, clockwise. Unsanitary, certainly; the girl wished she had asked for a cup, but they did seem a healthy lot. The drink itself was good, like beer but with a fresh quality that suggested hard cider. There were four more sets of four songs each, with a circuit of the pail after each set, and then the business of sprinkling a yellow powder and brushing the air with feathers. Everyone had sat still during the chant; the refreshment period was a break, when people changed positions. Pablo's women brought in food. The girl felt no noticeable lift from the small amount of the beer she had taken, but it did seem to have sharpened her appetite.

When she had eaten, Pablo said, "Young lady, where you come from?"

She said, "Ohio—Cleveland."

A young man, Uncle Juan's son, said, "I was there one time when I was in the Army. They got a good U.S.O." That took care of Cleveland.

An elderly man—Pablo's brother, she believed—asked, "How you like it here?"

"I like it. This is beautiful country."

Ralph took the trouble to translate that. Pablo said, "Yes. This is our country, Apache country." Then he went on at some length in Apache.

Juanita explained, "He's taken what you said as a kind of text, and he's telling how this is our country, and we must keep it, and we must live up to our Apache traditions."

More *tulapai* was brought in. The women were speaking up more than usual. There was an atmosphere of geniality and relaxation, but no ugliness, nothing one could call drunkenness.

The man she believed to be Pablo's brother, after a good draught of beer, launched upon a long story. Soon someone laughed. A little later, they all laughed. There were interruptions of laughter all through the latter part of the narration.

When he had finished, Ralph translated. "This is Tomás Horses speaking. He lives about five miles from here; in between Pablo's place and his there is a place called Yellow Spring, where people camp. That's important.

"He says there is a Pueblo Indian called Malaquias he knows pretty well, a smart trader. Three or four times, when Tomás has visited that Pueblo, Malaquias has given him wine, then traded with him when he was high, and outsmarted him. So he's been waiting for a chance to get even."

They were all listening eagerly. Hearing the story a second time, knowing the point, made it all the more delightful.

"Well, about a week ago Malaquias came trading jewelry, and he camped at Yellow Spring. Tomás had some whiskey, so he made his plan. He came and borrowed Pablo's buckskin; that's a fast strong horse and hard to hold once he gets going."

There were giggles.

"Then he drove to Yellow Spring in his wagon and told this man, 'My friend, put your goods in my wagon and come to my house. I'll give you a drink, and you can have supper with me, and perhaps we can do a little business.'"

This, it seemed, was hilarious.

"So he went along, and Tomás poured whiskey for him." More laughter. "Tomás went light. All the same, they traded, and the Pueblo traded him out of that buckskin for that string of turquoise he's wearing. The poor Apache had been gypped again." Ralph's own voice shook as he said this.

"So he gave the man some more whiskey, and kept him there for supper. Meantime, his two boys—this one here and another one, who's away now— went down the road about a mile and strung wire across between two trees."

The punctuations of laughter were almost continuous.

"So Tomás gave Malaquias a hackamore for the buckskin, and Malaquias started for his camp after dark, and good and tight. The buckskin was headed toward home, you understand, and Malaquias could not stop him when he started running. So they came to that wire, and it took him just right, under the chin, and threw him right off the horse. The horse came on back to Pablo's."

The telling had to stop for seconds of laughter.

"Then Tomás and the boys went and got the wire, and he sent this boy to the ranger station to tell how there was this foreign Indian lying in the road with his neck all torn and they'd better pick him up. By and by, they picked him up and took him to the hospital. He's still there."

Ralph looked about him, chuckling over the humor of it, feeling the successful narrator's glow. His audience was given over to laughter—all but the girl he loved, who seemed somehow alien, remote, so that he was unusually conscious of her paleness. He caught Juanita's eye, and she threw back her head to laugh again. Then he looked at the girl once more. She was so still, her eyes fixed on the ground. Wanting her to share in this as she had in so much else these last days, he forgot his satisfaction with his performance and studied her with concern, trying to reach what was in her mind, what was the matter. At that moment, she raised her eyes and looked directly at him. The last traces of pleasure left his face, because, as he read her now, her thoughts all laid open, he knew that this had ended it, and that she would start home the first thing tomorrow.

RICHARD SULLIVAN

IN A GLASS DARKLY*

HE GLARED at his image in the big mirror over the marble-top table in the hall: his thinning hair, his slightly puffy cheeks, his gaping mouth twitching furiously, his twisted necktie outflung over one sloping shoulder, his whole long skinny torso. One of his hands grabbed the brass candlestick on the marble-top table; his eyes in the mirror flickered white; slowly, slowly, he raised the candlestick. Face to face, he thought: There he is, the perfect husband; observe him well and note the markings, because now you see him, now you——

It had all been going nicely. Oh, he was lonesome, but not like this, not aware of himself. Never before in his life had he been so terribly aware of himself, so painfully, embarrassingly close to himself as now, glaring back with upraised brass candlestick and white eyes, in the mirror.

Edwina had started it. They were eating, and "Barry," she said, switching the conversation abruptly to him, "you can tell us now. Are you and Rita always really so happy? I mean, is it the same behind the scenes?" And she laughed, very inquisitively.

He looked from Edwina's opaque black marble eyes on his right to the steady cowlike brown gaze of Miss Sigfried, the psychologist, across the table from him, and, patting his thinning hair, he smiled nervously. "Well, I really—this is very interesting——" He turned to George on his left.

George was grinning. He bit with strong white teeth into a small radish. "This is the first time you've been away from her, Barry?"

"Well," said Barry, wishing he could invent quickly, "yes. Yes, it is. Oh, of course," he added quickly, "I've been away, but this is the first time Rita and John have been away together from me, from our home." Involved

---

* This story appeared originally in The Yale Review (Spring, 1943). Reprinted by permission of the author.

with words, he hoped he could change the talk to an elaborate explanation. "You understand what I mean, George?"

"I understand all right," said George, grinning.

"Barry is the perfect husband," explained Edwina to Miss Sigfried. "You see him."

"Well!" cried Miss Sigfried in a minor explosion of amazement.

"So attentive! Honestly, you'd think they were on their honeymoon."

Both women, smiling as if they shared an amusing secret, looked at Barry. He patted his hair. "Well, I must say," he stammered, "this is like seeing yourself in a new mirror. I never thought——"

"Seeing yourself with a dark eye glassily," said George. "Oh no! It's a glass eye darkily. Mark Twain."

"Is that Mark Twain?" exclaimed Barry eagerly. "I'd wondered. It's very good. A dark eye glassily!"

"No, a glass eye darkily, I think. Yes, a glass eye——"

Miss Sigfried tittered. Then with shrewd benevolence she asked, "And how long have you been married, Mr. Ferguson?" He remembered how she said it, accenting the first word: "And how long——?"

He twisted his face as if thinking hard. "Oh, six, well, almost seven years," he told her. He turned to George: "Let's see, you and Edwina were married after us, weren't you? Yes, sure——"

"They have a son—almost five years old," Edwina told Miss Sigfried. "You'd like Rita, she's little and dark. What did Margaret say about her? Oh, yes—Barry, Margaret says Rita looks like a woman well loved."

"Margaret, eh? Yes, well——!"

"Nobody says that about me!" complained Edwina in a whoop to Miss Sigfried, and both women laughed happily.

"You're lucky to have a provider, my girl," said George. He turned to Barry. "We can't all be old Romeos like this fellow."

"I don't know just how to take all this," protested Barry. "Look, do Rita and I impress everybody as being, well——?"

"Lovebirds," said Edwina.

"But how? I mean——?"

"Wherever you go you're always so attentive, and Rita treats you as if she just expected it. She's casual. You know. That's why I asked you if it was the same way behind the scenes. Don't you ever have fights?"

Barry's face twisted.

"His married life is one perpetual dream," said George, grinning, "a dream of fair woman. What's the matter with you, Barry? That's what you're supposed to say."

"Of course!" cried Barry. "That's it, of course!" He laughed strenuously, to block further comment, and then suddenly he remembered the dream he had had the night before.

After dessert and coffee they played bridge for a while, and he and Rita did not come up again as a subject; but all the time Barry felt that Miss

Sigfried was examining him like something smeared on a slide, and he was haunted by that dream of Rita; it came back now with overwhelming intensity: they were alone in a strange house, the children away someplace —there were several children and they were all away—Rita wore a new dress, misty-black, and a black unfamiliar hat; she came to him, a low music started, grew, spread, clear, very lilting, the piano strong and bright; she clung to him lightly, they danced, she was a faint familiar pressure against him as they whirled, whirled slowly, unearthly, like persons moving in water, the sweet growing force of the music around them like water; he was waked from the dream by the noise of the music; he sat up in bed, hearing still in the dark room the full round clarity of sound, so clear, so intense, that he sang aloud the shining wordless melody, determined to remember it, to tell it to Rita when she came back, to tell her this rich dream-strangeness.

But in the morning, though the dream was vivid, the sound of the music was unrecapturable; playing as Edwina's partner, he had strained again to hear it, forgotten music beyond the remembered fact; and it stayed beyond.

"Oh, but I really must go," Miss Sigfried had said at last, glancing with exaggerated concern at her wrist watch.

"Well, I can give you a lift too, Barry," George told him, after Edwina had said it was still early and Miss Sigfried had said yes, but her work got her up at five every morning.

"I think I'll walk, George. It's not far. I walked over."

"I have to take the car out for Siggy, anyhow."

"I'd rather walk, George. It's a nice night. Really."

"Full moon," said George, peering at him with rather ponderous slyness. "Don't know whether a romantic bachelor like you should walk in the full moon or not."

A cloud like a thick black snake had twisted across the moon as he walked. It was late summer; the night air was heavy; faraway thunder made the sky tremulous and vital. A few sudden drops of rain splashed on him just as he was turning into his own yard; he scooted to the porch.

Stuck in the screen door was a special-delivery from Rita. He scraped his forehead on the door edge in his anxiety to get inside quickly, to read the letter.

Rita asked him to remember that her ivy needed water, and to send her some money at once; she said John was being an absolute little devil. "Your letters are so mournful," she wrote. "Don't be silly. I'll be back in two weeks. You sound like a widower." She sent love from herself and his son.

He sat there with the letter on his lap. He patted his thinning hair. He had to admit, he told himself, that he was possibly more in love with Rita than she had ever been with him. Yes, he had to admit that. She had said nothing about missing him, nothing even to hint about loneliness. She wrote like a well-loved woman, confidently and casually.

He began to feel resentful. He went over to his desk. On it lay the letter he had started to Rita before he had gone out to dinner. He caught the final words—"most desolate." No use a man's making a fool of himself. He tore up the unfinished letter, then sat down at his desk. She wouldn't like it if he took up with some little blonde while she was gone, though, would she? No, she wouldn't like that. But she knew he wouldn't do it. He wouldn't either. No use trying to fool himself.

Opening his desk drawer, he took out his checkbook and wrote a check to her. "There," he said aloud in the empty house; the word sounded solemn and sharp—"There."

He loosened his necktie and opened his collar. The stale air in the room oppressed him. Outside, low in the sky, thunder rumbled. He went to the window. The moon had gone and slow thick rain streamed in the darkness; he could hear it beyond the glass, a stir out there, monotonous and insistent.

He was a comic figure, he supposed, the romantic husband with the thinning hair and the confident, beautiful wife. Plays had been written about him, songs, stories. As long as men had lived he had been funny.

He remembered something he had read somewhere about American husbands—that they were weak and complaisant while their wives were the hardest, shrewdest, most beautiful women on earth. He wondered if that was so; how would a writer get facts on a thing like that? He sniffed angrily: a writer wouldn't need any more facts than Edwina did; just look at Rita and himself—after six years, almost seven, he was still as devotedly, as slavishly, in love, no, more devotedly, more slavishly, in love with his wife than he had been when they were married. The perfect husband, no use denying it; nothing had worn off for him; it was all the same. Except that for Rita it had worn off. Except that.

Outside dark rain hissed steadily down; and thunder, very far away, was like a sound remembered, not heard; was dimly, illogically, like the sound of unremembered music from his dream.

He walked out into the hall and caught sight of himself in the mirror. There he was in the honest glass, darkly; and he thought of George and his ponderous wit, of George's white teeth biting down on the radish, of Edwina's black inquisitive eyes and the bovine placidity of Miss Sigfried, whose work got her up at five in the morning, and of—what was it Margaret said?—of the well-loved woman, his wife.

Suddenly he leaned forward, glaring at himself and hating the contamination which his very reflection seemed to him. For sheer, pure ignominy, the weak complaisant husband—the perfect husband!—brought face to face with himself was the most excruciating——

This was when, passionately, he grabbed the brass candlestick from the table. He raised it slowly, intending to smash the mirror, savoring bitterly all the urgent violence of the instant. "Now you see him, now you don't," he muttered. And then, as he glared into the whites of his close-up glaring eyes, he was suddenly overwhelmed with surprise at his own intensity. Peering at himself in the mirror, he was amazed. He gaped and blinked.

All at once his customary discretion returned to him in a good familiar rush of common sense. He snorted almost contemptuously at his threatening image, brandishing that great brass weapon in the glass. Carefully he set the candlestick down; it made a heavy clink on the marble-top table. Why, with it he could kill a man, he could have smashed that mirror into a thousand chips. He felt a kind of weary admiration at himself, at his display of temperament. He had never before in his life felt the way he did tonight, or rather the way he had felt tonight; for it was all over now, he realized ruefully, all over. To be so full of angry blood, so revengeful—he had rather liked it. Certainly no one who knew him would ever suspect his real interior violence. He smiled and shook his head at himself in the glass. It had been insane and very satisfying, but, well, to smash an expensive mirror like this one, which, he now remembered, had been Rita's mother's—well, he thought, to do that——!

Turning to go upstairs, he felt a little puzzled. But it was all fidgets, of course. Nervous nonsense. He had been lonely and sensitive; Edwina had hurt his feelings. Must be careful about showing such things—he wondered if his embarrassment had been noticeable during the evening. He'd call Edwina tomorrow.

As he snapped off lights on the stair landing, he heard the faint uneasy roll of far-off thunder. It seemed to him very peaceful and soothing. Maybe that writer was right about American husbands and wives—but, well, it didn't make much difference, did it? Not much difference, he decided, not much. And walking up the final three stairs, he wondered hopefully if tonight he would dream.

EDWARD J. McTAGUE

THE PASTOR'S PRIVATE EYE*

"THIS IS a rather unusual case."

The Bishop spoke in an undertone.

"Fantastic," whispered the Chancellor.

The Bishop and the Chancellor stood beside each other and gazed out the office window. Several stories below heavy traffic thundered along Cathedral Parkway. They saw nothing; they did not hear the policeman's shrill whistle. They were totally absorbed with a problem.

Behind them and in front of the Chancellor's desk sat a curate. He was visibly disturbed. He had written to the Bishop requesting a transfer, and stated that to remain any longer in his present assignment might impair general health and effectiveness. He included in his letter a brief statement

* "The Pastor's Private Eye" appeared in *Pastoral Life* (May-June, 1956). Reprinted by permission of the author and the editor of *Pastoral Life*.

from his physician. He pointed out also that the pastor and the domestics were quite considerate of him and even went to extraordinary pains to make life pleasant for him in the rectory. But he added that there was a condition existing in the house that made life miserable and intolerable for him, and that it was the pastor's dog!

The Bishop and the Chancellor returned to the desk. The Bishop removed the zucchetto and placed it on the pad. He nodded to the Chancellor to continue interrogating the curate. The Chancellor, peering over his bifocals, began:

"Tell us, Father, does the pastor's dog molest you in any manner or form?"

The curate reflected a moment and answered: "If you mean, Monsignor, that he bites or snaps at me, I must say no."

"Then what is the trouble?"

"It's the dog's attitude, Monsignor."

The Bishop tugged at his pectoral cross and said: "Father, please explain the dog's attitude."

The curate moved his chair closer to the desk and in a confidential manner, said: "Your Excellency, every morning after breakfast, the dog follows me to my study, looks at me, shakes his head, and walks over to the pastor's room."

"I wouldn't consider that abnormal behavior for the dog," said the Bishop.

"But he carries tales about me, your Excellency."

"Who carries tales?"

"The dog."

The Bishop looked at the Chancellor. The Chancellor moved his head from side to side like a pendulum.

"Now, Father," the Chancellor proceeded, "you allege that this dog makes reports about you to the pastor. How do you know this?"

"The pastor tells me so," replied the curate, without the slightest hesitation.

"What sort of tales does he tell?" the Chancellor inquired.

The curate coughed nervously and said: "Last Tuesday, he reported me to the pastor for coming in after midnight."

"And did you come in at a late hour?"

"Yes, Monsignor, I visited mother and on the way back I was delayed with a flat tire."

"The dog should have overlooked that," the Chancellor stated. "You have a right to visit your mother."

"Thank you," said the curate, who felt quite relieved by the favorable comment. He continued: "The dog also turned me in for not wearing my biretta."

"Have you failed in this?" the Chancellor queried.

"Yes, I must confess," sighed the curate.

"You were in violation of a diocesan statute," admonished the Chancellor. With that he leaned back in his chair and picked a red book from the shelf.

He thumbed the pages quickly and continued: "Here it is, statute 4—'Clerics must wear the cassock in church and rectory' and so on and so on and so on, 'and provided with biretta.' " The Chancellor closed with a slam the diocesan articles of war and, like a C.O. about to throw the book at a soldier, concluded gravely: "Father, the dog is right!"

"And liturgically correct," added the Bishop.

"I quite agree with you," said the curate, "but it makes me feel inferior to have a dog standing between the pastor and me."

"Oh, tut, tut!" exclaimed the Bishop, "that's a matter of taste, not of ecclesiastical precedence."

The Bishop settled back in his chair and after a moment of reflection said: "Father, have you been under a doctor's care?"

"Oh, I've had the usual childhood diseases, mumps, measles and an occasional visit to the dentist. I really feel good, except for the dog."

The Bishop rose and walked over to the curate.

"Father," he said in a kindly tone, "I want you to return to the rectory and relax. As Teresa of Avila used to say: 'Let nothing disturb thee,' and I might add, not even a little dog."

"Thank you, your Excellency," said the curate. He went down on his right knee and kissed his Bishop's ring.

After the curate's departure, the Bishop said to the Chancellor: "What do you think of this?"

The Chancellor answered slowly and deliberately: "A borderline case, your Excellency. There seems to be an anxiety neurosis. I believe we should refer the case to a psychiatrist."

"Before doing so," said the Bishop, "let us call in the pastor."

The Chancellor reached for the telephone.

About two p.m. the pastor came into the Chancery office. The Bishop was very cordial in his greeting.

"Good afternoon, Father. I trust this sudden summons hasn't upset you."

"Oh, no," said the pastor, "my conscience is clear. I've paid all my assessments."

The Bishop removed his zucchetto and tossed it on the desk. Then he nodded to the Chancellor.

"Father," began the Chancellor, "your curate was in here this morning. He is apparently nervous and suffering from an obsession. Before recommending treatment we feel that you should first be consulted."

The pastor looked confused and panted like a sprinter after a quarter mile.

"I am sorry to hear this," he said with deep feeling. "My curate is really a good priest. Do you know the cause of his trouble?"

The Chancellor looked at the Bishop and his Excellency took up the questioning.

"Father, you have a dog?"

"Yes, I have."

"It is apparent," said the Bishop, "that you think more of this dog than you do of your curate."

"I wouldn't say that," said the pastor, "but I will go on record as saying that it's hard to get a good dog."

"But do you realize, Father, that your dog may be a contributing cause of nervousness in your curate?"

The pastor bowed his head and replied: "Your Excellency, I am amazed that you should entertain such a notion about my dog."

The Chancellor was now irritated and pointing a finger at the pastor, shouted, "Father, our primary concern is the curate and not this confounded beast. . . ."

The pastor leaped to his feet and leaning across the desk, exploded: "Young man, don't you refer to my dog as a beast. My dog is a purebred German dachshund. That's more than many of us can claim."

"Your dog is a tale-bearer," the Chancellor barked back.

"My dog is not a gossip, and he's not a juvenile delinquent. . . ."

"Gentlemen, gentlemen!" the Bishop pleaded, raising his arms like an umpire. "Please, please, remember there are people in the outer offices."

"Sorry," said the pastor through his teeth.

"Sorry," the Chancellor frowned.

The Bishop pushed his zucchetto back on his head and tugging at his pectoral cross said to the pastor: "Father, your poor assistant is apparently suffering from a persecutory delusion. He sincerely believes that your dog is making reports to you. . . ."

"That is quite correct," interrupted the pastor.

The Bishop's eyes popped. The Chancellor's mouth opened.

The pastor continued: "You see, your Excellency, my little dog reports to me daily. He keeps me well informed, and what he tells me is for the good of the parish and quite beneficial to me also."

"For instance?" asked the Bishop.

"The other day, he informed me that my assistant forgot to wash the purificators and bless water for the fonts. These, of course, are minor infractions. Moreover, my dog holds no grudges."

The Bishop and the Chancellor rose together and walked over to the window. The pastor drew out his pipe and filled it.

"Isn't this a nice basket of crabs!" murmured the Chancellor. "Two in one day and from the same house!"

The Bishop was in deep thought. He turned suddenly and moved over to the side of the pastor.

"Tell me, Father, have you had a medical check-up recently?"

"No, indeed," replied the pastor. "I feel as frisky as an Irish terrier."

"I assume," the Bishop went on, "that you haven't had a vacation. May I suggest a restful sea voyage. . . ."

"That's not for me," the pastor broke in, "I've just built a school and I have to put an addition to it. Besides, my dog gets seasick."

The Bishop straightened up. He felt like an autoist who had run out of gas.

"Father," he said softly, "please go home. I assure you that God and time will adjust matters."

After the pastor had left, the Chancellor said to the Bishop: "Shall we lower the net, your Excellency, and scoop them both in?"

"No," said the Bishop, "we must move slowly like Mother Church. I am going to visit that rectory at once."

The Chancellor was dumfounded.

"Bishop," he implored, "you cannot do that. These two men may be as nutty as a New Year's fruit cake."

"I am going," said the Bishop firmly.

The Chancellor stood between the door and the Bishop.

"Step aside, Monsignor. I am going to the rectory. I want to meet that dog!"

The Bishop arrived at the rectory in the late afternoon. As he stepped from his Volkswagen, the pastor, who had been sitting on the porch anticipating Matins and Lauds, came forward to greet him.

"You are welcome. I did not expect an ad limina so soon."

"Let's sit on the porch," suggested the Bishop. "I dislike climbing stairs."

The pastor pointed to a rocker, and the Bishop sat down.

On the floor between the Bishop and the pastor sat the dog. He was an ugly little animal with ears like a pair of open wallets. His long body resembled a torpedo and his short legs were each about the size of a Howard Johnson frankfurter. The school kids called him the little "hot dog." What he lacked in beauty he made up in brains. The pastor loved him and used to say that he had a higher I.Q. than some of the high-school boys.

The Bishop patted the dog, and the response was an incessant wagging of the tail.

"You see," said the pastor, "he knows you're an important person."

" 'Her conscious tail her joy declared,' " the Bishop mused.

"It's a he, your Excellency."

"I know. I was merely quoting a line from Gray's poem about a drowned cat."

"A cat would make a nice pet for you, Bishop."

"I prefer your dog."

The pastor squirmed. He wondered if the Bishop had a latent faculty whereby he could impound a dog within his jurisdiction.

"What is his name?" the Bishop asked.

"Chad. I called him after a saintly Bishop of the seventh century. The name means 'battler.' "

"Called after a Bishop, eh? All the more reason I should have him. He is sort of a confrere."

"Bishop, would you care for a cigar or a cup of tea?"

"No, Father, I am really interested in Chad."

There was a long pause. The pastor was thinking furiously.

"Your Excellency, have you ever considered a parakeet? Our Holy Father has a pair of finches."

The Bishop did not hear. The little dog was snuggling up to him. It was the first time that Chad had seen a priest wearing a ring and a sparkling cross.

"I take it," said the Bishop, "you wouldn't separate Chad from bed and board here for a little consideration?"

"Oh, no, your Excellency, I really couldn't dispense with his services. He's my private eye. He sits on this deck every Sunday and watches the parishioners go by. He has a remarkable memory for names and faces, and reports accurately on the Mass-missers."

"Uncanny!" exclaimed the Bishop.

"And he goes through the school every day, just like an inspector general."

The Bishop moved his chair closer to the pastor and inquired eagerly: "Does he give you a report on the nuns?"

"Unfortunately, no, Bishop. I am inclined to believe that the good Sisters bribe the little rascal with dainties."

The Bishop looked at his watch and rose to go. The pastor stood up instantly and handed the Bishop his hat. At the lowest step, the Bishop turned and said: "Father, and this is inter nos, Chad would be of invaluable service to me. My Vicar General and Chancellor keep a lot of things away from me."

The Bishop with his head drooping on his shoulders stepped into his car. He turned on the ignition and, leaning out the window, said: "Father, the life of a Bishop is a lonely one. God love you and Chad."

As the Bishop drove off, the pastor felt like that rich bumpkin in purple and fine linens who had ignored poor Lazarus. He turned to his pet and said: "Oh, Chad, the embarrassment of rank!"

As they walked up the steps together, the pastor remarked: "On second thought, my boy, would you care to do some part-time sleuthing for his Excellency?"

But the dog skipped through the doorway whistling the hit tune: "You can't be true to two. No, you can't be true to two. You can only be true to one. . . . !"

JOHN CAMPBELL SMITH

*RUN, RUN AWAY, BROTHER**

THE OTHER morning, as I was riding to work on the subway, I thought I saw my brother getting off at the station before mine. Like me, he was obviously on his way to work, filled with the early-morning tiredness, the

* "Run, Run Away, Brother" appeared originally in *The Yale Review* (June, 1956) and in *The Best American Short Stories 1957.* Reprinted by permission of *The Yale Review.*

gray-faced unwillingness that seems to characterize people who ride the
subway to work, and—for a moment—he turned and looked at me, sitting by
the window of the crowded, lighted car, staring at him across the platform
and the hurrying people. He was part of them, as I was—part of that crowd
—tall, corpulent, a little shabby. He stared at me, and I thought that he was
going to recognize me, but then he turned his head and pushed on up the
subway steps, and the train I was on began to glide out of the station. For
an instant—for a single instant—I had a wild impulse to spring to my feet
and run after him, though I knew it was too late.

That was the third or fourth time this year I have seen my brother. Twice
I have seen him in the subway. Once I was riding in a bus with my wife,
and he was crossing the street in a small town just outside Bethlehem,
Pennsylvania. The fourth time he was coming out of a movie, part of a
crowd, just as my wife and I were going in. Once or twice I thought he
saw me, as I did the other day, and each time he seemed just on the verge
of recognition, but each time he turned his head away.

I am thirty-one, and my brother, who was killed aboard an aircraft carrier
in the Pacific during the Second World War, would be twenty-nine if he
had lived. I see him as twenty-nine, as though Time, instead of stopping
for him when he was eighteen, had gone on as it has for the world, and I
imagine him as having married, as having a job, as being more a failure than
a success, vaguely rebellious and vaguely puzzled, anxious to be liked and
often betrayed and hurt. I imagine that he falls just short of that instant of
recognition because he is a little bit ashamed and does not wish me to know
what has happened to him. There is something queerly furtive about the
way he turns his head and hurries off to be lost in the crowd, or so it seems
to me. And of course I know that he is dead, that the men I see, quickly and
fleetingly, under these circumstances, are not my brother.

Actually, there is much about this that is, I must admit, a little bit specious,
made up. I am not obsessed by this notion: I know better. But that moment
—that split-second shock of recognition—is real. Something in that moment,
as my attention wanders, as I sit lost in daydreaming—something catches me
off guard, and the face emerges from the crowd, jostling against my memory
with his name: *Jimmy*.

But even as I turn my head to follow the figure, reality reasserts itself.
I realize, with a certain spurious nostalgia, that it is simply that this man
could have been my brother, that Jimmy would have looked and moved
like this. I manufacture the rest, the imagined life history, the almost-
recognition, and know that I do. My brother does not ride to work on the
same subway that carries me. We do not meet, and I know that the reality
of that moment is a function simply of the guilt I feel toward him.

There is nothing unusual about any of this. I suspect that many people
have had the same experience—have, in a crowd, thought they saw someone
they knew to be dead. They shrug it off with the reflection that it was a
remarkable resemblance, fight off the momentary poignance of remembrance,

and then forget the incident. And the guilt I feel is not an unusual thing either, not difficult to recognize for what it is, ordinary, not deeply repressed, revealing nothing particularly significant. A lot of people, I imagine, feel some such guilt toward the dead, whether they will admit it or not.

The only odd thing, I think, is the fact that in my fancy my brother should have gone on living, growing up, growing older. His shabbiness reflects, I am afraid, something of the truth about my opinion of him. I realize that the dead often go on living for people, but most such lives are exempt from change. The dead children remain forever children. The boy killed in war is forever a boy. And they are transformed in this existence of remembrance, become heroes, invested with all the excellences and virtues that were theirs and with all the flaws faded out, the sullenness, irresponsibility, unhappiness, whatever it might be, as missing from memory as the flaws removed by the photographer's skillful retouching are missing from the faces in photographs . . . are missing from the face in the photograph that stands on the table in one corner of the living room in my parents' house, next to my own picture.

I can look at that picture of myself, taken when I was in high school, and know that if I had died that is how I would have been remembered, as better than I am, clear-eyed and young, with nothing, surely, behind that face to feel sorry for, to conceal. Looking at my brother's picture, the question I find myself asking is why I cannot remember him like that and let it go. And it is this, perhaps, that is interesting, in need of explanation.

To begin with, though, in my own defense there is the mere fact that I was not there on that gray, overcast morning when a Japanese plane slipped through the curtain of protection that shrouded the aircraft carrier on which he served to drop a single bomb onto the middle of the flight deck and end the world. I have seen pictures of that flaming, exploding ship listing to one side like a huge dying thing, overtopped by a sombre, disaster-proclaiming cloud of black oily smoke; pictures of the antlike figures of men clambering down ropes into the oil-slicked water, clinging desperately to the sides of the vessel, jumping; but I am there only in imagination, as I am there when I read the account of an airplane crash in the newspapers, and my brother— that stout, uncertainly smiling, high school boy (I see him standing at a train window, waving goodbye)—is not there at all; it is unimaginable that he should be there.

It is hard to visualize as real a death that is far away, occurring in a way and under circumstances of which you have only heard, and even harder when that death is public, partaking of the kind of statistical abstraction that can be covered by the words "heavy casualties."

The reality—vivid, remembered—is driving my parents down to the station to see him off on the day he left. I had only recently learned to drive. We started a little too late and I got involved with the downtown traffic, then had difficulty finding a place to park. By the time we got to the platform, the train was already leaving, pulling slowly out of the station. My brother

was part of a group of boys who had enlisted at the same time, and the platform was crowded with people waving a last goodbye to sons, fathers,
brothers.

And at one of the crowded windows of the train we saw him momentarily,
his eyes searching the receding platform for us. He found us, raised his hand,
smiled as he waved, the uncertain smile of bravado that hides bewilderment and doubt, and his soft, unformed, seventeen-year-old features proclaimed that he was only a boy who had joined these other, older faces
at the window by mistake. It was an accident, one that he would admit if
he could.

And here it becomes important that you understand something about my
brother, so that you will know why he was standing there at that window,
how it happened to him, so fatal an accident. It was the sort of thing that
was always happening to my brother.

We went to the same high school, but whereas I was a prize student, author
of the class play, the class poem, editor of the class yearbook, he was a
truant, a failure, a rebellious liar. And while he had fought bitterly for my
parents' permission to quit school and join the navy, winning it finally as a
solution to the problem that by then he presented and with which they could
no longer cope, the original idea had not been his. Two of his friends had
suggested that they all join together and he had agreed on that basis, to be
with them. At the last moment his friends had backed out, but Jimmy, committed by then, had been unable to withdraw.

It is this that was typical. He was (let me say) a coward, big but physically
without grace, awkward, afraid of the jump over the edge of the bank, the
climb along the girders of the railroad bridge, but so anxious for friends that
they could always talk him into it. For them, as one of them, he would do it.
And when the owner of the apple trees from which they were stealing fruit
burst out into his backyard, my brother, who had climbed the tree to shake
down apples for the others, was the one caught, while—from a safe distance—
his friends stood and laughed at him. They laughed when, walking the log
across the river, he slipped and fell into the black turgid water and cut his
hand on a rusted tin can at the bottom. The trouble with Jimmy was that he
always cried when they laughed. I could have told him that it was a
mistake to cry.

But—the train pulling away, the people on the platform waving—he was
too old to cry. Perhaps that partially underlay his look of bewilderment, his
realization that it was too late.

And, of course, it was my fault that we had been late in getting to the
station, my fault that we had missed him, missed the opportunity to say
goodbye. My parents were hurt and angry. We drove home in almost complete silence, except for my mother, who cried a little.

That glimpse of him at the train window was the last I had of my brother.
He came home twice on leave before he finally joined a ship, and once after
that, after the ship had been damaged, while it was undergoing repairs. But

by the time he got home I was in the army. His leaves never coincided with mine.

I was in Europe when I received the telegram informing me of his death. The captain in charge of our company made a special trip up to our firing position to deliver it to me, and he made an awkward attempt to express his sympathy, but I did not, as I remember, feel much. The death of an only brother should perhaps have been more of an occasion, but there was something unreal about the meaning of the telegram under those circumstances, just as there was by then something unreal about home, that other world in which the news might have a significance that it did not have for me. My reality was all about me and as much as I could encompass. I felt sorry for my parents, but even that was abstract. The letter I wrote to them was full of clichés that I thought might be appropriate.

And, of course, this is only an excuse, far from sufficient as explanation. It does not explain my behavior once I was home. My brother's death had been a terrible event in my parents' lives, far more terrible than I would have supposed. The first thing they wanted to do was to tell me about it. My mother cried openly, my father's face flushed with grief as they tried to tell me, to assimilate me into their suffering, and with an anger and brutality that surprised me, I rejected every attempt on their part—rejected them until my mother exclaimed angrily, "You, you don't even want to hear about your brother. You don't want to hear anything about the way he died. You don't even want to remember him."

I denied it, but it was true. And it would, I know, have been a simple thing to have satisfied them, to have been kind, calling for nothing more than a conventional expression of sorrow and interest on my part.

They had of course an advantage over me in some respects. They had seen him after he had been in the navy for some time, just a few months before he was killed. I never knew that person he became, did not witness the transformation from the seventeen-year-old boy who could not pass algebra into the sailor who was killed. I visualize him standing at a train window. They know what he actually looked like, that he was thinner, taller, his voice deeper; my father claims that he was frightened and tired, did not want to go back to the ship although he would not admit it.

I have seen a picture of him taken a few months before his death, a picture taken with three of his friends aboard the ship, on which he had scrawled their names, "Frank, Joe, Steve and me." The features are recognizable, but it is not a picture of anyone I know. I do not know any of the four, although they are all familiar. They might be any of the figures in snapshots taken far away and a long time ago, now, those ordinary, ordinary faces that stare out of a certain, fixed unrecoverable moment in time to remind us . . . to remind us, if we knew them. . . . But I did not know them.

But there are other things, reasons, excuses, ways of justifying myself. The extravagance of my parents' grief has, I think, something to do with my rejection of it. I wanted to be welcomed, and felt, I suppose, a little as though I were being asked to mourn the fact that I was not my brother, that it could not have been he who returned.

My mother once told me that they had never worried about me. "It was always Jim we worried about," she said, "I suppose because he was the younger. Your dad always said that you could take care of yourself. And yet, it was you that we thought something would happen to. It was so terrible that it should have been your brother. We just weren't prepared for that."

And what she was saying, without realizing it, was that, with both of us gone, they steeled themselves against the possibility of the worst by mentally accepting half of disaster, by mentally making a sacrifice that would propitiate against worse sacrifice. They would, as it were, insure the return of one by relinquishing in anticipation the other.

I suppose I could be a little bit bitter about this, but I do not think that I am. Actually, I suspect that I am rather pleased by the melodramatic injustice of it. It is something I can point to, use in self-justification, and in fact perhaps I overinterpret my mother's remark because of this. I do not think so.

We were, people used to say, in front of us, when they shouldn't have, so unlike one another. You'd never think they were brothers, they'd say. They're not a bit alike.

It included everything. My brother was a fat child. I was painfully thin. He was slow, both physically and mentally; not unintelligent, but slow and bewildered, and then indifferent. Physically he could never keep up with any group, arrived last, panting, red-faced and out of breath, lacked the speed, coordination, and stamina that would have succeeded at any kind of sport. He was the kid who—when it came to choosing sides—was always chosen last or, if the sides were already even, was not chosen at all. In all of this I had the advantage over him.

When grownups made these comparisons between my brother and me, they were always in my favor. Tacked on to them, generally, was the admonition to my brother to be more like me, to do better at school, to be better behaved, less of a problem. The comparison, of course, did my brother nothing but harm. In my case, however, it was no unalloyed good, because—and this was the puzzling, unexplained fact—they admonished my brother with an affectionate, forgiving smile.

"You just can't stay angry with him," my mother often said. "He gets around you."

My accomplishments, on the other hand, were expected; my behavior, taken for granted, won no smiles. It puzzled and hurt me at the time, this difference. I felt then that Jimmy won more of affection and love than I, inexplicably, simply because he deserved it less, although I can rephrase it now to read because he needed it more.

He enjoyed no such advantage of course in that other, far more important world of childhood. There is one thing that children do that, looking back, appals me with its cruelty. Most children do not accept ostracism readily. Told that they are not wanted, they will not withdraw, remain behind, but will insist on tagging along, insist on being with the group if only as the mocked-at, rejected minority of one. Some of them attain to belonging by making for themselves a role, by playing the clown, insisting on their value as the butt of others' jokes. In this way they gradually win acceptance. Some, however, can never find such a role for themselves, any role that will do. The solution in such an instance is often to run away from the victim.

I have heard a boy propose, "Let's run away from Jimmy. What do you say?" I have even seen them purposely invite him to go along with us somewhere so that later we might run away from him, making of it an activity like marbles or swimming, something to do on a hot summer afternoon.

Suddenly, at a prearranged signal, the entire group begins to run, together, in a mass, in obvious premeditation to escape from one boy, to leave him behind, acting out abandonment. And why, I ask myself now, should anyone run to keep up under these circumstances, as though to be left behind were the worst possible fate, as though the world were winter, where the wolves, howling, close in on the straggler and tear him down and the only safety is with the herd?

"All right, you guys. All right." Running, panting, not to be lost. . . .

But even the swiftest runner, gray-faced and sick with the unevenness of such a contest, the realization that *he* runs alone, to nowhere, cannot keep up. Even the swiftest runner cannot surmount such a handicap and drops behind. And the fat boy runs against that fact too, heavily, lumbering, ashamed, until he is finally alone, slows to a walk, the blood pounding in his ears, his breath panting.

"Is he coming?"

"Nah, we lost him."

And, walking slowly in the hot summer sunlight, he begins to cry, truly lost, unable to find them, those others, disappeared into an alley, across a field, around another corner.

But let me go back, beyond this, to another time, to a time when we inhabited that small secure world that included only us and our parents, and beyond which, vast and vague and yet to be explored, there existed the whole other world, the Outside. At this stage there were the two of us. We communicated with one another as equals, shared our information and ideas about reality, existed together.

I remember that one of the things we used to do was to go to watch the railroad trains pass by. The railroad crossing was about five blocks from our house, on the same street, a dusty, unpaved street, and that five blocks was a vast distance from home, a long walk to the very edge of explored territory. We never crossed the railroad tracks or left the street to right or left.

My brother was so young (or is this imagination and not memory?) that he would occasionally have fallen if he had not held on to my hand; but he clutched my hand for protection too, so as not to be lost, because I, as his older brother, was there to take care of him, and I walked more slowly so that he could keep up.

I remember these trips as occurring in autumn, on a bright cold sunshiny day, my brother bundled up in a sweater and jacket and scarf, his cheeks red with the cold, his nose running, and wearing a miniature baseball cap with his name stitched on the brim.

We got to the railroad tracks and stood there, hand in hand, waiting for the gates to come down, a warning ringing of bells filling us with excited anticipation and a touch of fear, and then the train passed, running (it seemed to us) with terrible speed and power, the whistle deafening, followed, in dizzying, hypnotic succession, by the freight cars, one after another, passing and passing and passing.

We always waved as the train passed. Sometimes we waited to see two or three, and then we turned and walked back home again, satisfied, my brother's nose running more than ever, through the cold brilliance of the autumn afternoon.

My point is that I was my brother's protector and—more important—his friend. It was natural that I should be always there, always ready to take care of him. At this time there was not much real difference between us except the accidental one of age, which did not as yet matter. My brother was not fat then nor I thin. There is a picture of us together taken at that time. You can tell that we are brothers. You can see that I am older only because I am slightly taller.

But—and I cannot say exactly when it happened—we changed. I could not have been very conscious of the fact that it was happening, because I remember clearly another incident, and this—although it happened—makes me hesitate. It has a suspiciously fictional quality, is too pat, too neatly and dramatically sums up a situation.

It has no beginning, but simply starts. We are at a playground not very far from where we lived, there with a group of other boys. Suddenly, inexplicably, the others in the group reject my brother, begin mocking him because he is fat.

It is, I think, the first time that it can have happened, because I am unprepared, cannot understand this rejection of my brother, which is also (since we are together, inseparable) a rejection of me.

I fight back, angrily, with my own jeers and taunts, doubly stung because now they can mock me for fighting my brother's battles, accusing him of being unable to fight his own, and irritated with my brother for his sullenness, because—hurt—*he* will not fight back, but looks at me and whispers, "Let's go home, Steve."

I know that that is what will happen—that we will go home in the end, my brother crying, and I resist this conclusion, the necessity for it, say, "Don't be a crybaby."

It is the epithet that the others have already hurled at him, a sure pressing home of the advantage of strength over weakness, the chanting, "Crybaby. Crybaby. Jimmy's a crybaby."

And, now, unexpectedly, a boy makes the offer that surely can never have been made to me before then. "If he wants to go home, why don't you let him? He's too fat to keep up, anyway. He's just a crybaby."

It is inconceivable, and inconceivable, too, that I should be standing there, in the hot sunlight, hesitating, for the first time conscious of the possibility of our separateness, of my belonging without him.

"He—he doesn't know the way. He couldn't find his way home."

And my brother, staring at me incredulously, is really crying now, with hopeless despairing anger. And—and I see (but can this really be true, as I remember it? do I really remember this?), I see that he *is* fat; for the first time, I see that he is fat and that the others are right; he *is* too small to keep up and a crybaby who will not fight. Startled, I see him through the eyes of the others, from a distance, for the first time.

"I do. I know my own way home."

"All right. Go home then. I'm going to play."

And still he cannot believe it, hesitates, standing there. "Why—why can't I play too?"

I stare angrily into his tear-streaked face, his brother, until then automatically his protector, committed, on his side. "Because you can't. You can't run fast enough. You're too fat. You can sit and watch us."

And, suddenly, he is running—all alone—away from us, my brother, running through sunlight across that playground field (oh, will he ever run fast enough, fat, crying, runny-nosed little boy, finding his own way home for the first time, to get out of my memory? will you run out of my memory, brother? run home, run home, out of my conscience—not toward death, not that way, oh, not blindly because of the tears toward that shadow) and I have joined the others in our game of tag, one of them for the first time, having, at last, for the first time, rejected my brother. It is odd that he should have become fat and that—until that afternoon—I should not have noticed it, and have noticed it, suddenly, then.

And this of course set the pattern. In this way was my guilt established, and from that time on, I was, over and over again, to reject my brother. And having once decided, having once joined the others, I was never to return, was to be always among the first to agree that he could not play, could not come, should be abandoned.

Perhaps happiest in the end are those who of their own accord withdraw, retreating into themselves or books or some other interest that makes them —seemingly, at least—self-sufficient, those who fight back by becoming indifferent. This my brother could never do. He persisted, and eventually another change took place in our relationships to the world.

As we grew older our positions, oddly enough, became reversed. Again I cannot say exactly when it was that I ceased to be one of the group, while he gradually moved closer to it. School helped to set me apart, although I could not have been aware of what was happening, that I was slipping imperceptibly over a line of belonging into another world of official accomplishment and excellence, one with which most of the boys with whom I grew up would have no traffic.

And there were other things too: those hot, boredom-dazed afternoons of boyhood, of poking around, doing nothing in particular, with nothing to do, when suggestion after suggestion is inspected and then lackadaisically rejected—afternoons from which I would finally withdraw, going my own way back to the books that could so much better fill in the time. It seemed to me then that I lost nothing, gained in the process. I did not think of myself as resigning membership in anything.

(But, perhaps I did, in a sense, know, because—turning my back and walking away—I hesitated, afraid that the next moment, myself gone, something interesting *would* be suggested, *would* happen. And, whether or not it ever did is not the really important question. The fact is that I was not there.)

And Jimmy grew closer to them while I grew apart. Rejection of school became a passport, suddenly, to belonging. By the time he was in high school, Jimmy had found a role, that of rebellion, indifference, the taking of long chances with the authority of the world.

That much of this was spurious, undertaken only to impress his friends, did not matter. That in the end they would not stand with him, that *he* more often than not was the one caught, blamed, punished, and that then they cynically laughed at him did not matter. He was able now to rebel, because at last he had found someone to be with. And our estrangement was complete.

We fought often during this period, bitter verbal battles and physical battles too. By the time he was fourteen he was taller and heavier and stronger than I, should have been able to win. But I was older, his big brother, and this fact impressed him, caused him to crumple after a few minutes, to burst into tears, while he threw his hands over his face for protection, abandoning the fight. People wondered not only that brothers should be so unlike one another but that they should hate one another so much—blaming him, as they blamed him, for most of the differences between us.

But, as I have said, they admonished him with an affectionate, forgiving smile. And that is the point. Despite the differences between us (all of them in my favor) he won more of affection and love than I, not because (as I thought then) he simply deserved it less, nor (as I have since tried to justify it to myself) because he needed it more (although there is truth in this last), but because—and I hope that this is not confusing—he gave more, was more likable, because—quite simply—despite everything, he was nicer than I was.

I will not try to justify this judgment of mine that seems, perhaps, so at variance with the facts as I have presented them. (Remember, after all, that it is I who have chosen which facts to present.) I will say that there was in the end something warm and unchanged and possibly hopeless beneath that external rebellion and indifference to authority that my brother cultivated throughout adolescence. It was not a real change, a growing up, even a hardening. Underneath, there was still that little boy, as friendly, as rebuffed, as hopelessly unable to fight back as ever.

I remember that I did not write to him very often while I was in the army—that he wrote much more often to me, awkward, affectionate letters that seemed to deny our real relationship as it had existed, the enmity, indifference, dislike. After I received word of his death two of his letters, held up in transit, came through. I read them with an odd sense of wonder, incredulous that I could no longer, if I wished, answer—that the figure who had penned that childish scrawl now existed nowhere. He complained that I had not bothered to answer previous letters, mentioned a girl he had met in Hawaii ("Boy, if Mom could only have seen me"), kidded me about the great American novel I was going to write someday. "How about answering some of my letters, huh? You're not that busy. I know that. You should write home more, too. Mom says she hardly gets any letters from you. Anyway, write when you get a chance. I promise to answer."

He had signed it—*Your loving brother, Jimmy*.

And that is the typical thing—the mawkish display of affection. It is this that gives him away, gave him away, revealed him as unchanged. The back flap of every letter he sent my parents was lettered S. W. A. K. "Sealed with a Kiss," my mother said, when she told me about it, her voice becoming soft with the premonition of tears. "Every letter. Every letter he ever wrote us."

And because she knew that she was beginning to cry and that it irritated me, her display of grief, of sentimentality, she said, hoping to choke it off in anger, "You. Oh, you would never think of such a thing."

And she was right. And that, perhaps, gives me away.

But—but, after all, I do not wish to labor my point, the excuses I can offer for not wishing to believe in—for refusing to accept the fact of—my brother's death. They are simple, and mostly summed up in my recollection of that improbably fictional rejection of him, of responsibility for him, on that playground long ago. It is simply that if he is dead I can never call him back across that field where he runs, crying, never call him back and explain, retract, justify, never undo any part that I had in making him what he became. And I *should* have. I should have long ago, and I had many opportunities to do so. I feel (I suppose) in the final analysis that I should have been able to intervene between him and death, as I should have intervened in countless instances between him and the things that hurt him while we were growing up. I was his older brother and more competent. I was, in the end, one of the chief sources of his weakness.

And this explanation, which I have offered myself for a long time now, is a satisfying, even an ennobling one; this acceptance of guilt and its causes, in keeping with my own often denied sentimentality, reveals me as responsible to my brother even when I denied responsibility. It is even in many respects true.

But if it were wholly true, I do not think I would see my brother riding to work on the subway in the early weekday morning. He could rest, forgotten by me, the boy in the photograph on the table at home, the boy who died, forever eighteen, forever young, saved or unsaved by me, the ideal figure of my parents' remembering.

No, my real guilt, harder to perceive, to accept, is simply that I will not remember him as other than he was. I insist on the flaws, the weakness, cowardice, incompetent rebellion. I insist on him as he became, insist on not liking him, as I did not like him, and I suspect that I do so because of the affectionate, forgiving smiles that he so often won (I thought) unfairly —the smiles that I so often missed.

Yes, I know you, Brother, though you adopt the disguise of death that transforms you for everyone else, that gives you the unanswerable advantage over me. Tall and still fat after all these years, vaguely shabby, perplexed by failures that are your own fault and that you will not admit, you pause, for a moment, in the crowd pushing their way through the subway turnstiles, pause, and I recognize you across the people and the years that intervene.

You are not transformed for me, no success in any terms. You are still the minority of one, the coward, the cowed, the incompetent. And I see that you recognize my opinion, see it in your moment of hesitation, that moment when you almost recognize me, and then, furtively, ashamed that I should know what has happened to you, turn away. *You are the truth of the relationship between us, your presence, here, the final rejection on my part.*

But wait—wait, Brother, for just a moment. Again, look this way again. For just a moment, look up at me. Do not hurry away so fast, ashamed and furtive. Oh, Brother, turn again and recognize me, your brother, for just an instant, before you are lost forever in the tangled thickets of time and the jungle of the world.

RICHARD YOUNG THURMAN

THE CREDIT LINE*

"WHAT DID you say you studied in college?" I was hoping to avoid that question. On the basis of principle I was proud of what I had studied, but I knew it would have made a more effective impression right then if I could have said fly-tying or welding.

"English."

* Reprinted from *The Atlantic Monthly* (July, 1956). This story appears in the O. Henry Awards *Prize Stories of 1958*. Reprinted by permission of the author.

"Ah, English."

I didn't look up at him, but I imagined there was that smile on his face that showed how quaintly he regarded my four misspent years.

"English. Oh, how I envy you. Studying the poets, the great writers— Longfellow, Jack London, Emily Post, and the rest. I, too, have wanted to do all that, but I have had to work hard all my life. Be that as it may, we cannot possibly lend you any money. Personally, I'd like to. But you have no job; so how could we hope to get our money back?"

"But I am hungry. Doesn't that make any difference?"

"To me it makes a great difference, but it's not my money to lend. It's the Company's money. But maybe I have something for you better than money. Maybe I have a job for you that you'd like. In this job, I promise you, you'll meet people you've never even heard about in your books."

He described it to me. I gathered that I was to be called a Field Representative; I also gathered that this title was merely a shield I carried before me into the field while collecting delinquent payments.

"Well, it doesn't sound bad," I said, quite stunned by the horror of the job. "But how do I go about getting money out of people if they don't want to pay?"

"You just go out and pick it up."

"If it's that easy, why don't you already have it?"

This, I could see, hurt him. He looked at me gravely, making it apparent that I was too lighthearted about all of this for his taste. Then he asked me, implored me, never to strike any of the customers while collecting money.

"Feel free to let them beat you up a little, but, please, never hit back. Sometimes it works, but more often it just gives the Company a bad name."

"All right," I promised. "But I still don't know how to go about it. Where do I start?"

"I really don't want to tell you," he said after some thought. "I could tell you how I do it, of course, or how Leonard, our other Field man, does it, but I'd rather you found your own way."

He begged me a few more times not to hit anyone. I am big enough to kill a man without much trouble, and I guess he had some serious thoughts about turning me loose on the public. When I finally left his office, I left him with the pleasure of thinking that only his good advice would hold me back from breaking bones and drinking warm blood while in the field. Actually, of course, the thing holding me back was my paralyzing innocence at asking anyone for money, a thing I had always considered the grossest breach of good taste. I thumbed through the cards containing the case histories of my delinquent accounts until I came to one that stirred the most response. Compassion was what I had most of right then, and it was evident from the case history of Sam Deaks that everything but compassion had been tried and had failed.

While driving out to the Deaks place I drafted a rough speech in my mind, an eloquent apology, not only for my coming for the money they owed, but for the whole sad state of Man that made such indignities necessary.

My banging on the paint-peeled door of the apartment house finally brought out a small woman.

"Mrs. Deaks?"

She grunted a little and glared.

"Mrs. Deaks, I want you to know that I am not here to bully or harass. I am not here to continue the torment to which, judging from your case history here in my hand, you and your family have been put. I am here to help you in whatever way I can. In short, Mrs. Deaks, I am here to . . ."

By this time I was way off the script I had prepared. I had hoped to take her by sympathetic storm, but all I had done was to make her face harder with every word. Then she slammed the door on the foot I had moved into it.

"Now just a minute, Mrs. Deaks. You don't even know who I am."

"Oh, don't I? You're from Thrifty Finance, that's who you are. Last time it was a Cadillac I'd just won. Lord knows what you're pretending to sell or give away this time."

"Please, Mrs. Deaks, I didn't come for anything but to help you if I can."

"Okay. You can start helping me by getting your damn big foot out of the door."

She tried to slam it tighter against my foot. We were looking at each other through this small opening and there must have been something quite disarming in what she saw. The door opened just enough for the blood to start up again in my toes.

"You're lying to me," she said. "You're not from Thrifty Finance."

"I never said I was. But I am. And why would I say it if I weren't?"

"That's right. That's certainly not a thing you'd go around saying just for the sake of lying."

Then she looked at me very closely for a minute. She opened the door and looked at me all the way from my shoes up to my hat.

"Well, you may be with them, but haven't been with them long."

"Just three hours."

"I knew it. You're too fine a looking boy to have been around that place more than a few hours. It will get you. Watch and see. But right now, why don't you come in for a cup of coffee?"

"All right," I said, and she took me by the hand and led me down a long dark hallway lit only by a foggy skylight high above.

"Three hours, eh? Then I guess you don't know much about how they make their loans down there. Well, I'll tell you how they made this one. They snatched Sam right up off the street. They saw him walking past the office, and there was never a man looked more like he needed a dollar than Sam. So they smiled at him through the window. They even went over to open the door for him. And in he went, and they asked him where he worked, and how much furniture we had, and they wrote all of this down and handed him a hundred dollars and out he went, drunk for three days. And you know when I first heard about it?"

"No. When did you first hear about it?"

"The first time I heard about it was three months later when they backed the truck up in front of our house and moved out all the furniture. They took the couch right out from under Sam when he was down with the arthritis again. But that made me happy for a time, seeing him lying there on the floor after doing such a fool thing."

"Didn't they send notices?"

"Lots of them. But they didn't mean anything to me, and Sam kept saying they didn't mean anything to him."

I let my eyes drift around the room we had just come into at the end of the hall. I looked at the big television set, and at the couch and chairs, and at the bright green rug on the floor. Everything was so shining new that I could barely see beyond the glare to the shabby walls of the apartment.

"Oh, no you don't," she said. " I know just what you're thinking and you better stop it. Everything here's ours or being paid for, just like it would be with you if you weren't such a crook."

"But, Mrs. Deaks, I . . ."

"But Mrs. Deaks nothing. Every time I think of you dragging poor Sam in off the street. And that moving van . . ."

She picked up a dish of fruit and came halfway across the room at me. "Don't you dare sit on that couch," she yelled, pushing me back against it. "You vulture. Waiting till my back's turned to steal the rest of what we have. Now you just get out of here and never come back or you'll get hit in the face like that other one."

I made a grab for the fruit dish, and while I was holding it above her head she kept pounding me on the chest with both her fists. That's when I got a little mad and took her by the arm. "Now you just listen to me. I came here to help you, and I'm going to help you, no matter how nasty and uncoöperative you are."

I put the fruit back on the table and flung the door open and slammed it shut as I left.

I walked around the block a few times, choked with a righteousness so enormous that I hardly recognized it as mine. Then I went back to the apartment and pounded on the door again. Nobody came. But when I tried the door it pushed open and I walked quietly down the hall toward the living room. "I'm coming in for that cup of coffee," I said, standing close to the door and getting ready to dive for the bowl of fruit.

She looked at me; then she shrugged her shoulders and brought out the coffeepot from the kitchen. For more than an hour she and I and her son, a small boy who kept bumping into things whenever he moved more than two feet from his chair, sat around and talked about a little of everything, except the money I had come for.

"I can see it hasn't been easy for you."

"Take Will here as an example of how easy it's been. Will's a fine boy, but just look at him, trying his best to get some idea of what you look like across the room."

Will was about twelve years old, and he kept squinting at me and apologizing with his smiles for having to screw his face up so.

"Can't he wear glasses?"

"You ought to see them. As thick as diamonds and costing twice as much. We're saving for them, but as long as Will's without glasses for want of money, I'll not pay a blessed cent to a robber like you."

That's how it went during that hour. For a while she would forget that I was anyone but just me, and then she would go on and on, filling my ears with tales of unimaginable suffering and hard luck. But there was never a whine in the telling—only a fierce, towering pride in recounting all her family had borne up under. I found myself envying the Deaks family their heroic battle, and I left her apartment with no money but with a deep conviction that Thrifty was indeed the den of thieves she said it was.

I told the head thief about that part of my experience with the Deakses which I thought consistent with good taste and diplomacy.

"Phony baloney! They've been pulling that 'We've got it too tough to pay' routine ever since they hooked us for the money."

"Mrs. Deaks said you hauled Mr. Deaks in off the street and forced the money on him."

"That whole family, kids and all, came in here walking on their knees to get that money. She's plain crazy. How else you going to explain someone like that? Coming in and borrowing money with never a thought of paying it back! Well, I'll tell you what we're going to do. They think we're so tough, so we'll just show them they're right. We're going to get that money if it takes twenty-four hours a day."

From that time on the Deakses were never given a single day without some calculated reminder that Thrifty was on the job and determined. Sometimes I would make the telephone call, clutching my Adam's apple to disguise my voice; sometimes it would be the manager or the assistant manager. Taking our tip from other masters of terror in our time, we would usually make our calls at night so that the Deakses would have our warnings to sit up with the rest of the sleepless night. The manager took great delight in the strategy and energy of this campaign. "No one," he told me one morning after making a 3 A.M. call to them, "can stand up under this sort of pressure. You watch. They'll be breaking."

During this time, what with the coffee and the occasional lunch or dinner shared with them, I had become their good friend, and it was far beyond Mrs. Deaks's essential innocence to imagine that *I* might have been the one who had phoned the night before.

"They phoned me again last night," she would say to me, "and just as I was about to go crazy with Helga's poor leg. It's a funny thing, you know, but I've come to enjoy talking with that poor man at night. He seemed so desperate that it comforted me a little just trying to calm him down a bit."

What the manager, with his good salary, his trim wife, and the childless simplicity of his modern apartment, would never understand about the Deakses was the insignificance of a Thrifty threat when piled on top of the mountain of troubles they always had upon them. What could it add to the agony of the leg Helga had broken while bowling, or to Will's near blindness, or to Mr. Deaks's growing arthritis, or to Mrs. Deaks's gallstones, or to their married daughter's threat to return home with her three and a half children if her husband didn't stop beating her?

But even though I came to know intimately the cluttered landscape of the Deakses' life and knew that credit extended and credit withdrawn, purchase and repossession, were as impersonally regarded by them as the air I breathed, I still shared with the manager a certain blindness in regard to the way they really felt, or didn't feel, about the money they owed us. I had inherited from my father, and he from his, the black sense that debt was the gravest of all sins, beside which murder was no more than a high-spirited lark. And so I imagined the Deakses must have felt that way, too, even though they pretended not to. And I suppose that is why I did what I did.

The idea hit me one day just as I was coming away from breakfast at their house. I had seen the old man hobble off to work, his arthritis almost killing him, he said, but not nearly so much as Mrs. Deaks's badgering him to get out of the house and get to work.

"He's a good enough worker," she said. "But it don't come natural to him. It takes a prod now and then to remind him of his duties."

I guess there was something about the way he hobbled down the hall, or the way she said what she had, that gave me this idea of assuming the whole burden of the Deakses' debt to us, along with what I imagined to be their consequent guilt.

Down at the office I was a hero, of course, when I proudly announced that the Deakses had finally paid off in full. It took everything I had saved to pay it off, but it was worth every cent to hear them all wondering how I had done it. The manager inclined toward his midnight calls as an explanation, but the assistant manager reminded him that they had tried those same tactics several times before I had come to Thrifty, all of them unsuccessfully. So they wondered and I gloated. But my pleasure then was nothing compared with my excitement that evening when I went up to the Deakses' apartment.

Sitting around in their living room after our first cup of coffee, I pulled out the note the Deakses had signed so long before. Neither of them seemed to recognize it, so I explained what it was and then showed them the "Paid" stamped across the face of it.

"But how . . ."

"Now you won't have to worry about midnight calls or any more stupid letters."

I felt I must have overwhelmed them with my own joy, for there was none on their faces and no one said a word.

"*You* paid it," she finally said. "You paid it with your own money. Without even asking us how we felt about it, you went and paid it. Why? This way it makes it look like we really owed it."

"You did owe it, Mrs. Deaks."

"We never did. All I know is that Sam was drug in off the street, made to take that money, and then the furniture was moved away. What he did was to sell them the furniture as far as I can see. We never owed them a cent after they took that."

"Just like I've told you before, Mrs. Deaks, the furniture was just security for the loan. When the loan wasn't paid, the security was taken and sold and the sale price was applied to what you owed."

"So we ended up owing them almost as much as when Sam got it. That don't make any sense to me."

"Well, sense or not, it's behind you now."

"Willie," she said, her face harder than I had ever seen it, "go get me the cup. We'll take care of this right now."

"Get the cup. What'll we do about . . ."

"We'll do. We'll just do. Get it."

Will backed out of the room and into the kitchen, his eyes shooting out at me like wet peas from down the long barrel of those incredibly thick new glasses of his. He brought the cup back and handed it to her—a quite ordinary-looking cup, distinguished only by the flight of ducks that started near the handle and flew in wild abundance all around and back.

Mrs. Deaks reached into the middle of that flock of ducks and pulled out some money.

"Here's fifteen dollars," she said. "You'll get that much next week, and the week after, and so on until you're paid. Now I think you better go."

"Mrs. Deaks, please, listen."

"Don't talk now. Just go."

The next week was a busy one for me, but I thought of them often, mainly because I began to feel the pinch of putting out money I could ill afford. Then Mrs. Deaks phoned me on Friday and asked if I could pick her up at her place and ride over to the plant to get Mr. Deaks.

"We'll never get the money if he gets out of there with his check. He stops off for a while before coming home, and that's when he'll spend your money."

"Let him spend it, Mrs. Deaks. You know that what you're asking is not what I want. I did it simply because I'm fond of you folks."

"I didn't notice your caring about what we wanted when you went and paid. You be here at four-thirty. No later."

That's the way it went for the next few weeks. Every Friday she would phone me and I would pick her up and we would go over to the plant to wait for him. Innocent and unsuspecting at first, he became increasingly hard to find. But under Mrs. Deaks's generalship, and with the aid of Will, Helga, and the married daughter with her oldest boy, we were always a few moves ahead of him. With his new glasses, Will showed a particular flair for this sort of hunting, and found Mr. Deaks one Friday hiding beneath a pile of rope in the back of a truck that was pulling out of the plant.

During all those weeks when the Deakses were paying me back fifteen dollars each Friday, I imagined they must be undergoing some hardship, of course, but I was shocked sick when I called on them one evening and saw that all their bright, brassy new furniture was gone.

"I know this is all on account of me, but why do you put yourself through so much to pay me back money I don't want?"

"You're a smart boy. You can figure that out."

This, coming from Mr. Deaks, was a shock. His face ordinarily was a little loose, hanging in some vague halfway state between jolliness and petulance. But now he looked like Mrs. Deaks. In fact the whole family looked to me like some steel engraving from seventeenth-century New England; only the flintlocks, the hats, the buckled shoes, and the white bibs were missing from the tableau of fierce rectitude.

"I just came to tell you I won't take your money tomorrow. I absolutely refuse. I want you to wait at least another week before paying me anything."

"What you want and what you'll get are . . ."

"That's right, Sam. They're two different things. We'll go right on paying until we don't owe you a cent. How much do we owe you now? Fifty dollars? Sixty?"

I was shocked once more, and then it was just like being with old friends again. With their grim program of paying me back as soon as possible, I had naturally thought that Mrs. Deaks was keeping an exact accounting of what was owed me. But here was this new glimpse into the innocent, riotously disorganized soul of the Deaks family.

"You owe me just ten dollars," I said, telling about a ten-dollar lie.

"Good heavens! That little? Why, we can pay that easy tomorrow."

"Sure, we can pay that easy," he said. "I've made it this far, and who'll say I can't make it tomorrow?"

He was looking around and beaming with what they had done, and no one bothered to mention all those Fridays we had spent looking for him.

"You just tell me where you want the money brought tomorrow and I'll be there."

"Why not bring it here?" I said. "Why don't we have a little celebration tomorrow night? We've all earned it."

"Here? That's just the ticket. How about coming for dinner? We'll get a pot roast."

By the time I arrived the next evening the place was transformed. There was a new couch, a modern two-section affair with resplendent gold metallic thread shooting through the red frieze, matching chairs, two new tables, and new table lamps with shades like the swirling skirts of ballerinas.

"How do you like it?" she beamed. "Everything's here again."

"Everything but Pa," said Will. "And he won't be here. You can bet on that."

"Supper won't be a minute," she said. "Can I get you a glass of beer?"

"Please," I said, and when she had left I turned to Will. "What makes you think he won't be here?"

"What makes you think he will?"

"He said he would, didn't he?"

"So, he said he would," and I swear I could see the light come way down deep in his eyes before the phone even rang.

"That'll be Pa," he said. He answered the phone and held it out to me.

"Mr. Grishell? How the hell are you, Mr. Grishell? This is Sam Deaks talking. I just wanted you to know I hadn't forgotten about tonight. No, sir. In fact I was on my way home when I got dislocated a little and ended up here."

"Don't apologize, Mr. Deaks."

"Who's apologizing? I'm just telling you why I won't be home. I got this bottle, thinking it might be nice to have around tonight. And . . . Well, here I am. But I don't want you to do any worrying, Mr. Grishell. You'll get that money next Friday. You can count on that . . . this is Sam Deaks talking."

No one mentioned either him or the money for the rest of the evening, but with food costing what it does, and with what I ate that night, I made a pretty good nick in their balance with me.

Aside from a few other meals with them, all of them comfortably free from any talk about money, that was one of the last times I saw the Deakses except at a distance. I've seen them walking down the street a few times and I've waved at them and they've waved back. But then one day, just a few days ago, I was walking along on my collection rounds when a car pulled up alongside me. It was a Buick, shining and chromed from bumper to bumper. It wasn't the latest in Buicks, but it was new enough to move with inconspicuous respectability along any street in town. And there at the wheel was Sam Deaks, and there were all the rest of them.

"Mr. Grishell," they called out. I walked over to the car.

"What do you think of it?" he beamed at me. "Isn't she a beauty?"

"It sure is. What did you do? Rob a bank? Find a better job?"

"Neither," she said. "Sam lost his old job, in fact, and we're going down now to see about an ad for a job in the paper. But what do you think of the car?"

"It's a real beauty. But how . . ."

"How'd we get it?" she laughed. "Well, just a while ago, a little after we'd gotten paid up at your place, we got a letter from the manager of Thrifty telling us that our credit had now been established and for us to drop in any time. They're not really such bad folks down there. I guess we just had a misunderstanding. But it sure is nice having a car that really runs."

"Can we drop you anywhere, Mr. Grishell?" Mr. Deaks asked.

"No, thanks. I'm out for the exercise as much as anything."

"Well, all right," he said, more confident and more relaxed than I had ever seen him, and with all of them paying him more attention than they ever had. "But why don't you drop around and see us? Any time. There's always coffee, or a beer, or a bite to eat."

"I'll do that. I'd like to visit with you folks again."

"Well, you know how we feel about you, Mr. Grishell," she said, and then they were off like a rocket.

I watched them down the street, and fast as they were traveling, they were still in sight by the time I had decided to get another job. I couldn't afford to pay for that car, and I certainly wasn't up to taking it away from them.

MARY DEASY

MORNING SUN*

THE TRAIN curved away lonesomely down the track and disappeared into the morning mist. Standing on the platform, the five of us listened to the silence fold slowly back over the cobbled yard. It was early; even after the trip Halleck was still half asleep. He and Burney stood blinking along the wet shining rails, shivering a little in the morning air.

"Ma," Burney said. She didn't answer, and after a minute he said, "Ma—" again. She looked at him then. She had on the black silk dress that Pa had bought her before he'd gone down to Pittsburg Landing with General Grant's army, and her Sunday shawl, and the bonnet that she wore to go to church. "Where's it goin' now, Ma?" Burney said.

She was looking at him, but not the way she'd ever looked at any of us before the trouble about Rome. Her face was like the statue's face in the square at home, the eyes blank and clear and never moving, as if they were going to look on and on that way forever, without knowing or caring if it rained or shone or hailed or blew.

"Likely East," she said to Burney. "Likely to places where there's more sin and temptation than there is even here."

Her voice was queer too, the way it had sounded ever since she'd waked us up in black dark that morning to tell us we were going on a journey, and behind the sound of it you could hear the last long whistle that the train made dying off somewhere in the mist.

"We'll be on our way now," she said to us. "We've got a walk in front of us, and I don't want any laggin'."

That was for Thad; he was the one who never started off to go any place without finding something on the road that was a good bit more interesting to him than whatever it was he was supposed to do when he got there. He

* "Morning Sun" appeared originally in the Summer, 1953, issue of *The Virginia Quarterly Review*. Reprinted by permission of Paul R. Reynolds & Son.

could stand and watch a plain cabbage butterfly for half an hour at a stretch, on his way home from school with the chores still to do, and he liked listening to the men talking down at the square, and sometimes coming out with something himself that made people say he'd grown up too quick inside just the way he had outside, a boy only fourteen and almost as tall as a man, even if he was only half as broad.

He didn't say anything now; none of us said anything till we were in the street outside the station. It was quiet out there, with only a few early wagons clattering by, past the buildings that were so big and crowded so thick that they seemed to lean over us as we went up the steep cobblestoned hill. Our footsteps made sharp sounds on the cobblestones, and we walked steady and fast, listening to the sounds our footsteps made, till Burney said: "Are we goin' on a picnic, Ma? I thought we were goin' on a picnic." He was seven, too old to be a baby, like Halleck, but not old enough to know what Thad and I knew.

Ma didn't stop to look at him. "No," she said, "we're not goin' on any picnic. This is the Lord's day of wrath; we're not goin' on any picnic on this day."

"You said we were goin' to see Rome," Burney said. Ma always said he was the persistent one; he'd keep on worrying after something he wanted to know like a puppy after a bone. "And Rome said the next time we saw him he'd be drivin' a spankin' new buggy, and we'd all of us go on a picnic in it—."

Nobody answered him. Halleck was walking between Thad and me, and we each had hold of one of his hands, but he was having a hard time keeping up. When he stumbled the third time I stopped and said: "Wait a minute, Halleck, I'll carry you."

Ma turned around. "You've got no call to do that," she said to me. "He's big enough to walk to where he's goin'."

"Where is he goin', Ma?" Burney said.

Ma didn't answer him. She bent down and picked Halleck up herself.

"I'll carry him up this hill," she said. "Then he can walk the rest of the way on his own two feet."

There wasn't much farther to go, after the top of the hill. We began to meet people in the street, almost all of them men, and all going in the same direction that we were going. Then we came out on to an open square, and that was when we saw it—the wooden scaffolding, twice the height of a man, with a dozen steps leading up to it, and the crowd already growing thick and noisy around it. I stopped when I saw it, because you can tell yourself over and over and over again that something is so, that it's got to be so, and there's nothing you can do about it; but you don't really believe it.

"Ma—" I said. I couldn't say any more; my voice was queer in my throat and didn't sound right when it came out.

She turned around to me. "Yes," she said. "Now you know. Now you know what I brought you this way to see."

I looked at the wooden platform; I didn't want to, but I had to look.

There were two ropes. Two men came up and stood next to me and looked at them too.

"Strong and thick enough for a pair of bulls, by Harry!" one of them said, and laughed. "They ain't takin' no chances there."

"Ma," I said again, and this time it came out. "I can't stay here—"

I saw her breath suck in, sharp. "You're goin' to stay here and see what you've got to see," she said. "You're goin' to stay here and get a lesson that you'll remember all the days of your life. The Lord laid His hand of wrath on my first-born, for his sins, but He'll never lay it on any of the rest of you, if I can help it. You're goin' to see with your own eyes the wages of sin—"

I looked at Thad, but I knew before I looked at him that there was nothing he could do. Rome was the one who'd always been Ma's favorite, who could get anything he wanted out of her, especially after Pa had been killed at Vicksburg. He was like Pa, big and good-looking and full of talk and laughing, and even when he'd told Ma last year that she'd have to run the store alone from then on, because he was going to the county seat to live, it hadn't seemed to make any difference in the way she felt about him. He'd only been home once since then, at Christmastime, but she'd scraped every penny out of the till to make sure he'd have roast turkey and mince pie the way he liked it, and a new watch chain for Pa's gold watch that she'd kept ever since Vicksburg, and that she wanted to give him now for a Christmas present.

It hadn't seemed to make any difference either when the news came about his being in jail over at the county seat, and about the man dead in the tavern there; at least it hadn't made any difference at first. All she'd said was that it was a black lie that God Himself would punish, because Rome was a decent, God-fearing boy who couldn't have raised his hand in murdering rage against a fellow creature any more than she could herself. She'd tied her bonnet on that minute, and left Thad to look after the store, and walked three miles over to Perryville to take the late train to the county seat.

She didn't come home again till the evening after, and when she did, she hadn't a word to say about Rome. I had stew warming on the stove, but she never touched a bite; she just sat there in the kitchen, with her bonnet still on and her eyes like the statue's eyes in the square, till Burney waked up in the trundlebed behind the curtain where he and Halleck slept, and came out to see what was going on. When he saw her sitting there he said, "Did Rome come back with you, Ma? Did he? Did he?"—because he knew Ma's going away had had something to do about Rome, even if he didn't know just what it was.

Ma looked at him; it was the first she had seemed to take notice of any of us since she'd come in, though Thad and I had been there all the time.

"No, he didn't come back with me," she said. "And it'll be a long day before he steps inside this house again, and a black one before any of us sees his face again. If God was to strike him dead this minute, I'd give thanks to Him for His mercy, for sparing a son of mine the violent end that comes to those that lay violent hands on others—"

Burney stood there staring at her; he didn't understand what she was saying, but Thad and I did. It was like the whole world squeezing in on you and leaving you shut into one little room where nobody else can ever come; I could see from Thad's face that that was the way he felt too. But he only started to say, quiet and serious as always, "Ma, he didn't," before Ma turned on him like that statue moving, not fast, but the way you knew that nothing could stop her.

"No," she said. "You'd excuse him too. Because you think some day you may go the same way. Because you're the fruit of the same seed that he was fruit of, the sons of a father who couldn't settle down to a decent, quiet life even after he was past the time of youth, but had to go off seeking violence and a violent end—"

It wasn't fair for Thad, who wasn't any more like Rome than if they'd been strangers born instead of brothers; but it wouldn't have done any good telling that to Ma. It was that way with her after that night as if she couldn't tell him, or even Halleck and Burney, from Rome, as if they were all Rome at different ages, and would all grow up to be just what Rome was now when they were twenty-one. I was out of that, because I was a girl, but I looked more like Rome than any of the others, though I was quiet and thin and dark instead of big and laughing and dark, and so I would see her looking at me sometimes the same way she looked at the boys, as if she was thinking that there had been women before this too who had taken someone's life into their hands.

Thad listened to the men down at the square; when he came home he told me the talk was that it had been a fair fight, though Rome had struck the first blow, between him and the man who was dead now, till the time that a third man named Atzel, who'd come into the tavern with Rome, had joined in it too. Then, in a moment, the dead man was lying there, and nobody to say for sure who had struck the blow that had killed him. And he was the son, they told it, of a man who called the Governor of the state by his first name, and who had judges and congressmen to dinner at his home. There was going to be a trial, Thad said; it would be at the county seat, and till then Rome would have to stay there in jail.

We thought that Ma would go to the trial, but she didn't; the way we found out what had happened there was when Thad came home one evening and said he'd heard it at the square Rome and the man named Atzel had both been found guilty of murder. Ma was there when he told it, getting supper for me in the kitchen, but she didn't say a word, just went on laying out cups and plates as if there wasn't anybody else in the room. I looked at Thad.

I couldn't say it even then; I stopped there with my blood running cold in me, seeing Thad nod his head just enough for me to be able to be sure that I had to take it for a *Yes*. He looked queer and white, standing there with his hair falling over his eyes—it was always too long; Ma said it grew just as fast as the rest of him—and his breath coming quick because he'd run all the way home. I saw how he was looking at Ma, waiting for her to do something, or to say something. His eyes followed her hands, that were steadily setting the cups and plates on the table, as if he couldn't take them away from watching them, and all at once it seemed as though he couldn't stand there waiting in that quiet a minute longer, and he burst out, not like himself: "Ma—aren't you goin' to do somethin'?"

She straightened up then and stood there looking at him, still holding one of the cups in her hand.

"Yes," she said. "Yes, I'm goin' to do somethin'. I'm goin' to see to it, with the help of the Lord, that no other child of mine falls into the pit of violence that Satan has digged for my first-born—"

And that was every word that she would say about it. We had our supper then, but Thad didn't eat any; he sat there looking at his plate, and I could see his shoulders moving in quick jerks when he breathed. After it was over he went right on outside, and I slipped out as soon as I could and found him sitting on the steps with his head in his hands. It was chill dark out there, with the fall night coming on.

"Thad," I said. He looked up a little. "What're you goin' to do, Thad?" I said.

He didn't say anything for a minute. Then he said, in a low stubborn voice: "I'm goin' to run away to the county seat. I'm goin' to get a job there. Maybe if I can earn a little money, I can hire a lawyer to do somethin' for Rome."

"I'll go too," I said. "I'm near thirteen. I can hire out in somebody's kitchen."

He shook his head. "No," he said. "You've got to stay here. Who'd help Ma with the store if you went away? She can't manage all alone, and Halleck and Burney're more hindrance than help—" He sat there a little longer, not looking at me, thinking about things. "Rome won't be likin' it, cooped up there in that jail," he said then. "He was always a one for stretchin' his legs. 'Mornin' sun's like a fiddle playin' to set me feet dancin' on strange roads,' he used to say." He stood up. "I reckon if I'm goin' I'd better start now."

I watched him go off down the road, walking fast, looking back just once to wave me good-by. He looked mighty lonesome setting off in that darkness, and I felt scared and empty inside, watching him go, because I knew he was only fourteen years old, if he was near as tall as any grown man.

It was queer when Ma found out he was gone. She didn't cry, or take on at all, the way she'd done the year before when Burney'd run off one morning and followed a peddler clear over to Perryville. I didn't tell her where he'd gone, but she guessed it herself anyway, straight off; she said where one had fallen, the other would fall too. It was that way with her that she couldn't seem to see any difference at all between the reason Thad had gone to the county seat and the reason Rome had gone there. And when

Mr. Harkness drove over there two weeks later and came back the next day with Thad looking halfstarved and sick on the buggyseat beside him, you might have thought it was Rome that Ma saw walking in the door instead of Thad, with the tavern-fight that the man had been killed in fresh with all its guilt on his head.

After Mr. Harkness had gone, she sat there looking at Thad without saying a word. We were in the kitchen; Burney and Halleck were there. Burney said, "Did you see Rome, Thad? Did you? Did you?"

"No," Thad said. "I didn't see him."

His eyes looked big because his face was thinner. We'd been eating supper; it was still on the table, and I saw him looking at it and then looking quickly away again.

Ma got up and went over to the big oak chest in the corner. She took out the Bible and laid it, open, on the table.

"Put your hand here," she said to Thad. He did it. "Now swear on this Book you'll never run off from your home again till you're a full man and can carry your sins on your own head."

"Ma, I had to—" he started to say.

Halleck reached up and put his hand on the Bible. He could just reach it, standing tiptoe beside the table.

"I want to do it too," he began.

"Thaddeus—" Ma said. She didn't even look at Halleck.

"All right, Ma," Thad said. "I swear."

He looked as if somebody had beaten him. I hadn't ever seen Thad look that way before.

"I swear too," Halleck said. "Can I swear, Ma?"

"Hellfire," Burney said proudly. "I can swear."

He didn't know what it was all about any more than Halleck did, but Ma sent him off to bed that minute, though he'd hardly more than started on his supper. Thad looked at the table.

"Set another plate," Ma said to me.

I was so glad to have Thad back I was near crying. I sat there watching him eat his supper, and I wanted to ask him what had happened, but I couldn't ask while Ma was there. She didn't say another word about his having been away; she acted as if he was just sitting there eating the supper that he hadn't eaten the night he went away.

After supper he went outside to sit on the steps again, just the way he had that night, and I went out after a while and sat down beside him.

"Thad," I said. "What're you goin' to do now?"

He didn't look at me. He had his head down and his arms around his knees, and after a while I heard that he was crying. I hadn't seen Thad cry for almost as long as I could remember, and I didn't know what to do or say. I could feel a lump swelling up big in my own throat, and I sat there looking hard across the road and acting as if I didn't notice anything. After a little while he looked over at me and wiped his face on his sleeve, trying to do it so it wouldn't seem as if the wet that was on it came from crying.

"Nothin'," he said then. His voice sounded flat. "I can't do nothin'. I'm not a man grown; nobody'll pay any heed to me."

"There ought to be somethin'—" I said.

It's hard to make yourself believe there isn't any way out of a trouble that you can see coming a long way off; it's like standing under a tree that's falling on somebody you care about and not being able to run or call, seeing it start to move slow, and then faster and faster and faster, till you know the next minute it'll be down on them and you still standing there, doing nothing. But it seemed as though that was the way this had to be. I sat on the steps with Thad for a long time that night, and after a while he told me a little about what had happened to him when he was away, how he hadn't been able to earn enough money even to keep food in his mouth, and how the lawyers and the jailers had laughed at him, a fourteen-year-old boy in dusty clothes without one penny to rub against another in his breeches pockets.

"If I was a man—" he said.

I could feel his arm tense as he clenched his fist, hard, on his knee. But he wasn't a man yet, and it was too long to wait, so the days went on till it was the morning Ma waked us up early to tell us we were going on a journey, and then we both knew what it would be.

Only we didn't know then that we were going to the county seat, not to see Rome and talk to him just once more, but to watch what was going to happen to him. We stood there in the gray morning mist of the square, that was a solid crowd of people now, with some of them laughing and some of them shouting, but most of them just standing there watching the wooden scaffolding like people that are waiting for a show to begin, and I felt as though, if I could only close my eyes for a minute, it would all fade into nothing, like a dream. But I couldn't close my eyes, because Halleck was getting restless, standing there in the middle of all those people, with nothing around him to see but trouser legs and coattails, and I had to hold tight to his hand to keep him from straying off. People were looking at him and Burney; I suppose they were looking at all of us, because they were mostly grown men in the crowd, and we must have seemed a queer company to be coming to a place like this. There were women aplenty looking out the windows of the houses round about, though, and boys of Thad's age perched on ledges and roof-tops, till it seemed as if every brick and stone had eyes.

Then I heard it—the hoarse, murmuring sound that started across the square, at the edge of the crowd, and came sweeping toward us and over us like a wave till it died down suddenly to a dead quiet. Everybody was looking toward the north end of the square, and I looked too, but I couldn't see anything but a rough sea of hats, and I couldn't hear anything but a rattle of horses' hooves, very loud and sharp in the sudden stillness. Till somebody called, "There they are!"—and then I saw too; it was Rome coming up the steps to the wooden scaffolding. He was taller than any of the men around him, a head taller than the other bound man beside him, in the baggy gray breeches and the gray coat that looked too big for him, and he walked as if for him, too, it was all a part of a dream—the crowd, the platform, the hoarse noise and movement of the crowd, that surged and flowed beneath him like restless water.

"What're they doin' now, Ma? What's happenin'?" Burney said. He was standing on his tiptoes, nearly crying, he was so disappointed at not being able to see what was going on. Ma didn't answer him, but she reached down and picked him up, holding him high so that he could see the platform. She spoke to Thad without looking at him.

"Lift Halleck up," she said to him. I didn't even recognize her voice now; it was like something coming out of stone, like something coming out of the statue with the blank, still eyes: "I want him to see too—" she said.

Thad didn't move.

"Thad—" she said.

He wasn't looking at her either; he was staring straight ahead, breathing fast.

"No," he said. "No, Ma, I won't."

"Thaddeus—" she said.

He never turned his head. "It ain't any use askin', Ma," he said.

I thought she was going to ask me then, and I held on to Halleck's hand tighter; I'd never gone against Ma before, but now I was going to say what Thad had said to her. But she didn't get a chance to ask me, because just then somebody standing on the scaffolding beside Rome and the man in the gray coat began reading something from a paper that he held in his hand.

"It's Rome," Burney said; he said it so loud that everybody around us turned to look. "Ma, it's Rome! What's he doin' up there, Ma?"

Ma said, "Hush!" and Burney hushed. But maybe then some of the people around us had figured who we were, because they even stopped looking at the platform to look at us, and I heard one of them, a man with a big iron-gray beard, say to the man beside him: "My God, it ain't human—hoistin' the kid up to see like it was a reg'lar parade—"

But if Ma heard it, she never gave a sign. She stood there holding Burney up and looking straight ahead at the platform, and even Burney was quiet now, in the monstrous, breathing quiet that was laid over the square. It was as though that whole packed crowd was just one big slow single creature breathing, sucking its breath in and then letting it out slow, under the still gray morning sky, so that you carried the rasp of it in your ears, waiting for every new breath to come after it. The man in the gray coat and the baggy breeches was crying now; he was a grown man, with heavy oily black hair and a black stubble of beard on his face, and he stood there crying before all those people with his eyes staring out over them as if he was begging some of them, any of them, to come and help him. But there was Rome standing there just as though he was all alone, just the way I'd seen him stand a hundred times at home, only bigger somehow, as if every inch of him was stretched tall and wide to catch living in it, and the feel of the air, with the gray chill of the early winter morning in it.

I felt the cold drops coming out all over my body, and I closed my eyes tight, holding hard to Halleck's hand, as if, like Ma, I couldn't tell the difference between him and Rome, so that it was like holding Rome's hand too when I held Halleck's. I could still hear the breathing, heavy and harsh and regular, all around me, and a muttering of voices from the scaffolding that seemed to come from far away. Then it all stopped: it held its breath and stopped, and I knew what it was, and I held my breath too, not thinking or breathing or wanting to breathe or wanting to think, till a long sigh swept over the crowd and the man beside me said, "The poor bastard," and I felt him move and turn away.

I opened my eyes then but I didn't look; I opened my eyes because I heard Halleck's voice saying, "You're holdin' my hand too hard; let me go," and I stooped down in the middle of all those moving legs and coattails and put my arms around him tight and held on to him. I couldn't cry. I knew it was over, but I couldn't cry; all I could do was kneel there in the middle of the square with my arms tight around Halleck while the crowd about us broke into talk and even laughing and shouting, as though they had to taunt the dead with their own aliveness so they could be sure they were still breathing the chill morning air and seeing the morning sun that was just beginning now to break through the mist. It seemed like a long time; then I felt Thad's hand on my shoulder and heard his voice saying, not like his own voice, but flat and hoarse: "Come on. We're goin' now."

I stood up. Ma was standing there, as white as a ghost, with her eyes burning across the moving crowd toward the scaffolding, but I didn't look; I took Halleck's hand, and started across the square with Thad, walking away from the platform, toward the street that led to the railroad station.

The streets looked cheerful now, with the sun shining out brighter every minute, and the people walking along them, and the wagons and carriages rattling by. Only it was still like a dream; it still seemed as though I could walk straight through the brick walls if I wanted to, because they weren't really there, because none of it was really there—the people, or the square, or the town itself, or Rome who wasn't Rome any more, but only a quiet lonely silent hooded bundle without feeling or knowing. So I couldn't cry, because you can't cry in a dream; all you can do is wait for it to end. I looked over at Thad.

"Thad—" I said.

He kept right on walking, as though he'd never heard me. He was walking fast; it was all right for me, because I could keep up, but Halleck almost had to run; I was afraid he was going to fall.

"Thad—" I said again. "Wait for us. Halleck can't go fast."

He stopped then and looked at Halleck, and I saw the drops shining on his face that was as white as Ma's had been, and his shoulders shaking under his coat. He looked as though he was going to be sick, and all of a sudden he wheeled around and walked three steps into an alley and was sick, leaning against the brick wall, when it was over, with his shoulders still shaking and the cold sweat standing out clear on his forehead.

"Is Thad sick?" Halleck said.

Thad raised his head. There was a look on his face that wasn't like any look I had ever seen there before; it was like something inside him had got past the point where he could stand to keep it quiet there any more. All of a sudden he smashed his right fist as hard as he could against the wall.

"If I was a man—" he said. "If I was a man—! If I was a man—! If I was a man—!"

Every time he said it he smashed his fist again into the wall. Halleck began to cry and Thad stopped then; he stood there breathing deep, staring down at his knuckles, where the blood was beginning to run through the broken skin. In the morning sun it looked very bright and red and unreal, like blood in a dream, and I had to reach out and touch it and feel my hand come away wet before the lump pushed up scalding thick and hot in my throat and the tears came bursting from my eyes and I began, at last, to cry.

NANCY HALE

*A SLOW BOAT TO CHINA**

At Gettysburg, familiar to them as the halfway point between home and St. David's, Elvira Wilson and her son, nicknamed Pete, paused for lunch before turning south into Maryland and Virginia. Something was missing; this was the first time in five years that Pete's father, Jimmy Wilson, was not along to make of the return to school a gay, triumphant, almost riotous occasion; Jimmy had had to go to Detroit. They were rather subdued, Elvira felt anxiously, as they went into the short-order joint Jimmy always stopped at, and ordered hamburgers and milk and coffee. This would never do. Next year Pete would go away, in a more final sense, to college; how degrading to have his last return to school a depressing one alone with his mother. Elvira placed one teaspoon behind the other, on the counter, and with her fist pounded the rear spoon sharply, so that the front one jumped bowl first into the glass of water. Pete's face broke into a grin; the counterman laughed. Jimmy's old trick was always a success.

After lunch they turned south on Route 15 and tore down through the increasingly green, increasingly lush landscape. It was almost like being granted something normally forbidden—the page turned back to summer, a chance to live over again time that was actually finished. Thick green willows

* "A Slow Boat to China" appeared in *The Virginia Quarterly Review* (Winter, 1957). Reprinted by permission of Harold Ober Associates, Inc.

wept over the gingerbread balconies of brick houses deep in the country. Town by town the countryside became more Southern, relaxed, yearning. Elvira drove at a steady sixty-five, with style, the way her father had taught her to drive long ago in an old red Jordan roadster. She sat erect, her neat smooth head held very high, but Pete slouched, like all the young today, his head back against the seat, one foot propped on the dashboard. As they left Frederick, Maryland, he began to whistle an old haunting tune.

"What's that?" she asked.

He sang: " 'I'd love to get you. . . .' "

But her attention had been distracted by the appearance of the Blue Ridge Mountains to the west of them, running along parallel to their rapid passage. Heavy, looming, inscrutable, they abruptly appeared to her, for the first time frightening. She stepped the car's speed up to seventy and tipped her chin higher.

"Hey," Pete said mildly, taking his foot down off the dashboard.

She gave a little laugh and continued to hold the speed. It was a pretty pass, she thought, when one became afraid of inanimate objects. She supposed it might have something to do with what people called a resistance to Pete's leaving her; a dread of losing him. But she had *never* been that kind of sap. Jimmy always phrased it, that one held one's child solely in trust, against his becoming a man. When she thought how her own father had trained her for independence—the target practice, the flying lessons, the full allowance at sixteen. . . . But in the meantime the mountains traveled along beside them, high, perilous, and somehow terrible.

It occurred to her that perhaps the Blue Ridge really did look different today.

"Them there hoary pinnacles are quite something, aren't they?" she asked cautiously.

"Aw, shucks," Pete said. "Them ain't no hoary pinnacles. Them's just some little old country mountains."

But she thought it helped the way the mountains made her feel, to keep talking.

"Does anybody ever go skiing in them?" she continued, as she took a curve with a smooth turn of her thin wrists.

"Too forested," Pete said. "Some of the guys go climbing in them, though, with their families, weekends."

"I've never been attracted to mountain-climbing, have you?" she inquired conversationally.

"I don't know. Never gave it much thought."

"I read somewhere," she said, "what some mountain-climber said when he was asked why he climbed—Everest, I guess. He said, 'Because it's there.' "

"Seems kind of a dumb reason," Pete said. "You mean he didn't even want to?"

He went back to whistling. To their right the mountains marched along southwards, in sombre, mysterious ranks, the higher and the lower. They were more purplish than blue; they seemed almost to topple, but the mists sustained them. In the foreground the rich country ran, raw and red and bright green, over the rolling hills, and the road ran over the country like a white tape laid down ahead; but lift your eyes higher and there stood the mountains, waiting threatening with an ambiguous eloquence. Elvira looked away at her wrists as they controlled the wheel; from one of them hung a gold bracelet; the cuffs above them were heather-mixture tweed; she wore a white silk blouse with her suit, and the collar was pinned with a gold horse's bit.

"Hey, Mom," Pete said. He shifted his weight and recrossed his long, straight, skinny legs.

"Yessir," she said.

"Look," he said, and paused.

"Looking," she said.

"Pop said something," Pete said hesitantly, "about giving away some of my stuff to the Welles brat. I mean, I didn't want you to exactly clean out my room so I would hardly recognize it when I got home Christmas, or anything."

"I guess you'll have no trouble recognizing it," she said lightly. "You don't want us to leave it totally untouched by mortal hands, do you? Or you want it should be a shrine—James Wilson, Jr., slept here?"

Pete laughed.

"Heck no," he said. "I'm saving that."

They were crossing the Virginia line.

"But I was just thinking," Pete said.

"An excellent practice," she said.

"I was thinking about that Erector set you gave me way back. The thing is, I just didn't want Pop to give it to the Welles brat. That always was a super Erector set, Mom, I'd sort of like to hang on to it."

She glanced sidewise at him and, catching his eye, made a humorous face.

"You plan to clutch it in your hot little fist as you arrive at Dartmouth?" she said.

He shrugged his broad, flat, skinny shoulders.

"I guess it is sentimental," he allowed.

"Un tout petit peu," * she said.

"Which being translated?"

"You'll get it in first-year French," she said.

Pete put his head back against the seat again and, after a moment, began to whistle the same old, haunting tune that had followed them all the way down from the higher, more autumnal states. She knew that she associated it with something and was unwilling to plumb what.

" 'I'd love to get you. . . .' " Pete sang softly to himself.

As she listened, the car whirled past a weathered, paintless Virginia shack; two scrub pines in front, and a desolate old Ford pickup truck. The front

* A very little bit.

door of the shack stood open on darkness, and, in the instant they swept by, a hen came wandering, pecking, out of the door. They tore on down the long road to school. To the west the mountains still ranged, purplish, demanding, and inescapable.

It was with relief that Elvira took the turn into the narrower road running east, that led to St. David's and left the Blue Ridge behind them.

"It won't be long now," she remarked cheerfully.

"That's *right*," he replied in a nasal, mock-radio accent.

Soon the school appeared, crowning a low hill off across the rolling countryside like a minor Acropolis, with its classic buildings—the gymnasium, the Great Hall, Anderson Hall, and the white-columned dormitories.

"That's a fine sight," she said.

"Not half bad for a salt mine," he agreed.

They drew up with dash in front of Number Three dormitory, where most sixth-formers lived. Pete continued to lounge back, squinting speculatively at his future living-quarters.

"Brooding, my good man?" Elvira enquired briskly. "We've got to get cracking. Get this crate unloaded before we go into Mr. Harrison's office.

"Front and center," she ordered. Pete's abstracted expression broke into a grin.

"Right," he said, and, jumping out, began to pull the bags out of the back of their station-wagon.

"Put your back into it," she encouraged. She could hear Jimmy saying the words, in other years; gaily, inimitably.

A tall boy with red hair came around the side of the dormitory.

"If it isn't Wilson. I'll be switched," he remarked, approaching.

"Higgins, you old horror," Pete said.

Higgins reached out and snatched Pete's arm into a half-Nelson.

"Hey," Pete said. "If you're all that energetic you can just help me get some of this junk into the dump."

Smiling to herself, Elvira got out of the front seat and stretched her legs, shaking her skirt out; a tall erect woman in a good tweed suit, who looked all wiriness. She kept on smiling; Pete was so obviously a success at school.

Seated, alone, in the anteroom to the headmaster's office, Elvira undid her jacket, leaned back, and lit a cigarette, surveying the other waiting parents, some with their boys, some without. It was easy to tell the parents with new boys—the anxious brows, the whispered, ignored admonitions, the impatient glances thrown toward the closed door to Mr. Harrison's office. There was such a family just opposite to her.

She herself was an old hand at this. She had had her two minutes or so, together with Pete, in Mr. Harrison's office, while the broad, ruddy headmaster read off Pete's schedule and asked if there was anything she particularly wanted to speak about. "Not a thing," she had replied, conveying in the tone of her voice—gay, she hoped, resonant—the satisfaction the Wilsons felt at what St. David's was doing for Pete; her full confidence in Mr. Harrison's judgment. He had given her what she was sure was a relieved smile. Not every mother was so reasonable; some behaved year after year like wild cows whose calves are being taken from them. Elvira had been able to recognize, unaided, the moment when a mother became definitely de trop,* the moment for Mr. Harrison's little man-to-man talk with Pete. She knew the ropes, the system, and could sit here in a green cotton brocade chair without twitching or looking worried, in this square, stiff waiting-room with its green cotton brocade curtains and its copies of old school year-books.

The thought of the mountains waiting crossed her consciousness like a cloud; lifting her chin, she gave all her attention to the family opposite her.

The father was handsome; of a sanguine complexion, close-shaven, dressed in a well-cut Glen plaid suit. The mother had been a beauty—a Southern belle, Elvira guessed—and now was a soft-skinned, pretty, but ravaged brunette, unwisely made up. They must have been known after their marriage as a handsome couple; but no longer. Between them sat a boy of about fourteen who resembled his father. He was obviously a new boy, excited and impressed and covering it all up with a touching imitation of his father's self-assurance. There was, in addition, a wriggling girl, perhaps eight, brought along for the thrill of seeing Brother start boarding-school.

But in vain did the little girl squirm for attention against her mother's knees; the faded beauty had great, once-lovely eyes for nothing but that wonderful, that thrilling son—her pride, her delight, her beloved. She kept whispering to him. It was perfectly clear that she was unmoved, unimpressed, by the brisk masculinity that St. David's exuded like an aura; indifferent to its fine buildings and first-rate playing fields; she had obviously not been fooled for one instant by all the talk they had given her about building manhood, inculcating character, developing a sense of honor. What she knew, with animal sureness, was that this was the place where they took away your son from you.

She continued to lean, her elbow on the arm of his chair, and look longingly into the boy's impatient face. Just so must she once have leaned, years ago, toward some favored admirer, perhaps her future husband, when she was a young, beautiful, sought-after, indulged debutante at a Richmond German or, perhaps, a Bachelors' Cotillion.

Nobody now, however, paid the slightest attention to her. The boy ignored her whispers. He spoke occasionally to his father, who nodded and smiled with an air of masculine complicity. The mother might as well not have been there, except to the little girl, who rubbed pleadingly against her mother's knees and was, in her turn, ignored.

The door to Mr. Harrison's office opened and Pete came out. The headmaster's secretary stepped into the anteroom from her own office. She beckoned to the family of four, who rose and went into the headmaster's.

Elvira started to get up, but Pete came across to her and said:

* Superfluous.

"Got to get my classroom card checked through with Mr. Elkins. Mind waiting here? I won't be long."

He disappeared, and Elvira leaned back in her chair again and lit another cigarette. A new family entered the room, an extremely chic woman in black, with a much-older husband who looked as if he might be a diplomat. They had with them a small, timid-looking boy.

After a bit the door into Mr. Harrison's office opened again and the well-groomed father was to be seen shaking Mr. Harrison's hand. The mother was just beside him. She was looking back into the office where her son must be sitting. Her expression, the turn of her head, was so tragic that for a moment Elvira thought she might be going to make a scene.

Then the system took hold and the preparatory-school machinery, especially designed for separating mothers from their sons, went into action; you could almost see the synchronized meshing gears. Mr. Harrison took the woman's tragically uplifted hand and shook it. The husband, with mechanical gallantry, put his arm around his wife's shoulders and led her to a sofa. The door into the headmaster's office neatly closed, leaving the boy inside. "Mummy . . ." the little girl repeated. The woman's large, pretty eyes held an expression of primitive suffering. As Elvira watched, the husband said something soothing to his wife. When she turned her face to answer him, it wore a look of real hate.

Pete popped back into the room.

"All set," he said. Elvira got to her feet, and together they went out, and down the steps of the Great Hall into the warm September afternoon.

Pete's new room, on the ground floor of Number Three dormitory, was empty; his roommate had not yet arrived. Elvira went around the room doing all the appropriate maternal things; feeling the springs of the bed, inspecting the closet space, looking severely into drawers for signs of silverfish. She examined the view from the single window; this year it was of the main lawn, with two oak trees and a maple included in it. "Well," she said, "no use prolonging the agony."

"That's *right*," he said, doing his nasal imitation.

She took his young face between her hands and gave him two kisses—firm, official, unemotional, affectionate; the kind of kisses a boy could endure being caught getting.

"It's been nice knowing you," she said.

"Likewise," he replied, looking down at her. He must be a good two inches taller than she nowadays. The year he had first come to school, she thought, she had had to bend down to kiss him goodbye.

He strolled, long-legged, beside her out to the car, and, when she got in, slammed the door after her. They smiled at each other. She started up the motor.

"See you soon," he said.

"Not if I see you first," she replied. It was an old family joke; Jimmy Wilson always made it.

Elvira looked back through the rear-view mirror when she was half-way down the drive. Pete had joined a group of boys and was walking rapidly toward Anderson Hall, gesticulating. She settled down to drive.

But instead of fear, the view of the mountains dead ahead which she had dreaded filled her with sudden, unexpected, remorseless anger.

She was disconcerted to find herself boiling at the silliest things: at the school for giving Pete a room with only one window; at the garage at home for not properly fixing the tail-gate of the station-wagon, which had squeaked and rattled all day long. As her rage found its scope, it took wing. She found herself feeling—as she looked angrily ahead at the long, undulating line of mountains, blue in the gathering dusk—furious at those absurd men, those mountain-climbers, with their idiotic philosophy: "Because it's there." What a damn silly reason for climbing a mountain! She could just see them, jaws set, ropes and picks in hand, scaling their preposterous summits like insects driven by instinct, with no will of their own. She began revengefully to feel angry at the mountains themselves—large, purple, ponderous, monotonous, boring.

Her anger seemed to catch on anything in its way, like a dazzling light glancing off polished surfaces. The strength of her anger was so towering that she felt a sense of power toward the landscape, as though she could stride into those mountains, knock their heads together, topple them with a blow like ninepins.

She drew up with a jerk and a squeal of brakes at the red Stop sign before turning back on to Route 15. When she was straightened out on the main road, she sank her foot into the accelerator and let the car leap without glancing at the speedometer.

The car swept up toward a scene that, in its instant of visibility, struck her like a sharp, painful note in music: a weathered, paintless Virginia cabin, two tall scrub pines in front; an old, dilapidated Ford truck. The front door stood open upon darkness. Hens wandered, pecking, about the bare dirt yard. A hen ran out. . . .

There was an awful squawk and a bump, and she had jammed on the brakes without consciousness of doing so. She jerked the car door open and walked around to the back where the hen lay spread in blood and feathers upon the road.

Elvira stared blankly at the mess. She turned and walked automatically over to the shack. She had often agreed with Jimmy when he expressed himself on the subject of people who would kill an animal like an insect, sweep on uncaring, leave poorer people to wipe their livestock up off the road. She knocked on a board at the side of the open front door and waited. Nobody came. She walked around, a tall fine-drawn woman in a tweed suit, to the back of the cabin. A corrugated tin wash-tub was tipped on its side against the back step. The place was deserted.

She went back to the car and got in; shut the door with a slam beside her; put her hands on the wheel, stared straight ahead down the long straight road north, and burst into tears.

With her tears and as if a part of them, the memory she had resisted earlier erupted; like a dammed subterranean stream, like an abscess breaking. Pete was in bed recuperating from measles. His thin little neck stretched up eagerly like a bird's, his shoulders under the pajamas were narrow, a child's; his eyes were bright after the glaze of illness. The new Erector set lay scattered over the bedclothes, bits of it put together into an angle, a support.

"Is there anything you want before I go downstairs?" she asked. There were PTA envelopes to be addressed.

"Turn on the vic. I want—" But she knew what he wanted, the new record; the new tune. He began to sing it along with the record, in his high, clear voice: "'I'd love to get you . . . On a slow boat to China . . . All to myself, alone. . . .'"

As she stood beside his bed he reached out for her hand and pulled at it coaxingly.

"Don't go. Stay with me. Read."

"I've *been* reading. And I've got so much work to do."

"Read some more. I would love to get you on a slow boat to China, Mom," he said. "Wouldn't it be fun. Sailing along, for a long time. Mom, let's take a slow boat to China. I'd *love* to get you. . . ."

Looking down into his lively shiny eyes she felt dizzy; frightened. It was like standing high above a deep, shadowy valley, through which a river, slowly, ran down to the sea. What she felt was a kind of vertigo.

"Can it, kid," she said. "I can't spend my whole day lally-gagging around with the likes of you. Got to get cracking."

A car passed with a whine of the tires, and Elvira became once more aware of her surroundings, the motionless car enclosing her, the road, the cabin. The memory and the tears sank behind her eyes, out of mind. She waited for a moment, uncertainly, questioningly, with the feeling that something was expected of her.

Then she blew her nose briskly. It had been years, in her well-adjusted life, since she had cried and blown her nose and smelled that special smell that went with tears. It reminded her of her childhood. She thought of her mother, languid, with pre-Raphaelite nasturtium-colored hair, who always said, "Don't ask me. Ask your father. He'll know."

Elvira took a long breath. It was lucky, she thought, that she had never let herself go off the deep end, about Pete, the way some mothers did; she was rewarded by the knowledge that he was a great success.

She got out of the car again and walked back to the cabin. It wore an air of desertion, chilly, damp. But you couldn't really think of something as deserted, she thought, when there was still activity about it; and the hens ran busily, senselessly, about the dirt yard pecking. Somebody must live here; there was the truck. Elvira walked around to the back again and stood in the desolate yard staring past a board privy, set at a crazy cant under a redbud tree that dripped big yellow leaves, at the thin woods behind. She went over to the back door. "Hello," she called. "Hello?" But nothing from the house answered her. "I killed one of your hens," she called. But the deserted house gave out only a breath of mildew.

She walked around to the front and stood fumbling in her purse; took out two dollars and laid them on the floor just inside the open door. She returned to the car, got in, and turned the ignition key; the motor came back to life.

Though it was a little humiliating to find that she was, after all, the sort of mother who cried over her son's childhood, the experience seemed to have done her good. She felt drained but calm, as she let the car's speed mount to her accustomed dashing rate, and she saw with relief that her tears had washed the mountains clean of the dark conflict of emotions that had soiled them for her all day. Now they had resumed their acceptable aspect of beautiful and majestic. Letting her eyes stray west from time to time into the late afternoon shadows settling in the deep places where mountains and valley became one, she imagined what it would be like to climb the mountains: up narrow trails, between thick green walls of forest, until the top was attained, from which the lovely and still sunlit valley could be overlooked. It was an academic reflection, since brisk sets of tennis were the Wilsons' game, but she found herself thinking, as the car tore northward toward Gettysburg, that mountain-climbing would be a wonderfully rewarding sport, if you had the time and could choose.

MARK VAN DOREN

NOBODY SAY A WORD*

AFTER THE children stopped asking she told them. "I don't know where your father is," she said quietly during supper on the sixth day. They were all at the table—neither of the girls had gone to the kitchen for anything, and their small brother hadn't bolted yet to resume playing in the yard. They sat, paralyzed, and listened.

"I simply don't know." The strain of saying this was nothing to what it had been when Madie, the first evening he wasn't there, kept running to the door and reporting that he hadn't come in sight yet up the walk; or when Arthur, always a hard one to satisfy, had insisted every night when he went

* Reprinted from *Nobody Say a Word and Other Stories*, Henry Holt & Company, 1953. Copyright 1953 by Mark Van Doren. Reprinted by permission of Mark Van Doren.

to bed: "Papa's on a business trip. He'll be back tomorrow." He would say it the next night as if he had never said it before, and Margaret learned soon enough to nod and say nothing, as if of course the child knew.

But the worst thing had been the anticipation, of what Madie asked now. She was the directest of the three, though she wasn't the oldest. "What did he say, Mother, the last time he—what did he *say?*"

The worst thing was to have to answer, "Nothing," for in a way it wasn't true. George hadn't ever said: "I'm going, and I'm not coming back," but she had always known he would leave her, and so he didn't need to say so. He knew she knew.

But here was Madie looking at her, accusing her of holding something back. And a deep, sudden blush was her way of admitting that she had; only, what was there to tell, and how could it be told to these three? To Sarah most of all, who never had really asked. Sarah was the serious one who didn't like things to go wrong or change. No child does, said Margaret to herself; but the others had talked and Sarah hadn't—except, of course, with her strange large eyes. They had got larger every day, under the fine hair she insisted on combing straight back from her forehead. Young as she was, she knew the effect of that—knew it gave her authority, as if she weren't young after all; and in a sense she never had been.

"He didn't say anything," said Margaret, "about not—I mean, about not ever—"

"Not ever!" Madie was scowling in the odd way that made everybody love her. She looked near-sighted, though the doctor said she wasn't. She looked fierce; whereas she was the fondest of them all.

The words had given too much away. "Not ever" sounded—well, as fatal as the fact. And Margaret felt that she must have grown all at once very pale, for the children stared at her with a new intentness, and Arthur barely mumbled, "Papa's on a business trip—we know that," as if he had lost confidence that this was so.

But Sarah's face had altered less, and her eyes not at all. Did Sarah understand that some men did what George had done? Some women, too? But the men. That father of five children years ago when *she* was a child, that meek neighbor man, she forgot his name, who did so poorly and was so apologetic—"No force," her own father said—who disappeared one day and didn't come home for years. But he came home, and the town never knew how he made it up with his family: what he said to them, or they to him, or whether there was bitterness and quarreling. Not a sound or a sign from the house into which he walked one night and—well, what then? The next day he was in his leather shop as usual, and nobody had the nerve to ask him where he had been. He had so little nerve himself, it would have been torture on both sides.

Sarah had never heard of him, but she looked now as if she might have. Margaret was startled by the suspicion, yet there it was: Sarah's mind was on the same track as her own. She was even thinking—

Then she said it.

"When he does come"—Sarah closed her eyes a moment, imagining—"I know what we should do. Act just the same as if he never went anywhere. No talk, no questions. Not a word. I know."

Madie shook her brown hair out of her eyes. "I couldn't. I'd have to tell him I was glad."

Arthur merely stared down at his napkin.

They were all trying to help, they were all trying to seem undeserted, unafraid.

"You wouldn't have to tell him," Sarah said. "Wouldn't he know? *He'd* be glad. He'd like it best if none of us said a word."

At least, thought Margaret, motionless in her chair, it's confessed now. They realize he *did* desert me—and them. But me first of all. They are sorry for me. They are trying to be good children. And they are, they are.

Madie and Arthur, flying from their place across the table, reached her at the same moment. Neither one of them had ever seen her weep like this. But Sarah didn't come.

What was she saying? She had been right—she really had, except of course that George would never—

What was she saying? The two others were so close about, it was almost impossible to hear.

"Listen! Mother, Madie, Arthur—listen! Nobody say a word."

For there was George.

Sarah must have seen him out of the back of her head; the hall door was behind her. Margaret, facing him with Madie and Arthur, started to her feet, but the two children clutched her close and she sat down again, trembling. They hadn't looked up yet. When they did—

"Madie!" she managed to whisper. "You and Arthur—don't say anything. Don't go to him—not yet. Your father's come. He's here."

Now she had to clutch at them, they were so wild in her two arms. They all had to wait till Sarah spoke. Sarah hadn't been wrong about *one* thing. George couldn't stay away. And her heart struggled with itself, not knowing how the whole of her should feel. It was bad, it was good. She was still hurt, yet she was happy—in a strange way, as if she were asleep; in a bitter way, as if this new sweet taste—it might be so, it might—were the taste of poison.

The two children were quieter than she would have believed possible. They were minding her, they were waiting for Sarah. Or was it because George looked so terribly tired? Standing in the door, his shoulders drooping, he must have shocked them too. His eyes were the biggest thing about him. They seemed to want to look away; to close and stay closed; but they couldn't. They were for Margaret entirely, they saw no children there, no chairs, no table, no dishes, no clock.

"Hello," said Sarah, turning halfway round. "You're late. Was it a hard day at the shop?" It was scarcely her voice they heard. "Was Mr. Meeker mean, and kept you? Did somebody have an accident? You know, I was the one that set the table and I counted wrong. You go wash up, I'll fix a place." It was as if she were reciting from memory. "All of us helped get supper, even Arthur. He mashed the potatoes—partly."

But her father, if he listened to a single word, gave no sign that he did. His dark eyes traveled for a moment, impartially, over the three young faces that separated him from Margaret, then returned to her where she sat, half guilty because of her silence, in her walnut armchair that matched his across the room. His stood against the wall, in shadow, as it had stood all week.

"Arthur," she said, "get Papa's chair for him." She spoke slowly, as if it were a deep wrong to mention only this. "Go on."

For the boy was staring at the man. A business trip, a business trip—he must be fighting the temptation to say those words and prove he had been right. A business trip. But he looked sidewise at Sarah and said nothing; then, embarrassed, ran to drag the armchair into place.

Madie's face burned with excitement, and her body shook all the way down; Margaret's arm felt the straight, strong back trembling as if in terror. But it wasn't terror. It was doubt that she ought to be where she was. It wasn't like Madie to keep this distance from someone she adored.

She only said: "Hello, Dad. We had a test in history today. I think I did all right. I'll tell you about it later. Miss Martingale—"

She stopped because he didn't seem to hear. He hadn't shifted a foot, he hadn't twitched a finger, since he came.

Margaret thought: He's a ghost, he isn't really there. It's like a game—all of us pretending to see him. It's like children who play family, and make up uncles and cousins. They're making up a father. That isn't him, that isn't George.

And suddenly she screamed—not loud, not long, but she knew she screamed. The sound was worse because it was so weak—she was ashamed, and reached for Arthur who had jumped away.

But he was already at his father's knees, and Madie, her face streaming tears, had hold of one of George's arms, which she embraced as if it had once been wounded in a war. It was veritable flesh. She hung upon it with all her weight.

Sarah came around the table, defeated, and stood while Margaret kissed her pale forehead. "All right, dear," said the mother. "It was a good thing to try, even if I broke down. You go over there with them. Quick, now."

For still George had not said a word. His hands strayed over two young heads, then three; but even while they did this they seemed to be thinking of the wife they had not touched. Never had touched, maybe, or else might never touch again. As if *she* were the ghost.

Margaret settled it. "All three of you," she said, standing straight up at last, "go somewhere else now. Outdoors, or anywhere. Don't stay long, I mean, but—oh, I don't need any help with Papa's supper. Madie—really—I don't need help."

"Are you sure?" asked Sarah. She was so responsible.

"Yes, dear. You take Arthur."

Sarah led them both out, never looking back, while Margaret waited for him to come close, to touch her flesh with him, to make one sound she could hear.

He didn't soon enough. He was still all eyes, mournful and ashamed. He was still a man come out of a new grave.

So she went close to him.

MARTIN ARMSTRONG

ALLOW ME TO SUGGEST*

Mr. BEPTON, a friendly, talkative old gentleman much interested in human nature, found himself, on a pleasant morning in October, in the town of Rockington with a couple of hours on his hands. He had come there on legal business, connected with the death of a brother-in-law, and had expected a long and tedious morning in a solicitor's office. But the affair had turned out to be unexpectedly simple, and to his surprise and delight he had found himself flung on the streets, as it were, with nothing whatever to do until his train left at one-thirty. Mr. Bepton loved to prowl in strange towns, inspecting the people, the shops and the buildings, and it had been a matter of regret to him that this tiresome legal business would prevent him from taking advantage of his visit to Rockington to immerse himself for a few hours in the life of the town. Rockington, as a matter of fact, was not entirely new to him. Many years before he had spent a day there, and he remembered, though vaguely, the cathedral, the docks, the two noble gates—relics of the old fortifications—and many fine examples of Georgian work in the squares and terraces of Upton, the high-lying western suburb of the town.

He remembered, too, the Upton suspension-bridge that hung, airy and delicate as a spider's web, over the deep valley of the river Tarve, and he decided that he would begin by taking a train to the suspension-bridge and then, when he had renewed his acquaintance with it, wander back at leisure to the railway station. He remembered vividly the extraordinary impression that the suspension-bridge had produced on him. It was, or seemed to be, such a flimsy thing compared with its huge span and the depth of the gorge below it that, when he had left the bank and launched out on its thin slab of roadway, he had had a delicious feeling of insecurity, and when he had reached the centre and had paused to glance down into the deep valley under his feet his brain had reeled delightfully and he had been grateful for the strong iron rail of the parapet.

Accordingly Mr. Bepton boarded a tram. In a quarter of an hour it

* "Allow Me to Suggest" appeared originally in *John O'London's Weekly* (July 29, 1938) and later in *Best British Short Stories 1939*. Reprinted by permission of A. D. Peters, literary agent.

deposited him about fifty yards from the bridge, and as he made his way towards it he was aware, gleefully aware, of a timorous tingling of the nerves. It was a gorgeous morning and just the very morning for the occasion, because although the air was full of sunshine the morning mists had not yet evaporated: they still hung in the gorge, giving to it an effect of enormous depth. As he advanced on to the bridge, he saw that the trees that clothed the steep slope of the opposite bank were ablaze with every tint from the palest lemon to a flaming copper. In the misty air they seemed to be not trees, not material objects, but mere colour itself, stationary billows of colour, built up out of the obscure depths into the clearer but still misty upper air of the October morning. And as he trotted along towards the centre of the bridge, Mr. Bepton felt a pleasant quailing of the entrails and a titillation of the soles of his feet, as if feet and entrails were aware, through the thin slab of roadway, of the formidable depth below. As before, too, his brain was agreeably affected: he felt light-headed, stimulated, as if he had been drinking a light but excellent wine.

When he had reached the middle of the span he paused, as he had done on the former occasion, and holding firmly on to the rail of the parapet plunged his gaze daringly into the abyss. Vaguely, through the semi-transparent mist, he could see the river, a faint, luminous, indeterminate ribbon made of a substance more subtle than water. Vague shapes, mere blurs, loomed here and there at its edges: it was impossible to see what they were and whether they were real objects or merely reflections in the water. He raised his eyes, and for a moment his brain turned slowly round as he rediscovered himself, readjusted himself to his position, suspended there in mid-air.

And as he regained his faculties, he became aware of a gentle, monotonous, rhythmical sound which seemed to come from a point not far below where he was standing. What could it be? Since he had come on to the bridge he had had it to himself, and glancing to the right and left he saw that it was still deserted. It might, of course, be some mechanical sound, or perhaps, down in the valley, someone was sawing wood. But no, there could be no doubt that the sound did not come from so far below: it came from under the bridge, only a few feet from where he was standing, and with a sudden thrill of terror Mr. Bepton was convinced that it was the bridge itself, the sound of a girder which, after seventy years of ceaseless strain, was cracking, cracking, cracking under its load. For a moment he had an impulse to set off at a full gallop in a frantic attempt to reach safety before the bridge collapsed. But before he could move he had found relief. It was impossible that such a mild, mechanical sound should be dangerous. Whatever it might be, there was no cause for panic. And now Mr. Bepton's curiosity was aroused; he was determined to solve the mystery, and leaning his arms along the parapet he stood on tiptoe and glanced over the edge in the direction of the noise.

About six feet to the right of where he was standing he saw, just below the level of the roadway, the head and shoulders of a man. He was perched, it appeared, on a little platform slung by chains from the parapet. His shoulders were bent, and from his movements and the sounds he was making he seemed to be at work with a file. Mr. Bepton watched him and a shiver ran up his spine, for the fellow was working away within a foot of the edge of his miserable little platform. If, in a moment of inadvertence, he were to take a step backwards, he would simply . . . !

Abruptly Mr. Bepton checked the thought. Even to think of such a thing, with the fellow precariously poised there, absorbed in his work, was dangerous. The mere thought might—who could say?—be transferred from his own mind to the man's, and then, gracious heavens . . . ! Once again Mr. Bepton resolutely checked the thought, refused to allow it to take shape. But just at that moment the noise of filing stopped and the man straightened himself, raised his head and discovered Mr. Bepton.

'Good morning!' said Mr. Bepton.

'Morning!' said the man.

'Lovely day!' said Mr. Bepton.

'Not so bad for the time of the year!' said the man.

'You seem pretty cool,' said Mr. Bepton.

'Cool?' said the man. 'Not me! I'm sweatin'.'

'I mean,' said Mr. Bepton, 'it seems to me pretty cool to be able to stand on that little platform and not turn a hair.'

'Why, what's the matter with the platform?' said the man.

Mr. Bepton shuddered. 'Nothing, I hope. But to be able to stand there with nothing between you and a three-hundred-foot drop. . . . Well, I feel none too secure, even with this parapet in front of me.'

The man laughed. 'If you was to come down here and do my job, you'd never notice it after the first week.'

'It really doesn't bother you at all?' said Mr. Bepton.

'Not a bit!' said the man. 'When you're busy workin', it don't much matter where you are. You don't have no time for lookin' at the view.'

'Just as well!' said Mr. Bepton with another shudder.

'Hm! So you don't like the view?' said the man. 'It's reckoned to be rather special.'

'Oh, it's a magnificent view,' said Mr. Bepton; 'quite magnificent. What I mean is, it's just as well not to look at it when you're hanging in mid-air, as *you* are. As a matter of fact, I suppose you *are* pretty careful not to look down.'

'Never given it a thought,' said the man. 'If there was any reason for lookin' down, no doubt I'd look down.'

'Allow me to suggest that you don't,' said Mr. Bepton. 'There's no harm in being on the safe side. *I* looked down just now, right down as far as I could see, and I don't mind telling you it gave me the most horrible sensations.'

'Indeed!' said the man.

'Yes!' said Mr. Bepton, warming to his subject. 'I felt—how shall I describe it?—I felt a curious tingling in the soles of my feet, as if my very feet were aware of the horrible depth beneath me. It was a strange sensation. And then I felt it creep up my spine and it was just as if my brain turned round once and for a moment I lost touch with my surroundings. Those are the sort of feelings I had, despite the fact that I have this solid parapet between me and . . . and death. And I must say, it seems to me monstrous that that platform of yours shouldn't be fitted with a stout rail at least three feet high. I have half a mind to write to the authorities about it.'

The man smiled sardonically. 'Well, you're a great one for talk if you'll excuse my sayin' so. If you was to talk less and think less about it, you'd feel right enough. You see, you're just standin' there and lookin' down for pleasure, as you might say. You ain't got nothin' else to do. But if you was to come over and do a job of work along of me. . . .'

'I couldn't,' said Mr. Bepton, agitated at the mere suggestion. 'I simply couldn't do it. If I were to find myself where you are now, my brain would reel and I would be seized with that horrible feeling—you know—that I'd lost touch with things, that my feet weren't secure, that if I reached out my hand, just to restore my balance, just to steady myself by taking hold of a girder, I should miss it, it wouldn't be there, and I should give a lurch, an appalling lurch, sway, plunge forward and . . .'

He was interrupted by a frantic expostulation from the man. ''Ere! 'Ere! Steady, gov'ner!' and next moment the fellow shot him a wild glance, flung out a hand, reeled slowly, and then, to Mr. Bepton's unutterable horror, plunged like a heavy sack over the edge. His size diminished with appalling rapidity under Mr. Bepton's horrified gaze; in less than three seconds he was no bigger than a doll, and then, on the misty mirror of the stream, far below, Mr. Bepton saw a sudden many-pointed star, like a star made by a stone flung at a thick plate of glass—a brief explosion of radiating silver shafts which, a moment later, had died away into vaguely winking concentric circles.

EVELYN WAUGH

THE MAN WHO READ DICKENS*

Although Mr. McMaster had lived in Amazonas for nearly sixty years, no one except a few families of Shiriana Indians was aware of his existence. His house stood in a small savanna, one of those little patches of sand and grass that crop up occasionally in that neighborhood, three miles or so across, bounded on all sides by forest.

The stream that watered it was not marked on any map; it ran through

* Reprinted from *A Handful of Dust*. Copyright 1934 by Evelyn Waugh. Reprinted by permission of Little, Brown and Company. Permission for Canada granted by A. D. Peters, literary agent.

rapids, always dangerous and at most seasons of the year impassable, to join
the upper waters of the River Uraricuera, whose course, though boldly
delineated in every school atlas, is still largely conjectural. None of the
inhabitants of the district, except Mr. McMaster, had ever heard of the
republics of Colombia, Venezuela, Brazil and Bolivia, each of which had at
some time claimed possession of it.

Mr. McMaster's house was larger than those of his neighbors, but similar
in character—a palm-thatch roof, breast-high walls of mud and wattle, and a
mud floor. He owned the dozen or so head of puny cattle which grazed in
the savanna, a plantation of cassava, some banana and mango trees, a dog and,
unique in the neighborhood, a single-barreled breech-loading shotgun. The
few commodities which he employed from the outside world came to him
through a long succession of traders, passed from hand to hand, bartered for
in a dozen languages at the extreme end of the longest threads in the web
of commerce that spreads from Manáos into the remote fastness of the
forest.

One day while Mr. McMaster was engaged in filling some cartridges, a
Shiriana came to him with the news that a white man was approaching
through the forest, alone and very sick. He closed the cartridge and loaded
his gun with it, put those that were finished into his pocket and set out in
the direction indicated.

The man was already clear of the bush when Mr. McMaster reached him,
sitting on the ground, clearly in a very bad way. He was without hat or
boots, and his clothes were so torn that it was only by the dampness of his
body that they adhered to it; his feet were cut and grossly swollen; every
exposed surface of skin was scarred by insect and bat bites; his eyes were
wild with fever. He was talking to himself in delirium but stopped when
Mr. McMaster approached and addressed him in English.

"I'm tired," the man said, then. "Can't go any farther. My name is Henty,
and I'm tired. It must be several months since I had anything to eat."

Mr. McMaster hoisted him to his feet and, supporting him by the arm,
led him toward the farm. They went very slowly but at length reached the
house.

"Lie there in the hammock. I will fetch something for you."

Mr. McMaster went into the back room of the house and dragged a tin
canister from under the heap of skins. It was full of a mixture of dried leaf
and bark. He took a handful and went outside to the fire. When he returned
he put one hand behind Henty's head and held up the concoction of herbs
in a calabash for him to drink. He sipped, shuddering slightly at the bitterness. At last he finished it. Mr. McMaster threw out the dregs on the floor.
Henty lay back in the hammock quietly. Soon he fell into a deep sleep.

"Ill-fated" was the epithet applied by the press to the Anderson expedition
to the upper Uraricuera region of Brazil. Every stage of the enterprise was
attacked by misfortune. It was due to one of the early setbacks that Paul
Henty became connected with it.

He was not by nature an explorer; an even-tempered, good-looking young man of fastidious tastes and enviable possessions, unintellectual, but appreciative of fine architecture and the ballet, well traveled in the more accessible parts of the world, a collector though not a connoisseur, popular among hostesses, revered by his aunts. He was married to a lady of exceptional charm and beauty, and it was she who upset the good order of his life by confessing her affection for another man, for the second time in the eight years of their marriage. The first occasion had been a short-lived infatuation with a tennis professional; the second was with a captain in the Coldstream Guards, and was rather more serious.

Henty's first thought under the shock of this revelation was to go out and dine alone. He was a member of four clubs, but at three of them he was liable to meet his wife's lover. Accordingly, he chose one which he rarely frequented, a semi-intellectual company composed of publishers, barristers and men of scholarship awaiting election to the Athenaeum.

Here he fell into conversation with Professor Anderson and heard of the proposed expedition to Brazil. The particular misfortune that was retarding arrangements at that moment was the defalcation of the secretary with two-thirds of the expedition's capital. The principals were ready—Professor Anderson, Dr. Simmons the anthropologist, Mr. Necher the biologist, Mr. Brough the surveyor, wireless operator and mechanic—the scientific and sporting apparatus was packed up in crates ready to be embarked, the necessary facilities had been stamped and signed by the proper authorities, but unless twelve hundred pounds was forthcoming the whole thing would have to be abandoned.

Henty, as has been suggested, was a man of comfortable means; the expedition would last for nine months or a year; he could shut his country house—his wife, he reflected, would want to remain in London near her young man—and cover more than the sum required. There was a glamour about the whole journey which might, he felt, move even his wife's sympathies. There and then, he decided to accompany Professor Anderson.

When he went home that evening he announced to his wife: "I have decided what I shall do."

"Yes, darling?"

"You are certain that you no longer love me?"

"Darling, you know I adore you."

"But you are certain you love this guardsman, Tony Whatever-his-name-is, more?"

"Oh, yes; ever so much more. Quite a different thing altogether."

"Very well, then. I do not propose to do anything about a divorce for a year. You shall have time to think it over. I am leaving next week for the Uraricuera."

"Golly, where's that?"

"I am not perfectly sure. Somewhere in Brazil, I think. It is unexplored. I shall be away a year."

"But, darling, how ordinary! Like people in books—big game, I mean, and all that," his wife protested.

"You have obviously already discovered that I am a very ordinary person."

"Now, Paul, don't be disagreeable—oh, there's the telephone. It's probably Tony. If it is, d'you mind terribly if I talk to him alone for a bit?"

But in the ten days of preparation that followed she showed greater tenderness, putting off her soldier twice in order to accompany Henty to the shops where he was choosing his equipment and insisting on his purchasing a worsted cummerbund. On his last evening she gave a supper party for him at the Embassy, to which she allowed him to ask any of the friends he liked; he could think of no one except Professor Anderson, who came oddly dressed, danced tirelessly and was something of a failure to everyone. Next day, Mrs. Henty came with her husband to the boat train and presented him with a pale blue, extravagantly soft blanket in a suede case of the same color with a zip fastener and monogram. She kissed him goodbye and said, "Take care of yourself in wherever it is."

Had she gone as far as Southampton she might have witnessed two dramatic incidents. Mr. Brough got no farther than the gangway before he was arrested for debt—a matter of £32; the publicity given to the dangers of the expedition was responsible for the action. Henty settled the account.

The second problem was harder. Mr. Necher's mother was on the ship before them; she carried a missionary journal in which she had just read an account of the Brazilian forests. Nothing would induce her to permit her son's departure; she would remain on board until he came ashore with her. If necessary, she would sail with him, but go into those forests alone he should not. All argument was unavailing with the resolute old lady who eventually, five minutes before the time of embarkation, bore her son off in triumph, leaving the company without a biologist.

Nor was Mr. Brough's adherence long maintained. The ship in which they were traveling was a cruising liner taking passengers on a long voyage. Mr. Brough had not been on board a week and had scarcely accustomed himself to the motion of the ship before he was engaged to be married; he was still engaged, although to a different lady, when they reached Manáos and refused all inducements to proceed farther, borrowing his return fare from Henty and arriving back in Southampton engaged to the lady of his first choice, whom he immediately married.

In Brazil the officials to whom their credentials were addressed were all out of power. While Henty and Professor Anderson negotiated with the new administrators, Dr. Simmons proceeded upriver to Boa Vista, where he established a base camp with the greater part of the stores. These were instantly commandeered by the revolutionary garrison, and he himself was imprisoned for some days and subjected to various humiliations which so enraged him that, when released, he made promptly for the coast, stopping at Manáos only long enough to inform his colleagues that he insisted on laying his case personally before the central authorities at Rio.

Thus, while they were still a month's journey from the start of their labors, Henty and Professor Anderson found themselves alone and deprived of the greater part of their supplies. The ignominy of immediate return was not to be borne. For a time they considered the advisability of going into hiding for six months in Madeira or Tenerife, but even there detection seemed probable; there had been too many photographs in the illustrated papers before they left London. Accordingly, in low spirits, the two explorers at last set out alone for the Uraricuera, with little hope of accomplishing anything of value to anyone.

For seven weeks they paddled through green, humid tunnels of forest. They took a few snapshots of naked, misanthropic Indians; they overtaxed their digestions imbibing nauseous intoxicants at native galas; they were robbed of the last of their sugar by a Guianese prospector. Finally Professor Anderson fell ill with malignant malaria, lapsed into coma and died, leaving Henty alone with a dozen Maku oarsmen, none of whom spoke a word of any language known to him.

They reversed their course and drifted downstream with a minimum of provisions and no mutual confidence. One day a week or so after Professor Anderson's death, Henty awoke to find that his boys and his canoe had disappeared during the night, leaving him with only his hammock and pajamas some two or three hundred miles from the nearest Brazilian habitation. He set himself to follow the course of the stream, at first in the hope of meeting a canoe; later, when the whole forest became peopled for him with frantic apparitions, for no conscious reason whatsoever.

He plodded on, wading in the water, scrambling through the bush. Vaguely at the back of his mind he had assumed that the jungle was a place full of food; that there was danger of snakes and savages and wild beasts but not of starvation. Lately, he observed that this was far from being the case; it consisted solely of immense tree trunks, embedded in a tangle of thorn and vine rope, all far from nutritious. On the first day he suffered hideously. Later, he seemed anaesthetized and was chiefly embarrassed by the behavior of the inhabitants who came out to meet him in footman's livery, carrying his dinner, and then irresponsibly disappeared or raised the covers of their dishes and revealed live tortoises.

Many people were there who had treated him kindly in London, but here they ran around with derisive cries and asked him questions to which he could not possibly know the answers. His wife came too, and he was pleased to see her, assuming that she had got tired of her guardsman and was there to fetch him back; but she wore a cap and gown and spoke only of quadratic equations, and soon disappeared.

It was then that he remembered that it was imperative for him to reach Manáos that afternoon, as he had to take part in a football match; he redoubled his energy, stumbling against boulders in the stream and getting caught up among the vines. "But I mustn't waste my strength," he reflected, "or I shall be no good in the match." Then he lost interest in that, too, and was conscious of nothing more until he found himself lying in a hammock in Mr. McMaster's house.

His recovery was slow; at first, days of lucidity alternated with delirium; then his temperature dropped and he was conscious, even when most ill; the days of fever grew less frequent, finally occurring between long periods of comparative health. Mr. McMaster dosed him regularly with herbal remedies.

"It's very nasty," said Henty, "but it does do good."

"There is medicine for everything in the forest," said Mr. McMaster, "to make you well and to make you ill. My mother was an Indian and she taught me many of them. I have learned others from time to time from my wives. There are plants to cure you and give you fever, to kill you and send you mad. There are medicines even I do not know. They say it is possible to bring dead people to life, but I have not seen it done."

"But surely you are English?"

"My father was—at least, he was a Barbadian. He came to British Guiana as a missionary. First he was married to a white woman but he left her in Guiana to look for gold. Then he took my mother. Shiriana women are ugly but very devoted; I have had many. Most of the men and women living in this savanna are my children. That is why they obey. For that reason, and because I have the gun. My father lived to a great age. It is not twenty years since he died. He was a man of education. Can you read?"

"Yes, of course."

"It is not everyone who is so fortunate. I cannot."

Henty laughed apologetically. "But I suppose you haven't much opportunity here."

"Oh, yes, that is just it. I have a great many books. I will show you when you are better. Until five years ago there was an Englishman—a black man but he was well educated in Georgetown. He died. He used to read to me every day until he died. You shall read to me when you are better."

"I shall be delighted to."

"Yes, you shall read to me," Mr. McMaster repeated, nodding.

During the early days of his convalescence Henty had little conversation with his host; he lay staring up at the thatched roof and thinking about his wife, rehearsing over and over again different incidents in their life together, most often the affair with the tennis professional and the latest scenes about the soldier; the days, exactly twelve hours each, passed without distinction. Mr. McMaster retired to sleep at sundown.

The first time that Henty left the house Mr. McMaster took him for a little stroll around the farm.

"I will show you the black man's grave," he said, leading him to a mound between the mango trees. "He was very kind to me. Every afternoon until he died, he used to read to me for two hours. I think I will put up a cross to commemorate his death and your arrival—a pretty idea. Do you believe in God?"

"I've never thought about it much."

"You are perfectly right. I have thought about it a great deal, and I still do not know . . . Dickens did."

"I suppose so."

"Oh, yes; it was apparent in all his books. You will see."

That afternoon Mr. McMaster began the construction of a headpiece which he intended to place on the Negro's grave.

At last, when Henty had passed six or seven consecutive days without fever, Mr. McMaster said, "Now I think you are well enough to see the books."

At the end of the hut there was a loft formed by a platform erected in the eaves of the roof. Mr. McMaster propped a ladder against it and mounted. Henty followed, still unsteady after his illness. Mr. McMaster sat on the platform and Henty stood at the top of the ladder looking over. There was a heap of small bundles there, tied up with rag, palm leaf and rawhide.

"It has been hard to keep out the worms and ants. Two are practically destroyed. But there is an oil the Indians know how to make that is useful."

He unwrapped a parcel and handed down a calf-bound book. It was an early American edition of *Bleak House*.

"It does not matter which we take first."

"You are fond of Dickens?"

"Why, yes, of course. More than fond, far more. You see, they are the only books I have ever heard. My father used to read them, and then, later, the black man—and now you. I have heard them all several times by now but I never get tired; there is always more to be learned and noticed, so many characters, so many changes of scene, so many words. I have all Dickens' books here except those that the ants devoured. It takes a long time to read them all—more than two years."

"Well," said Henty lightly, "they will well last out my visit."

"Oh, I hope not. It is delightful to start again. Each time I think I find more to enjoy and admire."

They took down the first volume of *Bleak House*, and that afternoon Henty had his first reading.

He had always rather enjoyed reading, aloud, and Mr. McMaster was a unique audience. The old man sat astride his hammock opposite Henty, fixing him with his eyes and following the words, soundlessly, with his lips. Often when a new character was introduced he would say, "Repeat the name. I have forgotten him," or "Yes, yes, I remember her well. She dies, poor woman."

He would frequently interrupt with questions; not, as Henty would have imagined, about the circumstances of the story—such things as the procedure of the Lord Chancellor's Court or the social conventions of the time, though they must have been unintelligible, did not concern him—but always about the characters. "Now, why does she say that? Does she really mean it? Did she feel faint because of the heat of the fire or of something in that paper?"

He laughed loudly at all the jokes, and at some passages which did not seem humorous to Henty, asking him to repeat them two or three times, and later, at the description of the sufferings of the outcasts in "Tom-all-Alone's," tears ran down his cheeks into his beard. His comments on the story were usually simple. "I think that Dedlock is a very proud man," or "Mrs. Jellyby does not take enough care of her children." Henty enjoyed the readings almost as much as he did.

At the end of the first day the old man said, "You read beautifully, with a far better accent than the black man. And you explain better. It is almost as though my father were here again." And always at the end of a session he thanked his guest courteously. "I enjoyed that very much. It was a distressing chapter. But, if I remember rightly, it will turn out well."

However, by the time they were well into the second volume, the novelty of the old man's delight had begun to wane, and Henty was feeling strong enough to be restless. He touched more than once on the subject of his departure, asking about canoes and rains and the possibility of finding guides. But Mr. McMaster seemed obtuse and paid no attention to these hints.

One day, running his thumb through the remaining pages of *Bleak House*, Henty said, "We still have a lot to get through. I hope I shall be able to finish it before I go."

"Oh, yes," said Mr. McMaster. "Do not disturb yourself about that. You will have time to finish it, my friend."

For the first time Henty noticed something slightly menacing in his host's manner. That evening at supper, a brief meal of farina and dried beef eaten just before sundown, Henty renewed the subject.

"You know, Mr. McMaster, the time has come when I must be thinking about getting back to civilization. I have already imposed myself on your hospitality for too long."

Mr. McMaster made no reply.

"How soon do you think I shall be able to get a boat? . . . I said, How soon do you think I shall be able to get a boat? I appreciate all your kindness to me more than I can say but—"

"My friend, any kindness I may have shown you is amply repaid by your reading of Dickens. Do not let us mention the subject again."

"Well, I'm very glad you have enjoyed it; I have, too. But I really must be thinking of getting back."

"Yes," said Mr. McMaster. "The black man was like that. He thought of it all the time. But he died here . . ."

Twice during the next day Henty opened the subject, but his host was evasive. Finally he said, "Forgive me, Mr. McMaster, but I really must press the point. When can I get a boat?"

"There is no boat."

"Well, the Indians can build one."

"You must wait for the rains. There is not enough water in the river now."

"How long will that be?"

"A month; two months."

They had finished *Bleak House* and were nearing the end of *Dombey and Son* when the rain came.

"Now it is time to make preparations to go."

"Oh, that is impossible. The Indians will not make a boat during the rainy season; it is one of their superstitions."

"You might have told me."

"Did I not mention it? I forgot."

Next morning, Henty went out alone while his host was busy, and looking as aimless as he could, strolled across the savanna to the group of Indian houses. There were four or five Shirianas sitting in one of the doorways. They did not look up as he approached them.

He addressed them in the few words of Maku he had acquired during the journey but they made no sign. Then he drew a sketch of a canoe in the sand. He went through some vague motions of carpentry, pointed from them to him, then made motions of giving something to them and scratched out the outlines of a gun and a hat and a few other recognizable articles of trade. No one gave any sign of comprehension, and he went away unsatisfied.

At their midday meal Mr. McMaster said, "Mr. Henty, the Indians tell me that you have been trying to speak to them. It is easier that you say anything you wish through me. You realize, do you not, that they would do nothing without my authority? They regard themselves, quite rightly in most cases, as my children."

"Well, as a matter of fact, I was asking them about a canoe."

"So they gave me to understand. And now, if you have finished your meal, perhaps we might have another chapter. I am quite absorbed in the book."

They had finished *Dombey and Son*. Nearly a year had passed since Henty had left England, and his gloomy foreboding of permanent exile became suddenly acute when between the pages of *Martin Chuzzlewit* he found a document written irregularly in pencil.

Year 1919.

I, James McMaster of Brazil, do swear to Barnabas Washington of George-town that if he finish this book in fact Martin Chuzzlewit *I will let him go away back as soon as finished.*

There followed a heavy pencil X and after it, *Mr. McMaster made this mark signed Barnabas Washington.*

"Mr. McMaster," said Henty, "I must speak frankly. You saved my life, and when I get back to civilization I will reward you to the best of my ability. I will give you anything within reason. But at present you are keeping me here against my will. I demand to be released."

"But my friend, what is keeping you? You are under no restraint. Go when you like."

"You know very well that I can't get away without your help."

"In that case, you must humor an old man. Read me another chapter."

"Mr. McMaster, I swear by anything you like that when I get to Manáos I will find someone to take my place. I will pay the man to read to you all day."

"But I have no need of another man. You read so well."

"I have read for the last time."

"I hope not," said Mr. McMaster politely.

That evening at supper only one plate of dried meat and farina was brought in, and Mr. McMaster ate alone. Henty lay without speaking, staring at the thatch.

Next day at noon a single plate was put before Mr. McMaster but with it came his gun, which he held on his knees as he ate. Henty resumed the reading of *Martin Chuzzlewit*.

Weeks passed hopelessly. They read *Nicholas Nickleby* and *Little Dorrit* and *Oliver Twist*. Then a stranger arrived in the savanna, a half-caste prospector, one of that lonely order of men who wander for a lifetime through the forests tracing the little streams, sifting the gravel and ounce by ounce filling little leather sacks with gold dust. Mr. McMaster was vexed at his arrival, gave him farina and passo and sent him on his journey within the hour, but in that hour Henty had time to scribble his name on a slip of paper and put it into the man's hand.

From now on there was hope. The days followed their unvarying routine; coffee at sunrise; a morning of inaction while Mr. McMaster pottered about on the business of the farm; farina and passo at noon; Dickens in the afternoon; farina and passo and sometimes some fruit for supper; silence from sunset to dawn—but Henty lived in quiet confidence and expectation. Sometime the prospector would arrive at a Brazilian village with news of his discovery.

The disasters to the Anderson expedition would not have passed unnoticed. Henty could imagine the headlines that must have appeared in the popular press; even now, probably, there were searching parties working over the country he had crossed; any day English voices might sound over the savanna and a dozen friendly adventurers come crashing through the bush. Even as he was reading, while his lips mechanically followed the printed pages, his mind wandered away from his eager, crazy host opposite, and he began to narrate to himself incidents of his home-coming: he shaved and bought new clothes at Manáos, telegraphed for money, received wires of congratulation; he enjoyed the leisurely river journey to Belém, the big liner to Europe; savored good claret and fresh meat and spring vegetables. He was shy at meeting his wife and uncertain how to address her. . . . "Darling, you've been much longer than you said. I quite thought you were lost. . . ."

And then Mr. McMaster interrupted. "May I trouble you to read that passage again? It is one I particularly enjoy."

The weeks passed with no sign of rescue but Henty endured the day for hope of what might happen on the morrow; he even felt a slight stirring of cordiality toward his jailer and was, therefore, quite willing to join him when one evening after a long conference with an Indian neighbor, he proposed a celebration.

"It is one of the local feast days," he explained, "and they have been making piwaree. You may not like it but you should try some. We will go across to this man's home tonight."

Accordingly, after supper they joined a party of Indians who were assembled round the fire in one of the huts at the other side of the savanna. They were singing in a monotonous manner and passing a calabash of liquid from mouth to mouth. Separate bowls were brought in for Henty and Mr. McMaster, and they were given hammocks to sit in.

"You must drink it all without lowering the cup. That is the etiquette."

Henty gulped the dark liquid, trying not to taste it. But it was not unpleasant; hard and muddy on the palate like most of the beverages he had been offered in Brazil, but with a flavor of honey and brown bread. He leaned back in the hammock, feeling unusually contented. Perhaps at that very moment the party searching for him was in camp a few hours' journey away . . . Meanwhile, he was warm and drowsy.

The cadence of song rose and fell interminably, liturgically. Another calabash of piwaree was offered him, and he handed it back empty. He lay watching the play of shadows on the thatch as the Shirianas began to dance. Then he shut his eyes and thought of England and his wife and fell asleep.

He awoke, still in the Indian hut, with the impression that he had outslept his usual hour. By the position of the sun he knew it was late afternoon. No one else was about. He looked for his watch and found to his surprise that it was not on his wrist. He had left it in the house, he supposed, before coming to the party.

"I must have been tight last night," he reflected. "Treacherous drink, that." He had a headache and feared a recurrence of fever. When he set his feet on the ground he found that he stood with difficulty; he walked unsteadily. On the way across the savanna he was obliged to stop more than once. When he reached the house he found Mr. McMaster sitting there.

"Ah, my friend, you are late for the reading this afternoon. There is scarcely another half-hour of light. How do you feel?"

"Rotten. That drink doesn't seem to agree with me."

"I will give you something to make you better. The forest has remedies for everything, to keep you awake and to make you sleep."

"You haven't seen my watch anywhere?"

"You have missed it?"

"Yes. I thought I was wearing it. I say, I've never slept so long."

"Not since you were a baby. Do you know how long? Two days."

"Nonsense! I can't have."

"Yes, indeed. It is a long time. It is a pity because you missed our guests."

"Guests?"

"Why, yes. I have been quite gay while you were asleep. Three men from outside. A pity you missed them. Pity for them, too, as they particularly wished to see you. But what could I do? You were so sound asleep. They had come all the way to find you, so—I thought you would not mind—as you could not greet them yourself, I gave them a little souvenir, your watch.

"They wanted something to take home to your wife, who is offering a great reward for news of you. They were very pleased with it. And they took some photographs of the little cross I put up to commemorate your coming. They were pleased with that, too. They were very easily pleased.

"But I do not suppose they will visit us again; our life here is so retired—no pleasures except reading. I do not suppose we shall ever have visitors again.

"Well, well, I will get you some medicine to make you feel better. Your head aches, does it not? We will not have any Dickens today—but tomorrow, and the day after that, and the day after that. Let us read *Little Dorrit* again. There are passages in that book I can never hear without the temptation to weep."

JAMES PLUNKETT

*THE HALF-CROWN**

THE MAN in the bookshop was suspicious. He had his hands in the pockets of his grey overall and he looked at you in a sharp knowing way which made you feel guilty.

"*A Hall and Knight's Algebra*," Michael, embarrassed, said.

The eyes, cold and commercial, looked from the book to Michael. "Hocking it. Slipping it out of the house to flog it for cigarettes and the pictures," said the eyes. The hand took the book.

"A shilling," the man said, and sucked his tooth.

"That's not enough," Michael said, "it's worth more than that. It's worth three bob at least." The man turned the book over, pretending to examine it. He saw that Michael's sports jacket was too small for him and the ends of his flannel trousers were turned down in an attempt to conceal their shortness.

"Name and address?" he asked, as though absent-mindedly. That was written inside the cover. But if they really inquired and they got to know at home?

"What's that necessary for?" Michael countered. "You don't think I stole it?"

"I'm entitled to ask that," the man said. "Lots of books is pinched this time of the year. Besides," he added, "maybe your mammy doesn't know you're selling it." He used the word "mammy" very deliberately as an insult to Michael's self-esteem. "Well," he said, "how about one and sixpence?"

* From *The Trusting and the Maimed and Other Irish Stories*, published 1955 by the Devin-Adair Co., New York. Reprinted by permission of the publishers.

"It's worth more than one and six," Michael persisted doggedly. The man handed it back. "There you are," he said without interest, "take it or leave it." That was that.

The previous evening he had been so certain of getting at least half a crown that he had told Anne Fox he would meet her at the station. He had been out swimming with Mark, her brother, at Sandycove and when they came back she stood on the steps to talk to them. He had leaned over the borrowed bicycle with the togs and towel wrapped about the handlebars, enticed by her dark eyes, her slim bare knees, and moved by the cool and salty odour of his own body. He would risk a lot to be with her. Getting half a crown had seemed a small enough task. He thought she was very beautiful. At one point the thought so absorbed him that she said to him smiling, "A penny for them, Michael." But he had no words as yet for graciousness.

It had been the first thought to come into his mind when he was wakened too early that morning by his mother's hand stirring his shoulder. She was taking the child to the dispensary and wanted to be down early to be well placed in the queue.

"Michael son," she said at a quarter to eight. "Michael!" But the sun even at that hour was so strong in the bedroom he found it difficult to open his eyes. Without any intention of moving he said he was coming. At half past eight she again called him. "Your father has gone ages ago. You promised me you'd get up early," she said. But he pulled his shoulder away to show her how he hated her to touch him. Gradually over the past year he had felt hatred of her growing in him.

"I'm coming," he said angrily, "go and leave me alone." And when she had closed the door he turned over deliberately on his side. She had to be shown that shaking him would get her nowhere. But after a while, his anxiety to ask her for money had overcome his anger and he got up. She had fried bread for breakfast because it would save the butter, and when he sat down at table she served him with her hat and coat on. She had the baby in the pram. The rest of the children were with her married sister in the country. He said to her:

"We're going on an outing to-day. I want to know if you can give me half a crown."

"Half a crown," she said unhappily. "You got your pocket money on Saturday."

"You don't call one-and-sixpence pocket money."

That rebuffed her for a moment. She made another effort.

"Can't you borrow a bicycle somewhere?"

"We're going to Bray," he said. "The rest are going on the three o'clock train."

"Couldn't you arrange to meet them out there?"

Meet them out there? Tell them he had finished with school and could find no work and he couldn't help it if it meant being short of cash? He flung fried bread across the table.

"Keep your lousy half-crown," he had said, rising to go into the bathroom.

"Michael," she called after him, "you know if I had it I'd give it to you." He refused to answer. Then in a hurt tone she called to him, "I gave you two shillings last week." But he banged the door loudly. Later he had heard her take the pram down the steps by herself.

He stuffed the book back in his pocket. The sun, high over the tall buildings and the summer crowds, beat down on his bare head. Even under the striped awnings outside the shops in Grafton Street it was intolerably hot. There was an aroma of coffee in the air to stir his appetite, and flowers blazed yellow and red in vendors' baskets. Near the Green two girls on bicycles looked at him with interest. One was a tidy piece but she wasn't as nice as Anne Fox. He wouldn't think of Anne Fox in that way. None of the girls was as nice as Anne Fox. She was different. She wouldn't do that—no—she wouldn't let you—no. But if he couldn't go to Bray maybe Dorgan would see her home. He got on easily with girls and when he knew Michael was soft on Anne he would make sure to cut in on him. Dorgan loved to do that. He would invent stories for the rest of the gang, which he could tell in a way that made it hard not to believe them. If he did he would break his bloody neck. Then of course the rest would think it was sour grapes, but it wasn't that at all. Anne wouldn't let you do that; she was a nice girl but she was soft on him too. He knew by the way she looked at him last night on the steps, and the way she leaned her head back a little so that he could see her soft warm shapely throat and the way she laughed at what he said to show she liked him to talk to her. So nice it had been last night on the high steps under the green-gold, cloud-crossed evening sky to ask her; and now it was all being bagged-up because of a lousy half-crown.

His father and mother were both at table. He walked through quietly to sneak the book back on the shelf. The baby was asleep in the pram. It had blobs of white ointment on its face. Bits of bun lay on its dress and coverlet. He took his place and his mother rose immediately to fetch his meal for him. The tassels of a faded green cover hung down beneath the tablecloth. There was a hole worn in the centre when the tablecloth was not on but you covered it with a fern pot and that was more or less all right. He looked at his father slyly with the idea of putting out a hint for some money but his father's face was not a good-humoured one—in fact—no—it wasn't. His father's face was moist and flabby. Though it was so warm he wore a dark suit and a butterfly collar which was respectable because of his calling. He was a clerk in the office of Joshua Bright & Son, Timber Merchants. In good humour he told stories which always ended in Mr. Bright saying, "Kavanagh, you're a man after my own heart. How on earth did you fix it? I'm certainly indebted," or words to that effect. It always made you want to kick both of them in the fanny. But Bright was not on the menu to-day. There was something else.

"If I've told you once," began his father, "I've told you a dozen times that a razor should be dried and cleaned when you've finished with it. No one with manners a cut above those of a pig would leave a razor in the condition mine was left in. I've never objected to you using it—though what in God's name you have to shave is beyond me—all I ask is that you dry it after you."

He remembered he had not dried it. He had left it down to put water in his hair in the absence of hair dressing and of course he forgot—well, he didn't exactly forget but he was in a bad humour over his mother.

"Razor?" he lied, pointlessly and brazenly. "I never touched your razor."

His father turned to his mother. "There's your rearing for you now," he said; "the lie springs easy to his lips. If he's going to sit there——"

His mother immediately tried to conciliate them. Too quickly, in her desire to placate them his mother said, "You might have left it yourself, you were in such a hurry this morning."

"That's right," his father shouted, and let the knife and fork fall with a clatter on the plate, "stick up for him. Encourage him to deceive and defy his own father. I'll be a bloody lunatic before long between the pair of you."

"You can think what you like," Michael persisted. "It wasn't me."

"Michael," put in his mother.

"Then I suppose it was the cat," his father said with childish sarcasm, "or maybe it walked out of the case by itself. But I'll tell you one thing, you'll use it no more. You can get a razor of your own."

"I suppose you'll tell me how."

"Buy one. Do a little study to fit yourself for earning your keep."

"You must have studied a bit yourself in your day." Michael sneered. "You earn such a hell of a lot now."

He left the table. As he entered the next room a cup flew past his ear and shattered against the wall. It was unexpected and he jumped.

"You impertinent brat," his father yelled after him. He locked the door hastily.

He came out when he was certain his father had gone. His mother took his meal from the oven where she had put it to keep it hot. She had been crying. That sort of thing had never happened before.

"Have your meal, child," she said. "I don't know what's to become of us."

"I don't want it."

"It isn't right to answer your father like that; you should respect him. He works hard for what he gets."

"He knows how to hold on to it too."

She was silent. Then she said, "You know you'd get the half-crown if we had it. What were you ever denied that we had to give?"

"You can buy that baby in there sweet cake."

"A little penny bun. I'm ashamed of you, Michael."

That, unaccountably, slipped under his guard and stung him.

"You mind your own bloody business," he lashed back.

In St. Stephen's Green, children, their nurses watching them, were feeding the ducks from paper bags. And at the pond with the artificial sprays which spurted threads of pearly bright water into the thirsty air, children were sailing a boat. Michael lounged with his hands in his pockets. They were catching the train now.

"Michael Kavanagh is awful to be late like this," the girls were saying with angry little jerks of their heads, and the fellows were saying, "Oh, he'll come, don't bother, let's get a carriage." They were going to Bray to swim and after to lie in the bracken. They were going to eat ice cream and drink lemonade which the boys would buy for the girls, and eat sandwiches and make tea which the girls would bring for the boys. Anne would lie in the bracken. For the length of his own afternoon he could watch the people sleeping with newspapers over their faces and look at the flowers which blazed with a barren and uncommunicative joyousness. The sculptured face of Mangan brought some lines to his mind. "I could scale the blue air. I could walk . . . climb . . . I could . . ." How the hell did it go? That was school. You knew these things when you sat for Leaving Cert. and then after a while you wondered how the hell did it go. You left school and watched the advertisements.

"Junior clerk reqd. rep. firm Hons. Leaving Cert. Knowledge book-keeping asset. 15/-weekly to start. Good prospects."

Queue with the rest; don't stammer—oh—don't stutter—think, oh, think. Cool—be cool and smile respectfully. Self-possession is nine-tenths of the law.

Your mother had pressed your suit and sat up into the small hours ironing and darning. She had already begun a Novena to Saint Anthony. (O please, Saint Anthony, send him work: O please. O sweet and good Saint Anthony intercede for my boy.) Your father gave you advice. He told you, take off your hat and smile easily and pleasantly. Don't fidget or sit on the edge of the chair, which wasn't to say, of course, that you were to put your feet on the desk. He had had a word with Gussy Gallagher who was said to have tons of influence since he hit it lucky in the auctioneering business. He was reputed to be a brigadier-general or something in the Knights of Columbanus. Now and then your mother looked across.

"Pay attention to what your father is telling you," she would say. When she ironed late at night like that her hair fell in straggles over her face, her breath caught her now and then, her forehead so white showed moistly in the streamy light.

As you sat waiting to be interviewed you kept saying like an idiot over and over again something silly—like:

"When Richelieu attained to office he was faced with the task of building a French navy."

Like when you were a child you went to the shop repeating in case you might forget: A pint of milk—a tin of beans—a duck loaf—and a half-pound of margarine and say the margarine is for baking. (That was a lie, but it was only a little white lie if your mother told you to tell it.)

But in the end someone else, like Harte or Joe Andrews, always got the job. Joe Andrews didn't know much about Richelieu, but he knew someone on the selection board with a bit more pull than Gussy Gallagher or Saint Anthony.

Knowledge weakened with winter, sickened with spring, withered and died in the hot July sun, giving place to new growths, to the contemplation of women, to long vacant hours, to quick greeds and slow lusts and jealous incessant neediness.

He sat down on one of the benches which were placed at secluded intervals along the quiet path. His mother was a silly bitch and his father a skinflint. His mother went out with his father to the pictures once a week and this was the night. It was the only night they went out but they could stay at home to-night because the other children were away and he was damned if he was going to stay in to mind the baby. That would be one way of getting his own back. The whole set-up was a bloody cod.

There was a thin white line running down the right side of his face, from his nose to the corner of his lips. He tried to relieve the tautness from time to time by rubbing his face with his hands, but failed because it welled up from inside him. Over him hung a wealth of almond blossom and opposite to him was a laburnum tree. It showered with perfect grace of movement to the tips of its trailing branches. Near it sat an old man and a child. He was a white-haired, serene-faced old man, whose ample waistcoat was crossed by two golden chains. On one end of the chain hung a watch. The little child was playing with it. She put it to her ear, listened, laughed. "Tick tock, tick tock," the old man said, making an attempt to imitate the sound. Frequently he bent down to chuck her under the chin or smile at her. Growing tired of the watch, she put her hand in his pocket to pull out a pair of glasses, a white handkerchief and a silver coin. The glasses and handkerchief were discarded, but she kept the coin. When she threw it, it flashed in the sun; when it fell, it rang musically on the path and rolled round and round. It staggered in circles before flopping down. The old man, whom you knew to be old more by the stringy looseness of the neck behind his white butterfly collar than by any sign of age in the bright face, smiled an invitation to Michael to enjoy the antics of the child. But Michael only hated the child. He hated the child because a foolish and indulgent old man allowed it to play carelessly with a precious piece of silver. The milled edges of a half-crown were strong and comforting. You could stand a girl's fare and buy her ice cream, or buy cigarettes to smoke after a swim, and fish and chips to eat from a paper bag on the way home with the lads at night. The coin went up and down and he followed it greedily with his eyes. Sometimes it fell, a bright though tiny star, out of the child's reach, and the child would toddle across innocently to retrieve it. Sometimes when it fell, it staggered clumsily towards Michael. When the game had gone on for some time the old man lost interest and began to nod. Michael looked up and down the path. A keeper was examining a flower bed some distance away. There was nobody near. But to rise, take up the coin and walk away quickly—that would be too obvious. The child might cry, or the old man open his eyes at the wrong moment. With half-closed eyes he followed the course of the coin.

To steal a half-crown could be mortal or venial. Three conditions were required for mortal sin and these were: (1) grave matter; (2) perfect knowledge; (3) full consent. It would be mortal to steal it from a poor man, but venial to steal it from a rich man, because it was dependent on the gravity of the injustice done. Not that he cared whether it was mortal or venial because he had committed sins of impurity which were always mortal and killed the soul, and it was eight months since his last confession. Automatically he almost said, "and I accuse myself of my sins." When the slide went click in the darkness the priest didn't say a penny for them he said well my child and with tongue stuck to roof and sweat of shame you had to tell. If you were caught you were a (not-nice-word) thief.

The coin fell and rolled towards him. He watched it. It curved, glittering, towards his left. Gingerly he reached out his foot and stopped it. Then he looked sharply at the old man, whose eyes were still closed. He bent and picked it up.

"Go on," he whispered to the child when she came near him, "hump off." The face upturned to him was tiny and questioning. He could have raised his boot and crushed it without caring. But her bewilderment frightened him. When she began to cry he jumped up and said to her: "Here—we'll look for it in the grass."

He was earnestly searching along the verge when the old man stood beside him.

"Poor little pet," he said, "what's the matter now?"

"She lost her half-crown. I think it rolled in here."

They hunted for a considerable time. Michael kept his face averted. His heart thumped. He was afraid the old man might see it there thumping against his ribs, pulsing in his neck, calling out thief, thief, so loudly that it must surely be heard. But the child began to sob and the old man comforted her by promising to bring her off to buy ice cream. After some time he told Michael he would have to leave it for the sweeper. "Finders keepers," he said regretfully but pleasantly as he was going.

Waiting impatiently while the old man and the child went off, Michael sat down again. He had no notion of the time. He should have asked the old fool before he went. They had gone in the direction of the station, but he would not dare to go that way lest they should meet again. The old man would want to chat. Where did he live? Was he still at school? What were his intentions? Suitable openings were hard to find for a young man standing on the threshold of life. A grunt, A stammer. There were no other answers to these things, none that he had found. They were simple expressions of amiability which always made the machinery of his mind lumber and clank, defeated and chaotic. He could never find responses. He was afraid if the old man spoke to him, he would blurt out, "I took the half-crown and I'm sticking to it. You can do what you like about it." So he sat for half an hour and then went off in the opposite direction, taking a roundabout way to the station. He passed the university where Mark would soon begin to study to be a doctor. He always had money. Mark would never need to put his foot on a half-crown dropped by a child in a public park.

The street was so quiet he could hear his own footsteps echoing, and the building itself seemed peacefully asleep. There was a smell of dust and a sunlit silence. He thought of cool waters, of Anne Fox in her red bathing costume raising her round arms to let cool water fall from them glitteringly. She would climb Bray Head in her light cotton frock, slim knees bending, a sea-fragrance about her. It would not be easy to find them. She might go anywhere about the Head to lie in the bracken. She might lie in the bracken with Dorgan. He would have to search and search.

He hastened up the steps to the station, as though by hastening he could persuade the train to leave any earlier, or be with her any sooner. But when he reached the top he stood still. Just turning away from the booking office, holding the child by the hand, was the old man. The child wanted to carry the tickets. On the steps, an impassable barrier, stood guilt and terror. Instinctively and immediately he moved away.

At the corner of the Green, leaning against one of the pillars which had held the ornamental chains that one time bordered the pavement, he remained for a long time. He knew it was after six o'clock because people were passing in clusters on bicycles, and the hunger pains in his belly were worse. He should have taken his dinner. He was staring at the sky, golden and tranquil behind barred clouds, when his mother stopped beside him. She had been shopping and was pushing the pram with the baby in it. He knew it was she but barely moved to acknowledge her. Let her see him miserable. Let her see that he had only a corner to stand at and a sky to stare into. It would hurt her and that was something to know. Once he had loved them. When he was young, before the other children came along, he and his mother had often waited for his father at that very corner with a flask of tea and sandwiches and hot currant buns. They used to go into the Green to sit on the grass and have a picnic. But now he hated them. He had nothing to say to them. He had hated them for a long time now but they refused to recognise it. His mother waited. Then she said, "A penny for them, Michael."

Anne Fox had said that too, and now she was lying in the bracken with Dorgan. He made a sullen mask of his face and refused to answer. After a while, this time more urgently, she said, "Michael."

He grunted and shrugged.

"The baby isn't well," she began, once again placating him, trying to soften him, to bring him back to her. "I think I'll stay in to-night. You can go to the pictures instead. Make it up with your father at tea and then the pair of you can go off together."

"What is there to make up?" he asked. "You make me sick."

Hesitantly she suggested: "You weren't very nice to him at dinner."

"He wasn't very nice to me—was he?"

He looked around as he asked and was shocked to see tears in her eyes. But she averted her head and began to walk. He lagged behind, refusing to walk beside her. He saw in hunger and misery the squat steeple of the Methodist church, and over in the sky crossed regularly with clouds—a painted sea. Girls in the sea were slim and lovely. Girls in the sea had straight slim shapely legs. He looked at his mother's legs. They were very thin. They were encased in cheap unfashionable stockings, woolly, yellow in colour, wrinkled above the calves, much darned and dragged at the ankles. Her skirt was uneven as it swung about them. He watched the effort of her short step-by-step movement. He could not remember ever having looked at his mother's legs before. Now it stabbed him like a sword. His throat contracted. He searched for something brutal to say, something to protect himself against this fresh and unexpected onslaught of pain. She walked with her thin back towards him, her hands guiding the pram.

"We'll have to hurry home," she said brightly; "your poor father will be ages waiting."

He hoped to God she had wiped her eyes. He did not want people to see her. She quickened her pace and panted with the initial push.

"I have an egg for your tea," she added.

The brutality in him subsided. An egg for his tea. It made him want to laugh. But it also made him want to stretch out his hand to her, to touch her, to tell her he was sorry. But there were no words. He cast around for words. But when he even tried to think of them the grinding and turmoil in his head only became worse. Then his fingers touched the stolen half-crown. A flush of shame and unworthiness crept sullenly into his cheeks. It was suddenly without value. It could not buy what he wanted. Because he hardly knew what he wanted. He struggled with his own tears. He watched her now with immense tenderness, sorry for her, aching with love for her. But still something, his pride or his great shyness, would not permit him to speak to her or even to walk beside her.

In that way they went home; she walking ahead and unwitting, and he, who had no words for anything except churlishness or anger, followed silently.

MICHAEL McLAVERTY

THE WILD DUCK'S NEST*

THE SUN was setting, spilling a gold light on the low western hills of Rathlin Island. A small boy walked jauntily along a hoof-printed path that wriggled between the folds of these hills and opened out into a crater-like valley on the cliff-top. Presently he stopped as if remembering something; then suddenly he left the path, and began running up one of the hills. When he reached the top he was out of breath and stood watching streaks of light radiating from golden-edged clouds, the scene reminding him of a picture he had seen of the Transfiguration. A short distance below him was the cow standing at the edge of a reedy lake. Colm ran down to meet her waving his stick in the air, and the wind rumbling in his ears made him give an exultant whoop which splashed upon the hills in a shower of echoed sound. A flock of gulls lying on the short grass near the lake rose up languidly, drifting like blown snowflakes over the rim of the cliff.

The lake faced west and was fed by a stream, the drainings of the semi-circling hills. One side was open to the winds from the sea and in winter a little outlet trickled over the cliffs making a black vein in their grey sides. The boy lifted stones and began throwing them into the lake, weaving web after web on its calm surface. Then he skimmed the water with flat stones, some of them jumping the surface and coming to rest on the other side. He was delighted with himself and after listening to his echoing shouts of delight he ran to fetch his cow. Gently he tapped her on the side and reluctantly she went towards the brown-mudded path that led out of the valley. The boy was about to throw a final stone into the lake when a bird flew low over his head, its neck a-strain, and its orange-coloured legs clear in the soft light. It was a wild duck. It circled the lake twice, thrice, coming lower each time and then with a nervous flapping of wings it skidded along the surface, its legs breaking the water into a series of silvery arcs. Its wings closed, it lit silently, gave a slight shiver, and began pecking indifferently at the water.

Colm with dilated eyes eagerly watched it making for the farther end of the lake. It meandered between tall bulrushes, its body, black and solid as stone against the greying water. Then as if it had sunk it was gone. The boy ran stealthily along the bank looking away from the lake, pretending indifference. When he came opposite to where he had last seen the bird he stopped and peered through the sighing reeds whose shadows streaked the water in a maze of black strokes. In front of him was a soddy islet guarded by the spears of sedge and separated from the bank by a narrow channel of water. The water wasn't too deep—he could wade across with care.

Rolling up his short trousers he began to wade, his arms outstretched, and

* From *The Game Cock and Other Stories*, Devin-Adair Co., New York, 1948. Reprinted by permission of the publishers.

379

his legs brown and stunted in the mountain water. As he drew near the islet, his feet sank in the cold mud and bubbles winked up at him. He went more carefully and nervously. Then one trouser fell and dipped into the water; the boy dropped his hands to roll it up, he unbalanced, made a splashing sound, and the bird arose with a squawk and whirred away over the cliffs. For a moment the boy stood frightened. Then he clambered on to the wet-soaked sod of land, which was spattered with sea gulls' feathers and bits of wind-blown rushes.

Into each hummock he looked, pulling back the long grass. At last he came on the nest, facing seawards. Two flat rocks dimpled the face of the water and between them was a neck of land matted with coarse grass containing the nest. It was untidily built of dried rushes, straw and feathers, and in it lay one solitary egg. Colm was delighted. He looked around and saw no one. The nest was his. He lifted the egg, smooth and green as the sky, with a faint tinge of yellow like the reflected light from a buttercup; and then he felt he had done wrong. He put it back. He knew he shouldn't have touched it and he wondered would the bird forsake the nest. A vague sadness stole over him and he felt in his heart he had sinned. Carefully smoothing out his footprints he hurriedly left the islet and ran after his cow. The sun had now set and the cold shiver of evening enveloped him, chilling his body and saddening his mind.

In the morning he was up and away to school. He took the grass rut that edged the road for it was softer on the bare feet. His house was the last on the western headland and after a mile or so he was joined by Paddy McFall; both boys dressed in similar hand-knitted blue jerseys and grey trousers carried home-made school bags. Colm was full of the nest and as soon as he joined his companion he said eagerly: "Paddy, I've a nest—a wild duck's with one egg."

"And how do you know it's a wild duck's?" asked Paddy slightly jealous.

"Sure I saw her with my own two eyes, her brown speckled back with a crow's patch on it, and her yellow legs—"

"Where is it?" interrupted Paddy, in a challenging tone.

"I'm not going to tell you, for you'd rob it!"

"Aach! I suppose it's a tame duck's you have or maybe an old gull's."

Colm put out his tongue at him. "A lot you know!" he said, "for a gull's egg has spots and this one is greenish-white, for I had it in my hand."

And then the words he didn't want to hear rushed from Paddy in a mocking chant, "You had it in your hand! . . . She'll forsake it! She'll forsake it! She'll forsake it!" he said, skipping along the road before him.

Colm felt as if he would choke or cry with vexation.

His mind told him that Paddy was right, but somehow he couldn't give in to it and he replied: "She'll not forsake it! She'll not! I know she'll not!"

But in school his faith wavered. Through the windows he could see moving sheets of rain—rain that dribbled down the panes filling his mind with thought of the lake creased and chilled by wind; the nest sodden and black with wetness; and the egg cold as a cave stone. He shivered from the thoughts and fidgeted with the inkwell cover, sliding it backwards and forwards mechanically. The mischievous look had gone from his eyes and the school day dragged on interminably. But at last they were out in the rain, Colm rushing home as fast as he could.

He was no time at all at his dinner of potatoes and salted fish until he was out in the valley now smoky with drifts of slanting rain. Opposite the islet he entered the water. The wind was blowing into his face, rustling noisily the rushes heavy with the dust of rain. A moss-cheeper, swaying on a reed like a mouse, filled the air with light cries of loneliness.

The boy reached the islet, his heart thumping with excitement, wondering did the bird forsake. He went slowly, quietly, on to the strip of land that led to the nest. He rose on his toes, looking over the ledge to see if he could see her. And then every muscle tautened. She was on, her shoulders hunched up, and her bill lying on her breast as if she were asleep. Colm's heart hammered wildly in his ears. She hadn't forsaken. He was about to turn stealthily away. Something happened. The bird moved, her neck straightened, twitching nervously from side to side. The boy's head swam with lightness. He stood transfixed. The wild duck with a panicky flapping, rose heavily, and flew off towards the sea. . . . A guilty silence enveloped the boy. . . . He turned to go away, hesitated, and glanced back at the bare nest; it'd be no harm to have a look. Timidly he approached it, standing straight, and gazing over the edge. There in the nest lay two eggs. He drew in his breath with delight, splashed quickly from the island, and ran off whistling in the rain.

BRYAN MacMAHON

*THE CORN WAS SPRINGING**

THE BOY heard the young footsteps behind and beneath him. Then he heard the tittering like tearing paper. When the footsteps stopped he dared not turn round though he was aware that the eyes behind and beneath him were gimleting holes in his shoulder-blades. As he turned, a fistful of spalls was thrown in his face: a sharp stone caught him on the cheek bone. He blinked his eyes protectively. When he opened them again he had a memory of two dresses whisking beneath his little scaffold and vanishing through the chapel door. He heard the inner glass door swish open. Within the chapel the first footsteps of his attackers were excited and irreverent. The door was a long while closing, as it was controlled by an apparatus designed to prevent it slamming. Then he heard the footsteps within grow reverent

* From *The Lion-Tamer and Other Stories*. Copyright, 1949, by Bryan MacMahon. Reprinted by permission of E. P. Dutton Co., Inc. For Canada, permission granted by The Macmillan & Co., Ltd., London, and The Macmillan Company of Canada, Limited.

and meek and innocent. The boy put the back of his hand to his cheek where the spall had nicked him; when he withdrew it there was a small sign of blood on the point of the knuckle. He resumed his carving on the hood moulding around the doorway. As he worked he hummed menacingly through his teeth:

> I'm sitting on the stile, Mary, where we sat, side by side,
> On a bright May morning long ago when first you were my bride.
> The corn was springing fresh and green . . .

Through the song and the noise of the mallet his ears were most alert.

The convent, with the chapel to the right of it and the schools to the left, was wonderfully clear in the pure air of the May morning. The three buildings formed a quadrangle with an open side or mouth. This mouth was turned to the south: thus the sunlight of the young summer was trapped in the garden beds before the convent door. In the middle of the beds was a statue of Our Lady. Around the base of the statue was a bed of tulips, already alight with vivid blooms which leaped up from a carpet of forget-me-nots. The façade of the convent proper was scrawled over by the angry cords of Virginia creeper which in autumn whooshed the sober building into a red-gold blaze. The high convent peeped over the ivied wall into the village, the single street of which fell downhill to peter out in a mutter of thatched cottages at the base of the hill.

The planks on which the boy was seated were supported by two six-foot trestles. The youngster appeared to be about seventeen years of age. He was wearing a soiled white coat. A pair of goggles was pushed high up on his forehead. He had an open, even a merry face. Soon his anger ebbed in him and he began to forget that he was waiting for his assailants to emerge. He focused his attention on the mallet and chisel. This was the first time the foreman had entrusted him with important work of this nature and it behoved him to be careful. He continued to sing softly, but the malice had now vanished from his song; "The lark's loud song is in my ear and the corn is green again." The mallet wasn't a whit too heavy for his hand: it was accurate, obedient, and kind, going where he asked it to go. Funny to listen to the old stone-cutters talking of mallets. Holly was good, American hickory better, but neither the one nor the other could hold candlelight to the wood of the female crab-tree. The old fellows on the job were a study. Matthews was so accurate that the others said jokingly that he could carve faces on the shoulders of a lemonade bottle; Flanagan was peerless at lettering a tombstone. But they had their faults: Matthews was deplorable at foliage and Flanagan was hopeless at the angle-cut to get shadows. The foreman, Finucane, was the best all-around man in the province but he was unpredictable in mood, and if he were ill-tempered he couldn't carve soap. They were all superstitious to an extraordinary degree, and if a mallet fell from a scaffold every man on the job watched to see if its handle pointed to the gateway, for if it did there was trouble ahead. Their conversation was invariably trade-proud and esoteric; to a man they were contemptuous of tailors.

The boy again heard the footsteps behind him. Crunching on the limestone spalls, He knew immediately it was the foreman. The man stayed watching him for a moment before he spoke gruffly. His cap hid his eyes.

"Well, how're you doing?" The foreman was as lean as a mustang. He had a small brown moustache.

"Fine, sir."

"That's it! Go on, go on! What are you afraid of? You're working on the freeway." Finucane put his hand in behind one of the trestles and with his fingers caressed the foliage carved on one of the terminal bosses. This was his own work. On the boss were the letters I.H.S. on a bed of leaves. The caressing appeared to afford him keen satisfaction. Coming out in front of the doorway again he kicked the spalls away. "Keep the path clean underneath you and don't let people be dragging that stuff up the middle of the chapel," he said. Then he gave a grunt indicative of a grudged satisfaction of the boy's work.

As the foreman turned to go away he spoke with a half-smile. "Mother Xavier is in the garden—she's gathering more leaves." He turned down the short cement pathway that led to the road. As he walked away he kicked more of the spalls aside.

Finucane must have heard the nun coming, for scarcely had he gone than Mother Xavier came round the corner of the chapel with a great ado of hissing and trundling. She was a gigantic woman with an enormous, bespectacled face. It was almost impossible to determine her expression, as she had a trick of sealing up her eyes by reflecting the sunlight on the lenses of her spectacles. Her face was pale and the mouth indeterminate. The tremendous girth of her body made playthings of her rosary and girdle. Through the creakings of her approach the boy made a last effort to sift the noises that he fancied were coming from within the chapel. His effort was unavailing, for no sound could be heard above the clacking of the nun's rosary and the great rustle of her moving garments. The boy looked down into the twin circles of reflected sunlight that hid her eyes. Then he saw that the old nun was carrying a handful of leaves.

"Aha, young man!" Mother Xavier wheezed. The boy stopped working, and as a mark of respect dipped his goggled forehead toward his mallet-head.

"Well, did you find out what kind of leaves they were?"

"I did, ma'am—I think they're hop leaves."

"Hop leaves?" she complained. Grumbling, she moved to one side and peered through the stilts of the trestles at the foliage carved on the terminal boss. Then, "They don't look like hop leaves to me. I don't know much about hop leaves. Why didn't he put vine leaves or some other kind of leaves on them?"

"I couldn't exactly say, ma'am."

"Tck-tck! Well, maybe he knows his own business. And maybe he doesn't! Now isn't that a nice leaf?" She was handing him up a sycamore leaf that was splendid in its young green leaf and red stem. The boy took it gravely and, catching it by the stem, revolved it appraisingly between his thumb and forefinger.

"That's a lovely leaf, ma'am."

"And that?" She handed up another leaf.

"That's a grand leaf, too, ma'am."

"And that?—and that?—and that?"

The boy said they were all beautiful leaves.

"And will you tell me why he didn't put those leaves on the boss instead of his old hop leaves?"

The young stone-cutter said he couldn't exactly say.

Suddenly the great nun became conscious of the boy as a boy. Her face grew a shade softer.

"What's your name, sonny?" she asked.

"Jamesy Dunphy, ma'am."

"And where are you from?"

He told her that. Also his age. That his father and mother were alive. That he was the eldest of six. That his mother had had an operation for gall-stones. That the baby was as good as gold, except the time that he had the whooping-cough, when he got up any amount of phlegm. That he had an aunt a radiologist in an hospital in Lancaster. That his father had bound him to a stonemason. That he pulled the goggles down on his eyes when he was working on a certain class of stone.

This information received, the old nun delivered judgment. "God bless you, Jamesy, but you're a great boy altogether. Your father and mother should be proud of you!"

The boy had no reply to this, except to attempt a faint smile. This smile was killed decisively as he heard a low squeak from the chapel door. His sudden tautness communicated itself to the old nun, who immediately moved herself to a position where she could peer in the doorway. She continued to look in suspiciously. Just as she was about to investigate the squeak further two other nuns came walking out of the pathway that wandered through the flower-beds. One was a tall, graceful nun of thirty-five or so, who had the accurate features of statuary allied to the capital complexion of rude health. Her companion was a tiny old nun with a bright scarlet face so pointed that it instantly reminded one of a small song-bird. On catching sight of Mother Xavier this small old nun sprang to the attack. She turned her face to the tall nun beside her.

"There she is now, Reverend Mother, pestering the poor little boy," said tiny Mother Catherine.

Mother Xavier gathered herself for attack. Herself and Mother Catherine were old friends who played at being old foes. For many years they had taken every second term at being Reverend Mother. At last they had been successful in their pleadings for a younger nun in command. They were now testing the new Reverend Mother, playing at being enemies in her presence, simulating contrariness and even dotage; not infrequently taking refuge behind barriers of obtuseness in order to witness her reactions of perplexity. It was all a game, and the new Reverend Mother thoroughly understood the rules. She knew that the two old nuns were probing her for that kernel of royalty that must of necessity be present in every woman who seeks to rule a community of women.

So Mother Xavier, playing according to the rules of the game, bridled in the midst of her fat. She employed her old subterfuge of taking refuge behind the light-laden lenses of her spectacles. She tucked her leaves up her capacious sleeves, and mock-fumed at the venom of the little woman's onslaught.

"The Lord give me patience!" she breathed.

The young Reverend Mother extended her arms in a wholly delightful gesture. "Hush, mothers, hush!" she chided. The boy was tapping softly, one eye on the newcomers so as to be ready with his salute if they addressed him.

Then two traitorous leaves began to sneak down out of Mother Xavier's sleeves. They were buoyant and took a long time to fall to the ground. Mother Xavier saw their treachery reflected faithfully on Mother Catherine's face. Mother Catherine opened her mouth and made the preparatory noises of a song-bird who hears singing afar. Her opponent pursed her mouth as a prelude to retaliation. The young Reverend Mother took them by the arms and drew them softly away. "Something I wish to ask you both . . ." she said. She guided them as a dancer moves a partner. They seemed unwilling to part company with their anger. As the three nuns moved among the flower-beds the boy watched them curiously. In his own mind he compared them to a hillock of black serge on the move. He heard the two old voices clash on one another; then the oil of the young nun's speech was poured between.

When they had gone, the girls came out of the chapel.

One, a black-haired girl of fifteen or so, scurried skittishly out beneath the scaffold and rushed to the doorway that led to the road. The other, a tall girl of about seventeen, with ripe-corn hair brushing on her shoulder blades, walked out slowly. She was obviously a disdainful but graceful minx. Despite the apparent valour of her carriage, the indefinable impression of unsureness in calves and ankles was unmistakable.

Jamesy Dunphy lowered his hammer and eyed her fully and severely. Watching her move away from him he said nothing, for he was shrewd enough to know that if he stayed motionless the girl would turn around. She did so, a good deal sooner than he had expected. Finding herself fully apprehended, she faced him as bold as brass. The boy ran his hands down the moulding in the direction of the terminal boss, thereby subtly implying that the carving of the foliage was his unaided work. The tall girl was still staring. Their glances were locked for a little while.

"D'you see me?" asked Jamesy. The words of themselves seemed harsh, but the intonation was soft.

"I do."

"You'll know me again when you see me."

More than a hint of her tongue appeared. "A cat can look at a queen," she said.

"Can a cat fire stones at a queen?"

She looked around at the light spalls. "Stones!" she said contemptuously.

A pause. The boy over-earnestly returned to his work. Again the sound of young footsteps behind him, picking their way among the spalls.

"What are you doing?" she asked.

"Can't you see what I'm doing?"

She was about four yards from him now. She was peering at the boss on the left-hand side of the doorway. "Did you do that?"

"Huh-huh!"

"You did in your eye!"

The boy said evenly, "And who do you think did it so?"

"You didn't do it—that's one sure thing!"

A pause. Then the boy spoke out of the corner of his mouth.

"Run away, little girl, and do your lessons!"

"Lessons? I'm in Intermediate!"

The boy's face creased in its film of powder. He said a curious thing. "Trace the character of Banquo."

Her eyebrows lifted in genuine amazement. "Did you do Inter?"

"Uh-huh!"

"An' what are you doing picking old stones if you did Intermediate?"

The boy gave her a look of concentrated scorn.

"Here, buzz off!" he said.

"I'll buzz off if I like."

There was a sudden agitated whisper from the doorway at the roadway. "Kitty! Kitty Kavanagh! Reverend Mother is over in the playground. She's watching you!"

A momentary wiggle of fear came into Kitty's eyes. She looked across the flower-beds and saw Reverend Mother walking up and down on the nearer edge of the school playground. She stepped backwards and placed the head of a bush in the line of vision between herself and the nun. "Ah, she can't see me at all." She threw the defiant words across her shoulder.

"She's after looking over at you, Kitty," wailed the dark girl. Then in terror and uprighteousness, "I'm going away."

"Who's stopping you, cowardy-cat?"

But the young Reverend Mother had seen the girl. The speed of her gait increased as she debated within herself whether or not she should reprove Kitty Kavanagh for her forwardness. She found it difficult to reach a decision, for her own memory was harrying her without respite. Then, as now, it was a bright May morning. The slow, soft effervescence of the apple-blossom was foaming in the vat of the orchard; Bernard had come striding through the trees, his head every now and again was bending engagingly. She was picking rust off the garden seat with her finger-nail. Bernard came nearer and nearer, bringing with him the treasures of his carriage and eyes and hair. Again and again the vision sprang out from the ambush of the years. The young Reverend Mother groped for her beads and ran them through her fingers as she walked.

The Great Parlour was on the second story of the convent. The lower half of the windows had been raised to their full extent so as to let in the May air. Within, the two old nuns were seated behind the table watching the young Reverend Mother and Kitty Kavanagh. Mechanical impulses of their lips compelled them to call the girl "Baggage! Minx! Madcap! Hussy!" but their imprecation had no validity. They continued to watch, with such immobility that they might have been sleepers. They were independent of eagerness and anger and surprise. Their souls were beyond invasion. Long ago they had made a truce with life, and life had respected the terms of the bargain. Now they were two old gentlewomen of God who were superior to the memories of tulle and music and huzzas. From their holy stupor they continued to watch as they had watched the village below them for more than fifty years. They knew themselves for what they were—two old leaks by which the tremendous confidences of tormented wives had been vented. They continued to watch, with such an extraordinary concentration as almost passed muster for obtuseness. But they were not obtuse. They had seen too many novices with smiling distances in their eyes, and finger-tips for ever seeking their ear-lobes. They had seen too many ringleted cherubs grow up and meet seduction, too many angular imps enlarge and become country empresses. They had strong precedents to guide them: they themselves had distilled lamplight on far hills and the litmus bloom of rhododendrons to inadequate drops in the eye-corners. They had recognized themselves in everyone with whom they came in contact, until personal pain was lessened by division and subdivision. A shot in the boundary elms would have startled them: a rat gnawing in the partition would have terrified them. But the remoter phenomena of people's emotions they perfectly understood.

Mother Xavier had now no sunlight to gild her glasses, and there behind the lenses was discovered the reason why she herself had been selected Reverend Mother. Now more than ever was Mother Catherine a bird of God. But what kind of bird was she? She was neither His falcon nor His magpie nor even His beloved black hen. Age had granted her the boon of interpreting aright the authenticity of curious hallelujahs. A slow, sad smile slitted her beak. She continued to regard Kitty Kavanagh, and, as she watched, she saw the girl's dead mother and dead grandmother stand behind, directly behind, the flirting child. Just so they had coquetted and pirouetted and flirted. And had they been the worse for it all? No, a thousand times no. (The soft silver gongs of first love were ringing through the sunny convent and were strangely welcome.)

The two old nuns continued to watch in stubby pattern; their etiolated faces framed in the black passe-partout of their veils and their facial bones thrown into relief by the light reflected from the inverted fans of their gamps. Their amazing power of self-identification was now being exerted to the full.

Just then the foreman stole past the dark-haired sentry at the gateway and took in the situation at a glance. He saw the boy and girl, the nuns behind the open window and the striding Reverend Mother. His decision was swift. "Hey, come off it!" he roared at the boy.

The girl stood, a cool spectator, enjoying the youngster's shame. The foreman did not intimidate her. Her sense of amusement heightened as the boy went round the corner of the chapel, to work on large rough stones lying beside the gooseberry bushes. As he went he had the wit to hum to himself, "And I'll not forget you, darling, in the land I'm going to. . . ."

A breeze came up out of the good green fields. It prinked and pranced like a flighty filly. Suddenly it stood stock-still, and instantly the bright May morning was motionless. The young Reverend Mother moved up through the tulip beds on her way to the main door. Her face had the lustre of prayer-book gilt. The old nuns remained regardant until such time as the approaching nun was out of sight beneath them. Then each awoke to find that her mind had been a box within a box within a box.

SAKI

THE SCHARTZ-METTERKLUME METHOD*

LADY CARLOTTA stepped out on to the platform of the small wayside station and took a turn or two up and down its uninteresting length, to kill time till the train should be pleased to proceed on its way. Then, in the roadway beyond, she saw a horse struggling with a more than ample load, and a carter of the sort that seems to bear a sullen hatred against the animal that helps him to earn a living. Lady Carlotta promptly betook her to the roadway, and put rather a different complexion on the struggle. Certain of her acquaintances were wont to give her plentiful admonition as to the undesirability of interfering on behalf of a distressed animal, such interference being "none of her business." Only once had she put the doctrine of non-interference into practice, when one of its most eloquent exponents had been besieged for nearly three hours in a small and extremely uncomfortable may-tree by an angry boar-pig, while Lady Carlotta, on the other side of

* Reprinted from *The Short Stories of Saki* by H. H. Munro. By permission of the Viking Press, Inc. For Canada, permission granted by The Bodley Head, Publishers, London.

the fence, had proceeded with the water-colour sketch she was engaged on, and refused to interfere between the boar and his prisoner. It is to be feared that she lost the friendship of the ultimately rescued lady. On this occasion she merely lost the train, which gave way to the first sign of impatience it had shown throughout the journey, and steamed off without her. She bore the desertion with philosophical indifference; her friends and relations were thoroughly well used to the fact of her luggage arriving without her. She wired a vague non-committal message to her destination to say that she was coming on "by another train." Before she had time to think what her next move might be she was confronted by an imposingly attired lady, who seemed to be taking a prolonged mental inventory of her clothes and looks.

"You must be Miss Hope, the governess I've come to meet," said the apparition, in a tone that admitted of very little argument.

"Very well, if I must I must," said Lady Carlotta to herself with dangerous meekness.

"I am Mrs. Quabarl," continued the lady; "and where, pray, is your luggage?"

"It's gone astray," said the alleged governess, falling in with the excellent rule of life that the absent are always to blame; the luggage had, in point of fact, behaved with perfect correctitude. "I've just telegraphed about it," she added, with a nearer approach to truth.

"How provoking," said Mrs. Quabarl; "these railway companies are so careless. However, my maid can lend you things for the night," and she led the way to her car.

During the drive to the Quabarl mansion Lady Carlotta was impressively introduced to the nature of the charge that had been thrust upon her; she learned that Claude and Wilfrid were delicate, sensitive young people, that Irene had the artistic temperament highly developed, and that Viola was something or other else of a mould equally commonplace among children of that class and type in the twentieth century.

"I wish them not only to be taught," said Mrs. Quabarl, "but interested in what they learn. In their history lessons, for instance, you must try to make them feel that they are being introduced to the life-stories of men and women who really lived, not merely committing a mass of names and dates to memory. French, of course, I shall expect you to talk at mealtimes several days in the week."

"I shall talk French four days of the week and Russian in the remaining three."

"Russian? My dear Miss Hope, no one in the house speaks or understands Russian."

"That will not embarrass me in the least," said Lady Carlotta coldly.

Mrs. Quabarl, to use a colloquial expression, was knocked off her perch. She was one of those imperfectly self-assured individuals who are magnificent and autocratic as long as they are not seriously opposed. The least show of unexpected resistance goes a long way towards rendering them cowed and apologetic. When the new governess failed to express wondering admiration of the large newly purchased and expensive car, and lightly alluded to the superior advantages of one or two makes which had just been put on the market, the discomfiture of her patroness became almost abject. Her feelings were those which might have animated a general of ancient warfaring days, on beholding his heaviest battle-elephant ignominiously driven off the field by slingers and javelin throwers.

At dinner that evening, although reinforced by her husband, who usually duplicated her opinions and lent her moral support generally, Mrs. Quabarl regained none of her lost ground. The governess not only helped herself well and truly to wine, but held forth with considerable show of critical knowledge on various vintage matters, concerning which the Quabarls were in no wise able to pose as authorities. Previous governesses had limited their conversation on the wine topic to a respectful and doubtless sincere expression of a preference for water. When this one went as far as to recommend a wine firm in whose hands you could not go very far wrong Mrs. Quabarl thought it time to turn the conversation into more usual channels.

"We got very satisfactory references about you from Canon Teep," she observed; "a very estimable man, I should think."

"Drinks like a fish and beats his wife, otherwise a very lovable character," said the governess imperturbably.

"My dear Miss Hope! I trust you are exaggerating," exclaimed the Quabarls in unison.

"One must in justice admit that there is some provocation," continued the romancer. "Mrs. Teep is quite the most irritating bridge-player that I have ever sat down with; her leads and declarations would condone a certain amount of brutality in her partner, but to souse her with the contents of the only soda-water syphon in the house on a Sunday afternoon, when one couldn't get another, argues an indifference to the comfort of others which I cannot altogether overlook. You may think me hasty in my judgments, but it was practically on account of the syphon incident that I left."

"We will talk of this some other time," said Mrs. Quabarl hastily.

"I shall never allude to it again," said the governess with decision.

Mr. Quabarl made a welcome diversion by asking what studies the new instructress proposed to inaugurate on the morrow.

"History to begin with," she informed him.

"Ah, history," he observed sagely; "now in teaching them history you must take care to interest them in what they learn. You must make them feel that they are being introduced to the life-stories of men and women who really lived——"

"I've told her all that," interposed Mrs. Quabarl.

"I teach history on the Schartz-Metterklume method," said the governess loftily.

"Ah, yes," said her listeners, thinking it expedient to assume an acquaintance at least with the name.

"What are you children doing out here?" demanded Mrs. Quabarl the next morning, on finding Irene sitting rather glumly at the head of the stairs, while her sister was perched in an attitude of depressed discomfort on the window-seat behind her, with a wolf-skin rug almost covering her.

"We are having a history lesson" came the unexpected reply. "I am supposed to be Rome, and Viola up there is the she-wolf; not a real wolf, but the figure of one that the Romans used to set store by—I forget why. Claude and Wilfrid have gone to fetch the shabby women."

"The shabby women?"

"Yes, they've got to carry them off. They didn't want to, but Miss Hope got one of father's fives-bats and said she'd give them a number nine spanking if they didn't, so they've gone to do it."

A loud, angry screaming from the direction of the lawn drew Mrs. Quabarl thither in hot haste, fearful lest the threatened castigation might even now be in process of infliction. The outcry, however, came principally from the two small daughters of the lodge-keeper, who were being hauled and rushed towards the house by the panting and dishevelled Claude and Wilfrid, whose task was rendered even more arduous by the incessant, if not very effectual, attacks of the captured maidens' small brother. The governess, fives-bat in hand, sat negligently on the stone balustrade, presiding over the scene with the cold impartiality of a Goddess of Battles. A furious and repeated chorus of "I'll tell muvver" rose from the lodge children, but the lodge-mother, who was hard of hearing, was for the moment immersed in the preoccupation of her washtub. After an apprehensive glance in the direction of the lodge (the good woman was gifted with the highly militant temper which is sometimes the privilege of deafness) Mrs. Quabarl flew indignantly to the rescue of the struggling captives.

"Wilfrid! Claude! Let those children go at once. Miss Hope, what on earth is the meaning of this scene?"

"Early Roman history; the Sabine women, don't you know? It's the Schartz-Metterklume method to make children understand history by acting it themselves; fixes it in their memory, you know. Of course, if, thanks to your interference, your boys go through life thinking that the Sabine women ultimately escaped, I really cannot be held responsible."

"You may be very clever and modern, Miss Hope," said Mrs. Quabarl firmly, "but I should like you to leave here by the next train. Your luggage will be sent after you as soon as it arrives."

"I'm not certain exactly where I shall be for the next few days," said the dismissed instructress of youth; "you might keep my luggage till I wire my address. There are only a couple of trunks and some golf-clubs and a leopard cub."

"A leopard cub!" gasped Mrs. Quabarl. Even in her departure this extraordinary person seemed destined to leave a trail of embarrassment behind her.

"Well, it's rather left off being a cub; it's more than half-grown, you know. A fowl every day and a rabbit on Sundays is what it usually gets.

Raw beef makes it too excitable. Don't trouble about getting the car for me, I'm rather inclined for a walk."

And Lady Carlotta strode out of the Quabarl horizon.

The advent of the genuine Miss Hope, who had made a mistake as to the day on which she was due to arrive, caused a turmoil which that good lady was quite unused to inspiring. Obviously the Quabarl family had been woefully befooled, but a certain amount of relief came with the knowledge.

"How tiresome for you, dear Carlotta," said her hostess, when the overdue guest ultimately arrived; "how very tiresome losing your train and having to stop overnight in a strange place."

"Oh, dear, no," said Lady Carlotta; "not at all tiresome—for me."

GRAHAM GREENE

A CHANCE FOR MR. LEVER*

Mʀ. Lᴇᴠᴇʀ knocked his head against the ceiling and swore. Rice was stored above, and in the dark the rats began to move. Grains of rice fell between the slats onto his Revelation suitcase, his bald head, his cases of tinned food, the little square box in which he kept his medicines. His boy had already set up the campbed and mosquito net, and, outside in the warm damp dark, his folding table and chair. The thatched pointed huts streamed away toward the forest and a woman went from hut to hut carrying fire. The glow lit her old face, her sagging breasts, her tattooed, diseased body.

It was incredible to Mr. Lever that five weeks ago he had been in London.

He couldn't stand upright; he went down on hands and knees in the dust and opened his suitcase. He took out his wife's photograph and stood it on the chop box; he took out a writing pad and an indelible pencil: the pencil had softened in the heat and left mauve stains on his pajamas. Then because the light of the hurricane lamp disclosed cockroaches the size of black beetles flattened against the mud wall, he carefully closed the suitcase. Already in ten days he had learned that they'd eat anything, socks, shirts, the laces out of your shoes.

Mr. Lever went outside; moths beat against his lamp; but there were no mosquitoes; he hadn't seen or heard one since he landed. He sat in a circle of light carefully observed. The blacks squatted outside their huts and watched him; they were friendly, interested, amused, but their strict attention irritated Mr. Lever. He could feel the small waves of interest washing around him, when he began to write, when he stopped writing, when he wiped his damp hands with a handkerchief. He couldn't touch his pocket without a craning of necks.

Dearest Emily, he wrote, I've really started now. I'll send this letter back with a carrier when I've located Davidson. I'm very well. Of course, everything's a bit strange. Look after yourself, my dear, and don't worry.

"Massa, buy chicken," his cook said, appearing suddenly between the huts. A small stringy fowl struggled in his hands.

"Well," Mr. Lever said, "I gave you a shilling, didn't I?"

"They no like," the cook said. "These low bush people."

"Why don't they like? It's good money."

"They want king's money," the cook said, handing back the Victorian shilling. Mr. Lever had to get up, go back in to his hut, grope for his money box, search through twenty pounds of small change: there was no peace.

He had learned that very quickly. He had to economize (the whole trip was a gamble which scared him); he couldn't afford hammock carriers. He would arrive, tired out after seven hours of walking, at a village of which he didn't know the name and not for a minute could he sit quietly and rest. He must shake hands with the chief, he must see about a hut, accept presents of palm wine he was afraid to drink, buy rice and palm oil for the carriers, give them salts and aspirin, paint their sores with iodine. They never left him alone for five minutes on end until he went to bed. And then the rats began, rushing down the walls like water when he put out the light, gamboling among his cases.

I'm too old, Mr. Lever told himself, I'm too old, writing damply, indelibly, I hope to find Davidson tomorrow. If I do, I may be back almost as soon as this letter. Don't economize on the stout and milk, dear, and call in the doctor if you feel bad. I've got a premonition this trip's going to turn out well. We'll take a holiday, you need a holiday, and staring ahead past the huts and the black faces and the banana trees toward the forest from which he would come, into which he would sink again next day, he thought, Eastbourne. Eastbourne would do her a world of good, and continued to write the only kind of lies he'd ever told Emily, the lies which comforted. I ought to draw at least three hundred in commission and my expenses. But it wasn't the sort of place he'd been accustomed to sell heavy machinery in; thirty years of it, up and down Europe and in the States, but never anything like this. He could hear his filter dripping in the hut, and somewhere somebody was playing something (he was so lost he hadn't got the simplest terms to his hand), something monotonous, melancholy, superficial, a twanging of palm fibers which seemed to convey that you weren't happy, but it didn't matter much, everything would always be the same.

Look after yourself, Emily, he repeated. It was almost the only thing he found himself capable of writing to her; he couldn't describe the narrow steep lost paths, the snakes sizzling away like flames, the rats, the dust, the naked, diseased bodies. He was unbearably tired of nakedness. Don't forget. . . . It was like living with a lot of cows.

"The chief," his boy whispered, and between the huts under a waving torch came an old stout man wearing a robe of native cloth and a battered

bowler hat. Behind him his men carried six bowls of rice, a bowl of palm
oil, two bowls of broken meat. "Chop for the laborers," the boy explained,
and Mr. Lever had to get up and smile and nod and try to convey without
words that he was pleased, that the chop was excellent, that the chief would
get a good dash in the morning. At first the smell had been almost too much
for Mr. Lever.

"Ask him," he said to his boy, "if he's seen a white man come through
here lately. Ask him if a white man's been digging around here. Damn it,"
Mr. Lever burst out, the sweat breaking on the backs of his hands and on
his bald head, "ask him if he's seen Davidson?"

"Davidson?"

"Oh hell," Mr. Lever said, "you know what I mean. The white man I'm
looking for."

"White man?"

"What do you imagine I'm here for, eh? White man? Of course white
man. I'm not here for my health." A cow coughed, rubbed its horns against
the hut, and two goats broke through between the chief and him, upsetting
the bowls of meat scraps; nobody cared, they picked the meat out of the
dust and dung.

Mr. Lever sat down and put his hands over his face, fat, white, well-cared
for hands with wrinkles of flesh over the rings: I'm too old for this.

"Chief say no white man been here long time."

"How long?"

"Chief say not since he pay hut tax."

"How long's that?"

"Long, long time."

"Ask him how far is it to Greh tomorrow."

"Chief say too far."

"Nonsense," Mr. Lever said.

"Chief say too far. Better stay here. Fine town. No humbug."

Mr. Lever groaned. Every evening there was the same trouble. The next
town was always too far. They would invent any excuse to delay him, to
give themselves a rest.

"Ask the chief how many hours——?"

"Plenty, plenty." They had no idea of time. "This fine chief. Fine chop.
Laborers tired. No humbug."

"We are going on," Mr. Lever said.

"This fine town. Chief say——"

He thought: if this wasn't the last chance, I'd give up. They nagged him
so, and suddenly he longed for another white man (not Davidson, he daren't
say anything to Davidson) to whom he could explain the desperation of his
lot. It wasn't fair, that a man after thirty years' commercial traveling should
need to go from door to door asking for a job. He had been a good traveler,
he had made money for many people, his references were excellent, but the

world had moved on since his day. He wasn't streamlined; he certainly wasn't streamlined. He had been ten years' retired when he lost his money in the depression.

Mr. Lever walked up and down Victoria Street showing his references. Many of the men knew him, gave him cigars, laughed at him in a friendly way for wanting to take on a job at his age ("I can't somehow settle at home. The old warhorse you know . . ."), cracked a joke or two in the passage, went back that night to Maidenhead silent in the first class carriage, shut in with age and ruin and how bad things were and poor devil his wife's probably sick.

It was in the rather shabby little office off Leadenhall Street that Mr. Lever met his chance. It called itself an engineering firm, but there were only two rooms, a typewriter, a girl with gold teeth, and Mr. Lucas, a thin narrow man with a tic in one eyelid. All through the interview the eyelid flickered at Mr. Lever. Mr. Lever had never before fallen so low as this.

But Mr. Lucas struck him as reasonably honest. He put "all his cards on the table." He hadn't got any money, but he had expectations, he had the handling of a patent. It was a new crusher. There was money in it. But you couldn't expect the big trusts to change over their machinery now. Things were too bad. You'd got to get in at the start, and that was where—why, that was where this chief, the bowls of chop, the nagging and the rats and the heat, came in. They called themselves a republic, Mr. Lucas said, he didn't know anything about that, they were not as black as they were painted, he supposed (ha ha, nervously, ha ha); anyway this company had slipped agents over the border and grabbed a concession: gold and diamonds. He could tell Mr. Lever in confidence that the trust was frightened of what they'd found. Now an enterprising man could just slip across (Mr. Lucas liked the word slip, it made everything sound easy and secret) and introduce this new crusher to them: it would save them thousands when they started work, there'd be a fat commission, and afterward, with the start. . . . There was a fortune for them all.

"But can't you fix it up in Europe?"

Tic, tic, went Mr. Lucas's eyelid. "A lot of Belgians; they are leaving all decisions to the man on the spot. An Englishman called Davidson."

"How about expenses?"

"That's the trouble," Mr. Lucas said. "We are only beginning. What we want is a partner. We can't afford to send a man. But if you like a gamble . . . 20 per cent commission."

"Chief say excuse him." The carriers squatted round the basins and scooped up the rice in their left hands. "Of course. Of course," Mr. Lever said absentmindedly. "Very kind, I'm sure." He was back out of the dust and dark, away from the stink of goats and palm oil and whelping bitches, back among the Rotarians and lunch at Stone's, "the pint of old," and the trade papers; he was a good fellow again finding his way back to Golders Green just a little lit; his masonic emblem rattled on his watch chain; and he bore with him from the tube station to his house in Finchley Road a sense of companionship, of broad stories and belches, a sense of bravery.

He needed all his bravery now; the last of his savings had gone into the trip. After thirty years he knew a good thing when he saw it, and he had no doubts about the new crusher. What he doubted was his ability to find Davidson. For one thing there weren't any maps; the way you traveled in the Republic was to write down a list of names and trust that someone in the villages you passed would understand and know the route. But they always said "Too far." Good fellowship wilted before the phrase.

"Quinine," Mr. Lever said. "Where's my quinine?" His boy never remembered a thing; they just didn't care what happened to you; their smiles meant nothing, and Mr. Lever, who knew better than anyone the value of a meaningless smile in business, resented their heartlessness, turned toward the dilatory boy an expression of disappointment and dislike.

"Chief say white man in bush five hours away."

"That's better," Mr. Lever said. "It must be Davidson. He's digging for gold?"

"Ya. White man dig for gold in bush."

"We'll be off early tomorrow," Mr. Lever said.

"Chief say better stop this town. Fever humbug white man."

"Too bad," Mr. Lever said, and he thought with pleasure: my luck's changed. He'll want help. He won't refuse me a thing. A friend in need is a friend indeed, and his heart warmed toward Davidson, seeing himself arrive like an answer to prayer out of the forest, feeling quite biblical and *vox humana*. He thought: Prayer. I'll pray tonight, that's the kind of thing a fellow gives up, but it pays, there's something in it, remembering the long agonizing prayer on his knees, by the sideboard, under the decanters, when Emily went to hospital.

"Chief say white man dead."

Mr. Lever turned his back on them and went into his hut. His sleeve nearly overturned the hurricane lamp. He undressed quickly, stuffing his clothes into a suitcase away from the cockroaches. He wouldn't believe what he had been told; it wouldn't pay him to believe. If Davidson was dead, there was nothing he could do but return; he had spent more than he could afford; he would be a ruined man. He supposed that Emily might find a home with her brother, but he could hardly expect her brother—— He began to cry, but you couldn't have told in the shadowy hut the difference between sweat and tears. He knelt down beside his campbed and mosquito net and prayed on the dust of the earth floor. Up till now he had always been careful never to touch a floor with his naked feet for fear of jiggers; there were jiggers everywhere, they only waited an opportunity to dig themselves in under the toenails, lay their eggs, and multiply.

"O God," Mr. Lever prayed, "don't let Davidson be dead; let him be just sick and glad to see me." He couldn't bear the idea that he might not any longer be able to support Emily. "O God, there's nothing I wouldn't do." But that was still an empty phrase; he had no real notion yet of what he would do for Emily. They had been happy together for thirty-five years; he had never been more than momentarily unfaithful to her when he was lit after a Rotarian dinner and egged on by the boys; whatever skirt he'd been with in his time he had never for a moment imagined that he could be happy married to anyone else. It wasn't fair if, just when you were old and needed each other most, you lost your money and couldn't keep together.

But, of course, Davidson wasn't dead. What would he have died of? The blacks were friendly. People said the country was unhealthy, but he hadn't so much as heard a mosquito. Besides you didn't die of malaria; you just lay between the blankets and took quinine and felt like death and sweated it out of you. There was dysentery, but Davidson was an old campaigner; you were safe if you boiled and filtered the water. The water was poison even to the touch; it was unsafe to wet your feet because of guinea worm, but you didn't die of guinea worm.

Mr. Lever lay in bed and his thoughts went round and round and he couldn't sleep. He thought: you don't die of a thing like guinea worm. It makes a sore on your foot, and if you put your foot in water you can see the eggs dropping out. You have to find the end of the worm, like a thread of cotton, and wind it round a match and wind it out of your leg without breaking; it stretches as high as the knee. I'm too old for this country, Mr. Lever thought.

Then his boy was beside him again. He whispered urgently to Mr. Lever through the mosquito net, "Massa, the laborers say they go home."

"Go home?" Mr. Lever said wearily; he had heard it so often before. "Why do they want to go home? What is it now?" but he didn't really want to hear the latest squabble: that the Bande men were never sent to carry water because the headman was a Bande, that someone had stolen an empty treacle tin and sold it in the village, that someone wasn't made to carry a proper load, that the next day's journey was "too far." He said, "Tell 'em they can go home. I'll pay them off in the morning. But they won't get any dash. They'd have got a good dash if they'd stayed." He was certain it was just another try-on; he wasn't as green as all that.

"Yes, massa. They no want dash."

"What's that?"

"They frightened fever humbug them like white man."

"I'll get carriers in the village. They can go home."

"Me too, massa."

"Get out," Mr. Lever said; it was the last straw; "get out and let me sleep." The boy went at once, obedient even if he was a deserter, and Mr. Lever thought: sleep, what a hope. He lifted the net and got out of bed (barefooted again: he didn't care a damn about the jiggers) and searched for his medicine box. It was locked, of course, and he had to open his suitcase and find the key in a trouser pocket. His nerves were more on edge than ever by the time he found the sleeping tablets and he took three of them. That made him sleep, heavily and dreamlessly, though when he woke he found that something had made him fling out his arm and open the net. If there had been a single mosquito in the place, he'd have been bitten, but, of course, there wasn't one.

He could tell at once that the trouble hadn't blown over. The village—he didn't know its name—was perched on a hilltop; east and west the forest flowed out beneath the little plateau: to the west it was a dark unfeatured mass like water, but in the east you could already discern the unevennesses, the great gray cotton trees lifted above the palms. Mr. Lever was always called before dawn, but no one had called him. A few of his carriers sat outside a hut sullenly talking; his boy was with them. Mr. Lever went back inside and dressed; he thought all the time, I must be firm, but he was scared, scared of being deserted, scared of being made to return.

When he came outside again the village was awake: the women were going down the hill to fetch water, winding silently past the carriers, past the flat stones where the chiefs were buried, the little grove of trees where the rice birds, like green and yellow canaries, nested. Mr. Lever sat down on his folding chair among the chickens and whelping bitches and cow dung and called his boy. He took "a strong line"; but he didn't know what was going to happen. "Tell the chief I want to speak to him," he said.

There was some delay; the chief wasn't up yet, but presently he appeared in his blue and white robe, setting his bowler hat straight. "Tell him," Mr. Lever said, "I want carriers to take me to the white man and back. Two days."

"Chief no agree," the boy said.

Mr. Lever said furiously, "Damn it, if he doesn't agree, he won't get any dash from me, not a penny." It occurred to him immediately afterward how hopelessly dependent he was on these people's honesty. There in the hut for all to see was his money box; they had only to take it. This wasn't a British or French colony; the blacks on the coast wouldn't bother, could do nothing if they did bother, because a stray Englishman had been robbed in the interior.

"Chief say how many?"

"It's only for two days," Mr. Lever said. "I can do with six."

"Chief say how much?"

"Sixpence a day and chop."

"Chief no agree."

"Ninepence a day then."

"Chief say too far. A shilling."

"All right, all right," Mr. Lever said, "a shilling then. You others can go home if you want to. I'll pay you off now, but you won't get any dash, not a penny."

He had never really expected to be left, and it gave him a sad feeling of loneliness to watch them move sullenly away (they were ashamed of themselves) down the hill to the west. They hadn't any loads, but they weren't singing; they dropped silently out of sight, his boy with them, and he was alone with his pile of boxes and the chief who couldn't talk a word of English. Mr. Lever smiled tremulously.

It was ten o'clock before his new carriers were chosen; he could tell that none of them wanted to go; and they would have to walk through the heat of the middle day if they were to find Davidson before it was dark. He hoped the chief had explained properly where they were going; he couldn't tell; he was completely shut off from them, and when they started down the eastward slope, he might just as well have been alone.

They were immediately caught up in the forest. Forest conveys a sense of wildness and beauty, of an active natural force, but this Liberian forest was simply a dull green wilderness. You passed, on a path a foot or so wide, through an endless back garden of tangled weeds; it didn't seem to be growing round you, so much as dying. There was no life at all, except for a few large birds whose wings creaked overhead through the invisible sky like an unoiled door. There was no view, no way out for the eyes, no change of scene. It wasn't the heat that tired so much as the boredom; you had to think of things to think about; but even Emily failed to fill the mind for more than three minutes at a time. It was a relief, a distraction, when the path was flooded and Mr. Lever had to be carried on a man's back. At first he had disliked the strong bitter smell (it reminded him of a breakfast food he was made to eat as a child), but he soon got over that. Now he was unaware that they smelt at all; any more than he was aware that the great swallow-tailed butterflies, which clustered at the water's edge and rose in green clouds round his waist, were beautiful. His senses were dulled and registered very little except his boredom.

But they did register a distinct feeling of relief when his leading carrier pointed to a rectangular hole dug just off the path. Mr. Lever understood. Davidson had come this way. He stopped and looked at it. It was like a grave dug for a small man, but it went down deeper than graves usually do. About twelve feet below there was black water, and a few wooden props which held the sides from slipping were beginning to rot; the hole must have been dug since the rains. It didn't seem enough, that hole, to have brought out Mr. Lever with his plans and estimates for a new crusher. He was used to big industrial concerns, the sight of pit heads, the smoke of chimneys, the dingy rows of cottages back to back, the leather armchair in the office, the good cigar, the masonic handgrips, and again it seemed to him, as it had seemed in Mr. Lucas's office, that he had fallen very low. It was as if he was expected to do business beside a hole a child had dug in an overgrown and abandoned back garden; percentages wilted in the hot damp air. He shook his head; he mustn't be discouraged; this was an old hole. Davidson had probably done better since. It was only common sense to suppose that the gold rift which was mined at one end in Nigeria, at the other in Sierra Leone, should pass through the republic. Even the biggest mines had to begin with a hole in the ground. The company, he had talked to the directors in Brussels, were quite confident: all they wanted was the approval of the man on the spot that the crusher was suitable for local conditions. A signature, that was all he had to get, he told himself, staring down into the puddle of black water.

Five hours, the chief had said, but after six hours they were still walking. Mr. Lever had eaten nothing, he wanted to get to Davidson first. All through the heat of the day he walked. The forest protected him from the direct sun, but it shut out the air, and the occasional clearings, shriveled though they were in the vertical glare, seemed cooler than the shade because there was a little more air to breathe. At four o'clock the heat diminished, but he began to fear they wouldn't reach Davidson before dark. His foot pained him; he had caught a jigger the night before; it was as if someone held a lighted match to his toe. Then at five they came on a dead black.

Another rectangular hole in a small cleared space among the dusty greenery caught Mr. Lever's eye. He peered down and was shocked to see a face return his stare, white eyeballs like phosphorus in the black water. The black had been bent almost double to fit him in; the hole was really too small to be a grave, and he had swollen. His flesh was like a blister you could prick with a needle. Mr. Lever felt sick and tired; he might have been tempted to return if he could have reached the village before dark; but now there was nothing to do but go on; the carriers luckily hadn't seen the body. He waved them forward and stumbled after among the roots, fighting his nausea. He fanned himself with his sun helmet; his wide fat face was damp and pale. He had never seen an uncared-for body before; his parents he had seen carefully laid out with closed eyes and washed faces; they "fell asleep" quite in accordance with their epitaphs, but you couldn't think of sleep in connection with the white eyeballs and the swollen face. Mr. Lever would have liked very much to say a prayer, but prayers were out of place in the dead drab forest; they simply didn't "come."

With the dusk a little life did waken: something lived in the dry weeds and brittle trees, if only monkeys. They chattered and screamed all round you, but it was too dark to see them; you were like a blind man in the center of a frightened crowd who wouldn't say what scared them. The carriers, too, were frightened. They ran under their fifty-pound loads behind the dipping light of the hurricane lamp, their huge flat carriers' feet flapping in the dust like empty gloves. Mr. Lever listened nervously for mosquitoes; you would have expected them to be out by now, but he didn't hear one.

Then at the top of a rise above a small stream they came on Davidson. The ground had been cleared in a square of twelve feet and a small tent pitched; he had dug another hole; the scene came dimly into view as they climbed the path: the chop boxes piled outside the tent, the syphon of soda water, the filter, an enamel basin. But there wasn't a light, there wasn't a sound, the flaps of the tent were not closed, and Mr. Lever had to face the possibility that after all the chief might have told the truth.

Mr. Lever took the lamp and stooped inside the tent. There was a body on the bed. At first Mr. Lever thought Davidson was covered with blood, but then he realized it was a black vomit which stained his shirts and khaki shorts, the fair stubble on his chin. He put out a hand and touched Davidson's face, and if he hadn't felt a slight breath on his palm he would have taken him for dead; his skin was so cold. He moved the lamp closer, and now the lemon-yellow face told him all he wanted to know: he hadn't thought of that when his boy said fever. It was quite true that a man didn't die of malaria, but an old piece of news read in New York in '98 came back to mind: there had been an outbreak in Rio and 94 per cent of the cases had been fatal. It hadn't meant anything to him then, but it did now. As he watched, Davidson was sick, quite effortlessly; he was like a tap out of which something flowed.

It seemed at first to Mr. Lever to be the end of everything, of his journey, his hopes, his life with Emily. There was nothing he could do for Davidson, the man was unconscious, there were times when his pulse was so low and irregular that Mr. Lever thought that he was dead until another black stream spread from his mouth; it was no use even cleaning him. Mr. Lever laid his own blankets over the bed on top of Davidson's because he was so cold to the touch, but he had no idea whether he was doing the right, or even the fatally wrong, thing. The chance of survival, if there was any chance at all, depended on neither of them. Outside his carriers had built a fire and were cooking the rice they had brought with them. Mr. Lever opened his folding chair and sat by the bed. He wanted to keep awake: it seemed right to keep awake; he opened his case and found his unfinished letter to Emily. He sat by Davidson's side and tried to write, but he could think of nothing but what he had already written too often: Look after yourself; don't forget the stout and milk.

He fell asleep over his pad and woke at two and thought that Davidson was dead. But he was wrong again. He was very thirsty and missed his boy. Always the first thing his boy did at the end of a march was to light a fire and put on a kettle; after that, by the time his table and chair were set up, there was water ready for the filter. Mr. Lever found half a cup of soda water left in Davidson's syphon; if it had been only his health at stake he would have gone down to the stream and drunk, but he had Emily to remember.

There was a typewriter by the bed and it occurred to Mr. Lever that he might just as well begin to write his report of failure now; it might keep him awake; it seemed disrespectful to the dying man to sleep. He found paper under some letters which had been typed and signed but not sealed. Davidson must have been taken ill very suddenly; Mr. Lever wondered whether it was he who had crammed the black into the hole; his boy perhaps, for there was no sign of a servant. He balanced the typewriter on his knee and headed the letter, In Camp near Greh.

It seemed to him unfair that he should have come so far, spent so much money, worn out a rather old body to meet his inevitable ruin in a dark

tent beside a dying man when he could have met it just as well at home with
Emily in the plush parlor. The thought of the prayers he had uselessly uttered
on his knees by the campbed among the jiggers, the rats, and the cockroaches
made him rebellious. A mosquito, the first he had heard, went humming
round the tent. He slashed at it savagely; he wouldn't have recognized himself among the Rotarians. He was lost and he was set free. Moralities were
what enabled a man to live happily and successfully with his fellows, but
Mr. Lever wasn't happy and he wasn't successful, and his only fellow in the
little stuffy tent wouldn't be troubled by Untruth in Advertising or by Mr.
Lever coveting his neighbor's oxen. You couldn't keep your ideas intact
when you discovered their geographical nature. The Solemnity of Death:
death wasn't solemn; it was a lemon-yellow skin and a black vomit. Honesty
is the Best Policy: that he saw quite suddenly was palpably false. It was an
anarchist who sat happily over the typewriter, an anarchist who recognized
nothing but one personal relationship, his affection for Emily. Mr. Lever
began to type: I have examined the plans and estimates of the new Lucas
crusher. . . .

Mr. Lever thought with savage happiness: I win. This letter would be the
last the company would hear from Davidson. The junior partner would open
it in the dapper Brussels office; he would tap his false teeth with a Waterman
pen and go in to talk to M. Golz. Taking all these factors into consideration
I recommend acceptance. . . . They would telegraph to Lucas. As for Davidson, that trusted agent of the company would have died of yellow fever
at some never accurately determined date. Another agent would come out,
and the crusher. . . . Mr. Lever carefully copied Davidson's signature on a
spare sheet of paper. He wasn't satisfied. He turned the original upside down
and copied it that way, so as not to be confused by his own idea of how a
letter should be formed. That was better, but it didn't satisfy him. He
searched until he found Davidson's own pen and began to copy and copy
the signature. He fell asleep copying it and woke again an hour later to find
the lamp was out; it had burned up all the oil. He sat there beside Davidson's
bed till daylight; once he was bitten by a mosquito in the ankle and clapped
his hand to the place too late: the brute went humming out. With the light
Mr. Lever saw that Davidson was dead. "Dear dear," he said. "Poor fellow."
He spat out with the words, quite delicately in a corner, the bad morning
taste in his mouth. It was like a little sediment of conventionality.

Mr. Lever got two of his carriers to cram Davidson tidily in his hole. He
was no longer afraid, of them or of failure or of separation. He tore up his
letter to Emily. It no longer represented his mood in its timidity, its secret
fear, its gentle fussing phrases, "Don't forget the stout," "Look after yourself." He would be home as soon as the letter, and they were going to do
things together now they'd never dreamed of doing. The money for the
crusher was only the beginning. His ideas stretched further now than Eastbourne, they stretched as far as Switzerland; he had a feeling that if he really
let himself go, they'd stretch as far as the Riviera. How happy he was on

what he thought of as "the trip home." He was freed from what had held him back through a long pedantic career, the fear of some conscious fate that notes the dishonesty, notes the skirt in Piccadilly, notes the glass and too many of Stone's special. Now he had said Boo to that goose.

But you on the other hand who are reading this, who know so much more than Mr. Lever, who can follow the mosquito's progress from the dead swollen black to Davidson's tent, to Mr. Lever's ankle, you, I say, may possibly believe in fate, a kindly fate tender toward human frailty, ready to give Mr. Lever three days of happiness, three days off the galling chain, as he carried back through the forest his amateurish forgeries and the infection of yellow fever in the blood. The story may very well confirm your faith in that loving merciful omniscience if it has not been shaken by personal knowledge of the drab empty forest through which Mr. Lever now went so merrily, where it is impossible to believe in any spiritual life, in anything outside the nature dying round you, the shriveling of the weeds. There are two opinions about everything; it was Mr. Lever's favorite expression, drinking beer in the Ruhr, Pernod in Lorraine, selling heavy machinery.

ERNEST HEMINGWAY

IN ANOTHER COUNTRY*

In the fall the war was always there, but we did not go to it any more. It was cold in the fall in Milan and the dark came very early. Then the electric lights came on, and it was pleasant along the streets looking in the windows. There was much game hanging outside the shops, and the snow powdered in the fur of the foxes and the wind blew their tails. The deer hung stiff and heavy and empty, and small birds blew in the wind and the wind turned their feathers. It was a cold fall and the wind came down from the mountains.

We were all at the hospital every afternoon, and there were different ways of walking across the town through the dusk to the hospital. Two of the ways were alongside canals, but they were long. Always, though, you crossed a bridge across a canal to enter the hospital. There was a choice of three bridges. On one of them a woman sold roasted chestnuts. It was warm, standing in front of her charcoal fire, and the chestnuts were warm afterward in your pocket. The hospital was very old and very beautiful, and you entered through a gate and walked across a courtyard and out a gate on the other side. There were usually funerals starting from the courtyard. Beyond the old hospital were the new brick pavilions, and there we met every afternoon and were all very polite and interested in what was the matter, and sat in the machines that were to make so much difference.

The doctor came up to the machine where I was sitting and said: "What did you like best to do before the war? Did you practice a sport?"

I said: "Yes, football."

"Good," he said. "You will be able to play football again better than ever."

My knee did not bend and the leg dropped straight from the knee to the ankle without a calf, and the machine was to bend the knee and make it move as in riding a tricycle. But it did not bend yet, and instead the machine lurched when it came to the bending part. The doctor said: "That will all pass. You are a fortunate young man. You will play football again like a champion."

In the next machine was a major who had a little hand like a baby's. He winked at me when the doctor examined his hand, which was between two leather straps that bounced up and down and flapped the stiff fingers, and said: "And will I too play football, captain-doctor?" He had been a very great fencer, and before the war the greatest fencer in Italy.

The doctor went to his office in a back room and brought a photograph which showed a hand that had been withered almost as small as the major's, before it had taken a machine course, and after was a little larger. The major held the photograph with his good hand and looked at it very carefully. "A wound?" he asked.

"An industrial accident," the doctor said.

"Very interesting, very interesting," the major said, and handed it back to the doctor.

"You have confidence?"

"No," said the major.

There were three boys who came each day who were about the same age I was. They were all three from Milan, and one of them was to be a lawyer, and one was to be a painter, and one had intended to be a soldier, and after we were finished with the machines, sometimes we walked back together to the Café Cova, which was next door to the Scala. We walked the short way through the communist quarter because we were four together. The people hated us because we were officers, and from a wineshop someone called out, "A basso gli ufficiali!"* as we passed. Another boy who walked with us sometimes and made us five wore a black silk handkerchief across his face because he had no nose then and his face was to be rebuilt. He had gone out to the front from the military academy and been wounded within an hour after he had gone into the front line for the first time. They rebuilt his face, but he came from a very old family and they could never get the nose exactly right. He went to South America and worked in a bank. But this was a long time ago, and then we did not any of us know how it was going to be afterward. We only knew then that there was always the war, but that we were not going to it any more.

We all had the same medals, except the boy with the black silk bandage across his face, and he had not been at the front long enough to get any medals. The tall boy with a very pale face who was to be a lawyer had been

* Down with the officers!

a lieutenant of Arditi and had three medals of the sort we each had only one of. He had lived a very long time with death and was a little detached. We were all a little detached, and there was nothing that held us together except that we met every afternoon at the hospital. Although, as we walked to the Cova through the tough part of town, walking in the dark, with light and singing coming out of the wineshops, and sometimes having to walk into the street when the men and women would crowd together on the sidewalk so that we would have had to jostle them to get by, we felt held together by there being something that had happened that they, the people who disliked us, did not understand.

We ourselves all understood the Cova, where it was rich and warm and not too brightly lighted, and noisy and smoky at certain hours, and there were always girls at the tables and the illustrated papers on a rack on the wall. The girls at the Cova were very patriotic, and I found that the most patriotic people in Italy were the café girls—and I believe they are still patriotic.

The boys at first were very polite about my medals and asked me what I had done to get them. I showed them the papers, which were written in very beautiful language and full of *fratellanza** and *abnegazione*,† but which really said, with the adjectives removed, that I had been given the medals because I was an American. After that their manners changed a little toward me, although I was their friend against outsiders. I was a friend, but I was never really one of them after they had read the citations, because it had been different with them and they had done very different things to get their medals. I had been wounded, it was true; but we all knew that being wounded, after all, was really an accident. I was never ashamed of the ribbons, though, and sometimes, after the cocktail hour, I would imagine myself having done all the things they had done to get their medals; but walking home at night through the empty streets with the cold wind and all the shops closed, trying to keep near the street lights, I knew that I would never have done such things, and I was very much afraid to die, and often lay in bed at night by myself, afraid to die and wondering how I would be when I went back to the front again.

The three with the medals were like hunting-hawks; and I was not a hawk, although I might seem a hawk to those who had never hunted; they, the three, knew better and so we drifted apart. But I stayed good friends with the boy who had been wounded his first day at the front, because he would never know now how he would have turned out; so he could never be accepted either, and I liked him because I thought perhaps he would not have turned out to be a hawk either.

The major, who had been the great fencer, did not believe in bravery, and spent much time while we sat in the machines correcting my grammar. He had complimented me on how I spoke Italian, and we talked together very easily. One day I had said that Italian seemed such an easy language to me that I could not take a great interest in it; everything was so easy to

* Brotherhood.
† Sacrifice.

say. "Ah, yes," the major said. "Why, then, do you not take up the use of grammar?" So we took up the use of grammar, and soon Italian was such a difficult language that I was afraid to talk to him until I had the grammar straight in my mind.

The major came very regularly to the hospital. I do not think he ever missed a day, although I am sure he did not believe in the machines. There was a time when none of us believed in the machines, and one day the major said it was all nonsense. The machines were new then and it was we who were to prove them. It was an idiotic idea, he said, "a theory, like another." I had not learned my grammar, and he said I was a stupid impossible disgrace, and he was a fool to have bothered with me. He was a small man, and he sat straight up in his chair with his right hand thrust into the machine and looked straight ahead at the wall while the straps thumped up and down with his fingers in them.

"What will you do when the war is over if it is over?" he asked me. "Speak grammatically!"

"I will go to the States."

"Are you married?"

"No, but I hope to be."

"The more of a fool you are," he said. He seemed very angry. "A man must not marry."

"Why, Signor Maggiore?"

"Don't call me 'Signor Maggiore.' "

"Why must not a man marry?"

"He cannot marry. He cannot marry," he said angrily. "If he is to lose everything, he should not place himself in a position to lose that. He should not place himself in a position to lose. He should find things he cannot lose."

He spoke very angrily and bitterly, and looked straight ahead while he talked.

"But why should he necessarily lose it?"

"He'll lose it," the major said. He was looking at the wall. Then he looked down at the machine and jerked his little hand out from between the straps and slapped it hard against his thigh. "He'll lose it," he almost shouted. "Don't argue with me!" Then he called to the attendant who ran the machines. "Come and turn this damned thing off."

He went back into the other room for the light treatment and the massage. Then I heard him ask the doctor if he might use his telephone and he shut the door. When he came back into the room I was sitting in another machine. He was wearing his cape and had his cap on, and he came directly toward my machine and put his arm on my shoulder.

"I am so sorry," he said, and patted me on the shoulder with his good hand. "I would not be rude. My wife has just died. You must forgive me."

"Oh—" I said, feeling sick for him. "I am so sorry."

He stood there biting his lower lip. "It is very difficult," he said. "I cannot resign myself."

He looked straight past me and out through the window. Then he began to cry. "I am utterly unable to resign myself," he said and choked. And then crying, his head up looking at nothing, carrying himself straight and soldierly, with tears on both his cheeks and biting his lips, he walked past the machines and out the door.

The doctor told me that the major's wife, who was very young and whom he had not married until he was definitely invalided out of the war, had died of pneumonia. She had been sick only a few days. No one expected her to die. The major did not come to the hospital for three days. Then he came at the usual hour, wearing a black band on the sleeve of his uniform. When he came back, there were large framed photographs around the wall, of all sorts of wounds before and after they had been cured by the machines. In front of the machine the major used were three photographs of hands like his that were completely restored. I do not know where the doctor got them. I always understood we were the first to use the machines. The photographs did not make much difference to the major because he only looked out of the window.

F. SCOTT FITZGERALD

BABYLON REVISITED*

1

"And where's Mr. Campbell?" Charlie asked.

"Gone to Switzerland. Mr. Campbell's a pretty sick man, Mr. Wales."

"I'm sorry to hear that. And George Hardt?" Charlie inquired.

"Back in America, gone to work."

"And where is the Snow Bird?"

"He was in here last week. Anyway, his friend, Mr. Schaeffer, is in Paris."

Two familiar names from the long list of a year and a half ago. Charlie scribbled an address in his notebook and tore out the page.

"If you see Mr. Schaeffer, give him this," he said. "It's my brother-in-law's address. I haven't settled on a hotel yet."

He was not really disappointed to find Paris was so empty. But the stillness in the Ritz bar was strange and portentous. It was not an American bar any more—he felt polite in it, and not as if he owned it. It had gone back into France. He felt the stillness from the moment he got out of the taxi and saw the doorman, usually in a frenzy of activity at this hour, gossiping with a *chasseur*† by the servants' entrance.

Passing through the corridor, he heard only a single, bored voice in the

* From *Taps at Reveille*. Copyright 1935 by Charles Scribner's Sons. Reprinted by permission of the publishers.
† Uniformed attendant.

once-clamorous women's room. When he turned into the bar he travelled the twenty feet of green carpet with his eyes fixed straight ahead by old habit; and then, with his foot firmly on the rail, he turned and surveyed the room, encountering only a single pair of eyes that fluttered up from a newspaper in the corner. Charlie asked for the head barman, Paul, who in the latter days of the bull market had come to work in his own custom-built car—disembarking, however, with due nicety at the nearest corner. But Paul was at his country house today and Alix giving him information.

"No, no more," Charlie said, "I'm going slow these days."

Alix congratulated him: "You were going pretty strong a couple of years ago."

"I'll stick to it all right," Charlie assured him. "I've stuck to it for over a year and a half now."

"How do you find conditions in America?"

"I haven't been to America for months. I'm in business in Prague, representing a couple of concerns there. They don't know about me down there."

Alix smiled.

"Remember the night of George Hardt's bachelor dinner here?" said Charlie. "By the way, what's become of Claude Fessenden?"

Alix lowered his voice confidentially. "He's in Paris, but he doesn't come here any more. Paul doesn't allow it. He ran up a bill of thirty thousand francs, charging all his drinks and his lunches, and usually his dinner, for more than a year. And when Paul finally told him he had to pay, he gave him a bad check."

Alix shook his head sadly.

"I don't understand it, such a dandy fellow. Now he's all bloated up——" He made a plump apple of his hands.

Charlie watched a group of strident queens installing themselves in a corner.

"Nothing affects them," he thought. "Stocks rise and fall, people loaf or work, but they go on forever." The place oppressed him. He called for the dice and shook with Alix for the drink.

"Here for long, Mr. Wales?"

"I'm here for four or five days to see my little girl."

"Oh-h! You have a little girl?"

Outside, the fire-red, gas-blue, ghost-green signs shone smokily through the tranquil rain. It was late afternoon and the streets were in movement; the *bistros** gleamed. At the corner of the Boulevard des Capucines he took a taxi. The Place de la Concorde moved by in pink majesty; they crossed the logical Seine, and Charlie felt the sudden provincial quality of the Left Bank.

Charlie directed his taxi to the Avenue de l'Opéra, which was out of his way. But he wanted to see the blue hour spread over the magnicent façade, and imagine that the cab horns, playing endlessly the first few bars of *Le Plus que Lent*,† were the trumpets of the Second Empire. They were closing the

* Small wineshop or restaurant.
† A waltz by Claude Debussy.

iron grill in front of Brentano's Bookstore, and people were already at dinner behind the trim little bourgeois hedge of Duval's. He had never eaten at a really cheap restaurant in Paris. Five-course dinner, four francs fifty, eighteen cents, wine included. For some odd reason he wished that he had.

As they rolled on to the Left Bank and he felt its sudden provincialism, he thought, "I spoiled this city for myself. I didn't realize it, but the days came along one after another, and then two years were gone, and everything was gone, and I was gone."

He was thirty-five, and good to look at. The Irish mobility of his face was sobered by a deep wrinkle between his eyes. As he rang his brother-in-law's bell in the Rue Palatine, the wrinkle deepened till it pulled down his brows; he felt a cramping sensation in his belly. From behind the maid who opened the door darted a lovely little girl of nine who shrieked "Daddy!" and flew up, struggling like a fish, into his arms. She pulled his head around by one ear and set her cheek against his.

"My old pie," he said.

"Oh, daddy, daddy, daddy, daddy, dads, dads, dads!"

She drew him into the salon, where the family waited, a boy and a girl his daughter's age, his sister-in-law and her husband. He greeted Marion with his voice pitched carefully to avoid either feigned enthusiasm or dislike, but her response was more frankly tepid, though she minimized her expression of unalterable distrust by directing her regard toward his child. The two men clasped hands in a friendly way and Lincoln Peters rested his for a moment on Charlie's shoulder.

The room was warm and comfortably American. The three children moved intimately about, playing through the yellow oblongs that led to other rooms; the cheer of six o'clock spoke in the eager smacks of the fire and the sounds of French activity in the kitchen. But Charlie did not relax; his heart sat up rigidly in his body and he drew confidence from his daughter, who from time to time came close to him, holding in her arms the doll he had brought.

"Really extremely well," he declared in answer to Lincoln's question. "There's a lot of business there that isn't moving at all, but we're doing even better than ever. In fact, damn well. I'm bringing my sister over from America next month to keep house for me. My income last year was bigger than it was when I had money. You see, the Czechs——"

His boasting was for a specific purpose; but after a moment, seeing a faint restiveness in Lincoln's eye, he changed the subject.

"Those are fine children of yours, well brought up, good manners."

"We think Honoria's a great little girl too."

Marion Peters came back from the kitchen. She was a tall woman with worried eyes, who had once possessed a fresh American loveliness. Charlie had never been sensitive to it and was always surprised when people spoke of how pretty she had been. From the first there had been an instinctive antipathy between them.

"Well, how do you find Honoria?" she asked.

"Wonderful. I was astonished how much she's grown in ten months. All the children are looking well."

"We haven't had a doctor for a year. How do you like being back in Paris?"

"It seems funny to see so few Americans around."

"I'm delighted," Marion said vehemently. "Now at least you can go into a store without their assuming you're a millionaire. We've suffered like everybody, but on the whole it's a good deal pleasanter."

"But it was nice while it lasted," Charlie said. "We were a sort of royalty, almost infallible, with a sort of magic around us. In the bar this afternoon"—he stumbled, seeing his mistake—"there wasn't a man I knew."

She looked at him keenly. "I should think you'd had enough of bars."

"I only stayed a minute. I take one drink every afternoon, and no more."

"Don't you want a cocktail before dinner?" Lincoln asked.

"I take only one drink every afternoon, and I've had that."

"I hope you keep to it," said Marion.

Her dislike was evident in the coldness with which she spoke, but Charlie only smiled; he had larger plans. Her very aggressiveness gave him an advantage, and he knew enough to wait. He wanted them to initiate the discussion of what they knew had brought him to Paris.

At dinner he couldn't decide whether Honoria was most like him or her mother. Fortunate if she didn't combine the traits of both that had brought them to disaster. A great wave of protectiveness went over him. He thought he knew what to do for her. He believed in character; he wanted to jump back a whole generation and trust in character again as the eternally valuable element. Everything else wore out.

He left soon after dinner, but not to go home. He was curious to see Paris by night with clearer and more judicious eyes than those of other days. He bought a *strapontin** for the Casino and watched Josephine Baker go through her chocolate arabesques.

After an hour he left and strolled toward Montmartre, up the Rue Pigalle into the Place Blanche. The rain had stopped and there were a few people in evening clothes disembarking from taxis in front of cabarets, and *cocottes* prowling singly or in pairs, and many Negroes. He passed a lighted door from which issued music, and stopped with the sense of familiarity; it was Bricktop's, where he had parted with so many hours and so much money. A few doors farther on he found another ancient rendezvous and incautiously put his head inside. Immediately an eager orchestra burst into sound, a pair of professional dancers leaped to their feet and a maître d'hôtel swooped toward him, crying, "Crowd just arriving, sir!" But he withdrew quickly.

"You have to be damn drunk," he thought.

Zelli's was closed, the bleak and sinister cheap hotels surrounding it were dark; up in the Rue Blanche there was more light and a local, colloquial French crowd. The Poet's Cave had disappeared, but the two great mouths

* Reserved seat.

of the Café of Heaven and the Café of Hell still yawned—even devoured, as
he watched, the meagre contents of a tourist bus—a German, a Japanese, and
an American couple who glanced at him with frightened eyes.

So much for the effort and ingenuity of Montmartre. All the catering to
vice and waste was on an utterly childish scale, and he suddenly realized the
meaning of the word "dissipate"—to dissipate into thin air; to make nothing
out of something. In the little hours of the night every move from place to
place was an enormous human jump, an increase of paying for the privilege
of slower and slower motion.

He remembered thousand-franc notes given to an orchestra for playing
a single number, hundred-franc notes tossed to a doorman for calling a cab.

But it hadn't been given for nothing.

It had been given, even the most wildly squandered sum, as an offering
to destiny that he might not remember the things most worth remembering,
the things that now he would always remember—his child taken from his
control, his wife escaped to a grave in Vermont.

In the glare of a *brasserie** a woman spoke to him. He bought her some
eggs and coffee, and then, eluding her encouraging stare, gave her a twenty-
franc note and took a taxi to his hotel.

II

He woke upon a fine fall day—football weather. The depression of yesterday was gone and he liked the people on the streets. At noon he sat opposite
Honoria at Le Grand Vatel, the only restaurant he could think of not remi-
niscent of champagne dinners and long luncheons that began at two and
ended in a blurred and vague twilight.

"Now, how about vegetables? Oughtn't you to have some vegetables?"

"Well, yes."

"Here's *épinards* and *chou-fleur* and carrots and *haricots*."†

"I'd like *chou-fleur*."

"Wouldn't you like to have two vegetables?"

"I usually only have one at lunch."

The waiter was pretending to be inordinately fond of children. "*Qu'elle
est mignonne la petite! Elle parle exactement comme une française.*"‡

"How about dessert? Shall we wait and see?"

The waiter disappeared. Honoria looked at her father expectantly.

"What are we going to do?"

"First, we're going to that toy store in the Rue Saint-Honoré and buy
you something you like. And then we're going to the vaudeville at the
Empire."

She hesitated. "I like it about the vaudeville, but not the toy store."

"Why not?"

"Well, you brought me this doll." She had it with her. "And I've got lots
of things. And we're not rich any more, are we?"

* Bar.
† Here's spinach and cauliflower . . . and beans.
‡ What a darling little girl she is! She speaks precisely like a French child.

"We never were. But today you are to have anything you want."

"All right," she agreed resignedly.

When there had been her mother and a French nurse he had been inclined to be strict; now he extended himself, reached out for a new tolerance; he must be both parents to her and not shut any of her out of communication.

"I want to get to know you," he said gravely. "First let me introduce myself. My name is Charles J. Wales, of Prague."

"Oh, daddy!" her voice cracked with laughter.

"And who are you, please?" he persisted, and she accepted a rôle immediately: "Honoria Wales, Rue Palatine, Paris."

"Married or single?"

"No, not married. Single."

He indicated the doll. "But I see you have a child, madame."

Unwilling to disinherit it, she took it to her heart and thought quickly: "Yes, I've been married, but I'm not married now. My husband is dead."

He went on quickly, "And the child's name?"

"Simone. That's after my best friend at school."

"I'm very pleased that you're doing so well at school."

"I'm third this month," she boasted. "Elsie"—that was her cousin—"is only about eighteenth, and Richard is about at the bottom."

"You like Richard and Elsie, don't you?"

"Oh, yes. I like Richard quite well and I like her all right."

Cautiously and casually he asked: "And Aunt Marion and Uncle Lincoln—which do you like best?"

"Oh, Uncle Lincoln, I guess."

He was increasingly aware of her presence. As they came in, a murmur of ". . . adorable" followed them, and now the people at the next table bent all their silences upon her, staring as if she were something no more conscious than a flower.

"Why don't I live with you?" she asked suddenly. "Because mamma's dead?"

"You must stay here and learn more French. It would have been hard for daddy to take care of you so well."

"I don't really need much taking care of any more. I do everything for myself."

Going out of the restaurant, a man and a woman unexpectedly hailed him.

"Well, the old Wales!"

"Hello there, Lorraine. . . . Dunc."

Sudden ghosts out of the past: Duncan Schaeffer, a friend from college. Lorraine Quarrles, a lovely, pale blonde of thirty; one of a crowd who had helped them make months into days in the lavish times of three years ago.

"My husband couldn't come this year," she said, in answer to his question. "We're poor as hell. So he gave me two hundred a month and told me I could do my worst on that. . . . This your little girl?"

"What about coming back and sitting down?" Duncan asked.

"Can't do it." He was glad for an excuse. As always, he felt Lorraine's passionate, provocative attraction, but his own rhythm was different now.

"Well, how about dinner?" she asked.

"I'm not free. Give me your address and let me call you."

"Charlie, I believe you're sober," she said judicially. "I honestly believe he's sober, Dunc. Pinch him and see if he's sober."

Charlie indicated Honoria with his head. They both laughed.

"What's your address?" said Duncan sceptically.

He hesitated, unwilling to give the name of his hotel.

"I'm not settled yet. I'd better call you. We're going to see the vaudeville at the Empire."

"There! That's what I want to do," Lorraine said. "I want to see some clowns and acrobats and jugglers. That's just what we'll do, Dunc."

"We've got to do an errand first," said Charlie. "Perhaps we'll see you there."

"All right, you snob. . . . Good-by, beautiful little girl."

"Good-by."

Honoria bobbed politely.

Somehow, an unwelcome encounter. They liked him because he was functioning, because he was serious; they wanted to see him, because he was stronger than they were now, because they wanted to draw a certain sustenance from his strength.

At the Empire, Honoria proudly refused to sit upon her father's folded coat. She was already an individual with a code of her own, and Charlie was more and more absorbed by the desire of putting a little of himself into her before she crystallized utterly. It was hopeless to try to know her in so short a time.

Between the acts they came upon Duncan and Lorraine in the lobby where the band was playing.

"Have a drink?"

"All right, but not up at the bar. We'll take a table."

"The perfect father."

Listening abstractedly to Lorraine, Charlie watched Honoria's eyes leave their table, and he followed them wistfully about the room, wondering what they saw. He met her glance and she smiled.

"I like that lemonade," she said.

What had she said? What had he expected? Going home in a taxi afterward, he pulled her over until her head rested against his chest.

"Darling, do you ever think about your mother?"

"Yes, sometimes," she answered vaguely.

"I don't want you to forget her. Have you got a picture of her?"

"Yes, I think so. Anyhow, Aunt Marion has. Why don't you want me to forget her?"

"She loved you very much."

"I loved her too."

They were silent for a moment.

"Daddy, I want to come and live with you," she said suddenly.

His heart leaped; he had wanted it to come like this.

"Aren't you perfectly happy?"

"Yes, but I love you better than anybody. And you love me better than anybody, don't you, now that mummy's dead?"

"Of course I do. But you won't always like me best, honey. You'll grow up and meet somebody your own age and go marry him and forget you ever had a daddy."

"Yes, that's true," she agreed tranquilly.

He didn't go in. He was coming back at nine o'clock and he wanted to keep himself fresh and new for the thing he must say then.

"When you're safe inside, just show yourself in that window."

"All right. Good-by, dads, dads, dads, dads."

He waited in the dark street until she appeared, all warm and glowing, in the window above and kissed her fingers out into the night.

III

They were waiting. Marion sat behind the coffee service in a dignified black dinner dress that just faintly suggested mourning. Lincoln was walking up and down with the animation of one who had already been talking. They were as anxious as he was to get into the question. He opened it almost immediately:

"I suppose you know what I want to see you about—why I really came to Paris."

Marion played with the black stars on her necklace and frowned.

"I'm awfully anxious to have a home," he continued. "And I'm awfully anxious to have Honoria in it. I appreciate your taking in Honoria for her mother's sake, but things have changed now"—he hesitated and then continued more forcibly—"changed radically with me, and I want to ask you to reconsider the matter. It would be silly for me to deny that about three years ago I was acting badly——"

Marion looked up at him with hard eyes.

"——but all that's over. As I told you, I haven't had more than a drink a day for over a year, and I take that drink deliberately, so that the idea of alcohol won't get too big in my imagination. You see the idea?"

"No," said Marion succinctly.

"It's a sort of stunt I set myself. It keeps the matter in proportion."

"I get you," said Lincoln. "You don't want to admit it's got any attraction for you."

"Something like that. Sometimes I forget and don't take it. But I try to take it. Anyhow, I couldn't afford to drink in my position. The people I represent are more than satisfied with what I've done, and I'm bringing my ·ster over from Burlington to keep house for me, and I want awfully to have

Honoria too. You know that even when her mother and I weren't getting along well we never let anything that happened touch Honoria. I know she's fond of me and I know I'm able to take care of her and—well, there you are. How do you feel about it?"

He knew that now he would have to take a beating. It would last an hour or two hours, and it would be difficult, but if he modulated his inevitable resentment to the chastened attitude of the reformed sinner, he might win his point in the end.

Keep your temper, he told himself. You don't want to be justified. You want Honoria.

Lincoln spoke first: "We've been talking it over since we got your letter last month. We're happy to have Honoria here. She's a dear little thing, and we're glad to be able to help her, but of course that isn't the question——"

Marion interrupted suddenly. "How long are you going to stay sober, Charlie?" she asked.

"Permanently, I hope."

"How can anybody count on that?"

"You know I never did drink heavily until I gave up business and came over here with nothing to do. Then Helen and I began to run around with——"

"Please leave Helen out of it. I can't bear to hear you talk about her like that."

He stared at her grimly; he had never been certain how fond of each other the sisters were in life.

"My drinking only lasted about a year and a half—from the time we came over until I—collapsed."

"It was time enough."

"It was time enough," he agreed.

"My duty is entirely to Helen," she said. "I try to think what she would have wanted me to do. Frankly, from the night you did that terrible thing you haven't really existed for me. I can't help that. She was my sister."

"Yes."

"When she was dying she asked me to look out for Honoria. If you hadn't been in a sanitarium then, it might have helped matters."

He had no answer.

"I'll never in my life be able to forget the morning when Helen knocked at my door, soaked to the skin and shivering, and said you'd locked her out."

Charlie gripped the sides of the chair. This was more difficult than he expected; he wanted to launch out into a long expostulation and explanation, but he only said: "The night I locked her out——" and she interrupted, "I don't feel up to going over that again."

After a moment's silence Lincoln said: "We're getting off the subject. You want Marion to set aside her legal guardianship and give you Honoria. I think the main point for her is whether she has confidence in you or not."

"I don't blame Marion," Charlie said slowly, "but I think she can have entire confidence in me. I had a good record up to three years ago. Of course, it's within human possibilities I might go wrong any time. But if we wait much longer I'll lose Honoria's childhood and my chance for a home." He shook his head, "I'll simply lose her, don't you see?"

"Yes, I see," said Lincoln.

"Why didn't you think of all this before?" Marion asked.

"I suppose I did, from time to time, but Helen and I were getting along badly. When I consented to the guardianship, I was flat on my back in a sanitarium and the market had cleaned me out. I knew I'd acted badly, and I thought if it would bring any peace to Helen, I'd agree to anything. But now it's different. I'm functioning, I'm behaving damn well, so far as——"

"Please don't swear at me," Marion said.

He looked at her, startled. With each remark the force of her dislike became more and more apparent. She had built up all her fear of life into one wall and faced it toward him. This trivial reproof was possibly the result of some trouble with the cook several hours before. Charlie became increasingly alarmed at leaving Honoria in this atmosphere of hostility against himself; sooner or later it would come out, in a word here, a shake of the head there, and some of that distrust would be irrevocably implanted in Honoria. But he pulled his temper down out of his face and shut it up inside him; he had won a point, for Lincoln realized the absurdity of Marion's remark and asked her lightly since when she had objected to the word "damn."

"Another thing," Charlie said: "I'm able to give her certain advantages now. I'm going to take a French governess to Prague with me. I've got a lease on a new apartment——"

He stopped, realizing that he was blundering. They couldn't be expected to accept with equanimity the fact that his income was again twice as large as their own.

"I suppose you can give her more luxuries than we can," said Marion. "When you were throwing away money we were living along watching every ten francs. . . . I suppose you'll start doing it again."

"Oh, no," he said. "I've learned. I worked hard for ten years, you know—until I got lucky in the market, like so many people. Terribly lucky. It didn't seem any use working any more, so I quit. It won't happen again."

There was a long silence. All of them felt their nerves straining, and for the first time in a year Charlie wanted a drink. He was sure now that Lincoln Peters wanted him to have his child.

Marion shuddered suddenly; part of her saw that Charlie's feet were planted on the earth now, and her own maternal feeling recognized the naturalness of his desire; but she had lived for a long time with a prejudice—a prejudice founded on a curious disbelief in her sister's happiness, and which, in the shock of one terrible night, had turned to hatred for him. It had all happened at a point in her life where the discouragement of ill health and adverse circumstances made it necessary for her to believe in tangible villainy and a tangible villain.

"I can't help what I think!" she cried out suddenly. "How much you were responsible for Helen's death, I don't know. It's something you'll have to square with your own conscience."

An electric current of agony surged through him; for a moment he was almost on his feet, an unuttered sound echoing in his throat. He hung on to himself for a moment, another moment.

"Hold on there," said Lincoln uncomfortably. "I never thought you were responsible for that."

"Helen died of heart trouble," Charlie said dully.

"Yes, heart trouble." Marion spoke as if the phrase had another meaning for her.

Then, in the flatness that followed her outburst, she saw him plainly and she knew he had somehow arrived at control over the situation. Glancing at her husband, she found no help from him, and as abruptly as if it were a matter of no importance, she threw up the sponge.

"Do what you like!" she cried, springing up from her chair. "She's your child. I'm not the person to stand in your way. I think if it were my child I'd rather see her——" She managed to check herself. "You two decide it. I can't stand this. I'm sick. I'm going to bed."

She hurried from the room; after a moment Lincoln said:

"This has been a hard day for her. You know how strongly she feels——" His voice was almost apologetic: "When a woman gets an idea in her head."

"Of course."

"It's going to be all right. I think she sees now that you—can provide for the child, and so we can't very well stand in your way or Honoria's way."

"Thank you, Lincoln."

"I'd better go along and see how she is."

"I'm going."

He was still trembling when he reached the street, but a walk down the Rue Bonaparte to the *quais* set him up, and as he crossed the Seine, fresh and new by the *quai* lamps, he felt exultant. But back in his room he couldn't sleep. The image of Helen haunted him. Helen whom he had loved so until they had senselessly begun to abuse each other's love, tear it into shreds. On that terrible February night that Marion remembered so vividly, a slow quarrel had gone on for hours. There was a scene at the Florida, and then he attempted to take her home, and then she kissed young Webb at a table; after that there was what she had hysterically said. When he arrived home alone he turned the key in the lock in wild anger. How could he know she would arrive an hour later alone, that there would be a snowstorm in which she wandered about in slippers, too confused to find a taxi? Then the aftermath, her escaping pneumonia by a miracle, and all the attendant horror. They were "reconciled," but that was the beginning of the end, and Marion, who had seen with her own eyes and who imagined it to be one of many scenes from her sister's martyrdom, never forgot.

Going over it again brought Helen nearer, and in the white, soft light that steals upon half sleep near morning he found himself talking to her again. She said that he was perfectly right about Honoria and that she wanted Honoria to be with him. She said she was glad he was being good and doing better. She said a lot of other things—very friendly things—but she was in a swing in a white dress, and swinging faster and faster all the time, so that at the end he could not hear clearly all that she said.

IV

He woke up feeling happy. The door of the world was open again. He made plans, vistas, futures for Honoria and himself, but suddenly he grew sad, remembering all the plans he and Helen had made. She had not planned to die. The present was the thing—work to do and someone to love. But not to love too much, for he knew the injury that a father can do to a daughter or a mother to a son by attaching them too closely: afterward, out in the world, the child would seek in the marriage partner the same blind tenderness and, failing probably to find it, turn against love and life.

It was another bright, crisp day. He called Lincoln Peters at the bank where he worked and asked if he could count on taking Honoria when he left for Prague. Lincoln agreed that there was no reason for delay. One thing—the legal guardianship. Marion wanted to retain that a while longer. She was upset by the whole matter, and it would oil things if she felt that the situation was still in her control for another year. Charlie agreed, wanting only the tangible, visible child.

Then the question of a governess. Charlie sat in a gloomy agency and talked to a cross Bernaise and to a buxom Breton peasant, neither of whom he could have endured. There were others whom he would see tomorrow.

He lunched with Lincoln Peters at Griffons, trying to keep down his exultation.

"There's nothing quite like your own child," Lincoln said. "But you understand how Marion feels too."

"She's forgotten how hard I worked for seven years there," Charlie said. "She just remembers one night."

"There's another thing." Lincoln hesitated. "While you and Helen were tearing around Europe throwing money away, we were just getting along. I didn't touch any of the prosperity because I never got ahead enough to carry anything but my insurance. I think Marion felt there was some kind of injustice in it—you not even working toward the end, and getting richer and richer."

"It went just as quick as it came," said Charlie.

"Yes, a lot of it stayed in the hands of *chasseurs* and saxophone players and maîtres d'hôtel—well, the big party's over now. I just said that to explain Marion's feeling about those crazy years. If you drop in about six o'clock tonight before Marion's too tired, we'll settle the details on the spot."

Back at his hotel, Charlie found a *pneumatique** that had been redirected

* Letter or message sent by pneumatic tube.

from the Ritz bar where Charlie had left his address for the purpose of finding a certain man.

> DEAR CHARLIE: You were so strange when we saw you the other day that I wondered if I did something to offend you. If so, I'm not conscious of it. In fact, I have thought about you too much for the last year, and it's always been in the back of my mind that I might see you if I came over here. We *did* have such good times that crazy spring, like the night you and I stole the butcher's tricycle, and the time we tried to call on the president and you had the old derby rim and the wire cane. Everybody seems so old lately, but I don't feel old a bit. Couldn't we get together some time today for old time's sake? I've got a vile hang-over for the moment, but will be feeling better this afternoon and will look for you about five in the sweatshop at the Ritz.
>
> Always devotedly,
>
> LORRAINE.

His first feeling was one of awe that he had actually, in his mature years, stolen a tricycle and pedalled Lorraine all over the Étoile between the small hours and dawn. In retrospect it was a nightmare. Locking out Helen didn't fit in with any other act of his life, but the tricycle incident did—it was one of many. How many weeks or months of dissipation to arrive at that condition of utter irresponsibility?

He tried to picture how Lorraine had appeared to him then—very attractive; Helen was unhappy about it, though she said nothing. Yesterday, in the restaurant, Lorraine had seemed trite, blurred, worn away. He emphatically did not want to see her, and he was glad Alix had not given away his hotel address. It was a relief to think, instead, of Honoria, to think of Sundays spent with her and of saying good morning to her and of knowing she was there in his house at night, drawing her breath in the darkness.

At five he took a taxi and bought presents for all the Peterses—a piquant cloth doll, a box of Roman soldiers, flowers for Marion, big linen handkerchiefs for Lincoln.

He saw, when he arrived in the apartment, that Marion had accepted the inevitable. She greeted him now as though he were a recalcitrant member of the family, rather than a menacing outsider. Honoria had been told she was going; Charlie was glad to see that her tact made her conceal her excessive happiness. Only on his lap did she whisper her delight and the question "When?" before she slipped away with the other children.

He and Marion were alone for a minute in the room, and on an impulse he spoke out boldly:

"Family quarrels are bitter things. They don't go according to any rules. They're not like aches or wounds; they're more like splits in the skin that won't heal because there's not enough material. I wish you and I could be on better terms."

"Some things are hard to forget," she answered. "It's a question of confidence." There was no answer to this and presently she asked, "When do you propose to take her?"

"As soon as I can get a governess. I hoped the day after tomorrow."

"That's impossible. I've got to get her things in shape. Not before Saturday."

He yielded. Coming back into the room, Lincoln offered him a drink.

"I'll take my daily whisky," he said.

It was warm here, it was a home, people together by a fire. The children felt very safe and important; the mother and father were serious, watchful. They had things to do for the children more important than his visit here. A spoonful of medicine was, after all, more important than the strained relations between Marion and himself. They were not dull people, but they were very much in the grip of life and circumstances. He wondered if he couldn't do something to get Lincoln out of his rut at the bank.

A long peal at the door-bell; the *bonne à tout faire* passed through and went down the corridor. The door opened upon another long ring, and then voices, and the three in the salon looked up expectantly; Richard moved to bring the corridor within his range of vision, and Marion rose. Then the maid came back along the corridor, closely followed by the voices, which developed under the light into Duncan Schaeffer and Lorraine Quarrles.

They were gay, they were hilarious, they were roaring with laughter. For a moment Charlie was astounded; unable to understand how they ferreted out the Peters' address.

"Ah-h-h!" Duncan wagged his finger roguishly at Charlie. "Ah-h-h!"

They both slid down another cascade of laughter. Anxious and at a loss, Charlie shook hands with them quickly and presented them to Lincoln and Marion. Marion nodded, scarcely speaking. She had drawn back a step toward the fire; her little girl stood beside her, and Marion put an arm about her shoulder.

With growing annoyance at the intrusion, Charlie waited for them to explain themselves. After some concentration Duncan said:

"We came to invite you out to dinner. Lorraine and I insist that all this shishi, cagy business 'bout your address got to stop."

Charlie came closer to them, as if to force them backward down the corridor.

"Sorry, but I can't. Tell me where you'll be and I'll phone you in half an hour."

This made no impression. Lorraine sat down suddenly on the side of a chair, and focussing her eyes on Richard, cried, "Oh, what a nice little boy! Come here, little boy." Richard glanced at his mother, but did not move. With a perceptible shrug of her shoulders, Lorraine turned back to Charlie:

"Come and dine. Sure your cousins won' mine. See you so sel'om. Or solemn."

"I can't," said Charlie sharply. "You two have dinner and I'll phone you."

Her voice became suddenly unpleasant. "All right, we'll go. But I remember once when you hammered on my door at four A.M. I was enough of a good sport to give you a drink. Come on, Dunc."

Still in slow motion, with blurred, angry faces, with uncertain feet, they retired along the corridor.

"Good night," Charlie said.

"Good night!" responded Lorraine emphatically.

When he went back into the salon Marion had not moved, only now her son was standing in the circle of her other arm. Lincoln was still swinging Honoria back and forth like a pendulum from side to side.

"What an outrage!" Charlie broke out. "What an absolute outrage!"

Neither of them answered. Charlie dropped into an armchair, picked up his drink, set it down again and said:

"People I haven't seen for two years having the colossal nerve——"

He broke off. Marion had made the sound "Oh!" in one swift, furious breath, turned her body from him with a jerk and left the room.

Lincoln set down Honoria carefully.

"You children go in and start your soup," he said, and when they obeyed, he said to Charlie:

"Marion's not well and she can't stand shocks. That kind of people make her really physically sick."

"I didn't tell them to come here. They wormed your name out of somebody. They deliberately——"

"Well, it's too bad. It doesn't help matters. Excuse me a minute."

Left alone, Charlie sat tense in his chair. In the next room he could hear the children eating, talking in monosyllables, already oblivious to the scene between their elders. He heard a murmur of conversation from a farther room and then the ticking bell of a telephone receiver picked up, and in a panic he moved to the other side of the room and out of earshot.

In a minute Lincoln came back. "Look here, Charlie. I think we'd better call off dinner for tonight. Marion's in bad shape."

"Is she angry with me?"

"Sort of," he said, almost roughly. "She's not strong and——"

"You mean she's changed her mind about Honoria?"

"She's pretty bitter right now. I don't know. You phone me at the bank tomorrow."

"I wish you'd explain to her I never dreamed these people would come here. I'm just as sore as you are."

"I couldn't explain anything to her now."

Charlie got up. He took his coat and hat and started down the corridor. Then he opened the door of the dining room and said in a strange voice, "Good night, children."

Honoria rose and ran around the table to hug him.

"Good night, sweetheart," he said vaguely, and then trying to make his voice more tender, trying to conciliate something, "Good night, dear children."

V

Charlie went directly to the Ritz bar with the furious idea of finding Lorraine and Duncan, but they were not there, and he realized that in any case there was nothing he could do. He had not touched his drink at the Peters', and now he ordered a whisky-and-soda. Paul came over to say hello.

"It's a great change," he said sadly. "We do about half the business we did. So many fellows I hear about back in the States lost everything, maybe not in the first crash, but then in the second. Your friend George Hardt lost every cent, I hear. Are you back in the States?"

"No, I'm in business in Prague."

"I heard that you lost a lot in the crash."

"I did," and he added grimly, "but I lost everything I wanted in the boom."

"Selling short."

"Something like that."

Again the memory of those days swept over him like a nightmare—the people they had met travelling; then people who couldn't add a row of figures or speak a coherent sentence. The little man Helen had consented to dance with at the ship's party, who had insulted her ten feet from the table; the women and girls carried screaming with drink or drugs out of public places——

——The men who locked their wives out in the snow, because the snow of twenty-nine wasn't real snow. If you didn't want it to be snow, you just paid some money.

He went to the phone and called the Peters' apartment; Lincoln answered.

"I called up because this thing is on my mind. Has Marion said anything definite?"

"Marion's sick," Lincoln answered abruptly. "I know this thing isn't altogether your fault, but I can't have her go to pieces about it. I'm afraid we'll have to let it slide for six months; I can't take the chance of working her up to this state again."

"I see."

"I'm sorry, Charlie."

He went back to his table. His whisky glass was empty, but he shook his head when Alix looked at it questioningly. There wasn't much he could do now except send Honoria some things; he would send her a lot of things tomorrow. He thought rather angrily that this was just money—he had given so many people money. . . .

"No, no more," he said to another waiter. "What do I owe you?"

He would come back some day; they couldn't make him pay forever. But he wanted his child, and nothing was much good now, beside that fact. He wasn't young any more, with a lot of nice thoughts and dreams to have by himself. He was absolutely sure Helen wouldn't have wanted him to be so alone.

BIOGRAPHICAL DATA

J. DONALD ADAMS conducts the "Speaking of Books" column for *The New York Times* Book Review Section. For some years he has been making eminently sound comments on realism, naturalism, the scope of the novel, and the possible value or fatuity of today's experiments in writing.

JOHN ARLOTT has held various positions with the British Broadcasting Corporation. Previously, he had been a police detective for nine years. He has written several books about sports, his primary interest for the past decade.

MARTIN ARMSTRONG has been a poet, a novelist, and a short-story writer since the 1920's. More recently, he has been doing critical work in *The Listener*, the weekly publication of the British Broadcasting Corporation.

ROGER BANNISTER, now a physician in London, is the first athlete in history to run the mile in less than four minutes.

Although born in France and always characterized by a French clearness in his thinking, HILAIRE BELLOC became an English citizen and even served in Parliament for seven years. Pugnacious and learned, satiric and whimsical, he wrote history, biography, essays, and poetry. He and Chesterton are frequently regarded as a team—called the Chesterbelloc —because of the vigor of their common insistence on the importance and value of Christianity.

EMILY BRONTË, nineteenth-century English poet and novelist, won literary immortality for her only novel, *Wuthering Heights*. This is a gripping story of love and hate, cruelty and revenge, acted out by an unbelievable but unforgettable cast of characters, against the background of the wild, purple English moors.

Chiefly a dramatic critic, IVOR BROWN has written books on politics as well and has edited *The Observer* in London for six years. In his essays he has consistently made himself, in the words of one critic, "a foe of jargon and the muddy phrase."

A political columnist for The Philadelphia *Bulletin*, JOHN C. CALPIN has long been interested in Matt Talbot and is presently contemplating writing a biography of him.

JOYCE CARY was an English author, who died in 1957. His novels, noted for brilliant characterization, include *Herself Surprised*, *To Be a Pilgrim*, and *The Horse's Mouth*. He was also an essayist and critic of considerable importance.

A distinguished historian, BRUCE CATTON won the Pulitzer Prize for his book, *A Stillness at Appomattox*, a study of the Civil War. He combines fidelity to history with a cursive style.

JOHN CHAPMAN has been the drama editor of the New York *Daily News* for thirty years. He edited annual anthologies of the best plays on the American stage during the period 1947 to 1953.

G. K. CHESTERTON was a prolific and versatile writer of the essay, short story, poetry, biography, and philosophy. His best-known work includes *The Everlasting Man*, *The Wisdom of Father Brown*, and *St. Thomas Aquinas*.

JOHN CIARDI, poet, critic, and poetry editor of *The Saturday Review*, is a director of the Bread Loaf School of English. He is also professor of English at Rutgers University.

SAMUEL LANGHORNE CLEMENS, "the Lincoln of our literature," contributed extensively to American fiction during the latter part of the nineteenth century. His memorable and nostalgic stories include *Tom Sawyer* and *Huckleberry Finn*. In non-fiction he is to be remembered for his humorous and satiric *Innocents Abroad*.

SAMUEL TAYLOR COLERIDGE, critic, essayist, and the most philosophical of the English Romantic Poets, will be recalled for his poems "Christabel," "Kubla Khan," and "The Rime of the Ancient Mariner." He collaborated with Wordsworth in writing *The Preface to the Lyrical Ballads*.

Professor of English at Fordham University, FRANCIS X. CONNOLLY has edited two excellent anthologies which have been widely used in college classes.

JEAN DIETRICK CONNORS, an alumna of Immaculata College, has written for *Perspective*. She presently lives in Philadelphia.

Polish-born JOSEPH CONRAD became a master of the English language and one of the greatest writers of sea stories. He is remembered for *Lord Jim* and *Victory*.

Born in Ceylon and educated at the University of London, ANANDA K. COOMARASWAMY lived in India before becoming curator of Indian art at the Boston Museum of Fine Arts in 1917. A specialist in Oriental art and philosophy, who lectured at Harvard and Boston College, he was unusually well acquainted with the writings of St. Augustine and St. Thomas Aquinas.

An architect by training, RALPH ADAMS CRAM has helped design buildings at West Point and Bryn Mawr. He revised the original plans for the Cathedral of St. John the Divine. He also "changed the style to thirteenth century French Gothic with a strong final accent on English Gothic." Fond of the medieval, an original thinker in politics, and a strangely imaginative writer, he has produced a tour de force in "White Magic."

R. B. CUNNINGHAME GRAHAM was born in 1852 and during his twenties lived among American and Mexican cowboys and Argentine gauchos. Largely of Scottish ancestry, he had one Spanish forebear who seems to have influenced a taste for South American life. He wrote biographies of the important Conquistadores and a variety of sketches, some bitter, some sentimental, but all quite animated, about his experiences in South America and even in Africa.

ARTHUR DALEY succeeded John Kieran as sports columnist in *The New York Times* about a decade ago. The box in which his daily report appears is possibly the most literate sports commentary in the United States. He has no superior in the writing of biographical sketches.

THE REV. MARTIN C. D'ARCY is an English Jesuit, whose philosophical and critical writings have been respected by scholars for three decades. He has been principal of Campion Hall at Oxford University and a rather frequent lecturer in this country.

CHRISTOPHER DAWSON is a philosopher of history in the most complete Christian tradition. His books explain history in the light of Christian development, and his evaluation of medieval life and literature is cogent and persuasive. He is presently professor of Catholic studies at Harvard.

A pianist of professional competence and training, MARY DEASY has, for the past decade or so, turned with rewarding success to the writing of novels and short stories. Of "Morning Sun" Martha Foley says: "It has all the dimensions of a classic." Miss Deasy's stories have been selected for reprinting in the O. Henry Awards *Prize Stories* and in *The Best American Short Stories*. She lives in Cincinnati.

A nineteenth-century English novelist, CHARLES DICKENS created a gallery of vivid characters. His novels have delighted generations of readers. Among his creations are *The Tale of Two Cities*, *Oliver Twist*, and *A Christmas Carol*.

JOHN EARLE, seventeenth-century Anglican bishop and tutor of Charles II, wrote a book of *Characters*, which is the most successful work in its field.

World-famous poet, critic, and poetic dramatist, T. S. ELIOT has always been received with mixed reactions because of his erudite and esoteric style. His poems include "The Love Song of J. Alfred Prufrock," "Ash Wednesday," and "The Hollow Men." Some of his poetic dramas are *Murder in the Cathedral*, *The Cocktail Party*, and *The Elder Statesman*.

F. SCOTT FITZGERALD, born in St. Paul, Minnesota, in 1896, and educated at Princeton, became a symbol of the "Jazz Age." His eye-catching titles include the novels: *This Side of Paradise*, *The Beautiful and Damned*, *Tender Is the Night*, and *The Great Gatsby*. *Tales of the Jazz Age* and *All the Sad Young*

Men are collections of short stories. His style, poetic and hypnotic, contains some of the most hauntingly beautiful and memorable prose to be written in this century. Today there is as much interest in Fitzgerald the dramatic personality as in Fitzgerald the author.

JAMES ANTHONY FROUDE was at first much influenced by John Henry Newman and the Tractarian Movement. His enthusiasm for the latter slackened off to zero. In succeeding years he became an ambitious historian, more brisk perhaps than reliable.

JACK GOULD is radio and television critic for *The New York Times*. His criticism, invariably keen and fair, has brought him four significant awards.

GRAHAM GREENE was born in England in 1904. His early novels were considered "shockers," but he later turned to Catholic themes, using sin and redemption in *The Heart of the Matter* and *The End of the Affair*. He has also written some powerful short stories.

NANCY HALE is the wife of the professor of English literature at the University of Virginia. She was born in Boston of a family long distinguished in American writing.

JOSEPH HALL was an Anglican bishop, first of Exeter, later of Norwich. His satirical and ecclesiastical writings occasioned warm controversy in the troubled years of the seventeenth century. His *Characters of Virtue and Vice* is an early work.

A nineteenth-century English art critic of peculiar fervor and determined opinion, PHILIP GILBERT HAMERTON was deeply interested in the techniques of art, though not a first-class artist himself. He had an unfortunate habit of annoying the never very patient Whistler and became that gentleman's Number One target for scorn.

Born in Russia in 1905, MANYA HARARI has been a publisher in England since 1946 and a translator of French and Russian literatures. Among his translations have been Gabriel Marcel's *The Philosophy of Existence* and, with Max Hayward, Boris Pasternak's *Dr. Zhivago*.

RICHARD HAYES has been the drama editor of *The Commonweal* since 1952. Earlier, he had written several articles and reviews for that publication.

ERNEST HEMINGWAY, the son of a physician, was born in Chicago in 1898. He served in an ambulance unit in Italy during World War I and, when he returned home, began a career as a journalist, later turning to literature. Mr. Hemingway, a Nobel Prize winner, has given us some of the best-known titles in modern literature—*The Sun Also Rises, A Farewell to Arms, For Whom the Bell Tolls*, and *The Old Man and the Sea*. His swift and laconic prose set a style in the writing of his time which has received both the compliment of imitation and the flattery of parody. In his best work there is a taut and terse perfection which few have been able to attain.

WASHINGTON IRVING, a short-story writer and biographer, was the first major writer of the American Romantic Movement. "Rip Van Winkle" and "The Legend of Sleepy Hollow" are his most popular stories. To American fiction he contributed humor, graphic characterization, and definite geographical locales such as the Hudson River Valley.

HENRY JAMES, the son of an aristocratic and affluent family, received a cosmopolitan education. In writing his international novels, such as *The Americans* and *Daisy Miller*, his purpose was to delineate the American character abroad and to present contrasting social backgrounds, rather than conflicting loyalties. James was also a master craftsman in the art of the short story.

RUSSELL KIRK is the editor of *Modern Age*. Active as a commentator on American life, he is research professor of political science at Post College and a member of the faculty of politics at the New School for Social Research.

The late MONSIGNOR RONALD KNOX was among the most versatile writers of his time. Before his death he had spent a dozen or more years in rendering the Bible into modern idiom. During his long career he published satire, criticism, devotional works, and detective stories. Monsignor Knox spent many years as Newman Chaplain at Oxford, where as a young man he had entered the Church.

OLIVER LA FARGE, anthropologist and fiction writer, lives in Santa Fe, close to the Indians whose lives he records so vividly. His novel, *Laughing Boy*, won the Pulitzer Prize in 1929.

CHARLES LAMB, English essayist, is the author of *The Essays of Elia*, a truly significant work specially noted for its charm, humor, pathos, and warm affection for mankind.

Evelyn Waugh believes that "the Danes are the most exhilarating people in Europe." Perhaps some of the non-Danes on the Continent will question that statement, but MOGENS LIND, himself a Danish writer, gives considerable strength to Waugh's view. Surely Lind shares with Will Rogers and Victor Borge a genuinely humorous temperament. And his travel book underscores an amiable Danish manner.

JAMES RUSSELL LOWELL was a nineteenth-century scholar, critic, and for many years a professor at Harvard. He also tried writing poetry, but he was less successful. His best-known work is *The Biglow Papers*.

MICHAEL MCLAVERTY is a teacher in Belfast. He has just published his seventh novel, *The Choice*. There is a pronounced poetic mood in the generality of his short stories.

BRYAN MACMAHON, Irish short-story writer and novelist, incorporates the folk tradition of his native Ireland, using modern settings, a variety of themes, and creating many delightful characters.

THE REV. EDWARD J. MCTAGUE is pastor of the Holy Spirit parish at Sharon Hill, Pennsylvania. For ten years he was an army chaplain. There is a refined humor in all the stories and poems he has written.

JACQUES MARITAIN, internationally known Thomistic philosopher, author, and critic, has written scores of books and articles. Perhaps his most famous work is *Art and Scholasticism*. For a time he served as French Ambassador to the Vatican and until his recent retirement was professor of philosophy at Princeton University.

HARRIET MARTINEAU was a nineteenth-century novelist, political economist, journalist, and travel writer. Her reputation as an economist was high and somewhat unique because no woman before her had turned to this type of specializing. The account of Mrs. Wordsworth incorporated in the text is a typical example of the excellent obituary writing which is, and has been, quite common in British journalism.

W. SOMERSET MAUGHAM, who resides on the French Riviera, is the dean of British novelists and short-story writers. His most moving and powerful novel, the story of the moral degradation of a human soul, is *Of Human Bondage*.

ALICE MEYNELL, brilliant English Catholic essayist of the last century, is the author of many collections of essays including *The Rhythm of Life* and *The Second Person Singular*.

ELIZABETH MONGAN is curator of prints at the Alverthorpe Gallery and the National Gallery at Washington. An authority on the graphic arts, she has done considerable research on the drawings, engravings, water colors, and other art works of William Blake.

JOHN HENRY CARDINAL NEWMAN was the genius of the Oxford Movement, and its great prose document is his fascinating *Apologia*. This nineteenth-century literary giant also wrote *The Grammar of Assent* and *The Idea of a University*.

Born in Teheran, Iran, HAROLD NICOLSON has become a noted English essayist and biographer. For several years he served in the British foreign service, and he has conducted a column in *The Spectator*. He is married to V. Sackville West, the witty novelist.

SEAN O'FAOLAIN, Irish short-story writer and critic, uses Cork as the locale for his skilfully contrived stories. His very successful work includes *Midsummer Night Madness*, *The Man Who Invented Sin*, and *Simple Folk*. He is presently teaching literature at Princeton.

Popular British critic and eminent biographer, HESKETH PEARSON is a frequent narrator for the British Broadcasting Corporation and a contributor to *The Listener* magazine. He has written an excellent biography of George Bernard Shaw.

JOSEPH PENNELL and his wife ELIZABETH were friends of Whistler and his most detailed biographers. Joseph was an artist, especially proficient in lithography. His drawings of Philadelphia scenes are among his best.

NOEL PERRIN, a graduate of Williams College and Duke University, took a Master's degree in literature at Cambridge. He is presently an instructor in English at Dartmouth. He has written articles for *The New Yorker, Punch,* and *The New Statesman.*

A union official and a professional viola player on occasion, JAMES PLUNKETT is now an energetic writer of short stories. His 1955 collection entitled *The Trusting and the Maimed,* in which "The Half-Crown" appeared, contains half a dozen stories of high merit.

CHARLES ROLO is Book Review Editor for *The Atlantic Monthly.* Born in Egypt of British parents, he is a graduate of Oxford. He has written *Wingate's Raiders,* a war book, and has edited the works of Aldous Huxley.

SAKI is the pen name for H. H. MUNRO, an English short-story writer with a light, charming, urbane touch. He was an author who wrote to be enjoyed, not to be criticized or studied. In all his stories he succeeds in delighting the reader with his felicitous style. Like O. Henry, he favors the unexpected or surprise ending.

ROBERT SENCOURT is the pen name for Robert Esmonde Gordon George. A New Zealander by birth, he has taught English literature in such assorted places as Lisbon and Lahore, India. His writings are largely biographical and historical.

THE REV. JOHN W. SIMONS is one of three brothers who are priests in the Archdiocese of Philadelphia. He is presently teaching at St. Charles Seminary. A poet and a critic, who is especially well informed in English, American, and Spanish literatures, he has published verse and articles in *America, The Commonweal, Perspective,* and *Thought.*

JOHN CAMPBELL SMITH is an alumnus of the University of Pennsylvania. He lives in Philadelphia and works for an advertising agency.

FREYA STARK was born in England but after wide travels in the Far East now lives in Asolo, Italy. Her books on Arabia, Iran, and Iraq reflect her knowledge of the history of these lands as well as the personal experiences of the author, who has been called a traveler of genius. Her style is among the finest in twentieth-century prose.

ROBERT LOUIS STEVENSON, Victorian novelist, was also well-known as a romancer, poet, critic, and short-story writer. Among his interesting contributions are his *South Seas* stories and *Dr. Jekyll and Mr. Hyde.*

STRIX is the pseudonym of Colonel Robert Peter Fleming. Before World War II he traveled widely as a correspondent for *The Times* of London. He has been a frequent contributor to *The Spectator* magazine.

JOSEPH STRUTT was an antiquary with a keen interest in the costumes, armor, and customs of earlier centuries. At the time of his death he was writing a romance, *Queenhoo Hall,* the last chapter of which was supplied by Walter Scott.

RICHARD SULLIVAN, novelist and short-story writer, is a contributor to many leading magazines and is a professor of English at the University of Notre Dame. He is best remembered for *The World of Idella May.*

ALLEN TATE, American poet and critic, helped found the magazine *Fugitive* to express Southern agrarian views. He has taught at many universities including Princeton. In 1943 he held the chair of poetry at the Library of Congress. His work *On the Limits of Poetry* was well received.

Born in India, WILLIAM MAKEPEACE THACKERAY, nineteenth-century essayist and novelist, is the author of *Vanity Fair,* a novel of manners, but his greatest work is *Henry Esmond*, an historical novel bristling with wit and sentimentalism concerning the days of the good Queen Anne.

A Greek philosopher, THEOPHRASTUS, student of Plato, succeeded Aristotle as head of the Peripatetic school of philosophy. His interests were in natural history and botany, but his *Characters* is a series of sketches which shows his deep interest in human beings.

HENRY DAVID THOREAU, American literary recluse, arch individualist, and lover of nature, wrote *Walden*, a rich, poignant record of human experience, and the insurgent essay "Civil Disobedience."

After infantry combat in World War II, RICHARD YOUNG THURMAN received his degree from Utah State Agricultural College. He has sharpened his capacity for writing by a succession of positions in such diversified fields as truck driving, banking, sheepherding, and salesmanship. The humor and the skill of "The Credit Line" obviously justify its inclusion in the O. Henry Awards *Prize Stories of 1957*.

MARK VAN DOREN received his Ph.D. degree at Columbia University in 1920 and taught English there until his retirement in 1958. A brother of the equally famous Carl (deceased), he has published numerous volumes of short stories.

EVELYN WAUGH has satirized the follies of wealthy irresponsibles since the publication of *Vile Bodies*. A novelist with a preference for the humor of the absurd and for the creation of excellent caricature, he has shown a power for more realistic portrayal in such a book as *Brideshead Revisited*.

GERALD WEALES is a book reviewer for *The Commonweal* and a member of the faculty of the University of Pennsylvania.

EDWARD WEEKS has an academic background of Cornell, Harvard, and Cambridge and is one of the most discerning critics in the United States today. Since 1938 he has been editor of *The Atlantic Monthly*.

JOHN T. WINTERICH, a contributing editor of *The Saturday Review* and a widely known bibliophile, is one of the foremost American authorities on first editions. His mellow style makes his work very readable and enjoyable.

WILLIAM BUTLER YEATS, poet and dramatist, was the main inspiration for the energy and achievement of the Irish Renaissance at the end of the century. By all standards Yeats is a major poet of the modern period.

Arrangement by Categories

(In justice to the variety of theme in some instances, occasional items are indexed under two headings.)

Index of Authors and Titles

431